BNFN
Fer

Principles of Corporate Finance Law

Second Edition

EILÍS FERRAN
and
LOOK CHAN HO

OXFORD
UNIVERSITY PRESS

Great Clarendon Street, Oxford, OX2 6DP,
United Kingdom

Oxford University Press is a department of the University of Oxford.
It furthers the University's objective of excellence in research, scholarship,
and education by publishing worldwide. Oxford is a registered trade mark of
Oxford University Press in the UK and in certain other countries

© E Ferran and L C Ho 2014

The moral rights of the authors have been asserted

Second edition published in 2014

Impression: 1

Published in the United States of America by Oxford University Press
198 Madison Avenue, New York, NY 10016, United States of America

British Library Cataloguing in Publication Data
Data available

Library of Congress Control Number: 2013949382

ISBN 978-0-19-967134-2 (Hbk)
978-0-19-967135-9 (Pbk)

Printed in Great Britain by
CPI Group (UK) Ltd, Croydon, CR0 4YY

Preface

In the period since the previous edition, the financial markets have experienced an unprecedented degree of strain. Whilst banks and other financial institutions have been at the eye of the storm, their problems have had repercussions for the financing of the ordinary commercial companies as well. Deficiencies in the legal and regulatory framework governing corporate finance have been exposed, leading to a multiplicity of private lawsuits and to wide-ranging regulatory reforms.

In other words, there has been much to do in producing this new edition. I am especially grateful to my co-author Look Chan Ho for coming on board and taking responsibility for chapters 11 and 12. I am also grateful to numerous Cambridge LLM Corporate Finance students for their feedback on draft chapters, and to Demetrio Maltese (LLM, 2012-13) for specific research assistance. I would like also to record my gratitude to the trustees of the JM Keynes Fellowship in Financial Economics, Cambridge University, for funding to support the research.

The manuscript was delivered to the publishers in August 2013 and reflects our knowledge and understanding of the law, regulation and practice at that time. We have been able, however, to include brief references to significant developments that occurred during the period between delivery of the manuscript and the final proofs.

The professionalism and dedication of the editors and others at OUP have been much appreciated.

EVF,
November 2013

The law and practice of debt finance respond to and thus develop from financial crisis. Two financial crises this book has now spanned. The original version of the book, entitled *Company Law and Corporate Finance*, was published just after the Asian financial crisis, and this edition is to be published when the world economy is beginning to recover from the global economic crisis.

As an admirer of the book since its inception as *Company Law and Corporate Finance*, I am delighted to be able to contribute to two chapters in the book relating to debt financing.

I am most grateful to Professor Ferran for all her kindness and echo her comments about OUP.

Look Chan Ho
London
November 2013

Contents

II. LEGAL CAPITAL

III. DEBT CORPORATE FINANCE

IV. CAPITAL MARKETS FINANCE

Table of Cases

AUSTRALIA

FRANCE

GERMANY

HONG KONG

IRELAND (REPUBLIC OF)

NEW ZEALAND

SINGAPORE

UNITED STATES OF AMERICA

Table of Legislation

AUSTRALIA

CANADA

List of Abbreviations

ABI	Association of British Insurers
ABL	Asset-backed Lending
ADR	American Depositary Receipt
AGM	Annual General Meeting
AIM	Alternative Investment Market
ASIC	Australian Securities and Investments Commission
BBA	British Bankers Association
BCBS	Basel Committee on Banking Supervision
BIS	Department for Business, Innovation and Skills
CAPM	Capital Asset Pricing Model
CDO	Collateralized Debt Obligation
CESR	Committee of European Securities Regulators
CJEU	Court of Justice of the European Union
CoCo	Contingent Convertible Bond
CRA	Credit Rating Agency
CSD	Central Securities Depository
D&O	Directors and Officers
DR	Depositary Receipt
DTI	Department of Trade and Industry
DTR	Disclosure and Transparency Rules
ECLE	European Company Law Experts
ECOFIN	Economic and Finance Ministers
EEA	European Economic Area
EGC	Emerging Growth Company
EMIR	European Market Infrastructure Regulation
ENRC	Eurasian Natural Resources Corporation plc
ESA	European Supervisory Authority
ESMA	European Securities and Markets Authority
EU	European Union
FASB	Financial Accounting Standards Board
FCA	Financial Conduct Authority
FEE	Federation of European Accountants
FLS	Funding for Lending Scheme
FRC	Financial Reporting Council
FRSSE	Financial Reporting Standard for Smaller Entities
FSA	Financial Services Authority
FSAP	Financial Services Action Plan
FSMA	Financial Services and Markets Act 2000
GAAP	Generally Accepted Accounting Principles
GDR	Global Depositary Receipt
HMT	HM Treasury
IAIS	International Association of Insurance Supervisors
IAS	International Accounting Standards
IASB	International Accounting Standards Board
ICAEW	Institute of Chartered Accountants in England and Wales
ICAS	Institute of Chartered Accountants of Scotland
ICE	Intercontinental Exchange Inc
ICMA	International Capital Market Association
ICSD	International Central Securities Depository
IDS	International Disclosure Standards
IFRS	International Financial Reporting Standards

IMA	Investment Management Association
IMS	Interim Management Statements
IOSCO	International Organization of Securities Commissions
IPO	Initial Public Offering
ISDX	ICAP Securities & Derivatives Exchange
JOBS	Jumpstart Our Business Startups
LIBOR	London Inter-Bank Offered Rate
LMA	Loan Market Association
LR	Listing Rules
LSE	London Stock Exchange
MAC	Material Adverse Change
MAD	Market Abuse Directive
MiFID	Markets in Financial Instruments Directive
MJDS	Multijurisdictional Disclosure System
MM	Modigliani-Miller
MRSO	Mutual Recognition of Securities Offerings
MTF	Multilateral Trading Facility
NAPF	National Association of Pension Funds
Nomad	Nominated adviser
OFT	Office of Fair Trading
ORB	Order book for Retail Bonds
OTC	Over-the-Counter
OTF	Organized Trading Facility
PAL	Provisional Letter of Allotment
PDR	Prospectus Directive Regulation
PIK	Payment In Kind
PIRC	Pensions Investments and Research Consultants
PLC	Public Limited Company
PR	Prospectus Rules
PSM	Professional Securities Market
QIB	Qualified Institutional Buyer
RIE	Recognized Investment Exchange
RIS	Regulated Information Service
RoT	Retention of Title
SQC	Small Quoted Company
SFC	Securities and Futures Commission
SIV	Special Investment Vehicle
SLIM	Simpler Legislation for the Internal Market
SME	Small and Medium-sized Enterprises
SPE	Societas Privata Europaea
SPV	Special Purpose Vehicle
SUSMI	Substantial US Market Interest
T2S	Target2-Securities
UKLA	UK Listing Authority
WACC	Weighted Average Cost of Capital

PART I
OVERVIEW

1

The Regulatory Framework

Scope of the Book

The legal forms for business in the UK range from the unincorporated sole trader, association, partnership, or trust[1] through to the incorporated limited or unlimited company, limited liability partnership, community interest company (for social enterprises), and charitable incorporated organization. Mutual organizational forms, such as industrial and provident societies run for the benefit of their members or of the community, are also available. Of these numerous possibilities, the limited company is the most popular organizational form for modern businesses of economic significance.[2] The company occupies this pre-eminent position because it has advantages over other types of business vehicle as an organizational form through which to limit financial risks and to raise large amounts of finance from investors whilst keeping the day-to-day running of the business concentrated in the hands of a relatively small group of managers.[3] These advantages are supplied by the state through its system of company law.[4] These special features of company law act as incentives to trade and commerce and can play a critical role in promoting enterprise and investment.[5]

Since it is company law that provides the basic features that make the company an especially attractive organizational form for the channelling of finance to business, this book begins with company law and then branches out into other areas of law that are relevant to corporate finance. Part I, which includes this chapter, provides an introduction to the regulatory and business framework governing corporate finance in the UK and examines ways in

---

[1] The business trust has recently undergone a resurgence as a finance-raising vehicle in Singapore: TH Wu, "The Resurgence of 'Uncorporation: The Business Trust in Singapore' [2012] JBL 683. On the use of the business trust in the United States: GC Walsh and MJ Michaels, 'The State of Statutory Business Trusts in the United States' (2013) 19 *Trusts & Trustees* 681.

[2] At the end of 2010/11 there were 2,455,400 companies on the register in the UK of which only 0.3 per cent were public companies, and 6,000 were unlimited companies. Near to two million of the companies on the register at 31 March 2011 had an issued share capital of £100 or less. Only just less than 14,000 had an issued share capital of £10 million or more. There were over 18,000 limited partnerships and around 43,000 limited liability partnerships on the register at the end of 2010/11. All of the preceding figures are taken from Companies House, *Statistical Tables on Companies Registration Activities 2010/11* (2011). The Small Business Survey 2012 conducted on behalf of the Department for Business, Innovation and Skills (BIS), found that the main legal statuses of small and medium-sized enterprise (SME) employers were private limited companies (52%), sole proprietorships (27%), and partnerships (12%): BMG Research, *Small Business Survey 2012: SME Employers* (April 2013). In 2013 there were approximately 1.2 million micro-businesses in the UK, defined as small incorporated companies, and qualifying partnerships, to which two of the three following criteria could be applied: balance sheet total: £289,415 (€350,000); net turnover: £578,830 (€700,000); or an average of ten employees during the financial year: BIS, *Simpler Financial Reporting for Micro-Entities: The UK's Proposal to Implement the 'Micros Directive'* (BIS, 2013) 9.

[3] The limited liability partnership, which also has certain advantages as an organizational structure suited to raising finance, was introduced by the Limited Liability Partnerships Act 2000. This structure was embraced first by some large professional firms, such as accountants and lawyers, but took more time to achieve recognition among small commercial businesses, possibly because of a rather unwieldy legal framework: M Lower, 'What's on Offer? A Consideration of the Legal Forms Available for Use by Small- and Medium-sized Enterprises in the United Kingdom' (2003) 24 *Company Lawyer* 166; J Freedman and V Finch, 'The Limited Liability Partnership: Pick and Mix or Mix-up?' [2002] JBL 475.

[4] These features, in particular the shielding of the firm's assets from claims by personal creditors of its shareholders (which is important to those dealing with companies because it gives them confidence that they alone have a claim on the firm's assets) could not be fully replicated by contracts: H Hansmann and RR Kraakman, 'The Essential Role of Organizational Law' (2000) 110 *Yale Law Journal* 387.

[5] HM Treasury and BIS, *The Plan for Growth* (March 2011).

which the corporate form can be used to limit financial risks. Part II is also about company law, with an emphasis on the parts of company law that are particularly concerned with the ways in which limited companies are financed through share issues. Part III reviews some major legal issues arising in relation to the debt financing of companies. Corporate finance theory establishes that companies fund their operations through a combination of funding obtained through share issues, retained earnings, and debt. A book on the law relating to corporate finance would therefore be incomplete if it did not include a section on the law relating to corporate borrowing, even though this is a very large subject in its own right. The final section of the book, Part IV, considers aspects of securities law. The capital markets constitute a rich source of corporate finance but, in order to gain access to them, companies must submit to an extensive array of obligations, particularly disclosure requirements, that are intended to support the operation of the markets as a mechanism for the efficient allocation of resources and to bolster investor confidence.

Throughout the book, the discussion relates to companies formed and registered under the Companies Act 2006, the Companies Act 1985, or former Companies Acts.[6] Although it is possible under the companies legislation to form an unlimited company[7] or a company limited by guarantee,[8] the book concentrates mainly on companies limited by shares.

Types of Company Limited by Shares

Companies limited by shares are either public companies or private companies. Less than 1 per cent of the total number of registered companies are public companies, although in terms of size of operations, market capitalization, number of employees, and the like, public companies tend to be much larger than private companies. The distinction between public and private companies is enshrined in the companies legislation. It is a requirement of the legislation that, subject to certain limited exceptions, every company must make plain its status by its suffix: 'public limited company' ('plc' for short) or 'private limited company' ('Ltd' for short).[9] The fundamental point of distinction between public and private companies is that only public companies are allowed to raise capital by offering their shares and other securities to the investing public at large.[10] This is a limitation that 'crowdfunding' platforms, which seek to raise finance for innovative purposes by securing relatively small contributions from many parties, must work around.[11] The companies legislation also distinguishes between public and private companies with regard to the rules relating to the raising and maintenance of share capital where, broadly speaking, private companies operate under a more relaxed regime than public companies.[12] The more stringent rules applying to public companies are commonly derived from European Union (EU) laws, which Member States are obliged to incorporate into their domestic legislation. Private companies are also relieved of some of the administrative obligations imposed by the companies legislation, such as the requirements to hold an annual general meeting (AGM) and to have a company secretary.[13]

---

  [6] Companies can also be formed by Royal Charter or by specific Acts of Parliament but incorporation by these methods is now uncommon.

  [7] An unlimited company is not subject to the maintenance of capital rules and is therefore free to return capital to its members.

  [8] This form of corporate structure tends to be adopted by non-profit making organizations.

  [9] Companies Act 2006, ss 58–65.   [10] Companies Act 2006, s 755.

  [11] O Stacey, S Lovegrove, and D Murphy, 'Crowdfunding: Possibilities and Prohibitions' (2012) 23(1) PLC 18.

  [12] Companies Act 2006, Pts 17–18, considered in detail in Part II of this book.

  [13] Companies Act 2006, s 336 (requirement for public companies to hold AGMs) and s 270 (private company not required to have a secretary).

For the purposes of exposition, it is often convenient to contrast a public company with a large number of shareholders, each of whom holds only a tiny fraction of its shares and virtually all of whom perform no managerial functions, with a private company which has a few shareholders, all or most of whom are also involved in the management of the company. This practice should not be allowed to obscure the fact that there are many different types and sizes of company that can be accommodated under the 'public' and 'private' banners. In the UK, there is no upper limit on the number of shareholders in a private company. It is possible to have private companies which have managerial structures similar to those of the paradigm public company, ie where most shareholders are investors who do not participate directly in the management of the company. On the other hand, the shareholder base of a public company can be very small; the minimum number of shareholders in a public company has been progressively relaxed over the years and now stands at one, which is the same as for a private company.[14] However, the burden of complying with more onerous requirements would usually deter the operators of a small business from seeking public company status at least until such time as it has established a sufficient reputation to make raising capital from external investors a viable financing option. In the context of public companies, it is important to recognize that there can be some companies where the shareholding is so widely dispersed that no one shareholder or group of shareholders holds more than a tiny fraction of its shares and others where one shareholder, or a group of shareholders, holds a significant portion of the share capital.[15] A widely-dispersed shareholder base is regarded as the typical ownership structure for the largest public companies in the US and the UK but elsewhere in the world public companies are often controlled by a single shareholder or by a concentrated group of shareholders.[16] As dispersal of share ownership increases, the percentage shareholding that any one shareholder needs in order to exercise some form of practical control decreases.[17]

Companies where all, or most, of the shareholders participate in management are sometimes described as 'quasi-partnership' companies, reflecting the fact that the management structure is akin to that of a partnership. Quasi-partnership companies tend to be private companies with just a few shareholders. The companies legislation does not specifically recognize the category of quasi-partnership companies but, in relieving private companies from certain administrative requirements, it acknowledges that there may be companies for which the demarcations between one group of corporate actors (the directors) and another group (the shareholders) are unnecessary and inappropriate. Quasi-partnership companies have achieved recognition in case law concerned with the protection of minority shareholders. A petitioner may be entitled to relief where the conduct complained of is contrary to what the parties have actually agreed.[18] The judicial House of Lords (now the Supreme Court) has said that the promises that the parties have actually exchanged in the case of a quasi-partnership company will usually be found in the understandings between the members at the time they entered into association.[19]

In its accounting, filing, and audit requirements, the companies legislation contains a lighter regime for 'small' and 'medium-sized' companies and groups of companies, with the relevant criteria for this purpose being turnover, balance sheet totals, and number of

---

[14] Companies Act 2006, s 7.

[15] ES Herman, *Corporate Control, Corporate Power* (Cambridge: CUP, 1981) ch 3; BR Cheffins, *Corporate Ownership and Control: British Business Transformed* (Oxford: OUP, 2008).

[16] RJ Gilson, 'Controlling Shareholders and Corporate Governance: Complicating the Comparative Taxonomy' (2006) 119 *Harvard Law Review* 1641.

[17] JE Parkinson, *Corporate Power and Responsibility* (Oxford: OUP, 1993) 59–63.

[18] *O'Neill v Phillips, Re a company (No 00709 of 1992)* [1999] 2 BCLC 1, [1999] 1 WLR 1092, HL.

[19] *O'Neill v Phillips, Re a company (No 00709 of 1992)* [1999] 2 BCLC 1, [1999] 1 WLR 1092, HL.

employees.[20] Many quasi-partnership companies will satisfy the criteria to be small companies for the purposes of the statutory accounting rules and for exemption from audit requirements. The accounting and filing rules also distinguish between 'quoted'[21] and 'unquoted' companies, with more extensive financial disclosure obligations attaching to those companies that are quoted.[22] Other parts of the legislation, particularly those concerned with transparency and shareholder rights, also single out quoted companies for a heavier burden of regulation.[23] Another type of company that is recognized by the companies legislation is the company that is part of a larger group of companies. Corporate groups are subject to specific regulation in the context of accounting requirements. Certain other legislative rules also have a particular application to companies within a group. However, the UK companies legislation does not contain a specialized part that is dedicated to the comprehensive regulation of corporate groups.

Despite the recognition of different types of company for various specific purposes, in broad terms the underlying approach to company law in the UK is that the same legal framework applies to all companies regardless of the number of shareholders or employees, managerial structure or size of financial operations. From time to time there have surfaced proposals for a separate form of incorporation for small businesses[24] but that option was specifically rejected in the major review of company law that preceded the Companies Act 2006.[25] In that debate, a powerful argument against adopting a special and distinct corporate regulatory framework for small businesses was that thresholds established for the scope of the special regime could operate as barriers to growth.[26] Instead, the government sought to address the needs of small businesses by using the Companies Act 2006 as an opportunity to refashion company law so as to make it more accessible to small businesses.[27] This Act did not go as far as to structure the entirety of the companies legislation so as to give priority to the needs of small businesses ('think small first'). Radical restructuring had been considered as part of the review but some of the more ambitious plans were scaled back during the legislative process, with the result that the basic design remained the same as before but provisions that were of particular importance to small companies were significantly revised and, throughout the legislation as a whole, efforts were made to express the law in more accessible language.

---

[20] Companies Act 2006, ss 381–4, ss 444–5, ss 465–7; Small Companies and Groups (Accounts and Directors' Report) Regulations 2008, SI 2008/409; Large and Medium Sized Companies and Groups (Accounts and Reports) Regulations 2008, SI 2008/410; The Companies Act 2006 (Strategic Report and Directors' Report) Regulations 2013, SI 2013/1970 (accounting and filing requirements); ss 477–9 and Companies and Limited Liability Partnerships (Accounts and Audit Exemptions and Change of Accounting Framework) Regulations 2012, SI 2012/2301 (conditions for exemption from audit).

[21] Defined in Companies Act 2006, s 385 as a company that is officially listed in the UK or another EEA State or admitted to dealing on either the New York Stock Exchange or NASDAQ.

[22] See Companies Act 2006, Pt 15, ch 6 (directors' remuneration report required of quoted companies), ch 7 (publication requirements in respect of financial statements), and ch 9 (members' approval of directors' remuneration reports). The provisions relating to directors' remuneration were amended in 2013 to revise the contents of the directors' remuneration report and to give members a binding voting on remuneration policy: Enterprise and Regulatory Reform Act 2013 and Large and Medium Sized Companies and Groups (Accounts and Reports) (Amendment) Regulations 2013, SI 2013/1981. The Companies Act 2006 (Strategic Report and Directors' Report) Regulations 2013, SI 2013/1970 also impose new disclosure obligations on quoted companies with regard to greenhouse gas emissions.

[23] See eg Companies Act 2006, Pt 13, ch 5 (provisions relating to company meetings) and Pt 16, ch 5 (members' rights to raise audit concerns).

[24] eg *A New Form of Incorporation for Small Firms* (Cmnd 8171, 1981). See WJ Sandars, 'Small Businesses—Suggestions for Simplified Forms of Incorporation' [1979] JBL 14. BIS once again floated this possibility in January 2011 with a view to reducing costs for small entrepreneurs but more detailed proposals on this particular matter have not been forthcoming. However, as discussed in the following text, certain provisions of the legislation have been relaxed under initiatives aimed at reducing 'red tape'.

[25] DTI, *Modernising Company Law* (Cm 5553, 2002) paras 1.5–1.6.

[26] DTI, *Modernising Company Law*, paras 1.5–1.6.

[27] DTI, *Company Law Reform Small Business Summary*, (URN 05/927).

An evaluation of the impact of the Companies Act 2006 that was conducted in 2010 for the Department for Business, Innovation and Skills (BIS), the relevant government department, found that despite high awareness, and in some instances high compliance or adoption, companies had largely neutral perceptions of added value in terms of flexibility and cost savings.[28] Changes for private companies on internal decision-making processes (resolutions and meetings) were identified as being especially beneficial in terms of flexibility and costs savings. However, overall, over a third of companies disagreed that company law had been simplified, perhaps indicating that further time was needed for changes to become more embedded and for benefits to be realized.

Making the UK one of the best places in Europe to start, finance, and grow a business remains a political priority. With the UK slipping from 4th in the World Economic Forum's Global Competitiveness Index in 1998 to 12th in 2010, politicians, perhaps rather predictably, identified the regulatory burden as a contributory factor in this decline.[29] So far as company law is concerned, the so-called 'red tape challenge' launched by the Prime Minister in April 2011 has resulted in changes to the regime governing company and business names, the proposed relaxation of certain accounting requirements for companies with less than ten employees (micro-businesses), and the streamlining of certain other detailed requirements.[30] However, these developments are more directed at fine-tuning details than aiming at ambitious and far-reaching reforms.

The Regulatory Framework for Corporate Finance

A range of actors, including the domestic and regional (ie EU) legislatures, national and international standard-setting bodies, and private and voluntary sector organizations, supply the legal and non-legal norms, principles, standards, guidelines, and rules that go to make up the regulatory framework governing corporate finance activity in the UK. The common purpose underlying this vast body of regulatory activity is to establish an optimal package of commands and incentives to stimulate desirable behaviour and to curb undesirable behaviour by affected parties. Some of the main elements of the regulatory framework are as follows.

Legislation

The Companies Act 2006 is the principal piece of primary legislation relating to the formation, operation, and control of companies. This Act applies to companies incorporated in Great Britain (England, Wales, and Scotland) and also to companies incorporated in the remaining region of the UK, Northern Ireland.[31]

---

[28] ORC International, *Evaluation of the Companies Act 2006* (BIS, 2010).

[29] HM Treasury and BIS, *The Plan for Growth*.

[30] <http://www.redtapechallenge.cabinetoffice.gov.uk/2013/02/27-02-13-businesses-to-be-cut-free-from-company-red-tape/> accessed July 2013.

This initiative in part reflects developments at EU level: Directive 2012/6/EU of the European Parliament and of the Council of 14 March 2012 amending Council Directive 78/660/EEC on the annual accounts of certain types of companies as regards micro-entities [2012] OJ L81/3 simplifies the position for micro-businesses. Directive 2012/6/EU has since been subsumed by more comprehensive changes to the EU accounting framework which are to be implemented into domestic law by July 2015: Directive 2013/34/EU of the European Parliament and of the Council of 26 June 2013 on the annual financial statements, consolidated financial statements, and related reports of certain types of undertakings, amending Directive 2006/43/EC of the European Parliament and of the Council and repealing Council Directives 78/660/EEC and 83/349/EEC, [2013] OJ L182/19.

[31] Companies Act 2006, Pt 45 extends the mainland legislation to Northern Ireland (this was not previously the case).

The Companies Act 2006 was enacted with the aim of bringing company law more into line with the realities of modern business. Extensive changes made by this legislation were largely based on an independent review of company law which was conducted between 1998 and 2001 by a group of experts appointed by the government. This group of experts, known as the Company Law Steering Group, produced a series of consultation documents and helped to build a broad consensus in favour of reform.[32] Not all of the Companies Act 2006 was entirely new, however. Some sections were simply re-stated versions of provisions that were in the Companies Act 1985 and brought into the 2006 Act because it was deemed preferable, as a government spokesperson put it, 'to make the new legislation much closer to a complete code of company law for the majority of users'.[33] The aim of making the Companies Act 2006 a near complete code has been achieved. The Companies Act 1985 remains in force only for certain specialized purposes that are outside the scope of this work.

The Financial Services and Markets Act 2000 provides, among other things, the regulatory framework for issuing securities to the public and for the admission of securities to trading on a regulated market. As a framework Act, it contains fundamental elements of the regulatory regime but much of the detail is to be found in delegated legislation. Relevant delegated legislation under the Financial Services and Markets Act 2000 comes in the form of both statutory instruments (made by HM Treasury (HMT)) and rules made by the Financial Conduct Authority (FCA) in the FCA *Handbook*. The FCA *Handbook* includes the *Prospectus Rules*, the *Listing Rules*, and the *Disclosure Rules and Transparency Rules*. When acting as the competent authority for listing, the FCA may refer to itself as the UK Listing Authority (UKLA).

Corporate insolvency is regulated by the Insolvency Act 1986 and detailed rules made thereunder. Provisions relating to the winding up of solvent companies are also contained in this Act. The Insolvency Act 1986 has been amended on a number of occasions, including far-reaching reforms made by the Enterprise Act 2002 that, among other things, imposed significant restrictions on the availability of the insolvency procedure of administrative receivership.

As a Member State of the EU, the UK is obliged to give effect within its domestic laws to legislation that is adopted at the European level. A considerable amount of the domestic company law that is relevant to corporate finance has its roots in EU law. The influence of Europe is stronger still in the regulation of public offers of securities and the admission of securities to trading. Establishing a regulatory framework to facilitate the development of a genuinely integrated pan-European capital market has been a priority for EU policymakers in recent years and a large body of centralized legislation has been adopted in pursuit of that goal. Member States retain a limited discretion to impose their own additional requirements but the major decisions on the shape of regulatory policy relating to the capital markets are now taken at the European, rather than the domestic, level.

Internal constitutional instruments

Companies are permitted considerable flexibility in the internal constitutional regulation of their own affairs. Historically, companies were required to have a constitution set out in two documents: the memorandum of association and the articles of association. The Companies Act 2006 retains the concept of a memorandum of association but it no longer has constitutional significance as all that is required (and permitted) as its contents is a statement that the subscribers wish to form a company, agree to become members of the company, and, in the case of a

---

[32] The work of the Steering Group and the company law reform process generally are reviewed in E Ferran, 'Company Law Reform in the UK' (2001) 5 *Singapore Journal of International and Comparative Law* 516.
[33] Lord Sainsbury, *Hansard*, HL vol 682, col 795 (23 May 2006).

company that is to have a share capital, to take at least one share each. For companies incorporated before the Companies Act 2006 that had detailed constitutional provisions in their memoranda, those provisions are now treated as provisions of the company's articles.[34] A company's objects are unrestricted unless a company's articles specifically provide otherwise.[35] A company, once registered, is capable of exercising all the functions of an incorporated company.[36]

It is thus the articles of association that now constitute a company's main constitutional document, although they can be supplemented by certain shareholder resolutions or agreements.[37] Separate model form articles for public companies, private companies limited by shares, and private companies limited by guarantee are provided in delegated legislation made under the Companies Act 2006.[38] The relevant model form will apply by default if articles are not registered as part of a company's constitution or, if articles are so registered, in so far as they do not exclude or modify the relevant model articles.[39] However, subject to certain constraints under the general law, companies can depart from the model forms.

The companies legislation gives legal effect to the articles as a contract between the company and its shareholders and between the shareholders among themselves.[40]

Case law

The judiciary has made an immense contribution to the development of company law in the UK. One of the main functions of company law is to regulate conflicts of interest between directors and shareholders and, historically, it was the courts that played the major role in discharging that function by applying to directors a range of duties analogous to those they had developed in relation to trustees. Over the years, additional statutory rules were added as well but case law remained the primary source for the law on the general duties of directors. The Companies Act 2006 made a significant break with the past in this respect by introducing a statutory statement of directors' duties.[41] This statutory statement of general duties replaced the corresponding common law and equitable rules made by the judiciary[42] but the general duties are to be interpreted and applied in the same way as the common law rules or equitable principles, and regard is to be had to the corresponding common law rules and equitable principles in interpreting and applying the general duties.[43] It was indicated by a government spokesperson in Parliamentary scrutiny of the Bill that became the Companies Act 2006 that it was intended that the courts should continue to have regard to developments in the common law rules and equitable principles applying to other types of fiduciary relationships so that the statutory duties could develop in line with relevant developments in the law as it applies elsewhere.[44] The extent to which authorities on the common law and equitable principles remain relevant and the scope left for the judiciary to play a 'developmental' role in relation to directors' duties remain uncertain.

The justification put forward by the government for this shift in approach was that a statutory statement should make directors' duties more consistent, certain, accessible, and comprehensible.[45] The 2010 survey of the impact of the Companies Act 2006 reported that most stakeholders and businesses interviewed in the case studies were indeed positive about the

---

[34] Companies Act 2006, s 28.   [35] Companies Act 2006, s 31.
[36] Companies Act 2006, s 16(3).   [37] Companies Act 2006, s 17.
[38] The Companies (Model Articles) Regulations 2008, SI 2008/3229, amended by the Mental Health (Discrimination) Act 2013, s 3.
[39] Companies Act 2006, s 20.   [40] Companies Act 2006, s 33.
[41] Companies Act 2006, Pt 10, ch 2.   [42] Companies Act 2006, s 170(3).
[43] Companies Act 2006, s 170(4).   [44] Lord Goldsmith, *Hansard*, vol 678, GC col 243 (6 February 2006).
[45] DTI, *Company Law Reform* (Cm 6456, 2005) para 3.3.

codification of directors' duties and the focusing of directors' minds on their responsibilities and obligations.[46] However, less encouragingly, it also noted that the impact of the codification on corporate behaviour had been marginal.

Codes and guidelines

For a full view of the regulatory environment in which companies with a dispersed shareholder base operate within the UK, it is necessary also to look beyond the traditional legal sources, as a few well-known examples can quickly demonstrate. The UK Corporate Governance Code sets out standards of good practice in relation to issues such as board composition and structure, remuneration, accountability and audit, and relations with shareholders. The Corporate Governance Code, which began life as a private sector initiative and which is now maintained by the Financial Reporting Council, the body responsible for the oversight of financial reporting and corporate governance in the UK, is not legally enforceable in any direct way, although it is underpinned by requirements in the FCA *Listing Rules* whereby premium listed companies, including overseas companies, and standard listed issuers that are incorporated in the UK must report in their annual report and accounts on how they have applied the Code.[47] Despite the lack of direct enforceability, the Corporate Governance Code is an important element of the UK's regulatory framework. It has been said that 'for the director of a listed company the precepts of the [Corporate Governance] Code may well dominate his thinking, to the virtual exclusion of any question of law'.[48]

For directors of companies involved in mergers and acquisitions activity, the historically self-regulatory Takeover Code has a similar degree of significance. The Takeover Code, which governs offers for companies which have their registered offices in the UK, the Channel Islands, or the Isle of Man if any of their securities are admitted to trading on a regulated market in the UK or on any stock exchange in the Channel Islands or the Isle of Man, and certain other companies and entities, also began life as a private sector initiative that was not supported by direct legal sanctions. Over time, however, the Takeover Code acquired increasingly significant legal underpinning. As a result of implementation of the EU Takeover Directive,[49] the Takeover Code and the Panel on Takeovers and Mergers, an independent body, first established in 1968, whose main functions are to issue and administer the Takeover Code and to supervise and regulate takeovers and other matters to which the Code applies, now operate on a statutory footing.[50]

Non-binding but nevertheless important institutional guidelines also play a significant role in shaping corporate activity in the UK, particularly with regard to decisions relating to the raising of finance. The UK companies legislation gives shareholders a say in financing decisions that involve the issuance of new equity or equity-related financial instruments. Standing guidelines from the major institutional investors indicate their preferences on these matters. Whilst corporate managers are not bound to adhere rigidly to these preferences when putting forward financing proposals that require shareholder approval, they will know that they risk criticism, and even possible failure to obtain the required consents, if the reasons for deviation are not convincing.[51]

---

[46] ORC International, *Evaluation of the Companies Act 2006*.
[47] *LR* 9.8.6–9.8.6A (premium listing); *DTR* 7.2.1 (standard listing).
[48] LS Sealy, 'Directors' Duties Revisited' (2001) 22 *Company Lawyer* 79, 83.
[49] Directive (EC) 2004/25 of the European Parliament and of the Council of 21 April 2004 on takeover bids [2004] OJ L142/12.
[50] Companies Act 2006, Pt 28.   [51] See further ch 5.

2

Use and Abuse of the Corporate Form as a Vehicle for Raising Finance and Managing Financial Risk

Issues Considered in this Chapter

It is easy to incorporate a company in the UK. There is an administrative process involving form-filling and the disclosure of information but the requirements are not burdensome. Making the corporate form so readily available is a deliberate policy choice, which is intended to encourage entrepreneurship and enterprise.[1] Old-fashioned notions of incorporation as a privilege or concession granted by the state are thus very far removed from the modern legal reality.[2] Not only can people who operate businesses set themselves up within a company with a minimum of fuss, they can also sub-divide the business into a number of different companies within a group so as to enjoy many times over the advantages of the corporate form.

This chapter considers the standard features of the company that help to explain why, either in single entity form or as multiple entities linked within a corporate group, it is the organizational form chosen by most businesses that want to raise large amounts of capital. The advantages of the corporate form as a mechanism for shielding those who run or own a business from personal financial exposure are outlined. The shielding effect of the corporate form supports business innovation because it provides room for the kind of risk-taking that is often needed to get new ventures off the ground. At the same time, however, the fact that the operators of a business in corporate form do not shoulder all of the financial exposure is potentially problematic because it means that they may be tempted into excessive risk-taking, which if it is unsuccessful and the business fails, will result in creditors of the company being left with worthless claims. In its ability to allow the operators of a business to benefit fully from its success but not to absorb the full costs of its failure, the corporate form thus contains a deeply-embedded moral hazard problem. The policy challenge, therefore, is to strike a sensible balance between encouraging entrepreneurial risk-taking and preventing reckless or abusive conduct. How lawmakers in the UK have responded to this challenge and how the choices they have made compare with those made in certain other developed economies are also issues considered in this chapter. These issues go to the heart of what company law is really about, as debate in Europe has recognized:[3] if company law's primary goal is to be facilitative and helpful to those who establish and operate businesses, the policy

---

[1] E Ferran, 'Company Law Reform in the UK' (2001) 5 *Singapore Journal of International and Comparative Law* 516.

[2] On the historical development of English company law, see PL Davies, *Gower's Principles of Modern Company Law* 6th edn (London: Sweet & Maxwell, 1997) chs 2–3. (More recent editions do not include the historical material.) On the decline of the theory that incorporation should be regarded as a concession or privilege awarded by the State, see WW Bratton, 'The New Economic Theory of the Firm: Critical Perspectives from History' (1989) 1 *Stanford Law Review* 1471; M Stokes, 'Company Law and Legal Theory' in S Wheeler (ed), *The Law of the Business Enterprise* (Oxford: OUP, 1994) 80, 89 (reprinted from W Twining (ed), *Legal Theory and Common Law* (Oxford: Blackwell, 1986) 155). Wheeler's own comments on the concession theory are at 6–8. See also JE Parkinson, *Corporate Power and Responsibility* (Oxford: OUP, 1993) 25–32; J Taylor, *Creating Capitalism: Joint-Stock Enterprise in British Politics and Culture 1800-1870* (London: Royal Historical Society and Boydell Press, 2006).

[3] European Commission, *Report of the High Level Group of Company Law Experts on a Regulatory Framework for Company Law in Europe* (Brussels, November 2002) 29–31.

choices on striking the balance between competing concerns may be quite different from those that would be made from the starting point that company law's essential role is to protect people who deal with businesses whose operators benefit from the shielding effect of the corporate form.

Distinctive Features of the Company Limited by Shares

An incorporated company limited by shares has two distinctive features that are of particular significance in relation to corporate finance: separate legal personality and limited liability.

Separate legal personality

An incorporated company is a legal person separate and distinct from the people who hold shares in it and the people who manage it. This has been a foundation stone of company law in the UK ever since the decision of the judicial House of Lords in *Salomon v Salomon & Co Ltd*.[4] Mr Salomon was a boot and shoe manufacturer who had been in business for over thirty years as a sole trader. He then converted his business into the newly fashionable company limited by shares incorporated under the companies legislation of the time. Mr Salomon financed the company partly by investing in its shares and partly by lending to it and taking security. The incorporated business failed and the company became insolvent. An action brought by the company's liquidator gave the House of Lords the opportunity to consider fully for the first time the consequences of incorporation. It held that an incorporated company was a legally different person from the persons who had formed the company. Accordingly, even though Mr Salomon controlled all the shares in the company, it was legally distinct from him and he could not be made personally liable to make good the shortfall in the company's assets.

Various consequences follow from the fact that a company has a separate legal personality. A company continues in existence even though managers and shareholders may come and go.[5] It is the company, not its managers or shareholders, that acquires the contractual rights and undertakes the contractual liabilities that are involved in the running of the business. A contract between a company and a substantial shareholder, even one who controls all of the shares in the company, is a valid bilateral contract.[6] A company can have as one of its employees the controller of all its shares.[7] As a legal person, a company can incur tortious liability and can be prosecuted for committing crimes. The property of the business is owned by the company, and its shareholders do not have an insurable interest in it.[8] If shareholders misappropriate the company's property they may be guilty of theft.[9]

The designation of a pool of assets that belongs to the business rather than to its operators personally, which is achieved through incorporation, has been described as 'affirmative asset partitioning'.[10] Affirmative asset partitioning shields the assets of the business from the people behind it and, importantly, from the personal creditors of those people. Affirmative

---

[4] [1897] AC 22, HL.

[5] *Standard Chartered Bank v Pakistan National Shipping Corp and Ors (Nos 2 and 4)* [2003] 1 AC 959, HL, [36] *per* Lord Rodger.

[6] *Salomon v Salomon & Co Ltd* [1897] AC 22, HL.

[7] *Lee v Lee Air Farming Ltd* [1961] AC 12, HL. But whether a controlling shareholder can be viewed as an employee will depend on the context: *Buchan v Secretary of State for Employment* [1997] BCC 145; *Secretary of State for Trade and Industry v Bottrill* [1999] BCC 177; *Secretary of State for Business, Enterprise and Regulatory Reform v Neufeld* [2009] BCC 687, CA.

[8] *Macaura v Northern Assurance Co* [1925] AC 619, HL.

[9] *Re AG's Reference (No 2 of 1982)* [1984] QB 624, CA.

[10] H Hansmann and RR Kraakman, 'The Essential Role of Organizational Law' (2000) 110 *Yale Law Journal* 387.

asset partitioning is a feature that makes the corporate form attractive as a vehicle for raising finance: financiers can concentrate their risk-assessment processes and investigative and monitoring efforts on the particular entity to which they are supplying capital, thereby avoiding costs that would otherwise be passed through to the operators of the business that is seeking external finance.

Piercing the veil of incorporation

Piercing (or lifting) the veil of incorporation means looking through the corporate form to its shareholders.[11] It involves disregarding the separate personality of the company.[12] The vital commercial significance of incorporation is respected by the law and it is therefore exceptional for the veil to be pierced[13] In *Barclay Pharmaceuticals Ltd v Waypharm LP* Gloster J expressed the orthodox position when she noted that the corporate form is a structure that facilitates the raising of necessary capital for business and that, for this reason, only in exceptional circumstances does the law allow the creditor of a company to pierce the veil of incorporation.[14] In *VTB Capital plc v Nutritek International Corp* the Supreme Court even considered the argument that there is no jurisdiction at all for a court to lift the veil except where a statute provides, but determined that it was unnecessary and inappropriate to resolve that issue because the case for piercing the veil could not succeed on the facts.[15] Soon afterwards in *Prest v Petrodel Resources Ltd*[16] members of the Supreme Court stepped back from discarding outright the power to pierce the veil, accepting that there was a consensus in the case law that the veil could be pierced in limited circumstances involving impropriety and not wishing for the law 'to be disarmed in the face of abuse.'

In the *VTB* decision Lord Neuberger P acknowledged that 'the precise nature, basis and meaning of the principle [of veil piercing] are all somewhat obscure, as are the precise nature of circumstances in which the principle can apply.'[17] This point has also been made by commentators.[18] The position in the UK on this point is not dissimilar to that in other countries.[19] Veil piercing has been described as 'rare, unprincipled, and arbitrary' by one US commentator, who has suggested that it should be abolished altogether.[20] Another has described it as a 'mangled and muzzy doctrine' that would benefit from principled simplification.[21]

---

[11]　*VTB Capital plc v Nutritek International Corp* [2013] UKSC 5, [118] *per* Lord Neuberger.

[12]　*Prest v Petrodel Resources Ltd* [2013] UKSC 34, [16] *per* Lord Sumption.

[13]　*Standard Chartered Bank v Pakistan National Shipping Corp and Ors (Nos 2 and 4)* [2003] 1 AC 959, HL,[37] *per* Lord Rodger.

[14]　[2012] EWHC 306 (Comm).　　　[15]　[2013] UKSC 5.

[16]　*Prest v Petrodel Resources Ltd* [2013] UKSC 34, [28] *per* Lord Sumption. Lord Neuberger P [80] agreed that, on reflection, it would be wrong to discard the doctrine. Lady Hale acknowledged its existence [92]. Lord Mance [100] referred to the possibility of a 'final fall-back' in very rare circumstances, and Lord Clarke [103] reasoned in similar terms. For Lord Walker [106], however, piercing the veil was not a doctrine at all, but simply a label to describe certain disparate outcomes that superficially appeared to disregard separate legal personality. His Lordship noted 'If there is a small residual category in which the metaphor operates independently no clear example of it has yet been identified'.

[17]　[2013] UKSC 5, [123].

[18]　The plea 'is it not time to know just when a company is a "sham" and when the veil of incorporation *can* be "torn aside"?' (Lord Wedderburn, 'Multinationals and The Antiquities of Company Law' (1984) 47 MLR 87) has never been comprehensively answered. S Ottolenghi, 'From Peeping Behind the Corporate Veil to Ignoring it Completely' (1990) 53 MLR 338 reviews the authorities and the earlier literature in an attempt to provide a structure based on four categories. The article acknowledges that the authorities cannot be organized into a closed list of the circumstances in which the court can pierce the veil.

[19]　A point made by Lord Neuberger himself in *Prest v Petrodel Resources Ltd* [2013] UKSC 34, [75]–[78].

[20]　SM Bainbridge, 'Abolishing LLC Veil Piercing' [2005] *University of Illinois Law Review* 77; SM Bainbridge, 'Abolishing Veil Piercing' (2001) 26 *Journal of Corporation Law* 479.

[21]　PB Oh, 'Veil-Piercing' (2010) 89 *Texas Law Review* 81, 145.

One matter that is clear so far as the UK is concerned is that the courts do not have a discretionary power to lift the veil in the interests of justice.[22] Judicial veil piercing is a 'fall-back' principle with limited application, which has been developed pragmatically for the purpose of providing a practical solution in particular factual circumstances where all other more conventional remedies have proved to be of no assistance.[23] Recent authorities have described the circumstances in which judicial veil piercing is possible in very narrow terms, as being triggered by the misuse of the company structure by its controllers in order to immunize themselves from liability for wrongdoing outside the company.[24] The following principles have been outlined:

1. Ownership and control of a company are not of themselves sufficient to justify piercing the veil.

2. The court cannot pierce the veil, even when no unconnected third party is involved, merely because it is perceived that to do so is necessary in the interests of justice.

3. The corporate veil can only be pierced when there is some impropriety.

4. The company's involvement in an impropriety will not by itself justify a piercing of its veil: the impropriety must be linked to use of the company structure to avoid or conceal liability.

5. If the court is to pierce the veil, it is necessary to show both control of the company by the wrongdoer and impropriety in the sense of a misuse of the company as a device or facade to conceal wrongdoing.

6. A company can be a facade for such purposes even though not incorporated with deceptive intent.[25]

Veil piercing is a mechanism that may allow a court to grant discretionary equitable relief but it does not extend to enabling a claimant to pursue a contractual claim against a person other than the original contracting party.[26]

In *Prest v Petrodel Resources Ltd*,[27] the latest and now the leading Supreme Court decision on the issue, Lord Sumption summarized the position succinctly in the following terms: 'there is a limited principle of English law which applies when a person is under an existing legal obligation or liability or subject to an existing legal restriction which he deliberately evades or whose circumstances he deliberately frustrates by interposing a company under his control.'[28] According to Lord Sumption, use of the corporate form for the purposes of concealment or evasion is required.

---

[22] *Woolfson v Strathclyde Regional Council* 1978 SLT 159, HL; *Adams v Cape Industries plc* [1990] Ch 433, CA; *Yukong Lines Ltd of Korea v Rendsburg Investments Corp of Liberia* [1998] 1 WLR 294; (noted J Payne, 'Reaching the Man Behind the Company' [1998] *Company, Financial and Insolvency Law Review* 147); *HR v JAPT* [1997] *Pensions Law Review* 99 (noted C Mitchell, '"Beneficiaries" Rights Against Trustee Company Directors' [1998] *Company, Financial and Insolvency Law Review* 133); *Ord v Belhaven Pubs Ltd* [1998] BCC 607, CA; *Trustor AB v Smallbone and Ors (No 2)* [2001] 3 All ER 987; *Ben Hashem v Abdulhadi Ali Shayif* [2009] 1 FLR 115, [160].

[23] *Prest v Petrodel Resources Ltd* [2013] UKSC 34. *Woolfson v Strathclyde Regional Council* 1978 SLT 159, HL, 161 *per* Lord Keith; *Adams v Cape Industries plc* [1990] Ch 433, CA, 544 *per* Slade LJ; *Re Polly Peck plc* [1996] 2 All ER 433, 447; *Trustor AB v Smallbone (No 2)* [2001] 2 BCLC 436; *Kensington International Ltd v Republic of the Congo* [2006] 2 BCLC 296.

[24] *Ben Hashem v Abdulhadi Ali Shayif* [2009] 1 FLR 115, [162]; *Lindsay v O'Loughnane* [2010] EWHC 529 (QB), [137]; *Linsen International Ltd v Humpuss Sea Transport PTE Ltd* [2012] 1 BCLC 651.

[25] *Ben Hashem v Abdulhadi Ali Shayif* [2009] 1 FLR 115, [159]–[164].

[26] *VTB Capital plc v Nutritek International Corp* [2013] UKSC 5.   [27] [2013] UKSC 34.

[28] [2013] UKSC 34, [35]. Lord Neuberger agreed with this formulation: [81]. Lord Mance [100] and Lord Clarke [103] wished to leave the position open so as not to foreclose all possible future situations.

Whilst the courts may as a last resort pierce the veil in circumstances where a company is used to evade an existing obligation that was incurred by a shareholder personally, they are not receptive to piercing the veil where the corporate form is adopted in order to limit the exposure of its shareholders for the debts of the business. The freedom to use incorporation as a means of reducing future legal liability is an inherent part of company law.[29]

The implications of the very narrow confines of judicial veil piercing are examined further later in this chapter in the context of piercing the veil of incorporation between companies that are in the same corporate group.

Limited liability

Shareholders in a company limited by shares are liable to contribute only a limited amount to its assets. The minimum amount of the contribution in respect of each share is its par value—ie its fixed nominal value[30] —because that constitutes the minimum allotment price.[31] Where a share is allotted at a price higher than its par value (described as an issue at a premium), then the required contribution is par value plus the premium.[32] Company law does not set mandatory par values for shares, nor does it require companies to issue their shares at specific premiums. These are matters for companies to decide on an individual basis.[33] Many private companies start life with a nominal share capital of £100 divided into 100 £1 shares. The par value of shares in public companies is often much less than £1 because this can enhance liquidity, the argument being that, for example, ten shares of 10p each will be easier to sell than one share of £1. The mandatory rule that shares cannot be allotted by the company at less than par provides another explanation for low par values. When a company is planning to raise capital by offering its shares for investment it will have in mind the price at which it intends to offer the shares but must take into account that the offer price may have to be adjusted downwards in response to market conditions at the time when the offer is made. To enable this fine-tuning to take place, the par value of shares must be practically irrelevant, which means that there must be a large margin between the intended premium at which the shares are to be offered and their par value.

Limited liability does not follow automatically from the principle of separate legal personality.[34] Corporate personality means that the company, not its shareholders, is the person responsible for the debts of the business. The extent to which the company can require its shareholders to provide the finance to meet the liabilities of the business is a logically distinct issue. The legislation of 1844[35] that first established the procedure for incorporating a company by an administrative registration process did not provide for limited liability of the shareholders. Limited liability did not become part of the law relating to companies incorporated by registration[36] until over ten years later, when the Limited Liability Act 1855 was passed.[37] Initially, not all industries enthusiastically embraced the opportunity to limit

---

[29] *Prest v Petrodel Resources Ltd* [2013] UKSC 34, [34] *per* Lord Sumption; *Adams v Cape Industries plc* [1990] Ch 433, CA, 544 *per* Slade LJ. See also *Multinational Gas and Petrochemical Co v Multinational Gas and Petrochemical Services Ltd* [1983] Ch 258, CA, noted Lord Wedderburn, 'Multinationals and The Antiquities of Company Law.'

[30] Companies Act 2006, s 542.   [31] Companies Act 2006, s 580.   [32] Companies Act 2006, s 582.

[33] It may be a breach of duty by directors if they fail to offer new shares at the best price obtainable (*Shearer v Bercain* [1980] 3 All ER 295) but this would not put the company in breach of any general requirement of company law.

[34] PI Blumberg, *The Multinational Challenge to Corporation Law: The Search for a New Corporate Personality* (Oxford: OUP, 1993) 7.

[35] Joint Stock Companies Act 1844.

[36] The principle of limited liability already applied to companies incorporated by Charter or by specific Act of Parliament.

[37] On the struggle for limited liability in the UK: PL Davies, *Gower's Principles of Modern Company Law* 6th edn (London: Sweet & Maxwell, 1997) 40–6; A Muscat, *The Liability of the Holding Company for the Debts of its Insolvent*

liability.[38] Reluctance among banks was especially noticeable: for some time unlimited share-holder liability was regarded in the banking sector as a badge of prudence, but this attitude did not survive the collapse of the City of Glasgow bank in 1878, which was ruinous for most of the bank's shareholders.[39]

People who lend to companies also have limited exposure: they, too, are liable to contribute no more than the principal amount that they agree to lend. The basic distinction between the shareholder and the lender is that, whilst both contribute a fixed amount, only the shareholder hopes for open-ended capital gain in respect of the investment. This distinction can easily become blurred—preference shares can resemble debt finance by offering the investor only a limited capital return, lenders may make their profit on a loan by advancing less than the agreed principal on the basis that the full amount of the principal is to be repaid, and debt instruments may be structured so as to convert to equity at the option of the holder or issuer, or automatically on insolvency or other specified trigger events—but it suffices as a point of departure for the present discussion.[40] Provided the company remains solvent, lenders get back what they lent, but no more; it is the shareholders of a solvent company who are entitled to claim the residue remaining after all liabilities and claims have been met (hence shareholders can be described as the 'residual claimants'). The flip side of the contrast between a lender and a shareholder is the position in an insolvent company: there, in simple terms,[41] the order of repayment is: first, creditors who have taken security on the company's property, secondly, unsecured creditors and, finally, shareholders. Shareholders, at the bottom of the pile, have the least chance of recovering their investment but, because they benefit from limited liability, they do not have to make good any shortfall in the company's assets. The risk of corporate insolvency is thus borne in part by a company's creditors. This has led to the view that limited liability can be regarded as a device for shifting risk from shareholders to creditors.[42]

For shareholders, limited liability operates as a shield against having to contribute over and above the fixed amount of the investment they agree to make in return for their shares. This aspect of the shielding effect of limited liability leads to a number of positive consequences, which, for convenience, can be considered under the following headings, although they are in fact inter-related: promotion of entrepreneurial activity; passive investment; portfolio diversification; cost of capital; transferability of shares; and insulation from tort liabilities.

Subsidiaries (Aldershot: Dartmouth, 1996) 103–6. The Limited Liability Act 1855 contained various safeguards, including regulated minimum par values (£10), but most of these disappeared almost immediately when that Act was repealed and replaced by the Joint Stock Companies Act 1856. The historical background to limited liability in the US is explored in SB Presser, 'Thwarting the Killing of the Corporation: Limited Liability, Democracy and Economics' (1992) 87 *Northwestern University Law Review* 148, 155–6 and Blumberg, *The Multinational Challenge to Corporation Law*, 10–4.

[38] *Barclay Pharmaceuticals Ltd v Waypharm LP* [2012] EWHC 306 (Comm), [37].

[39] A Haldane, 'The Doom Loop' (2012) 34 *London Review of Books* 21; BR Cheffins, *Corporate Ownership and Control* (Oxford: OUP, 2008) 164–6 and 232–3. As Cheffins notes, banks were initially excluded from the 1855/6 legislation but were brought within its scope by amendments in 1857/8.

[40] It has been argued that capital markets would nullify the practical impact of any widescale attempt to withdraw shareholders' limited liability by devising synthetic securities which replicated all of the advantages of shares but which did not adopt that legal form: JA Grundfest, 'The Limited Future of Unlimited Liability: a Capital Markets Perspective' (1992) 102 *Yale Law Journal* 387.

[41] This rank order ignores such matters as the costs of the insolvency process, priorities between secured creditors (see ch 12), subordinated creditors (see ch 11), and different classes of shareholders (see ch 6).

[42] See DW Leebron, 'Limited Liability, Tort Victims, and Creditors' (1991) 91 *Columbia Law Review* 1565, 1584; but contrast BR Cheffins, *Company Law Theory, Structure and Operation* (Oxford: OUP, 1997) 497.

Promotion of entrepreneurial activity

Limited liability encourages entrepreneurial activity because it allows people to limit the risks involved in conducting business. This is the main function of limited liability in quasi-partnership type companies where raising share capital from persons other than the controllers of the business, or their families, is usually not a realistic option.[43] The importance of this aspect of limited liability should not be overstated because in a real-life situation it is likely to be whittled away by unlimited personal guarantees which some providers of debt finance to the business may demand from its controllers, who are likely to be both shareholders and directors simultaneously. To the extent that personal guarantees are given, contractual stipulation in effect overrides the limited-liability position established by company law.[44] Yet not all creditors of the business will be in a position to demand personal guarantees: some will lack the necessary bargaining strength whilst others may have no opportunity to bargain because they are the victims of a tort committed by the company. The controllers can thus still derive some benefit from limited liability.[45]

Passive investment

Limited liability facilitates passive investment, ie investment on the basis that the investor will not play a part in management. The fact that there is a cap on the amount at risk is an encouragement to investors to allow other people to run a business using their money. Without such a cap, a prudent[46] investor might be disinclined to invest in shares at all or, at least, would undoubtedly expect a very high return to compensate for the risks involved. The investor might also want to monitor more closely the way in which the managers of the business conduct its affairs, and that would lead to additional costs.[47]

There is a risk that, because they enjoy limited liability, shareholders may allow the managers of their company to take greater risks in the running of the business than they would have permitted if they had to face the prospect of being personally liable without limit for the failure of that business. In the event of such failure, it is the creditors who will have to absorb the loss over and above the amount of share capital that has been invested. Here we begin to see a problem with limited liability (sometimes described as a 'moral hazard'): it is the shareholders who reap the benefit from success because they get capital gains but they do not bear all the risk of failure.[48] The moral hazard aspects of limited liability are considered further in this chapter in the context of groups of companies because they can arise in an especially strong form in that context. Here the emphasis is on the upside. Successful risk-taking, which may be funded by passive investment, is a positive outcome facilitated by limited liability. As well as benefiting shareholders and ensuring that debts to creditors can be paid when due, successful risk-taking, funded by passive investment, may also produce new jobs for employees

---

[43] Presser, 'Thwarting the Killing of the Corporation,' 163 argues that limited liability was developed in the 19th century to facilitate investment in smaller firms and that it 'reflects a traditional American policy to favour the small-scale entrepreneur.'

[44] FH Easterbrook and DR Fischel, *The Economic Structure of Corporate Law* (Cambridge, Mass: Harvard University Press, 1991) 55–6.

[45] Cheffins, *Company Law Theory, Structure and Operation*, 500–1.

[46] A reckless investor, especially if he or she is virtually insolvent anyway, might not mind taking on such a degree of risk because there is always the option of bankruptcy.

[47] Easterbrook and Fischel, *The Economic Structure of Corporate Law*, 41–2. But the extent to which shareholders would intensify their monitoring of management could depend on the potential return. If high enough, they might still adopt a fairly passive role: Presser, 'Thwarting the Killing of the Corporation,' 159.

[48] Cheffins, *Company Law Theory, Structure and Operation*, 497–8; P Halpern, M Trebilcock, and S Turnbull, 'An Economic Analysis of Limited Liability in Corporation Law' (1980) 30 *University of Toronto Law Journal* 117, 144–5.

and contribute to general economic prosperity. Thus there is a public interest in the facilitation of passive investment through the provision of limited liability.[49]

Passive investment means that companies can expand their capital base whilst retaining a cohesive managerial structure involving relatively few individuals who, between them, own only a small portion of the company's issued share capital: in other words, ownership (through shareholding) and control (through managing the business) are able to separate. It was exactly because large businesses, such as railway companies, needed to expand their capital base in this way that there was such pressure for the enactment of limited liability for the shareholders of registered companies in the middle of the nineteenth century.[50] When limited liability became available, it immediately prompted a spate of new incorporations.[51] The limited liability company rapidly became the means whereby businesses could raise large amounts of finance from a large pool of investors.[52]

Portfolio diversification

Limited liability also facilitates portfolio diversification. This is the process whereby an investor can reduce the risks involved in investing in volatile securities by constructing a portfolio of investments in which those securities are balanced by others that are lower risk and which offer a lower return. Portfolio diversification does not eliminate systematic risk—ie the risk of variability in returns on investments because of the way that capital markets in general respond to macro-economic developments, such as changes in the tax regime, or exchange-rate and interest-rate swings. Portfolio diversification is all about reducing the specific risks arising from factors which are unique to the individual companies whose shares are included in the portfolio.[53]

Without limited liability, portfolio diversification could not eliminate or reduce the risks associated with investing in specific companies.[54] It would have the opposite effect of increasing risk because every time an investor added a new share to his portfolio that would create exposure to the risk of being personally liable for all of that company's debts.[55] Without portfolio diversification, and in the absence of some alternative way of dealing with risk such as the purchase of insurance,[56] companies seeking to raise share capital from investors would have to offer them a return that compensated them for taking on specific risk as well as systematic risk, with the result that share capital would become a more expensive form of finance. Some investors might be prompted to withdraw altogether from holding shares, which could cause the costs associated with raising capital by issuing shares to increase still further because of the diminution in the size of the pool of finance available in that form.[57]

---

[49] PL Davies, *Introduction to Company Law* (Oxford: Clarendon Press, 2002) 63–5.

[50] JB Baskin and PJ Miranti, *A History of Corporate Finance* (Cambridge: CUP, 1997) 138–45 trace the 19th-century development of limited liability in the UK and the US.

[51] PL Davies, *Gower's Principles of Modern Company Law* 6th edn (London: Sweet & Maxwell, 1997) 46, n 64; Blumberg, *The Multinational Challenge to Corporation Law*, 17–9.

[52] Halpern, Trebilcock, and Turnbull, 'An Economic Analysis of Limited Liability in Corporation Law', 118–9; M Radin, 'The Endless Problem of Corporate Personality' (1983) 32 *Columbia Law Review* 643, 654; HG Manne, 'Our Two Corporation Systems: Law and Economics' (1967) 53 *Virginia Law Review* 259, 260.

[53] Manne, 'Our Two Corporation Systems: Law and Economics', 262.

[54] Easterbrook and Fischel, *The Economic Structure of Corporate Law*, 43.

[55] This assumes a rule of joint and several personal liability. For an analysis of portfolio diversification under a pro rata personal liability rule, see Leebron, 'Limited Liability, Tort Victims, and Creditors', 1597–1600.

[56] On insurance as an alternative to limited liability, see Easterbrook and Fischel, *The Economic Structure of Corporate Law*, 47–9.

[57] Though if investors simply switched to synthetic securities devised by companies to replicate the features of share capital, query whether the overall cost of capital would increase significantly. On the response of the capital markets to the withdrawal of limited liability, see Grundfest, 'The Limited Future of Unlimited Liability'.

Other investors might concentrate their investment on one or two companies and engage in closer monitoring and control of the management of those companies, which could generate inefficiencies.

Cost of capital

The return required by the providers of a company's share capital and debt constitutes its cost of capital. Minimizing the cost of capital is a crucial part of running a business, and corporate finance decisions such as how much debt or share capital to have in the balance sheet, or how much profit to pay out by way of dividend, are all fundamentally about cost of capital.[58] It might be argued that limited liability should not affect cost of capital because all it does is to cause part of the risk of insolvency to fall on creditors rather than shareholders. Thus, to the extent that shareholders can limit their risk, the creditors' risk is increased and that will be reflected in the interest rates charged in respect of debt finance.[59] This argument is superficially appealing but it begins to break down on closer examination.

First, if shareholders did not have limited liability and were personally liable for all of the company's debts, that would still not eliminate the risk to creditors because their chances of being repaid would depend on the creditworthiness of all of the shareholders. Checking the creditworthiness of a large number of persons would be time-consuming and costly, as would enforcing claims against a large number of shareholders in the event of default. Limited liability reduces the costs that creditors have to incur in transacting with companies because they need to check only the creditworthiness of the company itself and, in the event of default, need to sue the company only. In theory, the reduction in transaction costs that follows from limited liability should impact positively on the rates at which the company can borrow.[60]

Secondly, a bank or other professional lender that is considering lending a large amount of money to a company can be expected to investigate the company closely. Specific investigation, in combination with the lender's accumulated general knowledge and experience of lending to companies, should put it in a strong position to assess the risks involved, with the consequence that a professional lender may price more accurately the risk for which it requires compensation than potential equity investors would have done had the company sought additional finance in that form.[61]

Another possible reason why the savings in cost of capital that flow from limited liability may not necessarily be cancelled out by higher interest rates charged by creditors to compensate them for bearing part of the risk of insolvency is that interest rates are not the only risk-management tool available to creditors. Depending on respective bargaining positions, creditors may be able to reduce their risk by taking security or imposing contractual restrictions on the operation of the business. However, some caution is appropriate here: if one creditor accepts a lower rate of interest in return for security, another unsecured creditor may charge a higher rate to compensate it for the risk that, in insolvency, it will rank behind the secured creditor and will have to absorb loss remaining after the shareholders' funds (the equity cushion) have been wiped out. Whether alternative risk-management mechanisms that are available to creditors reduce the total amount of interest charged to a borrowing

---

[58] See ch 3.

[59] Halpern, Trebilcock, and Turnbull, 'An Economic Analysis of Limited Liability in Corporation Law,' 126–9.

[60] RC Clark, *Corporate Law* (Boston: Little, Brown, 1986) 8–9; Halpern, Trebilcock, and Turnbull, 'An Economic Analysis of Limited Liability in Corporation Law,' 134–5.

[61] Clark, *Corporate Law*, 8.

company is thus a debatable point, which is considered further in chapter 3. Also considered in chapter 3 is the deductibility of interest charges, which is a further incentive for companies to opt for debt financing in order to minimize their cost of capital.

Transferability of shares

Unless the articles of association of a particular company restrict dealings, shares in limited companies are freely transferable. Shares which are admitted to CREST, the UK's mechanism for the electronic trading of securities, are bought and sold without a document of transfer. Otherwise shares are transferred by means of an instrument of transfer in accordance with the formalities prescribed in the Stock Transfer Act 1963 (where the shares have been paid for in full) or the company's articles (where they are not fully paid).[62]

If shareholders had joint and several personal liability for all of their company's debts,[63] a relevant consideration for a person investing in shares would be the ability of other shareholders to pay the company's debts. Prudent shareholders would engage in costly monitoring of each other's wealth[64] and they would want to restrict the transfer of shares so as to ensure that any new shareholders were at least as wealthy as the persons whose shares they acquired. Moreover, share prices would not be uniform: the wealth of the person acquiring the shares would affect the price because a wealthy investor could expect to pay less for the same shares than an impecunious one on the basis that he or she would be taking on more of the risk in the event of corporate default.[65] With limited liability, shares are fungible securities and trading can take place on an anonymous basis.

Tort liabilities

Another function of limited liability is that it insulates shareholders from tort liabilities that may be incurred by their company. If, say, a company pollutes a river or one of its factories blows up, then the persons who are injured or who suffer physical damage to their property can seek compensation from the company. Depending on the seriousness of the accident and the number of victims involved, the compensation costs may be very large. Limited liability means that the shareholders do not have to meet the claims from their personal resources. The victims of the tort will be unsecured creditors in the company's insolvency. They may also have a claim against the company's directors or senior managers as joint tortfeasors but, for this to succeed, they will need to establish a distinct personal liability in tort attaching to those individuals.[66]

---

[62] Companies Act 2006, Pt 21.

[63] This is only one of the ways in which an unlimited-liability regime might operate. Another is that shareholders might incur liability pro rata to their investment: see Leebron, 'Limited Liability, Tort Victims, and Creditors,' 1578–84; H Hansmann and RR Kraakman, 'Towards Unlimited Shareholder Liability for Corporate Torts' (1991) 100 *Yale Law Journal* 1879, 1892–4. Pro rata liability would remove the incentive to monitor other shareholders' wealth: Leebron, 'Limited Liability, Tort Victims, and Creditors,' 1607–8; Hansmann and Kraakman, 'Towards Unlimited Shareholder Liability for Corporate Torts,' 1903–6; Presser, 'Thwarting the Killing of the Corporation,' 160–1.

[64] Easterbrook and Fischel, *The Economic Structure of Corporate Law*, 42.

[65] Halpern, Trebilcock, and Turnbull, 'An Economic Analysis of Limited Liability in Corporation Law,' 130–1. Again, the position would be different under a rule of pro rata personal liability: Leebron, 'Limited Liability, Tort Victims, and Creditors,' 1608–10.

[66] *Williams v Natural Life Health Foods Ltd* [1998] 1 WLR 830, HL. See further R Grantham and C Rickett, 'Directors' 'Tortious' Liability: Contract, Tort or Company Law?' (1999) 62 MLR 133. For the liability of company officers for fraud see *Standard Chartered Bank v Pakistan National Shipping Corp and Ors* [2003] 1 AC 959, HL.

The present practice of the courts in the UK is not to view tort claimants (or other categories of non-adjusting creditors) more favourably than contractual creditors in relation to piercing the veil.[67] However, whether the law should be more willing to favour tort claimants is an issue that is much debated in the literature.[68] Some commentators consider that the veil of incorporation should not be allowed to shield those involved in a company from the consequences of its hazardous activities. It is argued that preserving the veil of incorporation in this situation may encourage excessive risk-taking by companies and operate unfairly in relation to the victims of the tort who, unlike contractual creditors of the company, do not have an opportunity to adjust and protect their position through a bargaining process. The debate on this topic is particularly concerned with the situation where the tortfeasor is a subsidiary within a corporate group. The corporate group is the structure that exploits the advantages of the corporate form (separate personality and limited liability) to the fullest extent. It is also the structure that often provides the starkest manifestation of the disadvantages of the corporate form for those who come into contact with it. Accordingly, before moving on to consider those disadvantages, it is appropriate now to look more closely at corporate groups as an organizational arrangement for the conduct of business activity.

The Corporate Group

Complex corporate groups, sometimes comprising thousands of subsidiaries, have become a dominant force in the world economy.[69] The structure of the international financial sector provides a good example of the modern reality: one recent study found that among the international financial conglomerates identified by regulators as 'large, complex financial institutions,' each had several hundred majority-owned subsidiaries and eight had more than 1,000 subsidiaries.[70]

Key drivers of corporate group organizational structures include asset shielding, tax planning, risk management (a group structure may provide protection against the risks involved in operating in politically unstable countries and serve to limit the jurisdiction of the courts of a particular country to certain entities within the group), administrative efficiency, and regulatory requirements.[71] The banking industry can again be referred to in order to illustrate regulation as a driver of organizational structure: the UK's new retail banking ring-fence

---

[67] *Adams v Cape Industries* [1990] Ch 433, CA.

[68] The literature includes the following: Leebron, 'Limited Liability, Tort Victims, and Creditors'; Hansmann, and Kraakman, 'Towards Unlimited Shareholder Liability for Corporate Torts'; Presser, 'Thwarting the Killing of the Corporation,' 166–72; D Goddard, 'Corporate Personality—Limited Recourse and its Limits' in R Grantham and C Rickett (eds), *Corporate Personality in the 20th Century* (Oxford: Hart, 1998) 11, 39–40.

[69] UNCITRAL, *Legislative Guide on Insolvency Law Part Three: Treatment of Enterprise Groups in Insolvency* (United Nations, 2012); PI Blumberg, KA Strasser, NL Georgakopoulos and EJ Gouvin, *Blumberg on Corporate Groups: Jurisdiction Practice and Procedure* 2nd edn (New York: Aspen Publishers, 2012); PI Blumberg, 'The Transformation of Modern Corporation Law: The Law of Corporate Groups' (2005) 37 *Connecticut Law Review* 605; T Hadden, *The Control of Corporate Groups* (London: Institute of Advanced Legal Studies, 1983); PI Blumberg, 'The American Law of Corporate Groups' in J McCahery, S Piccoitto, and C Scott (eds) *Corporate Control and Accountability* (Oxford: Clarendon Press, 1993) 305; JE Antunes, *Liability of Corporate Groups* (Deventer: Kluwer, 1994) ch 1; T Hadden, 'Regulating Corporate Groups: International Perspective' in McCahery, Piccoitto, and Scott, *Corporate Control and Accountability*, 343.

[70] R Herring and J Carmassi, 'The Corporate Structure of International Financial Conglomerates: Complexity and its Implications for Safety and Soundness' in AN Berger, P Molyneux, and JOS Wilson (eds) *The Oxford Handbook of Banking* (Oxford: OUP, 2012) ch 8. See also J Fiechter, İ Ötker-Robe, A Ilyina, M Hsu, A Santos, and J Surti, *Subsidiaries or Branches: Does One Size Fit All?* (IMF Staff Discussion Note, SDN/11/04).

[71] UNCITRAL, *Legislative Guide on Insolvency Law Part Three*, 11–4; Company Law Review Steering Group, *Modern Company Law for a Competitive Economy: Completing the Structure* (DTI, 2000, URN00/1335) 177; J Harris and A Hargovan, 'Corporate Groups: The Intersection Between Corporate and Tax Law' (2010) 32 *Sydney Law Review* 723, 725–6.

rests on the foundation of a requirement for retail banking operations to be conducted by a separate entity within a wider group.[72] Sometimes the complexity of a group structure may be attributable more to the legacy effects of past acquisition policies than to being the positive outcome of deliberate organizational choices, ie companies may be brought into a corporate group by acquisition and then simply allowed by their new owner to retain their original corporate form as subsidiaries within the group.[73] Analysis of business structures suggests that enterprises which are divided into separate divisions operating as separate profit centres with responsibility for their own administration may be preferable to enterprises that have one central management because the divisional structure reduces the length of chains of command and facilitates the setting of goals and consequential monitoring.[74] However, although the legal rules concerning groups of companies would seem to fit well with the achievement of a multi-divisional management structure, evidence suggests that the divisionalization that occurs in practice within large organizations may be unrelated to the formal corporate structure of the group.[75]

The recognition of corporate groups in company law

There is no separate branch of company law in the UK that deals with corporate groups generally,[76] but for particular purposes the Companies Act 2006 does recognize and attach legal significance to two main types of corporate group: namely, the holding or parent company and its subsidiary companies, and the parent undertaking and its subsidiary undertakings.[77] The latter type of group is relevant for the purposes of consolidated group accounts; the former is relevant in other specific statutory contexts.

The definition of the corporate group for accounting purposes

The purpose of group accounts is to give the shareholders and creditors of the holding company a clearer picture of the use of their investment than could be gleaned from its individual accounts.[78] The process of drawing up group accounts involves treating the assets and liabilities of all of the companies in the group as if they were part of the assets and liabilities of the company that heads the group. This results in the financial statements of a group

---

[72] Independent Commission on Banking, *Final Report: Recommendations* (September 2011); Financial Services (Banking Reform) Bill 2013, expected to be enacted by end December 2013.

[73] RP Austin, 'Corporate Groups' in CEF Rickett and RB Grantham (eds), *Corporate Personality in the Twentieth Century* (Oxford: Hart, 1998) 741; A Wyatt and R Mason, 'Legal and Accounting Regulatory Framework for Corporate Groups: Implications for Insolvency in Group Operations' (1998) 16 *Corporate and Securities Law Journal* 424; Muscat, *The Liability of the Holding Company for the Debts of its Insolvent Subsidiaries*, 14.

[74] OE Williamson, 'The Modern Corporation: Origin, Evolution, Attributes' (1981) 19 *Journal of Economic Literature* 1537; N Kay, 'Corporate Governance and Transaction Costs' in J McCahery, S Piccoitto, and C Scott (eds), *Corporate Control and Accountability* (Oxford: Clarendon Press, 1993) 133.

[75] Herring and Carmassi, 'The Corporate Structure of International Financial Conglomerates'; Hadden, *The Control of Corporate Groups*, 10, 12–3; Muscat, *The Liability of the Holding Company for the Debts of its Insolvent Subsidiaries*, 8–10.

[76] Hadden, *The Control of Corporate Groups*, 2–3; A Tunc, 'The Fiduciary Duties of a Dominant Shareholder' in CM Schmitthoff and F Wooldridge (eds), *Groups of Companies* (London: Sweet & Maxwell, 1991) 1–3; DD Prentice, 'Some Comments on the Law Relating to Corporate Groups' in J McCahery, S Piccoitto, and C Scott (eds) *Corporate Control and Accountability* (Oxford: Clarendon Press, 1993) 371, 372.

[77] Although not developed in the text, it may be noted that other groupings are also recognized in certain contexts (such as associated companies where one has the right to control at least one-third of the voting rights in the other; and Companies Act 2006, s 823 (attribution of corporate interests for the purpose of disclosure obligations)).

[78] C Napier and C Noke, 'Premiums and Pre-Acquisition Profits: the Legal and Accountancy Professions and Business Combinations' (1991) 54 MLR 810, 811; KJ Hopt, 'Legal Issues and Questions of Policy in the Comparative Regulation of Groups' [1996] I *Gruppi di Società* 45, 54–5.

being presented as those of a single economic entity.[79] The production of annual consolidated group accounts is mandatory for parent companies that are incorporated in the UK, save for those that are subject to the lighter disclosure regime for small companies, and certain other limited exceptions.[80]

The informational value of consolidated accounts depends crucially on the rules defining the entities to be included in the consolidation (scope rules). The narrower the scope, the more room there is for reporting entities to establish off-balance sheet special purpose vehicles (SPVs) in which they have significant economic stakes and whose activities could have significant adverse ramifications for them. The notorious story of the Enron Corporation, which grew spectacularly during the 1900s and collapsed, equally spectacularly, in 2001 after announcing a US$1 billion plus adjustment to its published accounts, shows what can happen when scope rules are restrictive. The Enron group made significant use of special purpose entities to engage in 'off-balance sheet' activities.[81] These special purpose entities were not part of the Enron corporate group for accounting purposes which made it possible to conceal debt and to manipulate financial results.[82] Consolidation requirements were revised in order to take account of lessons from the Enron experience[83] but public authorities and standard-setters always face an uphill task in trying to keep pace with markets that are populated by actors who have considerable incentives to find loopholes in order to minimize regulatory burdens. In spite of Enron-related improvements, the off-balance sheet industry continued to flourish until everything came crashing down again in the financial crisis of 2007–9. The years leading up to the financial crisis had witnessed the rapid growth of structures that employed highly-leveraged off-balance sheet vehicles and the use of transactions that took transactions temporarily off balance sheets, both of which had the effect of materially under-reporting the true extent of the economic risks that had been undertaken by many institutions.[84] Addressing the use of off-balance sheet special investment vehicles (SIVs), one influential report on the financial crisis noted that 'At the individual bank level, the classification of these as off-balance sheet proved inaccurate as a reflection of the true economic risk, with liquidity provision commitments and reputational concerns requiring many banks to take the assets back on balance sheet as the crisis grew, driving a significant one-off increase in measured leverage. But even if this had not been the case, the contribution of SIVs and conduits to total system leverage ... would still have increased total system vulnerability.'[85] It is no surprise, therefore, that there has been another round of reform of the consolidation requirements as part of the regulatory response to the financial crisis.[86] This has involved a

---

[79] International Financial Reporting Standard 10, *Consolidated Financial Statements* (IFRS 10).

[80] Companies Act 2006, ss 399–402.

[81] *Arthur Andersen LLP v U.S.* 125 S.Ct. 2129, U.S., 2005, 2132.

[82] In *re Enron Corp Securities, Derivative & ERISA Litigation* 235 F Supp 2d 549 (SD Tex 2002), 618. SL Schwarcz, 'Enron and the Use and Abuse of Special Purpose Entities in Corporate Structures' (2002) 70 *University of Cincinnati Law Review* 1309.

[83] Directive 83/349/EEC on consolidated accounts, [1983] OJ L193/1 (Seventh Company Law Directive, as amended), Art 34(7)(a), which was added in response to concern about off-balance sheet activities. The EU Directives on individual and consolidated accounts have been overhauled: Directive 2013/34/EU of the European Parliament and of the Council of 26 June 2013 on the annual financial statements, consolidated financial statements, and related reports of certain types of undertakings, amending Directive 2006/43/EC of the European Parliament and of the Council and repealing Council Directives 78/660/EEC and 83/349/EEC, [2013] OJ L182/19. Member States must implement the new requirements by July 2015.

[84] The most notorious individual example being the 'Repo 105/108' transactions used by Lehman Bros to remove securities inventory from the balance sheet: AR Valukas, *In Re Lehman Brothers Holdings Inc* (United States Bankruptcy Court Southern District of New York, Chapter 11 Case No 08 13555, Examiner's Report), vol 3.

[85] A Turner, *The Turner Review: A Regulatory Response to the Global Banking Crisis* (FSA, March 2009) 20.

[86] eg IFRS 10 and International Financial Reporting Standard 12, *Disclosure of Interests in Other Entities* (IFRS 12), published in May 2011.

move away from 'bright line' rules to more open-textured standards but only time will tell whether the new requirements will fare better than their predecessors in ensuring that all material economic risks are properly represented in financial statements and that opportunities for creative structuring are appropriately contained.

The UK position on the scope of consolidation requirements is now found in the Companies Act 2006, which gives domestic effect to EU requirements,[87] and in accounting standards.[88] The Companies Act 2006, sections 404–5 provide that where a parent company prepares Companies Act group accounts, all the subsidiary undertakings of the company must be included in the consolidation, subject to limited exceptions. In this context, 'undertaking' means a body corporate, partnership, or unincorporated association carrying on a trade or business, with or without a view to profit.[89] An entity is a subsidiary undertaking (SU) of another entity (the parent or 'P') where: (1) P holds a majority of the voting rights in SU; (2) P is a member of SU and has the right to appoint or remove the majority of its board of directors; or (3) P is a member of SU and controls alone, pursuant to an agreement with other shareholders, a majority of the voting rights in SU.[90] P is treated as a member of an undertaking if any of its SUs is a member of that undertaking and it is also treated as a member of an undertaking in which shares are held by a person acting on its behalf or on behalf of any of its SUs.[91] References to voting rights in a company are to rights conferred on shareholders in respect of their shares or, in the case of a company not having a share capital, on members, to vote at general meetings of the company on all, or substantially all, matters.[92] The reference to the right to appoint or remove a majority of the board of directors is to the right to appoint or remove directors holding a majority of the voting rights at meetings of the board on all, or substantially all, matters.[93]

In addition, there exists a parent and subsidiary undertaking relationship giving rise to an accounting consolidation obligation where: (1) P has the right to exercise a dominant influence over SU by virtue of provisions contained in SU's articles or by virtue of a control contract (legal control);[94] or (2) P has the power to exercise or actually exercises dominant influence over SU, or P and SU are managed on a unified basis (factual control).[95] These tests recognize that a company can effectively control other entities even without majority voting control: for example, if the majority of the shareholders are diversified passive investors, each holding a small proportion of its shares, one shareholder with a more substantial shareholding may in practice (as a consequence of the voting apathy of other shareholders) be in a position to control the outcome of shareholder meetings notwithstanding that it does not formally control the majority of the votes.

The test based on factual control is more significant in practice because the criteria for legal control are quite formal and rigid.[96] Where the operators of a business want to avoid a consolidation obligation, they are unlikely to regard the legal control limb of the statutory scope rules as being a major impediment to the achievement of this goal. The factual control

---

[87] Currently the Companies Act 2006 implements Directive 78/660/EEC and Directive 83/349/EEC (Fourth and Seventh Company Law Directives on annual accounts and consolidated accounts). The EU requirements are replaced by Directive 2013/34/EU, which must be implemented by July 2015.

[88] Financial Reporting Standard 2, *Accounting for Subsidiary Undertakings* (FRS 2) (to be withdrawn for accounting periods beginning on or after 1 January 2015). The new domestic framework will comprise: FRS 100, *Application of Financial Reporting Requirements*; FRS 101, *Reduced Disclosure Framework*; FRS 102, *The Financial Reporting Standard applicable in the United Kingdom and Republic of Ireland*; and *Financial Reporting Standard for Smaller Entities* (FRSSE) (updated July 2013, with changes to be effective January 2015).

[89] Companies Act 2006, s 1161.   [90] Companies Act 2006, s 1162(a), (b), and (d) and Sch 7.

[91] Companies Act 2006, s 1162(3).   [92] Companies Act 2006, Sch 7, para 2.

[93] Companies Act 2006, Sch 7, para 3.   [94] Companies Act 2006, s 1162(2)(c) and Sch 7, para 4.

[95] Companies Act 2006, s 1162(4).

[96] These requirements are specified in Companies Act 2006, Sch 7, para 4.

test is less easy to circumvent. Actual exercise of a dominant influence implies the exercise of an influence that achieves the result that the operating and financial policies of the undertaking influenced are set in accordance with the wishes of the holder of the influence and for its benefit whether or not those wishes are explicit.[97] The power to exercise dominant influence is a power that, if exercised, would give rise to the actual exercise of dominant influence. The actual exercise of a dominant influence should be identified by looking at the effect in practice. A power of veto may amount to exercise of a dominant influence in an appropriate case. The actual exercise of dominant influence may be interventionist or non-interventionist. Intervention that occurs only rarely on critical matters could amount to the exercise of a dominant influence. Entities would be 'managed on a unified basis' where the whole of the operations of the undertakings are integrated and they are managed as a single unit.

Where an EU company has its securities admitted to trading on a regulated market in the EU, it is obliged to draw up its consolidated accounts in accordance with International Financial Reporting Standards (IFRS)/International Accounting Standards (IAS) rather than under its national accounting system.[98] The relevant definitions of entities to be included in the consolidation are set out in IFRS 10, *Consolidated Financial Statements*, supplemented by *Effect Analysis*, which identifies typical scenarios and provides guidance on the application of the applicable requirements. Under IFRS 10, a parent entity is defined as an entity that controls one or more other entities. Control exists when the investor is exposed, or has rights, to variable returns from its involvement with the investee and has the ability to affect those returns through its power over the investee. The *Effect Analysis* considers the assessment of control by reference to a series of examples in which no single investor holds more than 50 per cent of the voting rights of an investee.

The definition of the corporate group for other purposes

Outside the accounting context, other sections of the companies legislation also employ the concept of the corporate group for specific purposes: for example, a subsidiary is prohibited from holding shares in its parent (or holding) company[99] and financial assistance by a subsidiary for the acquisition of shares in a parent is prohibited where the subsidiary or the parent is a public company.[100] The definition of the corporate group that applies for the non-accounting provisions overlaps with, but is narrower than, the accounting definition. A company is a parent (or holding) company and another company is a subsidiary if (1) P holds a majority of the voting rights in S; (2) P is a member of S and has the right to appoint or remove the majority of its board of directors; or (3) P is a member of S and controls alone, pursuant to an agreement with other shareholders, a majority of the voting rights in S.[101] If S in turn has a subsidiary (SS), SS is also a subsidiary of P.[102] A wholly owned subsidiary is one in which S has no members apart from P or P and other wholly owned subsidiaries of P.[103] These tests are broadly the same as the first set of tests that are used for the accounting definition of the corporate group (but see later for discussion of one important technical difference) and thus, it is the control of the majority of the voting rights, not the majority in number of the shares or of the directors, that matters.[104] The Companies Act 2006 tests for

[97] The remainder of this paragraph is based on guidance in FRS 2.
[98] Regulation (EC) 1606/2002 of the European Parliament and of the Council of 19 July 2002 on the application of international accounting standards [2002] OJ L243/1 (IAS Regulation); Companies Act 2006, s 403.
[99] Companies Act 2006, s 136.   [100] Companies Act 2006, ss 677–80.
[101] Companies Act 2006, s 1159 and Sch 6.   [102] Companies Act 2006, s 1159 and Sch 6.
[103] Companies Act 2006, s 1159(2).   [104] Companies Act 2006, Sch 6.

the existence of a corporate group that are based on legal control and factual control do not apply outside the accounting context.

At the level of detail there is one difference between the definitions of a group for accounting and non-accounting purposes that has proved to be important. In the accounting context, there is a deeming provision whereby an undertaking is deemed to be a member of an undertaking in which shares are held by another person acting on its behalf.[105] There is no such deeming provision in the non-accounting definition. This was pertinent in *Enviroco Ltd v Farstad Supply A/S*[106] where shares in a group company had been pledged by way of security and the name of the pledgee bank had been entered in the company's register of members.[107] The Supreme Court held that the change of membership meant that the company in question was no longer a subsidiary of the pledgor under the limb of the definition whereby the relationship arises if P is a member of S and controls alone, pursuant to an agreement with other shareholders, a majority of the voting rights in S. This finding was notwithstanding that the deed of pledge provided that until the security became enforceable the full voting and other rights and powers in respect of the shares remained exercisable by the pledgor because the requirement also to be a 'member' was not satisfied. As a result, the company was not entitled to benefit from an indemnity in favour of the pledgor's group. The outcome in this case can be described as 'certainly odd and possibly absurd'[108] but it would have amounted to impermissible judicial legislation for the Supreme Court to have found otherwise. Where a company enters into a contract containing provisions that relate to it and other members of its group, or has such provisions in its articles, it is necessary to establish contextually how the group is defined. This is a matter of drafting and contractual interpretation and there is no presumption that any of the statutory definitions is imported into contracts or other arrangements to which a company is a party. In the *Enviroco* case the contractual documentation had expressly imported the definition of subsidiary from the companies legislation.

Substantive company law and the corporate group: a general overview

The fundamentals are clear: each company within a corporate group is a separate and distinct legal entity; assets and liabilities belong to the individual companies, not to the group as a whole; and directors of subsidiaries owe the duties that attach to their office to the particular companies on whose boards they serve, not to the parent company or to the group as a whole. However, the fact that companies are related to each other can affect the way in which general principles of company law, such as those relating to directors' duties, actually operate. For example, whilst it is technically correct to say that a director of a subsidiary company owes his duties to the subsidiary rather than the parent company,[109] the core obligation owed by directors is that, outside insolvency situations, they must promote the success of their company for the benefit of its *members*.[110] This means, in effect, that directors of a solvent subsidiary can discharge their duties to the subsidiary by acting for the benefit of the parent company, at least so long as the subsidiary is wholly owned or the interests of the parent company and any minority shareholders in the subsidiary coincide.[111] Where a subsidiary is in, or near, insolvency the position is different, however, because the directors of the subsidiary must consider

---

[105] Companies Act 2006, s 1162(3).   [106] [2011] 1 WLR 921, SC.
[107] Companies Act 2006, s 112 (definition of 'member' by reference to registration).
[108] *Enviroco*, [47] *per* Lord Collins of Mapesbury.   [109] *Lindgren v L & P Estates Ltd* [1968] Ch 572, CA.
[110] Companies Act 2006, s 172.
[111] *Commissioner of Taxpayer Audit and Assessment v Cigarette Company of Jamaica Ltd* [2012] STC 1045, PC, [14] *per* Lord Walker quoting S Mortimore (ed), *Company Directors* (Oxford: OUP, 2009) para 12.18.

creditors' interests rather than members' interests and, moreover, this means the creditors of their own particular company rather than of the group as a whole.[112] Creditors' interests intrude because they become prospectively entitled, through the mechanism of liquidation, to deal with the company's assets.[113] Insolvency concerns also affect the position of directors of subsidiary companies in another important respect: directors can usually protect themselves from breach of duty claims by having their actions ratified by the company's shareholders but shareholder ratification is ineffective when a company's solvency is in doubt.[114] The ineffectiveness of shareholder ratification in these circumstances can be rationalized on the basis that a dire financial situation gives rise to a control shift in favour of creditors. If shareholders were left in control they would have incentives to continue the business on a speculative basis since they have nothing left to lose (because of limited liability): if the gamble did not pay off, the additional losses would fall on the creditors.[115]

In the context of petitions for relief from unfairly prejudicial conduct under the Companies Act 2006, section 994 the courts have sometimes been willing to move away from a rigid, legalistic approach to the entities within a corporate group. To succeed under this section, a petitioner must show that the affairs of the company of which he or she is a member have been conducted in an unfairly prejudicial manner. It has been held that, in an appropriate case, the conduct of a parent company—or of such of its directors who happen to be directors of the relevant subsidiary—towards a subsidiary may constitute conduct in the affairs of that subsidiary[116] and that the conduct of a subsidiary—or of some or all of its directors who happen as well to be directors of the parent company—may be regarded as part of the conduct of the affairs of the parent company.[117]

Despite the fact that, as these examples illustrate, company law does not completely ignore intra-group relationships between companies and there is some 'legal adaptation to reality,'[118] the overriding general legal principle that all companies are separate and distinct entities and are not, in law, a single enterprise even where they are part of a group, continues to exert a powerful force. The emphasis on the separate entity principle is especially noticeable in situations where a group is affected by insolvencies at entity level: the directors of the failed entity may be personally liable for breach of their duties but, generally speaking, the parent company and other companies in the group can walk away with no financial

---

[112] Companies Act 2006, s 172(3); *West Mercia Safetywear Ltd v Dodd* [1988] BCLC 250, 252; *Facia Footwear v Hinchliffe* [1998] 1 BCLC 218, 228; *MDA Investment Management Ltd* [2004] 1 BCLC 217.

[113] *Re Idessa (UK) Ltd* [2012] 1 BCLC 80, [54].

[114] *Moore Stephens v Stone Rolls Ltd* [2009] AC 1391, HL, [236] *per* Lord Mance; *Re New World Alliance Pty Ltd; Sycotex Pty Ltd v Baseler* (1994) 122 ALR 531, 550. See further A Keay, 'Directors Taking Into Account Creditors' Interests' (2003) 24 *Company Lawyer* 300; A Keay, 'Directors' Duties to Creditors: Contractarian Concerns Relating to Efficiency and Over-Protection of Creditors' (2003) 66 MLR 665; A Keay, *Company Directors' Responsibilities to Creditors* (London: Routledge-Cavendish, 2007); P Davies, 'Directors' Creditor-Regarding Duties in Respect of Trading Decisions Taken in the Vicinity of Insolvency' (2006) 7 *European Business Organization Law Review* 301.

[115] However, the efficiency of the imposition of a general creditor-facing duty can be debated: O Couwenberg and SJ Lubben, 'Solving Creditor Problems in the Twilight Zone: Superfluous Law and Inadequate Private Solutions' (24 June 2011), Seton Hall Public Law Research Paper No 1871745, available at <http://ssrn.com/abstract=1871745> accessed July 2013; F Tung, 'Gap Filling in the Zone of Insolvency' (2006-7) 1 *Journal of Business and Technology Law* 607; SM Bainbridge, 'Much Ado About Little? Directors' Fiduciary Duties in the Vicinity of Insolvency' (2006-7) 1 *Journal of Business and Technology Law* 335; RB Campbell and CW Frost, 'Managers' Fiduciary Duties in Financially Distressed Corporations: Chaos in Delaware (and Elsewhere)' (2007) 32 *Journal of Corporation Law* 491.

[116] *Scottish Co-operative Wholesale Society Ltd v Meyer* [1959] AC 324, HL; *Nicholas v Soundcraft Electronics Ltd* [1993] BCLC 3, CA.

[117] *Re Citybranch Group Ltd, Gross v Rackind* [2004] 4 All ER 735, CA. R Goddard and HC Hirt, 'Section 459 and Corporate Groups' [2005] JBL 247.

[118] J Dine, *The Governance of Corporate Groups* (Cambridge: CUP, 2000) 43.

consequences beyond writing off their equity investment and any intra-group debts that will not be repaid. Whilst the same is true of any individual or firm that holds shares in or is a creditor of a failed company, the downside consequences of limited liability often appear in a more acute form when they arise within the corporate group context. This issue merits closer examination.

Insolvency within a corporate group[119]

The starting point here is that companies that hold shares in other companies enjoy limited liability in respect of their investment. There is no legal distinction between the liability position of a parent company with respect to the debts of its subsidiaries and that of an individual investor who acquires shares: each is liable only up to the nominal amount of the shares which comprise the investment plus any premium charged in respect of the shares when they were first issued. This means that a network of companies can be formed in order to limit a group's contractual liability to outsiders and to create contractual liability between members of the group. It also means that it is possible to limit the group's potential exposure to tort victims by conducting hazardous activities through subsidiaries. Should the risky venture end in disaster, the parent will lose the value of its investment in the subsidiary but the creditors of the subsidiary cannot look to the parent to make good the shortfall in the subsidiary's assets.

An illustration of the use of the corporate form to create contractual liabilities within a group is provided by *Re Polly Peck plc*.[120] In this case a subsidiary, incorporated in the Cayman Islands, made a public issue of debt securities and lent the proceeds to its parent company. The parent company guaranteed the issue. It was held that the subsidiary was entitled to prove in the insolvency of its parent in respect of the on-loan. The court rejected the argument that the subsidiary was simply acting as the agent of its parent in issuing the debt securities, which would have meant that the on-loan had no legal significance, and also held that the arrangement was not a sham.

Whether a parent company should be held liable to make good shortfalls in its insolvent subsidiaries is an issue that is much discussed by academics.[121] An argument for preserving the veil of incorporation between companies within a group is that this facilitates managerial risk-taking, which is important if companies are to expand for the benefit of all of the constituencies who have an interest in them and for general economic prosperity.[122] According to this argument, investors will be encouraged to invest in the shares of a holding company which caps its potential losses in respect of particularly risky activities to the amount of share capital that it invests in the subsidiaries through which those activities are conducted.[123] Another argument for preserving the veil is that contractual creditors

---

[119] See generally, V Finch, *Corporate Insolvency Law Perspectives and Principles* 2nd edn (Cambridge: CUP, 2009) 581–96.

[120] [1996] 2 All ER 433.

[121] See in particular, JM Landers, 'A Unified Approach to Parent, Subsidiary, and Affiliate Questions in Bankruptcy' (1975) 42 *University of Chicago Law Review* 589; RA Posner, 'The Rights of Creditors of Affiliated Corporations' (1976) 43 *University of Chicago Law Review* 499; JM Landers, 'Another Word on Parents, Subsidiaries and Affiliates in Bankruptcy' (1976) 43 *University of Chicago Law Review* 527. For an English law perspective, see CM Schmitthoff, 'The Wholly Owned and the Controlled Subsidiary' [1978] JBL 218; Lord Wedderburn, 'Multinationals and the Antiquities of Company Law'; DD Prentice, 'Some Comments on the Law Relating to Corporate Groups'; H Collins, 'Ascription of Legal Responsibility to Groups in Complex Patterns of Economic Integration' (1990) 53 MLR 731; R Rhee, 'Bonding Limited Liability' (2010) 51 *William and Mary Law Review* 1417.

[122] Leebron, 'Limited Liability, Tort Victims and Creditors,' 1617–8.

[123] Presser, 'Thwarting the Killing of the Corporation,' 174–5; Blumberg, *The Multinational Challenge to Corporation Law*, 130–3.

assume that each company will be liable for its own debts but no more, and bargain accordingly. If piercing the veil within a corporate group were to become commonplace, thereby eroding the principle that a company's assets are only available to pay the debts owing to its own creditors, that would be likely to add to companies' costs of borrowing because creditors would need to extend their investigations into the creditworthiness of the group as a whole.[124]

The primary argument for piercing the veil within a corporate group relates to control: a corporate group is, ultimately, an integrated economic enterprise and the parent controls, or has the power to control, its subsidiaries' activities for the benefit of the group as a whole; therefore, the parent should be exposed to liability for the activities of its subsidiaries.[125] Whilst the individuals who hold shares in a small private company may also be its controllers, it can be argued that their position is not analogous to that of a parent company because they could be personally ruined in the event of veil-piercing to make them liable for the company's debts; piercing the veil between parent and subsidiary companies might make the parent insolvent but the shareholders in the parent would still be shielded from personal liability by the limited liability that they would continue to enjoy in respect of their investment.[126] In practical terms, moreover, the centralized group treasury arrangements and other enterprise-wide organizational arrangements that are commonly found in modern corporate groups mean that the relationships between the relevant entities are often very different from those between companies and human shareholders.[127] The point can also be made that the economic arguments about limited liability being necessary to enable companies to attract passive investment, to allow investors to engage in portfolio diversification, and to permit the functioning of capital markets do not apply in relation to a parent company's investment in a subsidiary.[128] Strict adherence to the preservation of the veil of incorporation may encourage excessive risk-taking by managers:[129] should an independent company which is not part of a group (or which is the holding company of a group) fail, the management will lose their jobs but that constraint against risk-taking is less powerful in relation to a subsidiary because there is always the possibility of its management being redeployed in other parts of the group in the event of its failure.[130] Moreover, although directors are legally obliged to act in the interests of their own company and not in the interests of the group of companies to which it may belong,[131] the distinction between group interests and those of the individual companies can easily become blurred in practice; and, except where there are insolvency concerns, irregularities, or breaches of duty by the directors of a group company in the movements of value around a corporate group can, in any event, be cured by the passing of a ratifying resolution by any other companies in the group which are the owners of its shares. The net result of these considerations is that companies within a group may deal with each other otherwise than on an arm's length basis to the detriment of creditors who cannot object unless they have imposed contractual restrictions on such activities and can monitor compliance effectively,[132] and of minority shareholders in the subsidiaries whose

---

[124] In other words, asset partitioning benefits, discussed earlier in this chapter, would no longer apply.

[125] Blumberg, *The Multinational Challenge to Corporation Law*, 123–4; Antunes, *Liability of Corporate Groups*, 131–2.

[126] Posner, 'The Rights of Creditors of Affiliated Corporations,' 511–2.

[127] UNCITRAL, *Legislative Guide on Insolvency Law Part Three*, 16–7, 48–51.

[128] Blumberg, *The Multinational Challenge to Corporation Law*, 133–40.

[129] Blumberg, *The Multinational Challenge to Corporation Law*, 134.

[130] Easterbrook and Fischel, *The Economic Structure of Corporate Law*, 56–7.

[131] *Lindgren v L & P Estates Ltd* [1968] Ch 572, CA.

[132] The complexity of group activities may in fact make it hard for creditors to follow the movement of assets around the group: Finch, *Corporate Insolvency Law Perspectives and Principles*, 584. For an example of intensely

only effective means of redress may be to allege that such dealing constitutes unfairly prejudicial relief from which they should be granted relief under section 994 of the Companies Act
2006.[133] A particular argument for piercing the veil within a corporate group is that limited
liability operates unfairly in relation to the victims of torts by subsidiaries since they cannot
negotiate around it.[134]

There is undoubtedly something troubling about the way in which corporate group structures can, seemingly, be used by those who control businesses to obtain the best of both
worlds—to exploit the benefits of formal legal structures and yet at the same time to benefit
from the synergies of an integrated enterprise-based operational model. However, balancing
the social benefits of the corporate structure against its costs is a large policy question that
the judiciary is not ideally positioned to address. For this reason, the resistance of the courts
in the UK to the adoption of an enterprise approach in relation to liability, even where tort
liability of companies within a corporate group is involved, is defensible.[135] The courts correctly emphasize the importance of maintaining the principle that the assets of a company
are available to pay its creditors and no others.[136] Closeness of companies within a group and
centralized managerial control are not deemed to be sufficient to justify the court disregarding the corporate structure.[137]

The leading case on corporate groups and piercing the corporate veil is the decision of the
English Court of Appeal in *Adams v Cape Industries plc*[138] which was an attempt by victims of
a tort (ie personal injuries suffered as a consequence of exposure to asbestos dust) to enforce
a judgment that had been obtained in the US. The company law point in issue was whether
the US courts could assert jurisdiction over an English company on the basis of the presence within the US of certain subsidiaries. The Court rejected the argument that the various
companies should be treated as one group enterprise. It reaffirmed the fundamental legal
principle that each company in a group of companies is a separate legal entity possessed of
separate rights and liabilities.[139] It distinguished earlier cases[140] appearing to support a group

---

complex inquiries into the location of ownership of assets around the entities of a failed corporate group, see *Re
Lehman Brothers International (Europe) (in administration) Pearson v Lehman Brothers Finance SA* [2012] 2 BCLC
151, CA, examined in M Bridge and J Braithwaite, 'Private Law and Financial Crises' [2013] *Journal of Corporate
Law Studies* 361.

[133] *Stein v Blake* [1998] 1 All ER 724, CA, illustrates the type of problems that can occur within a corporate group
(transfers of assets by the controlling shareholder). The Court of Appeal held that the other shareholder had no
personal common law claim arising from the facts.

[134] Hansmann and Kraakman, 'Towards Unlimited Shareholder Liability for Corporate Torts'; Leebron, 'Limited
Liability, Tort Victims, and Creditors', 1612–26; Blumberg *The Multinational Challenge to Corporation Law*, 135–6;
Rhee, 'Bonding Limited Liability'. However it is overly simplistic to regard all contract creditors in the same way.
Many contractual creditors have no real opportunity to engage in bargaining, junior employees being an example
that springs readily to mind. DD Prentice, 'Groups of Companies: The English Experience' in KJ Hopt (ed), *Groups
of Companies in European Laws* (Berlin: W de Gruyter, 1982) 99, 105 describes employees (and the revenue authorities) as 'quasi-involuntary creditors' who normally do not contract around limited liability. Prentice would also
include unsecured trading creditors in the category of those who do not normally engage in such bargaining.

[135] For a recent discussion of the English courts' response to the 'single economic unit' approach: *Linsen
International Ltd v Humpuss Sea Transport PTE Ltd* [2012] 1 BCLC 651. Compare AA Berle, 'The Theory of
Enterprise Entity' (1947) 47 *Columbia Law Review* 343 and Blumberg, *The Multinational Challenge to Corporation
Law*, ch 5, discussing the acceptance of enterprise principles in the US courts and legislation.

[136] See *Charterbridge Corp v Lloyd's Bank Ltd* [1970] Ch 62; *Ford & Carter Ltd v Midland Bank Ltd* (1979) 129 NLJ
543, HL, 544 *per* Lord Wilberforce.

[137] *Linsen International Ltd v Humpuss Sea Transport PTE Ltd* [2012] 1 BCLC 651, [39].

[138] [1990] Ch 433, CA.   [139] *The Albazero* [1977] AC 774, CA and HL, 807 *per* Roskill LJ.

[140] Including the notorious decision of the Court of Appeal in *DHN Food Distributors Ltd v Tower Hamlets LBC*
[1976] 1 WLR 852, CA. The judgment of Lord Denning MR in this case is probably the most positive endorsement
of the group enterprise approach in English law. The authority of the case is now slim: as well as being distinguished
in *Adams*, its correctness was doubted by the Scottish House of Lords in *Woolfson v Strathclyde Regional Council*
1978 SLT 159, HL.

enterprise approach as being concerned with specific statutes or contracts which justified the treatment of parent and subsidiary as one unit. Rather surprisingly, in view of the outright rejection of it in the *Adams* decision, a group enterprise argument resurfaced in *Re Polly Peck plc*.[141] The Court there regarded as 'persuasive' the argument that, in reality, the issue of debt securities was by the group rather than by the Cayman Islands subsidiary through which it had been channelled but ruled that it was precluded by *Adams*, a decision of a higher court, from accepting the group enterprise approach.[142]

The Court of Appeal in the *Adams* case confirmed that the court does not have a general discretion to disregard the veil of incorporation on grounds of justice. With regard to the argument that the corporate structure in that case was a façade, because it had been adopted to remove group assets from the USA to avoid liability for asbestos claims whilst at the same time continuing to trade in asbestos there, the Court concluded:

> We do not accept as a matter of law that the court is entitled to lift the corporate veil as against a defendant company which is the member of a corporate group merely because the corporate structure has been used so as to ensure that the legal liability (if any) in respect of particular future activities of the group (and correspondingly the risk of enforcement of that liability) will fall on another member of the group rather than the defendant company. Whether or not this is desirable, the right to use a corporate structure in this manner is inherent in our corporate law. [Counsel] urged on us that the purpose of the operation was in substance that Cape would have the practical benefit of the group's asbestos trade in the United States of America without the risk of tortious liability. This may be so. However, in our judgment, Cape was in law entitled to organise the group's affairs in that manner.[143]

Earlier in this chapter, the point was made that recent authorities have confined judicial veil piercing to a very narrow scope. The assessment of the doctrinal position does not change when the issues are examined specifically from a corporate group perspective:[144] even within the corporate group context, the scope for veil piercing is, at best, extremely limited and depends on a finding of improper use of the corporate form by its controllers to shield themselves from the consequences of their own wrongdoing.[145] Furthermore, if there is an impropriety that allows the court to pierce the veil, the effect will not be to make other group companies directly liable under the contracts of the failed entity but instead to allow for some other remedy such as the unravelling of intra-group transactions by which assets were stripped out of the defunct entity ahead of its failure.

---

[141] [1996] 2 All ER 433.

[142] [1996] 2 All ER 433, 447. Counsel's argument was based on the acceptance in *Adams v Cape Industries plc* [1990] Ch 433, CA that there were special cases where contract or statute permitted or required a group enterprise approach, but the court refused to put the insolvency rule against double proof into this special category.

[143] [1990] Ch 433, CA, 544.

[144] DD Prentice, 'Group Indebtedness' in CM Schmitthoff and F Wooldridge (eds), *Groups of Companies* (London: Sweet & Maxwell, 1991) 77: 'piercing the corporate veil is very much the exception to the rule and probably in the majority of cases the courts will refuse to do so.' The decisions of the Supreme Court in *VTB* [2013] UKSC 5 and *Prest* [2013] UKSC 34 confirm the accuracy of Prentice's observation.

[145] *Linsen International Ltd v Humpuss Sea Transport PTE Ltd* [2012] 1 BCLC 651. Judicial conservatism with regard to lifting the veil is not confined to the UK courts. Discussing the position in Australia and New Zealand, see R Baxt and T Lane, 'Developments in Relation to Corporate Groups and the Responsibilities of Directors—Some Insights and New Directions' (1998) 16 *Corporate and Securities Law Journal* 628; JH Farrar, 'Legal Issues Involving Corporate Groups' (1998) 16 *Corporate and Securities Law Journal* 184; The Australian High Court has generally held fast to an entity-based approach: Harris and Hargovan, 'Corporate Groups: The Intersection Between Corporate and Tax Law,' 726. For a view that the test for piercing the corporate veil propounded by Slade LJ in *Adams* is doctrinally unsustainable see: M Moore, 'A Temple Built on Faulty Foundations: Piercing the Corporate Veil and the Legacy of Salomon v Salomon' [2006] JBL 180.

Alternatives to piercing the veil: agency[146]

If it can be shown that a subsidiary acted as the agent of its parent, then, on ordinary agency principles, the liability will attach to the parent as principal.[147] However, there is no presumption that a subsidiary acts as the agent of its parent and this will depend on the facts pertaining to the relationship between parent and subsidiary.[148] Insufficient capital to engage in business independently can be an indicator that the subsidiary is an agent,[149] but capitalization needs to be considered in conjunction with the purpose for which the subsidiary exists: for example, if a subsidiary is established purely as a vehicle for the raising of debt, it may have a small amount of equity (with alternative forms of credit enhancement being built into the terms of the issue) but still be an independent operator rather than an agent.[150] Evidence that the subsidiary has a board of directors, all or most of whom are also directors or senior executives of the holding company, does not necessarily indicate an agency relationship between it and the parent company.[151]

Alternatives to piercing the veil: contractual guarantees

It is a trite observation that creditors of a failing company who are in the fortunate position of holding guarantees from other companies in its group may be able, in effect, to shift the liability around the group by enforcing their contractual claims.[152] There are some potential pitfalls that persons considering lending to a group company on the security of personal guarantees from other companies in its group need to look out for. One is that the other group companies may seek to resist giving guarantees and instead offer comfort letters in which they state that it is their policy to ensure that other companies in the group are, and will be, in a position to meet their liabilities. In *Kleinwort Benson Ltd v Malaysia Mining Corporation Bhd*[153] the Court of Appeal held that a comfort letter in these terms was merely a statement of present fact regarding intentions and that it was not a contractual promise as to future conduct.[154] Another potential difficulty stems from the fact that directors are required to serve their own company rather than the group as a whole. If directors of a guarantor company focus on the interests of the group and these do not coincide with the interests of their company, the guarantee may be tainted by breach of duty. Yet another potential pitfall is that if the solvency of the guarantor company is in doubt, the guarantee may be vulnerable under provisions of the Insolvency Act 1986 concerned with preferences and transactions at an undervalue.[155]

---

[146] Some form of trust-beneficiary or nominator-nominee relationship between companies in a group could also suffice to shift liability.

[147] *Canada Rice Mills Ltd v R* [1939] 3 All ER 991, PC; *Firestone Tyre and Rubber Co Ltd v Lewellin (Inspector of Taxes)* [1957] 1 All ER 561, HL; *Rainham Chemical Works v Belvedere Fish Guano Co* [1921] 2 All ER 465, HL.

[148] *Adams v Cape Industries plc* [1990] Ch 433, CA.

[149] *Re FG Films* [1953] 1 All ER 615. Landers, 'A Unified Approach to Parent, Subsidiary, and Affiliate Questions in Bankruptcy', 621.

[150] *Re Polly Peck plc* [1996] 2 All ER 433, 445–6.   [151] *Re Polly Peck plc* [1996] 2 All ER 433, 445–6.

[152] *Cattles plc v Welcome Financial Services Ltd* [2010] BCLC 712, CA.

[153] [1989] 1 WLR 379, CA. See also *Re Atlantic Computers plc* [1995] BCC 696.

[154] In *Wake v Renault (UK) Ltd* 15 Tr L 514, *The Times*, 1 August 1996, Robert Walker J noted that a comfort letter, even though not legally binding, may not be pointless since it may have important practical consequences: for instance in enabling a subsidiary company to borrow on more favourable terms than might otherwise be available, or in enabling auditors to sign off accounts on a going concern basis.

[155] Insolvency Act 1986, ss 238–41. The application of s 238 (transactions at undervalue) in the context of intra-group guarantees is considered by R Parry, *Transaction Avoidance in Insolvencies* (Oxford: OUP, 2001) ch 4.

Alternatives to piercing the veil: tort claims against other companies

A claimant will be able to obtain recompense from other group companies that are still viable if it can be established that those other companies are directly liable to the claimant in tort. Whether liability can be spread around a corporate group in this way depends on the application of the ordinary principles of the law of tort for the determination of liability.[156] An illustration is provided by *Chandler v Cape plc*, in which a parent company was held liable in negligence to a former employee of a defunct subsidiary for asbestosis contracted as a consequence of exposure to asbestos dust at work.[157] Applying the threefold test for a duty of care established by the seminal decision of the judicial House of Lords in *Caparo Industries Plc v Dickman*,[158] the court at first instance found that there had been a systemic failure to put in place proper safety arrangements, that the risk of an asbestos related disease from exposure to asbestos dust had been obvious, that the parent company had actual knowledge of the working conditions, that the parent was in a position of proximity to the claimant because health and safety policy had been dictated at group level, and that it was fair, just, and reasonable in the circumstances to impose a duty of care. This decision was upheld on appeal; Arden LJ emphatically rejected any suggestion that this involved piercing the corporate veil; she noted that a subsidiary and its parent were separate entities and that there was no imposition or assumption of responsibility by reason only that a company was the parent company of another company.[159]

A parent company which appoints its employees to serve as directors of its subsidiary companies is not vicariously liable for breaches of duty by those directors.[160]

Alternatives to piercing the veil: Insolvency Act 1986

Under section 213 of the Insolvency Act 1986, if it appears that any business of a company that is in the process of being wound up has been carried on with intent to defraud creditors or for any fraudulent purpose, the court, on the application of the liquidator, may declare that persons who were knowingly party to the carrying-on of the business in that manner are to be liable to make such contributions to the company's assets as the court thinks proper. A parent company could, depending on the facts, be knowingly a party to the carrying-on of the business of an insolvent subsidiary. However, a further requirement for liability to arise under this section is the presence of fraud. Fraud in this context means 'actual dishonesty, involving real moral blame'[161] and that can be difficult to establish.[162]

Section 214 of the Insolvency Act 1986 allows the court to order persons who knew or ought to have concluded that the company had no reasonable prospect of avoiding insolvent liquidation to contribute to the assets of a company in liquidation unless those persons can establish that they took every step that ought to have been taken with a view to minimizing the potential loss to the company's creditors. The judgment standards under this section are based on objective criteria rather than personal morality and honesty: a person is to be judged on the basis of his own knowledge, skill, and experience and also the knowledge,

---

[156] *Chandler v Cape plc* [2012] 3 All ER 640 (CA); *Lubbe v Cape plc* [2000] 4 All ER 268, HL; *Stocznia Gdanska SA v Latvian Shipping Co Latreefer Inc.* [2001] 1 Lloyd's Rep 537, affirmed [2002] 2 Lloyd's Rep 436, CA.

[157] [2012] 3 All ER 640, CA.   [158] [1990] 2 AC 605, HL.   [159] [2012] 3 All ER 640, [69].

[160] *Kuwait Asia Bank EC v National Mutual Life Nominees Ltd* [1991] 1 AC 187, PC.

[161] *Re Patrick and Lyon Ltd* [1933] 1 Ch 786.

[162] *Re Augustus Barnett & Son Ltd* (1986) 2 BCC 98904 where an attempt to make a parent company liable under the then equivalent of s 213 failed.

skill, and experience that could reasonably be expected of someone carrying out his func-tions in relation to the company.[163] For liability under section 214 to arise it must be shown that at the date of actual liquidation the company was in a worse position than it would have been if trading had ceased at the time it is contended it should have done. The appropriate comparison is between the net deficiency in the assets of the company as at the date at which it was contended that trading should have ceased and the date at which trading did in fact cease.[164] The amount of the contribution required of a director who is found to have engaged in wrongful trading is in the court's discretion; it has been said that the section is primarily compensatory rather than penal and that therefore the prima facie appropriate amount is the amount by which the company's assets can be said to have been depleted by the director's conduct.[165]

The Insolvency Act 1986, section 214 applies only to the directors of the failed com-pany. Directors for this purpose include de facto directors, a term whose meaning depends on the context in which it is used but which, broadly speaking, denotes persons who are part of a company's governance structure and who assume the powers and functions of a director but who have not been formally appointed.[166] A substantial shareholder who intervenes directly in running the affairs of the company runs the risk of being held to be a de facto director, and this represents a legal risk for parent companies.[167] It is also possible for wrongful trading liability to attach to shadow directors, ie persons on whose instructions or directions the actual directors[168] are accustomed to act.[169] A parent com-pany could potentially be caught as a shadow director. Four facts must be established in a shadow directorship allegation: (1) the identity of the actual directors; (2) that the alleged shadow director directed at least the governing majority[170] of the actual directors how to act in relation to the company or was one of the persons who did so; (3) that those directors acted in accordance with such directions; and (4) that they were accustomed so to act.[171] Relationships can be structured so as to minimize the risk of one party being held to be a shadow director of another: for example, a provider of finance to an ailing company should impose conditions on its offer of finance which the company is free to accept, rather than lending the money with instructions as to how it is to be used, because the former structure sits more comfortably with the principle that a lender is entitled to lay down terms relat-ing to the running of the business in the absence of which it would not be prepared to lend without constituting itself a shadow director.[172] Whether a parent company is a shadow director of its subsidiary will depend on the factual relationship between them.[173] It must

---

[163] Insolvency Act 1986, s 214(4).

[164] *Re Continental Assurance Co of London plc* [2001] BPIR 733; *Re Marini Ltd* [2004] BCC 172; *Re Idessa (UK) Ltd* [2012] 1 BCLC 80.

[165] *Re Produce Marketing Consortium Ltd* (1989) 5 BCC 569.

[166] *Re Hydrodam (Corby) Ltd* [1994] BCC 161; *Secretary of State for Trade and Industry v Tjolle* [1998] 1 BCLC 333; *Re Richborough Furniture Ltd* [1996] 1 BCLC 507; *Secretary of State for Trade and Industry v Hollier* [2007] BCC 11; *Ultraframe (UK) Ltd v Fielding* [2006] FSR 17, para 1254; *HMRC v Holland* [2011] 1 All ER 430, SC.

[167] *Secretary of State for Trade and Industry v Jones* [1999] BCC 336, 349–50.

[168] Including de facto directors: *Re Hydrodam (Corby) Ltd* [1994] BCC 161.

[169] Insolvency Act 1986, s 251. The meaning of the definition of shadow director was considered by the Court of Appeal in *Secretary of State for Trade and Industry v Deverell* [2001] Ch 340, CA, where Morritt LJ summarized the law in a series of propositions. There is an express exclusion of parent companies from the category of shadow director in respect of certain provisions of the Companies Act 2006 (see Companies Act 2006, s 251) but there is no such exemption under the Insolvency Act 1986. For further discussion of the shadow directorship category and its interrelationship with de facto directorship see ch 11.

[170] *Re Unisoft Group Ltd (No 2)* [1994] BCC 766, 775; *Ultraframe (UK) Ltd v Fielding* [2005] FSR 17, para 1272.

[171] *Re Hydrodam (Corby) Ltd* [1994] BCC 161.   [172] *Ultraframe (UK) Ltd v Fielding* [2005] FSR 17, para 1269.

[173] In an Australian case the factual evidence indicated that a 42 per cent shareholder controlled the affairs of a company to such an extent that it was liable under a provision extending liability to a person in accordance with

be shown that it was the regular practice of the subsidiary board to follow directions from the parent.[174]

Sections 238 and 239 of the Insolvency Act 1986 allow for the restoration of positions that would have existed had a failed company not entered into transactions at an undervalue or given voidable preferences. Orders under these sections may include requiring transferred property or its proceeds to be vested in the transferor company.[175] These sections are of general application but conditions that trigger grounds for an order may be more easily satisfied in the group context than in other situations because of certain presumptions and longer time limits that apply where parties are connected to each other.[176] Furthermore, since the interests of a failing company are identified with those of its own creditors rather than those of its shareholders or of the collective interests of the group's creditors, actions taken in the interests of the group will be particularly vulnerable under these sections.[177] The rules on transactions at an undervalue and on preferences thus act as a check on the freedom to move resources around a corporate group on non-commercial terms contrary to the interests of the creditors of specific companies within the group.[178]

Is the law on corporate groups deficient?

In the major economies of the world, including that of the UK, company law developed originally in relation to companies which had shareholders who were human beings and it was then applied by extension to companies whose share capital was owned by other companies.[179] Whether that extension, which permits corporate groups to exploit multiple tiers of limited liability, demands a specific response within company and insolvency law, in particular to provide explicitly for enterprise-based rather than entity-based liability to creditors, is a much debated issue,[180] on which lawmakers around the world have taken different views.[181]

Within the UK, the policy debate has shifted noticeably in recent years. Debate during the 1980s tended to suggest that corporate groups presented serious problems for creditors that demanded an interventionist legislative solution. That the law could be deficient in not

whose directions or instructions the directors were accustomed to act: *Standard Chartered Bank v Antico* (1995) 18 ACSR 1, NSW SC.

[174] *Re Unisoft Group Ltd (No 2)* [1994] BCC 766; *Secretary of State for Trade and Industry v Becker* [2003] 1 BCLC 555. DD Prentice, 'Corporate Personality, Limited Liability and the Protection of Creditors' in R Grantham and C Rickett (eds), *Corporate Personality in the 20th Century* (Oxford: Hart, 1998) 99, 115–8.

[175] Insolvency Act 1986, s 241.

[176] Insolvency Act 1986, s 239(6) (influence of desire to prefer presumed: *Re Oxford Pharmaceuticals Ltd* [2009] 2 BCLC 485); s 240(1)(a) (two-year time limit on review (it is usually six months in voidable preference cases)); s 240 (2) (inability to pay debts presumed in undervalue transaction situations). For the statutory definition of connected: Insolvency Act 1986, s 249 and s 435.

[177] eg, *Re Genosyis Technology Management Ltd* [2007] 1 BCLC 208, Ch.

[178] Parry, *Transaction Avoidance in Insolvencies*, 83–4 (intra-group guarantees as transactions at undervalue). Also at 238–9, considering the potential usefulness of Insolvency Act 1986, s 423 (transactions defrauding creditors) where assets have been transferred around a corporate group deliberately to put them out of reach of creditors. See also *Re Mea Corporation Ltd* [2007] 1 BCLC 618; I Mevorach, 'Transaction Avoidance in Bankruptcy of Corporate Groups' (2011) 8 *European Company and Financial Law Review* 235; UNCITRAL, *Legislative Guide on Insolvency Law Part Three*, 49–51.

[179] Antunes, *Liability of Corporate Groups*, 30–4; Muscat, *The Liability of The Holding Company for the Debts of its Insolvent Subsidiaries*, ch 4.

[180] Blumberg, *The Multinational Challenge to Corporation Law*, ch 11. The author advocates a general regime of enterprise law which would include, but not be limited to, enterprise liability. See also, Blumberg, 'The American Law of Corporate Groups,' 305, but contrast DD Prentice, 'Some Comments on the Law Relating to Corporate Groups'; Muscat, *The Liability of the Holding Company for the Debts of its Insolvent Subsidiaries*, 47, ch 7.

[181] RR Kraakman, J Armour, P Davies, L Enriques, H Hansmann, G Hertig, KJ Hopt, H Kanda, and EB Rock, *The Anatomy of Corporate Law* 2nd edn (Oxford: OUP, 2009) 135–41.

making special provision for group liability was judicially acknowledged.[182] An important contribution to this debate was the report of the Cork Committee, which reviewed insolvency law and practice in the UK in the early 1980s.[183] The Committee noted that 'some of the basic principles of company and insolvency law fit uneasily with the modern commercial realities of group enterprise.' Intra-group transfers of assets at an undervalue, lending between group companies on other than commercial terms, gratuitous guarantees by one group company of another group company's debts, and intra-group dividends paid without reference to the cash needs of the paying company were identified as the type of transactions that gave rise to concern.[184] Despite its concern and its acknowledgement that the law was defective,[185] the Committee mostly refrained from making detailed recommendations specifically relating to corporate groups. It outlined a number of justifications for its tentative stance.[186]

First, an alteration of the law so as to make a parent company liable for its insolvent subsidiary's debts would introduce a difference between types of shareholders (corporate or individual) with regard to the fundamental principle of limited liability. That could affect entrepreneurial activity as it might deter a prosperous company from embarking upon new ventures. Secondly, the Committee was concerned about the problems of allocating and apportioning liability. This concern had a number of facets: determining precisely what relationship between companies should trigger financial responsibility; the extent to which there might be financial responsibility for companies that were only partly-owned subsidiaries, and, if so, whether the parent could have any claims against the minority shareholders; whether financial responsibility for an insolvent subsidiary should lie only with its parent or with all the companies in the group; and to what extent there should be parental or group liability for debts incurred by an insolvent subsidiary at a time when it was not a member of the group. Thirdly, the Committee was also concerned about the foreign element, ie the extent to which, if at all, there should be parental or group liability for the debts of an insolvent foreign corporation. Fourthly, there were questions about the position of existing long-term creditors of companies when any changes in the law were introduced; the creditors of, say, a parent company, would be adversely affected by a law which made the parent responsible for the debts of a subsidiary unless complex transitional arrangements could be devised to prevent the legislation operating retrospectively to the detriment of those existing creditors. Taking all these factors into account, the Committee concluded that the implications of a change to some form of group enterprise liability would spread throughout company law and that a fundamental change to company law could not properly be introduced by means of proposals to change insolvency law. The Committee called for a wide review of the whole issue of group enterprise liability with a view to the introduction of reforming legislation within the foreseeable future.

By the 1990s, however, perceptions as to the key issues had changed. In part led by the work of the Cork Committee, the law restricting certain forms of abuse of limited liability had been tightened up, especially with the enactment of wrongful trading liability in section 214 of the Insolvency Act 1986 and the wide-ranging directors' disqualification regime in the Company Directors Disqualification Act 1986. These changes closed some perceived gaps in the regulatory framework and they helped to set the scene for a significant shift in the emphasis of the policy debate. Promoting enterprise and investment were the themes that dominated

---

[182] *Re Southard & Co Ltd* [1979] 1 WLR 1198, CA; *Re Augustus Barnett & Son Ltd* (1986) 2 BCC 98904, 98908. See also in Australia *Qintex Australia Finance Ltd v Schroeders Australia Ltd* (1990) 3 ACSR 267, NSW SC ComD; *Re Spargos Mining NL* (1990) 3 ACSR 1, WA SC.

[183] *Insolvency Law and Practice* (Cmnd 8558, 1982) ch 51.   [184] *Insolvency Law and Practice*, para 1922.

[185] *Insolvency Law and Practice*, para 1926.   [186] *Insolvency Law and Practice*, para 1934.

the company law reform debate that preceded the Companies Act 2006. Promoting rescue, rather than sorting out the consequences of financial failure, became increasingly influential in discussions about the philosophy underpinning insolvency law.[187] Although risks that people faced in dealing with businesses in corporate form were not ignored, clamping down on the freedom to establish a number of linked limited liabilities entities or restricting significantly the advantages of operating a business in that way never took hold as ideas with gathering momentum. There was no significant outcry against the Company Law Review Steering Group's strongly-stated view that there was no merit in imposing a more integrated regime on groups of companies because such a regime would take away flexibility in the way businesses organized themselves and would strike at the limited liability basis for company law.[188] Nor was there a significant outcry against its refusal to propose reform in the controversial area of parent company liability for its subsidiaries' torts.[189] In fact the Company Law Review Steering Group seemed more concerned to facilitate corporate groups by allowing the parent of a wholly-owned subsidiary formally to elect to guarantee the obligations of that subsidiary, with the effect that, for as long as the election remained in force, that subsidiary would enjoy specified exemptions from the requirements of the companies legislation. However, that proposal did not attract support and it was not included in the final reform package.[190]

The problem of the insolvent subsidiary can be sketched in emotive terms:

> A parent company may spawn a number of subsidiary companies, all controlled directly or indirectly by the shareholders of the parent company. If one of the subsidiary companies, to change the metaphor, turns out to be the runt of the litter and declines into insolvency to the dismay of its creditors, the parent company and other subsidiary companies may prosper to the joy of the shareholders without any liability for the debts of the insolvent company.[191]

However, there is a danger of overestimating the problem by overlooking commercial considerations and a range of specific creditor protection mechanisms that are in the general law. In many cases, a prosperous parent company will not abandon a failing subsidiary and its creditors, even though it could do so as a matter of law, because it is anxious not to damage the commercial reputation of the group or its credit rating.[192] There are detailed rules in company law that seek to protect creditors by requiring companies to maintain their capital, which apply to corporate groups as well as to individual companies. These rules are problematic and, as will be argued in Part II of this book, there are good grounds for saying that they should be abandoned because they do more harm than good, but, so long as they remain, they cannot be overlooked in addressing the question of whether the law should do more to respond to the 'problem' of corporate groups. Another important consideration is that many creditors can protect themselves by contract and, for them at least, there is no need for the law to adopt a paternalistic stance. To the extent that responsibility for the failure of a subsidiary can be placed on the shoulders of the subsidiary's directors, they will be liable to contribute to

---

[187] V Finch, 'The Recasting of Insolvency Law' (2005) 68 MLR 713.

[188] Company Law Review Steering Group, *Modern Company Law for a Competitive Economy: Completing the Structure*, paras 10.19–10.20.

[189] Company Law Review Steering Group, *Modern Company Law for a Competitive Economy: Completing the Structure*, paras 10.58–10.59. However, for a view that too little attention was given to this issue: PT Muchlinski, 'Holding Multinationals to Account: Recent Developments in English Litigation and the Company Law Review' (2002) 23 *Company Lawyer* 168.

[190] Company Law Review Steering Group, *Modern Company Law for a Competitive Economy: Final Report* (URN 01/942) paras 8.23–8.28.

[191] *Re Southard* [1979] 1 WLR 1198 CA.

[192] Hadden, *The Control of Corporate Groups*, 23–4; KJ Hopt, 'Legal Issues and Questions of Policy in the Comparative Regulation of Groups.'

its assets and, depending on the coverage of directors' liability insurance policies and indemnity arrangements, this may augment the assets available for distribution by the insolvency practitioner quite significantly. The 'shadow directorship' concept has at least the potential to bring parent companies within the scope of personal liability to contribute to the assets of a failed subsidiary in circumstances where it has controlled its operations. General directors' duties and the special liabilities that can arise in insolvency situations can have a significant deterrent effect. Insolvency rules on preferences and on transactions at an undervalue, as well as equitable principles that facilitate the tracing of misappropriated assets, including unlawful dividends, are mechanisms that can be used to reverse the movement of assets around a corporate group without due regard to the separate entity status of the various companies. Although not concerned directly with asset-augmentation, laws that permit the state to disqualify directors who have participated in wrongful or fraudulent trading, or who have shown themselves to be unfit to be concerned in the management of a company, reinforce the seriousness of the obligations on directors and act as incentives to pay proper attention where preferring group interests to those of individual corporate entities could be a breach of duty.[193]

Cumulatively, there is therefore much regulation in place that operates as a check on abuse within corporate groups. Nevertheless, the fact remains that in the absence of contractual guarantee obligations, a shadow directorship relationship, a tort claim, or an agency or analogous relationship, under UK law a parent company is generally free to walk away from failure within its group: where the debts of the subsidiary are of such magnitude as to threaten the solvency of the parent, the advantages of abandonment may outweigh the damage to the reputation of the group. Substantive consolidation, whereby assets of companies that are in law separate legal entities may be pooled, is not part of the law in the UK.[194] Nor is equitable subordination, whereby intra-group debts are subordinated to other debts of the insolvent entity.[195] Depending on your policy stance, this is either a deficiency in the law or a consequence of adherence to the principle of limited liability which should be accepted because, in overall terms, the economic advantages of permitting free access to limited liability outweigh the problems and it is therefore appropriate not to draw the regulatory regime too tightly in case this inhibits value-creating entrepreneurial activity.

It is increasingly likely that the policy debate about the regulation of corporate groups will be influenced by developments at the EU level because the creation and functioning of groups of companies are matters that are on the agenda for Community-wide company law.[196] In not having specific substantive group laws in either its legislation or its case law, the position in the UK is notably different from that in some other major Member States of the EU.[197] This is significant because, the variety of approaches to group law at Member State level

    [193] Company Directors Disqualification Act 1986.
    [194] Finch, *Corporate Insolvency Law Perspectives and Principles*, 587–8. cf the New Zealand Companies Act 1993, s 271, which provides for the court to order contributions or the pooling of assets of related companies where it considers it just and equitable to do so (applied in *Mountfort v Tasman Pacific Airlines of NZ Ltd* [2006] 1 NZLR 104, H Ct Auckland) and the Republic of Ireland Companies Act 1990, ss 140–141, which are in broadly similar terms to the New Zealand legislation (see G McCormack, 'Ireland: Pooling of Assets and Insolvency in Ireland' (1992) 13 *Company Lawyer* 191).
    [195] Finch, *Corporate Insolvency Law Perspectives and Principles*, 586–7.
    [196] KJ Hopt, 'Legal Issues and Questions of Policy in the Comparative Regulation of Groups'; C Windbichler, 'Corporate Group Law for Europe: Comments on the Forum Europaeum's Principles and Proposals for a European Corporate Group Law' (2000) 1 *European Business Organization Law Review* 165; European Commission, *Report of the High Level Group of Company Law Experts*, ch V; European Commission, *Action Plan: European Company Law and Corporate Governance—A Modern Legal Framework for More Engaged Shareholders and Sustainable Companies* (COM(2012) 740) para 4.6.
    [197] In particular Germany. On the relevant German provisions: A Dorresteijn, T Monteiro, C Teichmann, and E Werlauff, *European Corporate Law* 2nd edn (Alphen Aan Den Rijn: Wolters Kluwer, 2009) 284–9.

can be expected to feed into future EU initiatives, which could eventually require the UK to change its approach in key respects. An important structural difference is also noteworthy. In Continental Europe, it is common to find listed companies that are partly-owned subsidiaries, which is not the case in the UK. Subsidiaries with minority shareholders, and especially those that are listed companies, give rise to a wider range of policy concerns than wholly-owned subsidiaries, because minority shareholders, corporate governance, and investor protection issues must be considered as well as the interests of creditors, and those issues may be regarded as giving rise to more pressing concerns than creditor-related matters.[198]

The most prominent European example of special laws on corporate groups is found in Germany in the law relating to joint stock companies.[199] Under the German *Konzernrecht* a parent and its subsidiaries may conclude an enterprise contract. This allows the parent to direct the running of the group on an enterprise basis but only at the price of providing indemnities for losses stemming from the running of the business in the interests of the group rather than on an entity basis. This type of special arrangement for corporate groups is formal and arises only where the operators of a group choose to opt into it. Experience has shown it to be unpopular and it is little used. German joint stock company law also has special standards for de facto groups, whereby a parent company can be held liable to compensate subsidiaries which it has caused to act in a manner contrary to the subsidiaries' own interests.[200] However, satisfying the conditions for this liability to arise has proved to be difficult.[201] Judicial activism to extend enterprise liability beyond joint stock companies was checked by the *Bremer Vulkan* case in 2001, and instead principles relating to wrongful behaviour of shareholders that threaten the existence of a company have been applied to determine the circumstances in which a parent can be held liable for losses at subsidiary level.[202] The classic German statutory rules on indemnification within corporate groups have been said to be based on a valid theoretical concept but to be unworkable in practice.[203]

The German *Konzernrecht* model historically carried much weight in discourse at the EU level on Community-wide company law. The draft Ninth Directive on company law[204] proposed the introduction of a regime in Member States whereby, broadly, corporate groups could choose between a form of integrated operation which would entail group liability, or a form of operation in which the financial and managerial independence of the companies within the group would have to be respected and there would be no group liability.[205] The

---

[198] E Wymeersch, 'Do We Need a Law on Groups of Companies?' in KJ Hopt and E Wymeersch (eds), *Capital Markets and Company Law* (Oxford: OUP, 2003) 573; C Windbichler, 'Corporate Group Law for Europe: Comments on the Forum Europaeum's Principles and Proposals for a European Corporate Group Law' (2000) 1 *European Business Organization Law Review* 165; KJ Hopt, 'Legal Issues and Questions of Policy in the Comparative Regulation of Groups'; Reflection Group on the Future of EU Company Law, *Report* (European Commission, April 2011); European Company Law Experts, 'Response to the European Commission's Consultation on the Future of European Company Law' (1 May 2012) <http://ssrn.com/abstract=2075034> accessed July 2013.

[199] Dorresteijn, Monteiro, Teichmann, and Werlauff, *European Corporate Law*, 284–9; R Reich-Graefe, 'Changing Paradigms: The Liability of Corporate Groups in Germany' (2005) 37 *Connecticut Law Review* 785.

[200] Dorresteijn, Monteiro, Teichmann, and Werlauff, *European Corporate Law*, 287–8.

[201] R Reich-Graefe, 'Changing Paradigms: The Liability of Corporate Groups in Germany' (2005) 37 *Connecticut Law Review* 785, 792 (noting one successful case in forty years).

[202] Dorresteijn, Monteiro, Teichmann, and Werlauff, *European Corporate Law*, 288–9; A Daehnert, 'Lifting the Corporate Veil: English and German Perspectives on Group Liability' [2007] *International Company and Commercial Law Review* 393; M Shillig, 'The Development of a New Concept of Creditor Protection for German GmbHs' (2006) 27 *Company Lawyer* 348.

[203] Wymeersch, 'Do We Need a Law on Groups of Companies?' 588.

[204] Commission Document III/1639/84-EN.

[205] T Hadden, 'Insolvency and the Group—Future Developments' in RM Goode (ed), *Group Trading and the Lending Banker* (London: Chartered Institute of Bankers, 1988) 101, 103–8.

draft, which was loosely based on German law,[206] received a hostile reception when it was introduced, and the proposal was eventually abandoned due to lack of support. The German approach has, however, had influence at the Member State level: inspired by Germany, Italy has amended its legislative framework to regulate corporate group relationships,[207] and there are also dedicated provisions in Portuguese law.[208]

In 2003, the European Commission ruled out as unnecessary the enactment of an autonomous body of law specifically dealing with groups.[209] Its preference was for better financial and non-financial information about corporate groups to be mandated. It also suggested that Member States should be required to provide for a framework rule for groups that would allow those concerned with the management of a company belonging to a group to adopt and implement a coordinated group policy, provided that the interests of that company's creditors were effectively protected and that there was a fair balance of burdens and advantages over time for that company's shareholders. In broad terms, this proposal for recognition of a 'group interest' amounted to an endorsement of the *Rozenblum* doctrine by the Commission. The *Rozenblum* doctrine is derived from a decision of the French criminal courts whereby, under certain conditions, it is considered to be legitimate for the directors of subsidiaries to act in the overall interest of the group.[210] The conditions in French law for the safe harbour are: (1) the firm structural establishment of the group; (2) the existence of a coherent group policy; and (3) an equitable distribution of the revenue and costs of the business among the members of the group. It has been said of the French position that no group transaction is forbidden so long as there is some 'quid pro quo,' though not necessarily an exact counterbalance.[211] However, support provided by a group company must not exceed what can reasonably be expected from it, so that where support is beyond the provider's financial capacity, it will be considered unlawful. The Commission saw the introduction of such a rule as an important step towards improved business efficiency and competitiveness, but it stressed that appropriate safeguards would have to be carefully designed. The Commission's stated intention in 2003 was for a proposal for a framework Directive to this effect to be presented in the medium term. This proposal as yet remains unadopted.[212] However, ideas of this nature have not been abandoned completely.[213] Support remains for the idea of at least a recommendation from the European Commission to Member States to amend their company law to recognize the interest of the group as such. It has been suggested that cross-border trade

---

[206] On which see: KJ Hopt, 'Legal Elements and Policy Decisions in Regulating Groups of Companies' in CM Schmitthoff and F Wooldridge (eds), *Groups of Companies* (London: Sweet & Maxwell, 1991) ch V, and F Wooldridge, *Groups of Companies: The Law and Practice in Britain, France and Germany* (London: Institute of Advanced Legal Studies, 1981).

[207] P Fasciani, 'Groups of Companies: The Italian Approach' (2007) 4 *European Company and Financial Law Review* 195.

[208] M Andenas and F Wooldridge, *European Comparative Company Law* (Cambridge: CUP, 2009) 451–70.

[209] European Commission, *Modernising Company Law and Enhancing Corporate Governance in the European Union—A Plan to Move Forward* (COM (2003) 284) 18–20.

[210] From the decision of Cour de Cassation, 1985 *Revue des Sociétés* 648.

[211] Wymeersch, 'Do We Need a Law on Groups of Companies?' 591.

[212] T Baums, 'European Company Law Beyond the 2003 Action Plan' (2007) 8 *European Business Organization Law Review* 144.

[213] Note also a parallel debate on harmonization of insolvency law: European Parliament, *Harmonisation of Insolvency Law* (2010). This report notes that harmonization of insolvency law could drive harmonization of company law in a number of areas, including directors' liabilities, rules on lifting the veil, and on a clear definition of the individual company v corporate group interest. See further European Parliament Resolution with recommendations to the Commission on insolvency proceedings in the context of EU company law (T7-0484/2011); European Commission, *A New European Approach to Business Failure and Insolvency* (COM(2012) 742); European Commission, *Proposal for a Regulation of the European Parliament and of the Council amending Council Regulation (EC) No 1346/2000 on insolvency proceedings* (COM(2012) 744); European Commission, *Report on the Application of Council Regulation (EC) No 1346/2000 on insolvency proceedings* (COM(2012) 743).

would be enhanced if there were a European framework rule for groups that allowed those concerned with the management of a group company to adopt and implement a coordinated group policy, provided that the interest of the company's creditors were effectively protected and that there was a fair balance of burdens and advantages over time for the company's shareholders.[214] In December 2012 the European Commission indicated its receptiveness to these ideas by announcing as part of a Company Law Action Plan that it would, in 2014, come up with an initiative to improve both the information available on groups and recognition of the concept of 'group interest'.[215] How ambitious this initiative will be remains to be seen.

In the specialized context of bank recovery and resolution, EU legislation has now recognized the concept of the 'group interest' in the context of intra-group financial support.[216] The proposed Bank Recovery and Resolution Directive envisages that financial support may be provided in accordance with a group financial support agreement so long as: (a) there is a reasonable prospect that the support provided will redress the financial difficulties of the entity receiving the support; (b) the provision of financial support has the objective of preserving or restoring the financial stability of the group as a whole and is in the best interests of the group entity providing the support; (c) the financial support is provided on terms that include consideration; (d) there is a reasonable prospect, on the basis of the information available to the management of the group entity providing financial support at the time when the decision to grant financial support is taken, that the consideration for the support will be paid and, if the support is given in the form of a loan, that the loan will be reimbursed by the group entity receiving the support; (e) the provision of the financial support would not jeopardize the liquidity or solvency of the entity providing the support; (f) the provision of the financial support would not create a threat to financial stability in the Member State of the group entity providing support; (g) the entity providing the support complies at the time the support is provided, and shall continue to comply after the support is provided, with specified regulatory requirements; and (h) the provision of the financial support would not undermine the resolvability of the group entity providing the support.[217] This is, broadly speaking, an application of the 'quid pro quo' principle found in the *Rozenblum* doctrine, though in a very conditional form. The Commission refrained from going further in recognizing the 'group interest' in this Directive, its reasoning being that whilst the adoption of the notion of 'group interest' would be very effective in reaching the goal of legal certainty around intra-group asset transfer, this benefit would not satisfy a proportionality test because of the extent to which it would undermine the traditional separate entity approach of company laws and insolvency laws, and could require also a review of contract law.[218] A proportionality test will also apply to any future initiatives in company law that touch on this issue.

---

[214] European Company Law Experts, 'Response to the European Commission's Consultation on the Future of European Company Law' (1 May 2012). Available at SSRN: <http://ssrn.com/abstract=2075034> or <http://dx.doi.org/10.2139/ssrn.2075034>.

[215] Commission, *Action Plan: European Company Law and Corporate Governance—a Modern Legal Framework for More Engaged Shareholders and Sustainable Companies* (COM(2012) 740) para 4.6.

[216] European Commission, *Proposal for a Directive of the European Parliament and of the Council establishing a framework for the recovery and resolution of credit institutions and investment firms and amending Council Directives 77/91/EEC and 82/891/EC, Directives 2001/24/EC, 2002/47/EC, 2004/25/EC, 2005/56/EC, 2007/36/EC, and 2011/35/EC, and Regulation (EU) No 1093/2010.*

[217] Proposal for a Directive of the European Parliament and of the Council establishing a framework for the recovery and resolution of credit institutions and investment firms and amending Council Directives 77/91/EEC and 82/891/EC, Directives 2001/24/EC, 2002/47/EC, 2004/25/EC, 2005/56/EC, 2007/36/EC, and 2011/35/EC, and Regulation (EU) No 1093/2010, Art 19 (Council General Approach, June 2013).

[218] European Commission, *Impact Assessment Accompanying Proposal for a Directive Establishing a Framework for the Recovery and Resolution of Credit Institutions and Investment Firms* (SWD(2012) 167) 22.

3

Capital Structure—Fundamental Legal, Accounting, and Financing Considerations

Scope of this Chapter

The legal rules governing the financing of companies are the primary focus of this book. As a prelude to the more detailed examination that follows in later chapters, the purpose of this chapter is to outline the basic components of the capital structure of a company and to consider, in a rudimentary way, some of the factors that may be taken into account by the managers of a company when making financing choices. Simple illustrations of the way in which financing choices have to be recorded in a company's accounts are provided. A company's accounts (individual and consolidated) play a key role in determining compliance with legal requirements on corporate capital. By giving historical information about previous financing choices and the performance of the company, the accounts also provide important investment information.

There are basically three ways for a company to finance its operations: share issues, debt, and retained profits. In an introductory exposition such as this, it is convenient to take the simplest type of share and to compare its standard features with those of the simplest type of debt instrument. This should not be allowed to obscure the great flexibility that exists in practice with regard to the characteristics of financial instruments issued by companies. It is possible to issue shares which, by their terms of issue, deviate significantly from the standard case, to structure debt so as to mimic the characteristics of share capital, and to devise instruments which combine some of the features of share capital and of debt. Devising innovative financial instruments that tap into particular investor preferences in changing market conditions is a significant part of corporate finance advisory activity.

Share Capital Terminology

There are many different types of share, including ordinary shares, preference shares, and redeemable preference (or ordinary) shares. The ordinary share is the most straightforward type of share.

The **allotted share capital** of a company is the amount of share capital that has been allotted by a company at any time. This amount may also be described as the company's *issued* **share capital**. Allotted share capital/allotted shares and issued share capital/issued shares are not precisely synonymous terms but, save for certain specific contexts where the differences may matter (such as the interpretation of a tax concession available in respect of 'issued' share capital), they can, and frequently are, used interchangeably. The terms **shareholder** and **member** are also often used interchangeably even though, again, there are certain technical differences between them.[1] The same is true of **equity share capital**: this term carries a precise meaning in particular contexts (such as certain provisions of the Companies Act 2006)[2] but it is often used in a looser sense to mean the same as share capital

---

[1] Companies Act 2006, s 112 defines who are the members of a company.

[2] Companies Act 2006, s 548. This definition generally excludes preference shares, except where such shares are also participating with respect to dividends and/or capital. Another context where 'equity' carries a technical

or, in the shortened form of *equity*, to mean share capital, other undistributable reserves, and retained earnings.

A company limited by shares, whether public or private, is formed by one or more persons subscribing their names to a memorandum of association and complying with the requirements of the Companies Act 2006 with regard to registration.[3] The effect of these requirements is that the minimum number of allotted (or issued) shares in a company limited by shares is one. There is no regulation in the UK of the minimum overall amount of a private company's allotted share capital but for a public company there is a minimum of £50,000.[4]

Shares must have a *par* (or nominal) value ascribed to them in the statement of capital that a company must file with the registrar of companies on formation and whenever its capital is altered thereafter.[5] The par value sets the minimum allotment price.[6] Shares may be allotted at a price that is more than their par value. The difference (if any) between the par value of a share and the allotment price is known as a *share premium*.

Shares may be allotted on a fully, partly, or nil paid basis.[7] The amount paid up in respect of the par value of shares (ie excluding premiums) represents a company's *paid up share capital*. Where shares are allotted otherwise than on a fully-paid basis, payment dates may be set by the terms of allotment or the company's constitution (ie its articles of association); alternatively, it may be left to the discretion of the directors to call for payment in accordance with the articles. A company's *called up share capital* is made up of the share capital that has been paid up plus any amounts in respect of share capital (ie excluding premiums) that have been called up or are due on specified future dates. Allotted share capital which has not been called up is *uncalled share capital*.

In respect of private companies, company law in the UK does not require a specific minimum amount of share capital actually to be invested in the business before trading commences. During the 2000s, this feature of the law briefly gave the UK a competitive advantage over some other European countries whose laws imposed minimum capital requirements on private companies because it made the UK a relatively cheap incorporation venue for businesses that could then operate elsewhere in the Community under EU Treaty freedoms in respect of cross-border activities.[8] The advantage faded as other countries took steps to relax their requirements and as incidental drawbacks flowing from being incorporated in one Member State but conducting business mostly elsewhere began to emerge.[9] To the extent that there is a direct *ex ante* constraint on UK private companies trading on minimal amounts of share capital, it is lending practice rather than law: banks may be reluctant to lend to a private company if its proprietors have not themselves demonstrated their confidence in the company's prospects by taking the risk of investing a substantial amount in its share capital. UK law relies more on *ex post* constraints: should a company that has started trading with an inadequate equity capital base fail, the adequacy

meaning is in accounting: see IAS 32, *Financial Instruments: Presentation*; IAS 39, *Financial Instruments: Recognition and Measurement* (superseded by IFRS 9, *Financial Instruments* from January 2015); IFRS 7, *Financial Instruments: Disclosures*. Depending on their specific terms, preference shares may be classified as equity instruments or financial liabilities for accounting purposes.

[3] Companies Act 2006, s 7.   [4] Companies Act 2006, ss 761 and 763.
[5] Companies Act 2006, s 10 refers to the statement of capital that must be filed on formation.
[6] Companies Act 2006, s 580.
[7] These, and other terms mentioned in this paragraph, are considered in more detail in ch 4 below.
[8] See further ch 4 below.
[9] M Becht, L Enriques, and V Korom, 'Centros and the Cost of Branching' [2009] *Journal of Corporate Law Studies* 171.

(or not) of its financing structure is a factor that the court may take into account in proceedings against its directors.[10]

The position is different in relation to public companies, which are required to have a paid up share capital of at least £12,500 before they start trading.[11] Whilst not completely trivial, this is hardly a significant amount. More powerful factors in determining the actual size of a public company's equity capital base stem from commercial pressures to maintain a balance between debt and equity ('gearing' or 'leverage') that is acceptable to lenders and investors.

Accounting for an Allotment of Ordinary Shares

When a company allots ordinary shares for cash at their par value, this will be recorded as an increase in the company's current assets and as an increase in share capital.[12] In numerical terms, the action will look like Table 3.1.

The amount shown in a company's accounts as its share capital is subject to the legal rules on maintenance of capital.[13] The maintenance of capital principle operates as a trade-off for limited liability: shareholders cannot be held liable to contribute to the company's assets for more than they have undertaken to subscribe in respect of their shares, but in return the amounts subscribed must be maintained. 'Maintenance' in this context essentially means 'not returned to the shareholders.'[14] It is not a breach of the maintenance of capital principle for a company's share capital to be wiped out by improvident trading or bad investment decisions, although such events may trigger insolvency proceedings in relation to the company.

Table 3.1 Accounting for an Allotment of Shares at Par Value

Pre-allotment of new shares		
Assets	£m	£m
Cash	5,000	5,000
Financing		
Share capital	1,000	
Reserves	4,000	5,000
Post-allotment of 10m new £1 shares at par to investors who pay cash		
Assets		
Cash	5,010	5,010
Financing		
Share capital	1,010	
Reserves	4,000	5,010

---

[10] *Re Purpoint Ltd* [1991] BCC 121, 127 *per* Vinelott J.

[11] This requirement follows from the combination of the minimum capital requirement of £50,000 (Companies Act 2006, s 761) and the rule that shares in public companies must not be allotted except as paid up at least as to one-quarter of nominal value (Companies Act 2006, s 586): ie 50,000/4 = 12,500.

[12] This discussion is limited to ordinary shares or other shares that for accounting purposes are classified as equity instruments. The position is more complex in relation to shares that for accounting purposes are classified as financial liabilities: P Holgate, *Accounting Principles for Lawyers* (Cambridge: CUP, 2006) 151–4.

[13] Discussed later in ch 7.

[14] *Trevor v Whitworth* (1887) 12 App Cas 409, HL, 414 *per* Lord Herschell; this analysis is echoed by Lord Watson at 423–4.

Table 3.2 Accounting for an Allotment of Shares at a Premium

Pre-allotment of new shares		
Assets	£m	£m
Cash	8,000	8,000
Financing		
Share capital	2,000	
Other reserves	6,000	8,000
Post-allotment of 10m new £1 shares at £2 per share		
Assets		
Cash	8,020	8,020
Financing		
Share capital	2,010	
Share premium	10	
Other reserves	6,000	8,020

When shares are allotted at a premium to their par value, the share premium must be credited to a separate account, as illustrated by Table 3.2.

With only a few exceptions, sums credited to a share premium account are subject to the maintenance of capital principle in the same way as paid up share capital.[15]

Characteristics of Ordinary Shares (Common Equity)

The standard characteristics of an ordinary share relate to entitlements in respect of dividends, capital growth, and participation in internal governance through voting.[16]

Dividends

Dividends are distributions to shareholders that are made out of the company's distributable profits. A company that does not have profits available for distribution cannot pay dividends. Moreover, even where distributable profits are available, the holders of ordinary shares have no absolute entitlement to demand that dividends be paid. The payment of dividends is governed by a company's articles, which normally authorize the directors to pay interim dividends at their discretion where they consider that this is justified by the company's profits, and provide for final dividends to be declared by the shareholders in general meeting on the basis of a recommendation from the directors.[17] As a matter of legal theory, it is possible for a company to pay dividends on its ordinary shares which fluctuate widely from year to year. It is also open to a company not to pay any dividends at all and to plough back the entire profits into the future funding of its operations. Both of these possibilities give way, in practice, to commercial considerations which may, depending on factors such as its nature or the sector in which it operates, require a company to pay steady dividends out of its distributable profits in order to satisfy the expectations of investors.[18] Dividends are paid out of a company's post-tax profits.

---

[15] Companies Act 2006, Pt 17, ch 7. The implications of this are discussed further in ch 4.
[16] The financial incidents of ordinary shares are considered in more detail in ch 6. This chapter provides an overview.
[17] Model Articles (plc), art 70; Model Articles (ltd), art 30.   [18] See further ch 9.

Capital gains and risk

When a company is wound up, the holders of its ordinary shares are entitled to any surplus that remains after all the liabilities have been paid. This means that the ordinary shareholders of a company may be described as its 'residual claimants' or, in legal terms, as its owners. The entitlement to eventual capital gains is reflected in the price at which its shareholders can sell their shares during the life of the company. On the other hand, however, as residual claimants or owners, investors in ordinary shares assume significant risks because they are the last to be paid in a winding up and, hence, will be the first to absorb any shortfall in the company's assets. Investors in ordinary shares will expect a return that is adequate to compensate them for the risk that they will not be repaid in the event of winding up.

Voting rights

Ordinary shares usually entitle their holders to one vote per share. It is possible to have non-voting ordinary shares or ordinary shares which carry multiple votes but their distorting effect on the operation of the market for corporate control (ie voting control of the company does not necessarily follow from acquiring the majority in number of its shares) and on corporate governance mechanisms, which are based on the control that shareholders can exercise through their votes, means that weighted voting shares are unpopular with institutional investors in the UK.[19] Participants in quasi-partnership type companies or joint venture companies may favour multiple voting rights as a means of entrenching their original bargain. One familiar form of multiple voting provision used for entrenchment purposes is a clause that is triggered by a proposal to remove a shareholder from the office of director and which provides that, in that event, the votes attaching to the shares held by that shareholder will be multiplied to an extent that is sufficient to defeat the motion.[20]

Common equity and financial regulation

In the context of the prudential regulation of banks there is a departure from the general stance in company law of not regulating the amount of equity capital that a business must hold. This departure from the general rule is justified because of the need to protect the safety and stability of the financial system. As was manifest in the financial crisis of 2007–9, bank failure can have a major destabilizing effect.

The international standards on bank capital (known generally as 'Basel III') now contain a very detailed list of the features that financial instruments must have in order to qualify as common shares for regulatory capital purposes.[21] Whilst this list is directed towards a specific purpose, it is also of more general interest because it captures the features that most people would tend to associate with equity. The Basel III list sets out the criteria for classification as common shares as follows:[22]

1.   Represents the most subordinated claim in liquidation of the bank.

---

[19] See generally Institutional Shareholder Services, Shearman & Sterling and European Corporate Governance Institute, *Report on The Proportionality Principle in the European Union* (May 2007) (study commissioned by the European Commission) <http://www.ecgi.org/osov/documents/final_report_en.pdf>> (accessed July 2013). Issues relating to 'one share—one vote' (the 'proportionality principle') are considered further in ch 13.

[20] This is commonly described as a *Bushell v Faith* clause after the House of Lords decision that sanctioned it: [1970] AC 1099, HL.

[21] Basel Committee on Banking Supervision, *Basel III: A Global Regulatory Framework for More Resilient Banks and Banking Systems* (December 2010, revised June 2011).

[22] *Basel III*, para 53.

2. Entitled to a claim on the residual assets that is proportional with its share of issued capital, after all senior claims have been repaid in liquidation (ie has an unlimited and variable claim, not a fixed or capped claim).

3. Principal is perpetual and never repaid outside of liquidation (setting aside discretionary repurchases or other means of effectively reducing capital in a discretionary manner that is allowable under relevant law).

4. The bank does nothing to create an expectation at issuance that the instrument will be bought back, redeemed or cancelled nor do the statutory or contractual terms provide any feature which might give rise to such an expectation.

5. Distributions are paid out of distributable items (retained earnings included). The level of distributions is not in any way tied or linked to the amount paid in at issuance and is not subject to a contractual cap (except to the extent that a bank is unable to pay distributions that exceed the level of distributable items).

6. There are no circumstances under which the distributions are obligatory. Non payment is therefore not an event of default.

7. Distributions are paid only after all legal and contractual obligations have been met and payments on more senior capital instruments have been made. This means that there are no preferential distributions, including in respect of other elements classified as the highest quality issued capital.

8. It is the issued capital that takes the first and proportionately greatest share of any losses as they occur. Within the highest quality capital, each instrument absorbs losses on a going concern basis proportionately and *pari passu* with all the others.

9. The paid in amount is recognised as equity capital (ie, not recognised as a liability) for determining balance sheet insolvency.

10. The paid in amount is classified as equity under the relevant accounting standards.

11. It is directly issued and paid-in and the bank can not directly or indirectly have funded the purchase of the instrument.

12. The paid in amount is neither secured nor covered by a guarantee of the issuer or related entity or subject to any other arrangement that legally or economically enhances the seniority of the claim.

13. It is only issued with the approval of the owners of the issuing bank, either given directly by the owners or, if permitted by applicable law, given by the Board of Directors or by other persons duly authorized by the owners.

14. It is clearly and separately disclosed on the bank's balance sheet.

Debt Finance Terminology

A company can borrow from banks or other lenders or can tap the capital markets by issuing debt securities to investors. The raising of capital by an issue of debt securities is sometimes described as direct financing because the company appeals directly to investors; bank borrowing is in turn described as indirect financing because the bank stands between the company and the providers of the funds, namely the bank's depositors and persons from whom it has raised capital via the capital markets.

There are many different types of debt instrument that companies use to raise funds from the capital markets. The terminology used to describe debt instruments tends to be driven more by market practice than by legal definition and is thus liable to fluctuate from market to market and from time to time in response to practical developments. Markets devise terms to distinguish debt securities by reference to certain key characteristics such as duration (for example, the term 'commercial paper' is commonly used to describe short-term debt securities, whilst long-term debt securities are often called 'bonds') and whether they are secured (sometimes described as 'debentures') or unsecured (often known as 'loan stock'). Terminological variety is a particular feature of the markets in specialist debt securities which are normally bought and traded in by limited numbers of expert investors.

The term *debenture* also crops up in the context of bank financing for companies. Here it tends to be used to describe a loan which is secured on the company's property. In confining the use of the term debenture to secured loans, practice is narrower than legal usage. There is no exhaustive legal definition of the term debenture[23] but a commonly cited description is that it encompasses any document which creates or acknowledges a secured or unsecured debt.[24]

Borrowing from banks and other lenders and issuing debt securities to investors are not the only ways in which companies can raise external non-equity finance to fund their operations. Companies can obtain short-term trade credit by acquiring goods on credit terms; sellers may supply goods on an open account or may require assurance as to payment in the form of documentary credits issued by banks and/or security by means of provisions that reserve title to the goods in the seller until payment.[25] Other asset financing mechanisms include finance leases, hire purchase, and arrangements such as 'repos,' which are transactions in which a company sells assets but with an option to re-acquire them, that in functional or economic terms are the same as loans but which are in a different legal category.[26] In addition there are many types of receivables financing that companies can use to improve their cash flow by enabling them to obtain funds more quickly than through awaiting payment from customers for goods supplied on credit. One type of receivables financing is debt factoring, where receivables (trade debts) are sold to a factor which then collects the debts, either on a recourse basis (where the factor has recourse to the company should customers fail to pay) or a non-recourse basis (where the factor in effect provides bad debts protection); another is block discounting, where debts are sold for an immediate cash payment by the discounter but ordinarily the company continues to collect the debts, acting as agent for the discounter.[27] Certain types of businesses are not thought suitable for receivables financing: it is useful for businesses operating in sectors that generate trade debtors, such as manufacturing and wholesale distribution, but less so for businesses that sell to the general public or otherwise for immediate settlement.[28] Reasons of space preclude separate consideration of asset and trade financing in this book.[29]

---

[23] Companies Act 2006, s 738 lists various instruments which are debentures but the list is not closed. The absence of a precise definition has given rise to few practical problems: *Re SH & Co (Realisations) 1990 Ltd* [1993] BCC 60, 67.

[24] *Levy v Abercorris Slate and Slab Co* (1887) 37 Ch D 260. See also *Edmonds v Blaina Furnaces Co* (1887) 36 Ch D 215; *Lemon v Austin Friars Investment Trust Ltd* [1926] 1 Ch 1, CA; *Knightsbridge Estates Trust v Byrne* [1940] AC 613, HL; *R v Findlater* [1939] 1 KB 594, CCA; *NV Slavenburg's Bank v Intercontinental Natural Resources Ltd* [1980] 1 All ER 955.

[25] On retention of title (RoT) clauses generally, see G McCormack, *Secured Credit under English and American Law* (Cambridge: CUP, 2004) ch 6.

[26] Asset sales achieve the same economic effect as secured loans but currently avoid the Companies Act 2006 requirements for the registration of charges. An attempt to avoid the registration requirements by labelling a structure as a sale will not work if the legal substance of the arrangement is in fact a secured loan: *Welsh Development Agency v Export Finance Co Ltd* [1992] BCC 270, CA. On the form and substance debate in the context of Companies Act registrations see further ch 12.

[27] Law Commission, *Registration of Security Interests: Company Charges and Property Other Than Land* (Law Com CP No 164, 2002) paras 6.24–6.29.

[28] Competition Commission, *The Supply of Banking Services by Clearing Banks to Small and Medium-sized Enterprises* (2002) paras 3.111–3.117.

[29] See RM Goode, *Commercial Law* 4th edn (London: Penguin, 2009) Pt 5; LS Sealy and RJA Hooley, *Commercial Law Text, Cases and Materials* 4th edn (Oxford: OUP, 2008) Pt VII.

Characteristics of Simple Debt

Interest

The rate of interest payable in respect of a loan is determined by the contract between the company and the lender. The rate of interest may be fixed or may be floating and, as such, liable to be adjusted in specified circumstances. Unlike dividends, interest is normally payable whether or not the company makes profits. Interest is deductible from the company's pre-tax profits and thus goes to reduce the profits on which the company is liable to pay tax. The favourable tax treatment is one factor that makes debt a potentially cheaper source of finance for a company than share capital. Judged well, a company can use the tax shield on debt to reduce its tax bill and increase its overall payout to providers of capital. Table 3.3 illustrates the point.

Table 3.3 Tax Shield Provided by Debt

	Co A	Co B
Earnings	100,000	100,000
Interest	0	30,000
Taxable earnings	100,000	70,000
Tax at 30%	30,000	21,000
Net earnings	70,000	49,000

These figures indicate that Co B could pay out 79,000 to investors (30,000 + 49,000) whereas Co A could pay out only 70,000. Put another way, Co B benefits from a tax shield of £9,000.

Capital gain and risk

A creditor is entitled to the repayment of the principal amount of the loan at the end of its term, but this is normally the limit of the creditor's claim against the company. Creditors do not share in a company's capital growth. The opportunity for capital gains for investors in debt securities lies in exploiting differences between the yield on the securities, measured by reference to their cash flows in the form of interest payments and principal repayment at maturity, and the interest rates prevailing in the market. Where the yield on debt securities is higher than market interest rates, an investor may be able to sell the securities at a premium to their face value and thereby obtain a capital gain.

Providers of debt finance rank above shareholders for repayment in the event of winding up. There is also a ranking order between debts depending on whether they are secured or unsecured and, if secured, the type of security. Certain types of debt are given a preferential ranking status by the insolvency legislation,[30] whilst others are deferred.[31] Priority over share capital in winding up is another factor that reduces the cost of debt finance in comparison to share capital: providers of debt finance accept less risk and that is reflected in the return that the company has to pay for financing in this form. However, in a highly leveraged firm, low ranking holders of debt occupy a residual position akin to that of shareholders because they will be first to absorb losses after the equity has been exhausted.

Control

Covenants, which are contractual restrictions imposed by the terms on which debt capital is provided, are in a broad sense the debt finance equivalent to the control that shareholders are

[30] Insolvency Act 1986, Sch 6 sets out the categories of preferential debt.
[31] Insolvency Act 1986, s 74(2)(f) (sums due to a member of the company). This section was considered in *Soden v British & Commonwealth Holdings plc* [1998] AC 298, CA and HL.

entitled to exercise via the votes attaching to their shares. The precise extent of the restrictions imposed contractually through covenants is fact-specific and likely to depend on a range of variables, including the length of the period for which the finance is to be available, whether it is privately negotiated or is raised directly from the capital markets, and whether it is secured or unsecured. General economic conditions are also relevant, as evidenced by 'covenant lite' financing transactions entered into in 2006–7, a period of great buoyancy in credit markets.[32] Covenants may include limitations on the company's borrowing levels, restrictions on the payment of dividends, negative pledge clauses whereby the company promises not to grant any new security on its property, and provisions restricting disposals of the company's property or major changes in the nature of its business.[33]

Hybrid Securities in Outline

A hybrid security combines some of the features generally associated with share capital with some of those of debt capital.[34] It can also be described as a form of mezzanine finance, occupying a mid-way position between debt and equity. A preference share is a form of hybrid security. Preference shares differ from ordinary shares in that they carry the right to a fixed annual dividend and/or to a return of a fixed principal amount. Preference shares normally carry limited voting rights. The fixed dividend and/or principal is payable in priority to the return on ordinary shares but (unless the terms on which the preference shares are issued otherwise provide) there is no right to participate over and above the fixed amount (hence they are typically described as being non-participating). The fixed return and the priority to ordinary shares are characteristics that resemble loan capital. Nevertheless, preference shares are still at law shares, although whether for accounting purposes they are equity instruments or financial liabilities depends on their specific terms. The legal constraints that flow from the maintenance of capital principle apply as much to preference shares as they do to ordinary shares: thus dividends on preference shares can be paid only from distributable profits and, accordingly, unlike interest, will not be paid if the company does not have these profits (but so long as the entitlement is cumulative it can be carried forward until such time as the company does have distributable profits); and holders of preference shares rank below creditors for the purposes of repayment.

It has been held in Australia that a company that has no ordinary shares in issue can nevertheless validly issue preference shares.[35] Since, in practical terms, there must be something for preferential shares to be preferential to, the preferential rights must remain potential only, without effective content, unless and until the directors issue ordinary shares.

A more sophisticated version of a preference share is the convertible preference share which, in addition to the rights of a normal preference share, also entitles the holder at some point in the future to convert it into another security such as an ordinary share in the company or in its holding company. A convertible preference share combines the benefits of being preferential (in particular ranking ahead of ordinary shares for dividends and for repayment of capital) with the opportunity to share, via conversion, in capital growth, which is a key benefit associated with ordinary shares.

Debt capital can also be raised on terms that provide for the investor to be able to convert the debt into a share (of the borrower company or some other company) at some later date.

---

[32] G Moore, 'Europe's Second Cov-lite Loan' (2007) 26(5) *International Financial Law Review* 8.

[33] See further chs 11 and 15.

[34] R McCormick and H Creamer, *Hybrid Corporate Securities: International Legal Aspects* (London: Sweet & Maxwell, 1987).

[35] *Weinstock v Beck* [2013] HCA 15.

This type of financial instrument is described as convertible debt. Convertible debt instruments can also be structured so that the issuer rather than the investors holds the conversion option or so that conversion is automatic upon the occurrence of specified trigger events. Similar to a convertible debt security is a debt instrument with an attached warrant. The warrant gives the holder the option to subscribe shares. The debt-plus-warrant structure differs from convertible debt in that exercise of the warrant does not bring the debt instrument to an end, whereas the debt instrument disappears when a conversion right is exercised. The characteristic shared by convertible debt securities and warrants, and which makes them both hybrid securities, is that, unlike straight debt, they offer the investor the opportunity to participate in capital growth or (if the conversion is at the issuer's, rather than the holder's, option) expose the investor to the loss-absorption risks associated with equity financing.

Another form of debt that is regarded as being hybrid is subordinated debt. Broadly speaking, when debt is subordinated its terms include provision for the principal amount of the loan (and sometimes interest as well) not to be repaid until some or all of the company's other debts have been paid in full. To compensate for the subordination, a company may have to pay a higher rate of interest than it would pay on its unsubordinated debt. To enhance the attractiveness of the investment opportunity for investors still further, it may also have to offer share options or conversion rights. Subordinated debt is similar to share capital in that it ranks for payment behind other debts and, if share options or conversion rights are attached, it offers the opportunity to participate in capital growth. Yet it remains debt on which interest may be payable even if the company does not have distributable profits and, prior to conversion, it ranks higher on the repayment ladder than share capital.[36]

Valuation of Securities[37]

Shares

The value of a share ultimately comes down to what someone is willing to pay for it, and this can depend on precisely what it is that the purchaser seeks to acquire. Thus, a bidder who wants to take over a company may have to pay more for its shares than an investor who seeks to acquire a small parcel of its shares, the difference in price here being the premium that the bidder has to pay for control. Valuation is not an exact science but where shares are quoted, the starting point in any valuation process is to look at the price at which they are trading in the market. For some unquoted companies it may be possible to arrive at an estimate of the value of their shares based on empirical evidence of the market value of shares in analogous quoted companies. The market price of shares may then be compared with their value on the basis of other methods of valuation. This comparison may, in different contexts, assist professional investment analysts in arriving at their recommendations on whether to buy or sell securities, and enable bidders to determine the control premium they are prepared

---

[36] *Collins v G Collins & Sons* (1984) 9 ACLR 58, NSW SC EqD illustrates this point. A corporate rescue scheme involving the subordination of certain debts was not approved by the court but, because of the technical differences between share capital and loan capital, it was prepared to sanction an alternative arrangement in which the relevant debts would be converted into preference shares. Query, however, whether it would be possible to structure subordinated debt which ranks behind preference shares. In principle, an arrangement whereby receipts in respect of subordinated debt are turned over to the preference shareholders should be possible but, depending on the structure used, this type of arrangement could raise financial assistance concerns or might be vulnerable as an indirect unlawful return of capital.

[37] HS Houthakker and PJ Williamson, *The Economics of Financial Markets* (Oxford: OUP, 1996) ch 6; RA Brealey, SC Myers, and F Allen, *Principles of Corporate Finance* 10th edn (New York: McGraw-Hill, 2011) ch 19; WL Megginson, SB Smart, and BM Lucey, *Introduction to Corporate Finance* (London: South-Western Cengate Learning, 2008) ch 5.

to pay. Other valuation techniques must necessarily be used to value the shares of unquoted companies where there are no appropriate quoted comparators.

The main methods of valuing shares otherwise than at the price at which they are trading in the market are set out later. All of these methods have limitations and some are more appropriate than others for particular purposes. Where they involve assumptions or projections, there is scope for different valuers to take different views. This means that the sensible course for, say, a potential bidder, is to use a combination of valuation methodologies in order to derive a valuation range in respect of a target company.[38]

Net asset value

A valuation based on net asset value involves dividing the total market or book value of the company's net assets by the number of shares in issue. Where the book values of the company's assets are out of date, it may be necessary to conduct a revaluation exercise in order to bring these into line with market values. This method of valuation is the primary tool for valuing property companies. It is inappropriate where much of the value of the business is attributable to factors that do not appear in the balance sheet, such as the skills of the staff of an advertising or design company.

Dividend valuation

The principle underlying the dividend valuation method is that the value of a share lies in the flow of income that an investor can expect from it during its life, including any dividend paid on the liquidation of the company. Although the return to the holder of a share from time to time comes in the form of dividend plus the capital gain on the disposal of the share, the price that a purchaser is willing to pay for that share is based on expectation of future dividends, with the result that it is the value of the stream of dividends over the life of the share that represents its value. Dividend valuation methodology arrives at the present value of a share by looking at the expected flow of dividends during the life of the company and discounting future returns to reflect the time value of money and the risk that the expected cash flows may not in fact be forthcoming.

Free cash flow valuation

Instead of looking at just one component of the return to shareholders (ie dividends), the free cash flow valuation method proceeds on the basis that the company's entire free cash flow (ie its income remaining net of all operating costs and investment outlays) belongs to the shareholders. Discounted cash flow methodology involves discounting future cash flows at an appropriate discount rate and relies upon projections of future cash flows.

Debt securities

The value of a debt security lies in the present-day value of the stream of income payable in respect of the security. In the case of a simple debt security which has a fixed interest rate and a

---

[38] In a different context, note *Re Macro (Ipswich) Ltd* [1994] BCC 781, where the court employed both net-asset and dividend-yield methods of valuation as the basis for arriving at the price at which a minority holding in a private company should be bought out under (now) Companies Act 2006, s 994. Generally, on the valuation of shares in unquoted companies, see N Eastaway, H Booth, and K Eames, *Practical Share Valuation* 5th edn (Haywards Heath: Tottel, 2009).

fixed maturity date, its value is thus the discounted value of the interest that is payable during the life of the loan and of the principal amount that is repayable on maturity.

Cost of capital

The preceding discussion about valuation of shares and debt securities glossed over a fundamentally important point, namely, the appropriate discount rate to apply when determining the present value of expected future cash flows. The rate that is used must account for the time value of money and must reflect the risk that is inherent in any expectation of payments to be made in the future. A key element, therefore, is the valuation of risk. There are two forms of risk that are present in investing in corporate securities: risks relating to the particular companies whose securities are included in a portfolio (specific risks) and risks stemming from factors, such as the potential for changes in fiscal policy or interest rates, that are generally applicable (systematic risk). Portfolio theory dictates than an investor can eliminate specific risks by forming a diversified portfolio of investments in which risks attaching to particular securities are counterbalanced by the characteristics of other securities.[39] On this basis, it is only for systematic risk that investors can properly expect to receive compensation from the companies whose securities they hold. Accordingly, it is the valuation of systematic risk that is the focus of concern.

The Capital Asset Pricing Model (CAPM) is the most widely used technique for measuring systematic risk in equity investment and, hence, for estimating investors' required rate of return. In broad terms, the CAPM assesses the required rate of return on an equity investment by reference to the risk-free rate of return available to an investor, the premium required by investors to compensate them for the general systematic risk of investing in the equity market, and the undiversifiable systematic risk of a particular investment relative to the equity market. Although no investment is entirely risk-free, the rates of return on government securities (gilts) are the closest available comparator. The premium that investors require for holding a fully diversified portfolio of equity securities is determined by looking at the difference between historical gross returns on the equity market and on risk-free investments in gilts. The undiversifiable risk inherent in holding a particular share is known as its beta. Equity betas are calculated by reference to their historical returns and the corresponding returns on the market.

In theory, the CAPM can also be used to assess the required rate of return on debt securities but debt betas are not readily available. Instead, the rate of return required by investors in debt securities tends to be determined by reference to the rate of return on the existing debt securities of the company and of similar issuers. A similar process, involving examination of the company's borrowing history and comparison with analogous companies, may be used in determining the rate of return on debt finance provided by banks or other lenders.

The returns required by the providers of a company's share capital and debt constitute its cost of capital. The company's cost of capital is a driving factor in decisions on whether to invest in new projects because these will only be worthwhile investments where they are expected to generate returns at least equal to the company's cost of capital. Put another way, the company's cost of capital represents the cut-off rate for new projects. The average rate of a company's cost of capital is determined by the cost of its capital weighted by the proportion of funding obtained from each source (weighted average cost of capital, or WACC).

---

[39] H Markowitz, 'Portfolio Selection' (1958) 7 *Journal of Finance* 77.

Capital Structure

In modern economics literature, the analysis of corporate capital structures usually starts with the Modigliani-Miller (MM) theorem as a benchmark.[40] The main elements of the original MM theory are that (a) the total value of a company is independent of its capital structure, and (b) the cost of a company's equity capital is a linear increasing function of its debt to equity ratio, keeping the overall cost of capital constant. In other words, increasing the amount of debt would lead to an offsetting increase in the cost of equity and vice versa.[41] This theorem as to the irrelevance of financial leverage was developed on the basis of certain restrictive assumptions, including the absence of taxes and insolvency and transaction costs, and the existence of perfect capital markets in which all investors have equal access to information. Much of the subsequent literature has re-evaluated MM with more realistic assumptions.[42] Once the assumptions on which the original theory was based are relaxed, in particular to take into account the fact that interest is tax deductible whereas dividends are not (thus giving rise to a tax shield as illustrated earlier in this chapter), it appears that it may be possible to add some debt to a company's capital structure without affecting the expected return to shareholders. Against this, the relaxation of the assumption of no insolvency costs points away from reliance on debt because, the greater the proportion of debt, the more likely it is that the company will default and enter into one of the corporate insolvency procedures within the framework of insolvency law. These procedures are costly to implement and, as the risk of insolvency grows with the addition of more and more debt to a company's capital structure, this can eventually outweigh the tax benefit of debt. The upshot of these competing considerations is that the addition of debt to a company's capital structure will be beneficial up to the point where the benefit of the tax shield resulting from debt are eclipsed by the costs of financial distress. On that basis, the focus then shifts to the making of a trade-off between the benefits of debt and the expected costs of financial distress to determine the optimal long-term target capital structure. Subsidiary questions about the design of particular securities and about the public (capital markets) and private (banks) sources from which external finance may be available also assume considerable importance.

The trade-off theory of optimal capital structure implies that the correct mix of debt and equity for any particular company is dependent on a range of variables, including its age, its size, and the nature of its business and assets. Where companies are incorporated is another relevant variable because differences in applicable legal, tax, and institutional regimes can be expected to have some impact.[43] Gearing ratios do in fact vary across industries in ways that

---

[40] F Modigliani and MH Miller, 'The Cost of Capital, Corporation Finance and the Theory of Investment' (1958) 48 *American Economic Review* 433. For an appraisal of the theorem and some of the literature spawned by it, see MH Miller, 'The Modigliani-Miller Propositions After Thirty Years' (1988) 2 *Journal of Economic Perspectives* 99, and the other symposium papers published in that edition of the journal. Another overview that provides an introduction to decades of research on capital structure is SC Myers, 'Capital Structure' (2001) 15 *Journal of Economic Perspectives* 81. For a major review of the literature, see also M Harris and A Raviv, 'The Theory of Capital Structure' (1991) 46 *Journal of Finance* 297; S Frydenberg, 'Theory of Capital Structure—a Review' in G Arntzen, L Fallan, and O Gustafsson (eds), *Frihet og mangfold: festskrift til Odd G. Arntzen* (Tapir Academic Press) (version in English revised to January 2011 at: <http://ssrn.com/abstract=556631> accessed July 2013).

[41] RJ Gilson and RR Kraakman, 'The Mechanisms of Market Efficiency Twenty Years Later: The Hindsight Bias' (2003) 28 *Journal of Corporation Law* 715, 719.

[42] The original authors themselves relaxed some of the original assumptions in later papers: eg F Modigliani and MH Miller, 'Corporate Income Taxes and the Cost of Capital: a Correction' (1963) 53 *American Economic Review* 261.

[43] F Bancel and UR Mittoo, 'Cross-Country Determinants of Capital Structure Choice: A Survey of European Firms' (2004) 33(4) *Financial Management* 103.

are broadly consistent with the theory: companies with steady cash flows or readily realizable assets, such as utility companies, tend to have higher gearing ratios;[44] and companies with relatively few current tangible assets but with considerable future growth prospects, such as exploration companies, tend to have lower gearing ratios, as do innovative technology companies where the reliability of profit growth is uncertain.[45] Some country-by-country differences can also be discerned.[46] At particular times—such as when a substantial new investment project is undertaken—there may temporarily be an abnormally high reliance on debt finance but some empirical evidence suggests that high gearing levels do not persist and that there is a strong reversion in leverage over the longer term as companies take steps to reduce their indebtedness.[47] However, evidence on the speed with which firms adjust towards target leverage does not all point in the same direction.[48]

More generally, the trade-off theory does not fully explain real-life capital structures because in fact many profitable companies operate with much lower levels of tax-deductible debt than the theory would predict.[49]

A different point of view on corporate capital structures is provided by the 'pecking order' theory.[50] The basis of the pecking order theory is that asymmetric information between managers and investors gives rise to mispricing risks, which vary in scale depending on the information sensitivity of the financial instrument in question and which are therefore more severe in relation to equity than to debt. 'Good' managers will seek to minimize the risk of mispricing so as to maximize value and therefore will opt for forms of financing that are least affected by problems of asymmetric information. This implies a 'pecking order' capital structure in which internally-generated funds are preferred to external sources of finance and, as between external sources, debt is preferred to new equity.[51] Evidence of large projects being primarily financed externally from debt is consistent with the pecking order theory's identification of a preference for debt over equity but, at the same time, evidence that firms do not exhaust internal resources before turning to external sources to finance such projects is not consistent with the theory.[52] Nor does the pecking order theory explain evidence of reversions to initial capital structures in the longer term.[53]

While the trade-off and pecking order theories of capital structure both have some explanatory power, neither provides all the answers. The same can also be said of other theories on corporate capital structure that have developed alongside the two main theories or as refinements of them. One such theory, which is associated with the trade-off theory, is based on 'agency costs.' There are agency costs in corporate finance that flow from the potential conflicts of interest between debt and equity investors and also from the

---

[44] Myers, 'Capital Structure,' 82–4.   [45] Myers, 'Capital Structure,' 82–4.

[46] F Degeorge and EG Maug, 'Corporate Finance in Europe: A Survey,' in X Freixas, P Hartmann and C Mayer (eds), *Handbook of European Financial Markets and Institutions* (Oxford: OUP, 2008) ch 7; Bancel and Mittoo 'Cross-Country Determinants of Capital Structure Choice,' 103. Differences in accounting rules complicate the process of attempting country-by-country comparative studies of capital structure.

[47] C Mayer and O Sussman, 'A New Test of Capital Structure,' CEPR Discussion Paper No 4239 (February 2004) <http://ssrn.com/abstract=509022> accessed July 2013; P Bunn and G Young, 'Corporate Capital Structure in the United Kingdom: Determinants and Adjustment' (August 2004). Bank of England Working Paper No 226 (August 2004) <http://ssrn.com/abstract=641281> accessed July 2013.

[48] R Huang and JR Ritter, 'Testing Theories of Capital Structure and Estimating the Speed of Adjustment' (2009) 44 *Journal of Financial and Quantitative Analysis* 237

[49] Myers, 'Capital Structure,' 88–91.

[50] SC Myers, 'The Capital Structure Puzzle' (1984) *Journal of Finance* 575; SC Myers and NS Majluf, 'Corporate Financing and Investment Decisions When Firms Have Information Investors Do Not Have' (1984) 13 *Journal of Financial Economics* 187.

[51] Myers, 'Capital Structure,' 92–3.

[52] Mayer and Sussman, 'A New Test of Capital Structure.'

[53] Mayer and Sussman, 'A New Test of Capital Structure.'

absence of a perfect alignment between managers' and investors' interests.[54] When considering from an agency cost perspective the trade-offs involved in using debt as a source of finance, it becomes necessary to add to the financial distress side of the equation the costs associated with risks that managers will prefer the interests of shareholders to those of creditors by transferring value from one group to the other or by engaging in excessive risk-taking. Agency cost analysis of the implications of conflicts of interest between debt and equity investors may be a factor that helps to explain why many companies operate with more conservative debt ratios than would be warranted by comparing the benefits of interest tax shields against the costs involved in insolvency procedures.[55] On the other side of the equation, however, debt can be beneficial when it is examined through the lens of the misalignment between managers' and investors' interests because it acts as a discipline on management by forcing firms to commit cash to debt interest payments; as such, it reduces opportunities for managers to use the free cash flow to engage in 'empire building' for their own reputational advantage or in other activities that benefit themselves rather than investors.[56] From this perspective, some of the explanation for why managers do not exploit the tax advantages of debt as fully as the trade-off theory would imply may lie in their reluctance to submit to the disciplining effect of adding more debt to the capital structure.[57]

Yet another line of analysis suggests a 'market timing' theory of capital structure, which is to the effect that firms' capital structures can be understood as the cumulative result of efforts to time the equity market—ie to issue shares when market prices are high and to repurchase them when market values are low.[58] The market timing theory posits that financing decisions that depend on the time-varying relative costs of equity and debt have long-lasting effects on capital structure because the observed capital structure at any given date is the outcome of prior period-by-period securities issuance decisions.[59]

Despite considerable advances made by a rich body of literature, it is widely acknowledged that corporate capital structure decisions involve complex, multidimensional problems that are not yet fully understood and explained. Thus it has been said that: 'In any case, understanding the determinants of the evolution of capital structure is arguably the most important unresolved question in corporate finance, and only time and additional empirical work will tell where the answer lies.'[60] According to an empirical study involving a comprehensive survey of corporate financing decision-making in UK listed companies, published in 2006, firms were heterogeneous in their capital structure policies: about half of the firms sought to maintain a target debt level, consistent with the trade-off theory, but 60 per cent claimed to follow a financing hierarchy, consistent with the pecking order theory.[61] These two theories were not viewed by respondents as either mutually exclusive or exhaustive.

[54] M Jensen and W Meckling, 'Theory of the Firm: Managerial Behavior, Agency Costs and Ownership Structure' (1976) 3 *Journal of Financial Economics* 305.

[55] Myers, 'Capital Structure,' 98.

[56] MC Jensen, 'Agency Costs of Free Cash Flow, Corporate Finance and Takeovers' (1986) 76(2) *American Economic Review* 323.

[57] Myers, 'Capital Structure,' 99.

[58] M Baker and J Wurgler, 'Market Timing and Capital Structure' (2002) 57 *Journal of Finance* 1.

[59] Huang and Ritter, 'Testing Theories of Capital Structure and Estimating the Speed of Adjustment.'

[60] Huang and Ritter, 'Testing Theories of Capital Structure and Estimating the Speed of Adjustment.'

[61] V Beattie, A Goodacre, and SJ Thomson, 'Corporate Financing Decisions: UK Survey Evidence' (2006) 33(9) & (10) *Journal of Business Finance & Accounting* 1402. See also Degeorge and Maug, 'Corporate Finance in Europe: A Survey'; Bancel and Mittoo, 'Cross-Country Determinants of Capital Structure Choice.'

Sources of Corporate Finance in the UK

Bank lending and its importance for SMEs

Smaller companies (which represent a large component of the group of businesses classified as small and medium-sized enterprises (SMEs[62])) are heavily dependent on internal sources of finance, ie equity provided by their owners, retained profits, and loans from directors and shareholders. Apart from short-term trade credit (including finance leases and hire purchase arrangements) and credit cards, bank finance is the main source of external finance for SMEs.[63] The heavy dependency of SMEs on bank financing is an issue that has been the focus of concern in a number of official reports stretching back many years.[64] Thus, while deleveraging by banks in the aftermath of the global financial crisis of 2007–9 has recently made the financing needs of SMEs a matter of high political priority, the fundamental issues are not new.[65] Effective solutions to the problem, which many consider to be rooted at least in part in lack of competition in a very concentrated banking industry, remain elusive: thus in 2011 the final report of the Independent Commission on Banking recorded that the largest four banks in the UK accounted for 85 per cent of SME current accounts, and observed that most of the competition problems highlighted during the 2000s by previous reports on UK banking still remained.[66] A number of official interventions to ease access to credit in the very difficult economic conditions that followed in the wake of the financial crisis 2007–9 have sought to put pressure on banks to increase their lending to business,[67] and also to support business by providing public guarantees for bank funding and establishing alternative sources of finances.[68] However, these efforts have met with limited success.[69] One important report published in 2012 warned: 'As things stand, there is a risk that the supply of finance for investment and working capital will not match demand as firms seek to increase production. Banks remain essential in providing credit to the economy, but the stock of bank lending has

---

[62] SMEs is a defined category for certain regulatory purposes, but in loose terms can be thought of as businesses (not necessarily incorporated) with a turnover of less than £25m.

[63] M Lund and J Wright, 'The Financing of Small Firms in the United Kingdom' (May 1999) *Bank of England Quarterly Bulletin* 195; T Breedon, *Boosting Options for Business* (Report for BIS, March 2012). Generally, see BDRC, *SME Finance Monitor* <http://www.sme-finance-monitor.co.uk> accessed July 2013, but regularly updated.

[64] Official reports noting the particular financing difficulties faced by small firms reports include: *Report of the Committee on Finance and Industry* (Cmnd 3897, 1931) (Macmillan Report); *Report of the Committee on the Workings of the Monetary System* (Cmnd 827, 1959) (Radcliffe Report); *Report of the Committee of Inquiry on Small Firms* (Cmnd 4811, 1971) (Bolton Report). A general review of the financial structure of SMEs is provided by A Hughes, 'Finance for SMEs: A UK Perspective' (1997) 9 *Small Business Economics* 151.

[65] A Davis, *Beyond the Banks: Innovative Ways to Finance Britain's Small Businesses* (NESTA, 2011). See also Breedon, *Boosting Finance Options for Business*, and the Government response to this Report: BIS, *Boosting Finance Options for Business: Government Response to the Industry Taskforce* (March 2012).

[66] Independent Commission on Banking, *Final Report* (September 2011). The banking industry established its own taskforce to address the issues: British Bankers Association, *Supporting UK Business* (BBA, October 2010).

[67] Following a period of discussion between the Government and the major UK banks on an initiative known as 'Project Merlin,' a statement was made by the banks on 9 February 2011 whereby the banks stated a capacity and willingness to lend £190 billion of new credit to business in 2011, with £76 billion of this lending capacity allocated to small and medium-sized enterprises. However, Project Merlin was not regarded as a success. It was followed in July 2012 by the launch by the Bank of England and HM Treasury of the Funding for Lending Scheme (FLS). The FLS is designed to incentivize banks and building societies to boost their lending to UK households and non-financial companies. It will do this by providing funding to banks and building societies for an extended period, at below current market rates, with both the price and quantity of funding provided linked to their performance in lending to the UK non-financial sector.

[68] HM Treasury, *Autumn Statement* (Cm 8231, November 2011) (announcing a new National Loan Guarantee Scheme of up to £20bn, and making available an initial £1bn through a Business Finance Partnership to invest in smaller businesses through non-bank channels).

[69] Bank of England, *Trends in Lending* (October 2012) (reporting contraction in the stock of lending to both SMEs and large businesses). Net lending to SMEs by all monetary financial institutions had been negative since the second quarter of 2011 and net lending to large businesses had been negative since the fourth quarter of 2011.

reduced over the last three years, and there remains a significant funding challenge for banks as a result of regulation at national and international level which is likely to further restrict the availability of credit.[70]

Sources of External Equity for SMEs and the Role of Venture Capital

External equity plays only a small role in the financing of smaller businesses.[71] This is substantiated by data summarized by the British Bankers Association as shown in Table 3.4:

Table 3.4 Use of Business Finance Across Different Sized Firms[72]

	Turnover	Broad characteristics	Use of regular finance	Use of specialist finance	Typical providers
Smallest Micro-businesses	Below £50k	Cash-based firms, often part-time business; few tangible assets; local operations	Limited mainly to overdraft, loans, and credit cards or personal finance products	Limited. Some asset-backed lending (ABL)— mainly vendor finance	Banks, credit card providers, and point of sale (vendor) finance
Micro-businesses	£50k to £1m	Increasingly full-time firms with staff, premises, and assets; local activity normally limited to a single region; occasional exporting	Overdraft, loans, and credit cards	Increased use of structured ABL. Occasional use of trade finance products	Banks, credit card providers, specialized providers for ABL and trade products
SMEs	£1m to £25m	Full-time, larger multiregional and national firms; increasing export/import activity	Overdraft, loans	Still some use of ABL, factoring and invoice discounting, export finance, some equity finance	Banks, credit card providers, specialized providers, business angels, private equity
Mid-sized companies	£25m up to £500m	Larger national and international firms, often multinational operations	Overdraft (or a revolving credit facility), some loans	Export finance, invoice finance, asset finance and equity funding	Banks, venture funds, equity funds and stock market listing

Government analysis in 2012 indicated that only around 1–2 per cent of SMEs looking for external finance sought equity finance, although venture capital, which is long-term equity-based capital invested by specialist funds, and business angels, that is wealthy individuals willing to invest in shares of start up or expanding businesses, remained an important niche source of 'start up' and 'early stage' finance for some businesses with high growth potential.[73]

---

[70] Breedon, *Boosting Options for Business*, 2.

[71] M Lund and J Wright, 'The Financing of Small Firms in the United Kingdom', *Bank of England Quarterly Bulletin* (May 1999) 195, 199.

[72] British Bankers Association, *Supporting UK Business*, 14.

[73] BIS, *SME Access to External Finance* (BIS Economics Paper No 16, January 2012).

Venture capital and private equity (generally 'later stage' financing) activity had grown dramatically in the UK during the 2000s in the period before the financial crisis, but contracted in the difficult economic conditions of the post-crisis period.[74] Overall, there remain significant gaps in the supply of long-term growth capital to smaller firms.[75] Moreover, this situation is not confined to the UK: the economic crisis has created a bleak short-term climate for new supplies of money from sources such as business angels and venture capital funds for early stage SMEs across Europe as a whole.[76]

Capital Markets: A Funding Source for Large Companies

Large, profitable companies unsurprisingly have the widest range of financing options available to them. The largest businesses can access the equity and debt capital markets directly, thereby reducing their dependency on bank-based financing. As for the balance between debt and equity in large, prosperous companies, the trade-off theory may suggest a positive relationship between profitability and gearing because there is a low risk of financial distress and the tax benefits of debt should increase as profits rise.[77] The agency costs theory would also appear to point in the same direction because of the disciplining effect of debt servicing commitments and of restrictive covenants.[78] On the other hand, the pecking order theory would suggest a negative relationship because highly profitable companies will have less need than other companies for any type of external finance.[79] Survey data indicated a sharp rise in UK corporate gearing between 1999 and 2002, with rises in gearing being concentrated among the largest and most profitable companies.[80] The debt to assets ratio of private non-financial companies in the UK peaked at 46.7 per cent in 2007–8, although the build up of debt was concentrated in certain areas, in particular commercial real estate companies and companies that had been the subject of leveraged buyouts.[81] The crisis led to a contraction in bank lending, and a reduction in the overall stock of corporate debt. Large companies, which had the capacity to replace bank loans with the proceeds of bond and equity issuance, were primarily responsible for the net repayment of bank lending during this period.[82]

The very largest companies can access both domestic and international capital markets. It is not essential for a company that is in search of capital from the domestic or international securities markets to do so via a formally organized stock exchange or other trading facility. However, admission of securities to trading on an exchange or other trading system may offer significant benefits, including access to bigger pools of capital, better liquidity, and an enhanced corporate profile.

The Main Market of the London Stock Exchange is the UK's most prestigious organized securities market.[83] It is open to UK companies and also to companies from other countries.

---

[74] BIS, *SME Access to External Finance*.

[75] BIS, *SME Access to External Finance*; C Rowlands, *The Provision of Growth Capital to UK Small and Medium Sized Enterprises* (Report for BIS, 2009).

[76] European Commission, *Report of the Chairman of the Expert Group on the Cross-border Matching of Innovative Firms with Suitable Investors* (November 2012, group chaired by Anthony Clarke).

[77] P Brierley and P Bunn, 'The Determinants of UK Corporate Capital Gearing' (Autumn 2005) *Bank of England Quarterly Bulletin* 356, 362.

[78] Brierley and Bunn, 'The Determinants of UK Corporate Capital Gearing.'

[79] Brierley and Bunn, 'The Determinants of UK Corporate Capital Gearing.' See also RG Rajan and L Zingales, 'What Do We Know About Capital Structure: Some Evidence From International Data' (1995) 50(5) *Journal of Finance* 1421.

[80] Brierley and Bunn, 'The Determinants of UK Corporate Capital Gearing.'

[81] Financial Services Authority, *Prudential Risk Outlook 2011*, 21–3.

[82] Financial Services Authority, *Prudential Risk Outlook 2011*, 21–3.

[83] This section on the Main Market is based on information on the London Stock Exchange's website<http://www.londonstockexchange.com>, in particular its publication *Listing on the London Stock Exchange* (2010).

Companies can list different types of shares and debt securities on the Main Market. Other financial instruments can also be listed, including securitized derivatives and securitized commodities. The Alternative Investment Market (AIM) is the London Stock Exchange's second-tier market. It describes itself as 'the most successful growth market in the world.'[84] Since its establishment in 1995, AIM has attracted over 3,100 companies, which between them have raised over £67 billion. AIM has a strong international focus. Compared to the Main Market, AIM has less stringent admission criteria and less wide-ranging continuing obligations. The London Stock Exchange also operates the Professional Securities Market (PSM), which is a market that enables domestic and overseas companies to raise capital through the issue of specialist securities, such as debt, convertibles, and depositary receipts, to professional or institutional investors.[85] The regulatory requirements governing the PSM are different from those for the Main Market and AIM because they are tailored for a specialist, professionals-only market segment.

The London Stock Exchange (LSE) competes internationally for business from issuers. 'Home bias,' whereby issuers offer and/or list their securities exclusively in their country of origin has become less prevalent, and this has enabled the LSE to expand its international coverage very significantly. In one of its publications, the LSE proclaims that 'More than any other major global exchange, London is where the world comes to market. During the past decade, over a third of the initial public offerings (IPOs) issued on the London Stock Exchange have been launched by international companies. And, of the more than 2,500 companies listed on the Exchange, almost 600 are international firms that are either headquartered outside the UK or derive a significant proportion of their business from overseas. These companies are attracted to London by the world's largest pool of investors dedicated to international assets, with over $1,100 billion (£697 billion) under management from institutions based in the capital.'[86] The implications of the London Stock Exchange being a capital market for the world are examined further in the last part of this book.

Within the UK, other market infrastructure providers have attempted to challenge the London Stock Exchange in the provision of capital markets services to issuers, but with limited success. The ICAP Securities & Derivatives Exchange (ISDX) provides two options for companies wishing to enter its markets: the ISDX Main Board (which like the London Stock Exchange's Main Market is an EU regulated market and a market for listed securities[87]) and the ISDX Growth Market (which is more geared towards the needs of earlier stage entrepreneurial companies).[88] These markets, previously known as the Plus Markets, had faced closure in 2012 after a series of loss-making years and survived only by being sold for a modest price to ICAP plc, an interdealer broker firm. The long-term plans of the new owner remain to be seen.

Efficient Capital Markets

Efficient capital markets theory underpins the conventional understanding of the pricing of securities in financial markets.[89] In general terms, the theory is concerned with whether prices at any point in time 'fully reflect' available information.[90] Ever since a classic review

---

[84] This section on AIM is based on information on the London Stock Exchange website, in particular its publication, *A Guide to AIM* (2010).

[85] This section on the PSM is based on information on the London Stock Exchange's website.

[86] A Jameson, 'The World Comes to Market' in LSE, *Perspectives on the Global Markets* (London: Yearbook 2012) 41.

[87] Excluding its High Growth Segment, which is a regulated market for unlisted securities.

[88] <http://www.isdx.com/regulation/default.aspx> accessed July 2013.

[89] For an overview of classic literature on this topic, see HS Houthakker and PJ Williamson, *The Economics of Financial Markets* (Oxford: OUP, 1996) 130–40.

[90] EF Fama, 'Efficient Capital Markets: A Review of Theory and Empirical Work' (1970) 25 *Journal of Finance* 383.

published in 1970, it has been usual to distinguish between three degrees of efficiency: weak-form efficiency, semi-strong-form efficiency, and strong-form efficiency.[91] In a weak-form efficient market, the current prices of securities reflect all relevant historical information. A semi-strong efficient capital market is one where prices adjust rapidly in response to information as soon as it becomes available. A strong-form efficient capital market is one where the prices reflect all relevant information, including information that has not yet been made public. Empirical research supports weak-form efficiency and semi-strong efficiency as explanations of how securities markets actually work in major jurisdictions, with the semi-strong version being the one that is most favoured.[92] That markets do not normally conform to the strong-form efficiency hypothesis is demonstrated by the (illegal) profits that can be made by insider trading: the opportunity for profit exists because market prices have not yet absorbed the information that has not been made public or, to put it another way, because the market is not conforming to the model of strong-form efficiency.

A distinction must be drawn between *informational* efficiency, that is the speed with which information is impounded into prices, and *fundamental* efficiency, by which is meant that prices represent the best current estimate of the present value of the future cash flows associated with a security. The market will be fundamentally efficient only when the market price equals the fundamental price. If prices in an informationally efficient market are inaccurate in a fundamental sense, this implies a potential problem with regard to allocative efficiency, meaning that scarce resources may fail to be allocated to their most productive use.[93]

However, in spite of the important theoretical distinction between informational and fundamental efficiency, financial regulatory policy has for a long time rested on the assumption that market prices are 'good indicators of rationally evaluated economic value' and that efficient and liquid financial markets 'deliver major allocative efficiency benefits.'[94] Fundamental value in a more abstract sense than the sum total of the market's evaluation of all the known information about a security is hard to pin down.

For many years the efficient capital market hypothesis therefore provided the intellectual context for capital market regulation.[95] It has been said that: 'Almost all issues are discussed against the background of market efficiency: whether issuers should be required to make duplicative disclosures; whether company insiders should be permitted to speak privately with institutional investors and analysts; and how damages can be inferred from stock price movements. Market efficiency and the mechanisms of market efficiency factor into all of these policy debates—and quite appropriately.'[96] As Adair Turner, the last Chairman of the Financial Services Authority before it was disbanded, put it: 'The predominant assumption behind financial market regulation—in the US, the UK and increasingly across the world— has been that financial markets are capable of being both efficient and rational and that a key goal of financial market regulation is to remove the impediments which might produce

---

[91] EF Fama, 'Efficient Capital Markets: A Review of Theory and Empirical Work' 383.

[92] EF Fama, 'Efficient Capital Markets: II' (1991) 46(5) *Journal of Finance* 1575.

[93] Although some contend that the connection between prices in the public trading markets for stocks and the allocation of real resources is a weak one, and that stock markets may have far less allocative importance than has generally been assumed: L Stout, 'The Unimportance of Being Efficient: An Economic Analysis of Stock Market Pricing and Securities Regulation' (1988) 87 *Michigan Law Review* 613.

[94] These quotations are from A Turner, *The Turner Review: A Regulatory Response to the Global Banking Crisis* (FSA, 2009) 39–40.

[95] RJ Gilson and RR Kraakman, 'The Mechanisms of Market Efficiency' (1984) 70 *Virginia Law Review* 549, 550.

[96] HE Jackson, 'To What Extent Should Individual Investors Rely on the Mechanisms of Market Efficiency: A Preliminary Investigation of Dispersion in Investor Returns' (2003) 28 *Journal of Corporation Law* 671.

inefficient and illiquid markets.'[97] Mandatory disclosure requirements targeted at correcting the market failure of information asymmetries were a central element of regulatory strategies for the capital markets.[98]

However, the hegemony of the efficient capital market hypothesis has never gone unquestioned and doubts have intensified in the aftermath of crises in which markets and market participants did not behave as theories based on efficiency and investor rationality would suggest. It is not new to acknowledge that financial markets are prone to 'bubbles' but the turmoil in the markets since 2007 has refocused critical attention on this crucial fact. The exposure of the limits of the assumptions of rationality that underpin the efficient capital markets hypothesis has led policymakers in search of new insights to turn increasingly to the work of behavioural economists who have stressed the need to take more account of socio-psychological factors that may lead investors to engage in irrational trading activities that affect share prices.[99] Although supporters of the efficient capital markets theory contend that arbitrage will quickly eliminate pricing inaccuracies caused by investor irrationality,[100] others point out that arbitrage is risky and subject to limitations, and that even professional investors cannot be relied upon to act with perfect rationality.[101]

The deep debate on these issues makes it hard now to claim, as was done in 1978, that 'there is no other proposition in economics which has more solid empirical evidence supporting it than the efficient market hypothesis.'[102] However, recognizing that disclosure on its own is an inadequate response to financial market failures because faulty market mechanisms cannot always be relied upon to process information efficiently or that badly designed disclosure requirements can be counterproductive does not mean rushing inexorably to the conclusion that disclosure-based regulatory strategies should be abandoned outright.[103] Since there is overwhelming empirical evidence that share prices react quickly, in the expected direction, to the release of information, overall the theory of efficient capital markets can continue to contribute usefully to the analytical framework even if it is demoted from the position of being *the* defining intellectual approach.

Measuring and assessing financial performance: company accounts

The definition of a semi-strong efficient capital market as one in which market prices shift rapidly in response to new information as soon as it becomes public, puts the spotlight

---

[97] Turner, *The Turner Review*, 39.

[98] JC Coffee, 'Market Failure and the Economic Case for a Mandatory Disclosure System' (1984) 70 *Virginia Law Review* 717; R La Porta, F Lopez-de-Silanes, and A Shleifer, 'What Works in Securities Laws?' (2006) 61 *Journal of Finance* 1.

[99] FB Cross and RA Prentice, *Law and Corporate Finance* (Cheltenham: Edward Elgar, 2007) ch 3 provide an overview of behavioural analysis of law and corporate finance. Behavioural economics is a discipline that has grown out of seminal work by the cognitive psychologists Kahneman and Tversky for which Kahneman was awarded the Nobel Prize in 2002. Their classic papers include A Tversky and D Kahneman, 'Judgment under Uncertainty: Heuristics and Biases' (1974) 185 *Science* 1124; D Kahneman and A Tversky, 'Prospect Theory: An Analysis of Decisions under Risk' (1979) 47 *Econometrica* 263; A Tversky and D Kahneman, 'The Framing of Decisions and the Psychology of Choice' (1981) 211 *Science* 453. The literature on behavioral economics is now vast. An important post-crisis critique is GA Akelof and RJ Shiller, *Animal Spirits: How Human Psychology Drives the Economy, and Why it Matters for Global Capitalism* (Princeton University Press, 2010).

[100] RJ Gilson and R Kraakman, 'The Mechanisms of *Market Efficiency* Twenty Years Later: The Hindsight Bias' (2003) 28 *Journal of Corporation Law* 715.

[101] A Shleifer and L Summers, 'The Noise Trader Approach to Finance' (1990) 4 *Journal of Economic Perspectives* 19; A Shleifer and R Vishny, 'The Limits of Arbitrage' (1997) 52 *Journal of Finance* 35.

[102] MC Jensen, 'Some Anomalous Evidence Regarding Market Efficiency' (1978) 6 *Journal of Financial Economics* 95.

[103] Although wariness about placing too much reliance on disclosure is certainly justified: SM Davidoff and CA Hill, 'Limits of Disclosure' (2013) 36 *Seattle University Law Review* 599.

onto the operation of processes whereby information is conveyed to the market and then impounded into prices. It has been said that: 'Since efficiency in the capital market depends on the distribution of information, it is ultimately a function of the cost of information to traders. The lower the cost of particular information, the wider will be its distribution, the more effective will be the capital market mechanism operating to reflect it in prices, and the more efficient will be the market with respect to it.'[104] Mandatory disclosure obligations eliminate the repetitive costs of individual acquisition of information by each market participant and, as such, they can be regarded as an efficiency-enhancing mechanism.[105] Regular reporting of financial performance is the central mandatory disclosure obligation to which all companies are subject. This section therefore provides an overview of the UK mandatory financial disclosure obligations for companies and of the institutional framework within which they operate.

Statutory financial disclosure framework for UK companies: an overview

The directors of a company must prepare individual accounts for the company for each of its financial years.[106] The accounts may be prepared in accordance with the requirements of the Companies Act or in accordance with international accounting standards/international financial reporting standards (IFRS).[107] Companies Act accounts comprise a balance sheet (statement of the financial position) as at the end of the relevant financial period and a profit and loss account (income statement) covering that period.[108] These fundamental statutory requirements are amplified by accounting standards (UK GAAP), which include a requirement for additional statements on income cash flow and changes in equity. Responsibility for UK GAAP lies with the Financial Reporting Council (FRC). A complete set of IFRS financial statements comprises a statement of financial position (balance sheet) at the end of the period, a statement of comprehensive income for the period (or an income statement and a statement of comprehensive income), a statement of changes in equity for the period, a statement of cash flows for the period, and notes comprising a summary of accounting policies and other explanatory material.[109] International Accounting Standards and International Financial Reporting Standards are the responsibility of the International Accounting Standards Board (IASB).[110]

Before approving the accounts the directors must be satisfied that they give a true and fair view of the assets, liabilities, financial position and profit or loss of the company.[111] This requirement applies both to Companies Act accounts and accounts drawn up in accordance with IFRS. The FRC takes the view that fair presentation under IFRS is equivalent to a true

---

[104] RJ Gilson and RR Kraakman, 'The Mechanisms of Market Efficiency' (1984) 70 *Virginia Law Review* 549, 593.

[105] RJ Gilson and RR Kraakman, 'The Mechanisms of Market Efficiency', 597–601.

[106] Companies Act 2006, s 394. There is an exemption for dormant subsidiaries: Companies Act 2006, s 394A-C.

[107] Companies Act 2006, s 395.

[108] Companies Act 2006, s 396. Detailed requirements are set out in Regulations made under Companies Act 2006, s 396 (individual accounts) and s 404 (group accounts): The Small Companies and Groups (Accounts and Directors' Report) Regulations 2008, SI 2008/409; The Large and Medium-sized Companies and Groups (Accounts and Reports) Regulations 2008, SI 2008/41 (as amended). These Regulations will be revised to implement (by July 2015) Directive 2013/34/EU of the European Parliament and of the Council of 26 June 2013 on the annual financial statements, consolidated financial statements and related reports of certain types of undertakings, amending Directive 2006/43/EC of the European Parliament and of the Council and repealing Council Directives 78/660/EEC and 83/349/EEC, [2013] OJ L182/19.

[109] IAS 1, *Presentation of Financial Statements*.

[110] Standards issued by the IASB are designated International Financial Reporting Standards but earlier pronouncements made by a predecessor body that remain in force are designated International Accounting Standards.

[111] Companies Act 2006, s 393.

and fair view.[112] A legal Opinion by George Bompas QC which was widely in circulation during 2013 takes issue with this view. This Opinion regards it as questionable whether statutory accounts prepared in accordance with IFRS will always give a true and fair view. If correct, this uncertainty would have implications for the legality of dividends and other distributions that depend on the existence of supporting accounts that give a true and fair view of the pay-or's company's financial position.[113] However, another Opinion obtained by the FRC from Michael Moore QC and published in October 2013 provides a more convincing analysis of the interaction between IFRS, as adopted in the EU, and the concept of a true and fair view under UK and EU law, and concludes that there is simply no reasonable basis for denying the existence of a true and fair override.

Subject to certain exemptions, directors of parent companies must also prepare consolidated group accounts for each year.[114] As a matter of European law, the consolidated group accounts of an issuer with securities admitted to trading on a 'regulated market' must be drawn up in accordance with IFRS as adopted in the EU.[115] This requirement is applicable to issuers on the London Stock Exchange's Main Market but not directly to issuers on AIM which is an 'exchange-regulated market' rather than an EU regulated market. (However, under the rules governing admission to trading on AIM, there is a requirement for AIM companies incorporated in European Economic Area (EEA) countries to prepare and present their annual consolidated accounts in accordance with IFRS.[116]) The group accounts of other companies may be drawn up as Companies Act group accounts or as IFRS group accounts.[117] The financial statements required to be included in Companies Act or IFRS accounts are the same as for individual accounts but on a consolidated rather than an individual basis. The individual accounts of a parent company and each of its subsidiary undertakings must all be prepared using the same reporting framework except where there are good reasons not to do so.[118]

In addition to the financial statements, the directors of a company must prepare a directors' report for each financial year of the company.[119] For a parent company that prepares group accounts, the directors' report must be a consolidated report.[120] Except for companies that are subject to a special regime for small companies, companies must also produce a further report known as the strategic report (which replaces a previous requirement for the inclusion of a business review in the directors' report).[121] The strategic report must contain a fair review of the company's business and a description of the principal risks and uncertainties facing the company.[122] The prescribed contents of strategic reports are more demanding for quoted companies than for unquoted companies and include a forward looking element.[123] They include requirements to describe the company's strategy and business model, to give information about board diversity and to refer to relevant human rights issues.[124] A 'quoted company' for

---

[112] FRC, *True and Fair* (July 2011).   [113] See further ch 9.   [114] Companies Act 2006, s 399.

[115] Regulation (EC) 1606/2002 of the European Parliament and of the Council of 19 July 2002 on the application of international accounting standards [2002] OJ L/243. This requirement is directly applicable in the UK. Companies Act 2006, s 403(1) notes its impact.

[116] AIM *Rules*, r 19.   [117] Companies Act 2006, s 403(2).   [118] Companies Act 2006, s 407.

[119] Companies Act 2006, s 415.   [120] Companies Act 2006, s 415.

[121] Companies Act 2006 (Strategic Report and Directors' Report) Regulations 2013, SI 2013/1970 revoking Companies Act 2006, s 417 and inserting Companies Act 2006, s 414A–D.

[122] Companies Act 2006, s 414C.

[123] Companies Act 2006, s 414C(7)–(8). There are also modifications for medium-sized enterprises: s 414C(6) (use of key performance indicators).

[124] The European Commission has proposed revisions to the EU Accounting Directive that also touch on these issues: European Commission, Proposal for a Directive amending Council Directives 78/660/EEC and 83/349/EEC as regards disclosure of non-financial and diversity information by certain large companies and groups (COM(2013) 207). In due course the UK requirements may require some adjustment to conform to new EU rules.

the purposes of the accounting requirements of the Companies Act 2006 includes companies whose equity share capital has been admitted to the London Stock Exchange's Main Market, or any other EEA market for officially listed securities, or which are admitted to dealing on the New York Stock Exchange or NASDAQ.[125] The directors of a quoted company are also required to prepare a directors' remuneration report for each financial year of the company.[126] Specific statutory liability falls on directors to compensate the company for false or misleading statements in, or omissions from, the directors' report, remuneration report, or strategic report. The liability standard is knowledge or recklessness.[127]

Subject to certain exemptions (including exemptions for small companies and dormant companies) annual accounts must be independently audited.[128] The auditor's report must state clearly whether, in the auditor's opinion, the annual accounts give a true and fair view, have been properly prepared in accordance with the relevant financial reporting framework, and have been prepared in accordance with the Companies Act 2006 and the IAS Regulation, where that is applicable.[129] The auditor must also state whether, in his or her opinion, the information given in the directors' report and strategic report is consistent with the accounts.[130] For quoted companies, the auditor's report must include a report on the auditable part of the directors' remuneration report and must state whether it has been properly prepared.[131]

The process under the Companies Act 2006 for putting annual accounts and reports into the public domain is that they must be sent to every shareholder and debenture holder, and every other person who is entitled to receive notice of the general meetings.[132] The Companies Act 2006 makes provision for documents and other information to be validly sent in hard copy form, in electronic form, or by being made available on a website.[133] Quoted companies must, in addition, make their annual accounts and reports available on a website which is accessible by the general public and not just members and debenture holders.[134] There is also provision for the strategic report and supplementary material to be sent to shareholders, debenture holders, and other entitled persons instead of the full accounts and reports but the full accounts and reports must be sent to any such person who so requests.[135] Public (but not private) companies must then within a specified period lay their accounts and reports before a general meeting.[136] Finally, all limited companies must file their annual accounts and reports with the registrar of companies.[137] Exactly what has to be filed depends on the type of company.[138]

The time limits for fulfilment of these requirements are important because a long time-lag is likely seriously to diminish the value of the information provided by the accounts. Under the Companies Act 2006, the time limit within which a public company must lay its accounts before the general meeting and then file them with the registrar is six months from the end of the relevant accounting reference period.[139] For private companies the time period for

---

[125] Companies Act 2006, s 385. The detailed requirements relating to remuneration reports were amended by the Enterprise and Regulatory Reform Act 213 and The Companies Act 2006 (Large and Medium-sized Companies and Groups (Amendment) Regulations 2013, SI 2013/1981). There may be further changes in the pipeline as a result of EU-level initiatives: European Commission, *Action Plan: European Company Law and Corporate Governance—A Modern Legal Framework for More Engaged Shareholders and Sustainable Companies* (COM(2012) 740).

[126] Companies Act 2006, s 420.   [127] Companies Act 2006, s 463.

[128] Companies Act 2006, s 475, as amended by the Companies and Limited Liability Partnerships (Accounts and Audit Exemptions and Change of Accounting Framework) Regulations 2012/2301.

[129] Companies Act 2006, s 495.   [130] Companies Act 2006, s 496 (as amended).

[131] Companies Act 2006, s 497.   [132] Companies Act 2006, s 423.

[133] Companies Act 2006, ss 1144–1148 and Schs 4–5.

[134] Companies Act 2006, s 430. Access can be restricted so far as necessary to comply with any enactment or regulatory requirement (in the UK or elsewhere): s 430(3)(b).

[135] Companies Act 2006, s 426–426A (as amended).

[136] Companies Act 2006, s 437.   [137] Companies Act 2006, s 441.

[138] Companies Act 2006, ss 444–448.   [139] Companies Act 2006, s 442.

delivery of accounts to the registrar is nine months.[140] Even though the publication time-scales were shortened by the Companies Act 2006, they still remain quite generous.

Additional financial disclosure framework under FCA *Disclosure and Transparency Rules*

The EU Transparency Obligations Directive requires Member States to impose disclosure requirements in relation to annual accounts and half-yearly financial reports. The original Transparency Obligations Directive also required interim financial statements (which were broadly equivalent to quarterly reports).[141] However, the obligation to publish quarterly financial information is abolished by the 2013 revising Directive.[142] The European Commission based the initiative to abolish mandatory quarterly reporting on findings indicating that it was not necessary for investor protection. Within the UK the abolition has also been viewed positively as a step that may reduce corporate short-termism.

The UK implements the Transparency Obligations Directive via the FCA *Disclosure Rules and Transparency Rules* (DTR). The issuer disclosure requirements in the *DTR* apply (with some exemptions) to issuers whose transferable securities are admitted to trading on a 'regulated market' and whose 'home State' is the UK. 'Regulated market' and 'home State' are regulatory concepts with considerable significance in EU securities law. For the purposes of this chapter, it can suffice to note that companies incorporated in the UK that have their equity share capital admitted to trading on the Main Market of the London Stock Exchange (which is a regulated market) are subject to the *DTR* issuer disclosure rules but AIM companies, even if UK incorporated, are not; this is because AIM is an 'exchange-regulated,' rather than an EU regulated, market.[143] The *DTR* are also the vehicle for the implementation in the UK of the requirement in the EU accounting framework for companies to include a corporate governance statement in their directors' report.[144]

Under the *DTR*, audited annual reports must be published within four months of the year end (rather than the more generous six months permitted by the Companies Act 2006).[145] Annual reports must contain a statement from each responsible person within the issuer that to the best of his or her knowledge the financial statements give a true and fair view and the management report includes a fair review of performance together with a description of principal risks and uncertainties.[146] Half-yearly financial reports (which need not be audited) must be made public as soon as possible, but no later than two months after the end of the period to which the report relates.[147] The contents of half-yearly reports are prescribed in outline by the *DTR* as comprising a condensed set of financial statements, an interim management report, and responsibility statements.[148]

The *DTR* also address the process whereby information is disseminated to the public.[149] All regulated information must be disseminated in a manner ensuring that it is capable of

---

[140] Companies Act 2006, s 442.

[141] Directive (EC) 2004/109 of the European Parliament and of the Council of 15 December 2004 on the harmonization of transparency requirements in relation to information about issuers whose securities are admitted to trading on a regulated market and amending Directive (EC) 2001/34, [2004] OJ L390/38, Arts 4–6.

[142] Directive 2013/50/EU of the European Parliament and of the Council of 22 October 2013 amending Directive 2004/109/EC, [2013] OJ L294/13.

[143] The significance of these categories is considered in further detail in ch 13.

[144] *DTR*, 7.2, which in due course presumably will also implement Directive 2013/34/EU of the European Parliament and of the Council of 26 June 2013 on the annual financial statements, consolidated financial statements and related reports of certain types of undertakings, amending Directive 2006/43/EC of the European Parliament and of the Council and repealing Council Directives 78/660/EEC and 83/349/EEC, [2013] OJ L182/19, Art 20.

[145] *DTR* 4.1.3.   [146] *DTR* 4.1.12.   [147] *DTR* 4.2.2. The filing period will be extended to three months when the revisions to the Transparency Obligations Directive are implemented.

[148] *DTR* 4.2.3.   [149] *DTR* 6.3.

reaching as wide a public as possible, and as close to simultaneously as possible throughout the EEA. It must also be communicated to the media in unedited full text (save for annual financial reports which can, generally, be edited). When regulated information is disclosed it must at the same time be filed with the FCA.[150] However, there is no requirement in the *DTR* for financial statements to be sent directly to shareholders (or others). The Transparency Obligations Directive also requires Member States to appoint at least one official mechanism for storing regulated information. In the UK, Morningstar, a commercial provider of independent financial research, performs this function.

Market efficiency (and investor protection) aims underpin the Transparency Obligations Directive. Its first recital declares that:

> Efficient, transparent and integrated securities markets contribute to a genuine single market in the Community and foster growth and job creation by better allocation of capital and by reducing costs. The disclosure of accurate, comprehensive and timely information about security issuers builds sustained investor confidence and allows an informed assessment of their business performance and assets. This enhances both investor protection and market efficiency.

These sentiments owe much to the intellectual framework provided by the efficient capital markets theory.

Additional financial disclosure framework for other publicly traded companies

The rules of the market on which a company's securities are admitted to trading may impose financial disclosure obligations in addition to those under the general law. Under the AIM *Rules for Companies*, for example, AIM companies must prepare half-yearly reports, which must be published without delay and in any event not later than three months after the end of the relevant period.[151] The information contained in a half-yearly report must include at least a balance sheet, an income statement, and a cash flow statement. The half-yearly report must be presented and prepared in a form consistent with that which will be adopted in the company's annual accounts. AIM companies have never been required to publish public quarterly reports or other interim financial statements.

---

[150] *DTR* 6.2.2.   [151] AIM *Rules*, r 18.

PART II
LEGAL CAPITAL

4

Formation of Share Capital

Scope of this Part

This part of the book is concerned with legal capital. Legal capital is a broad concept that embraces the rules relating to the raising of capital through share issuance, the maintenance of share capital, and the returning of value to shareholders in circumstances that do not infringe the maintenance of capital requirements. This chapter deals with 'pay in' rules, ie the regulation of the amount of share capital that is put into a company and the forms of consideration that a company can accept in return for its shares. The basic idea that underpins the pay in rules is that investors should in fact put into the company the amount in cash or non-cash consideration that they have agreed to invest in return for their shares. However, the rules in the Companies Act 2006 that give effect to this straightforward principle are quite complex, especially for public companies where they implement requirements derived from EU law in the form of a Directive that, notwithstanding a degree of modernization followed by consolidation in 2012, continues to be known as the Second Company Law Directive.[1]

Minimum Price of Individual Shares: Par Values

Every share in a limited company having a share capital must have a fixed nominal or par value.[2] An allotment of a share that does not have a fixed nominal value is void and, in the event of a purported allotment, criminal sanctions attach to every officer of the company who is in default.[3] The par value must be a monetary amount but it does not have to be an amount that is capable of being paid in legal tender.[4] This means that it can be a fraction or percentage of a monetary amount. The par value of any one share cannot be stated in two currencies—ie a share cannot have a par value of, say, US$1 or £1—but different shares in the same company can have par values stated in different currencies.[5] The nominal value of the shares taken on formation is part of the information that must be included in the statement of capital that is filed with the registrar when a new company is incorporated.[6] The statement of capital gives a snapshot of the company's share capital at the point in time to which it relates. Elsewhere in the Companies Act 2006, there are obligations to file an updated statement of capital when the share capital is altered, such as when new shares are allotted.[7]

There is no prescribed minimum par value in respect of the shares of public or private companies and thus any monetary amount can be selected for this purpose. To encourage

---

[1] Directive 2012/30/EU of the European Parliament and of the Council of 25 October 2012 on coordination of safeguards which, for the protection of the interests of members and others, are required by Member States of companies within the meaning of the second paragraph of Article 54 of the Treaty on the Functioning of the European Union, in respect of the formation of public limited liability companies and the maintenance and alteration of their capital, with a view to making such safeguards equivalent (Recast) [2012] L315/74 (Second Company Law Directive).

[2] Companies Act 2006, s 542.   [3] Companies Act 2006, s 542(2) and (4)–(5).

[4] *Re Scandinavian Bank Group plc* [1987] 2 All ER 70, [1987] BCC 93.

[5] Companies Act 2006, s 542(3), which is consistent with earlier authority: *Re Scandinavian Bank Group plc* [1987] 2 All ER 70, [1987] BCC 93. This is subject to rules on denomination of minimum capital: Companies Act 2006, s 765 discussed later.

[6] Companies Act 2006, ss 9–10.   [7] Companies Act 2006, s 555 (return of allotments).

liquidity, the ordinary shares of public companies tend to have low par values, such as 25p or lower. Liquidity is generally a less important issue in relation to the shares of a private company and larger par values, typically £1, are common. That it is for companies themselves to fix the par values of their shares softens considerably the impact of the seemingly mandatory rule that par values must be stated.

The legal consequence of giving a par value to a share is that this is the minimum price at which shares of that class can be allotted.[8] However, shares can, and often are, allotted at a price in excess of their par value. When this occurs, shares are said to be allotted at a premium. When the par value requirement was first established in the law in the UK it was thought to be important because it allowed creditors to ascertain the fixed and certain amount of capital that they were entitled to regard as their security.[9] However, ever since the 1940s, when rules were adopted that required companies to treat all amounts raised through share issuance as if they were capital, the significance of par values as a measure of the creditors' security disappeared because from that point onwards premiums as well as nominal amounts were to be counted as part of that security.

The concept of the par value of share capital might have significance if it gave some indication of the market value of a company's assets. However, it usually does not and instead may be a source of confusion. Where shares are issued at a premium, this creates an imbalance from the outset: an issue of 100,000 £1 shares at a premium of £1 each, gives the company a cash asset of £200,000 but the nominal value of its share capital (assuming no other issues) is £100,000. As time goes on, the overall net worth of the company and the value of individual shares in the company depend on the success of the company's business ventures and also on general economic factors.[10] In practice, the par value of a share commonly bears little relation to the price at which it trades in the market.

Par value requirements have been criticized frequently by review bodies. In 1945, as part of a general review of company law, the Cohen Committee reported that it saw much logic in the arguments put forward in support of having shares of no par value but because there was no public demand for, and considerable opposition to, the proposal, as well as some concerns about possible abuse, it refrained from recommending any change.[11] Less than ten years later, in 1954, a Board of Trade Committee under the chairmanship of Mr Montagu Gedge QC reported specifically on the question whether shares with no par values should be allowed.[12] On this occasion, the Committee found that there was general support for the proposal[13] and it recommended that shares with no par value should be permitted. The Gedge Committee accepted the following advantages claimed for no par value shares.

1. They represent the share for what it is—a fraction or aliquot part of the equity—and they do not import a notional token of value.

---

[8] Companies Act 2006, s 580. This statutory rule applies to all companies limited by shares. For public companies it gives effect to the Second Company Law Directive, Art 8.

[9] *Ooregum Gold Mining Co of India v Roper* [1892] AC 125, 133–4, HL.

[10] See ch 3 for an outline of approaches to the valuation of equity securities.

[11] *Report of the Committee on Company Law Amendment* (Cmd 6659, 1945). Previous company law amendment committees had also considered the issue: Wrenbury Committee (Cd 9138, 1918) and Greene Committee (Cmd 2657, 1926). For a detailed historical review of the debate in the UK on no par value shares, see C Noke, 'No Value in Par: a History of the No Par Value Debate in the United Kingdom' (2000) 10 *Accounting, Business & Financial History* 13.

[12] *Report of the Committee on Shares of No Par Value* (Cmd 9112, 1954).

[13] It was, however, opposed by the General Council of the Trades Union Congress: *Report of the Committee on Shares of No Par Value* (Cmd 9112, 1954) paras 29–31. Also, a minority report annexed to the main report recorded one member of the committee's opposition to the proposal.

2. As there is no nominal capital and the share has no nominal value, they make it impossible to relate a dividend to a nominal capital and thus avoid a potential source of misunderstanding and misrepresentation.[14]

3. It is the capital employed and not the paid up share capital which is the true value of the undertaking; an ordinary share of no par value does not purport to be anything but a share of the equity.

4. Where shares do not have par values, capital reorganizations are simplified.

5. Shares of no par value would in certain cases facilitate the raising of additional equity capital. The par value rules can hinder a company in financial difficulties that wants to raise new share capital where the par value of these shares is greater than the amount that anyone would be willing to pay for them.

The Gedge Committee acknowledged the need for safeguards against abuse but concluded that, provided the whole of the proceeds of any issue of shares having no par value were treated as capital money and not as distributable reserves, the position would be neither more nor less open to abuse than in respect of shares having a par value. The Jenkins Committee, in 1962, also recommended that legislation should be introduced to permit shares with no par values.[15] This Committee went one step further than the Gedge Committee by recommending that no par value preference shares, as well as no par value ordinary shares, should be permitted. Despite this support in principle for reform, an attempt to include provision for no par value shares in the Companies Act 1967 failed.

The Company Law Review Steering Group that spearheaded the review that led to the Companies Act 2006 returned to the issue. By 1999, when the Steering Group issued its first consultation specifically on the issue, the UK was already lagging behind other parts of the common law world, where the trend of permitting no par value shares, and in some cases positively abolishing the concept of par value in its entirety, had already become firmly established. For example, section 38 of the New Zealand Companies Act 1993 provides in simple, uncompromising terms that 'a share must not have a nominal or par value'. Reform to similar effect was introduced in Australia in 1998: section 254C of the Corporations Act 2001 now states succinctly that shares of a company have no par value. The Steering Group recommended that the UK should move to this position but only for private companies.[16] The reason for the limitation was that the Steering Group felt that the UK's hands were tied in relation to public companies because Article 8 of the Second Company Law Directive requires public companies to attribute par values to their shares. Although Article 8 provides a no par share alternative, this alternative, which is based on a Belgian model, is generally considered, at least in the UK, to be unattractive because in essence it retains much of the distinction between par value and premium. Article 8 introduces the concept of 'accountable par' as an alternative to nominal value, by which is meant that the fixed value of individual shares is determined by reference to the percentage or fraction of the subscribed (nominal value) capital that they represent. It has been noted that the accountable par approach in effect performs the same function as the par value system 'except that the basis of denomination is by

---

[14] Articles normally provide for dividends to be paid on the amount paid up on shares: eg, Model Articles (plc), art 71. Where, as is the usual case, shares are fully paid up (the position envisaged in Model Articles (Ltd), art 21), the dividend can be calculated simply as a monetary amount per share (ie the amount available for distribution is divided by the number of shares in issue).

[15] *Report of the Company Law Committee* (Cmnd 1749, 1962) paras 32–4.

[16] Company Law Review Steering Group, *Modern Company Law for a Competitive Economy—Company Formation and Capital Maintenance* (URN 99/1145) para 3.8.

reference to the fraction of the aggregate of share capital contributed which they represent' and that 'these shares are still denominated by reference to a fraction of a capital fund the amount of which is fixed at any point in time.'[17] So, whilst several European countries have introduced 'no par value' shares, this development has to be understood in a special sense as referring to the exploitation of the accountable par alternative.[18] Such shares are not 'true' no par value shares, as that term is generally understood outside the EU.

The proposal to abandon par values for private companies did not make it into the Companies Act 2006. Consultation revealed concern that having different regimes for private and public companies in this respect could act as a barrier to growth, as it could complicate the process of conversion from a private to a public company.[19] The long overdue full-scale reform to remove an anachronism must therefore await change at the European level. In 2000 a working group, established by the European Commission under its Simpler Legislation for the Internal Market (SLIM) project with the remit of examining the Second Company Law Directive, concluded that the suggestion to introduce no par value shares was worthy of further study.[20] This view was endorsed by the High Level Group of Company Law Experts which was set up by the European Commission in September 2001 to make recommendations on a modern regulatory framework in the EU for company law.[21] In its final report, the High Level Group recommended that the accommodation of no par value shares within the Second Company Law Directive should be further reviewed.[22] Yet reforms to the Second Company Law Directive in 2006 did not touch on the requirement for no par value shares.[23] The overall value of the Second Company Law Directive remains questionable but a strong body of opinion that it is outdated has yet to translate into meaningful change.[24]

Abolition of par values would have ramifications for existing rights in contracts, deeds, and other instruments that are determined by reference to par values but suitable transitional provisions could be enacted to minimize the upheaval.[25]

[17] J Rickford et al, 'Reforming Capital: Report of the Interdisciplinary Group on Capital Maintenance' (2004) 15 *European Business Law Review* 919, 929.

[18] P de Tarso Domingues, 'No Par Value Shares in the Portuguese Legal System' (2012) 13 *European Business Organization Law Review* 125 (discussing developments in Portuguese company law that follow the example set by Germany, France, and Italy in adopting 'no par value' shares).

[19] Company Law Review Steering Group, *Modern Company Law for a Competitive Economy—Capital Maintenance: Other Issues* (June 2000) para 9 notes this concern and other more technical points raised in the consultation exercise. The decision to drop the proposal is noted at Company Law Review Steering Group, *Modern Company Law for a Competitive Economy—Completing the Structure* (URN 00/1335) para 7.3.

[20] European Commission, *Results of the Fourth Phase of SLIM* (COM(2000) 056).

[21] High Level Group of Company Law Experts, *A Modern Regulatory Framework for Company Law in Europe: Final Report* (Brussels, November 2002) 1.

[22] High Level Group of Company Law Experts, *A Modern Regulatory Framework for Company Law in Europe: Final Report*, 82–3.

[23] Reforms to the Second Company Law Directive by Directive 2006/68/EC, [2006] OJ L 264/32 are now incorporated into the 2012 recast version of the Second Company Law Directive.

[24] Discussion on the Second Company Law Directive continues: European Commission, *Communication on a Simplified Business Environment for Companies in the Areas of Company Law, Accounting and Auditing* (COM(2007) 394); KPMG, *Feasibility Study on an Alternative to the Capital Maintenance Regime Established by the Second Company Law Directive* (European Commission, 2008); European Commission, *Consultation on the Future of European Company Law* (2011). But the most recent indications suggest that the Commission does not regard reform of the Second Company Law Directive as a priority and that in the general company law field it is intending to confine its attentions to making the law more accessible through codification: European Commission, *Action Plan: European Company Law and Corporate Governance—A Modern Legal Framework for More Engaged Shareholders and Sustainable Companies* (COM(2012) 740). The academic literature is divided on the need for reform of the par value requirement: compare, eg, P Santella and R Turrini, 'Capital Maintenance in the EU: Is the Second Company Law Directive Really That Restrictive' (2008) 9 *European Business Organization Law Review* 427, 444–6, with Rickford, 'Reforming Capital,' 929–30.

[25] Company Law Review Steering Group, *Capital Maintenance: Other Issues*, paras 13–21.

Minimum Capital

Company formation requirements mean that there must be at least one person who agrees to become a member of the company and, in the case of a company that is to have a share capital, to take at least one share.[26] As we have seen, the allotment price of any shares taken on formation must be not less than their par value but the founders can fix the par value at whatever level they choose. In the case of a private company a share can be allotted on a nil paid, partly paid, or fully paid basis.[27] The combination of these rules means that there is no legal bar in the UK to a private company starting to trade with little or no equity actually invested in the business. According to statistical information compiled by Companies House, as at 31 March 2011 over 100,000 companies on the register had no issued share capital and over 1.9 million (of the just short of 2.7 million total number on the register) had up to £100.[28]

The position used to be markedly different elsewhere in Europe as, historically, many countries imposed in their national laws minimum capital requirements on their equivalents to UK private limited companies.[29] As of 2005, the private company minimum capital requirements in Member States that required a substantial (€10,000+) amount, ranged from just over €10,000 in Sweden to €25,000 in Germany and €35,000 in Austria.[30]

However, on this matter at least, the position in Europe has not been static but the primary instigator of change has been the Court of Justice of the EU rather than the EU legislative bodies. Putting the point another way, this is a sphere in which negative harmonization (the removal of barriers to integration in domestic laws) has proved to be rather more significant than positive harmonization (the imposition of pan-EU standardized rules).[31]

In a series of important decisions during the late 1990s and 2000s the Court of Justice established that it is not a fraud or a breach of EU Treaty freedoms for the founders of a business to incorporate a private company in a Member State that does not impose minimum capital requirements in order to bypass such requirements in the domestic laws of the Member State in which the controllers of the business are located and where the company is intended wholly or mainly to trade.[32] The breakthrough decision, *Centros Ltd v Erhvervs-og Selskabsstyrelsen*,[33] involved an English company, Centros, that never traded in the UK and

---

[26] Companies Act 2006, s 8.

[27] Model Articles (Ltd), art 21 provides for shares to be fully paid up. Companies that want to retain flexibility can depart from the model form in this respect.

[28] Companies House, *Statistical Tables on Companies Registration Activities 2010/11*.

[29] M Becht, C Mayer, and HF Wagner, 'Where Do Firms Incorporate? Deregulation and the Cost of Entry' (2008) 14 *Journal of Corporate Finance* 241.

[30] M Becht, C Mayer, and HF Wagner, 'Where Do Firms Incorporate? Deregulation and the Cost of Entry.'

[31] J Armour, 'Who Should Make Corporate Law? EC Legislation *versus* Regulatory Competition' (2005) 58 *Current Legal Problems* 369; W-G Ringe, 'Company Law and Free Movement of Capital' [2010] *Cambridge Law Journal* 378.

[32] The landmark decisions are C-212/97 *Centros Ltd v Erhvervs- og Selskabsstyrelsen* [1999] ECR I-1459; C-208/00 *Uberseering BV v Nordic Construction Co Baumanagement GmbH* (NCC) [2002] ECR I-9919; C-167/01; *Kamer van Koophandel en Fabrieken voor Amsterdam v Inspire Art Ltd* [2003] ECR I-10155; C-411/03 *Sevic Systems AG v Amtsgericht Neuwied* [2005] ECR I-10805; C-196/04 *Cadbury Schweppes Plc v Inland Revenue Commissioners* [2006] ECR I-7995; C-210/06 *Cartesio Oktato es Szolgaltato bt* [2008] E.C.R. I-9641; C-378/10 *Vale Építési kft* [2013] 1 WLR 294; C-371/10 *National Grid Indus BV v Inspecteur van de Belastingdienst Rijnmond/Kantoor Rotterdam* [2012] 1 CMLR 49; C-38/10 *European Commission v Portuguese Republic (Kingdom of Denmark and others, intervening)* [2013] 1 CMLR 8. And see WH Roth, 'From *Centros* to *Uberseering*: Free Movement Of Companies, Private International Law, and Community Law' (2003) 52 *International and Comparative Legal Quarterly* 177; A Johnston and P Phil Syrpis, 'Regulatory Competition in European Company Law after Cartesio' [2009] *European law Review* 378; L Ceroni, 'The Cross-border Mobility of Companies within the European Community after the Cartesio Ruling of the ECJ' [2010] *Journal of Business Law* 311; J Borg-Barthet, 'Free at Last? Choice of Corporate Law in the EU Following the Judgment in *Vale*' [2013] *International and Comparative Legal Quarterly* 503; J lau Hansen, 'The *Vale* Decision and the Court's Case Law on the Nationality of Companies' (2013) *European Company and Financial Law Review* 1.

[33] Case C-212/97, [1999] ECR I-1459.

whose controllers were Danish residents. The decision to use an English company as the corporate vehicle was driven by the difference in approach to minimum capital between the UK and Denmark. The Court held that it was contrary to EU law for Erhvervs-og Selskabsstyrelsen (a Danish authority) to refuse to register in Denmark a branch of Centros.

In *Kamer van Koophandel en Fabrieken voor Amsterdam v Inspire Art Ltd*,[34] which again involved an English limited company which was used to conduct business in another Member State (the Netherlands) that had substantial minimum capital requirements for private companies in its domestic law, the Court confirmed that it was immaterial, having regard to the application of the rules on freedom of establishment, that a company was formed in one Member State only for the purpose of establishing itself in a second Member State, where its main, or even entire, business was to be conducted. The reasons why a company chose to be formed in a particular Member State were, save in the case of fraud, irrelevant with regard to the application of the rules on freedom of establishment. The fact that a company was formed in a particular Member State for the sole purpose of enjoying the benefit of more favourable legislation did not constitute abuse even if that company conducted its activities entirely or mainly in a second state. In this case the Court determined that it was contrary to EU law for the Netherlands to seek to restrict the exercise of freedom of secondary establishment by an English company by requiring it to comply with requirements of Dutch law relating to minimum capital and directors' liability.

In the period immediately after *Centros* there was a noticeable trend for small firms to opt for incorporation as an English private limited company even though, in terms of the residence of their directors and owners and the location of their main centre of activity, their nationality was that of another EU Member State. An empirical study of UK incorporations between 1997 and 2005 found that between 2002 and 2005 over 55,000 new UK private limited companies were set up from other EU Member States.[35] Using statistical analysis, the study established a link between the outflow of private limited companies to the UK from a number of EU Member States and minimum capital requirements and other incorporation costs in those states. In absolute numbers, firms obtaining *Centros*-style incorporations after 2002 came mainly from Germany, the Netherlands, and France. Germany and the Netherlands were among the countries that, at the time of the study, imposed substantial minimum capital requirements on private limited companies. France also did so until 2003, when it reformed its law so as to cancel the mandatory minimum capital requirement for private companies.[36] The study noted that, after that change in its laws, France experienced much lower outflows. Thereafter, Germany and the Netherlands also reconsidered their positions.

Following the example of France, the Netherlands opted for bold reform. In 2012 the Dutch legislature completed the procedure for the adoption of legislation for the simplification and 'flexibilization' of private company law. The package of measures (known, in short, as the Flex-BV Act) came into force in October 2012. The Flex-BV Act dropped the requirement for a minimum capital (which previously stood at €18,000), thereby making it possible for a Dutch BV to be incorporated with a capital of €1 or even less. Associated requirements for capital to be paid up on issue were also abolished.

---

[34] Case C-167/01, [2003] ECR I-10155.

[35] M Becht, C Mayer, and HF Wagner, 'Where Do Firms Incorporate? Deregulation and the Cost of Entry' (2008) 14 *Journal of Corporate Finance* 241.

[36] I Urbain-Parléane, 'Working Group on the Share Capital in Europe—French Answers to the Questionnaire,' in M Lutter (ed), *Legal Capital in Europe* (Berlin: De Gruyter Recht, 2006) 480, a special volume of the *European Company and Financial Law Review*.

Germany's response was more tentative. Reforming legislation in force from November 2008 provides for a new type of 'entrepreneur company' (*Unternehmergesellschaft (haftungsbeschränkt) (UG)*), which can be established with a minimum capital of €1.[37] A UG must retain 25 per cent of its annual profits and not distribute that portion to the shareholders. Once capital reserves reach €25,000, which is the minimum capital for an ordinary German private limited company (*Gesellschaft mit beschränkter Haftung (GmbH)*), the UG reaches full GmbH status and the mandatory retentions rule falls away.

Even Denmark, whose national legal requirements gave the European Court its first opportunity to rule on the compatibility of minimum capital requirements and Treaty freedoms, has changed its position. However, like Germany, its response has been cautious: a mandatory minimum capital requirement has been retained but the amount required has been reduced.[38]

It is possible to characterize these post-*Centros* developments in Europe as an example of regulatory competition at work.[39] Regulatory competition is a theoretical model in which states are seen as suppliers in a competitive product market, with the product supplied being regulation, and market participants who choose between different sets of national law being the consumers of the product. A precondition to the operation of regulatory competition is that the consumers must have freedom of choice: this was supplied by the European Court in the *Centros* case, which put beyond doubt the legal validity of corporate mobility with regard to incorporation. Theorists suggest that regulatory competition is a reliable mechanism to enable policymakers to discover what people actually want.[40] Applying this line of reasoning, it can be said that, post-*Centros*, entrepreneurs made it clear that mandatory minimum capital requirements were not in line with their preferences and that in opting for a deregulatory response when faced with a choice between losing incorporations or changing their laws, Member States were, in effect, responding to competitive pressures. Those States could not continue to impose their existing laws on companies that were exercising cross-border freedoms because the Court had made it clear that there was nothing about minimum capital requirements that could be regarded as a public interest justification for Member States to restrict Treaty freedoms by imposing them on companies incorporated elsewhere in the Community; adequate protection for those dealing with such companies was provided instead under the company laws of the country of incorporation.[41]

The post-*Centros* learning on the weakness of minimum capital as a creditor protection mechanism has also exerted influence at the EU legislative level, although the practical impact of this influence in terms of shaping the legislative framework has been relatively weak. In 2008 the European Commission proposed the introduction of a European private company

---

[37] Gesetz zur Modernisierung des GmbH-Rechts und zur Bekämpfung von Missbräuchen (MoMiG—Law for the Modernization of the GmbH and to Stop its Misuse).

[38] From DKK 125,000 (€16,780) to DKK 80,000 (€10,740): J lau Hansen, 'The New Danish Companies Act of 2009' (2010) *European Business Organization Law Review* 87, 91–2. Lau Hansen notes that Sweden has also taken a cautious approach but suggests that developments in both jurisdictions may be regarded as steps on the way to full abolition of mandatory minimum capital.

[39] L Enriques and M Gelter, 'Regulatory Competition in European Company Law and Creditor Protection' (2006) 7 *European Business Organization Law Review* 417.

[40] JM Sun and J Pelkmans, 'Regulatory Competition in the Single Market' (1995) 33 *Journal of Common Market Studies* 67, 82–8.

[41] This analysis relates to the *Gebhard* test, that is to the four factors that must be satisfied to justify national restrictions on the exercise of a Treaty freedom, namely: (i) the restrictions are applied in a consistent and non-discriminatory manner, (ii) the restrictions are justified by imperative requirements of public interest, (iii) the restrictions secure the attainment of their objective, and (iv) the restrictions are not disproportionate in their effect: C-55/94 *Gebhard v Colsiglio dell'Ordine degli Avvocati e Procuratori di Milano* [1995] ECR I-4165.

(Societas Privata Europaea or SPE) to complement the European public company.[42] The underlying aim of the proposal was to create a new European legal form that would enhance the competitiveness of small and medium-sized enterprises by facilitating their establishment and operation in the single market. A trivial €1 minimum capital was proposed. The European Commission explained this aspect of the proposal in the following terms:

> In order to facilitate start-ups, the Regulation sets the minimum capital requirement at €1. The proposal departs from the traditional approach that considers the requirement of a high minimum of legal capital as a means of creditor protection. Studies show that creditors nowadays look rather at aspects other than capital, such as cash flow, which are more relevant to solvency. Director-shareholders of small companies often offer personal guarantees to their creditors (e.g. to banks) and suppliers also use other methods to secure their claims, e.g. providing that ownership of goods only passes upon payment. Moreover, companies have different capital needs depending on their activity, and thus it is impossible to determine an appropriate capital for all companies. The shareholders of a company are the best placed to define the capital needs of their business.[43]

Yet the fate of the SPE proposal has also demonstrated the limits of learning from experience and the scope for still divergent national responses in spite of a degree of the convergence being fostered by negative harmonization. By 2011 it had emerged that the absence of a meaningful minimum capital requirement in the Commission's proposal, although welcomed by some, was for others a stumbling block to securing political agreement on the proposal.[44] A solution to the impasse on minimum capital and certain other matters (the location of the registered office or seat, and employee participation) has not yet been found and the European private company proposal is effectively stalled.[45]

Whereas for private companies minimum capital requirements are a matter governed by domestic laws, all EU incorporated public companies are subject to a minimum capital requirement derived from Article 6 of the Second Company Law Directive. The amount of the minimum capital as specified in the Directive is not less than €25,000. The UK 'over-implements' the Directive by specifying a minimum allotted capital requirement of £50,000 in nominal value or its euro equivalent.[46] Under the Companies Act 2006 newly-formed public companies are required to have an allotted capital of at least €50,000 before they can obtain the trading certificate that allows them to do any business or exercise any borrowing powers.[47] Having an allotted capital of at least €50,000 is also a condition that must be satisfied before a private company can re-register as a public company.[48] However, not all of the £50,000 in nominal value needs to be paid up at the time of obtaining a trading certificate or, as the case may be, re-registration. The rules relating to payment for shares in a public company

---

[42] European Commission, *Proposal for a Council Regulation on the Statute for a European Private Company* (COM(2008) 396).

[43] European Commission, *Proposal for a Council Regulation on the Statute for a European Private Company*, p. 7.

[44] Council, *Proposal for a Council Regulation on a European Private Company—Political Agreement* (10611/11, 23 May 2011). This text was not accepted: Council Meeting on Competitiveness (Internal Market, Industry Research and Space) 30/31 May 2011 (10547/11). Discussing the variety of different proposals and unsuccessful attempts to find agreement: K Fuchs-Mtwebana, 'The Regulation of Companies' Capital in the EU' [2011] *European Business Law Review* 237, 247–9; PL Davies, 'The European Private Company (SPE): Uniformity, Flexibility, Competition and the Persistence of National Laws' (1 May 2010). Oxford Legal Studies Research Paper No. 11/2011; ECGI—Law Working Paper No. 154/2010 <http://ssrn.com/abstract=1622293> accessed July 2013; MM Siems, L Herzog and E Rosenhäger, 'The Protection of Creditors of a European Private Company (SPE)' (2011) 12 *European Business Organization Law Review* 147.

[45] European Commission, *Action Plan*, suggests that the Commission no longer intends to pursue the SPE proposal.

[46] Currently specified as €57,100: Companies (Authorised Minimum) Regulations 2009, SI 2009/2425, reg 2.

[47] Companies Act 2006, s 761.   [48] Companies Act 2006, ss 90–91.

include a requirement that at least one-quarter of the nominal value must always be paid up on allotment,[49] so the minimum amount that must actually be put in is £12,500 (50,000 x ¼). It has been pointed out that a reading of the requirement for shares to be at least one-quarter paid up in conjunction with the statutory definition of 'payment in cash' appears to lead to the conclusion that the company does not actually have to receive hard cash on allotment of its shares because payment in cash includes an undertaking to pay cash at a later date.[50] Although surprising at first blush, the Companies Act 2006 and the underlying provisions of the Second Company Law Directive do not appear to rule out this reading.

Denomination of minimum capital

By way of a qualification to the general freedom with regard to having a multi-currency share capital,[51] the minimum share capital requirement must be satisfied by reference either to allotted share capital denominated in sterling or to allotted share capital denominated in euros (but not partly in one and partly in the other).[52] In determining whether a company has satisfied the minimum capital requirement, no account is to be taken of any of its allotted share capital that is denominated in a currency other than sterling or, as the case may be, euros.[53] Once a company has obtained its trading certificate or re-registered, it can subsequently redenominate its share capital, including that part of it that constituted its minimum capital, into any other currency.[54] In several respects these requirements with regard to minimum capital are more flexible than was the case prior to the Companies Act 2006. By expressly permitting sterling or its euro equivalent and allowing redenomination, the 2006 Act departs from some very cautious interpretations of Article 6 of the Second Company Law Directive that were held previously. There was a concern that Article 6 could oblige the UK to require public companies to have and retain a tranche of their capital denominated in sterling in order to satisfy the minimum capital requirement. Yet, even though the Companies Act 2006 strips the minimum capital currency denomination requirement down to a relatively unburdensome form, the position remains unsatisfactory because it forces public companies that do not want to have a tranche of sterling or euro denominated shares to go through a series of procedural steps that are of no apparent substantive benefit to anyone in order eventually to achieve that result.

Why might a company want to have a share capital denominated in a currency other than sterling or in a mixture of currencies, of which sterling is only one? One reason, which was relevant in *Re Scandinavian Bank Group plc*,[55] where the pre-2006 Act position was considered, is capital adequacy considerations.[56] Banks and other financial firms are subject to capital adequacy requirements that measure their capital against their assets. Where the capital and the assets are expressed in different currencies, the proportion of capital to assets may

---

[49] Companies Act 2006 s 586. This gives effect to Second Company Law Directive, Art 9 and Art 30. There is an exception from s 586 for shares allotted in pursuance of an employees' share scheme (s 586(2)) but such shares do not count for the purposes of the minimum capital requirement unless they have actually been paid up to at least one-quarter of their nominal value and any premium (s 761(3)). The same requirements apply to private companies seeking to re-register as public companies: Companies Act 2006, s 91(1)(b) and (2)(b).

[50] Companies Act 2006, s 583(3)(d). I am grateful to Daniel Illhardt (LLM (Cantab, 2011)) for drawing this point to my attention.

[51] See Companies Act 2006, s 542(3).   [52] Companies Act 2006, s 765.

[53] Companies Act 2006, s 765(3).

[54] The redenomination procedure is contained in Companies Act 2006, ss 622–8. Note also Companies Act 2006, s 766.

[55] [1987] 2 All ER 70, [1987] BCC 93.

[56] N Daubney and N Cannon, 'Converting to Multi-currency Share Capital in the UK' (1987) 6(5) *International Financial Law Review* 7.

be eroded simply through exchange rate fluctuations. This problem can be eliminated by matching the denomination of the capital to that of the assets. All companies, including those that are not subject to capital adequacy requirements, face a similar problem if they have covenanted in loan agreements or other contractual documents to maintain certain debt to equity ratios and the debt and equity are denominated in different currencies. Companies in this position may want to match the denomination or denominations of their capital to that of their debts. A company may also want to have a multi-currency share capital in order to attract foreign investors, or to encourage foreign vendors to accept the company's shares as consideration.[57] More generally, companies with extensive international operations may wish to have a multi-currency share capital not only to facilitate the raising of capital from the international equity market but also to match their capital base to their international earnings, or to reflect their status as significant international businesses.[58]

Is any valuable purpose served by minimum capital requirements?

The thinking behind mandatory minimum capital requirements is that they are intended to protect creditors by ensuring that companies have some substance behind them in the form of permanent equity capital that cannot be withdrawn at will by the shareholders. However, a simple rule such as that in the Second Company Law Directive in reality fails to deliver meaningful creditor protection because it is not tailored to the financial needs of specific companies and does nothing to prevent capital being lost in the course of business.[59] The High Level Group of Company Law Experts that, in 2002, advised the European Commission on European company law reform, explicitly noted the limitations of the Second Company Law Directive in this respect: that Group concluded that the only function actually performed by the minimum capital requirement was to deter individuals from 'lightheartedly starting a public limited company.'[60]

It is not difficult to think of ways in which minimum capital requirements could be reinforced with a view to increasing their effectiveness as a creditor protection mechanism but the potential negative consequences of imposing more stringent capital requirements also need to be kept in mind. For instance, one apparently straightforward reinforcement step would be to increase the amount of mandatory minimum capital. However, if the level were to be set too high, that could operate as a barrier to growth and entrepreneurship and could impede beneficial competition. To minimize that risk, policymakers contemplating the imposition of higher minimum capital requirements would need to take on the complex task of designing a carefully calibrated set of requirements that achieved a degree of commensurability between the specific risks undertaken by individual companies and the amount of capital that each of them was required to hold. Whilst it is certainly possible for policymakers to come up with very detailed frameworks of this sort, as is demonstrated by the sophisticated and complex

---

[57] The use of foreign currency denominated shares for this purpose is discussed by D Lewis, 'Foreign Currency Share Capital' (1993) 4(10) *Practical Law for Companies* 23.

[58] These were among the factors identified as being reasons to consider redenomination in response to the introduction of the euro: DTI, *The Euro: Redenomination of Share Capital, Consultative Document* (1998) para 1.6; G Yeowart, 'The Equity Markets and Company Share Capital: Planning for the Euro' [1998] 8 *Journal of International Banking Law* 269; C Proctor, 'Share Capital and the Euro' (1998) 9(3) *Practical Law for Companies* 17.

[59] The role of minimum capital requirements as a creditor protection mechanism is much discussed. Contributions include: W Schön, 'The Future of Legal Capital' (2004) 5 *European Business Organization Law Review* 429; M Miola, 'Legal Capital and Limited Liability Companies: the European Perspective' (2004) 4 *European Company and Financial Law Review* 413; J Armour, 'Legal Capital: An Outdated Concept?' (2006) 7 *European Business Organization Law Review* 5.

[60] High Level Group, *Final Report*, 82.

capital adequacy frameworks within which banks and other financial institutions must operate, to devise such a scheme for general commercial companies would involve a huge investment in regulatory design and in the establishment of an accompanying supervisory regime, as well as very significant compliance costs for the corporate sector. Whilst an outlay of this magnitude is justifiable in the banking context where the soundness and stability of the financial system are at stake, few would regard it as being an acceptable price to pay to counter the risks that creditors face in dealing with ordinary commercial companies. That there are market mechanisms whereby creditors can influence the amount of permanent equity capital invested in a company should not be overlooked, nor should the fact that the market can operate much more flexibly than any regulatory regime could ever be designed to do (although this is not to deny that market mechanisms have imperfections too).[61] Companies in different sectors and at different stages of their development will have different financing needs and the ratio of debt to equity in their capital structure will represent the cumulative effect of financing arrangements entered into over time by reference to their then current stage of development and market conditions at that time.[62] For instance, companies at an early stage of development that have few physical assets to offer as collateral to banks and no credit ratings to access bond markets, are likely to have to rely heavily on equity to finance their business.

Another option for reinforcement of minimum capital requirements would be to require capital to be topped up by an injection of fresh equity when it is no longer represented by assets. The Second Company Law Directive does not contain a requirement to this effect and there is none in the UK Companies Act 2006. All that the Directive does is to require that in the event of a serious loss of subscribed capital, a general meeting of shareholders must be called to consider whether the company should be wound up or any other measures taken.[63] As this requirement is applied in the UK, the obligation to hold a meeting is triggered only when the net assets of a public company have fallen to half or less of the value of the nominal value of its capital.[64] As such, it is likely to operate only in very extreme circumstances when a company's financial difficulties may already be becoming obvious, thus rendering redundant any disclosure functions that the obligation to convene a shareholders' meeting might serve, and the location of real decision-making power about its future may well have already shifted from the shareholders to the creditors. Some European countries go further and impose 'recapitalize or liquidate' obligations.[65] However, such rules have to be viewed with caution from a policy perspective because they are liable to distort corporate rescue efforts and have the potential to be used opportunistically in situations where shareholders are in dispute with each other, as one group could manipulate things to dilute the control of another group that cannot afford to contribute to the recapitalization.[66]

Rather than pondering on ways in which minimum capital requirements could be made more effective, it is more in line with current policy thinking in the UK, and

---

[61] Ch 7 discusses further the interplay between the market and regulation in creditor protection.

[62] On theories that seek to explain corporate capital structure, see further ch 3.

[63] Second Company Law Directive, Art 19 and Companies Act 2006, s 656.

[64] Companies Act 2006, s 656 refers to 'called up' share capital and the definition of called up share capital (s 547) points towards the conclusion that this does not include share premiums. This interpretation is consistent with Second Company Law Directive, Art 19, which refers only to 'subscribed capital.'

[65] M Miola, 'Legal Capital Rules in Italian Company Law and the EU Perspective' in Lutter, *Legal Capital in Europe* 515, 527–8 (discussing the Italian rule and describing it as less strict than that elsewhere, eg France). Spain also has stringent recapitalize or liquidate rules: JME Irujo, 'Capital Protection in Spanish Company Law' in Lutter, *Legal Capital in Europe*, 582, 593–4.

[66] L Enriques and J Macey, 'Creditors Versus Capital Formation: The Case Against the European Legal Capital Rules' (2001) 86 *Cornell Law Review* 1165.

increasingly elsewhere in Europe as well (although, as noted earlier in discussing the SPE, some deeply-rooted national preferences continue to exert a hold),[67] to suggest that minimum capital has lost credibility as a creditor protection mechanism and that for public companies either it should be abolished outright or left to wither away gradually by not adjusting the amount in line with inflation so that over time the amount that needs to be invested becomes increasingly trivial.[68] In declining to accept arguments that sought to justify national minimum capital requirements on public interest grounds, the European Court, in the *Centros* line of cases, has made it impossible to argue that minimum capital is an indispensable cornerstone of creditor protection and has indicated that, in so far as creditor protection is part of company law's role, the requisite level of protection can be delivered in other ways.

Allotted, Issued, and Equity Share Capital

This section considers the interpretation of the terms 'allotted' and 'issued' and outlines key procedural formalities that are associated with the share allotment and issuance process.

Allotted share capital

References in the Companies Acts to 'allotted share capital' are to shares of a company that have been allotted.[69] Generally the term allotment when used in respect of shares is not a term of art.[70] In *Spitzel v The Chinese Corporation Ltd*[71] Stirling J answered the general question 'What is an allotment of shares?' by saying: 'Broadly speaking, it is an appropriation by the directors or the managing body of the company of shares to a particular person.' In *Nicol's Case*[72] Chitty J, however, equated allotment with the forming of a binding contract to take shares. The key distinction between these two interpretations is that, in limited circumstances, appropriation could take place before a contract is concluded: it could happen when an offer to subscribe for shares is accepted but before the acceptance is communicated so as to form a contract, or it could even take place before acceptance where, as in a rights issue, the directors resolve that certain shares are to be allotted to particular persons and make an offer of those shares.[73] In line with the view that allotment may take place before there is a binding contract to take shares is *Re The Saloon Stream Packet Co Ltd, Fletcher's Case*,[74] where three stages in a contract to take shares were identified, namely an application for shares, an

---

[67] See also a German study that suggests that, from a legal policy point of view, a reasonable increase of the minimum capital as an allowance for inflation must be considered with regard to possible revision of the Second Company Law Directive: H Eidenmüller, B Grunewald, and U Niack, 'Minimum Capital in the System of Legal Capital' in Lutter, *Legal Capital in Europe*, 17, 40. Yet these authors do not appear to have a strong conviction about the practical merits of mandatory minimum capital: 'it must be stressed that the symbolic significance of this issue for the (supposed) modernisation of corporate law far exceeds its economic relevance' (at 30). Some other contributors to the same volume also express views that are moderately in favour of retention of mandatory minimum capital requirements: see, eg, A Kidyba, S Soltysiński, and A Szumański, 'A Report on Selected Aspects of Legal Capital under Polish Code of Commercial Companies' in Lutter, *Legal Capital in Europe*, 597, 618.

[68] High Level Group, *Final Report*, 82 inclines towards the 'do nothing' option. Compare Rickford, 'Reforming Capital,' 931 n 33: 'In our view useless provisions are always worth repealing' (Jonathan Rickford was a member of the High Level Group).

[69] Companies Act 2006, s 546(1)(b).

[70] *Re Florence Land and Public Works Co, Nicol's case* (1885) 29 Ch D 421, Ch D and CA, 427 *per* Chitty J; *Re Ambrose Lake Tin and Copper Co (Clarke's Case)* (1878) 8 Ch D 635, CA; *Re Compania de Electricidad* [1980] 1 Ch 146, 182; *Whitehouse v Carlton Hotel Pty Ltd* (1987) 70 ALR 251, H Ct of Aust, 271 *per* Brennan J.

[71] (1899) 80 LT 347.

[72] *Re Florence Land and Public Works Co, Nicol's case* (1885) 29 Ch D 421, Ch D and CA.

[73] *Spitzel v Chinese Corp Ltd* (1899) 80 LT 347; *Re Compania de Electricidad* [1980] 1 Ch 146, 182.

[74] (1867) 17 LT 136. See also *Re Scottish Petroleum Co* (1883) 23 Ch D 413, CA.

allotment and, finally, communication of and acquiescence in the allotment. In relation to timing, for the purposes of the Companies Acts a share in a company is taken to be allotted when a person acquires the unconditional right to be included in the company's register of members in respect of it.[75] A right to be included in the company's register of members would usually be derived from a contract to take shares. A contract to take shares is in essence no different from any other contract and the normal contractual rules, including those of offer and acceptance, apply. Accordingly, it would be possible for an offer of shares to be withdrawn before a contract is formed by communication of acceptance, in which case no entitlement to be entered in the register of members would arise.

One case where a person may acquire the right to be included in the company's register of members otherwise than by contract is in a bonus issue of shares.[76] A bonus issue of shares means an issue of new shares to the existing shareholders where the subscription price is met by the company out of funds which it is permitted to apply for that purpose. In *Re Cleveland Trust plc*[77] Scott J held that the relationship between company and shareholder vis-à-vis an authorized bonus issue may not be strictly contractual; but unless the issue is for some reason fundamentally flawed,[78] the person to whom the shares are offered, or the person to whom he has renounced the offer, acquires a right to be included in the company's register of members in respect of the bonus shares.

Authority to allot shares

Issues relating to the authority of directors to allot shares and the pre-emption rights of existing shareholders in respect of any new share issue are considered in chapter 5.

Registration of allotment and return of allotments

A company is obliged to register an allotment of shares as soon as practicable and in any event within two months after the date of allotment.[79] Non-compliance with this obligation constitutes a criminal offence by the company and every officer who is in default.[80]

Under section 555 of the Companies Act 2006, within one month after the making of an allotment, a limited company must deliver to the registrar of companies for registration a return of the allotment which notifies details of the allotment, again under penalty of criminal sanctions attaching to the company and defaulting officers in the event of non-compliance.[81] The return must be accompanied by a statement of capital stating with respect to the company's share capital at the date to which the return is made up:

(1) the total number of shares of the company;
(2) the aggregate nominal value of those shares;
(3) for each class of shares:
    (a) prescribed particulars of the rights attaching to the shares,
    (b) the total number of shares of that class, and
    (c) the aggregate nominal value of shares of that class, and

---

[75] Companies Act 2006, s 558.
[76] The term 'issue' is used here because 'bonus issue' is common parlance. It is not meant to have any particular technical significance.
[77] [1991] BCLC 424, 434–5.
[78] As it was in the *Cleveland* case where the purported issue was held to be void for mistake. *Cleveland* was applied in *EIC Services Ltd v Phipps* [2005] 1 All ER 338, CA where a bonus issue was held to be void for mistake.
[79] Companies Act 2006, s 554.   [80] Companies Act 2006, s 554(3).   [81] Companies Act 2006, s 557.

(4) the amount paid up and the amount (if any) unpaid on each share (whether on account of the nominal value of the share or by way of premium).[82]

The prescribed information for a return of an allotment by a limited company is the number of shares allotted, the amount paid up and the amount unpaid on each allotted share, whether on account of the nominal value or by way of premium, and the consideration for allotment if it is in non-cash form.[83] The prescribed particulars in respect of classes of shares relate to voting rights, dividend and capital participation rights, and whether the shares are redeemable.[84]

Issued share capital and issued shares

References in the Companies Act 2006 to 'issued share capital' are to shares of a company that have been issued.[85] What constitutes the issue of a share? In *Levy v Abercorris Slate and Slab Co*,[86] a case that concerned an issue of debentures, Chitty J said:[87] ''issued' is not a technical term, it is a mercantile term well understood.' This comment is equally applicable to an issue of shares. It is very common in practice for the terms 'issued' and 'allotted' to be used interchangeably, as if they meant the same thing and as if both events happened at precisely the same time. However, since the word 'issued' takes its colour from the context in which it is used, in particular situations it may be used to mean something different from 'allotted.' In particular, in certain contexts a share which has been allotted may not be regarded as an issued share. The converse is generally not true—a share is normally taken to be issued at some point after it has been allotted; exceptionally, however, in *Mosely v Koffyfontein Mines Ltd*,[88] a case which concerned the construction of articles of association dealing with increase of share capital, Farwell LJ put the order of the three separate steps in the life of a new share as being creation, issue, and allotment.[89]

In *Ambrose Lake Tin and Copper Co (Clarke's Case)*[90] a reference in the Companies Act 1867 to the issue of shares was taken to mean something different from, and later than, their allotment. Also, in various cases concerned with construction of tax legislation employing the term, the term 'issue' has been interpreted to mean something other than, and subsequent to, allotment.[91] But what does 'issued' mean where it is used to mean something other than 'allotted,' and where issue is thought to be subsequent to allotment? Again the answer to this question ultimately depends on the context in which the term is used[92] but a view that has attracted considerable support is that the distinction between allotment and issue of a share mirrors that between being a shareholder and being a member of a company. A person to whom a share has been allotted may be a shareholder[93] but

---

[82] Companies Act 2006, s 555(4). Identifying the amount of premium paid up on each share can cause problems for certain companies that have a complex history of allotting shares and managing their capital structure. Companies are expected to address this issue pragmatically and can draw upon guidance from the Institute of Chartered Secretaries and Administrators in doing so: ICSA, *Guidance on Statement of Capital* (2009).

[83] The Companies (Shares and Share Capital) Order 2009, SI 2009/388, art 3.

[84] The Companies (Shares and Share Capital) Order 2009, SI 2009/388, art 2.

[85] Companies Act 2006, s 546(1)(a).   [86] (1887) 37 Ch D 260.

[87] At 264. See also *Spitzel v Chinese Corp Ltd* (1899) 80 LT 347; *National Westminster Bank plc v IRC* [1995] 1 AC 119, HL.

[88] [1911] 1 Ch 73, CA.

[89] At 84. See also *Whitehouse v Carlton Hotel Pty Ltd* (1987) 70 ALR 251, H Ct of Aust, 271 *per* Brennan J.

[90] (1878) 8 Ch D 635.

[91] eg, *Oswald Tillotson Ltd v IRC* [1933] 1 KB 134, CA; *Brotex Cellulose Fibres Ltd v IRC* [1933] 1 KB 158; *Murex Ltd v Commissioners of Inland Revenue* [1933] 1 KB 173.

[92] In *Central Piggery Co Ltd v McNicoll* (1949) 78 CLR 594, H Ct of Aust, 599 Dixon J interpreted the word 'issue' to mean a step after allotment whereby the shareholder is put in control of the shares allotted.

[93] *Central Piggery Co Ltd v McNicoll* (1949) 78 CLR 594, H Ct of Aust, 599 *per* Dixon J.

that person does not become a member until registered as such on the company's register of members.[94] A shareholder is entitled to dividends in respect of the shares but rights such as attending meetings and voting on resolutions are membership rights which are held by members and not by mere shareholders.[95] Thus in *Oswald Tillotson Ltd v IRC*[96] the Court of Appeal equated the word 'issue', as used in certain tax legislation, with the creation of a registered shareholder. In *Agricultural Mortgage Corp v IRC*[97] Walton J, at first instance, and Goff LJ in the Court of Appeal, also inclined to the view that for the purpose of certain tax legislation 'issue' took place on registration.[98] The meaning of 'issue' for the purpose of certain tax legislation was considered by the judicial House of Lords (now the Supreme Court) in *National Westminster Bank plc v IRC*.[99] As in the earlier tax cases, it was held that issue followed allotment and was completed by the entry of the names of the holders of the shares on the company's register of members. Lord Lloyd (in the majority) agreed that the interpretation of the term depended on its context and considered that the interpretation favoured by the majority was appropriate for the context of company law.

Except in this section (or where specifically indicated) the common practice of using the terms 'issued' and 'allotted' interchangeably is adopted in this chapter and elsewhere in this book.

Equity share capital

For the purposes of the companies legislation, 'equity share capital' means issued share capital excluding any part of that capital that, neither as respects dividends nor as respects capital, carries any right to participate beyond a specified amount in a distribution.[100]

Payment for Shares

Introduction

The next part of this chapter is concerned with the rules governing payment for shares. This is a very detailed and complex area of company law, especially for public companies where the forms of consideration that they may accept for their shares are very closely regulated. These rules are intended to protect creditors and shareholders against companies accepting consideration that is in fact worth less than the issue price of their shares.[101] It is debatable whether such extensive regulation of public company share capital as is now contained in the companies legislation is necessary or desirable, but many of the requirements are derived from the Second Company Law Directive and, barring changes at the European level, this precludes meaningful change to the domestic law. In 2006, certain modest changes were made to the Second Company Law Directive in the interests of simplification and modernization but the revising Directive largely left it to Member States to decide

---

[94] For registration as a member, see Companies Act 2006, s 112.
[95] *Spitzel v Chinese Corp Ltd* (1899) 80 LT 347.   [96] [1933] 1 KB 134, CA.   [97] [1978] Ch 72, CA.
[98] 'Or possibly some other act' 85 *per* Walton J, or 'the issue of a certificate' 101 *per* Goff LJ. However, the view that a share is only issued when registration *and* the issue of a share certificate takes place has been rejected: *Re Heaton's Steel and Slab Co (Blyth's Case)* (1876) 4 Ch D 140, CA explaining *Re Imperial River Co (Bush's Case)* (1874) 9 Ch App 554, CA; *Re Ambrose Lake Tin and Copper Co (Clarke's Case)* (1878) 8 Ch D 635, CA.
[99] [1995] 1 AC 119, HL.   [100] Companies Act 2006, s 548.
[101] Second Company Law Directive, recital 3 provides: 'in order to ensure minimum equivalent protection for both shareholders and creditors of public limited liability companies, the co-ordination of national provisions relating to their formation, and to the maintenance, increase or reduction of their capital is particularly important.'

whether to apply the revised rules.[102] The UK was sceptical as to the value of the changes and implemented only some of them, not including those relevant to the regulation of payment for shares.[103]

Paid up share capital

A company's paid up share capital means the amount of capital money it has received in respect of its issued shares. Unless the context indicates otherwise, it does not include share premiums.[104] As noted earlier, there is no minimum amount that must be paid up on the allotment (or issue) of a share in a private company. Except for shares allotted in pursuance of an employees' share scheme, public companies must not allot a share except as paid up at least as to one-quarter of its nominal value and the whole of any premium on it.[105] If a share is allotted in contravention of this requirement, the allottee is liable to pay the minimum amount the company should have received (less any amount actually paid), with interest.[106] Subsequent holders of a share allotted in breach of this rule may also incur liability.[107] Subsequent holders (but not original allottees) may apply to the court to be relieved of their liability.[108]

Called up share capital

Called up share capital means so much of a company's share capital as equals the aggregate amount of the calls made on its shares (whether or not those calls have been paid), together with:

(1) any share capital paid up without being called; and

(2) any share capital to be paid on a specified future date under the articles, the terms of allotment, or any other arrangements for payment of those shares.[109]

It is common for shares to be issued fully paid. This means that, in the ordinary case, the amount of a company's called up share capital will thus equal that of its paid up share capital. However, the called up share capital could be a larger amount where shares are issued partly paid. For example, where shares are issued on a partly paid basis and the terms of the allotment provide for payment of the balance by instalments, limb (2) of the definition would mean that the outstanding amount of the capital that remains to be paid is included in the company's called up share capital. Note that the definition refers only to 'share capital'. Share premiums are not part of the share capital and therefore the share premium account does not constitute part of the called up capital.

---

[102] Directive 2006/68/EC, now incorporated into the recast version of the Second Company Law Directive.

[103] Companies (Reduction of Capital) (Creditor Protection) Regulations, SI 2008/719; Companies (Share Capital and Acquisition by Company of its Own Shares) Regulations, SI 2009/2022.

[104] This follows from Companies Act 2006, s 610(4) which requires the share premium account to be treated *as if it were* part of the paid up share capital (emphasis added).

[105] This rule is derived from the Second Company Law Directive, Art 9 and (in respect of premiums) Art 30. Article 30 relates only to increases in subscribed capital, which makes it possible to say that, as a matter of EU law, the requirement for premiums to be paid up does not apply to the first allotment of shares by a newly formed plc. The Companies Act 2006 does not make this distinction. Since most plcs begin life as private companies and are later converted, in practice most companies will already be well beyond the first allotment stage by the time these rules apply to them.

[106] Companies Act 2006, s 586(3). In the case of an allotment of bonus shares, this liability does not apply except where the allottee knew or ought to have known of the contravention (s 586(4)).

[107] Companies Act 2006, s 588.   [108] Companies Act 2006, s 589.   [109] Companies Act 2006, s 547.

Cash consideration for shares

A share is deemed to be paid up in cash or allotted for cash if the consideration is:

(1) cash received by the company;

(2) a cheque received by the company in good faith which its directors have no reason for suspecting will not be paid;

(3) a release of a liability of the company for a liquidated sum;

(4) an undertaking to pay cash to the company at a later date; or

(5) payment by some other means giving rise to a present or future entitlement (of the company or of a person acting on the company's behalf) to a payment, or a credit equivalent to payment, in cash.[110]

It is expressly provided that 'cash' in this context includes foreign currency.[111] Also expressly stated in the legislation is that the payment of cash, or any undertaking to pay cash, to any person other than the company is a form of non-cash consideration.[112]

Payments through an electronic settlement system are deemed to be payments in cash within (5).[113]

Case law has shed some further light on the meaning of cash in this context. It has been held that an undertaking to pay cash at a later date in (4) means an undertaking given to the company in return for the allotment; it does not include the assignment of a pre-existing debt to the company as consideration for the allotment.[114] The scenario of a company that acquires assets on credit and then pays for them by allotting shares to the vendor has also been judicially considered. Because 'cash' includes the release of a liability for a liquidated sum, the shares would prima facie be allotted for cash in this case. In *Re Bradford Investments plc (No 2)*[115] Hoffmann J, referring to this type of situation, commented: 'I would not wish to give the impression that an artificial resort to two documents instead of one could be used to avoid the provisions [requiring independent valuation of non-cash consideration for shares].'[116] However, whilst the courts may be expected to be vigilant to ensure that statutory requirements are not evaded, where there is no question of the two stages of the transaction being artificial or a sham, it appears that the shares will be treated as having been allotted for cash.[117]

Shares must not be issued at a discount

Shares may not be allotted at less than their par value. Originally this rule was established by case law[118] and it is now enshrined in section 580 of the Companies Act 2006.[119] If the rule is contravened, the allottee is liable to pay the company an amount equal to the amount of the discount, together with interest.[120] Subsequent holders of shares that were allotted at less than par may also be liable to pay up the shares in full.[121] Section 589 of the Companies Act 2006,

---

[110] Companies Act 2006, s 583(3).   [111] Companies Act 2006, s 583(6).
[112] Companies Act 2006, s 583(5).
[113] Companies Act 2006, s 383(4) and The Companies (Shares and Share Capital) Order 2009, SI 2009/388, art 4.
[114] *System Controls plc v Munro Corporate plc* [1990] BCC 386.   [115] [1991] BCC 379.
[116] Independent valuation requirements are considered further later.
[117] *Re Harmony and Montague Tin and Copper Mining Co, Spargo's Case* (1873) 8 Ch App 407, CA.
[118] *Ooregum Gold Mining Co of India v Roper* [1892] AC 125, HL; *Re Eddystone Marine Insurance Co* [1893] 3 Ch 9 CA; *Welton v Saffery* [1897] AC 299, HL.
[119] For public companies this implements Second Company Law Directive, Art 8.
[120] Companies Act 2006, s 580(2).   [121] Companies Act 2006, s 588.

which permits applications to court for relief from liability arising from failure to comply with certain of the requirements of the Act regarding the allotment of shares, does not apply in the case of the liability of the allottee to pay the amount of the discount, but subsequent holders may apply for relief from this liability. The directors who authorized the allotment at a discount may also be liable to the company for breach of duty.[122] A contract to allot shares at a discount at a later date is void and cannot be enforced by either party.[123]

The no-discount rule and convertible securities

In *Mosely v Koffyfontein Mines Ltd*[124] the Court of Appeal analyzed a proposal to issue convertible debentures at a discount to their par value where the debentures could immediately be converted into fully paid shares having a par value equal to the par value of the debentures. The Court of Appeal held that the issue of the debentures on the proposed terms was open to abuse as it could be used to circumvent the no-discount rule and, on that basis, granted an injunction to restrain the making of the issue. Cozens-Hardy LJ expressly left open the question of a debenture issued at a discount to its par value which conferred a right at some future date to demand a fully paid share in exchange for the par value of the debenture.[125] This situation is different from that where debentures issued at a discount are immediately convertible into fully paid shares having a par value equal to the par value of the debentures: in the former case the discount can be explained because it represents the investors' return without which they would (presumably) have demanded a higher rate of interest; in the latter case it is difficult to find any explanation for the discount other than it being a backhanded way of allowing shares to be allotted at a discount. So interpreted, the decision in the *Mosely* case does not prevent the issue of convertible debentures at a discount where the conversion right is not immediately exercisable. There can be no hard and fast rule governing the length of time that would have to elapse between issue of the debentures and permitted exercise of the conversion rights. It would presumably depend on whether there is a genuine reason for the discount: if there is, even a short delay might suffice.

When shares are allotted on conversion of convertible debentures, are they allotted for cash? Ultimately the answer to this question depends on the conversion mechanism in the terms of the debentures. In the *Mosely* case Vaughan-Williams LJ thought that shares allotted upon conversion of convertible debentures were allotted for money's worth,[126] but Cozens-Hardy LJ explained the conversion as involving the cancellation of a liquidated debt.[127] Where the issuer of the convertible securities and of the shares into which they convert is the same company, an allotment of shares in exchange for the release of the liquidated debt represented by the convertibles would be an allotment for cash according to the definition of that term in section 583(3)(c) of the Companies Act 2006.

Companies sometimes issue preference shares, or other shares carrying special rights, that are convertible at some point in the future into ordinary shares either of the same company or of another company in its group. A subscriber for shares does not become a creditor in respect of the amount subscribed and the conversion of a share would not constitute the release of a liability of the company for a liquidated sum. The conversion terms may provide for a return of capital to the shareholders (perhaps by the redemption of their shares) and subsequent application of the redemption proceeds to the subscription of new ordinary shares, in which case the conversion would involve an allotment of new shares for cash consideration.

---

[122] *Hirsche v Sims* [1894] AC 654, PC.   [123] *Re Almada and Tirito Co* (1888) 38 Ch D 415, CA.
[124] [1904] 2 Ch 108, CA.   [125] [1904] 2 Ch 108, CA, 120.   [126] [1904] 2 Ch 108, CA, 116.
[127] [1904] 2 Ch 108, CA, 119.

The no-discount rule and underwriting commissions

A company is permitted, to a limited extent,[128] to use capital to pay underwriting commissions. This exemption would permit, for example, the use of £2 per £100 subscribed for new £1 shares to pay a 2 per cent commission to the underwriters of the issue, provided this is consistent with the company's articles. If no subscribers can be found for the shares so that the underwriter has to take them itself, this means, in effect, that for an issue of shares having an aggregate par value of £100 the underwriter only has to pay £98. This scenario is sometimes said to be an exception to the rule that shares may not be issued at a discount. This is a convenient shorthand but the strict technical position is that the company and the underwriter have mutual obligations—the underwriter to pay the full subscription money and the company to pay the commission—and to the extent of the level of the commission these obligations cancel each other out.[129]

Regulation of non-cash consideration for shares

The Companies Act 2006, section 582(1) provides that shares of public and private companies may be paid up either in money or in money's worth (including goodwill and know-how). There is one exception: shares taken by a subscriber to the memorandum of a public company in pursuance of an undertaking in the memorandum must be paid up in cash.[130]

At common law, despite stressing the importance of the maintenance of capital doctrine as a device for protecting creditors and shareholders, the courts were reluctant to examine the adequacy of non-cash consideration for shares. In *Re Wragg Ltd*[131] the Court of Appeal accepted that the no-discount rule applied where a company allotted shares in consideration for the acquisition of property. But:

> …if, however, the consideration which the company has agreed to accept as representing in money's worth, the nominal value of the shares be a consideration not clearly colourable nor illusory, then, in my judgement, the adequacy of the consideration cannot be impeached…unless the contract can also be impeached; and I take it to be the law that it is not open to a [petitioner], unless he is able to impeach the agreement, to go into the adequacy of the consideration to show that the company have agreed to give an excessive value for what they have purchased.[132]

The Court of Appeal's approach in *Re Wragg Ltd* followed dicta in the opinions of the House of Lords in *Ooregum Gold Mining Co of India v Roper*[133] and also decisions in earlier cases[134] that established that a court could not interfere merely on the grounds that a company had, by issuing shares, overpaid for property and that only a dishonest or colourable transaction would allow the court to intervene.

Whether the consideration is colourable or illusory is a factual matter to be decided by reference to the facts of each case.[135] Consideration that is clearly bad, such as past consideration[136]

---

[128] Companies Act 2006, ss 552–3. The payment must be authorized by the articles and must not exceed 10 per cent of the issue price of the shares or the amount or rate authorized by the articles, whichever is the less. The use of capital in this way is sanctioned by the Second Company Law Directive, Art 8. The Model Articles (plc), art 44 provides for the payment of commissions on shares but does not prescribe an amount or rate.

[129] *Metropolitan Coal Consumers Association v Scrimgeour* [1895] 2 QB 604, CA. The Court of Appeal had no doubt that using capital to pay commissions did not infringe the rule prohibiting the issue of shares at a discount.

[130] Companies Act 2006, s 584.   [131] [1897] 1 Ch 796, CA.

[132] At 836 *per* ALS Smith LJ; see also at 830 *per* Lindley LJ.   [133] [1892] AC 125, HL.

[134] Cited in the judgments in *Re Wragg* [1897] 1 Ch 796, CA. See also *Re Theatrical Trust Ltd* [1895] 1 Ch 771.

[135] *Re Innes & Co Ltd* [1903] 2 Ch 254, CA, 262 *per* Vaughan Williams LJ.

[136] *Re Eddystone Marine Insurance Co* [1893] 3 Ch 9, CA (although in Scotland past consideration for shares has been accepted: *Park Business Interiors Ltd v Park* [1990] BCC 914, Court of Session, Outer House).

or consideration which permits an obvious money measure to be made showing that a discount was allowed,[137] will not be allowed to stand. The courts will not necessarily insist on a separate action to impeach a transaction involving the allotment of shares if the facts which go to establish that it is a colourable transaction are sufficiently plain to demonstrate that such an action would be little more than a technicality.[138] However, notwithstanding these cases, an overall assessment is that attempts to demonstrate that an agreement to issue shares in return for payment in kind rather than cash should be set aside as colourable or illusory have not often succeeded.[139]

Where shares of a public company are allotted for a non-cash consideration, the traditional reluctance to interfere has been replaced by stringent statutory rules derived from the Second Company Law Directive. Some of the requirements applicable to public companies are also relevant to a private company that is hoping to convert to a public company because the conversion may not proceed if those requirements have not been observed in respect of share issues in the period leading up to the proposed conversion.[140] The structure of the Second Company Law Directive is to prohibit forms of non-cash consideration for shares in a public company that are thought to be incapable of economic assessment,[141] namely undertakings to do work or perform services and long-term undertakings, and to permit other forms of non-cash consideration subject to independent valuation requirements. In the Companies Act 2006 the outright prohibitions are in chapter 5 of Part 17, whilst the independent valuation requirements are in chapter 6 of Part 17. The essence of the approach of the Directive is that the subscribed capital must be formed only of assets that are capable of economic assessment. 'Subscribed capital' equates to the nominal value of the issued share capital, and does not extend to share premiums. In not limiting its requirements to nominal value, in certain respects the UK Companies Act 2006 therefore goes beyond the minimum required by Community obligations.

Public companies must not accept an undertaking to do work or perform services as consideration for shares

Under section 585 of the Companies Act 2006 a public company is prohibited from accepting in payment up of its shares, or any premium on them, an undertaking given by any person that he, she, or another person should do work or perform services for the company or any other person. If a company accepts such an undertaking in payment up of its shares or any premium on them, the holder of the shares when they or the premium is treated as paid up (in whole or in part) by the undertaking is liable to pay to the company in respect of those shares an amount equal to the amount treated as paid up by the undertaking, together with interest.[142] The enforceability of the undertaking is unaffected.[143] Subsequent holders of the shares may also incur liability.[144] It is open to any person who is liable as a result of a breach of the rule against such undertakings being an acceptable form of consideration for shares in a public company, to apply to the court for relief.[145]

A holder of shares for the purposes of this rule includes a person who has an unconditional right to be included in the register of members in respect of the shares or to have an instrument of transfer of them executed in his favour.[146] If shares are allotted as fully paid in return

[137] *Re Theatrical Trust Ltd* [1895] 1 Ch 771.   [138] *Re White Star Line Ltd* [1938] 1 Ch 458.
[139] As noted in *Pilmer v Duke Group Ltd (in liquidation)* [2001] 2 BCLC 773, H Ct Aust, para 35.
[140] Companies Act 2006, s 93.   [141] Second Company Law Directive, Art 7.
[142] Companies Act 2006, s 585(2).   [143] Companies Act 2006, s 591.   [144] Companies Act 2006, s 588.
[145] Companies Act 2006, s 589.   [146] Companies Act 2006, s 585(3) and s 588(3).

for an undertaking by the allottee, or another person, to do work or to perform services, liability under this rule will attach to the allottee. However, if the shares are allotted on a partly paid basis (which would be rare in practice) and the company later accepts from their then holder an undertaking to do work or perform services in payment up of the shares, that person would then incur liability under the statutory rule but previous holders of the shares, including the original allottee, would not incur statutory liability.

Most UK-listed companies offer some form of share scheme incentives to their employees, which, at first blush, suggests an apparent friction between the legal position and the realities of practice. However, there are, in fact, many ways of structuring employee share schemes in order to circumvent the ban on accepting future services as consideration for shares (including the very common practice of using share options that give employees the right to acquire shares for cash at a favourable price, and also arrangements whereby the employee share scheme trust purchases previously issued shares in the market in order to satisfy employee entitlements to 'free' shares). Accordingly, the ban has the potential to operate more as a trap for the unwary or under-advised than as a worthwhile creditor protection mechanism.[147]

Public companies must not accept undertakings to be performed in the future as consideration for their shares

In addition to the absolute bar on accepting undertakings to do work or perform services in consideration for their shares, public companies are also restricted with regard to accepting other types of undertaking as consideration for their shares. Under section 587 of the Companies Act 2006 a public company must not allot shares as fully or partly paid up (as to their nominal value or any premium on them) otherwise than in cash if the consideration for the allotment is, or includes, an undertaking which is to be, or may be, performed more than five years after the date of the allotment.[148] The effect of contravening this rule is that the allottee is still liable to pay to the company an amount equal to the amount treated as paid up by the undertaking, with interest at the appropriate rate.[149] The enforceability of the undertaking is not affected.[150] Subsequent holders of the shares may also incur liability.[151] It is open to any person, whether an allottee or a subsequent holder, who incurs liability resulting from a contravention of the ban on long-term undertakings being good consideration for shares in a public company, to apply to the court for relief under section 589 of the Companies Act 2006.

The prohibition in section 587 of the Companies Act 2006 extends to the variation of a contract where, had the varied terms been the original terms, the contract would have contravened the section.[152] Also caught is the case where a share is allotted in consideration of an undertaking which is to be performed within five years of the allotment where the undertaking is not actually performed within the period allowed by the contract: at the end of the period allowed by the contract, the allottee then becomes liable to pay the company the amount which was treated as paid up by the undertaking, with interest.[153] Subsequent holder liability and applications to court for relief provisions apply here just as they would to a straightforward contravention of the section.

---

[147] It could also be added that it is really only the professional advisers that stand to benefit from this rule. However, the revenue to be generated from advising on the relatively simple matter of avoiding the s 585 trap is likely to be a drop in the ocean when viewed in the context of the overall fees that can be charged for advising on the very wide range of legal, tax, and accounting issues that need to be addressed in setting up and maintaining an employee share scheme

[148] This rule is derived from Second Company Law Directive, Arts 9 and 31(1).

[149] Companies Act 2006, s 587(2).   [150] Companies Act 2006, s 591.   [151] Companies Act 2006, s 588.

[152] Companies Act 2006, s 587(3).   [153] Companies Act 2006, s 587(4).

Valuation of non-cash consideration for shares in a public company

Section 593 of the Companies Act 2006 imposes a general requirement for independent valuation of any non-cash consideration for shares in a public company. A public company must
not allot shares as fully or partly paid up (as to their nominal value or any premium on them)
otherwise than in cash, unless the consideration has been independently valued and a valuation report has been made to the company in the six months preceding the allotment.[154]
A copy of the valuation report must be sent to the proposed allottee before the allotment.[155]
A copy of the valuation report must also be delivered to the registrar of companies when
the company files the return of allotment of the shares required by section 555 of the Act.[156]
The requirement for independent valuation of non-cash consideration is derived from the
Second Company Law Directive.[157] Under the Directive, the expert's report shall contain at
least a description of the assets comprising the consideration and of the methods of valuation
used, and shall state whether the values arrived at by the application of these methods correspond at least to the number and nominal value and, where appropriate, to the premium
on the shares to be issued for them.

The details of the valuation and report required by section 593 of the Companies Act 2006
are set out in sections 596 and 1149 to 1153 of the Act.[158] The company must appoint as the
independent valuer a person who would be qualified to be its auditor; it may appoint its current auditor.[159] The independent valuer so appointed may delegate the task of carrying out
the valuation,[160] but has a non-delegable duty to produce a report stating a range of matters
including a description of the consideration, the method used to value it, and the date of the
valuation.[161] The independent valuer and the delegate (if any) are entitled to require from the
officers of the company such information and explanations as they think necessary to enable
them to carry out their responsibilities.[162] The sanction for knowingly or recklessly making
a misleading, false, or deceptive statement in response to a proper inquiry is imprisonment,
or a fine (or both).[163]

If the valuation requirements are not complied with, penal liability can attach to the allottee and also to subsequent holders of the shares. Even though the allottee may have duly conveyed assets of considerable value to the company, if the assets have not been duly valued, he
can still be required to pay an amount equal to the aggregate of the nominal value and share
premium that was treated as paid up by the non-cash consideration, together with interest.
This liability attaches where the requirements for valuation have not been complied with and
either (a) the allottee has not received the valuer's report; or (b) he knew or ought to have
known that what has occurred amounted to a contravention of the statutory requirements
relating to the valuation process.[164] Subsequent holders of shares allotted in contravention
of the section 593 requirement of the Companies Act 2006 for independent valuation may
also incur statutory liability.[165] However, there is the possibility of applying to the court to be
relieved of liability.[166]

The broad legislative policy underlying the penal liability that attaches to allottees and
subsequent holders of shares in a public company that have been allotted for a non-cash consideration which has not been valued is to prevent public companies from issuing shares at a

---

[154] Companies Act 2006, s 593(1)(a)–(b).　　[155] Companies Act 2006, s 593(1)(c).
[156] Companies Act 2006, s 597.　　[157] This implements Second Company Law Directive, Arts 10 and 31(2).
[158] In *Re Ossory Estates plc* (1988) BCC 461, 463 Harman J described these requirements as 'curious and arcane.'
[159] Companies Act 2006, ss 1150–1151.　　[160] Companies Act 2006, s 1150.
[161] Companies Act 2006, s 596.　　[162] Companies Act 2006, s 1153.
[163] Companies Act 2006, s 1153(2) and (4).　　[164] Companies Act 2006, s 593(3).
[165] Companies Act 2006 s 605.　　[166] Companies Act 2006 s 606.

discount.[167] The liability is harsh because, prima facie, allottees can be required to pay twice over, once in cash and once in money's worth. Subsequent holders are also in what appears to be an invidious position because they can be obliged to pay for the shares in cash even though the company may have already received, from someone else, valuable non-cash consideration in respect of them. This harshness is mitigated by section 606 of the Companies Act 2006, which allows the court to grant relief from liability in certain circumstances. The onus is on the person, whether allottee or subsequent holder, seeking relief to apply to the court, and the burden is on the applicant to satisfy the court that a case for relief is made out.[168] The circumstances in which the court may grant relief are considered in a later section of this chapter.

There are two important statutory exemptions from the general rule requiring non-cash consideration for the shares of public companies to be independently valued. These are the *takeover* exemption and the *mergers* exemption, considered later.[169] These exemptions are derived from Article 31(3) of the Second Company Law Directive, which permits Member States not to apply the valuation requirement to increases in capital made in order to give effect to a merger, division, or a public offer. It is also expressly provided in section 593(2) of the Companies Act 2006, presumably for the avoidance of doubt, that bonus issues fall outside the valuation requirements. In addition to the statutory carve-outs, it may be possible to structure transactions so as to fall outside the valuation rules, for example, by the company agreeing to purchase an asset for cash and the vendor then agreeing to release the company from its obligation to pay for the asset in return for an allotment of shares.[170] It has been suggested that use of such structures means that in practice the valuation requirements are relatively easy to avoid.[171] However, the possibility that such structures might not withstand close judicial scrutiny cannot be completely discounted as there is room in this context for a court to look through an artificial arrangement.[172] One basis on which a court can depart from the legal form of a transaction is where it is a fraud or a sham but it is quite hard to persuade an English court to intervene on this ground. Another basis is where, as a matter of statutory interpretation, the particular provision in question requires (or permits) the court to look beyond its immediate legal form to its economic substance in order to ensure that the underlying statutory purpose is met.[173] A composite two-stage transaction designed to avoid the statutory valuation requirement could be vulnerable on this ground.[174] Since the requirement is derived from an EU Directive, views from elsewhere in Europe are worth noting. For example, there is a noticeable contrast between the view expressed by some British commentators on the ease with which the valuation requirement can be evaded and the position under German law, where the well-established doctrine on hidden contributions in kind is intended to prevent avoidance of the rules through the use of composite transactions.[175]

---

[167] *Re Bradford Investments plc (No 2)* [1991] BCC 379.
[168] *Re Bradford Investments plc (No 2)* [1991] BCC 383.   [169] Companies Act 2006, ss 594–5.
[170] The shares are allotted for cash in this case because 'cash' includes the release of a liability for a liquidated sum (Companies Act 2006, s 583(3)(c)).
[171] Rickford, 'Reforming Capital,' 935.   [172] *Re Bradford Investments plc (No 2)* [1991] BCC 379.
[173] J Vella, 'Departing From the Legal Substance of Transactions in the Corporate Field: the Ramsay Approach Beyond the Tax Sphere' [2007] *Journal of Corporate Law Studies* 243.
[174] J Vella, 'Departing From the Legal Substance of Transactions in the Corporate Field: the Ramsay Approach Beyond the Tax Sphere.'
[175] A Pentz, H-J Priester, and A Schwanna, 'Raising Cash and Contributions in Kind When Forming a Company and for Capital Increases,' in Lutter, *Legal Capital in Europe* 42, 52–3; S Grundmann, *European Company Law* 2nd edn (Cambridge: Intersentia, 2012) 224–5.

Takeover exemption

For the takeover exemption to apply there must be an arrangement providing for the allotment of shares in a public company ('company A') on terms that the whole or part of the consideration for the shares allotted is to be provided by the transfer to that company (or the cancellation) of some or all of the shares of another company ('company B') (or of a class of shares in that company).[176] The arrangement must allow for participation by all of the holders of the shares in company B (or, where the arrangement is in respect of a class of shares, all of the holders of the shares in that class) save that, for this purpose, shares held by the offeror company or by its nominees, or by other companies in its group or by their nominees, are ignored.[177] Shares allotted 'in connection with'[178] an arrangement satisfying these criteria are exempt from the usual valuation requirements. This exemption is apt to cover takeover situations where the consideration offered to the shareholders of the target is, or includes, shares in the offeror. However, its scope arguably extends beyond straightforward share-for-share allotments of this sort. Since the exemption applies to allotments 'in connection with' qualifying arrangements, it is possible to argue that no valuation is required so long as the assets to be acquired in exchange for shares include the entire share capital of another company. Applying this line of argument, it appears that a public company could avoid the valuation requirements in circumstances where it uses its shares as consideration for the acquisition of non-cash assets of substantial value by the simple expedient of ensuring that the assets acquired include the entire share capital of a company, even though the value of that company may be insignificant in relation to the overall size of the transaction.[179]

Mergers exemption

For the purposes of this exemption, a merger means a proposal by one company to acquire all the assets and liabilities of another company in exchange for the issue of shares or other securities of the first company to the shareholders of the other company.[180] Shares allotted by a company in connection with such a merger are not subject to the valuation requirement.[181]

Relaxation of the independent valuation requirement by the 2006 amending Directive

The mandatory requirement for independent valuation of non-cash consideration for shares attracts criticism as being time-consuming and expensive. Although the basic idea—that there should be some check that the value of the consideration accepted in return for shares really does match the issue price—is sound, the argument is that the idea is put into effect in a disproportionately heavy-handed manner.[182] The 2006 Directive responded to these criticisms by making it possible for Member States to dispense with the requirement for independent valuation of non-cash consideration for shares in a public limited company in certain circumstances.[183] These circumstances include where the consideration in question is transferable securities that are valued by reference to the price at which they have been trading on

---

[176] Companies Act 2006, s 594.   [177] Companies Act 2006, s 594(5).
[178] Companies Act 2006, s 594(1).
[179] Second Company Law Directive, Art 31(3) permits Member States to disapply the requirement for independent valuation in the event of an increase in subscribed capital made in order to give effect to a public offer.
[180] Companies Act 2006, s 595(2).   [181] Companies Act 2006, s 595.
[182] High Level Group, *Final Report*, 83 summarizes the arguments, describing the valuation requirements as 'one of the real problems of the system of capital formation created by the Second Company Law Directive.'
[183] Directive 2006/68/EC, now in the 2012 recast Second Company Law Directive, Arts 10–12, and Art 31.

a regulated market or assets that have been subject to a recent independent expert's report or valuation for the purpose of audited accounts. The Directive is limited in its deregulatory effect, however, because instead of the independent valuation obligation there is a requirement for publication of various matters (including a description of the consideration, its value and, where applicable, the source of valuation, and a statement that no new 'qualifying circumstances' affecting value have occurred since the valuation). In addition, there is provision for shareholders holding at least 5 per cent of issued share capital still to request an independent expert's report. The UK government took the view that it was not worthwhile to take advantage of the option provided by the amending Directive in this respect.[184]

Liability of subsequent holders

Generally speaking, where there is a breach of any of the statutory rules relating to payment for shares (ie the no-discount rule (section 580); the work/services undertaking rule for plc shares (section 585); the one-quarter paid up rule for plc shares (section 586); the long-term undertaking rule for plc shares (section 587); the valuation requirement for plc shares (section 593)), statutory liability attaches to subsequent holders of the shares as well as to the original allottee or person who is holding the shares at the time when the liability first arises.[185] Subsequent holders are jointly and severally liable with any other person so liable. A 'holder' of shares for the purpose of subsequent holder liability includes a person who has an unconditional right to be included in the company's register of members in respect of the shares or to have an instrument of transfer of the shares executed in his favour.[186] In *System Controls plc v Munro Corporate plc*[187] a company contracted to allot shares and fulfilled its obligation by issuing a renounceable letter of allotment. Hoffmann J held that the person in whose favour the letter had been renounced was a holder of the shares for the purposes of these sections.

Subsequent holders escape liability if they are purchasers for value who, at the time of the purchase, did not have actual notice of the contravention, or are persons who derive title to the shares (directly or indirectly) from such a person.[188] In the *System Controls* case the subsequent holder was not exempt where it knew that the allotment had been effected without valuation, even though it might have been unaware of the need for such a valuation to be obtained; Hoffmann J held that actual notice in this context meant notice of the facts and need not extend to an appreciation that they constituted a contravention.

Relief from liability

With two exceptions, those who incur liability by reason of a breach of the statutory rules relating to payment for shares can apply to the court to be relieved from liability. The exceptions relate to the no-discount rule and the one-quarter paid up rule for plcs where the allottee cannot apply to be relieved of the obligation to pay to the company an amount equal to the discount or the minimum amount, plus interest. However, it appears that a subsequent holder of a share that was allotted in breach of either of these rules may be relieved of liability.[189] It is for the person seeking to be relieved of liability to make the application to court rather than for the company to apply to the court for the imposition of liability. The applicant may seek to be relieved of the liability that arises under the companies legislation as a

---

[184] DTI, *Implementation of Companies Act 2006 Consultative Document* (February 2007) paras 6.8–6.26.
[185] Companies Act 2006, s 588 and s 605.   [186] Companies Act 2006, s 588(3) and s 605(4).
[187] [1990] BCC 386.   [188] Companies Act 2006, s 588(2) and s 605(3).
[189] Companies Act 2006, s 589(1).

consequence of the fact that there has been a breach of the statutory rules or of a liability arising from any undertaking given to the company in or in connection with payment for the shares.[190] Contractual undertakings remain enforceable notwithstanding a breach of the statutory rules regarding payment for shares.[191]

Relief from liability must be granted only where and to the extent that it appears to the court just and equitable to do so.[192] In making its determination, the court must have regard to two overriding principles:[193]

(1) that a company which has allotted shares should receive money or money's worth at least equal in value to the aggregate of the nominal value of those shares and the whole of any premium or, if the case so requires, so much of that aggregate as is treated as paid up; and

(2) subject to this, that where a company would, if the court did not grant the exemption, have more than one remedy against a particular person, it should be for the company to decide which remedy it should remain entitled to pursue.

In *Re Bradford Investments plc (No 2)*[194] Hoffmann J said that the designation of (1) as an overriding principle did not mean that the court would not have jurisdiction to grant an exemption unless it was satisfied that the company had received assets worth at least the nominal value of the allotted shares and any premium. However, it did mean that very good reasons would be needed before the court could accept that it would be just and equitable to exempt an applicant from liability in circumstances where the company had not received sufficient value in respect of its shares.

In determining whether it would be just and equitable to grant relief on an application for relief from liability under the Companies Act 2006, the court must take into account the following:

(a) whether the applicant has paid, or is liable to pay, any amount in respect of any other liability arising in relation to the shares under any of the relevant sections, or of any liability arising by virtue of any undertaking given in or in connection with payment of those shares;

(b) whether any person other than the applicant has paid or is likely to pay (whether in pursuance of an order of the court or otherwise) any such amount; and

(c) whether the applicant or any other person has performed in whole or in part, or is likely so to perform, any such undertaking, or has done or is likely to do any other thing in payment or part payment of the shares.[195]

Where the application is for relief from liability arising by virtue of an undertaking given to the company in, or in connection with, payment for shares, the court can grant an exemption only if and to the extent that it appears just and equitable to do so having regard to:

(1) whether the applicant has paid or is liable to pay any amount in respect of any liability arising in relation to the shares under any of the relevant provisions of the Companies Act; and

(2) whether any person other than the applicant has paid or is likely to pay (whether in pursuance of an order of the court or otherwise) any such amount.[196]

190 Companies Act 2006, s 589(2) and s 606(1).   191 Companies Act 2006, s 591 and s 608.
192 Companies Act 2006, s 589(3)–(4) and s 606(2)–(3).   193 Companies Act 2006, s 589(5) and s 606(4).
194 [1991] BCC 379, 384.   195 Companies Act 2006, s 589(3) and s 606(2).
196 Companies Act 2006, s 589(4) and s 606(3).

The burden is on the applicant to satisfy the court that a case for relief exists.[197] In *Re Ossory Estates plc*,[198] where the company had already re-sold at substantial profits properties which had been acquired in consideration for the allotment of shares and there was clear evidence that the vendor had so far complied with all of the undertakings arising from the conveyancing transactions and was likely to continue so to comply, Harman J was satisfied that a case for relief had been made out. However, in *Re Bradford Investments plc (No 2)*[199] the applicants were unable to establish that the assets transferred in consideration for shares had any net value and accordingly it was held that there was no case for relief.

Criminal liability for breach of rules relating to payment for shares

It is a criminal offence for a company to contravene any of the statutory rules relating to payment for shares. The company and any officer of it who is in default are liable to a fine.[200]

Share Premiums

The next part of this chapter looks at rules relating to share premiums. These rules would disappear under a no par value shares regime since, in that event, all of the consideration received by a company in return for an issue of its shares would simply be subject to the same rules.

Determining the issue price

Shares can be issued at a price that is higher than their nominal or par value, with any excess over the nominal value of the share being known as a share premium. It falls to the directors, as part of their general managerial power, to fix the price at which shares are allotted. Directors' duties serve as a safeguard against directors acting quixotically in setting issue prices. It has been judicially stated that directors have a prima facie duty to obtain the best price that they can for new share issues.[201] Rights issues are often made at a discount to the prevailing market price of the company's shares which is greater than is necessary to take account of the fact that the rights issues will increase the number of shares in the market. The purpose of the discount is to ensure the popularity of the issue and to prevent a commercially unacceptable proportion of it being left with the underwriters. Occasionally companies dispense with underwriting altogether and make the issue at a very substantial discount to the prevailing market price. In *Shearer v Bercain Ltd*[202] it was accepted that directors could legitimately offer a discount in order to ensure the success of a rights issue.[203]

Treatment of share premiums

Sums representing share premiums must be accounted for in a share premium account and, save for certain specified purposes, they must be treated as if they were part of the company's paid up share capital.[204] A rule to this effect was introduced into the domestic legislation

---

[197] *Re Bradford Investments plc (No 2)* [1991] BCC 379.   [198] (1988) 4 BCC 461.   [199] [1991] BCC 379.
[200] Companies Act 2006, s 590 and s 607.
[201] *Lowry v Consolidated African Selection Trust Ltd* [1940] AC 648, HL, 479 per Lord Wright; *Shearer v Bercain Ltd* [1980] 3 All ER 295, 307–8.
[202] [1980] 3 All ER 295. See also *Re Sunrise Radio Ltd* [2010] 1 BCLC 367.
[203] Ch 5 considers listing requirements and institutional investor expectations, which exert additional control over share allotments at discounted prices by publicly-quoted companies.
[204] Companies Act 2006, s 610.

following a recommendation from the Cohen Committee, which reported in 1945.[205] Prior to this change in the law, share premiums were seen as distributable and thus could be used for paying dividends or for writing off losses.[206]

The Second Company Law Directive does not require share premiums to be treated in the same way as share capital and it is thus open to the UK government to change the treatment of share premiums for both private and public companies in its domestic law.[207] The Companies Act 2006 presented an opportunity to do so but it was not taken. The possibility of deregulation free from Directive constraints with regard to the treatment of share premiums came to prominence only rather late in the policy formation process relating to the Companies Act 2006, by which time the agenda was more or less set and the government had decided to defer radical reform relating to legal capital except in certain specific areas until reform of the Second Company Law Directive had been thoroughly considered at the European level. Such is the degree of divergence between Member States in the treatment of share premiums in their national laws that it has been said of the law relating to share premiums in Europe that it has applied 'scant regard to any coherent or rational philosophy.'[208]

Permissible uses for share premiums

Sums representing share premiums represent a valuable source of corporate finance and they may be used by a company to fund its business operations in the same way as any other finance that it raises. In addition, the Companies Act 2006 authorizes the use of share premiums in a few other circumstances, and to this limited extent the treatment of share premiums differs from that in relation to share capital. The Companies Act 2006 narrowed the circumstances in which special use may be made of special premiums.[209]

Bonus issues

The share premium account may be applied by the company in paying up unissued shares to be allotted to members as fully paid shares.[210] Thus, if a company has issued 100 shares of £1 each at a premium of £1 per share, so that its share capital is £100 and it has a share premium account of £100, it may then issue a further 100 shares to its existing shareholders on the basis that the shares are to be issued fully paid by application of the share premium account; the end result is that the share premium account is reduced to zero but the company's paid up share capital increases to £200. As far as individual shareholders are concerned, the total value of their capital contribution remains constant but the investment is made potentially more liquid by being represented by two shares, each of which has a lower individual value than the one share held before the bonus issue. A bonus issue, also known as a capitalization issue, does not result in undistributable reserves leaving the company to the detriment of its creditors.

This statutory authorization in respect of the payment up of bonus shares from share premiums is limited to issues of fully paid bonus shares, and does not extend to issues of partly paid bonus shares or to issues of debentures.

---

[205] *Report of the Committee on Company Law Amendment* (Cmd 6659, 1945) para 108.
[206] *Re Duff's Settlement Trusts* [1951] Ch 721, and 923 (CA); *First Nationwide v Revenue and Customs Commissioners* [2011] STC 1540 (Upper Tribunal). MV Pitts, 'The Rise and Rise of the Share Premium Account' (2000) 10 *Accounting, Business & Financial History* 317.
[207] Rickford, 'Reforming Capital,' 939–41.   [208] Rickford, 'Reforming Capital,' 941.
[209] This narrowing of the permissible uses for share premiums broadly followed recommendations made by the Company Law Review Steering Group, *Company Formation and Capital Maintenance*, para 3.21.
[210] Companies Act 2006, s 610(3).

The authorization to use the share premium account in this way can be exploited by companies that want to return surplus cash to their shareholders. An established method of doing this is an arrangement generally known as a 'B share scheme' in which a company makes a bonus issue of a class of shares (B shares) that is fully paid up by application of the share premium account and then redeems (if the B shares were issued as redeemable) or buys back the B shares in accordance with the relevant provisions of the Companies Act 2006.[211] Redeemable shares and share buy-backs are considered in chapter 8.

Expenses and commissions on an issue of shares

Where a company has made an issue of shares at a premium, it may write off the expenses of that issue and any commission paid on that issue against the sum transferred to the share premium account in respect of that specific issue.[212] What would be included within the category of 'expenses of the issue' has not attracted judicial scrutiny but there is some guidance in accounting standards.[213] Expenses incurred by a company in order to put itself in the position to issue securities—such as restructuring costs—are unlikely to be included.[214]

Share premiums and non-cash consideration

Until 1980 it was unclear whether a company had to create a share premium account whenever it issued shares for a non-cash consideration that was more valuable than the nominal value of the issued shares. In *Henry Head & Co Ltd v Roper Holdings Ltd*[215] a holding company acquired two companies by means of a share-for-share exchange. The actual value of the shares acquired was much greater than the nominal value of the shares issued as consideration and the directors of the holding company were advised that they had to account for this excess by crediting it to a share premium account. This advice was upheld by the court. Notwithstanding this ruling, some practitioners continued to believe that the obligation to create a share premium account in this type of situation could be avoided.[216] The arguments on which that practice was based were finally considered by the court in *Shearer v Bercain Ltd*.[217] Essentially, those arguments were: (a) it was for the company to determine the terms of issue and it was not obliged to obtain a premium merely because investors might be willing to pay it; and (b) if the sale and purchase agreement provided for the assets to be sold at a price equal to the par value of the shares to be issued as consideration, there was no obligation on the company to create a share premium account.

Walton J rejected these arguments. In his view it was the prima facie duty of directors to obtain the best possible price for the shares.[218] Furthermore, the obligation to create a share premium account was not optional and could not be avoided by stating that the shares were issued at their nominal value; if the assets acquired in consideration of the issue of shares had an actual value greater than the nominal value of the consideration shares then, irrespective

---

[211] T Scott, 'Returning Value to Shareholders. Options for Companies' (1997) 8(3) *Practical Law for Companies* 19.

[212] Companies Act 2006, s 610(2).

[213] P Holgate, *Accounting Principles for Lawyers* (Cambridge: CUP, 2006) 149–50.

[214] P Holgate, *Accounting Principles for Lawyers*, 149–50.   [215] [1952] Ch 124.

[216] For an account of the development of market practice and corresponding regulation in relation to share premiums, see C Napier and C Noke, 'Premiums and Pre-Acquisition Profits: The Legal and Accounting Professions and Business Combinations' (1991) 54 MLR 810.

[217] [1980] 3 All ER 295.

[218] Following Lord Wright in *Lowry (Inspector of Taxes) v Consolidated African Selection Trust Ltd* [1940] AC 648, HL.

of the terms on which those shares had been issued, the company was subject to a mandatory requirement to create a share premium account.

As a result of the decision in *Shearer v Bercain Ltd*, pressure was brought to bear on Parliament to provide relief from the obligation to create a share premium account. This was done in the Companies Act 1981 and the relevant reliefs are now to be found in sections 611 (group reconstruction relief) and 612 (merger relief). Before looking at these reliefs in more detail, it should be noted that their interaction with the accounting requirements for acquisitions is complicated, and has become increasingly so as a consequence of the transition from the use of domestic accounting standards to international standards (International Financial Reporting Standards or IFRS).[219] At the root of these complications arguably lies the fact that IFRS are intended to serve the needs of investors rather than meet creditor protection aims of the legal capital/capital maintenance doctrines. In the UK, very lengthy and detailed guidance from the professional bodies for the accounting profession helps to bridge the divergence but this is unsatisfactory. The poor fit between modern accounting requirements and company law adds to the case for root and branch reform of the legal capital regime.[220]

Group reconstruction relief

Under the Companies Act 2006, relief from the obligation to create a share premium account is available where the issuing company:

(a) is a wholly-owned subsidiary of another company (the 'holding company'); and

(b) allots shares to its holding company or another wholly-owned subsidiary of its holding company in consideration for the transfer of non-cash assets to the issuing company—these assets may be assets of any company in the group comprising the holding company and all its wholly-owned subsidiaries.[221]

Where the shares in the issuing company are issued at a premium there is no obligation to carry the premium to a share premium account to the extent that it exceeds what is referred to as the minimum premium value.[222]

The minimum premium value means the amount by which the base value of the consideration for the shares allotted exceeds the nominal value of the shares.[223] The base value of the consideration is determined by reference to the value of the assets transferred to the acquirer minus the value of liabilities assumed by the acquirer. The Companies Act 2006 permits any amount over the minimum premium value to be disregarded in determining the amount at which any shares or other consideration provided for the shares issued is recorded in the issuing company's balance sheet.[224]

Merger relief

Merger relief is available in circumstances where one company acquires the share capital of another company by issuing its shares to the shareholders of the target company. In those circumstances, provided certain conditions are satisfied, there is no statutory obligation to

---

[219] ICAEW, *Guidance on the Determination of Realised Profits and Losses in the Context of Distributions under the Companies Act 2006* (TECH 02/10) para 9.43.

[220] E Ferran, 'The Place for Creditor Protection on the Agenda for Modernization of Company Law in the European Union' (2006) 3 *European Company and Financial Law Review* 178

[221] Companies Act 2006, s 611(1).   [222] Companies Act 2006, s 611(2).

[223] Companies Act 2006, s 611(3).   [224] Companies Act 2006, s 615.

credit to a share premium account the amount by which the value of the acquired shares exceeds the nominal value of the shares issued by way of consideration.[225] The Companies Act 2006 provides further that any amount not included in the issuing company's share premium account may also be disregarded in determining the amount at which the acquired shares (or other consideration) is shown in the issuer's balance sheet.[226]

The precise conditions which must be satisfied in order for merger relief to apply are that the issuing company must secure at least a 90 per cent equity holding in another company, and this holding must be secured pursuant to an arrangement[227] providing for the allotment of equity shares in the issuing company on terms that the consideration for the allotted shares is to be provided by the issue or transfer to the issuing company of equity shares in the other company; or by the cancellation of any such shares not held by the issuing company.[228] Thus if a company seeks to acquire all of the equity shares in a target company and offers the shareholders in the target its equity shares in exchange for each of the target's equity shares, merger relief will be available if and when the issuer acquires 90 per cent of the target's equity pursuant to the arrangement. Equity shares for this purpose are issued shares except those that neither as respects dividends nor as respects capital carry any right to participate beyond a specified amount in a distribution.[229] If a target company's equity share capital is divided into different classes of shares (for example, ordinary shares which are fully participating as to both dividends and capital and preference shares which are fully participating as to dividend but participating only for a fixed amount in any capital distribution), for merger relief to apply the conditions must be satisfied separately in respect of each class.[230] If non-equity shares of the target are also included in the arrangement, the acquisition of those shares does not go towards satisfying the conditions but, if the conditions are otherwise satisfied, merger relief is extended to any shares allotted in return for the non-equity shares of the target.[231]

What is meant by securing 'at least a 90 per cent equity holding in another company in pursuance of...an arrangement' is amplified by section 613 of the Companies Act 2006. The issuing company[232] must end up holding equity shares in the target of an aggregate nominal value equal to 90 per cent or more of the nominal value of the target's total equity share capital. However, whilst the holding must be arrived at as a consequence of an acquisition or cancellation of target company shares pursuant to the arrangement, it is not necessary for all, or indeed any, of the shares comprising the issuing company's holding of target company shares to be acquired pursuant to the arrangement.[233] Thus if the issuing company holds a number of target company shares prior to entering into an arrangement to issue its own shares in consideration for the cancellation of target company shares and, as a result of such cancellation, the size of the issuing company's original holding becomes equal to 90 per cent or more of the nominal value of the target's (diminished) equity share capital, merger relief conditions will have been satisfied. Similarly, where the arrangement is effected by means of a share-for-share exchange, the shares acquired by the issuing company pursuant to the exchange can be added to its prior holding of target company shares in order to ascertain whether the 90 per cent condition has been met.

---

[225] Companies Act 2006, s 612.   [226] Companies Act 2006, s 615.
[227] As defined in Companies Act 2006, s 616(1).   [228] Companies Act 2006, s 612(1).
[229] Companies Act 2006, s 616(1) and s 548.   [230] Companies Act 2006, s 613(4).
[231] Companies Act 2006, s 612(3).
[232] Shares held by the issuing company's holding company or subsidiary, or by other subsidiaries of its holding company, or by its or their nominees, are to be regarded as held by the issuing company (Companies Act 2006, s 613(5)).
[233] Companies Act 2006, s 613(3).

The conditions for merger relief to apply do not preclude the acquirer from offering the target company's shareholders a mixed consideration, which is partly in the form of shares and partly in the form of cash or other assets. To the extent that shares of the acquirer are issued by way of consideration, merger relief can apply in respect of those shares.

The operation of merger relief can be illustrated by the following example:

Company A makes a successful bid for 100% of the equity of Company B. The consideration is an issue to Company B's shareholders of 300 million equity shares in Company A, each of these shares having a nominal value of 5p and a fair value of £3. The transaction meets the conditions for statutory merger relief. Company A records the acquisition of B at fair value (£900 million).

Company A's balance sheet after the transaction is as follows:

Assets	£m
Investment in Company B	900
Other assets	440
Liabilities	
Creditors	(100)
Provisions	(40)
Net assets	1,200
Capital and reserves	
Ordinary shares of 5p each (120m existing + 15m (0.05 x 300 new))	135
Merger reserve (£2.95 x 300m)	885
Profit and loss reserve	180
	1,200

This example introduces the concept of a 'merger reserve', which serves as the balancing entry that is made necessary by reason of the fact that the company does not take advantage of the possibility provided by the Companies Act 2006 to record the value of the investment in B at the nominal value of the consideration A shares rather than at its fair value. To explain this example further, it is now necessary to look briefly, and in outline only, at the accounting position.

Statutory reliefs and accounting requirements

Guidance from the accountancy professional bodies notes that the accounting treatment adopted in the example in the previous section is not required as a matter of company law but that it is permissible and may in fact be necessary to satisfy accounting requirements.[234] As a general rule, companies that draw up their accounts in accordance with IFRS are required to record acquisitions at their fair value.[235] Since the entries on the shareholder funds side of the balance sheet must correspond with those on the assets side, there is therefore a need to have a reserve recording the difference between the nominal value of the consideration shares and the fair value of the acquired assets. Where merger relief is available, this function is performed by a merger reserve. A merger reserve is a non-statutory reserve that is not subject to the maintenance of capital principle. Although it is not a realized profit available for distribution immediately, it may become realized at a later date.[236]

---

[234] ICAEW, *Guidance on the Determination of Realised Profits and Losses*, para 2.11.

[235] ICAEW, *Guidance on the Determination of Realised Profits and Losses*, paras 9.43–9.44D (discussing some qualifications).

[236] ICAEW, *Guidance on the Determination of Realised Profits and Losses*, para 2.11. See also the discussion in the context of distributions in ch 9.

Importance of group reconstruction and merger relief

Why are group reconstruction and merger relief important? The last sentence of the previous section paves the way to the answer to this question: it is all to do with preserving as much flexibility as possible with respect to distributable profits. Distributable profits are considered further in chapter 9 but, in brief, the basic rule is that only net realized profits are available for distribution to shareholders by way of dividend. A merger reserve, unlike a share premium account, will become a realized profit when the related asset is disposed of by the acquirer for a 'qualifying consideration' such as cash.[237] A merger reserve will also become realized if the investment to which it relates is written down for impairment and a realized loss is thereby recognized.[238]

Other reliefs

The Secretary of State is empowered to make provision, by statutory instrument, for further relief from the requirement to create a share premium account in relation to premiums other than cash premiums, or for restricting or modifying any of the reliefs provided by the Companies Act itself.[239]

Other Capital Contributions

The Privy Council has held that there is nothing in the company law of England to render ineffective an agreement to finance a company by means of capital contributions without a formal allocation of shares.[240] Where shareholders of a company agree to increase its capital in this way, the amount invested becomes, like share premium, part of the owners' equity.[241] The Companies Act 2006 does not expressly envisage this type of financing arrangement and there is no specific statutory obligation requiring the filing of a statement of capital when capital is invested in this way.

Stock

This is really little more than a footnote to the chapter, as in recent times it has been rare for UK companies to convert their shares into stock and the Companies Act 2006 removed the possibility of doing so in future.[242] Historically, stock was thought to have two advantages over shares. First, it is possible to deal in fractions of stock but it is not possible to deal in fractions of shares. This advantage is, however, more theoretical than real. The market might want to be able to trade in a fraction of a share because the price of the whole unit is high. However, rather than converting its shares into stock, the company can meet this demand by sub-dividing its existing shares into new shares with lower par values than those which they replace. The second supposed advantage of stock is that stock does not have to be numbered. This makes stock administratively more convenient than shares, where a numbering

---

[237] ICAEW, *Guidance on the Determination of Realised Profits and Losses*, para 3.9(f)(ii). 'Qualifying consideration' is defined in the *Guidance*, paras 3.11–3.12. It includes cash, assets that are readily convertible to cash, and the release of liabilities.

[238] ICAEW, *Guidance on the Determination of Realised Profits and Losses*, paras 3.9(f)(iv) and 9.44.

[239] Companies Act 2006, s 614.

[240] *Kellar v Williams* [2000] 2 BCLC 390, PC; *Blackburn v Revenue and Customs Commissioners* [2008] EWCA Civ 1454.

[241] *Kellar v Williams* [2000] 2 BCLC 390, PC.   [242] Companies Act 2006, s 540(2).

obligation prima facie applies.[243] However, where all of the issued shares of a class are fully paid and rank *pari passu* for all purposes, none of those shares need thereafter have a distinguishing number so long as they remain fully paid and rank *pari passu* for all purposes with all shares of the same class for the time being issued and fully paid up.[244] It is uncommon for shares to be issued on a partly paid basis, which means that advantage can normally be taken of this exception. In 1962, the Jenkins Committee expressed the view that since the 1948 Companies Act had introduced the exception allowing fully paid shares not to be numbered, the advantages of converting from shares to stock had become negligible. The Committee recommended that references to stock should be eliminated from the companies legislation.[245] The Companies Act 2006 does not go quite so far but the remaining references to stock in the legislation are there simply to cater for the possibility that a few companies may still have stock in their capital structure. The 2006 Act retains the power that was also in predecessor legislation for companies to reconvert stock into shares.[246]

---

[243] Companies Act 2006, s 543(1).   [244] Companies Act 2006, s 543(2).
[245] *Report of the Company Law Committee* (Cmnd 1749, 1962) para 472.   [246] Companies Act 2006, s 540(3).

5

Share Allotments

Scope of this Chapter

This chapter is concerned with the corporate regulation of share issuance activity. Company law regulates matters of internal corporate governance with respect to share issues by specifically empowering shareholders in relation to equity financing decisions. For publicly listed companies, the company law shareholder empowerment rules relating to share issues are supplemented by listing requirements maintained by the Financial Conduct Authority (FCA), which in April 2013 succeeded the Financial Services Authority (FSA) as the UK's competent authority for listing.[1] The relevant listing requirements are also within the scope of this chapter. Also examined are the well-established guidelines from institutional investors that provide a degree of predictability about how shareholders will exercise their statutory and regulatory powers. The mandatory disclosure requirements triggered by new share issues are touched on only briefly in this chapter because the disclosure framework is considered in detail in the final Part of the book.

Regulating Share Issuance Activity: Striking a Balance

As a general rule, the management of a company's affairs is under the overall responsibility of its board and shareholders do not have a direct say in managerial decisions. Shares issues are an exception to this general rule because this is an area where potential agency problems between controllers (either managers or majority shareholders) and non-controllers are considered to be particularly significant. If left unregulated, there would be scope for controllers to use share issuance powers in ways that could adversely affect the interests of non-controlling shareholders in four key ways: (1) by effecting a transfer of wealth to new investors; (2) by diluting voting strength; (3) by distorting the operation of the market for corporate control or otherwise undermining mechanisms that are meant to promote managerial accountability to shareholders; (4) by being an instance of opportunistic exploitation of minority shareholders through misuse of majority shareholder power. Whilst the potential for abuse is held in check by directors' duties, in particular the proper purposes doctrine,[2] and statutory protection of minorities against unfair prejudice,[3] lawmakers at both national (UK) and regional (EU) level have seen fit to intervene more specifically by means of rules that empower shareholders by giving them a say in decisions to raise new finance through share issuance and protect minorities against controllers through mandatory pre-emption rights in favour of all shareholders.

The policy considerations that lie behind this approach are complex. On the one hand, it is indisputable that there are serious agency concerns that need to be addressed. On the other,

---

[1] In this chapter, the term 'listed' is used to denote a company that has an FCA premium listing and is admitted to dealings on the Main Market of the London Stock Exchange. The categories of 'premium' and 'standard' listing and the relationship between listing and admission to trading on a regulated market are examined in detail in ch 13.

[2] Codified as Companies Act 2006, s 171.

[3] Companies Act 2006, s 994. On the operation of the unfair prejudice remedy in the share issuance context, see *Re Sunrise Radio Ltd* [2010] 1 BCLC 367.

there is the obvious danger of undermining legitimate corporate financing objectives by imposing cumbersome rule-based requirements that may impede the efficiency of the capital-raising
process. The contrast between the EU, where pre-emption rights are mandatory, and the US,
where the principle of pre-emption has largely withered away as a form of shareholder protection, indicates that there is no single universally correct policy response to the agency conflicts
that are inherent in share issuance activity.[4] Nevertheless, the attachment to pre-emption rights
as a shareholder protection device is deeply engrained in European thinking: pre-emption
rights are regarded as an important part of the corporate governance accountability process
because they force management into a process of detailed dialogue with their shareholders
aimed at persuading those shareholders to take up their rights or to authorize a dispensation.[5]
As such, pre-emption rights are viewed as quite an effective form of discipline for underper-
forming managers.[6] In a review by the FSA that led eventually to the introduction of a requirement to offer pre-emption rights in the conditions for premium listing of an overseas company,
pre-emption rights were described as 'a key pillar of investor protection.'[7]

The Case for Special Protection of Shareholders' Interests

This section examines in more depth the agency problems that are said to justify special protection of shareholders' interests in the equity financing context.

Wealth transfers

When a company issues new shares it usually does so at a larger discount to the price at which
its existing shares are trading in the secondary market than is required to reflect the increase
in the number of issued shares. The extra discount element is intended to encourage investors
to acquire the new shares. Although directors have a duty to obtain the best price available
for new shares,[8] it may be justifiable for them to sanction a discount in order to ensure the
success of a new issue.[9] Pricing is a matter for the commercial judgment of the directors and
quite where the price will fall within the permissible range will depend on the particular circumstances of any given case.[10] To discharge their duties in exercising this power, directors
must consider the matters fairly in the interests of all shareholders and having regard to the
foreseeable range of responses.[11] The UK market has changed over the years from discounts
in the region of 15 to 20 per cent in the 1980s to deeper discounts of around 30 to 40 per cent
in more recent years.[12]

   If the discount element involved in a new issue of shares is not offered to existing shareholders this will necessarily result in the short term in an erosion in the value of their investment, as the following simplified example illustrates.[13]

---

[4] P Myners, *Pre-emption Rights: Final Report* (URN 05/679, February 2005) 16 notes that the UK and US systems both 'work' despite their differences.
   [5] Rights Issue Review Group, *A Report to the Chancellor of the Exchequer* (2008) 3.
   [6] J Franks, C Mayer, and L Renneboog, 'Who Disciplines Management in Poorly Performing Companies' (2001) 10 *Journal of Financial Intermediation* 209.
   [7] FSA, *Consultation on Amendments to the Listing Rules and Feedback on DP08/111* (CP 08/21).
   [8] *Shearer v Bercain* [1980] 3 All ER 295.
   [9] *Shearer v Bercain* [1980] 3 All ER 295, 307. See also Case C-338/06 *Commission v Spain* [2008] ECR I-10139.
   [10] *Re Sunrise Radio Ltd* [2010] 1 BCLC 367, [95].   [11] *Re Sunrise Radio Ltd* [2010] 1 BCLC 367, [95].
   [12] ABI, *Encouraging Equity Investment: Facilitation of Efficient Equity Capital Raising in the UK Market* (July 2013) 32.
   [13] This problem was perceived in early US decisions developing the concept of pre-emption rights: HS Drinker, 'The Pre-emptive Right of Shareholders to Subscribe New Shares' (1930) 43 *Harvard Law Review* 586. More recent expressions of this view can be found in the ABI/NAPF *Joint Position Paper on Pre-emption, Cost of Capital*

A shareholder owns 100 XYZ plc shares currently trading at £1.85 each. The value of the holding is £185. XYZ raises share capital by an issue of new shares which increases its share capital by 10 per cent. The new shares are offered to the market for subscription at £1.50 each.

The value of the shares in the company as a result of the issue is:

   (10 x 1.50 + 100 x 1.85)/110 = £1.818

   Value of holding = 100 x £1.818 = £181.80

Shareholder has lost over £3 in value.

Had the shareholder had been given the right to subscribe for a proportion of the new shares (one new share for every ten shares held) and had it taken up those rights, paying £15 to do so, the position would have been as follows:

Value of holding 110 x £1.818 = £200

Shareholder's position (200–15) = £185

Shareholders may not wish to, or may lack the funds to be able to, take up all or part of the shares that are offered to them on a pre-emptive basis. A right of pre-emption on its own thus can provide only limited protection against wealth transfer. Should the controllers of a company go through the motions of a pre-emptive offering knowing all the while that some shareholders will not be in a position to take up their rights, their actions would be open to challenge as a breach of directors' duties and/or as conduct that is unfairly prejudicial to shareholders' interests.[14] There is a particular responsibility on controllers to demonstrate even-handedness and fairness with respect to pricing in such circumstances in order to minimize the adverse impact on the value of the shareholdings of those who do not take up their rights.[15]

It is possible to bolster the structure of a pre-emptive offering in order to give shareholders firmer ex ante protection against wealth transfers than is provided by disciplines of directors' duties and shareholder remedies. This goal can be achieved by structuring the right to acquire the new shares at a discount as a tradable right in itself. This involves making the offer by means of a provisional letter of allotment (PAL) which is in renounceable form. The expected value of rights to acquire the shares can, using the same example, be calculated very roughly as the difference between the issue price of the new shares and the expected share price after issue, ie 32p. Provided the shareholder is able to sell those rights at a price at least equivalent to their expected value (which should be feasible so long as the reaction of the market to the issue is favourable and the shares trade after the announcement at a price at or above the theoretical ex-rights price) the shareholder's position should not be adversely affected. The following example illustrates.

A shareholder sells eight of its subscription rights for £2.56 and takes up the balance of the entitlement for two of those rights, paying £3 to do so, the eventual outcome for the shareholder is again unchanged because:

Value of holding 102 x £1.818 = £185.44

Shareholder's position 185.44–3 + 2.56 = £185.00

---

and Underwriting (July 1996); R Hinkley, D Hunter, M Whittell, and M Ziff, *Current Issues in Equity Finance* (London: ACT Publications, 1998) ch 4.

   [14] *Re a Company* [1985] BCLC 80 (upheld [1986] BCLC 430, CA); *West Coast Capital (Lios) Ltd, Petitioner* [2008] CSOH 72.

   [15] *Re Sunrise Radio Ltd* [2010] 1 BCLC 367.

In effect, the shareholder in the example sells part of the entitlement to fund the acquisition of the remaining part, a process that is sometimes described in practice as 'tail swallowing.' The example obviously ignores tax and dealing costs incurred in selling nil paid rights and taking up the balance of the entitlement and also market fluctuations in share prices but it serves nevertheless to demonstrate the importance of pre-emption rights accompanied by provision for the trading of subscription rights from the viewpoint of investors. From the company's viewpoint, by respecting pre-emption rights this structure secures the advantage of being able to offer new shares at a substantial discount and possibly therefore dispensing with underwriting and its associated costs.[16] However, the option of deep discounting and dispensing with underwriting is little used. This may be because deep discounting does not offer a company the same absolute certainty as underwriting. Another relevant consideration is that deeply discounted issues are sometimes associated with financial weakness and a lack of shareholder support; these negative connotations may deter managers of companies that are not in such a dire position from proposing the use of those structures.[17] However, there is support among institutional investors for the use of deep discount issues as a way to reduce the level of underwriting fees.[18]

Should the law intervene to protect shareholders against the risk of value transfers by making pre-emption rights mandatory? Should regulatory requirements go further and also mandate structures that facilitate the trading of rights to take up shares that are offered pre-emptively? The UK/EU approach broadly supports an affirmative answer to these questions and the way in which this pro-intervention stance is put into effect is discussed in more detail later in this chapter. Yet counterarguments also merit attention, not least because they help to explain why more extreme policy choices that would give shareholders very strong protection but at potentially too great a cost in terms of overall efficiency have been eschewed.

The overarching counterargument is that it is unduly short-termist to focus on the transfer of value resulting from the discount element in a new issue and that the longer-term financial interests of a company and its shareholders may be better served by allowing it more flexibility in the methods of raising capital. There are various facets to this argument. An issue of shares to a group of investors not limited to existing shareholders has the advantage of broadening the investor base in the company's shares, which may in the longer term open up further new sources of funding for the company. The ability to appeal to investors in jurisdictions outside those of the existing shareholders is one particular aspect of this analysis.[19] The costs and timescales involved in making an offer on a pre-emptive basis can also be compared unfavourably with a placing to external investors. Timing considerations have particular significance in volatile market conditions.

Protection against dilution

This argument for regulatory intervention in relation to share issuance is based on the idea of the shareholders' ownership rights: their proportionate share of the ownership of the company should not be diluted without their consent. Again there is a counterargument: to the extent that investors are concerned about holding an investment in a certain proportion of

[16] Myners, *Pre-emption Rights: Final Report*, 19.
[17] OFT, *Equity Underwriting and Associated Services* (OFT1303) 25.
[18] ABI, *Encouraging Equity Investment*, 39–41.
[19] 'Pre-emption Rights' (1987) 27(4) *Bank of England Quarterly Bulletin* 545, 547; E Haggar, 'Issuing Abroad is a Risky Venture' (1993) 108 *Corporate Finance* 22; E Haggar, 'Who Needs US Investors?' (1997) 148 *Corporate Finance* 42.

the share capital, they can always acquire shares in the market to maintain their holding.[20] However, this counterargument is not wholly persuasive. It clearly has no application in relation to companies whose shares are not openly traded.

Distortion of market for corporate control or other unconstitutional behaviour by directors

Another argument in favour of shareholder authorization requirements and pre-emption rights in respect of new share issues is that they help to curb unconstitutional behaviour by the directors of a company that is the target of a takeover bid, because they prevent the management from facilitating or blocking the bid by, as appropriate, issuing shares to a favoured bidder or to shareholders opposed to the bid. The counterargument here is that directors are subject to general duties to promote the success of their company and to use their powers only for proper purposes.[21] As a number of cases clearly demonstrate, it is an improper and unconstitutional use of power to issue shares so as to influence the outcome of a bid.[22] The issue for debate is thus whether general duties, supplemented by the requirements of the Takeover Code, amount to an adequate constraint on the perceived abuse or whether it is necessary in addition for there to be specific controls in the form of shareholder authorization requirements and pre-emption rights.

Abuse of majority shareholder power

Where control of a company lies with a majority shareholder rather than with its directors, minority shareholders are in a particularly vulnerable position because the majority shareholder may put pressure on the directors to exercise share issuance or other capital structuring powers in ways that are unfair to the interests of minority shareholders. Anti-dilution concerns may have particular resonance in this context, for example, in a company where the majority shareholders control sufficient votes to pass ordinary but not special resolutions, since a non-pre-emptive offering in this case could dilute the minority down to a level below that needed to block special resolutions.[23] Yet, in responding to majority/minority agency concerns, the law needs to be careful not to overprotect minorities by giving them powers that, in effect, allow them to hold the majority to ransom. Majority rule is a fundamentally important principle that runs through company law and any qualification to it needs to be carefully designed. The principle that no shareholder has the absolute right to expect their interest to remain constant forever is also well established in the law in the UK.[24] An Advocate-General to the Court of Justice of the EU has described the shareholders' right to retain unchanged their proportional share of their holding in the capital of the company as being a right that is inherent in being a shareholder.[25] However, in determining the precise scope of shareholder protections in the share issuance context, the Court has demonstrated due sensitivity to the wide range of economic factors that can arise in such situations.[26]

---

[20] 'Pre-emption Rights' (1987) 27(4) *Bank of England Quarterly Bulletin* 545, 547.
[21] Companies Act 2006, ss 171–172.
[22] *Hogg v Cramphorn Ltd* [1967] Ch 254; *Bamford v Bamford* [1970] Ch 212, CA; *Howard Smith Ltd v Ampol Petroleum Ltd* [1974] AC 821, PC.
[23] In *Re a company (No 005134 of 1986), ex p Harries* [1989] BCLC 383 a minority holding was diluted from 40 per cent to 4 per cent.
[24] *Mutual Life Insurance Co of New York v Rank Organisation Ltd* [1985] BCLC 11.
[25] Case C-42/95 *Siemens AG v Henry Nold* [1996] ECR I-6017, Opinion of Advocate-General Tesauro, para 15.
[26] C-338/06 *European Commission v Spain* [2008] ECR I-10139.

Shaping a balanced policy response

However persuasive the arguments for giving shareholders a say in equity financing decisions, the applicable regulatory framework needs to be focused and efficient because, as Paul Myners, the author of a report on the topic that was commissioned by the UK government, explained, this is an area where the need for balance is especially important:[27]

> Shareholders need to know that they are protected from any unwelcome dilution of their investment. And public companies need to be able to raise new money through the capital markets in as cheap and efficient a way as possible in order to grow and develop. Neither of these statements is particularly contentious—indeed they may appear self-evident. And yet the question of whether shareholders' pre-emption rights adversely impact on a company's ability to raise cash through the issuance of new shares is a complex and tricky issue.

There can be no question of giving minority shareholders an absolute veto over new share issues as that could be commercially disastrous. Therefore, if shareholders are to be specifically empowered to authorize share issues, this should be by way of a requirement for shareholder consent by means of either a simple or a super majority. To be consistent with the general law, this means either an ordinary resolution passed with a majority of the votes cast or a special resolution passed with at least 75 per cent of the votes cast. Secondly, and for the same reasons, rights of pre-emption in favour of existing shareholders should have an inbuilt waiver mechanism that can be activated by a simple or super majority vote of the shareholders and the rights should be structured so as to permit a company to offer shares to external investors if, or to the extent that, existing shareholders decline to take up their pre-emptive entitlements. Thirdly, acceptance of the first two considerations necessarily implies that minority shareholders will be vulnerable to the exercise of majority power, so policymakers have to be comfortable that the general law on directors' duties and shareholder remedies provides adequate supplementary protection against abuse. Fourthly, procedural aspects of shareholder empowerment and pre-emption rights need close attention to ensure that these are as streamlined as possible while still meeting their intended policy goals.

UK experience since 1980, when the UK first implemented shareholder allotment and pre-emption rights requirements in the Second Company Law Directive,[28] has demonstrated the scale of the challenge involved in striking an appropriate balance. The new EU requirements that were implemented by the Companies Act 1980 were added to the existing body of domestic law on shareholder rights with respect to share allotments without close examination whether they made any of the established rules effectively redundant. In addition, the new requirements were applied to private as well as public companies (in that respect going beyond the minimum required to comply with Community obligations). Only later did it come to be realized that elements of the law were duplicative and that bureaucratic procedures that were appropriate for public companies were often out of place in smaller private companies where the directors and shareholders were the same people, or at least closely connected groups. Learning from this experience, a more streamlined framework was put in place by the Companies Act 2006.

---

[27] Myners, *Pre-emption Rights: Final Report*, 3.

[28] Now recast as Directive 2012/30/EU of the European Parliament and of the Council of 25 October 2012 on coordination of safeguards which, for the protection of the interests of members and others, are required by Member States of companies within the meaning of the second paragraph of Article 54 of the Treaty on the Functioning of the European Union, in respect of the formation of public limited liability companies and the maintenance and alteration of their capital, with a view to making such safeguards equivalent (Recast) [2012] L315/74 (Second Company Law Directive).

However, the reforms enacted in 2006 still did not strip UK law down to the bare minimum required in order to comply with EU obligations. Further problems emerged during 2008 when several UK banks sought to strengthen their balance sheets by raising new equity. Against a background of increasingly adverse market conditions and plummeting share prices, the banks needed to act quickly, but the existing legal and regulatory framework put obstacles in their way.[29] It became apparent that certain well-meant shareholder protection mechanisms had not kept pace with dynamic modern securities markets and lagged behind the emergence of readily available, virtually instantaneous methods of communication. Compliance with the cumbersome regulatory framework threatened to undermine rather than foster shareholders' interests. The strains on the system that emerged during this period of crisis eventually prompted a further round of reforms, of both the Companies Act 2006 and of associated UK regulatory requirements and institutional investor guidelines.[30]

To go further would now require meaningful reform of the Second Company Law Directive, which is not a current priority at EU level. However, some related changes in EU capital market disclosure requirements and in financial regulation have occurred.[31] In 2013 the Association of British Insurers (ABI), the representative body of one major group of institutional investors, described the elements of the system in the UK for raising new equity capital that are within the scope of this chapter as being essentially 'fit for purpose.'[32] We can now turn to a closer examination of this system.

Shareholder Empowerment under the Companies Act 2006

Section 549(1) of the Companies Act 2006 provides that the directors of a company must not exercise any power of the company (a) to allot shares in the company, or (b) to grant rights to subscribe for, or to convert any security into, shares in the company, except in accordance with section 550 (private company with single class of shares) or section 551 (authorization by company). It is a criminal offence for a director knowingly to contravene or to permit or authorize a contravention of the section but nothing in the section affects the validity of an allotment.[33] If, in addition to failing to comply with the section, the directors act in breach of their general duties in making an allotment, its validity may be contested on that ground.[34]

The special authorization requirements imposed by this section apply to the allotment of all types of share, including ordinary, preference, and redeemable shares, save for shares allotted in pursuance of an employees' share scheme.[35] They also apply to the allotment of hybrid instruments such as warrants to subscribe for shares or bonds that are convertible into shares, save for allotments related to employees' share schemes.[36] However, where the

---

[29] E Ferran, 'What's Wrong with Rights Issues' (2008) 2 *Law and Financial Markets Review* 523.

[30] Rights Issue Review Group, *A Report to the Chancellor of the Exchequer*; FSA, *Rights Issue Subscription Periods* (CP09/4); FSA, *Report to HM Treasury on the Implementation of the Recommendations of the Rights Issue Review Group* (April 2010).

[31] Directive 2010/73/EU of 24 November 2010 amending Directives 2003/71/EC [201] OJ L327/1, inserting Art 7(2)(g) (a proportionate disclosure regime for share issues on a pre-emptive basis); Commission Delegated Regulation (EU) No 486/2012 amending Regulation (EC) No 809/2004 as regards the format and the content of the prospectus, the base prospectus, the summary and the final terms and as regards the disclosure requirements [2012] OJ L 150/1; European Commission, *Proposal for a Directive establishing a framework for the recovery and resolution of credit institutions and investment firms* (COM(2012) 280) (provision for shortening of notice periods for shareholder meetings to decide on an increase of capital in emergency situations, and for Member States to derogate from specified provisions (including increase of capital and pre-emption rights) that require shareholder consent or otherwise hinder effective and rapid resolution). On the prospectus requirements see further ch 13.

[32] ABI, *Encouraging Equity Investment*, 6.   [33] Companies Act 2006, s 549(4)–(6).

[34] *Hogg v Cramphorn* [1967] Ch 254; *Bamford v Bamford* [1970] Ch 212, CA; *Howard Smith Ltd v Ampol Ltd* [1974] AC 821, PC.

[35] Companies Act 2006, s 549(1)–(2).   [36] Companies Act 2006, s 549(1)–(2).

allotment of a hybrid instrument has been duly authorized, the special authorization requirements do not apply to the subsequent allotment of shares on the exercise of subscription or conversion rights.[37]

Private company with a single class of shares

The position under the Companies Act 2006 in relation to a private company with a single class of shares is permissive: the directors may exercise allotment powers except to the extent that they are prohibited from doing so under the company's articles.[38] Requiring private companies that have a straightforward capital structure to opt into restrictions via their articles was a significant policy change effected by the Companies Act 2006. Under the Companies Act 1985, as in force immediately before the 2006 Act, special authorization requirements for share issues applied to all companies but private companies (and not only those with a single class of shares) were permitted to opt out under certain conditions and subject to certain alternative requirements. This position had been introduced by the Companies Act 1980. Prior to that, the companies legislation had been silent on matters of constitutional authority to allot shares and this was left for companies to determine for themselves in their articles of association. The standard position was for the power to allot shares to be part of directors' general managerial powers. Directors' fiduciary duties served as the principal constraint against abuse of power. The Companies Act 1980 implemented Article 29 of the Second Company Law Directive, which provides that 'any increase in capital must be decided upon by the general meeting.'[39] The Second Company Law Directive applies only to public companies but the UK government chose initially to apply the new requirements also to private companies. The Companies Act 1980 was consolidated into the Companies Act 1985 without substantive change.[40] However, the policy choice with respect to private companies was subsequently revisited and the 'opt out' regime for private companies was inserted into the Companies Act 1985 by the Companies Act 1989.[41] The issue was examined again in the general review of company law that preceded the Companies Act 2006. The Company Law Review Steering Group concluded that the imposition of special requirements subject to an opt-out regime did not reflect the needs and practice of most private companies.[42] It recommended that statutory requirements for shareholder authorizations of share allotments should not apply to private companies, save for private companies with more than one class of share in order to prevent unauthorized change in the relative power of different classes of shares.[43] The Companies Act 2006 gave effect to this recommendation.

---

[37] Companies Act 2006, s 549(3).

[38] Companies Act 2006, s 550. Companies incorporated under the Companies Act 1985 have to pass a one-off opt-in ordinary resolution: The Companies Act 2006 (Commencement No 8, Transitional Provisions and Savings) Order 2008, SI 2008/2860, sch 2, para 43.

[39] The purpose of Art 29 is to provide a minimum level of protection to shareholders in all of the Member States: Joined Cases C-19/90 and C-20/90 *Karella v Karellas* [1991] ECR I-2691. See also Case C-381/89 *Syndesmos Melon tis Eleftheras Evangelikis Ekklisias* [1992] ECR I-2111; Case C-441/93 *Panagis Pafitis v Trapeza Kentrikis Ellados AE* [1996] ECR I-1347; C-338/06 *European Commission v Spain* [2008] ECR I-10139, para 23 and para 26.

[40] Companies Act 1985, s 80.

[41] Companies Act 2006, s 80A, inserted by Companies Act 1989, s 115(1), as from 1 April 1990.

[42] Company Law Review Steering Group, *Modern Company Law for a Competitive Economy: Final Report* (URN 01/942) para 4.5.

[43] Company Law Review Steering Group, *Modern Company Law for a Competitive Economy: Final Report*, para 4.5. An allotment of new shares may affect rights, eg by diluting existing voting control, but for the purposes of determining whether there is a variation of rights for which a specific class consent is required a distinction is drawn between a change to the right itself and a change to the enjoyment of the right. On class rights see further ch 6.

Authorization by company

The Companies Act 2006, section 551 regulates the exercise of share allotment powers by public companies and private companies with more than one class of shares. Its scope also extends to private companies with a single class of shares but as an alternative to the more relaxed procedure in the Companies Act 2006, section 550 that straightforward private companies can be expected to use in the ordinary case.

Section 551 provides that the directors of a company may exercise a power of the company to allot shares or to grant rights to subscribe for or to convert any security into, shares in the company if they are authorized to do so by the company's articles or by resolution of the company. It is common practice in public companies for authorization to be given by an ordinary resolution passed at the annual general meeting, although some companies adopt a composite approach whereby the articles contain parts of the authority that are unlikely to change from year to year and the resolution that is passed each year simply updates the amount of shares or other securities to which the authorization relates. An authorization under section 551 may be general or for a particular exercise of power and it may be unconditional or subject to conditions.[44] The maximum amount of shares that may be allotted under the authorization and its expiry date must be stated in the resolution.[45] In relation to the grant of rights to subscribe for, or to convert any security into, shares in the company, the maximum amount of shares that may be allotted under the authorization means the maximum amount of shares that may be allotted pursuant to the rights.[46] The requirement to state an amount may preclude the use of a formula.

It has long been established practice for the major UK institutional investors (the ABI and the National Association of Pension Funds (NAPF)) to view as routine requests for section 551 authorizations to allot new shares in an amount of up to one-third of the existing issued share capital.[47] The headroom afforded by this routine practice proved, however, to be too restrictive in the difficult market conditions of 2008 when banks, in urgent need of new equity, found that their ability to act quickly was compromised by the legal obligation to obtain shareholder approval for allotments in excess of their existing section 551 authorizations. Practice has adapted to that experience: under current ABI guidance, requests to authorize the allotment of a further one-third will now also be regarded as routine, provided that such additional headroom is applied to fully pre-emptive rights issues only, and subject to the condition that if the power is actually used and the aggregate actual usage of the authority exceeds one-third as regards nominal amount and also monetary proceeds exceed one-third of the pre-issue market capitalization, members of the board wishing to remain in office are expected to stand for re-election at the next following annual general meeting (AGM).[48]

The maximum statutory duration of a section 551 authorization is five years.[49] Under the Companies Act 2006, authorizations may be renewed for further periods not exceeding five years and they may be revoked at any time by an ordinary resolution.[50] The directors may continue to exercise powers after an authorization has expired if (a) the shares are allotted, or the rights are granted, in pursuance of an offer or agreement made by the company before

---

[44] Companies Act 2006, s 551(2).   [45] Companies Act 2006, s 551(3).
[46] Companies Act 2006, s 551(6).
[47] ABI, *Directors' Powers to Allot Share Capital and Dis-apply Shareholders Pre-emption Rights* (November 2009); NAPF, *Corporate Governance Policy and Voting Guidelines* (November 2011) 35.
[48] ABI, *Directors' Powers to Allot Share Capital.*   [49] Companies Act 2006, s 551(3).
[50] Companies Act 2006, s 551(4)–(5). Revocation by ordinary resolution is possible even where it amends the company's articles: s 551(8).

the authorization expired, and (b) the authorization allowed the company to make an offer or agreement which would or might require shares to be allotted, or rights to be granted, after the authorization had expired.[51] In practice, however, listed company authorizations are often updated annually to keep pace with developments in the company's capital over the course of the year and its changing needs, and also to meet the expectations of institutional investors.[52]

Statutory Pre-emption Rights under the Companies Act 2006

Mandatory pre-emption rights are enshrined in chapter 3 of Part 17 of the Companies Act 2006. The basic structure of chapter 3 of Part 17 is that, save for three main exemptions,[53] pre-emption rights apply in relation to all allotments of ordinary shares or rights to subscribe for, or to convert securities into, ordinary shares of the company by public and private companies. However, pre-emption rights can be disapplied and, in the case of a private company, completely excluded. It is worthwhile to note that pre-emption rights apply in relation to private companies, even those that have only one class of shares, unless positive steps are taken to opt out. Since pre-emption rights are a safeguard against dilution, which is a particular risk that minority shareholders in small closely-held companies face should the personal relationships between those involved in the company begin to break down, it is appropriate for the pre-emption rights regime to apply to all companies, and not just public companies, unless there is a positive decision of the shareholders to the contrary. The Companies Act 2006 re-enacted the substance of the statutory pre-emption regime that was previously in the Companies Act 1985[54] and, before that, in the Companies Act 1980,[55] but with a considerable number of drafting changes. For public companies, the provisions on pre-emption rights in the companies legislation fulfill the UK's obligation to implement Article 33 of the Second Company Law Directive, which requires shares to be offered on a pre-emptive basis to shareholders. Prior to the UK's accession to the European Community, the companies legislation did not impose pre-emption rights but there was such a requirement under listing rules for companies that were listed on the London Stock Exchange.

Pre-emption rights in relation to 'allotments' of 'equity securities': definitions

Statutory pre-emption rights under chapter 3 of Part 17 of the Companies Act 2006 apply in relation to allotments of 'equity securities.' Equity securities are defined as (a) ordinary shares in the company, or (b) rights to subscribe for, or to convert securities into, ordinary shares in the company.[56] 'Ordinary shares' are shares other than shares that, as respects dividends and capital, carry a right to participate only up to a specified amount in a distribution.[57] Preference shares would usually fall outside this definition but in a special case where the shares have a right to participate fully in respect of dividend or capital (or both) in addition to

---

[51] Companies Act 2006, s 551(7).
[52] NAPF, *Corporate Governance Policy and Voting Guidelines*, 36. Under ABI guidance, for a section 551 authorization with additional headroom for fully pre-emptive issues to be treated as routine, it must have a validity of one year only: ABI, *Directors' Powers to Allot Share Capital*.
[53] Companies Act 2006, s 564 (bonus shares), s 565 (non-cash issues), and s 566 (employees' share schemes). (Note also Companies Act 2006, s 576, not considered further in this chapter, which provides savings for certain older pre-emption procedures.)
[54] Companies Act 1985, s 89.   [55] Companies Act 1980, s 17.   [56] Companies Act 2006, s 560(1).
[57] Companies Act 2006, s 560(1).

capped preferential entitlements, they would be ordinary shares for this purpose. This definition of ordinary shares is relevant both to the determination of when a pre-emptive offer must be made and to the identification of the existing shareholders who are entitled to have such an offer made to them.

An 'allotment of equity securities' includes (a) the grant of a right to subscribe for, or to convert any securities into, ordinary shares in the company, and (b) the sale of ordinary shares in the company that immediately before the sale are held by the company as treasury shares.[58] Where statutory rights of pre-emption apply in relation to the grant of subscription or conversion rights, they do not apply in relation to the allotment of shares pursuant to those rights.[59] In other words, the procedures do not have to be followed twice.

The operation of the statutory pre-emption rights procedure

Section 561 of the Companies Act 2006 obliges a company that is proposing to allot new equity securities to offer the securities first to its existing holders of ordinary shares (disregarding the company in respect of shares held by it as treasury shares)[60] on the same or more favorable terms than they would be offered to others. The pre-emptive offer to each ordinary shareholder must be of a proportion of the new equity securities that is as nearly as practicable equal to the proportion in nominal value held by that shareholder of the ordinary share capital of the company (disregarding treasury shares).[61] The record date for determining the shareholders who are entitled to be made an offer and their proportional entitlements may be chosen by the company but it must be a date falling within the period of twenty-eight days immediately before the date of the offer.[62] Holders of warrants, convertible debt securities, or non-participating preference shares are not holders of ordinary shares and therefore are not within the group of persons to whom the offer can be made.[63] Before the company can allot securities otherwise than pursuant to the pre-emptive offer,[64] the period during which any such offer may be accepted must have expired or the company must have received notice of the acceptance or refusal of every offer so made.[65] The minimum statutory period of the pre-emptive offer is now fourteen days, which is the minimum required under EU law.[66] The offer period was reduced from twenty-one days in 2009, a change that had been recommended some years earlier[67] but which did not garner decisive support until the emergency equity fundraising efforts of the banks in 2008/9 brought home the seriousness of the pricing risk involved in extended offer periods.[68] Section 562(5) of the Companies Act 2006 specifically states that the period begins with the date on which the offer is sent or supplied (in the case of an offer made in hard copy form), the date when the offer is sent (in the case of an offer in electronic form), or the date of publication (in the case of an offer made by publication in the Gazette); it is thus not necessary to delay starting the clock until after receipt of the offer.

---

[58] Companies Act 2006, s 560(2)–(3).   [59] Companies Act 2006, s 561(2)(b).
[60] Companies Act 2006, s 561(4)(a).   [61] Companies Act 2006, s 561(1)(a) and (4)(b).
[62] Companies Act 2006, s 574.
[63] Extending the benefit of statutory pre-emption rights to bondholders, etc, would not be compatible with the Second Company Law Directive: *European Commission v Spain* [2008] ECR I-10139.
[64] Companies Act 2006, s 561(2) allows the company within the time limit to allot securities that have been offered to a holder of ordinary shares or anyone in whose favor the shareholder has renounced the right to their allotment. The 'offer' mentioned in s 561(2) appears to mean the pre-emptive offer required by s 561(1).
[65] Companies Act 2006, s 561(1)(b).
[66] Companies Act 2006, s 562(5) implementing Second Company Law Directive, art 33(3).
[67] Myners, *Pre-emption Rights: Final Report*, 33; Company Law Review Steering Group, *Final Report*, para 7.31.
[68] Ferran, 'What's Wrong with Rights Issues.'

The mechanics of the statutory pre-emption offer process are that an offer must be made to the holders of ordinary shares in hard copy or electronic form.[69] If the holder (a) has no registered address in a European Economic Area (EEA) state and has not given to the company an address in an EEA state for the service of notices on him, or (b) is the holder of a share warrant, the offer may be made by causing it, or a notice specifying where a copy of it can be obtained or inspected, to be published in the *London Gazette*.[70] Sending UK offer documentation into other countries is potentially problematic because the distribution of such documents may contravene the securities laws of those jurisdictions unless they are in a form that complies with the local law and any requisite approvals under that law have been obtained. The foreign law elements of the offer may add further to the time and costs involved in the offer process. The Gazette route offers a way round this problem. The distinction drawn between the EEA and third countries reflects the fact that foreign securities laws are less of a problem within the EEA than outside because of the harmonizing effect of EU prospectus and periodic disclosure requirements.[71] As discussed later in this chapter, companies that are fully listed may effectively have no option but to distribute rights issue documentation to shareholders throughout the EEA because they are subject to FCA requirements (implementing EU transparency laws) that mandate equality of treatment for all shareholders with respect to information and the effective dissemination of information on an EU-wide basis. For companies to which EU prospectus and transparency laws do not apply (for example, an unlisted company with relatively modest financing needs that can be accommodated within an exemption from prospectus requirements), the direct and indirect costs associated with sending offer documentation into other EEA countries may render the Companies Act 2006 pre-emption rights regime unattractive and may constitute a reason to consider the disapplication or (in the case of a private company) exclusion of that regime.

The Companies Act 2006 does not require offers to be made in the form of renounceable letters of allotment. In this respect, therefore, statutory protection is less than comprehensive. However, for listed companies the gap is filled by the FCA *Listing Rules*. When a listed company conducts a rights issue, which is the form of pre-emptive offering most favoured by investors, the issuer must make the offer to existing holders to subscribe or purchase further securities in proportion to their holdings by means of a renounceable letter (or other negotiable document) which may be traded (as 'nil paid' rights) during the offer period.[72]

Consequences of non-compliance with statutory rights

Failure to comply with the statutory pre-emption rights procedures results in the company and every officer of it who knowingly authorized or permitted the contravention being jointly and severally liable to compensate any person to whom an offer should have been made for any loss, damage, costs, or expenses which the person has sustained or incurred by reason of the contravention.[73] A two-year cut-off point applies to the bringing of claims for compensation under this section.[74] Failure to comply with the statutory pre-emption procedures does not in itself invalidate an allotment of shares but in appropriate cases the court may exercise its power under section 125 of the Companies Act 2006 to rectify the register of members by removing the names of persons to whom shares have been wrongly allotted. This was ordered in *Re Thundercrest Ltd*[75] where the court rectified the register of members of a small private company in order to remove the names of directors of the company to whom shares had

---

[69] Companies Act 2006, s 562(2).   [70] Companies Act 2006, s 562(3).   [71] See ch 14.
[72] FCA, *Handbook*, Glossary Definitions.   [73] Companies Act 2006, s 563.
[74] Companies Act 2006, s 563(3).   [75] [1995] BCLC 117.

been allotted in breach of the statutory pre-emption rights. The directors were the persons responsible for the breach and the court considered that not rectifying the register in those circumstances would have enabled the directors to profit from their own wrongdoing.

Shareholders who do not take up (or sell) subscription rights

Existing shareholders can still lose out in circumstances where the offer is conducted in full and exact compliance with the statutory requirements. This is because passive shareholders who do not respond to a pre-emptive offer of new securities run the risk of wealth erosion and dilution. The mandatory structure of a pre-emptive offering under the Companies Act 2006 does not address this risk specifically, although the possibility of challenging an offer of new shares that has been conducted in perfect conformity with the requirements of the Companies Act 2006 but which is, in truth, aimed at undermining the position of a minority shareholder as unfairly prejudicial conduct is open.[76] For shareholders in listed companies, much stronger ex ante protection is provided by the *Listing Rules*, which in relation to rights issues stipulate that if existing shareholders do not take up their rights to subscribe, the shares must be placed in the market at the end of the offer period and any premium obtained over the subscription or purchase price (net of expenses) is to be for the account of the holders, except that if the proceeds for an existing holder do not exceed £5, the proceeds may be retained for the company's benefit.[77] This protection for so-called 'lazy' shareholders is in addition to the *Listing Rules* requirement for rights issues to take the form of a renounceable letter of allotment, which enables active shareholders to engage in self-help. It has been noted that 'Rights issues therefore provide the non-accepting shareholders with two opportunities to receive compensation' and that 'Because rights issues provide shareholders with rights and benefits above that required by the statutory pre-emption requirements, they are favoured by shareholders.'[78]

When statutory pre-emption rights do not apply

The statutory pre-emption rights procedures do not apply in relation to the allotment of bonus shares,[79] equity securities paid up, wholly or partly, otherwise than in cash,[80] and securities under an employees' share scheme.[81] The exemption for allotments for non-cash consideration calls for particular comment.

Vendor placings

The fact that pre-emption rights do not apply to non-cash allotments facilitates share-for-share takeovers and other transactions in which companies use their shares as a form of currency for an acquisition.[82] However, the exemption can be used in more ingenious ways that, arguably, could be viewed as artificial structures that are designed to avoid the statute and whose legality is therefore open to question. The first such structure is the 'vendor

---

[76] Companies Act 2006, s 994; *Re Sunrise Radio Ltd* [2010] 1 BCLC 367; *McKillen v Misland (Cyprus) Investments Ltd* [2012] EWHC 2343 (Ch), [555].

[77] *LR.* 9.5.4.

[78] FSA, *Report to HM Treasury*, 6. On monetization as the key reason why institutional investors favour rights issues, see also ABI, *Encouraging Equity Investment*, 32–3.

[79] Companies Act 2006, s 564.   [80] Companies Act 2006, s 565.   [81] Companies Act 2006, s 566.

[82] HS Drinker, 'The Pre-emptive Right of Shareholders to Subscribe to New Shares' (1930) 43 *Harvard Law Review* 586, 607.

placing.' In a vendor placing, the purchaser technically allots new shares to the vendor as consideration for the asset acquired, thereby coming within the non-cash exemption from pre-emption rights, but the new shares are then immediately sold in the market on the vendor's behalf with the result that the vendor receives the cash proceeds of the new issue. The ultimate outcome is thus that the vendor receives cash in return for the asset it has sold without the company having to go to its shareholders either for the finance or for permission to raise it on a non pre-emptive basis.

Even though there is a degree of artificiality about this two-stage process, it can be argued that vendor placings are close enough to the purpose that underlies the relevant exemption, namely the facilitation of acquisitions, to make them acceptable. The company's balance sheet is expanded through the purchase of valuable assets and in that way existing shareholders' stakes in the enterprise are maintained. Furthermore, the decision to acquire specific business assets is, within appropriate limits, a matter of management and board judgment. Certainly, vendor placings are not regarded as controversial in practice provided institutional investors' views with regard to their structure are taken into account. Institutional investors take the view that existing shareholders are entitled to expect a right of clawback (ie a right for existing shareholders to subscribe for a share of an issue at the pre-agreed price) for any issues of significant size or which are offered at more than a modest discount to market price. However, vendor placings with clawback are not common.[83] Instead, vendor placings typically keep within ABI guidelines which provide that clawback will be expected only for placings involving more than 10 per cent of issued equity share capital[84] or a discount greater than 5 per cent.[85] In the case of listed companies, so far as pricing is concerned, investor expectations are bolstered by a specific requirement in the *Listing Rules* limiting the discount to a maximum of 10 per cent of the market price unless the issuer's shareholders have specifically approved a deeper discount.[86] Where 'clawback' is required, it would usually take the form of an 'open offer,' a variant form of pre-emptive offering structure. Differences between rights issues and open offers, and their significance, are examined later in the chapter.

Cashbox structures

A vendor placing implies the need for a vendor. One step beyond the vendor placing is the 'cashbox' structure where a third-party vendor has no direct involvement in the contractual structure. In a cashbox structure, the company in need of funds (Issuer) establishes a Newco and an offer of Newco ordinary and preference shares is made to an intermediary bank. The bank gives an undertaking to pay the subscription price (X). The bank then agrees to transfer the Newco (often a Jersey company for tax reasons) ordinary and preference shares to the Issuer in consideration for the allotment of shares in Issuer to placees found by the bank (which could include the Issuer's existing shareholders). The placing made by the Issuer is thus an issue for non-cash consideration. The bank then pays X to Newco and the Issuer can thereafter extract it, for example, by redeeming the preference shares or by an intra-group loan. Cashbox structures first emerged to enable companies to raise future acquisition finance without the costs, delays, and risks involved in pre-emptive offerings, and without the

---

[83] ABI, *Encouraging Equity Investment*, 33.
[84] An additional incentive to keep below the 10 per cent ceiling is that secondary offerings within this limit by issuers that are already admitted to trading do not require an admissions prospectus: *PR* 1.2.3(1). Nor will a public offers prospectus be needed provided the placing is structured so as to fall within an appropriate exemption (eg for qualified investors: FSMA, s 86(1)(a)). On prospectus requirements generally, see ch 13.
[85] ABI, *Shareholders' Pre-emption Rights and Vendor Placings* (1999); ABI, *Encouraging Equity Investment*, 33.
[86] *LR* 9.5.10.

potential complications inherent in a vendor placing of being linked to a specific acquisition. Over time, however, they have been used more widely, including, slightly counter-intuitively at first glance, for rights issues.[87] The advantage of a cashbox structure in a rights issue context is that the issue of issuer shares for a non-cash consideration in the form of shares in a Newco should qualify for merger relief under the Companies Act 2006, section 612, and when value is later extracted from the Newco this may give rise to distributable reserves in the hands of the issuer.[88]

The extended use of cashboxes has focused attention on the question whether the structure could be struck down as an artificial and improper circumvention of statutory requirements that, as provisions giving effect to EU law, should be interpreted purposively. EU jurisprudence does not shed any direct light on this question, and it has not been considered by the courts in the UK. Shareholder-led litigation to challenge the validity of a cashbox structure is an unlikely prospect, however, first because of the very limited role that litigation plays generally in UK corporate governance, and secondly because occasional attempts by shareholders to use litigation to challenge share offering structures outside the quasi-partnership company context have not tended to fare well.[89] A further reason for not dwelling further on the potential use of litigation in this context is that institutional investors have a different, and probably more powerful, weapon at their disposal: governance rights. In 2009 the ABI wrote to the chairs of listed companies stressing the importance that investors attach to pre-emption rights and indicating that boards would be held to account for their actions; although not spelt out, this missive hinted at the possibility of the ABI recommending its members to vote against the re-election of directors after a cashbox structure had been used.[90] The NAPF has also expressed concern about the increasing use of cashbox structures to circumvent requirements and expectations relating to pre-emption rights.[91] Further clarification of institutional investors' views on the acceptability or otherwise of the cashbox structure when not used as directly acquisition-linked financing is in the pipeline.[92]

Disapplication of Pre-emption Rights: All Companies

All companies, both public and private, can disapply pre-emption rights by a provision to that effect in their articles or by a special resolution.[93] This disapplication procedure operates by reference back to the authorization mechanisms under section 551 of the Companies Act 2006. First, where directors are generally authorized for the purposes of section 551, pre-emption rights may be disapplied by the articles or by special resolution for all allotments pursuant to that authorization, or the directors may be authorized to apply them to such allotments with such modifications as the directors may determine.[94] Secondly, where directors are generally or specifically authorized for the purposes of section 551, pre-emption rights may be disapplied by special resolution in relation to a specified allotment or may be

---

[87] ICAEW & ICAS, *Guidance on the Determination of Realised Profits and Losses in the Context of Distributions under the Companies Act 2006* (TECH 02/10) sec 12 include a useful outline of the cashbox structure and the increasing range of purposes for which it is used. See also ABI, *Encouraging Equity Investment*, 34.

[88] On the operation of merger relief, see ch 4. On whether a reserve arising in these circumstance would be a realized profit, see TECH 02/10, sec 12, especially para 12.7 (prima facie the reserve would be considered a realized profit).

[89] *Mutual Life Insurance Co of New York v Rank Organisation Ltd* [1985] BCLC 11; *Re BSB Holdings Ltd (No 2)* [1996] 1 BCLC 155.

[90] N Holmes and C Chambers, 'Recent Trends in Secondary Equity Offerings' in PLC, *Cross-border Capital Markets Handbook 2011* (PLC, 2011), <http://www.ashurst.com/doc.aspx?id_Content=5891> (accessed July 2012).

[91] NAPF, *Corporate Governance Policy and Voting Guidelines.*   [92] ABI, *Encouraging Equity Investment*, 36–7.

[93] Companies Act 2006, ss 570–1.   [94] Companies Act 2006, s 570.

applied to such an allotment with such modifications as may be specified in the resolution.[95] Special procedural requirements apply in relation to the obtaining of a special resolution in the second case.[96] A disapplication ceases to have effect when the section 551 authorization to which it relates is revoked or expires:[97] this means that the maximum period of a pre-emption rights disapplication under this procedure is five years. If a section 551 authorization is renewed, the disapplication may also be renewed for a period not longer than the renewed authorization.[98]

Disapplications for the purposes of making a rights issue or open offer

One of the superficially surprising features of UK corporate finance practice relating to publicly listed companies is that it is common to disapply statutory pre-emption rights in relation to rights issues and open offers (which are a variant form of pre-emptive offering).[99] Thus the standard disapplication resolution provides:

> THAT subject to the passing of the previous resolution the board be and it is hereby empowered pursuant to Section 570 of the Companies Act 2006 to allot equity securities (within the meaning of Section 560 of the said Act) for cash pursuant to the authority conferred by the previous resolution as if sub-section (1) of Section 561 of the said Act did not apply to any such allotment provided that this power shall be limited
>
> > (i) to the allotment of equity securities in connection with an offer (whether by way of a rights issue, open offer or otherwise) in favour of Ordinary Shareholders where the equity securities respectively attributable to the interests of all Ordinary shareholders are proportionate (as nearly as may be) to the respective numbers of Ordinary shares held by them,
> >
> > (ii) …
>
> but subject to such exclusions or other arrangements as the Directors may deem necessary or expedient in relation to treasury shares, fractional entitlements, record dates, legal or practical problems in or under the laws of any territory or the requirements of any regulatory body or stock exchange.

This practice prompts an obvious question: why disapply statutory pre-emption rights in relation to rights issues (and similar structures) when the purpose of the statutory scheme is exactly what is involved in a rights issue, namely the offering of new securities on a proportionate basis to existing shareholders? The key to solving this apparent puzzle lies in the detail of the statutory requirements, which can be inflexible in certain respects compared to the requirements in the *Listing Rules*.[100]

Timing

The minimum offer period for a *Listing Rules* rights issue is ten business days, with the first business day for the purposes of this calculation being the date on which the offer is first open for acceptance.[101] The equivalent period under the Companies Act 2006 is fourteen days.[102] Both periods were shortened as a result of the review of the efficiency of the rights issue

---

[95] Companies Act 2006, s 571.   [96] Companies Act 2006, s 571(5)–(7) and s 572.
[97] Companies Act 2006, s 570(3) and s 571(3).   [98] Companies Act 2006, s 570(3) and s 571(3).
[99] For a review of offering structures for secondary capital raising, including rights issues, open offers, placings, and cashbox structures, see W Pearce, C Haynes, and A Kirkby, 'Equity Financing of Acquisitions: Impact on Offering Structures' (2011) 22 PLC 23.
[100] *LR* 9.3.11–9.3.12.   [101] *LR* 9.5.6.   [102] Companies Act 2006, s 562(5).

process that was prompted by the emergency capital raising exercises conducted by financial institutions in the wake of the financial crisis.[103] In opting for business days, the *Listing Rules* are consistent with the approach adopted by the London Stock Exchange in its Admission and Disclosure Standards.[104] In its review of the position, the FSA found that market participants favoured ten business days as the more appropriate approach.[105] Although fourteen calendar days may create a shorter capital raising period where there are bank or public holidays, the interests of investors are thought to be better served by a longer period because at those times the transmission times of documents through the postal systems and transactions through the banking system are longer, the number of trading days on the stock market is smaller and so are the number of days on which electronic acceptance through CREST (the UK's securities settlement system) is possible.

Whether under a statutory pre-emptive offering or a *Listing Rules* rights issue, the timetable will be extended beyond the (broadly) two-week offer period if a shareholder general meeting needs to be convened. This could well be necessary, for instance, to refresh a section 551 authorization, to pass a new disapplication resolution, or if the rights issue is for the purposes of financing a large acquisition that itself requires shareholder approval. This extension to the timetable will have implications for the costs of the issue by increasing the underwriting commissions payable, because these are determined by reference to the period for which the underwriters are on risk. The FCA does not permit the offer period to run in parallel with the notice period for the meeting because of concerns about the complications that could arise if the required resolutions were not passed. If the time periods were to run concurrently, dealings in nil paid rights would in effect be conditional on the required shareholder approvals and, if not forthcoming, deals would either have to be unwound or purchasers would have to accept that they had purchased worthless instruments.[106] This problem could be avoided by dispensing with nil paid dealings (as is the case with open offers, discussed later) but a facility for dealing in nil paid rights is an important mechanism for preventing value transfers from existing to new shareholders and, as such, is a key reason why investors prefer rights issues to other, broadly similar, offer structures. There is, thus, a trade-off between the streamlining of the process from the company's perspective and the protection of investors' interests.

Fractions

Shareholders may have a technical entitlement to fractions of a share (for example a shareholder who holds seven shares will be technically entitled to a fraction of a share where the basis of the rights issue is that there will be one new share for every five shares held). Before the introduction of statutory pre-emption rights, the practice was to aggregate and sell the right to such fractions for the benefit of the company as soon as practicable after commencement of dealings in the new shares. This practice is not possible under section 561 of the Companies Act 2006 because it requires the company to make an offer which is as nearly as practicable in proportion to shareholders' existing holdings. It is practicable for fractions to be rounded up or down to the nearest whole number and it seems, therefore, that a company must do this in order to comply with the statutory requirements. This means that it may be practically impossible for the company to raise a round sum and the company would therefore lose the benefit that it would otherwise have had from the sale of the fractions.

---

[103] Rights Issue Review Group, *A Report to the Chancellor of the Exchequer*; FSA, *Rights Issue Subscription Periods* (CP 09/4).

[104] CP 09/4, 7.   [105] FSA, *Rights Issue Subscription Periods* (PS 09/2) 7.

[106] Rights Issue Review Group, *A Report to the Chancellor of the Exchequer* 25–7; FSA, *Report to HM Treasury*, 11–3.

Disapplying statutory pre-emption rights enables fractions to be sold for the company's benefit. The disapplication of pre-emption rights for the purposes of dealing with fractions is expressly mentioned in the *Listing Rules*[107] and, as can be seen from the sample resolution quoted earlier, it is usually expressly referred to in the disapplication resolution.

Overseas shareholders

Sending rights issue documentation to shareholders in other jurisdictions can be problematic because the distribution of such documents may contravene the securities laws of those jurisdictions unless the documents are in a form which complies with the local law and any requisite approvals under that law have been obtained. Although the Companies Act 2006 makes provision for this situation by allowing companies to publish offers to shareholders outside the EEA by means of a notice in the *London Gazette*, resolutions disapplying statutory pre-emption rights commonly permit the directors to make such arrangements as they think fit with regard to overseas shareholders who would, apart from such arrangements, be entitled to participate in a rights issue (see sample resolution quoted earlier). In practice, this means that overseas shareholders in jurisdictions where the relevant securities laws could be infringed by the offer of new shares may be excluded from the offer and, instead, new shares representing their entitlements may be sold on the market when dealings in the new shares commence, with the net proceeds of such sales being sent to them. For listed companies this practice is sanctioned by the *Listing Rules*.[108]

The exclusion of overseas shareholders in this way raises questions about the fair and equal treatment of shareholders. Directors of UK companies are under a general statutory duty to act fairly as between members of the company.[109] In addition, the FCA *Disclosure Rules and Transparency Rules* for listed companies giving effect to the EU Transparency Obligations Directive, provide for equality of treatment of shareholders in the same position with respect to information requirements.[110] Equality of treatment is also mandated by the Second Company Law Directive, Article 46 for shareholders in public companies for the purposes of the implementation of the Directive. However, there is no general principle of EU law mandating equal treatment of minority shareholders.[111]

Fairness and equality of treatment do not imply that all shareholders must be treated in exactly the same way, and thus there is no absolute bar on excluding certain shareholders from an offer of new securities and giving them the monetary equivalent instead. From the purely domestic law perspective, this point is supported by *Mutual Life Insurance Co of New York v The Rank Organisation Ltd*[112] where the exclusion of shareholders holding 53 per cent of the company's equity who were resident in the US and Canada from a rights issue was challenged as a breach of the contract between the company and its members contained in the articles. Specifically, it was alleged that the exclusion was contrary to a provision in the articles which required the company to treat all shareholders of the same class equally. Goulding J rejected the challenge for the following reasons: the directors had acted bona fide in the company's interests in making the allotment; the US and Canadian shareholders had not been treated unfairly since their exclusion from the right to acquire the new shares did

---

[107] *LR* 9.3.12(2)(a).   [108] *LR* 9.3.12(2)(b).   [109] Companies Act 2006, s 172(1)(f).
[110] *DTR* 6.1.3, implementing effect to Directive 2004/109/EC of the European Parliament and of the Council of 15 December 2004 on the harmonization of transparency requirements in relation to information about issuers whose securities are admitted to trading on a regulated market [2004] L390/38, Art 17 (Transparency Obligations Directive). Directive 2004/109/EC is amended by Directive 2013/50/EU, [2013] OJ L294/13.
[111] Case- 101/08 *Audiolux SA v Groupe Bruxelles Lambert SA (GBL)* [2009] ECR I-09823.
[112] [1985] BCLC 11.

not affect the existence of their shares or the rights attached to them; there was no suggestion that the terms of the offer were improvident; no shareholder in the company had the right to expect his interest to remain constant forever; and the reason for the exclusion of the North American shareholders was because of a difficulty relating to their own personal situation.

The nature of the statutory contract formed by a company's articles is somewhat obscure and the extent to which the courts will enforce provisions contained in those documents is uncertain.[113] Partly for these reasons, contractual actions by shareholders have tended to be eclipsed in recent years by actions under section 994 of the Companies Act 2006, which permits members of a company to seek relief from unfairly prejudicial conduct.[114] However, it is most unlikely that overseas investors who are excluded from a rights issue for the reasons that the court found persuasive in the *Mutual Life* decision would fare any better if they were to bring a claim under this section. Although it was not a section 994 case, in the *Mutual Life* decision Goulding J said that the exclusion was not 'unfair.' This was followed in *Re BSB Holdings Ltd (No 2)*[115] where, in reaching the conclusion that a complex capital reorganization was not unfairly prejudicial to the petitioner, Arden J expressly adopted as applicable to the case in hand three of the reasons given by Goulding J in the *Mutual Life* decision as indicating an absence of unfairness: (1) the restructuring did not affect the existence of the petitioner's shares or the rights attaching to them; (2) the terms on which a rights issue which was part of the restructuring was made were not improvident; and (3) the petitioner did not have any overriding right to obtain shares.

As for the requirements derived from EU law on the equal treatment of shareholders, the Court of Justice has rejected broad interpretations of specific Directive provisions.[116] The Advocate-General has explained with direct reference to the Second Directive, Article 46 that 'the principle of equal treatment of shareholders, which is recognised in the legal systems of several Member States of the Community, is not, according to the prevailing opinion, construed as an obligation on the part of the company to treat shareholders in the same way, but is understood to mean that unequal treatment needs sufficiently objective justification.' Reasoning similar to that used by Goulding J in the *Mutual Life* decision could thus be used to establish objective justification of the standard arrangements for the exclusion of overseas shareholders.

It is important at this juncture to clarify what is meant by an 'overseas shareholder' in this context. Historically, this would have meant any non-UK based shareholders, but it is now necessary to qualify the position as regards non-UK but EEA-based shareholders. So far as the regime for statutory pre-emption rights is concerned, UK and other EEA shareholders are now on the same footing: the Companies Act 2006 *London Gazette* route can only be used for non-EEA shareholders, which implies that all EEA shareholders, both in the UK and beyond, should be treated the same.[117] The *Listing Rules* (and standard disapplication

---

[113] It has generated extensive academic debate, including the following articles: KW Wedderburn, 'Shareholders' Rights and the Rule in *Foss v Harbottle*' [1957] CLJ 194; GD Goldberg, 'The Enforcement of Outsider Rights under Section 20 of the Companies Act 1948' (1972) 35 MLR 362; GN Prentice, 'The Enforcement of 'Outsider' Rights' (1980) 1 *Company Law* 179; R Gregory, 'The Section 20 Contract' (1981) 44 MLR 526; GD Goldberg, 'The Controversy on the Section 20 Contract Revisited' (1985) 48 MLR 158; RR Drury, 'The Relative Nature of a Shareholder's Right to Enforce the Company Contract' [1986] CLJ 219.

[114] The range of remedies open to the court on a successful petition under Companies Act 2006, s 994 is an important factor which encourages shareholders to seek relief under this section in preference to other claims that may be open to them: see, Law Commission, *Shareholder Remedies A Consultation Paper* (Law Com CP No 142, 1996) paras 20.2–20.4.

[115] [1996] 1 BCLC 155.

[116] Case C-101/08 *Audiolux SA v Groupe Bruxelles Lambert SA (GBL)* [2009] ECR I-09823; Case C-338/06 *Commission v Spain* [2008] ECR I-10139.

[117] Companies Act 2006, s 562.

resolutions) do not spell things out in such clear terms and instead authorize exclusions on grounds of necessity or expediency on account of the laws or regulatory requirements of a territory other than the issuer's country of incorporation (other than the UK).[118] But given the advanced state of harmonization of the EU capital markets law, it would be hard in normal circumstances to argue that the exclusion of non-UK EEA shareholders from a rights issue (or equivalent type of offer) is either necessary or expedient.

The achievement of an integrated internal securities market has long been a major policy goal for the EU and there is now a large body of EU law, implemented into UK domestic law, that is intended to facilitate and support its development. In particular, the process for cross-border offers of securities within the EEA has been streamlined by the harmonization of prospectus disclosure requirements and by the provision of a passporting facility whereby prospectuses that have been approved by the issuer's home state securities regulator are valid for use throughout the Community.[119] Although the rules relating to prospectuses still differ from Member State to Member State in certain respects, for example, with regard to liabilities for the inclusion of inaccurate information, the burden of compliance with multiple different sets of legal requirements has been significantly reduced. Furthermore, as noted already, EU capital markets law also requires that listed companies be positively obliged to treat shareholders equally with respect to information.[120] Regulated information must be disclosed on a non-discriminatory basis through the use of such media as may reasonably be relied upon for the effective dissemination of information to the public throughout the Community.[121] These requirements are reflected in the FCA *Disclosure Rules and Transparency Rules*.[122]

Excluding overseas shareholders located in EEA states outside the UK from participation in a pre-emptive offering would not sit comfortably with these requirements. As a matter of practice, the UK regulator, the FCA, normally expects all shareholders in EEA jurisdictions to be included in such an offer by a listed company.

Open offers

An open offer is a variant form of pre-emptive offer sanctioned by the FCA *Listing Rules*.[123] An open offer is defined as an invitation to existing holders to subscribe for or purchase securities in proportion to their holdings, which is not made by means of a renounceable letter (or other negotiable document). The fact that the offer is not made by means of a renounceable letter distinguishes the open offer from a rights issue. The absence of nil paid rights can be advantageous from a timetabling perspective (and hence from a costs perspective because of the shortening of the underwriting period) because the offer period can run concurrently with the notice period for any associated shareholder meeting that may be required.[124] The minimum offer period for a *Listing Rules* open offer is ten business days, and the timetable must also be approved by the recognized investment exchange on which the issuer's securities are traded.[125] A conventional open offer also differs from a rights issue in not providing protection for 'lazy' shareholders who do not take up their rights. However, in the aftermath of the financial crisis, the market developed a variant form 'compensatory' open offer, which is designed to compensate shareholders who do not subscribe for the new shares in the offer.[126] The *Listing Rules* have been updated to reflect this development and now provide that in an open offer with a compensatory element, the shares must be placed in the market

---

[118] *LR* 9.3.12(b).   [119] See further ch 13.   [120] Transparency Obligations Directive, Art 17.
[121] Transparency Obligations Directive, Art 21.   [122] *DTR* 6.1.3 and *DTR* 6.3.4.
[123] FCA, *Handbook*, Glossary Definitions. On open offers generally see *LR* 9.5.7–9.5.8.
[124] FSA, *Report to HM Treasury*, 15.   [125] *LR* 9.5.7.   [126] FSA, *Report to HM Treasury*, 14–8.

at the end of the offer period and any premium obtained over the subscription or purchase price (net of expenses) is to be for the account of the holders, except that if the proceeds for an existing holder do not exceed £5, the proceeds may be retained for the company's benefit.[127] Open offers (whether with compensation or not) are also subject to pricing restrictions that do not apply to full rights issues. The point underlying this difference is that in open offers there are no nil paid rights and so existing shareholders are exposed to a greater risk of value erosion than in a full-blown rights issue. This risk is especially pertinent for retail shareholders because they are less likely to be able to afford to take up their rights than institutional investors. The *Listing Rules* limit the discount in an open offer to not more than 10 per cent of the current market price at the time of announcing the terms of the offer, unless a deeper discount has been specifically approved by the issuer's shareholders.[128] In addition, the ABI has a preference for rights issues over open offers if the increase of share capital is more than 15 to 18 per cent or the discount is greater than 7.5 per cent.[129]

Disapplications for placings

A placing is an offer of securities that is not done on a pre-emptive basis. UK listed companies are expected to take account of the Pre-emption Group's publication *Disapplying Pre-emption Rights: A Statement of Principles* when they approach their shareholders for permission to disapply pre-emption rights for placings.[130] The *Statement of Principles* is an attempt to achieve a compromise between the desire of companies to have flexibility in the methods of raising capital which are open to them and institutional investors' interests in protecting pre-emption rights. The Pre-emption Group is comprised of representatives from the investment management industry and the corporate sector and its work has the backing of major institutional investor representative bodies. The *Statement of Principles* does not have legal force. It works by providing companies with an assurance that their major shareholders will, in principle, be favourably disposed towards a proposed disapplication of pre-emption rights so long as it is within specified limits. The *Statement of Principles* is not intended to be inflexible: companies can still seek disapplications in circumstances falling outside the specified limits but early dialogue with shareholders will be of particular importance in such cases. According to the *Statement of Principles*, critical considerations in non-routine cases are likely to include: the strength of the business case; the size and stage of development of the company and the sector within which it operates; the stewardship and governance of the company; other financing options; the level of dilution of value and control for existing shareholders; the proposed process following approval; and contingency plans in case the request is not granted.

Under the *Statement of Principles* a request for disapplication of pre-emption rights will generally be regarded as routine provided it seeks permission to offer non-pre-emptively no more than 5 per cent of ordinary share capital in any one year. Companies are also expected to have regard to cumulative limits. A company should not without (a) suitable advance consultation and explanation or (b) the matter having been specifically highlighted at the time at which the request for disapplication was made, issue more than 7.5 per cent of the company's ordinary share capital for cash other than to existing shareholders in any rolling three-year period. The *Statement of Principles* also addresses pricing:

---

[127] *LR* 9.5.8A.   [128] *LR* 9.5.10.   [129] ABI, *Encouraging Equity Investment*, 33.
[130] Pre-emption Group, *Statement of Principles* (2008). Companies listed on AIM are also encouraged to apply the principles. However, it has become common for AIM companies to seek a disapplication of at least 10 per cent and investors generally accept the need for this greater flexibility: ABI, *Encouraging Equity Investment*, 37.

Companies should aim to ensure that they are raising capital on the best possible terms, particularly where the proposed issue is in the context of a transaction likely to enhance the share price. Any discount at which equity is issued for cash other than to existing shareholders will be of major concern. Companies should, in any event, seek to restrict the discount to a maximum of 5 per cent of the middle of the best bid and offer prices for the company's shares immediately prior to the announcement of an issue or proposed issue.[131]

This stipulation is in addition to the backstop provision in the *Listing Rules* that generally limits discounts on placings (and open offers) to 10 per cent.[132] Placings within the 10 per cent ceiling can also benefit from an exemption from the requirement to produce a prospectus that would ordinarily be triggered by the admission of new securities to trading on a regulated market; provided the placing is structured appropriately, for example, by being made to qualified investors only, it can also benefit from exemptions in respect of public offer prospectuses.[133]

Accountability in respect of the use of the power to issue shares non-pre-emptively is also provided for: 'Once a request to disapply pre-emption rights has been approved, shareholders expect companies to discharge and account for this authority appropriately. It is recommended that the subsequent annual report should include relevant information such as the actual level of discount achieved, the amount raised and how it was used and the percentage amount of shares issued on a non-pre-emptive basis over the last year and three years.'[134]

Disapplication or Exclusion of Pre-emption Rights: Private Companies

The articles of a private company may exclude the statutory pre-emption rights regime, either generally or in relation to allotments of a particular description.[135] This power to exclude pre-emption rights is not limited to companies with one class of shares.

With respect to disapplication, the procedure considered in the previous section is also applicable to private companies. In addition, another provision of the Companies Act 2006 provides for the directors of a company with only one class of shares to be given power by the articles or by a special resolution of the company to allot equity securities of that class as if statutory pre-emption rights did not apply or applied with such modifications as the directors may determine.[136] Unlike the general disapplication route, disapplications under this provision are not tied to an allotment authorization under section 551 of the Companies Act 2006 (as none is required) and so need not be limited in duration to a maximum of five years.

Other Formalities in Relation to Share Allotments

A company must register in its books an allotment of shares as soon as practicable and in any event within two months after the date of the allotment.[137] Failure to comply constitutes a criminal offence by the company and every officer who is in default.[138] This requirement was introduced by the Companies Act 2006. Within one month of making an allotment of shares, a limited company must deliver to the registrar of companies a return of the allotment accompanied by a statement of capital.[139] The officers of the company who are in default in

---

[131] Pre-emption Group, *Statement of Principles*, para 20.   [132] *LR* 9.5.10.   [133] See further ch 13.
[134] Pre-emption Group, *Statement of Principles*, para 22.   [135] Companies Act 2006, s 567.
[136] Companies Act 2006, s 569.   [137] Companies Act 2006, s 554(1).
[138] Companies Act 2006, s 554(3)–(4).   [139] Companies Act 2006, s 555.

respect of this delivery requirement (but not the company itself) are liable to criminal sanctions.[140] Any person liable for the default can apply to the court for relief and the court, if satisfied that the omission was accidental or inadvertent or that it is just and equitable to grant relief, may make an order extending the time for delivery of the document for such period as the court thinks proper.[141] Responsible officers (but not the company itself) also commit a criminal offence if they fail to comply with the obligation to issue share certificates within two months after allotment where it is applicable.[142]

---

[140] Companies Act 2006, s 557. [141] Companies Act 2006, s 557(3). [142] Companies Act 2006, s 769.

6

Classes of Shares

Scope of this Chapter

It is common for UK companies to have complex capital structures involving several different classes of shares. The flexibility that is a hallmark of company law in the UK can be, and is, put to use creatively in a myriad range of circumstances, from the attachment of special rights to shares in order to create what is, in effect, a partnership of a small number of individuals within a corporate shell and to displace the ordinary company law principle of majority rule, through to the tailoring of a bundle of particular financial benefits attaching to a share that is designed so as to enable a listed company to appeal to certain rarefied investor preferences. The bank bailouts that followed in the wake of the collapse of Lehman Brothers in September 2008 provided high profile examples of this creativity at work: the bailouts of Lloyds and the Royal Bank of Scotland initially involved the government taking a combination of preference and ordinary shares; and the rights attaching to the preference shares included a block on the payment of dividends on ordinary shares. One type of complex capitalization arrangement that is encountered much less often in the UK than in some other countries is the publicly listed company with dual class ordinary shares, where one class of shares holds a dispropor-tionate share of the voting rights.[1] A government-initiated review explained the position in the UK as follows:

> UK companies are already legally free to create different share classes with differential voting rights. Two notable recent US flotations—those of Google and Facebook—have involved such a structure, and it is less likely that the founders of these companies, who are anxious to maintain their influence on the distinctive character of their organisations, would have agreed to an IPO if such an arrangement had not been possible.
>
> However multiple share classes are viewed with considerable hostility by UK institutional investors. The ABI, which led the historic opposition to these structures—a stance which led to the virtual elimination of dual class share structures amongst UK listed companies—told us that they remain strongly opposed.[2]

Nevertheless the review suggested that the issue should be a subject of continued review and discussion. Dual-class capitalization is a topic that has attracted considerable academic attention in the United States.[3] One recent article made the point that some of the country's most successful companies (including Berkshire Hathaway, Ford, and Google) have dual class structures and suggested that their success may indicate that the benefits can sometimes outweigh the costs that accompany dual-class capitalization.[4]

---

[1] Institutional Shareholder Services, *Report on the Proportionality Principle in the European Union* (Brussels: European Commission, 2007); PA Gompers, J Ishii, and A Metrick, 'Extreme Governance: An Analysis of Dual-Class Firms in the United States' (2010) 23 *Review of Financial Studies* 1051.

[2] BIS, *The Kay Review of UK Equity Markets and Long-term Decision Making: Final Report* (July 2012) 64. See ch 13 for discussion of the new premium listing principle on voting rights.

[3] Classic articles include R Gilson, 'Evaluating Dual Class Common Stock: The Relevance of Substitutes' (1987) 73 *Virginia Law Review* 807; J Gordon, 'Ties that Bond: Dual Class Common Stock and the Problem of Shareholder Choice' (1988) 76 *California Law Review* 1.

[4] EB Rock, 'Shareholder Eugenics in the Public Corporation' (2012) 97 *Cornell Law Review* 849, 900. But with the benefit of hindsight, the inclusion also of News Corporation on this list of successful companies tends to undermine the argument in that, for many, the scandals in its UK operations that were exposed during 2012 could be linked back to the dominance of its controlling shareholders, as facilitated by dual-class capitalization.

The many ways in which corporate finance practice in the UK already exploits the freedom to tailor capital structures to meet particular needs and preferences, and also the potential for further innovation, make it important to examine the legal implications of having several different classes of shares within a company's capital structure. The rights attaching to shares and the issues that arise when complexity is introduced into the capital structure by the issue of different classes of shares are the subject matter of this chapter.

The Legal Nature of a Share

There is no comprehensive legal definition of a share[5] but in *Borland's Trustee v Steel*[6] Farwell J described a share in the following terms:

> A share is the measure of a shareholder in the company measured by a sum of money, for the purposes of liability in the first place, and of interest in the second, but also consisting of a series of mutual covenants entered into by all the shareholders inter se. The contract contained in the articles is one of the original incidents of the share. A share is not a sum of money … but is an interest measured by a sum of money and made up of the various rights contained in the contract.

This description makes it clear that a shareholder is essentially an investor: he or she pays a sum of money in the hope of earning a return. The shareholder's financial interest is in the company itself and it does not amount to a direct interest in the company's assets. These assets belong to the company, which is a separate legal person. Thus in *Macaura v Northern Assurance Co Ltd*[7] it was held that a shareholder did not have an insurable interest in the company's property.[8] For corporate governance purposes, shareholders are typically regarded as the 'owners' of a company, a characterization that goes back to their position as the providers of the primary form of loss-bearing capital. As 'owners', shareholders are afforded a say in the running of a company, including with respect to decisions concerning the raising of new capital as well as on fundamental matters relating to a company's life, death, and major restructuring.[9] Nevertheless, the distinction between 'ownership' of the company by its shareholders and ownership of the business assets by the company itself is crucial. The asset partitioning benefits associated with the corporate form flow from this distinction.[10] A feature that is common to all forms of share capital is that mandatory company law rules on maintenance of capital that restrict distributions to shareholders always apply.[11] This inexorable rule gives all forms of share capital a permanent quality, in the sense that shareholders cannot insist on a return of capital that would infringe the maintenance of capital principle. This is so notwithstanding that for accounting purposes certain payments in respect of shares (such as dividends on non-participating redeemable preference shares) may be reported as expenses.[12]

---

[5] RR Pennington, 'Can Shares in Companies be Defined?' (1989) 10 *Company Lawyer* 140.

[6] [1901] 1 Ch 279, 288. This description was cited with approval in *IRC v Crossman* [1937] AC 26, HL, 66 *per* Lord Russell of Killowen.

[7] [1925] AC 619, HL.

[8] See also *Bank voor Handel en Scheepuaart NV v Slatford* [1953] 1 QB 248, CA (property held by a Dutch limited company bank with Hungarian shareholders did not fall within the scope of a provision concerned with property 'belonging to or held or managed on behalf of' a Hungarian); *John Foster & Sons Ltd v IRC* [1894] 1 QB 516, CA (conveyance of property from individuals to a company in which they held all of the shares was liable to stamp duty).

[9] Ch 5 examines the role of shareholders in decisions about new equity financing.

[10] Discussed in ch 2.   [11] See chs 7 and 9.

[12] Under IAS 32 this class of shares may be classified as a liability (debt).

Financial Incidents of Shares: Capital and Dividends

What financial entitlements do investors in shares acquire?
The position of holders of ordinary shares

An ordinary share is a share that carries full participation rights with respect to capital and dividends. For the purposes of statutory pre-emption rights, the category of 'ordinary share' is more broadly defined as 'shares other than shares that as respects dividends and capital carry a right to participate up to a specified amount in a distribution,' which would include shares that in commercial terms are viewed as preference shares but which are fully participating in respect of either dividends or capital, but not both.[13] However, the special case of the partly-participating preference share can be put to one side for the purposes of the discussion in this section. In commercial terms, ordinary shares are the 'equity' or 'risk' capital, with which is associated the greatest opportunity for capital growth but also the most financial exposure if the business is unsuccessful. Whilst for ordinary commercial companies market forces form the principal constraint on the amount of equity held in the business, the stability-enhancing features of equity, including its perpetual nature and its status as the most subordinated claim in liquidation, have led to mandatory requirements on minimum levels of equity becoming the central component of the prudential regulation of financial institutions.[14]

The full bundle of rights that is attached to any particular share is determined by contract (the company's articles and the terms of issue) rather than being exhaustively set out in the companies legislation.[15] However, in the absence of express provision to the contrary in the articles or terms of issue, there are certain default rules on capital and dividend entitlements established by case law that will take effect by implication as part of the terms of issue of ordinary shares. The Model Articles modify the default rules in some respects.

Default capital rights of ordinary shares

Investors in ordinary shares hope for capital growth, which, in ordinary circumstances, they will realize by selling their shares in the secondary markets or in private sales. As a matter of law, however, their ultimate entitlement is to any surplus that remains at the end of the process of winding up the company. The seminal case on the default rule applicable in respect of the distribution of any surplus that remains after paid up capital has been repaid is *Birch v Cropper*.[16] In this case it was held by the House of Lords that any such surplus is distributable equally among the ordinary shareholders in proportion to the nominal value of their shares. Lord Macnaghten explained:[17] 'Every person who becomes a member of a company limited

---

[13] Companies Act 2006, s 560(1).

[14] Basel Committee on Banking Supervision, *Basel III: A Global Regulatory Framework for More Resilient Banks and Banking Systems* (December 2010 (rev June 2011)). Basel III requires banks to have a minimum common equity Tier I capital of 4.5 per cent plus a common equity capital conservation buffer of 2.5 per cent. In addition, a surcharge is imposed on global systemically important banks, whereby they must hold an additional amount of common equity (between 1 and 2.5 per cent, with the possibility of a further 1 per cent) as a buffer against loss. Standard-feature ordinary shares satisfy the criteria for 'common equity' under the *Basel III framework* (para 52).

[15] Although there is now no doubt that a share is a species of intangible property and not merely a bundle of personal rights.

[16] (1889) 14 App Cas 525, HL. The default loss-sharing rule is also based on nominal values (*Re Hodges' Distillery, ex p Maude* (1870) 6 Ch App 51, CA) but this can be displaced by articles of association (*Re Kinatan (Borneo) Rubber Ltd* [1923] 1 Ch 124).

[17] (1889) 14 App Cas 525, HL, 543.

by shares of an equal amount[18] becomes entitled to a proportionate part in the capital of the company and, unless it be otherwise provided by the regulations of the company, entitled, as a necessary consequence, to the same proportionate part in all of the property of the company, including its uncalled capital.'

With respect to entitlements in respect of capital surpluses, the Model Articles for private and public companies do not modify the position that the nominal value of shares is the relevant denominator amount for the purposes of calculating individual claims. In theory the nominal value could be more than the amount paid up on the shares, that is in circumstances where the shares have been issued on a partly-paid basis. However, the Model Articles for private companies stipulate that all shares must be fully paid up[19] and it would be unusual for shares in a public company to be partly paid. Where shares are paid up in full, each shareholder's entitlement is easily calculated because it is found by dividing the surplus available by the number of shares in issue.

Default dividend rights of ordinary shares

The default rule established by case law is that the calculation of entitlements to distributions by way of dividend is also based on the nominal value of the ordinary shares held by each shareholder.[20] This rule can be displaced: if so authorized by its articles, a company can pay a dividend in proportion to the amount paid up on each share rather than its nominal amount.[21] The Model Articles for public companies do this.[22] In the normal case, where the ordinary shares in a company are all fully paid, the dividend can be expressed simply as the amount available for distribution to the holders of the ordinary shares divided by the number of shares in issue.

Dividends must be paid in cash unless the articles otherwise provide.[23] It is usual for articles to make provision for the payment of dividends in kind.[24]

The holder of an ordinary share does not have an absolute right to dividends in the way that a provider of debt finance is usually contractually entitled to receive interest. That there are no circumstances under which the declaration and payment of dividends or the making of other distributions are obligatory is of the essence of share capital.[25] At what point, if any, does the shareholder's expectation of a dividend crystallize into an enforceable entitlement? To address this question, it is necessary to turn, first, to the company's articles and, if relevant, the terms of issue of the shares in question. Articles of association typically distinguish between 'final' dividends declared by the shareholders in general meeting and 'interim' dividends paid on the authority of the board.[26] Where this is the case, the position is as summarized by Brightman J in *Potel v IRC* as follows:[27]

---

[18] 'Amount' in this context clearly means nominal amount: *Re Driffield Gas Light Co* [1898] 1 Ch 451.

[19] Art 21. 'Fully paid' under these Model Articles means that the nominal value and any premium has been paid: art 1. Ordinarily references to 'paid up' share capital relate only to the nominal amount and not to share premiums, as discussed in ch 4.

[20] *Oakbank Oil Co v Crum* (1882) 8 App Cas 65, HL.   [21] Companies Act 2006, s 581(c).

[22] Art 71. 'Paid up' in this context carries its ordinary meaning (ie excluding share premiums). It would not be feasible to measure an ordinary shareholder's entitlement to income and capital by reference to an amount which included a share premium paid when the share was first subscribed. Over time, it is likely that various share issues at different prices will have taken place and it would normally be impossible to trace back to the initial price at which a share was allotted because fully paid shares are not numbered and have no other individual distinguishing mark.

[23] *Wood v Odessa Waterworks Co* (1889) 42 Ch D 636.

[24] Model Articles (plc), art 76; Model Articles (Ltd), art 34.

[25] Under this *Basel III* framework, for example, this is part of the criteria for common equity.

[26] Model Articles (plc), art 70; Model Articles (Ltd), art 30.

[27] [1971] 2 All ER 504. See also ICAEW, *Guidance on the Determination of Realised Profits and Losses in the Context of Distributions under the Companies Act 2006* (TECH 02/10) paras 2.10–2.11.

    i. If a final dividend is declared, a date when such dividend shall be paid can also be specified.[28]

    ii. If a final dividend is declared by a company without any stipulation as to the date of payment, the declaration of the dividend creates an immediate debt.[29]

    iii. If a final dividend is declared and is expressed to be payable at a future date a shareholder has no right to enforce payment until the due date for payment arrives.[30]

    iv. In the case of an interim dividend which the board has resolved to pay, it is open to the board at any time before payment to review the decision and resolve not to pay the dividend.[31] The resolution to pay an interim dividend does not create an immediate debt.

    v. If directors resolve to pay an interim dividend they can, at or after the time of such resolution, decide that the dividend should be paid at some stipulated future date. If a time for payment is so prescribed, a shareholder has no enforceable right to demand payment prior to the stipulated date.

A shareholder is thus a creditor in respect of a dividend that has been declared but not paid by the due date for payment.[32] The six-year limitation period in respect of an unpaid dividend runs from the date when it is declared or any later date for payment.[33] However, when a company is in liquidation any sum due to a member of the company by way of dividend is deemed not to be a debt of the company in a case of competition between the member to whom it is due and any other creditor of the company who is not a member of the company. Any such sum is to be taken into account for the purpose of the final adjustment of the rights of the contributories among themselves.[34]

What financial entitlements do investors in shares acquire? The position of holders of preference shares

There is a presumption of equality with respect to shares.[35] To enable the displacement of this presumption, articles of association usually make provision for the issue of different classes of shares.[36] Companies with articles in the appropriate form can issue many different classes of shares, including multiple classes of ordinary share (eg voting and non-voting shares), preference shares, and redeemable shares. This section is concerned with preference shares. In commercial terms, preference shares are a hybrid security, akin to debt in the sense that the return is usually fixed or capped, but, as a share, they are still subject to the company law rules on share capital. Returns (income and capital) on preference shares usually rank ahead of the claims of ordinary shareholders, which may be beneficial in terms of the issuer's cost of capital. The appeal to investors can be further enhanced by the inclusion of provisions allowing for the conversion of preference shares into ordinary shares.

---

[28] *Thairwall v Great Northern Rly Co* [1910] 2 KB 509.
[29] *Re Severn and Wye and Severn Bridge Rly Co* [1896] 1 Ch 559.   [30] *Re Kidner* [1929] 2 Ch 121.
[31] *Lagunas Nitrate Co Ltd v Schroeder & Co and Schmidt* (1901) 85 LT 22.
[32] *Re Compania de Electricidad de la Provincia de Buenos Aires* [1980] 1 Ch 146.
[33] *Re Compania de Electricidad de la Provincia de Buenos Aires* [1980] 1 Ch 146, not following *Re Artisans' Land and Mortgage Corporation* [1904] 1 Ch 796. Money due from a member to the company is now regarded as an ordinary contract debt rather than a specialty debt (Companies Act 2006, s 33(2)) with the consequence that the ordinary contractual limitation period applies.
[34] Insolvency Act 1986, s 74(2)(f). *Soden v British & Commonwealth Holdings plc* [1998] AC 298, HL.
[35] *Re London India Rubber Company* (1868) 5 Eq 519; *Campbell v Rofe* [1933] AC 98, PC; *British and American Trustee and Finance Corporation v Couper* [1894] AC 399, HL, 417 *per* Lord Macnaghten.
[36] Model Articles (plc), art 43; Model Articles (Ltd), art 22.

The usual rules with respect to directors' authority to allot shares apply to preference share issues.[37] However, apart from the special case of partly-participating preference shares, preference shares are not within the scope of statutory pre-emption rights, which means that new issues of preference shares do not have to be offered first to existing ordinary (or preference) shareholders and also that preference shareholders are not entitled to a right of pre-emption in respect of allotments of new ordinary shares.

A preference share can be defined broadly as a share that, in respect of at least one of dividends or capital (but usually both), enjoys priority, for a limited amount, over the company's ordinary shares, but which is not otherwise participating. The precise extent of the preferential entitlement is, however, a matter of construction of the rights attached to the shares. It is not sufficient simply to designate shares as preference shares because that expression has no precise meaning. The preferential rights that are to be attached to the shares must be spelt out precisely as they will not be implied. Once the preferential entitlements are specified, there are certain secondary presumptions that apply unless contrary provision is made. The settling of the rights attaching to preference shares is a domestic matter in which neither creditors (unless they have specifically bargained for this) nor the outside public have an interest.[38]

As a matter of company law, preference shares are subject to the rules on maintenance of capital in the same way as ordinary shares. This means that dividends cannot be paid except from distributable profits and capital must not be returned otherwise than in accordance with reduction of capital procedures that are sanctioned by the companies legislation. For accounting purposes, however, many types of preference share are likely to meet the definition of financial liabilities and to be accounted for as such rather than as equity.[39] Whether an issue of preference shares would be regarded as a borrowing for the purposes of borrowing limits in articles of association or loan agreements is a matter of construction. The criteria for classification as common shares for bank regulatory capital purposes include being the most subordinated claim in liquidation of the bank and being entitled to an unlimited and variable claim in respect of both capital and dividends, which would exclude preference shares.

Default capital rights of preference shares

There is a presumption that all shares rank equally with regard to any distribution of assets.[40] Accordingly, any priority intended to be attached to a preference share must be expressly stated.[41] In particular, it is not to be presumed from the fact that a share has attached to it a preferential right in respect of dividend, that there is also a preferential entitlement in respect of capital.[42] A preferential entitlement with respect to capital implies priority to the extent of the nominal value of the share, unless some other amount (which could include a fixed or capped amount designated as a 'liquidation preference') is specified.[43] Where a preferential entitlement in respect of capital is specified, is that exhaustive or is there also an entitlement to participate *pari passu* in the distribution of any surplus? The position with respect to this matter could be spelt out in the terms of issue but, if not, the default position is as follows. In *Scottish Insurance Corp v Wilsons & Clyde Coal Co Ltd*[44] the articles provided that in the event

[37] Companies Act 2006, ss 549–55, discussed in ch 5.   [38] *Birch v Cropper* (1889) 14 App Cas 525, HL.

[39] See further IAS 32, *Financial Instruments: Presentation*; IAS 39, *Financial Instruments: Recognition and Measurement* (superseded by IFRS 9, *Financial Instruments* from January 2015); IFRS 7, *Financial Instruments: Disclosures*.

[40] *HSBC Bank Middle East v Clarke* [2006] UKPC 31, para 26; *Welton v Saffery* [1897] AC 299, HL, 309 *per* Lord Watson; *Birch v Cropper* (1889) 14 App Cas 525, HL.

[41] *Re London India Rubber Co* (1869) LR 5 Eq 519.   [42] *Birch v Cropper* (1889) 14 App Cas 525, HL.

[43] *Re Driffield Gas Light Co* [1898] 1 Ch 451.   [44] [1949] AC 462, HL.

of winding up, preference stock ranked before ordinary stock to the extent of repayment of the amounts called up and paid thereon. The House of Lords held that this amounted to a complete statement of the rights of the preference shares in the winding up and that they did not carry the further entitlement to share in any assets remaining after repayment of the capital paid up on the ordinary shares. Observations of Lord Macnaghten in *Birch v Cropper*[45] that had suggested that preference shares were entitled to share in surplus assets unless their terms contained an express and specific renunciation of that right were not followed.[46] Where it is claimed that preference shares are participating with regard to the distribution of a surplus, the onus is therefore on the person making that claim to point to some provision in the company's constitution or terms of issue that confers an entitlement to share in any surplus assets.[47]

In *Re Saltdean Estate Co Ltd*[48] the articles provided that preference shares issued by the company carried an entitlement to priority in respect of capital on a winding up, but that those shares were not to share in surplus assets remaining after all capital had been repaid. The articles were silent with regard to the position of preference shares in the event of a reduction of capital. Buckley J held that their position in a reduction of capital mirrored the rights that would apply in a winding up and that, accordingly, the first class of capital to be repaid was the class comprising the preference shares. The decision in *Re Saltdean Estate Co Ltd* was approved by the House of Lords in *House of Fraser plc v ACGE Investments Ltd*[49] although, in this case, the position was less uncertain because the articles expressly provided that the rights attached to the preference shares on a return of capital otherwise than on winding up were the same as the rights that they enjoyed on a winding up. Lord Keith of Kinkel thought fit to quote from Buckley J's judgment in the *Saltdean* case, including the following passage:[50]

> It has long been recognised that, at least in normal circumstances, where a company's capital is to be reduced by repaying paid-up share capital in the absence of agreement of the sanction of a class meeting to the contrary, that class of capital should first be repaid which would be returned first in a winding-up of a company … The liability to prior repayment on a reduction of capital, corresponding to their right to prior return of capital in a winding-up … is part of the bargain between the shareholders and forms an integral part of the definition or delimitation of the bundle of rights which make up a preferred share.

Lord Keith described this as 'an entirely correct statement of the law'.[51]

Default dividend rights of preference shares

Whether a preference share carries a preferential right to dividends as well as capital is a matter of construction of the terms of the share. There is no presumption that a share which carries a preferential right in respect of one financial aspect of shareholding (whether it be dividend or capital) also carries a preferential right in respect of the other.[52] It is usual for preferential entitlements to extend to both.

---

[45] *Birch v Cropper* (1889) 14 App Cas 525, HL, 546 *per* Lord Macnaghten.

[46] *Scottish Insurance Corp v Wilsons & Clyde Coal Co Ltd* [1949] AC 462, HL, 490 *per* Lord Normand.

[47] *Re National Telephone Co* [1914] 1 Ch 755, Ch D; *Re Isle of Thanet Electricity Supply Co Ltd* [1950] Ch 161, CA. In *Dimbula Valley (Ceylon) Tea Co Ltd v Laurie* [1961] Ch 353 preference shares were held to be participating and therefore entitled in a winding up to share in surplus assets remaining after all capital in respect of preference and ordinary shares had been repaid.

[48] [1968] 1 WLR 1844.   [49] [1987] AC 387, HL.

[50] *Re Saltdean Estate Co Ltd* [1968] 1 WLR 1844, 1849–50.

[51] *House of Fraser plc v ACGE Investments Ltd* [1987] AC 387, HL, 393. See also *Re Hunting plc* [2005] 2 BCLC 211. Note *Re Northern Engineering Industries plc* [1994] BCC 618, CA where the articles made special provision with regard to the rights of the preference shares.

[52] *Birch v Cropper* (1889) 14 App Cas 525, HL.

A preferential dividend is commonly expressed as a specified percentage of the nominal value of the share; sometimes, however, it can be expressed as a specified percentage of the amount paid up on the share or some other amount. Preferential dividends are usually expressed to be payable only when declared[53] but, if no dividend is declared in one year (or the dividend which is declared does not fully satisfy the preference shareholders' entitlements), it is presumed that the amount which is not paid is to be carried forward into subsequent years.[54] This well-established presumption that preferential dividends are cumulative can be displaced by provision to that effect in the company's articles or in the terms of issue.[55]

The following example, adapted from the actual terms of an issue of several classes of preference shares by Lloyds Bank plc in 2009, provides an illustration of terms relating to non-cumulative dividend entitlements attached to preference shares:

> Non-cumulative preferential dividends will accrue on the Preference Shares at a rate of 9.25 per cent. per annum on the liquidation preference of £1 per Preference Share from (and including) the Issue Date, and will be payable semi-annually in equal instalments in arrear on 31 May and 30 November in each year. Dividends will be paid only to the extent that payment of the same can be made out of profits of the Company available for distribution and permitted by law to be distributed as at each Dividend Payment Date.

Once the specified preferential dividend has been paid, can preference shareholders invoke the equality principle so as to rank equally with the ordinary shareholders in respect of any further distribution of profits to the extent that such distributions are not proscribed or otherwise regulated by the terms of the preference shares?[56] This question was answered in the negative in *Will v United Lankat Plantations Co*.[57] The shares in question had the right to a preferential dividend of 10 per cent and the House of Lords held that, as a matter of construction, that was the sum total of the holder's entitlement to dividends in respect of those shares. Articles or terms of issue could provide for preference shares to be participating with ordinary shares in respect of general dividends in addition to a fixed preferential dividend, although a provision to that effect would be relatively unusual.

Enfranchisement when preferential dividends are in arrears

Under the general law, a company cannot pay a preferential dividend if it does not have sufficient distributable profits available for that purpose. In such circumstances, the holder of a preference share cannot sue for breach of contract in the way that a creditor could sue in the event of a company failing to pay interest when due, for the reasons that have been discussed already. The way in which the interests of preference shareholders are typically protected in circumstances such as these is for articles to make provision for them to become entitled to participate in the internal governance of the company's affairs.

Preference shares are typically issued on terms specifying that they carry no or very limited voting rights in normal circumstances and only become fully enfranchised when the preferential dividend is deemed to be in arrear. Provided the drafting of the articles follows the usual form, exemplified by *Re Bradford Investments plc*[58] where the articles specified dates on

---

[53] *Bond v Barrow Haematite Steal Co* [1902] 1 Ch 362.

[54] *Henry v Great Northern Rly* (1857) 1 De G&J 606, 44 ER 858; *Webb v Earle* (1875) LR 20 Eq 556.

[55] *Staples v Eastman Photographic Materials Co* [1896] 2 Ch 303, CA.

[56] eg, in the RBS bank recapitalization in 2008, the terms of the preference shares subscribed by the government prohibited the payment of dividends on ordinary shares without the government's consent.

[57] [1914] AC 11, HL.   [58] [1990] BCC 740.

which preferential dividends were deemed to be payable and provided for enfranchisement of the shares when the dividend had not been paid in full for six months or more after the date for payment,[59] the dividend may be in arrear either because the company has chosen not to declare a dividend, even though sufficient distributable profits to cover that dividend are available, or because the requisite distributable profits are not available. The standard wording ensures that preference shares become enfranchised in either case and leaves no room for the argument that the dividend cannot be said to have become payable because of the lack of available distributable profits; Hoffmann J noted in the *Bradford* case that, with this wording, it is 'really beyond argument' that the preference shareholders become entitled to vote in these circumstances.

Payment of accumulated unpaid cumulative preferential dividends

Where cumulative preferential dividends have been in arrear for some time but distributable profits subsequently become available or the company goes into liquidation, special rules govern the entitlement of the holders of the shares in respect of those dividends (subject to anything to the contrary in the articles or terms of issue). When a cumulative preference dividend is finally declared, the whole of the accumulated amount is payable to the persons who are the holders of the preference shares at that time and it does not have to be apportioned between them and the other persons (if any) who held the shares during the time when the dividends were not declared.[60] Where preference shares of the same class have been issued over a period of time and the cumulative preferential dividend has not been declared over that period, the correct approach with regard to distributing any profits that do become available is to distribute them rateably among the shareholders according to the amount of dividend that has accumulated on each of the shares.[61] Where a company is in liquidation or is making a reduction of capital involving repayment, it is a question of the construction of the articles whether accumulated preferential dividends are payable.[62] Express provision is often made in the articles or terms of issue for the payment in a winding up or reduction of capital of a sum equal to the amount of preferential dividends (whether declared or not) on preference shares calculated up to the date of the winding up or of repayment of the capital in priority to any distribution to ordinary shareholders.[63]

What financial entitlements do investors in shares acquire? The position of holders of redeemable shares

Redeemable shares are shares issued on terms that provide for the company to redeem the shares at some point in the future. Both ordinary and preference shares can be issued on a redeemable basis provided certain conditions set out in chapter 13 of Part 18 of the Companies Act 2006 are complied with in connection with the issue. Companies were first allowed to issue redeemable preference shares by the 1929 companies legislation, and in 1981 the permission was extended so as to allow ordinary shares also to be issued on that basis. The background to the changes made by the 1981 legislation included a report by a committee under the chairmanship of Sir Harold Wilson that highlighted the difficulties faced by

---

[59] This is a customary provision, the practice of inserting it having developed after it was held in *Re Roberts & Cooper Ltd* [1929] 2 Ch 383 that, without such provision, preferential dividends which had not been declared could not be said to be in arrear.

[60] *Re Wakley* [1920] 2 Ch 205.   [61] *First Garden City Ltd v Bonham-Carter* [1928] 1 Ch 53.

[62] *Re EW Savory Ltd* [1951] 2 All ER 1036.   [63] eg see *Re Wharfedale Brewery Co Ltd* [1952] Ch 913.

smaller companies in raising share capital[64] and a government report on the purchase by a company of its own shares.[65]

An issue of redeemable shares allows a company to raise short-term capital. The reasons for seeking short-term capital in this form may vary from company to company. Smaller companies may favour redeemable shares because they ensure that any loss of control resulting from an issue of shares to outsiders is only temporary. Being able to offer either ordinary or preference shares on a redeemable basis gives such companies the flexibility to appeal to the widest possible range of potential investors; and, for their part, investors may be more willing to invest in redeemable shares than they would have been to invest in non-redeemable ordinary or preference shares of a company whose shares are not actively traded and for which there is no ready market. For a company whose shares are actively traded, giving potential investors a way of realizing their investment would tend to figure less prominently as a reason for issuing redeemable shares. When larger companies issue redeemable shares, they tend to be non-participating redeemable preference shares carrying a preferential entitlement in respect of dividends and capital. From an economic terms perspective, an issue of redeemable preference shares on such terms is very similar to raising fixed-rate, fixed-term debt financing.

Section 684 of the Companies Act 2006 allows a company to issue redeemable shares except where, or to the extent that, this is excluded or restricted by its articles of association. The Model Articles do not contain exclusions or restrictions. To avoid the situation of a company being left with no permanent share capital, no redeemable shares may be issued at a time when there are no issued shares of the company which are not redeemable.[66]

Section 685 of the 2006 Act permits the directors to determine the terms, conditions, and manner of redemption of shares if they are authorized to do so by the company's articles or by a resolution of the company. The Model Articles confer this power on directors.[67] This approach represents a departure from the previous position under the Companies Act 1985, which provided for the redemption of shares to be effected on such terms and in such manner as might be provided by the company's articles. The correct construction of this provision was a matter of some dispute because it was unclear whether the company's articles could give a measure of discretion to the directors with regard to the detailed aspects of the redemption, such as the redemption price and the date of redemption, or whether it required those details to be set out specifically in the articles. The Companies Act 2006 clarifies the position in favour of a flexible approach.

The financial terms of redeemable shares may include a provision for the payment of a redemption premium, ie an amount greater than the par value of the shares.

There are detailed rules concerning the financing of redemptions. Redeemable shares may be redeemed out of distributable profits of the company, or out of the proceeds of a fresh issue of shares made for the purpose of the redemption.[68] Redemption premiums must be paid from distributable profits, except that in respect of redeemable shares that were issued at a premium, redemption premiums may be paid out of the proceeds of a fresh issue of shares up to an amount equal to the aggregate of the premiums received by the company on the issue of the shares redeemed, or the current amount of the company's share premium account, whichever is the less.[69] Private companies are also permitted, subject to certain conditions, to redeem shares out of capital.[70] These requirements are considered further in chapter 8.

---

[64] Committee to Review the Functioning of Financial Institutions, *Interim Report on the Financing of Small Firms* (Cmnd 7503, 1979) para 17.

[65] Department of Trade, *The Purchase by a Company of its Own Shares* (Cmnd 7944, 1980).

[66] Companies Act 2006, s 684(4).   [67] Model Articles (plc), art 43(2); Model Articles (Ltd), art 22(2).

[68] Companies Act 2006, s 687(2).   [69] Companies Act 2006, s 687(3)–(4).

[70] Companies Act 2006, s 687(1).

Incidents of Shares: Transferability

A share is a chose in action.[71] Its transferability depends on the company's articles of association.[72] Transfer restrictions are commonly included in the articles of private companies, for example, a right of pre-emption in favour of the remaining shareholders or a power for the directors to refuse to register a transfer to a person of whom they do not approve. The purpose of such restrictions is not hard to detect: it is to prevent control of the company passing outside a limited circle.[73] To be fully listed, shares ordinarily must be free from any restriction on the right of transfer (except any restriction imposed for failure to comply with a notice under provisions of the Companies Act 2006 relating to company investigations).[74] The regulator, UK Listing Authority, a function performed by the Financial Services Authority until 2013 and then by the Financial Conduct Authority (UKLA), may in exceptional circumstances modify or dispense with this rule if it is satisfied that the power to restrict transfers would not disturb the market in those shares.[75]

Incidents of Shares: Voting Rights

The default position is one vote per share unless the articles make contrary provision.[76] Ordinary shares normally follow the default position, although it is possible to have non-voting ordinary shares and ordinary shares that carry multiple votes generally or in particular circumstances.[77] As discussed at the start of this chapter, one-share-one-vote is overwhelmingly the norm in UK listed companies. Preference shares normally carry only limited voting rights but, as discussed earlier, the shares may become fully enfranchised if the preference dividend is in arrear for longer than a specified period.

The Juridical Nature of the Relationship Between a Company and Its Registered Shareholders

By virtue of section 33 of the Companies Act 2006, a contractual relationship subsists between a company and its members and also between its members amongst themselves.[78] The persons who are members of a company are the subscribers to its memorandum whose names must be entered as such in the company's register of members and those persons who agree to become members of the company and whose names are entered on the register of members.[79] The terms of the statutory contract constituted by section 33 are contained in the company's constitution, and mainly in the articles. Articles of association are a commercial document and, within the confines of the language used, are to be construed in a manner giving them reasonable business efficacy in preference to a result which would or might prove

---

[71] *Colonial Bank v Whinney* (1886) 11 App Cas 426, HL.   [72] Companies Act 2006, s 544.
[73] Until 1980 there was an obligation on private companies to include restrictions on share transfers in their articles.
[74] *LR* 2.2.4.   [75] *LR* 2.2.6.   [76] Companies Act 2006, s 284.
[77] Institutional Shareholder Services, *Report on The Proportionality Principle*.
[78] Authorities on the contract between the company and its members include: *Oakbank Oil Co v Crum* (1882) 8 App Cas 65, HL; *Welton v Saffery* [1897] AC 299, HL; *Hickman v Kent or Romney Marsh Sheepbreeders Association* [1915] 1 Ch 881; *Bratton Seymour Service Co Ltd v Oxborough* [1992] BCC 471, CA. Authorities on the contract between the members among themselves include: *Wood v Odessa Waterworks Co* (1889) 42 Ch D 636, 642; *Rayfield v Hands* [1960] Ch 1. On the history of the statutory contract: Law Commission, *Shareholder Remedies A Consultation Paper* (Law Com CP No 142, 1996) paras 2.6–2.8.
[79] Companies Act 2006, s 112. The agreement to become a member need not be contractual: *Re Nuneaton Borough Association Football Club* (1989) 5 BCC 377.

unworkable.[80] The parol evidence rule generally precludes reference to a prospectus or listing particulars accompanying an issue of shares to determine their terms;[81] however, the parol evidence rule can be displaced, for example, where it can be shown that the prospectus contains a collateral contract.[82]

The statutory contract is of a special kind, its distinctive features being outlined by Steyn LJ in *Bratton Seymour Service Co Ltd v Oxborough*[83] as follows:

(i) it derives its binding force not from a bargain struck between the parties but from the terms of a statute;

(ii) it is binding only insofar as it affects the rights and obligations between the company and the members acting in their capacity as members;

(iii) it can be altered by a special resolution without the consent of all the contracting parties;

(iv) it is not defeasible on the grounds of misrepresentation, common law mistake, mistake in equity, undue influence or duress; and

(v) it cannot be rectified on the grounds of mistake.

To this list can be added the decision in *Bratton Seymour* itself: a term cannot be implied to articles of association from extrinsic circumstances on the grounds of business efficacy but this does not prevent the implication of a term purely from the language of the document itself.[84]

A further distinctive feature of the statutory contract is that not all of the provisions of the constitution can be enforced. There are two limitations. First, only those rights and obligations in the constitution that affect members in their capacity as members can be enforced as part of the section 33 contract.[85] Thus if an article purports to give someone the right to hold or make appointments to an office or position in the company, such as company solicitor[86] or director,[87] those articles will not ordinarily be enforceable as part of the statutory contract. Secondly, even a failure to comply with a provision of the constitution which does affect members in their capacity as members does not necessarily entitle an aggrieved party to seek a contractual remedy. The court will not act in vain, and if the failure amounts simply

---

[80] *Holmes v Keyes* [1959] 1 Ch 199, CA, 215 *per* Jenkins LJ; *BWE International Ltd v Jones* [2004] 1 BCLC 406, CA; *Hunter v Senate Support Services Ltd* [2005] 1 BCLC 175; *Attorney General of Belize v Belize Telecom Ltd* [2009] UKPC 10, [2009] 2 All ER 1127; *Thompson v Goblin Hill Hotels Ltd* [2011] UKPC 8.

[81] *Baily v British Equitable Assurance Co Ltd* [1906] AC 35, HL.

[82] *Jacobs v Batavia and General Plantations Trust Ltd* [1924] 2 Ch 329, CA.

[83] [1992] BCC 471, CA, 475 *per* Steyn LJ.

[84] See also *Stanham v NTA* (1989) 15 ACLR 87, NSW SC EqD, 90–1 *per* Young J; *Equitable Life Assurance Society v Hyman* [2002] 1 AC 408, HL; *Towcester Racecourse Co Ltd v The Racecourse Association Ltd* [2003] 1 BCLC 260; *HSBC Bank Middle East v Clarke* [2006] UKPC 31; *Attorney General of Belize v Belize Telecom Ltd* [2009] UKPC 10, [2009] 2 All ER 1127.

[85] *Hickman v Kent or Romney Marsh Sheepbreeders Association* [1915] 1 Ch 881; *Beattie v E & F Beattie Ltd* [1938] 1 Ch 708, CA. There is extensive academic literature debating the proposition that a member should be able to enforce all articles of association (see in particular KW Wedderburn, 'Shareholders' Rights and the Rule in *Foss v Harbottle*' [1957] CLJ 193; GD Goldberg, 'The Enforcement of Outsider Rights under Section 20 of the Companies Act 1948' (1972) 33 MLR 362; GN Prentice, 'The Enforcement of Outsider Rights' (1980) 1 *Company Lawyer* 179; R Gregory, 'The Section 20 Contract' (1981) 44 MLR 526; GD Goldberg, 'The Controversy on the Section 20 Contract Revisited' (1985) 48 MLR 121; and RR Drury, 'The Relative Nature of a Shareholder's Right to Enforce the Company Contract' [1986] CLJ 219). However, although there is a House of Lords decision which, on its facts, supports the proposition that members should be able to enforce all articles (*Quin & Axtens Ltd v Salmon* [1909] AC 442, HL), when specifically required to consider the point, the courts have tended to adopt a more restrictive approach and the accepted view is as stated by Steyn LJ in the *Bratton Seymour* decision.

[86] *Eley v Positive Government Security Life Assurance Co Ltd* (1875–6) 1 Ex D 88, CA.

[87] *Browne v La Trinidad* (1887) 37 Ch D 1, CA.

to a procedural irregularity, the court will stand back and allow the company to take steps to remedy the position itself. What amounts to a procedural irregularity has to be considered on a case-by-case basis as there is little consistency in the reported decisions.[88]

A member may seek a declaration or an injunction against the company for breach of the statutory contract.[89] In *Hunter v Senate Support Services Ltd*[90] flawed decisions by directors of a company in respect of the exercise of power in the company's articles to forfeit shares for non-payment of calls were held to be in breach of the claimant's individual rights as a shareholder. The directors' decision to forfeit the claimant's shares was therefore held to be voidable at the instance of the claimant and the resolutions to that effect were to be set aside.

A member may be able to claim damages from the company for breach of the statutory contract. However, the position on this point is not completely beyond doubt. Section 655 of the Companies Act 2006 provides that a person is not debarred from obtaining damages or other compensation by reason only of his holding or having held shares in the company. This reverses the decision of the House of Lords in *Houldsworth v City of Glasgow Bank*[91] where it was held that a person who had been induced to take shares in a company by a fraudulent misrepresentation could not claim damages for deceit whilst he remained a shareholder. However, whilst the reversal of the *Houldsworth* decision opens up the possibility of a damages claim, there is no clear authority establishing that damages may be claimed for breach of the statutory contract and, given the special nature of this contract, it should not be assumed that damages would necessarily be available. In any event, circumstances where damages for breach of the statutory contract would be more than nominal would probably be rare.

Since the statutory contract is bilateral, the company is entitled to seek contractual remedies against members who are in breach of, or may be proposing to breach, the contractual provisions of the constitution.[92]

Until the decision in *Rayfield v Hands*[93] there was a residual doubt regarding whether individual members could sue each other directly for breach of the statutory contract. Dicta in *Wood v Odessa Waterworks Co*[94] supported the view that such actions were permissible, but a comment (in a dissenting judgment) in *Welton v Saffery*[95] suggested that all actions in respect of the statutory contract had to be mediated through the company. In the *Rayfield* decision this comment was described as 'somewhat cryptic'[96] and it was held that, even where the company was not joined as a party to the action, petitioning members were entitled as against fellow members to a contractual remedy. The circumstances where a member might wish to sue fellow members for breach of the statutory contract are likely to be fairly limited. These days it is more likely that disputes between members that involve allegations relating to breach of the statutory contract would be ventilated through a claim for relief from unfair prejudice under section 994 of the Companies Act 2006.

---

[88]   eg of *MacDougall v Gardiner* (1876) 1 Ch D 13, CA where the court refused to declare that a poll was improperly refused and *Pender v Lushington* (1877) 6 Ch D 70 where a failure to allow certain votes to be cast was held to be remediable by way of injunction. On the same side of the line as the *MacDougall* decision are cases such as *Normandy v Ind Coope & Co Ltd* [1908] 1 Ch 84 (inadequate notice of general meeting) and *Devlin v Slough Estates Ltd* [1983] BCLC 497 (allegedly defective accounts). Cases on the *Pender* side of the line include *Kaye v Croydon Tramways Co* [1898] 1 Ch 358, CA (notice of meetings) and *Henderson v Bank of Australasia* (1890) 45 Ch D 330 (moving amendments to resolutions). It is not only the courts in the UK that produce decisions on the point that are not easy to reconcile: R Cheung, 'Shareholders' Personal Rights Under the Articles—Clarity and Confusion' [2011] *Journal of Business Law* 290 (discussing recent Hong Kong authorities).

[89]   *Pender v Lushington* (1877) 6 Ch D 70; *Johnson v Lyttle's Iron Agency* (1877) 5 Ch D 687, CA; *Wood v Odessa Waterworks Co* (1889) 42 Ch D 636.

[90]   [2005] 1 BCLC 175.   [91]   (1880) 5 App Cas 317, HL.

[92]   *Hickman v Kent or Romney Marsh Sheepbreeders Association* [1915] 1 Ch 881, 897.   [93]   [1960] Ch 1.

[94]   (1889) 42 Ch D 636.   [95]   [1897] AC 299, HL, 315 *per* Lord Herschell.   [96]   [1960] Ch 1, 5.

The rather anomalous nature of the statutory contract and the uncertainty about which rights are enforceable and which are not were considered in the review that preceded the Companies Act 2006. The Company Law Review Steering Group was against simple re-enactment of the equivalent position in the Companies Act 1985[97] but, save for a substantive amendment affecting limitation periods and some drafting improvements, this is what occurred. The government's view was that it was not convinced that there was anything better and clearer that could replace the established approach; it was wary of imposing radical solutions where it was not sure how much of a problem there really was in practice and, for that reason, the effect of a company's constitution was not an area in which it wanted to introduce substantive changes.[98]

Variation of Rights Attaching to Shares

The general rule governing the alteration of rights attaching to shares that are contained in the company's articles is that they can be changed by special resolution of the company.[99] This general rule is subject to two qualifications. First, the power to alter the articles by special resolution may be removed or restricted by a provision in the articles for entrenchment. Secondly, where a company's capital structure comprises more than one type of share, further consents in addition to the special resolution may be required because rights attaching to a class of share are specially protected and, generally speaking, can be changed only with the consent of the class.

Provision for entrenchment

A provision for entrenchment is a provision in the articles to the effect that specified provisions of the articles may be amended or repealed only if conditions are met or procedures are complied with that are more restrictive than those applicable in the case of a special resolution.[100] A provision for entrenchment may only be made in the company's articles on formation or by an amendment of the company's articles agreed to by all the members of the company.[101] A provision for entrenchment does not prevent amendment of the company's articles by agreement of all the members of the company or by order of a court or other authority having relevant authority.[102] Absolute entrenchment—no alteration in any circumstances, ever—is not possible.

Where there is a proposal to change a provision in the articles that sets out a right attaching to a particular class of shares, a class consent will need to be obtained as well as the special resolution of the general meeting to alter the articles. The mechanism for alteration of the class right may itself be contained in the articles. Is this a provision for entrenchment? On one interpretation, it may be possible to regard a provision in the articles providing for the variation of class rights as a 'condition' or 'procedure' that is more restrictive than in the case of a special resolution, depending on how the provision is drafted.[103] However, if that view is

---

[97] Companies Act 1985, s 14. See Company Law Review Steering Group, *Modern Company Law for a Competitive Economy: Completing the Structure* (URN 00/1335) para 5.64 and *Modern Company Law for a Competitive Economy: Final Report* (URN 01/942) paras 7.33–7.40.

[98] Lord Sainsbury, *Hansard*, HL vol 678, col GC37 (30 January 2006).   [99] Companies Act 2006, s 21.

[100] Companies Act 2006, s 22(1).   [101] Companies Act 2006, s 22(2).

[102] Companies Act 2006, s 22(3)–(4).

[103] However, if the provision provides simply for the obtaining of a special resolution of the class in accordance with normal procedures for special resolutions (see Companies Act 2006, s 283(1), which defines special resolutions including special resolutions of a class of members), the point does not arise because the procedure is no more restrictive than in the case of a special resolution.

correct, a consequence flowing from it is that companies may not be able to include certain types of variation of rights procedures in their articles post-formation otherwise than with the unanimous consent of the members. This view does not appear to be what is intended: the official Explanatory Notes on the Companies Act 2006 suggest that the variation of class rights procedure and a provision for entrenchment are different things.[104] On this basis, a mechanism for the variation of class rights can be added to articles post-formation without necessarily commanding the unanimous approval of all of the members.

Identifying a class of shares

Section 629(1) of the Companies Act 2006 provides that for the purposes of the Companies Acts shares are of one class if the rights attached to them are in all respects uniform.[105] The inclusion of this general statutory description of a class of shares was an innovation in the 2006 Act.[106] The statement of capital that a company must file on its formation and after changes in its capital structure must include for each class of shares: (a) prescribed particulars of the rights attached to the shares, (b) the total number of shares of that class, (c) the aggregate nominal value of shares of that class, and (d) the amount to be paid up and the amount (if any) to be unpaid on each share (whether on account of the nominal value of the share or by way of premium).[107] The prescribed particulars in respect of classes of shares relate to voting rights, dividend and capital participation rights, and whether the shares are redeemable.[108] It follows, therefore, that shares that have different rights attached to them are in different classes. This is clear from section 629 of the Companies Act 2006, and it was also the position established by earlier case law.[109] There are endless ways in which the rights attaching to shares could differ, but obvious examples of shares in different classes are preference and ordinary shares,[110] redeemable shares and non-redeemable shares,[111] and convertible shares and those which are not convertible. Separate series of preference shares carrying different rights to dividend and/or capital would be treated as being in different classes from each other; although one case on the interpretation of an investment clause of a settlement refers to 'sub-classes' of shares,[112] the concept of a sub-class is meaningless in relation to variation of rights procedures.

These examples focus on the financial aspects of shares but differences in the rights attaching to shares that result in the existence of separate classes of shares for the purposes of variation of rights procedures need not necessarily be financial. Thus, for instance, ordinary shares carrying limited or enhanced voting rights would comprise a class of shares separate from ordinary shares carrying a right to one vote per share. Non-voting or limited-voting

---

[104] Para 937.

[105] But rights attached to shares are not regarded as different from those attached to other shares by reason only that they do not carry the same rights to dividends in the twelve months immediately following allotment (s 629(2)).

[106] Other sections of the Companies Act 2006 that refer to classes of shares and to which this definition is therefore relevant include ss 334, 352, and 359 (application of provisions relating to shareholder meetings to class meetings); s 550 (power of directors to allot shares etc: private company with only one class of shares); s 569 (disapplication of pre-emption rights: private company with only one class of shares); and ss 947–985 (the takeover 'squeeze-out' and 'sell-out' provisions).

[107] See eg Companies Act 2006, s 10, which details the contents of the statement of capital filed on formation.

[108] The Companies (Shares and Share Capital) Order 2009, SI 2009/388, art 2.

[109] *Cumbrian Newspapers Group Ltd v Cumberland & Westmorland Herald Newspaper & Printing Co Ltd* [1987] Ch 1, 15.

[110] *Scottish Insurance Corp Ltd v Wilsons & Clyde Co Ltd* [1949] AC 462, HL; *White v Bristol Aeroplane Co* [1953] Ch 65, CA.

[111] *TNT Australia v Normandy Resources NL* [1990] 1 ACSR 1, SA SC.

[112] *Re Powell-Cotton's Resettlement* [1957] 1 Ch 159.

ordinary shares are not common in listed companies but are often used in quasi-partnership companies or joint venture companies in order to give effect to the particular arrangements between the parties. Another familiar provision in the articles of joint venture companies is for the shares held by each of the joint venturers to be designated as 'A' shares, 'B' shares, 'C' shares, and so forth; each group of shares enjoys the same rights save that only the holder of the A shares can appoint an A director, and likewise with the other designated shares. The purpose of these arrangements is to ensure that each joint venturer has the right to appoint one member of the board; the effect of the arrangements is to create separate classes of shares.

The process of establishing whether a company has more than one class of shares in its capital structure, and hence whether the need for class, as well as company, consents for alterations to the structure requires consideration, should usually be quite straightforward, as is evident from the preceding paragraphs. However, there are some circumstances in which the position is not necessarily so clear-cut.

Golden shares

Special rights may be attached to particular shares for so long as those shares are held by a named individual. In the UK during the 1980s this type of right was included in the articles of association of some privatized companies at the time when the businesses were first transferred from state to private ownership.[113] The government retained some control over the businesses for a period of time by taking a share (known as a 'golden share'), to which were attached certain rights such as the right to cast the majority of the votes on a poll at general meetings of the company in the event that any person offered to acquire more than 50 per cent of the ordinary shares; but the articles provided for the determination of these rights in the event of the sale of the golden share by the government.[114] In *Cumbrian Newspapers Group Ltd v Cumberland & Westmorland Herald Newspaper & Printing Co*[115] Scott J considered that the fact that the special rights would determine in the event of a transfer of the shares did not prevent the golden share from forming a special class. The reasoning on this point does not appear to be undermined by the adoption of the statutory definition of a class of shares in section 629 of the Companies Act 2006.

Rights conditional on holding a specified percentage shareholding

In the *Cumbrian Newspapers* case the articles conferred on a named individual the right to appoint a director, conditional upon that individual holding not less than 10 per cent in nominal value of the company's issued shares. This type of provision differs from the golden share structure because, although the right is dependent on holding a certain proportion of the company's shares, it is not attached to any particular shares. It was held that the special rights granted by the defendant's articles were rights that, although not attached to any particular shares, were conferred on the claimant in its capacity as a shareholder in the company

---

[113] C Graham, 'All that Glitters—Golden Shares and Privatised Enterprises' (1988) 9 *Company Lawyer* 23.

[114] The practice of including golden shares is now liable to be held to be in breach of EU Treaty principles relating to free movement of capital: C-463/00 *European Commission v Spain (supported by United Kingdom intervening)* [2003] ECR I-04581; C-98/01 *European Commission v United Kingdom* [2003] ECR I-04641; C-112/05 *European Commission v Germany* [2007] ECR-I-08995; C-326/07 *European Commission v Italy* [2009] ECR I-02291; C-274/06 *European Commission v Spain* [2008] ECR I-00026; C-207/07 *European Commission v Spain* [2008] ECR I-00111; C-171/08 *European Commission v Portugal* [2010] ECR I-06817. Generally, W-G Ringe, 'Company Law and Free Movement of Capital' [2010] *Cambridge Law Journal* 378.

[115] [1987] Ch 1.

and were attached to the shares for the time being held by the claimant without which it was not entitled to the rights; and that accordingly the claimant had 'rights attached to a class of shares.' This controversial decision, which, in effect, treated a 'class of members' as being synonymous with a 'class of shares' depended closely on the wording of particular sections of the legislation in force at the time (Companies Act 1985).[116] The wording of the Companies Act 2006 differs from the 1985 legislation in material respects in relation to this matter and it is open to question whether rights of the *Cumbrian Newspapers* type are still to be regarded as giving rise to a class of shares for the purposes of the variation of rights procedures. However, nothing was said explicitly in the parliamentary process leading up to the enactment of the Companies Act 2006 to suggest that a narrowing of the category of class rights to exclude *Cumbrian Newspaper*-style rights was intended.

Shares with different par values

In *Greenhalgh v Arderne Cinemas Ltd*[117] the company's share capital included ordinary shares with a par value of 50p (converting the relevant amount to decimals) and ordinary shares with a par value of 10p. It did not fall to the Court of Appeal to decide the point but Lord Greene MR indicated that he was inclined to agree with the view of the first instance judge, Vaisey J,[118] that the 10p shares formed a separate class from the 50p shares for the purpose of an article concerned with variation of rights attaching to a class of shares. The nominal value of the shares in a class is one of the matters that must be stated in any statement of capital filed under the Companies Act 2006.[119]

Shares on which different amounts have been paid up

It could happen that different amounts are paid up in respect of shares that have the same par value. If, say, some shares are fully paid and some are partly paid, does this give rise to two separate classes of shares? It is true to say that a person holding fully paid shares may be able to enjoy rights under the articles that a holder of partly paid shares does not enjoy—for example, assuming the articles follow the normal form, the fully paid shares will be freely transferable but the partly paid shares are likely to be subject to restrictions on transfer. Yet this difference is rooted in a factual matter, not a lack of uniformity in formal rights. Rather than viewing the shares as being in different classes (if the only difference between them is with regard to amounts paid up), it seems preferable to say that the rights attaching to them are in all respects uniform but the extent to which they can be actually enjoyed is fact-dependent. In the context of a scheme of arrangement under the companies legislation, shareholders holding partly paid shares were held to constitute a separate class of members from shareholders holding fully paid shares,[120] but, since the courts can consider economic interests as well as

---

[116] The 1985 Act (unlike the 2006 Act) made provision for class rights contained in the memorandum of association and referred (s 17) to 'the special rights of any class of members' contained in the company's memorandum. The variation of class rights procedure (Companies Act 1985, s 125, especially s 125(5)) cross-referred to Companies Act 1985, s 17. Scott J suggested that in relation to a company limited by shares, the expressions, 'rights of any class of members' and 'rights…attached to a class of shares,' had the same meaning.

[117] [1946] 1 All ER 512, CA.

[118] [1945] 2 All ER 719. It must be noted that the authorities that 'fortified' Vaisey J in his conclusion were scheme of arrangement cases: *Sovereign Life Assurance Co v Dodd* [1892] 2 QB 573, CA and *Re United Provident Assurance Co Ltd* [1910] 2 Ch 477. These cases may proceed on a different basis because consideration of economic interests as well as technical rights is permissible under Companies Act 2006, Pt 26, which governs schemes of arrangement.

[119] Companies Act 2006, s 555(4)(c)(iii).

[120] *Re United Provident Assurance Co Ltd* [1910] 2 Ch 477.

rights in that context, this decision is not determinative in relation to other provisions that are concerned with more formal procedures and rights.

When class distinctions matter

In *Greenhalgh v Arderne Cinemas Ltd*[121] it was accepted that shares could be in different classes for some purposes and in the same class for others. It is suggested that the way in which this should be understood is that it is only in respect of certain matters that class distinctions need to be taken into account. For example, in a company whose capital structures comprises two classes of ordinary voting shares (say A shares and B shares), the holders of the A shares and B shares should vote on ordinary governance matters, such as re-appointment of directors, as if they were a single undivided class, but on a matter that would involve a variation of rights attaching to either the A or B shares a separate class consent would be required. This example, however, prompts the following questions: When does a proposal for a constitutional change involve a variation of rights attached to a class of shares? Are all constitutional changes variations of the rights attached to a class of shares or only some of them? What is the position where the economic value of rights is eroded or otherwise affected but the formal rights remain the same? These questions are considered next.

Variation of class rights

The Companies Act 2006 contains a special procedure for the variation of class rights. The legislation provides that 'rights attached to a class of a company's shares' may only be varied in accordance with a provision in the articles for the variation of those rights or, if there is no such provision, in accordance with a procedure in the Act itself.[122]

What is a right attached to a class of shares for this purpose?

There are three possible ways of interpreting the concept of a right attached to a class of share (or, putting it more succinctly, a class right) for the purposes of variation of class rights procedures. The broadest interpretation is that once a company's share capital is divided into more than one class, all of the rights that flow from holding a share in the company—ie all the rights under the statutory contract—are 'rights attached to a class of shares.' However, that interpretation that would mean that all changes to the articles that modify the statutory contract would need to be regarded as a variation of class rights to which special protections apply; the principle of majority rule, which in relation to articles of association means that they can be altered by special resolution, would be very significantly curtailed. It has never been seriously maintained that the class rights protection procedure gives minorities such an extensive power of control over constitutional changes. In *Hodge v James Howell & Co Ltd* Jenkins LJ said: 'In general, one expects to find ordinary shares entitled to the whole of the profits and surplus assets remaining after preferences attached to any other class of shares are satisfied, and this residual right is not generally regarded as a special right or privilege or class right attached to the ordinary shares for the purposes of a modification of rights clause.'[123] Something more than the division of the capital into more than one class is required for particular rights attached to

---

[121] [1945] 2 All ER 719, [1946] 1 All ER 512, CA.

[122] Companies Act 2006, s 630. There is an equivalent procedure for variation of class rights in companies without a share capital (s 631).

[123] [1958] CLY 446, CA.

those shares to be regarded as class rights for the purposes of a modification of rights clause and, it is suggested, for the statutory procedure for the variation of class rights.

What is the something more? References to 'special' rights might be taken to suggest exclusivity[124] but it is apparent from the authorities that a right can be a right attached to a class of shares for the purposes of a variation of rights procedure even where it is common to more than one class: in *Greenhalgh v Arderne Cinemas Ltd*[125] voting rights that were common to two classes of shares were regarded as rights attached to a class of shares for the purposes of variation procedures (although the decision in the case was that there was in fact no variation of rights). Although there is no authority precisely on the point, the cases appear to proceed on the assumption that any rights that are exclusive to a particular class are rights attached to a class of shares but that, in addition, dividend and capital rights, rights to vote, and rights relating to protection of class rights[126] are rights attached to a class of shares even when they are not exclusive and the rights of the same nature and extent are also attached to other classes of shares in the company.

In essence, the matter in issue in this debate about the interpretation of the expression 'rights attached to a class of shares' is the extent to which minority interests are entitled to the special protection afforded to class rights. Investors in share capital take the risk that the rights which they acquire under the company's constitution by virtue of becoming members of the company will be changed by a resolution of the shareholders in general meeting; typically such rights are in the articles and, under section 21 of the Companies Act 2006, they can be changed by a special resolution (75 per cent of those voting) of the shareholders in general meetings. Where, however, a right attached to a class of shares is involved, the general power to alter the articles is qualified by a procedure that requires the consent of a specified majority of the class also to be obtained. The more broadly the expression 'rights attached to a class of shares' is interpreted, the more protection is afforded to minorities, and vice versa. The law therefore needs to achieve a balance that is consistent with rational expectations. Rights that rational investors would regard as fundamental to the investment—ie financial return and voting entitlements—should be treated as deserving of special protection even where they are not enjoyed exclusively by one class only, but more general rights derived from the articles should be capable of being changed more easily under the general power to alter articles without requiring compliance with the variation of class rights procedures. Whilst uncertainty remains, in practice it would thus be prudent for any company that has a complex capital structure comprising more than one class of shares to proceed on the basis that proposals to vary dividend, capital, or voting rights attaching to one class of shares will trigger variation of class rights procedures even where the rights in question are identical to those attached to another class of shares.

What is a 'variation' of a right attached to a class of shares?

Articles of association that contain provisions for the variation of class rights may specify what, for the purpose of those articles, is meant by the term 'variation'; in that case whether a

---

[124] *Cumbrian Newspapers Group Ltd v Cumberland & Westmorland Herald Newspaper & Printing Co Ltd* [1987] Ch 1, 15. See also *Re John Smith's Tadcaster Brewery Co Ltd* [1953] Ch 308, CA, 319–20 *per* Jenkins LJ.

[125] [1945] 2 All ER 719, [1946] 1 All ER 512, CA. Also note *Re Old Silkstone Collieries Ltd* [1954] 1 Ch 169, CA where two classes of preference shares were entitled to participate in a compensation scheme to be established under nationalization legislation. This entitlement though common to the two classes was held to be a special right that triggered a protective procedure under the company's articles relating to variation of class rights.

[126] Companies Act 2006, s 630(5) expressly provides that any alteration of a variation of rights clause in articles, or the insertion of such a clause into articles, is itself to be treated as a variation of rights attached to a class of shares.

particular proposal is a variation depends on construction of the particular articles. Section 630 of the Companies Act 2006 also makes provision for variation of rights attached to a class of shares to cover cases where the company's articles do not make provision for variation (and to provide certain minority protection and procedural requirements that are generally applicable). For the purposes of the statutory variation procedure, and also (unless the context otherwise requires) in relation to provisions for the variation of rights contained in articles, references to variation are to be read as including 'abrogation.'[127]

Straightforward examples of variations of class rights would include reducing the rate of a preferential dividend or decreasing the number of votes attached to a share. Since variation includes abrogation, removing a right to a preferential dividend would also amount to a variation of class rights. However, in *Re Schweppes Ltd*[128] it was held that an issue of ordinary shares did not vary the class rights of existing ordinary shares, nor those of existing preference shares. An issue of preference shares ranking *pari passu* with existing preference shares was held not to vary the class rights of the existing preference shares in *Underwood v London Music Hall Ltd*.[129] In *Dimbula Valley (Ceylon) Tea Co Ltd v Laurie*[130] the rights attached to preference shares included the right to participate in a winding up rateably with the ordinary shares in all assets remaining after paying creditors, costs, arrears of preference dividend, and repayment of all paid up capital. It was held that a bonus issue of shares did not vary this entitlement to participate even though it might reduce an individual shareholder's share of the surplus available on liquidation.

The distinction implicit in the *Dimbula* decision between varying a right and affecting the enjoyment of a right was developed in a trio of cases decided by the Court of Appeal in the 1940s and 1950s. In *Greenhalgh v Arderne Cinemas Ltd*[131] the Court of Appeal held that in respect of a share capital divided into 50p and 10p shares (using decimal equivalents for the sake of simplicity), a proposal to sub-divide the 50p shares into 10p shares did not amount to a variation of the class rights of the original 10p shares even though, as a result of the sub-division, the application of the provision in the articles which provided for each share (regardless of par value) to have one vote meant that the voting strength of the holders of the original 10p shares would be greatly diminished. Formally the rights attaching to the 10p shares were unchanged and it was simply that, through sub-division, those shareholders who could previously cast one vote in respect of each 50p share now could cast five, with a resulting diminution in the effectiveness of the votes cast by the holders of the original 10p shares. Lord Greene MR also commented on what the position might have been if the proposal had been to give the 50p shares five votes per share, rather than to sub-divide them. In that case, his Lordship considered that the rights attaching to the 10p shares might well have been varied because one of the rights attaching to those shares was that they should have voting powers *pari passu* with the other ordinary shares.[132]

The articles in the *Greenhalgh* decision imposed a special procedure to be followed on a 'variation' of rights. In *White v Bristol Aeroplane Co Ltd*[133] the relevant articles contained a more elaborate provision stipulating a procedure that was to be followed where rights attaching to a class of shares were to be 'affected, modified, varied, dealt with or abrogated in any manner.' The company's share capital comprised preference shares and ordinary shares and it proposed to increase its share capital by issuing new preference shares ranking *pari passu* with the existing preference shares and new ordinary shares ranking *pari passu* with existing ordinary shares. The question considered by the Court of Appeal was whether this clause

[127] Companies Act 2006, s 630(6).   [128] [1914] 1 Ch 322 CA.   [129] [1901] 2 Ch 309.
[130] [1961] 1 Ch 353.   [131] [1946] 1 All ER 512, CA.
[132] [1946] 1 All ER 512, CA, 515.   [133] [1953] 1 Ch 65, CA.

applied on the basis that the rights of the existing preference shares would be 'affected' by a new issue of *pari passu* shares. The court held that the rights would not be affected and that, accordingly, the procedure did not apply. The reasoning was that after the issue the rights attaching to the existing preference shares would, in formal terms, be precisely the same as they had been before the issue, the only change being in the enjoyment of, and the capacity to make effective, the voting rights attached to the shares.

In *Re John Smith's Tadcaster Brewery Co Ltd*[134] the Court of Appeal again restricted the application of special procedures for the variation of rights. In this case it was held that an issue of new ordinary shares did not 'affect' the voting rights attaching to preference shares so as to trigger special procedures under the company's articles. Evershed MR went so far as to express some dissatisfaction with the prolix drafting of variation of rights procedures in articles of the kind in question in *White v Bristol Aeroplane Co Ltd* and the particular case before him, commenting: 'it is perhaps unfortunate that those responsible for drafting these regulations seem apt... to string together words without pausing to reflect what their joint or separate significance might be.'[135] Evershed MR also sought to justify the court's restrictive stance by pointing out that a loose interpretation of a word such as 'affect' would mean that any activity on the part of the directors in pursuance of their powers which could be said to affect or touch the value of the preference shares would be rendered ineffective unless the special protective procedures were adhered to—a result which, in his Lordship's view, would be absurd.[136]

The distinction between varying a right and affecting the enjoyment of a right is now well established although on which side of the line a particular series of events falls can still be a disputed point.[137] It is justifiable for the special protection afforded to minorities by class rights protections to be kept within strict limits so as to avoid situations where the holders of a class of shares could hold an effective veto over virtually all of the company's activities.[138] Yet some of the cases seem to verge on an excessively restrictive interpretation of clauses that purport to extend variation procedures to situations where class rights are affected and such narrowness may be thought to defeat reasonable expectations.[139] As a matter of drafting, it is clear that if it is intended that proposals such as that involved in the *White* case should be subject to variation procedures, those procedures must be carefully drafted such as by providing that an issue of new shares ranking *pari passu* with existing shares will be a variation of class rights. Most favourable to the holders of a class of shares would be a provision drafted in general terms, such as one which provides for the protective procedure to apply where rights are 'affected as a business,'[140] but, from the company's perspective, a general formula such as this would probably be unacceptably vague and unpredictable.

There is one situation where there is a possibility of the literal approach not being followed in respect of articles that provide for protection in the event of class rights being 'affected.' This stems from a dictum in Evershed MR's judgment in *White v Bristol Aeroplane Co Ltd* where he said that:

> ...a resolution aimed at increasing the voting power of the ordinary stockholders by doubling it, so giving them twofold their present power, without altering any other of the privileges or rights attached to any class, might be said to be something so directly touching the position, and

---

[134] [1953] Ch 308, CA.   [135] [1953] Ch 308, CA, 312.   [136] [1953] Ch 308, CA, 316–7.

[137] eg *Re Smiths of Smithfield Ltd* [2003] BCC 769, especially para 57.

[138] RR Pennington, *Company Law* 7th edn (London: Butterworths, 1995) 283.

[139] Criticisms were voiced before the House of Lords in *House of Fraser plc v ACGE Investments Ltd* [1987] AC 387, HL but the House of Lords, in line with the earlier cases, adopted a narrow approach.

[140] As discussed in *White v Bristol Aeroplane Co* [1953] Ch 65, CA, 80 *per* Evershed MR.

therefore the rights, of the preference stockholders…albeit that there was no variation of their own individual rights.[141]

The context for this statement was that Evershed MR used this example to demonstrate that meaning could be given to the term 'affected' as distinct from 'variation.' However, he emphasized that he was not deciding the point and it is therefore uncertain how much weight should be attached to this comment. Departing from the literal rule for this particular case would seem to have little merit and would serve only to create further complexity and anomaly in this already difficult area.[142] However, applying normal principles, if the articles provide for two classes of shares to have *pari passu* voting rights and there is a subsequent proposal to increase the voting rights of one class, that would vary the *pari passu* voting right of the other class.[143]

Variation of rights by enhancement

Are class rights varied if the rights attached to that class are enhanced in some respect, for instance, if the rate of a preferential dividend is increased or if the number of votes attached to a share is multiplied? A dictum in *Dimbula Valley (Ceylon) Teas Co Ltd v Laurie*[144] suggests that increasing rights is a reinforcement rather than a variation of those rights but, in principle, it is difficult to see why the mere fact of a change being beneficial rather than adverse should preclude it from amounting to a variation of class rights. Notably, although the point was not specifically addressed, *Rights and Issues Investment Trust Ltd v Stylo Shoes Ltd*[145] proceeded on the assumption that an alteration increasing the voting rights attached to a class of shares required the consent of the relevant class. In *Unilever (UK) Holdings Ltd v Smith (Inspector of Taxes)*,[146] in considering tax issues relating to an alteration to the rights attaching to shares the Court of Appeal was of the view that the same test must apply whether the suggested alteration took the form of a restriction or an enhancement of rights.

The procedure for variation of class rights

In addition to the normal corporate consents required to change the company's constitution, the variation of rights attached to a class of shares also requires the consent of the class obtained in accordance with provisions in the company's articles for the variation of rights or, where the articles contain no such provision, in accordance with the statutory procedure in the companies legislation. The variation of rights procedure in the Companies Act 2006 is considerably simpler than the equivalent procedure in the Companies Act 1985. This is one of the consequences that follows from the simplification of the law on company constitutions by that Act, in particular, the fact that the option of setting out rights attached to shares in the memorandum rather than the articles is no longer available.[147]

---

[141] *White v Bristol Aeroplane Co* [1953] Ch 65, CA, 76–7.

[142] One further potential complication, not yet tested, is that Directive 2012/30/EU of the European Parliament and of the Council of 25 October 2012 on coordination of safeguards which, for the protection of the interests of members and others, are required by Member States of companies within the meaning of the second paragraph of Article 54 of the Treaty on the Functioning of the European Union, in respect of the formation of public limited liability companies and the maintenance and alteration of their capital, with a view to making such safeguards equivalent (Recast) [2012] L315/74 (Second Company Law Directive), Art 29(3) provides that where there are several classes of shares in a plc, an increase in capital shall be subject to a separate vote for each class of shareholders whose rights are *affected* (emphasis added) by the transaction. That 'affected' in this context could extend to a change in decision-making power has been suggested: S Grundmann, *European Company Law* 2nd edn (Cambridge: Intersentia, 2012) 236.

[143] *Greenhalgh v Arderne Cinemas Ltd* [1946] 1 All ER 512, CA.   [144] [1961] 1 Ch 353, 374.

[145] [1965] 1 Ch 250.   [146] [2003] STC 15, 76 TC 300, para 56.   [147] See Companies Act 2006, s 8.

The statutory procedure for the variation of a right attached to a class of shares is that:

1. the holders of three-quarters in nominal value of the issued shares of that class (excluding treasury shares) must consent in writing to the variation; or

2. a special resolution passed at a separate general meeting of the holders of that class must sanction the variation.[148]

Class meetings for a variation of class rights are governed by the procedural requirements applicable to company meetings generally (with appropriate modifications) except that: (a) the necessary quorum at any meeting (other than an adjourned meeting) is two persons holding, or representing by proxy, at least one-third in nominal value of the issued shares of the class in question (excluding treasury shares), and at an adjourned meeting one person holding shares of the class in question or his proxy; and (b) any holder of shares of the class in question present may demand a poll.[149] It is for the chairman of a class meeting to regulate its conduct but prima facie the meeting should be attended only by the members of the class so that they have an opportunity to discuss the matter privately and without their discussion being overheard by members of other classes.[150] Where rights attached to a class of shares are varied, the company must, within one month from the date when the variation is made, deliver to the registrar a notice giving particulars of the variation.[151]

Voting to alter class rights—a fettered power?

It is well established that a vote attached to a share is a property right to be exercised as its owner thinks fit.[152] In principle, a shareholder cannot be compelled to vote, nor can he be held to account for the way in which he chooses to exercise his vote. A line of authorities, however, imposes a qualification: in certain circumstances the courts will deny effect to a resolution if the shareholders who supported it were, in some sense, exercising their power inappropriately. Although some of the language in relevant judgments may suggest otherwise,[153] denying effect to a resolution is not the same thing as imposing a duty on the shareholders to vote in a particular way—shareholders may please themselves, knowing that even though the court may deny effect to their decisions, they will not be held to have breached a duty, or be liable to pay compensation, to anyone who may be aggrieved by their actions.[154] However, rational shareholders would want to avoid the trouble and expense of voting in circumstances where that vote may later be held to be ineffective by a court. Accordingly, if they vote at all, they may consider themselves to be under a practical, if not a legal, duty to cast their votes in a manner that will withstand judicial scrutiny.

A class consent to the variation of rights attached to the shares comprising the class is one of the (quite rare) situations in which the courts have been prepared to deny effect to the decision of the majority of the class. In *British American Nickel Corp Ltd v MJ O'Brien*[155] the company proposed a scheme for the reconstruction of the company involving mortgage bonds being exchanged for income bonds. The proposal was passed at a meeting of the mortgage bondholders but the sanction would not have been obtained but for the support of the holder

---

[148] Companies Act 2006, s 630(4).   [149] Companies Act 2006, s 334.
[150] *Carruth v Imperial Chemical Industries Ltd* [1937] AC 707, HL.   [151] Companies Act 2006, s 637.
[152] Leading authorities are *Pender v Lushington* (1877) 6 Ch D 70; *Northern Counties Securities Ltd v Jackson & Steeple Ltd* [1974] 1 WLR 1133; *North-West Transportation Co Ltd v Beatty* (1887) 12 App Cas 589, PC.
[153] eg *British American Nickel Corp v O'Brien* [1927] AC 369, PC, 378 *per* Viscount Haldane.
[154] LS Sealy, 'Equitable and Other Fetters on a Shareholder's Freedom to Vote' in NE Eastham and B Krivy (eds), *The Cambridge Lectures 1981* (Cambridge: Butterworths, 1982) 80.
[155] [1927] AC 369, PC.

of a large number of bonds who had been given an incentive to support the scheme that was not made available to other bondholders and which was not disclosed. The Privy Council held that the resolution was invalid, one reason for this invalidity being that the bondholder who had been given the incentive had not treated the interest of the whole class of bondholders as the dominant consideration. Viscount Haldane, delivering the judgment, explained the principle applied by the court:[156]

> There is, however, a restriction of such powers, when conferred on a majority of a special class in order to enable that majority to bind a minority. They must be exercised subject to a general principle, which is applicable to all authorities conferred on majorities of classes enabling them to bind minorities; namely, that the power given must be exercised for the purpose of benefiting the class as a whole, and not merely individual members only.

This principle was applied by Megarry J in *Re Holders Investment Trust Ltd*[157] where trustees who were the holders of the majority of the preference shares in a company had supported a proposal to convert the preference shares into loan stock. The trustees also held the majority of the company's ordinary shares and the evidence indicated that they had acted throughout on the basis of what was in the interests of the Trust (which, of course, as trustees they were obliged to do) and had not applied their minds to the question of what was in the interests of the preference shareholders as a class. In these circumstances, Megarry J held that the sanction given by the preference shareholders as a class was not effective.

Judicial control over the exercise of majority power was again in issue in *Assénagon Asset Management SA v Irish Bank Resolution Corporation Limited*.[158] The specific facts concerned the failure of the Anglo Irish Bank during the financial crisis of 2007–9. As in *British American Nickel* this case involved bondholders rather than shareholders but the principles articulated are not exclusive to any particular category of financial instrument.[159] The case involved the operation of a technique used by issuers of corporate bonds known as 'exit consent'. The technique is used when an issuer wants to persuade all the holders of a particular bond issue to accept an exchange of their bonds for replacement bonds on different terms. Bondholders are invited to offer their existing bonds for exchange on terms whereby they are required to commit themselves irrevocably to vote at a bondholders' meeting for a resolution amending the terms of the existing bonds. On the facts, the exchange asked bondholders to accept 20 cents in the euro and to bind themselves to vote for a resolution leaving holders who rejected the exchange offer to be redeemed at a rate of one cent per 1,000 euros. By authorizing the redemption at a nominal value of any bonds that remained outstanding on completion of the exchange offer, the resolution effectively destroyed the value of the rights arising from those existing bonds. The exchange offer and the associated exit consent mechanism were fully disclosed to all bondholders and there was no question of private negotiations and inducements to selected parties. Nevertheless, the court determined that it was not lawful for the majority to lend its aid to the coercion of a minority by voting for a resolution which expropriated the minority's rights under their bonds for a nominal consideration. This form of coercion was held to be entirely at variance with the purposes for which majorities in a class are given power to bind minorities.

Statutory protection of minorities in a class of shareholders

Under Section 633 of the Companies Act 2006, shareholders have the right to apply to court to have a variation of class rights cancelled. There are certain requirements that must be

---

[156] At 371.   [157] [1971] 1 WLR 583.

[158] [2012] EWHC 2090 (Ch). Compare *Azevedo v Imcopa Importação* [2013] EWCA Civ 364.

[159] Briggs J noted that it could be traced back to Justinian's *Institutes*: [41]. The basis for application arises from general principles of law and equity: [45].

satisfied in order to bring a claim under this provision and it is therefore limited in its effect. To have standing to bring a claim under this section, the petitioner or petitioners must hold not less in the aggregate than 15 per cent of the issued shares of the class in question. The petitioner or petitioners must not have consented to or voted in favour of the resolution for the variation; shareholders who have simply changed their minds may not invoke section 633. The application must be made within twenty-one days after the date on which the consent was given or the resolution was passed. If a claim is properly brought, the variation has no effect until it is confirmed by the court. The court may disallow the variation if it is satisfied, having regard to all the circumstances of the case, that the variation would unfairly prejudice the shareholders of the class represented by the applicant; if the court is not so satisfied, it must confirm the variation. The court's decision is final. A copy of the court's order must be filed with the registrar of companies.[160]

The remedy under section 633 of the Companies Act 2006 overlaps with the unfair prejudice remedy in section 994 of that Act. The general unfair prejudice remedy does not have a threshold condition in relation to a minimum shareholding nor does it impose a strict time limit within which claims must be brought. The court has considerable remedial flexibility under section 994 of the Companies Act 2006, which is in distinct contrast to the position under section 633 of the Act, where the court is empowered only to disallow the variation.

Class rights and reduction of capital

Cases concerning reduction of capital provide particularly useful examples of judicial consideration being given to the question of what constitutes a variation of rights attaching to a class of shares. Reductions of capital in accordance with section 645 of the Companies Act 2006 are subject to the approval of the court. In principle the court has jurisdiction to approve a reduction of capital notwithstanding that it is not in precise conformity with class rights,[161] but this discretion is qualified by the Companies Act 2006, section 641(6), which makes the statutory reduction procedures subject to any provision of the company's articles restricting or prohibiting the reduction of capital. In a case where the articles of association made provision for the variation of class rights, separate class consents were regarded as a 'prerequisite' of a proposed reduction of capital involving a variation of class rights and it was held that the court had, accordingly, no jurisdiction to confirm the reduction in the absence of such approval.[162] The procedure in the Companies Act 2006, section 642 for private companies to reduce their capital out of court by means of a special resolution of the shareholders supported by a solvency statement from the directors does not make specific reference to class rights.[163] However, since section 630 of the Companies Act 2006 makes it clear that rights attached to a class of shares can only be varied in accordance with the specified procedure, it is difficult to see how any out of court reduction of capital that involves a variation of class rights could validly proceed in the absence of appropriate class consents.

In determining whether a proposed reduction of capital varies the rights attached to a class of shares, the starting point is the company's articles of association or terms of issue of the

---

[160] Companies Act 2006, s 635.

[161] *British and American Trustee and Finance Corp v Couper* [1894] AC 399, HL.

[162] *Re Northern Engineering Industries plc* [1993] BCC 267. See also on the importance of class rights in reduction of capital situations: *Bannatyne v Direct Spanish Telegraph Co* (1887) 34 Ch D 287, CA, 300 *per* Cotton LJ; *Re Chatterley-Whitfield Collieries Ltd* [1948] 2 All ER 593, CA (affirmed *sub nom Prudential Assurance Co Ltd v Chatterley-Whitfield Collieries Ltd* [1949] AC 512, HL).

[163] Companies Act 2006, ss 642–4.

shares, as these may make specific provision in relation to the situation.[164] For example, in *Re Northern Engineering Industries plc*[165] the articles provided that any reduction of capital would be a variation of the class rights of the preference shares and an attempt to limit the application of this provision on the basis of an argument that 'reduction' for this purpose did not include cancellation of the preference shares was rejected. If the articles or terms of issue do not make express provision, the position is that the various classes of shares are to be treated as they would be treated in the event of a winding up. What this means is that if a company's share capital comprises ordinary shares and non-participating preference shares that carry a right to priority as to return of capital (but no right to share in any surplus remaining after payment of creditors, costs, accrued unpaid dividends on preference shares (if any), and the return of paid up capital plus any specified liquidation/redemption premium), a reduction of share capital involving the return of capital is effected in accordance with class rights where the preference shares are paid off first[166] —this is perfectly consistent with their entitlements because those shares would rank before the ordinary shares on a winding up. Conversely, where the reduction involves cancellation of nominal share capital as a result of losses, it is the ordinary shares (which would bear this loss in the event of winding up) that must be cancelled first.[167]

It is clear from the case law that the payment off and cancellation of non-participating preference shares as outlined in the last paragraph does not abrogate, affect, modify, or deal with the rights attached to those shares. In *Re Saltdean Estate Co Ltd*[168] Buckley J explained that the rights were not abrogated; rather, by paying off the preference shares first, the company was giving effect to the priority right attached to those shares. In *House of Fraser plc v ACGE Investments Ltd*[169] Lord Keith of Kinkel amplified this explanation. Paying off preference shares that were entitled to priority on a winding up or otherwise, gave effect to the entitlement and did not abrogate it; and the reduction did not 'modify, commute, affect or deal with' the rights attached to the shares within the meaning of the company's articles because those words all contemplated that, after the transaction, the shareholders in question would continue to hold some rights, albeit of a different nature from those that they previously held. The payment off and cancellation of non-participating preference shares will extinguish any further entitlement to whatever fixed dividend was previously attached to those shares.[170] It is not a variation of class rights to extinguish this entitlement; rather, this is something that the holders of the shares must be taken to have agreed to as a necessary consequence of their right to priority on a return of capital.[171]

Where a company's share capital consists of ordinary shares and participating preference shares that have a priority right in respect of dividends (calculated by reference to paid up amounts) but then rank *pari passu* with the ordinary shares in respect of capital, any reduction of capital must, to conform to class rights, be spread equally across both classes.

---

[164] A provision dealing with return of capital 'on a winding up or otherwise' will be taken to refer to repayment of capital in accordance with Companies Act 2006, s 645: *House of Fraser plc v ACGE Investments Ltd* [1987] AC 387, HL.

[165] [1993] BCC 267.

[166] *Re Chatterley-Whitfield Collieries Ltd* [1948] 2 All ER 593, CA (affirmed *sub nom Prudential Assurance Co Ltd v Chatterley-Whitfield Collieries Ltd* [1949] AC 512, HL); *Scottish Insurance Corp v Wilsons & Clyde Coal Co Ltd* [1949] AC 462, HL; *Re Saltdean Estate Co Ltd* [1968] 1 WLR 1844; *House of Fraser plc v ACGE Investments Ltd* [1987] AC 387, HL.

[167] *Re Floating Dock of St Thomas Ltd* [1895] 1 Ch 691.   [168] [1968] 1 WLR 1844.

[169] [1987] AC 387, HL. See also *Re Hunting plc* [2005] 2 BCLC 211; *Re Peninsula and Oriental Steam Navigation Co* [2006] EWHC 389 (Ch).

[170] *Re Chatterley-Whitfield Collieries Ltd* [1948] 2 All ER 593, CA (affirmed *sub nom Prudential Assurance Co Ltd v Chatterley-Whitfield Collieries Ltd* [1949] AC 512, HL).

[171] *House of Fraser plc v ACGE Investments Ltd* [1987] AC 387, HL.

A reduction involving capital repayment or cancellation will thus result in a reduction of the amounts paid up on both classes of shares, but the effect on the continuing enjoyment of the priority dividend right will be especially significant: although the rate of the dividend will remain the same, the amount that the holders of the shares actually receive will be potentially significantly less because of the reduction of the principal amount on which that dividend is based. In line with the restrictive approach that characterizes case law relating to the interpretation of the term 'variation,' a reduction in the amount of dividend actually received resulting not from a direct adjustment to the rate of dividend but indirectly from a reduction of the principal amount by reference to which it is calculated is not, in itself, regarded as a variation of class rights.[172]

Class rights and redemption of shares/share buy-backs

Class rights issues similar to those in reduction of capital situations can also arise in relation to share buy-backs and redeemable shares. Even where a redemption is funded from distributable reserves, from the investor's perspective its investment in the company's capital is returned. The buy back or redemption of one class of shares could therefore interfere with the priority entitlements of the holders of other classes of the company's shares.

In determining whether a repurchase of shares or issue of redeemable shares constitutes a variation of rights attached to another class of shares the starting point is, again, the articles of association or the terms of issue of the existing shares. For example, the terms on which preference shares are issued may expressly anticipate further issues of redeemable shares and specify whether or not those issues will constitute a variation of the rights of the preference shares. Where no such provision is made and the company has issued preference shares that are entitled to priority on a winding up or any return of capital, a subsequent issue of redeemable shares could constitute a variation of the class rights of the existing preference shares since, on redemption, capital could be returned first to the holders of the redeemable shares. Even if the terms of the preference shares simply provide for priority on a winding up and are silent with regard to returns of capital, the analysis should be the same by extension of the decisions on reduction of capital where the court held that it is to be implied that the position corresponds to the rights on winding up unless otherwise stated. Where there are preference shares that are entitled to priority on a return of capital in a winding up or otherwise, it would be a variation of their class rights for the company to purchase ordinary shares before the preference shares have been paid off unless (as is often the case) the terms on which the preference shares were issued expressly sanctioned buy-backs of ordinary shares.

---

[172] *Bannatyne v Direct Spanish Telegraph Co* (1887) 34 Ch D 287, CA; *Re Mackenzie & Co Ltd* [1916] 2 Ch 450. See also *Adelaide Electric Co Ltd v Prudential Assurance Co* [1934] AC 122, HL where the rate of dividend was unchanged but, because of a change in the place of payment and currency of payment (from English pounds to Australian pounds), shareholders actually received a much smaller amount. The House of Lords held that there was no variation of class rights. This case again illustrates the restrictive approach of the courts, but the decision does turn on the interpretation of 'pound' as used in the company's articles. A change of currency that is not within the scope of the language used in the articles could, it is suggested, constitute a variation of class rights.

7

Maintenance and Reduction of Capital

Protection of Creditors' Interests: Introduction

In modern systems of corporate regulation, the benefits to shareholders and controllers that flow from limited liability are counterbalanced by provisions that seek to protect creditors' interests. The main corporate regulatory strategies for the protection of creditors' interests are: mandatory disclosure rules, especially in relation to financial performance; detailed legal capital rules that throughout the life of a company govern the maintenance of its share capital and other quasi-capital reserves; and broad solvency-based standards underpinned by personal liability attaching to directors or controllers. These strategies can operate independently of each other or can be complementary, such as where mandatory financial statements are used as the basis for measuring compliance with legal capital rules.

UK company law, in common with that in all other EU Member States, still contains many detailed rules on the maintenance of capital, some of which are mandatory under the EU Second Company Law Directive;[1] elsewhere in the economically developed world, however, many countries have moved away from these rules in favour of more open-textured solvency-based standards.[2] There is a lively and detailed European debate on options for reform, which has gathered pace since landmark decisions of the (now) Court of Justice of the European Union (CJEU) that held that certain detailed legal capital rules in national laws that impeded the operation of Treaty freedoms could not be justified by reference to public interest imperatives[3] and which has deepened more recently, as changes in accounting have shifted the emphasis of financial disclosure from informing creditors to informing investors and, as a result, put in question the usefulness of published accounts as the yardstick for determining compliance with legal capital rules.[4]

Policymakers appear to be edging towards dismantling the detailed legal capital rules, although the pace of change at the European level is quite conservative, reflecting the fact that there is still a considerable divergence of views in Europe on fundamental questions about the role of company law, as opposed to insolvency law, in addressing creditors' interests and on whether this is an area where pan-European regulatory harmonization is appropriate in any event. The issues are complex and policymakers are aware that they require a nuanced and

---

[1] Directive 2012/30/EU of the European Parliament and of the Council of 25 October 2012 on coordination of safeguards which, for the protection of the interests of members and others, are required by Member States of companies within the meaning of the second paragraph of Article 54 of the Treaty on the Functioning of the European Union, in respect of the formation of public limited liability companies and the maintenance and alteration of their capital, with a view to making such safeguards equivalent (Recast), [2012] OJ L315/74 (Second Company Law Directive).

[2] J Armour, G Hertig, and H Kanda, 'Transactions with Creditors' in RR Kraakman, J Armour, P Davies, L Enriques, H Hansmann, G Hertig, KJ Hopt, H Kanda, and EB Rock, *The Anatomy of Corporate Law: A Comparative and Functional Approach* 2nd edn (Oxford: OUP, 2009) ch 5.

[3] Case C-212/97 *Centros Ltd v Erhvervs- og Selskabsstyrelsen* [1999] ECR I-1459; Case C-208/00 *Überseering BV v Nordic Construction Co Baumanagement GmbH (NCC)* [2000] ECR I-09919; Case C-167/01 *Kamer van Koophandel en Fabrieken voor Amsterdam v Inspire Art Ltd* [2003] ECR I-10155. See further ch 4.

[4] EV Ferran, 'The Place for Creditor Protection on the Agenda for Modernisation of Company Law in the European Union' [2006] *European Company and Financial Law Review* 178; G Strampelli, 'The IAS/IFRS After the Crisis: Limiting the Impact of Fair Value Accounting on Companies' Capital' (2011) 8 *European Company and Financial Law Review* 1.

careful response. Although the Second Company Law Directive was amended in 2006,[5] the changes made were so slight as to prompt the remark from a leading commentator that: 'The revision of the Second Company Law Directive has not even started.'[6] The Commission subsequently commissioned the accountancy firm KPMG to write a feasibility study on alternatives to the Second Directive.[7] Disappointingly for advocates of reform, on the basis of the findings in this study the Commission concluded that the Directive did not seem to be a source of significant operational problems for companies and announced that no follow-up measures or changes to the Directive were foreseen in the immediate future.[8] Nevertheless, pressure for change continues to be exerted. The European Company Law Experts (ECLE) group maintains that the case for a fundamental and comprehensible reform of the system of formation and maintenance of legal capital remains compelling.[9]

The UK is among the Member States that favour significant reform. In pursuit of this agenda, the Companies Act 2006 stripped out some elements of the legal capital regime and moved towards more reliance on solvency standards. However, even within the UK there are different views on the appropriate extent of the dismantling of the legal capital regime: notably, the Companies Act 2006 did not go quite as far in this direction as would be permissible without breaching EU law.[10] To the extent that the UK 'over' implements the Second Company Law Directive it is proceeding on the basis that the Directive is a minimum harmonization measure, a view which is supported by jurisprudence of the Court of Justice.[11]

Questioning the value of the legal capital doctrine

The essence of the legal capital doctrine is that share capital and certain other reserves must not be paid out to shareholders except in tightly constrained circumstances. The payout constraint is expressed in the following way in Article 17(1) of the Second Company Law Directive: 'Except for cases of reductions of subscribed capital, no distribution to shareholders may be made when on the closing date of the last financial year the net assets as set out in the company's annual accounts are, or following a distribution would become, lower than the amount of the subscribed capital plus those reserves which may not be distributed under the laws or the statutes.'

The effect of this provision is that only that portion of the net assets that exceeds the capital and undistributable reserves can be paid out to shareholders, notwithstanding that from a

---

[5] Directive 2006/68/EC of the European Parliament and of the Council of 6 September 2006 amending Council Directive (EEC) 77/91 as regards the formation of public limited liability companies and the maintenance and alteration of their capital [2006] OJ L264/32. The 2006 reforms are now incorporated into the 2012 recast version of the Second Directive.

[6] E Wymeersch, 'Reforming the Second Company Law Directive' (November 2006) <http://ssrn.com/abstract=957981> accessed July 2013.

[7] KPMG, *Feasibility Study on an Alternative to the Capital Maintenance Regime Established by the Second Company Law Directive 77/91/EEC of 13 December 1976 and an Examination of the Impact on Profit Distribution of the New EU Accounting Regime* (2008).

[8] European Commission, *Results of the External Study on the Feasibility of an Alternative to the Capital Maintenance Regime of the Second Company Law Directive and the Impact of the Adoption of IFRS on Profit Distribution* (2008).

[9] ECLE, 'The Future of European Company Law' (1 May 2012), Columbia Law and Economics Research Paper No. 420 <http://ssrn.com/abstract=2075034>. But it is apparent from European Commission, *Action Plan: European Company Law and Corporate Governance—A Modern Legal Framework for More Engaged Shareholders and Sustainable Companies* (COM(2012) 740) that reforming the Second Company Law Directive is not an immediate priority.

[10] See the rejection of a solvency-based regime for determining the ability of a private company to pay dividends discussed further later in this chapter and in Ch 9.

[11] C-338/06 *European Commission v Spain* [2008] ECR I-10139, para 23 and para 26; Case C-101/08 *Audiolux SA v Groupe Bruxelles Lambert SA (GBL)* [2009] ECR I-09823, para 39.

solvency perspective, which tests ability to pay debts as they fall due and/or by reference to the overall net asset position (total assets less total liabilities, not treating share capital as a liability), the company might well have capacity to make larger payouts without threatening its creditors' expectations of repayment. Article 17 carves out reductions of subscribed capital but under other provisions of the Directive these actions are subject to other formal requirements with regard to shareholder resolutions and the oversight of the court in relation to creditor protection.[12] As further exemplified by the Second Company Law Directive, the payout constraints that form the centrepiece of the legal capital doctrine may be reinforced by rules relating to the raising of capital, including minimum capital requirements and rules regulating the types of consideration that can be accepted in return for shares, and by requirements relating to share buy-backs and other corporate actions that could be indirect forms of payout to shareholders.

A large body of literature has grown up in which many failings of legal capital as a creditor protection device are outlined.[13] The criticisms (which are not necessarily always entirely consistent with each other) include the following:

1. legal capital rules are crude mechanisms that fail to protect creditors because they are poorly designed;

2. legal capital rules are unsophisticated and their intended protective effect is nullified by the efforts of astute legal and financial professionals who, with relative ease, can devise schemes to bypass the rules;

3. legal capital rules impose costs that are not outweighed by their benefits;

4. legal capital rules distort corporate finance decisions by preventing some economically worthwhile transactions or other steps;

5. creditors can protect themselves and there is no need for mandatory rules of company law to perform that function;

6. creditor protection should be addressed primarily through insolvency rather than company law; and

7. flexible *ex post* standards are inherently preferable to rigid *ex ante* rules.

On the other hand, counterarguments put forward by defenders of legal capital include:[14]

1. legal capital provides preventive protection;

2. legal capital has the same effect as a covenant with all the creditors and is thus of value to weaker creditors who cannot negotiate covenants for themselves—furthermore, for all creditors, it avoids the transaction costs involved in negotiating contractual protection;

3. legal capital rules prevent the plundering of a company, especially after a takeover;

---

[12] Arts 34–8.

[13] The literature includes: JA Armour, 'Share Capital and Creditor Protection: Efficient Rules for a Modern Company Law' (2000) 63 MLR 355; J Armour, 'Legal Capital: An Outdated Concept?' (2006) 7 *European Business Organization Law Review* 5; L Enriques and JR Macey, 'Creditors Versus Capital Formation: The Case Against the European Legal Capital Rules' (2001) 86 *Cornell Law Review* 1165; F Kübler, 'The Rules of Capital Under Pressure of the Securities Markets' in KJ Hopt and E Wymeersch (eds), *Capital Markets and Company Law* (Oxford: OUP, 2003) 95; J Rickford (ed), 'Reforming Capital. Report of the Interdisciplinary Group on Capital Maintenance' (2004) 15 *European Business Law Review* 919; EV Ferran, 'Creditors' Interests and 'Core' Company Law' (1999) 20 *Company Lawyer* 314; Ferran, 'The Place for Creditor Protection.'

[14] This list is drawn from the executive summary by Marcus Lutter of an Expert Group on Legal Capital in Europe that was published as a special issue of the *European Company and Financial Law Review*: M Lutter (ed), *Legal Capital in Europe* (Berlin: De Gruyter Recht, 2006).

4   restrictions on distributions protect the management against pressure from shareholders;

5   distributions limited by legal capital have a more long-term effect than a short-term solvency test;

6   a credible shift to greater reliance on solvency tests would require major expansion of liability rules for management and much more rigorous enforcement; and

7   legal capital is deeply rooted in the Continental European legal culture and any change would entail massive upheaval, with associated adaptation costs, for uncertain benefits.

The protection of the interests of long-term creditors is a particular sticking-point in considering options for change. Solvency-based standards operate by requiring the directors of a company to take a view on the company's solvency and to assume personal liability for that view. Solvency tests can be drafted in different ways but typically would require directors to certify that the company is solvent at the time of the payout and for some time thereafter. Since it is not feasible to expect directors to assume personal responsibility for the performance of the company long into the future (when they may no longer be in charge of directing its affairs), a limited time horizon, such as twelve months, is appropriate for the prospective limb of the solvency test. In any case, as Lord Walker noted in *BNY Corporate Trustee Services Ltd v Eurosail-UK 2007-3BL plc*, any attempt to apply a cash flow (ie debts as they fall due) test will become completely speculative once it moves beyond the reasonably near future.[15] How best to factor long-term liabilities into this assessment is a complex and controversial issue.[16] One approach would be to require directors simply to take account of long-term liabilities in determining their company's solvency thereby leaving considerable discretion with the directors as to the weight to be attached to long-term liabilities.[17] Another approach would be to require directors to determine solvency specifically by reference to an accounts-based balance sheet test of an excess of assets over liabilities but this would lead back to the problem that financial statements drawn up under accounting rules that were not designed with creditors' interests primarily in mind are not necessarily a reliable yardstick.[18]

Concerns about longer term solvency issues were an inhibiting factor when the possibility of shifting to a solvency-based payout regime for dividends by private companies was considered in the UK in the reform exercise that preceded the Companies Act 2006. There were worries that the proposed solvency test provided only an assurance of short-term solvency and that this was not a sufficient guarantee of a company's ability to meet its long-term debts, and therefore did not provide adequate protection for creditors. This concern was voiced in the Parliamentary debate on the Companies Bill where a spokesman for the government noted that:

> The solvency test proposed in the amendment would only require the directors to consider debts falling due in the next year, thus allowing the company to pay a dividend even though it had

---

[15]   [2013] UKSC 28, [2013] 1 WLR 1408, [37].

[16]   J Rickford, 'Legal Approaches to Restricting Distributions to Shareholders: Balance Sheet Tests and Solvency Tests' (2006) 7 *European Business Organization Law Review* 135; W Schön, 'Balance Sheet Tests or Solvency Tests— or Both' (2006) 7 *European Business Organization Law Review* 181; W Schön, 'The Future of Legal Capital' (2004) 5 *European Business Organization Law Review* 429.

[17]   That these are matters of judgment is accepted in the UK in the context of the Insolvency Act 1986, s 123 tests of inability to pay debts considered in *BNY Corporate Trustee Services Ltd v Eurosail-UK 2007-3BL plc* [2013] UKSC 28, [2013] 1 WLR 1408. Insolvency Act 1986, s 123(2) provides a so-called 'balance sheet' insolvency test (surplus of liabilities over assets) but this is not to be taken literally and there is no statutory provision which links section 123(2) to the detailed provisions of the Companies Act 2006 as to the form and contents of a company's financial statements.

[18]   Rickford, 'Legal Approaches.'

long term liabilities—such as for pensions—exceeding its assets. Directors would still, of course, need to consider their general duties under Chapter 2 of Part 10 of the [... Act], but there is a real question as to whether this would be sufficient protection for long term creditors.[19]

On the other hand, a solvency-based regime for reductions of capital by private companies was adopted in the Companies Act 2006 and that Act also continued a regime first enacted in predecessor legislation whereby private companies can use capital to fund share buy-backs so long as solvency requirements are satisfied.[20] The inconsistency as between the statutory controls on dividends, reduction of capital, and share buy-backs is odd given that, in economic terms, dividends, reductions of capital, and share buy-backs have much in common and can even be regarded simply as alternative methods of returning value to shareholders that differ only in their incidental features, such as tax treatment. The anomalous outcome in the Companies Act 2006[21] may be related to the fact that dividends are the principal way in which UK companies return value to shareholders and hence the procedures governing the payment of dividends attract particularly close scrutiny. The proposal to move to a solvency test for the determination of private companies' dividend-paying capacity surfaced quite late in the reform process leading up to the Companies Act 2006 and the government was not sure that important questions of principle had been fully addressed.[22] In so far as the pressure for change was linked to developments in accounting, it was felt that there was a case for waiting to see the practical impact of new accounting rules.[23] In addition, notwithstanding EU law did not preclude changes in the law relating to private companies, at the time of the Companies Act 2006 there was thought to be some merit in not rushing ahead of EU-level initiatives on reform of the Second Company Law Directive that might, in due course, overtake national level developments and permit a comprehensive, coherent reform of the rules on dividends for both public and private companies.[24] With the benefit of hindsight the last of these arguments looks unpersuasive: now that the European Commission has deprioritized changing the Second Company Law Directive, not going further in the Companies Act 2006 could be regarded as a missed opportunity.

The Development of the Maintenance of Capital Regime in the UK

In *Trevor v Whitworth*[25] Lord Watson explained that the law prohibits:

> ...every transaction between a company and a shareholder, by means of which the money already paid to the company in respect of his shares is returned to him, unless the Court has authorized the transaction. Paid up capital may be diminished or lost in the course of the company's trading; that is a result which no legislation can prevent; but persons who deal with, and give credit to a limited company, naturally rely upon the fact that the company is trading with a certain amount of capital already paid, as well as upon the responsibility of its members for the capital remaining at call; and they are entitled to assume that no part of the capital which has

---

[19] Lord Sainsbury, *Hansard*, vol 680, col GC48 (20 March 2006).   [20] Companies Act 2006, s 714.
[21] In fact anomalies in the legal procedures governing these variant mechanisms can be found in the laws of many countries: Rickford, 'Legal Approaches,' 144–5.
[22] Lord Sainsbury, *Hansard*, vol 680, col GC 48 (20 March 2006).
[23] Lord Sainsbury, *Hansard*, vol 680, col GC 48 (20 March 2006).
[24] The Appendix to the 'Twenty-Sixth Report of the Delegated Powers and Regulatory Reform Committee' (November 2006) contains a memorandum from the relevant government department (then the Department of Trade and Industry (DTI), now the Department for Business, Innovation and Skills (BIS)) explaining its policy of not making changes to the law in respect of private companies until the position in Europe becomes clearer.
[25] (1887) 12 App Cas 409, HL, 423–4.

been paid into the coffers of the company has been subsequently paid out, except in the legitimate course of its business.

Similarly in *Guinness v Land Corporation of Ireland*[26] Cotton LJ noted that paid up capital could not be returned to shareholders because that would 'take away from the fund to which the creditors have a right to look as that out of which they are to be paid.'

The common law rule prohibiting the return of capital is now reinforced by statutory rules relating to distributions and to reduction of capital. Under Part 23 of the Companies Act 2006, distributions of the company's assets to members must be made only out of profits available for the purpose. 'Profits available for the purpose of a distribution' is a precise statutory concept under Part 23 but, broadly speaking, it excludes share capital and other quasi-capital reserves. Part 23 and its effect are examined separately in Chapter 9. A reduction of capital is not a distribution for the purposes of Part 23.[27] Reductions of capital are regulated instead by chapter 10 of Part 17 of the 2006 Act and are permissible only when confirmed by the court or, in the case of a private company, when supported by a solvency statement given by the directors. The two statutory procedures for the reduction of capital are considered in detail later in this chapter.

Application of the common law rule prohibiting the return of capital to shareholders

Notwithstanding the intervention of statute, the courts continue sometimes to use the common law rule prohibiting the return of capital as the basis for looking through to the substance of corporate actions, howsoever labelled, and striking down those that are inappropriate in the sense that they amount to a fraud on the company's creditors. In the words of Pennycuick J in *Ridge Securities Ltd v IRC*[28] that are frequently cited in this context, the operative principle is that:

> The corporators may take assets out of the company by way of dividend or, with leave of the court, by way of reduction of capital, or in a winding up. They may of course acquire them for full consideration. They cannot take assets out of the company by way of voluntary disposition, however described, and, if they attempt to do so, the disposition is ultra vires the company.

The approach of the courts is illustrated by the following cases.

In *Re Halt Garage (1964) Ltd*[29] a family company was owned and managed by a husband and wife team. The company continued to pay the wife as a director of the company even after it had become apparent that she was seriously ill and would never again play an active role in the management of the company. The company later went into liquidation and, on the application of the liquidator, Oliver J held that the amount of remuneration so paid exceeded what could be regarded as a genuine exercise of the power to pay remuneration. To the extent that the payments exceeded genuine remuneration for the holding of the office of director, they were repayable to the liquidator because they amounted to a disguised return of capital.

---

[26] (1882) 22 Ch D 349, CA, 375. See also *Verner v General and Commercial Investment Trust* [1894] 2 Ch 239, CA, 264 *per* Lindley LJ; *Ammonia Soda Co Ltd v Chamberlain* [1918] 1 Ch 266, CA, 292 *per* Warrington LJ; *Hill v Permanent Trustee Co of New South Wales Ltd* [1930] 720, PC, 731 *per* Lord Russell of Killowen.
[27] Companies Act 2006, s 829(2)(b)(ii).   [28] [1964] 1 WLR 479, 495.
[29] [1982] 3 All ER 1016. See also *Ridge Securities Ltd v IRC* [1964] 1 All ER 275; *Jenkins v Harbour View Courts Ltd* [1966] NZLR 1, NZ CA; *Redweaver Investments Ltd v Lawrence Field Ltd* (1990–91) 5 ACSR 438, NSW EqD.

In *Aveling Barford Ltd v Perion Ltd*[30] the claimant company, at a time when it had no distributable profits, sold some of its property at a price considerably lower than that at which it had been valued by an independent valuer. The purchaser was a company, Perion Ltd, which was controlled by Dr Lee, who was also the controller of the vendor company. Within a year Perion Ltd re-sold the property for a significant profit. The liquidator of Aveling Barford successfully sought to recover the proceeds of sale on the grounds that Perion Ltd held it on constructive trust. The court held that Dr Lee had breached his fiduciary duty to Aveling Barford by selling the property at such a low price and that since Perion Ltd had known of the facts which made this transaction a breach of duty it was liable as a constructive trustee. Hoffmann J dealt with the argument that, if there had been a breach of fiduciary duty by Dr Lee, it was unchallengeable because it had been done with the consent of the shareholders of Aveling Barford by holding that the transaction was not a genuine exercise of the company's power under its memorandum to sell its assets, and that it amounted to an unlawful return of capital which could not be validated by shareholder authorization or ratification. In this case, the purchaser company was not itself a shareholder in the vendor company, although both companies shared the same controller. Hoffmann J held that the fact that the transaction was in favour of a company controlled by, rather than directly to, Dr Lee was irrelevant because the real purpose of the transaction was to benefit Dr Lee. The facts thus fell within the scope of the rule prohibiting the return of capital to shareholders because, by an indirect route, that was exactly the result in that case.[31]

An indirect return of capital was also in issue in *Barclays Bank plc v British & Commonwealth Holdings plc*[32] where a group of banks, acting through a corporate vehicle, was required to buy a company's redeemable preference shares in the event of the company failing to redeem those shares in accordance with their terms. The company gave financial covenants to the banks so that, if it found itself unable to redeem its preference shares, it would also be in breach of covenant to the banks. The economic effect of the arrangement was that the banks had to pay for the shares but could then prove in the company's liquidation as creditors for the amount that they had paid for the shares as the sum due for breach of contract. This arrangement was held to amount to an indirect return of capital, contrary to *Trevor v Whitworth*,[33] on the basis that the rule in that case was wide enough to catch an agreement which was only likely to be called upon in the event of the company's insolvency, and which enabled shareholders in that event to obtain from third parties a payment in an equivalent amount to the payment due from the company, and for the third parties thereupon to become entitled as creditors to seek repayment from the company. Had the decision been otherwise, the effect would have been to allow a claim by one group of shareholders to be converted into a claim by creditors ranking before general shareholders' claims and equally with other creditors.

An unlawful return of capital is ultra vires

In the quotation from the *Ridge Securities* case above, Pennycuick J describes the disposition as being *ultra vires* the company. Ultra vires is an appropriate term in this context because the disposition is contrary to what companies are permitted to do under the general law. Thus in

---

[30] [1989] BCLC 626. See also *Hickson Timber Protection Ltd (in receivership) v Hickson International plc* [1995] 2 NZLR 8, NZ CA, noted RI Barrett, 'Diversion to Shareholders of Proceeds of Sale of Corporate Asset' (1996) 70 ALJ 43; R Grantham, 'Corporate Groups and Informality' [1995] NZLJ 176.

[31] The High Court of Australia has held that a scheme from which shareholders benefit indirectly can amount to an unlawful return of capital: *Australasian Oil Exploration Ltd v Lachbery* (1958) 101 CLR 119, H Ct of Aust.

[32] [1995] BCC 19 (affirmed [1995] BCC 1059, CA) following *Re Walters' Deed of Guarantee* [1933] Ch 321.

[33] (1887) 12 App Cas 409, HL.

MacPherson v European Strategic Bureau Ltd[34] an arrangement involving payments to shareholders that were described as payments for consultancy services, which was entered into at a time when the company was insolvent, was held to be ultra vires because, according to Chadwick LJ:[35]

> In my view, to enter into an arrangement which seeks to achieve a distribution of assets, as if on a winding up, without making proper provision for creditors is, itself, a breach of the duties which directors owe to the company; *alternatively, it is ultra vires the company* (emphasis added). It is an attempt to circumvent the protection which the 1985 Act aims to provide for those who give credit to a business carried on, with the benefit of limited liability, through the vehicle of a company incorporated under that Act.

Buxton LJ agreed:

> It would need a considerable degree of cynicism to think that an arrangement whereunder the corporators depart with the future income leaving the creditors with the debts is for the benefit of the company, even if the beneficiaries hold the whole of the interest in the company; and for the reasons set out by Chadwick LJ such an arrangement is without question *ultra vires* the company.[36]

Ultra vires, in this wide sense, is to be distinguished from ultra vires in the sense of actions falling outside the scope of a company's stated objects. Historically, the ultra vires rule in the latter sense was used by the courts as a creditor protection device, in addition to the rule prohibiting the return of capital to shareholders. Thus in *Trevor v Whitworth* Lord Herschell said:[37]

> The capital may, no doubt, be diminished by expenditure upon and reasonably incidental to all the objects specified. A part of it may be lost in carrying on the business operations authorised. Of this all persons trusting the company are aware, and take the risk. But I think they have a right to rely, and were intended by the Legislature to have a right to rely, on the capital remaining undiminished by any expenditure outside these limits, or by the return of any part of it to the shareholders.

At the time when *Trevor v Whitworth* was decided, having stated objects that defined the limits of a company's capacity was one of the fundamental tenets of company law: anything that fell outside the objects was *ultra vires* and void. The modern position is very different. In practice, companies tend to have very wide objects and the Companies Act 2006 finally took this practice to its endpoint by permitting, for the first time, unrestricted objects.[38] Where objects are stated they 'do not need to be commercial; they can be charitable or philanthropic; indeed, they can be whatever the original incorporators wish, provided that they are legal. Nor is there any reason why a company should not part with its funds gratuitously or for non-commercial reasons if to do so is within its declared objects.'[39] Furthermore, even if a company has restricted objects under its constitution, the validity of an act done by the company cannot be called into question on the ground of lack of capacity by reason of those restricted objects.[40] Whilst constitutional restrictions may limit internally the authority of directors to act on the company's behalf, externally the Companies Act 2006 protects outsiders (as did predecessor companies legislation) by providing that in favour of a person dealing with a company in good faith, the power of the directors to bind the company or authorize

---

[34] [2000] 2 BCLC 683, CA.   [35] At para 48.   [36] At para 60.
[37] (1887) 12 App Cas 409, HL, 415. Also 424 *per* Lord Watson and 433 *per* Lord Macnaghten.
[38] Companies Act 2006, s 31.
[39] *Re Horsley & Weight Ltd* [1982] Ch 442, CA. See also *Rolled Steel Products (Holdings) Ltd v British Steel Corp* [1986] Ch 246, CA.
[40] Companies Act 2006, s 39.

others to do so is deemed to be free of any such constitutional limitation.[41] A person deals with a company for this purpose if he is a party to any transaction or other act to which the company is a party;[42] the inclusion of other acts indicates that this protection is not limited to commercial transactions. The net result of all of this is that the ultra vires rule, in the sense that is related to constitutional limitations, no longer plays a meaningful creditor protection role.

The doctrinal test for distinguishing between genuine transactions and disguised distributions

In *Progress Property Co Ltd v Moorgarth Group Ltd*[43] a company sold a wholly-owned subsidiary to another company. Since all three companies were indirectly controlled by the same individual there was some superficial similarity with the factual scenario in the *Aveling Barford* case. It was alleged that the sale had taken place at an undervalue and that it was therefore a disguised distribution. The sale price had been calculated on a basis that took into account an indemnity believed to have been given by the vendor and from which it was to be released. In fact there was no such indemnity liability and thus nothing from which the vendor could be released.

The Supreme Court determined that the essential issue was one of characterization, bearing in mind that the question was one of substance rather than form and that labels used by the parties were not conclusive. A relentlessly objective test was rejected as being oppressive and unworkable.[44] Lord Walker explained that the court's real task was to inquire into the true purpose and substance of the impugned transaction. This called for an investigation of all the relevant facts, which could include the state of mind of the human beings who were orchestrating the corporate activity. A corporate action structured in the form of an arm's length commercial transaction was the paradigm example of a situation in which subjective intentions were relevant. If the conclusion was that it was a genuine arm's length transaction that had been negotiated in good faith then it would stand, even if the transaction might, with hindsight, appear to have been a bad bargain. However, if the transaction was an improper attempt to extract value by the pretence of an arm's length sale, it would be held unlawful. Either conclusion would depend on a realistic assessment of all the relevant facts and would not be simply a retrospective objective valuation exercise in isolation from all other inquiries. A 'margin of appreciation' had to be allowed.[45] On the facts, even on the assumption that the sale had been at an undervalue, it had been a genuine sale and not an unauthorized disguised distribution.

Gratuitous dispositions to third parties and directors' duties

Gratuitous dispositions otherwise than to, or for the benefit of, shareholders by definition fall outside the scope of the prohibition on returning capital to shareholders but they are, of course, subject to the general framework of company law as well as to provisions of the insolvency legislation relating to voidable preferences and transactions at an undervalue.[46] In *Barclays Bank plc v British & Commonwealth Holdings plc*[47] it was asserted at first instance that there is a fundamental principle of company law established by the cases that

---

[41] Companies Act 2006, s 40.   [42] Companies Act 2006, s 40(2)(a).   [43] [2011] 1 WLR 1, SC.
[44] In favour of this approach, see E Micheler, 'Disguised Returns of Capital—An Arm's Length Approach' [2010] CLJ 151.
[45] At [28] and [31]–[32] *per* Lord Walker, approving *Clydebank Football Club Ltd v Steedman* 2002 SLT 109.
[46] In particular, Insolvency Act 1986, ss 238–9.   [47] [1995] BCC 19 (affirmed [1995] BCC 1059, CA).

no company may make truly gratuitous dispositions of its assets. The judge accepted as correct a submission from counsel that the principle that a company cannot make a gratuitous disposition of its assets save either for the benefit of its business or out of distributable profits with the approval of its shareholders applied very widely. However, in so far as this assertion of a fundamental principle appears to relate to corporate capacity to dispose of assets it is not consistent with other authority that supports the view that a company *can* give away its assets, provided this is permitted by its constitution:[48] the principle, such as it is, is defeasible at the option of the company. Moreover, where a company's constitution restricts gratuitous dispositions, such dispositions may stand where the recipients can claim the benefit of the statutory protection for outsiders provided by the Companies Act 2006, section 40, which, in favour of a person dealing with a company in good faith, deems the power of the directors to bind the company, or to authorize others to do so, to be free of any limitations under the company's constitution.

The so-called principle relating to gratuitous dispositions of assets may be more accurately regarded nowadays as a constraint on directors in the exercise of their powers.[49] Under the Companies Act 2006 directors must act to promote the success of their company for the benefit of its members,[50] subject to a duty developed by case law for directors of insolvent (or nearly insolvent companies) to consider creditors' interests.[51] Under the Companies Act 2006, directors must also act in accordance with the company's constitution and must only exercise powers for the purposes for which they are conferred.[52] For directors to make a gratuitous disposition of assets otherwise than for the benefit of the company would be a breach of these statutory and (in respect of having regard to creditors' interests, where applicable) common law duties.[53] It is generally possible for shareholders to ratify breaches of duty by directors[54] but this rule is subject to exceptions.[55] One exception is that shareholder ratification is not effective in relation to a transaction that constitutes a fraud on a company's creditors[56] and this exception would catch gratuitous dispositions made in breach of duty at a time when a company is insolvent.[57] Although the boundaries of what can (and cannot) be ratified are not entirely clear, in principle the exception should also catch gratuitous dispositions in breach of duty that are funded from undistributable reserves, even though overall solvency

---

[48] In particular *Brady v Brady* [1988] BCLC 20, 38 *per* Nourse LJ.

[49] *ANZ Executors & Trustee Co Ltd v Qintex Australia Ltd* (1990–1) 2 ACSR 676 where McPherson accepted that it was ultra vires in the sense of abuse of power rather than corporate capacity that was relevant in answering the question whether a disposition of the property of the company was made for the benefit and to promote the prosperity of the company. A similar distinction is drawn in *Rolled Steel Products (Holdings) Ltd v British Steel Corp* [1986] Ch 246, CA. See also *MacPherson v European Strategic Bureau Ltd* [2000] 2 BCLC 683, CA.

[50] Companies Act 2006, s 172.

[51] Companies Act 2006, s 172(3) and *West Mercia Safetywear Ltd v Dodd* [1988] BCLC 250. This duty is also recognized in a line of Commonwealth authority including: *Kinsela v Russell Kinsela Pty Ltd (in liq)* (1986) 4 NSWLR 722; *Spies v R* (2000) 201 CLR 603, 636, H Ct Aust; *Nicholson v Permakraft (NZ) Ltd* [1985] 1 NZLR 242, NZ CA. The Canadian Supreme Court has held that directors of a company in the zone of insolvency do not owe a fiduciary duty directly to creditors: *Peoples Department Store v Wise* [2004] 3 SCR 461; R Flannigan, 'Reshaping the Duties of Directors' (2005) 84 *Canadian Bar Review* 365. On the fluctuating situation in US law, see HTC Hu and JL Westbrook, 'Abolition of the Corporate Duty to Creditors' (2007) 107 *Columbia Law Review* 1321; SM Bainbridge, 'Much Ado about Little? Directors' Fiduciary Duties in the Vicinity of Insolvency' (2007) 1 *Journal of Business and Technology Law* 335; RB Campbell and CW Frost, 'Managers' Fiduciary Duties in Financially Distressed Corporations: Chaos in Delaware (and Elsewhere)' (2007) 32 *Journal of Corporation Law* 491.

[52] Companies Act 2006, s 171.

[53] However, note Companies Act 2006, s 247 which overrides s 172 to the extent of authorizing directors to make provision for employees on the cessation or transfer of the company's business.

[54] Companies Act 2006, s 239.

[55] *Aveling Barford Ltd v Perion* [1989] BCLC 626, 631. Companies Act 2006, s 239(7) provides that the section does not affect any rule of law as to acts that are incapable of being ratified by the company.

[56] *Rolled Steel Products Ltd v British Steel Corp* [1986] Ch 246, CA, 296 *per* Slade LJ.

[57] *West Mercia Safetywear Ltd v Dodd* [1988] BCLC 250.

may not be in doubt, because shareholders are not empowered to sanction gifts from capital otherwise than in accordance with the prescribed statutory procedures for reduction of capital.[58]

Reduction of Capital under the Statutory Procedures

A limited company having a share capital can reduce its capital only in accordance with prescribed statutory procedures. Section 641(1)(b) of the Companies Act 2006 provides a procedure for court-approved reductions of capital, which can be used by all limited companies that have a share capital. In addition, section 641(1)(a) provides a procedure for private companies only, whereby they can reduce their capital on the basis of a directors' statement of solvency and court approval is not required. The solvency statement procedure is not made available to public companies because of complications stemming from the UK's obligation to implement Community law. Articles 34 to 38 of the Second Company Law Directive regulate reductions of capital by public companies and Article 36 in particular requires Member States to provide for creditors to have the right in certain circumstances to challenge a reduction in court. Although consideration was given in the lead-up to the Companies Act 2006 to the possibility of extending the solvency statement procedure to public companies, this was eventually ruled out because of concern that the need for additional safeguards to be built into the procedure for public companies in order to satisfy the Second Directive would likely mean that few public companies would use the solvency statement procedure in practice.

Where a choice of procedures is available, that is in the case of private companies, the advantage of the solvency statement procedure is that it is easier, quicker, and cheaper.[59] However, it places a particular onus on the directors of the company through the requirement for a solvency statement, to which criminal sanctions apply if there are no reasonable grounds for the opinions expressed. Evidence from practice suggests that there is reluctance among directors of active trading companies, particularly those with large and/or complex businesses, to put their name to a solvency statement and that many companies continue to opt for the court approval procedure notwithstanding that it is slower and more costly.[60]

Why reduce capital?

A company may find itself in a position where it has assets that are excess to the needs of its business. For example, a rationalization programme may lead a company to decide to sell off certain divisions of the company's business in order to concentrate on its core activities. The cash generated by selling off the divisions may then not be needed by the company to finance what has become a smaller business. A reduction of capital is one of the methods whereby the company may return this surplus to its shareholders.[61] Other ways of returning value to shareholders are share buy-backs (considered in Chapter 8) and special dividends (considered in Chapter 9). The choice between the different methods of returning value will be affected by a range of considerations, including the differences in the tax treatment of the various options and the varying opportunities they offer for managing the shareholder base.[62]

---

[58] *Re George Newman and Co* [1895] 1 Ch 674.

[59] A Pearson and N Chisholm, 'Reductions of Capital: The New Order' (2010) 21 PLC 37.

[60] A Pearson and N Chisholm, 'Reductions of Capital: The New Order' (2010) 21 PLC 37.

[61] eg *Wilsons & Clyde Coal Co Ltd* [1949] AC 462, HL; *Prudential Assurance Co Ltd v Chatterley-Whitfield Collieries Co Ltd* [1949] AC 512, HL.

[62] R Moore, B Ward, B Phillips, and S Stewart, 'Returning Value to Shareholders: Giving Something Back' (2012) 23 PLC 23.

Reductions of capital and buy-backs, but not dividends, can be used to reduce the number of shares in issue. However, a reduction of capital is more formal and complex than other procedures for returning value to shareholders, particularly for public companies because of the requirement for court approval.

As between reductions and buy-backs, a difference, which may be crucial in some circumstances, is that the reduction of capital procedure has an expropriatory dimension—ie it has the potential to be used to pay off shareholders against their wishes—whereas buy-backs are only possible where there are willing sellers. Thus a reduction of capital may be useful in circumstances where the company wants to refinance by paying off a relatively expensive form of financing and replacing it with cheaper financing from a different source.[63]

Another situation where a company may want to reduce its capital is where the share capital recorded in the company's books is no longer reflected by the assets of the company because of trading or other losses that the company has suffered.[64] In this situation the company may want to cancel part of its stated capital without making any payment to its shareholders in order to restore reality to its balance sheet position. If a company in this position did not reduce its capital it would have to make good the losses before it could resume paying dividends to its shareholders.

Another use for the reduction of capital procedure is where the company wishes to convert an undistributable reserve, such as a share premium account, into a reserve that may be capable of being regarded as distributable.[65]

Forms of reduction of capital sanctioned by the Companies Act 2006

Section 641(3) of the Companies Act 2006 allows a limited company with a share capital to reduce its share capital in any way in accordance with the prescribed statutory procedures. In particular, but without prejudice to the general nature of the power, the company may:[66]

1. extinguish or reduce liability on any of its shares in respect of share capital not paid up;

2. either with or without extinguishing liability on any of its shares, cancel any paid up share capital that is lost or unrepresented by available assets; or

3. either with or without extinguishing liability on any of its shares, pay off any paid up share capital that is in excess of the company's wants.

Limitation on the use of solvency statement reduction of capital procedure

Generally speaking, a private company can choose between the court approval procedure and the solvency statement procedure. However, there is one qualification: the solvency statement reduction of capital procedure may not be used if as a result of the reduction there would no longer be any member of the company holding shares other than redeemable shares.[67] This qualification ensures that private companies cannot rely on relatively informal methods to reduce their capital to zero and that such an apparently extreme type of reduction must be overseen by the court. Many reductions of capital do involve the momentary reduction of capital to zero immediately followed by an increase in capital in a recapitalization.[68]

---

[63] As in *Re Hunting plc* [2005] 2 BCLC 211.
[64] eg *Re Jupiter House Investments (Cambridge) Ltd* [1985] BCLC 222, [1985] 1 WLR 975.
[65] As in *Re Ransomes plc* [1999] 1 BCLC 775 (affirmed [1999] 2 BCLC 591, CA).
[66] Companies Act 2006, s 641(4).   [67] Companies Act 2006, s 641(1)(2).
[68] eg *Re MB Group plc* [1989] BCC 684.

The Court Approval Procedure

Special resolution of the shareholders

The first step in a reduction of capital under the court approval procedure is the passing of a special resolution in accordance with the procedure for special resolutions generally.[69] The resolution may be passed as a resolution passed at a meeting or, in the case of a private company, as a written resolution. A special resolution may not provide for a reduction of capital to take effect later than the day on which it has effect in accordance with the 2006 Act.[70]

The oversight of the court in respect of creditors' interests

After the resolution has been passed, the company must then apply to the court for an order confirming the reduction.[71] The court has a discretion whether to confirm a reduction and on what terms, provided that statutory requirements in respect of creditors are satisfied.[72] The statutory creditor protection requirements apply, unless the court otherwise directs, where the reduction involves diminution of liability in respect of unpaid share capital or the payment to a shareholder of any paid up share capital.[73] They also apply in other types of reduction if the court so directs[74] but this would be unusual.[75]

The key statutory creditor protection requirement is that every creditor who would be entitled to prove in the company's liquidation is also entitled to object to the reduction of capital provided he or she can show that there is a real likelihood that the reduction would result in the company being unable to discharge his or her debt or claim when it fell due.[76] The court must settle a list of creditors who are entitled to object.[77] The assessment of a 'real likelihood' requires the objecting creditor to go some way up the probability scale, beyond the merely possible, but short of the probable; the creditor is not required to prove that a future event will happen.[78] The assessment must be grounded in the facts as they are known and should not be speculative (the factual element).[79] The assessment involves looking forward for a period in relation to which it is sensible to make predictions (the temporal element).[80] In *Re Liberty International plc* Norris J noted that for private companies directors are required to look forward for twelve months and without suggesting that implicitly the same period applies when the sanction of the court is necessary, indicated that in any given case there would be a natural temporal boundary beyond which sensible assessment of likelihood would not be possible.[81] The statutory procedure for drawing up the list of creditors is underpinned by criminal sanctions: an officer of the company commits an offence if intentionally or recklessly he or she conceals the name of a creditor entitled to object to the reduction or misrepresents the nature or amount of the debt or claim of any creditor, or if he or she is knowingly involved in any such concealment or misrepresentation.[82] If a creditor whose name is entered on the list does not consent, this blocks the court from confirming the reduction unless it is satisfied that

---

[69] Companies Act 2006, s 283.　　[70] Companies Act 2006, s 641(5).　　[71] Companies Act 2006, s 645(1).
[72] *British and American Corp v Couper* [1894] AC 399, HL, 403–6 *per* Lord Herschell LC; *Poole v National Bank of China* [1907] AC 229, HL, 239 *per* Lord Macnaghten.
[73] Companies Act 2006, s 645(2)–(3).　　[74] Companies Act 2006, s 645(4).
[75] *Re Meux's Brewery Ltd* [1919] 1 Ch 28 provides a rare example.　　[76] Companies Act 2006, s 646.
[77] Companies Act 2006, s 646(2).　　[78] *Re Liberty International plc* [2010] 2 BCLC 665.
[79] *Re Liberty International plc* [2010] 2 BCLC 665.　　[80] *Re Liberty International plc* [2010] 2 BCLC 665.
[81] *Re Liberty International plc* [2010] 2 BCLC 665. See also *BNY Corporate Trustee Services Ltd v Eurosail-UK 2007-3BL plc* [2013] UKSC 28, [2013] 1 WLR 1408, [37] *per* Lord Walker (that any attempt to apply a cash flow (ie debts as they fall due) test will become completely speculative once the court has to move beyond the reasonably near future).
[82] Companies Act 2006, s 647.

the creditor's debt or claim has been discharged, determined, or secured.[83] The court may dispense with a creditor's consent if the company secures payment of the creditor's debt or claim by appropriating the amount of the debt or, where the debt or claim is not admitted and the company is not willing to provide for it in full, or it is contingent or not ascertained, an amount fixed by the court.[84]

In practice, reductions of capital are typically structured with in-built creditor protection with a view to persuading the court to order the disapplication of the statutory protections where they would otherwise apply. One such form of in-built creditor protection is for the company to demonstrate that it has, and after the reduction will continue to have, sufficient cash and readily realizable investments to pay all of its existing creditors, including its contingent creditors. Another is for the company to arrange for a bank to guarantee repayment of its creditors' debts. The court will also dispense with the statutory creditor protection requirements where, or to the extent that, creditors have already consented to the reduction. Such is the prevalence of self-help arrangements that in *Royal Scottish Assurance plc, Petitioner*[85] Lord Glennie was prompted to remark that since 1949 it has been the invariable practice of the Scottish and English courts to disapply the requirement for a list of creditors on obtaining satisfactory assurances that their interests had been protected.

The oversight of the court in respect of shareholders' interests

Although not specifically mentioned in the Companies Act 2006, it is clear from case law that a court which is asked to confirm a reduction of capital will also be concerned to ensure that shareholders are properly treated. The court seeks to apply broad standards of fairness, reasonableness, and equity.[86] It will be concerned to see that the shareholders had the matter properly explained to them so that when it came to the general meeting at which they passed the special resolution they were fully informed about what they were doing.[87] The court will also be concerned to see that the reduction has a discernible purpose and, in establishing this, the applicant company has a duty of full and frank disclosure to the court.[88]

Where a company's share capital is divided into more than one class of shares, it is possible that a reduction of capital may impinge on class rights. Case law relating to the court approval reduction of capital procedure establishes that the court has jurisdiction to confirm a reduction notwithstanding that it involves a departure from the legal rights of the classes for the court's power to confirm a reduction is perfectly general.[89] However, this general power is qualified by the Companies Act 2006, section 641(6), which provides that the statutory procedure has effect subject to any provision of the company's articles restricting or prohibiting the reduction of share capital. In *Re Northern Engineering Industries plc*,[90] where the articles specifically provided that the rights attached to any shares were to be deemed to be varied by the reduction of the capital paid up on those shares, Millett LJ, with whom the other members of the Court of Appeal agreed, described the separate class consent of the preference shareholders as a 'prerequisite' of a proposed reduction of capital and held that the Court had no jurisdiction to confirm the reduction in the absence of such approval.

In the absence of an express deeming provision such as that in *Re Northern Engineering*, reference must be made to a body of case law on class rights to determine whether the structure of a proposed reduction of capital involves a variation or a fulfilment of the rights

---

[83] Companies Act 2006, s 648(2).   [84] Companies Act 2006, s 646(4)–(5).   [85] 2011 SLT 264, at [8].
[86] *Scottish Insurance Corp v Wilsons & Clyde Coal Co Ltd* [1949] AC 462, HL.
[87] *Re Ratners Group plc* [1988] BCLC 685, 688.   [88] *Re Ransomes plc* [1999] 2 BCLC 591, CA.
[89] eg, *British and American Corpn v Couper* [1894] AC 399.   [90] [1994] BCC 618, CA.

attaching to a particular class of shares. Where the company's share capital comprises ordinary shares and preference shares that carry rights to a preferential dividend at a specified rate and priority with regard to the return of capital but no further rights to participate and no special deeming terms, it accords with the class rights of the preference shares to repay those shares first on a reduction of capital.[91] The holders of the preference shares cannot therefore prevent the company from paying them off and refinancing more cheaply from an alternative source. The converse in respect of entitlements applies in a reduction of capital involving no repayment but merely a cancellation of shares: it accords with their respective class rights for the ordinary shares, rather than the preference shares, to absorb this loss.[92]

A class consent to a reduction of capital involving a variation of class rights may not be effective if those who voted in favour did not act in the interests of the class as a whole. In *Re Holders Investment Trust Ltd*[93] a class meeting of preference shareholders approved a reduction of capital that varied their class rights but this approval was held to be ineffective because the majority preference shareholders were held to have acted in what they considered to be their own best interests without asking themselves what was in the interests of the class as a whole. However, it is obviously difficult for the court to scrutinize too closely the motives that lead to votes being cast in any particular way and it is questionable how far this intervention by the court is compatible in any event with the principle that a vote attaching to a share is a right of property which the shareholder is free to exercise as he or she thinks fit.

General powers of the court

The court can confirm a reduction on such terms and conditions as it thinks fit. The court may order that the fact of reduction be indicated by the company adding to its name as its last words the phrase 'as reduced' for a specified period.[94] The court may also order the company to publish the reasons for the reduction of capital or such other reasons in regard to it as the court thinks expedient, with a view to giving proper information to the public, and (if the court thinks fit) the causes which led to the reduction.[95]

Registration

A copy of the order of the court, together with a statement of capital (approved by the court) setting out details of the company's altered share capital must be registered with the registrar of companies.[96] The registrar must certify registration of the order and statement of capital and this certificate is conclusive evidence that all the requirements of the Act with respect to the reduction of capital have been complied with and that the company's altered share capital is as stated in the statement of capital.[97] Notice of the registration must be published in such manner as the court may direct.[98] The reduction of capital takes effect ordinarily on the registration of the order and statement of capital but where the reduction of capital forms part of a scheme of arrangement under Part 26 of the Companies Act 2006, it takes effect either on delivery of the order and statement of capital to the registrar or, if the court so orders, on the registration of the order and statement.[99]

---

[91] *Scottish Insurance Corp v Wilsons & Clyde Coal Co Ltd* [1949] AC 462, HL; *Re Saltdean Estate Co Ltd* [1968] 1 WLR 1844; *House of Fraser plc v ACGE Investments Ltd* [1987] AC 387, HL.
[92] *Re Floating Dock of St Thomas Ltd* [1895] 1 Ch 691.   [93] [1971] 1 WLR 583.
[94] Companies Act 2006, s 648(4).   [95] Companies Act 2006, s 648(3).
[96] Companies Act 2006, s 649(1)–(2).   [97] Companies Act 2006, s 649(5)–(6).
[98] Companies Act 2006, s 649(4).   [99] Companies Act 2006, s 649(3).

Where allotted capital is reduced below the authorized minimum

Where a reduction of capital would bring the allotted share capital below the authorized minimum for a public company (currently set at £50,000), the normal procedures for registration of the reduction are modified. The registrar must not register the reduction whilst the company remains a public company unless the court otherwise directs.[100] The company should re-register as a private company. There is a special expedited procedure for the re-registration of a public company in these circumstances where the court oversees constitutional changes to be made in connection with the re-registration and a special resolution of the shareholders is not required.[101]

Effect of a court-approved reduction of capital

The effect of a reduction of capital is to relieve a member of the company (past or present) of any liability in respect of any share to any call or contribution exceeding the amount that remains unpaid on the share calculated by reference to the statement of capital showing the altered share capital.[102] This is qualified in one respect in order to protect creditors who, by reason of their ignorance of the proceedings or of their nature and effect, were not entered on the list of creditors. If, after the reduction of capital, the company is unable to pay the amount of such a creditor's debt or claim, members of the company at the time the reduction took effect are then liable to contribute for the payment of that debt or claim an amount not exceeding that which they would have been liable to contribute if the company had commenced to be wound up on the day before that date.[103]

Notwithstanding that the creation of distributable reserves is one of the key reasons for a company to choose to reduce its capital, the default position under the Companies Act 2006 is that a reserve arising from a reduction of capital is not distributable.[104] However, this is subject to provision to the contrary in a statutory instrument made under the primary legislation. The relevant Order provides that if a limited company having a share capital reduces its capital and the reduction is confirmed by order of court, the reserve arising from the reduction is treated as a realized profit unless the court orders otherwise.[105]

Reduction of Capital under the Solvency Statement Procedure: Private Companies Only

Special resolution of the shareholders and class consents

A special resolution is also required under the solvency statement procedure.[106] Since the possibility for the court to approve a reduction of capital that departs from the legal entitlements attaching to shares is not available under this procedure, class consents should be obtained where a reduction of capital is structured in such a way as to constitute a variation of class rights.

---

[100] Companies Act 2006, s 650. On the relevant calculations in circumstances in which a public company has allotted share capital denominated in more than one currency, see The Companies (Authorised Minimum) Regulations 2009, SI 2009/2425, reg 3.

[101] Companies Act 2006, s 651. The normal re-registration procedure, in Companies Act 2006, ss 97–101, requires a special resolution.

[102] Companies Act 2006, s 652.   [103] Companies Act 2006, s 653.   [104] Companies Act 2006, s 654(1).

[105] The Companies (Reduction of Share Capital) Order 2008, SI 2008/1915, art 3.

[106] Companies Act 2006, s 641(a).

Solvency statement

The special resolution must be supported by a solvency statement made by the directors not more than fifteen days before the date of the special resolution.[107] The solvency statement must be made available to members when they vote on the resolution. Where the resolution is proposed as a written resolution, a copy of the solvency statement must be sent to every eligible member at or before the time when the proposed resolution is sent or submitted.[108] Where the resolution is to be proposed at a meeting, a copy of the solvency statement must be made available for inspection by members of the company throughout the meeting.[109] Failure to observe the procedural requirements to make the solvency statement available to members will not affect the validity of the special resolution.[110] The sanction is that defaulting officers of the company commit an offence if they deliver a solvency statement to the registrar that was not provided to the members.[111] Furthermore, if directors choose to propose a resolution for the reduction of capital without making the solvency statement available, they run the risk of the resolution being vetoed by members.

Contents of solvency statement

A solvency statement for the purposes of the reduction of capital procedure is a statement in writing that each of the directors (a) has formed the opinion, as regards the company's position at the date of the statement, that there is no ground on which the company could then be found to be unable to pay (or otherwise discharge) its debts and (b) has also formed the opinion that the company will be able to pay (or otherwise discharge) its debts as they fall due during the year immediately following that date.[112] If it is intended to wind up the company within twelve months of the date of the statement, the prospective opinion in (b) is modified and must relate to the ability to pay debts in full within twelve months of the commencement of the winding up.[113] In forming their opinions, the directors must take account of all of the company's liabilities, including any contingent or prospective liabilities.[114] A requirement to 'take account' of contingent and prospective liabilities does not mean that the directors must simply take them at their full face value since future liabilities must be discounted for contingencies and deferment.[115] In particular a prospective liability that will not become due for a long time would not threaten the ability of a company (provided it is not wound up during the year) to pay its debts that are due or will become due in the year ahead. The solvency statement must be made by all the directors of a company. Thus a director who is unable or unwilling to join in the making of a solvency statement would have to resign or be removed from office before that procedure could be used.

---

[107] Companies Act 2006, s 642(1).   [108] Companies Act 2006, s 642(2).
[109] Companies Act 2006, s 642(3).   [110] Companies Act 2006, s 642(4).
[111] Companies Act 2006, s 644(7).
[112] Companies Act 2006, s 643 and The Companies (Reduction of Share Capital) Order 2008, SI 2008/1915, art 2.
[113] Companies Act 2006, s 643(1)(b)(i).   [114] Companies Act 2006, s 643(2).
[115] *BNY Corporate Trustee Services Ltd v Eurosail-UK 2007-3BL plc* [2013] UKSC 28, [2013] 1 WLR 1408. This case concerned the so-called 'balance sheet' test for winding up in Insolvency Act 1986, s 123(2). It was observed that the cash flow test in s 123(1)(e) involves an element of futurity even though a duty to take account of contingent or prospective liabilities does not appear on the face of the statute: [34] *per* Lord Walker. See also P Walton, ' "Inability to Pay Debts": Beyond the Point of No Return' [2013] JBL 212. In spite of the differences in the wording of the relevant statutory provisions, the *Eurosail* analysis of the appropriate treatment of contingent or prospective liabilities is instructive for the purposes of Companies Act 2006, s 643 which imposes an express duty to take account of such liabilities in the context of a cash flow test limited temporally to one year.

Sanctions in respect of false solvency statements

Making a statutory statement without having reasonable grounds for the opinions expressed in it is a criminal offence for which the maximum punishment is imprisonment for up to two years.[116] The Companies Act 2006 does not specify civil sanctions for making a false or inaccurate solvency statement. Since the provision of a defective solvency statement would mean that the statutory procedures for a lawful reduction of capital have not been followed, the common law rules that the reduction is void,[117] that the responsible directors are in breach of their duties to the company,[118] and that recipient shareholders may be held liable to repay any capital that has been distributed to them[119] presumably apply.

Registration requirements relating to the solvency statement procedure

The special resolution for the reduction of capital must be delivered to the registrar within fifteen days after it is passed or made in accordance with the general procedures governing the delivery of special resolutions.[120] In addition, the solvency statement and a statement of capital must also be delivered to the registrar within fifteen days of the passing of the resolution.[121] The registrar must register these documents on receipt and the resolution does not take effect until those documents are registered.[122] There must also be delivered to the registrar, within the same time period, a statement by the directors confirming that the solvency statement was made not more than fifteen days before the date on which the resolution was passed and was properly provided to members.[123] These various registration obligations are underpinned by criminal sanctions[124] but it is expressly provided that the validity of a resolution for the reduction of capital is not affected by compliance failures.[125]

Effect of a reduction of capital under the solvency statement procedure

After a reduction of capital, the members cease to be liable for calls or other contributions as regards the amount by which the nominal amount of their shares has been reduced.[126]

The prima facie statutory rule that a reserve arising from a reduction of capital is not distributable also applies to reductions effected under the solvency statement procedure, but as with court approved reductions, this is subject to any provision that may be made by order under section 654 of the Companies Act 2006. Under the relevant Order, a reserve arising from a reduction of capital under the solvency statement procedure is treated as a realized profit.[127]

Reductions of Capital and Schemes of Arrangement: Two Case Studies

A scheme of arrangement is a statutory procedure under the Companies Act 2006, Part 26, whereby a company may make a compromise or arrangement with its members or creditors (or any class of them). A scheme of arrangement under Part 26 involves several steps

---

[116] Companies Act 2006, s 643(4)–(5).
[117] *MacPherson v European Strategic Bureau Ltd* [2000] 2 BCLC 683, CA.
[118] *Aveling Barford Ltd v Perion Ltd* [1989] BCLC 626.　　　[119] *Re Halt Garage (1964) Ltd* [1982] 3 All ER 1016.
[120] Companies Act 2006, ss 29–30.　　　[121] Companies Act 2006, s 644.
[122] Companies Act 2006, s 644(3)–(4).　　　[123] Companies Act 2006, s 644(5).
[124] Companies Act 2006, s 644(8)–(9).　　　[125] Companies Act 2006, s 644(6).
[126] Companies Act 2006, s 652.
[127] The Companies (Reduction of Share Capital) Order 208, SI 2008/1915, art 3(2).

including the approval or sanction of the court. The court has an unfettered discretion and thus its sanction is not a formality or a rubber stamp. The subject matter of the scheme must be such that the court will approve it. There must be a genuine compromise or arrangement[128] and it must be such that an intelligent and honest person, a member of the class concerned and acting in respect of his or her own interest, might reasonably approve.[129] Procedural requirements relating to the holding of meetings of members/creditors must also be satisfied and there must be no coercing of the minority.[130] Subject to these considerations, a scheme of arrangement can be used to achieve a wide range of purposes, including acquisitions and demergers,[131] group reorganizations, for example, to insert a new holding company on top of an existing group, and other corporate restructurings that may involve, as part of a larger set of arrangements, a return of capital to shareholders. The use of a scheme of arrangement in conjunction with a reduction of capital merits examination in the context of this chapter.

In outline, the steps involved in a scheme of arrangement are as follows. After a compromise or arrangement is proposed between the company and its creditors or members (for the purposes of links with the reduction of capital procedures we are concerned with members' schemes), or any class of them,[132] the formal start of the procedure is the convening of a meeting of members by the court in accordance with sections 896–898 of the Companies Act 2006. The court is empowered to summon a meeting as it directs. With the notice summoning the meeting, a statement i) explaining the effect of the scheme; ii) setting out the material interests of directors, if any; and iii) explaining the effect of the scheme on those interests in so far as it differs from the effect on like interests of other persons, must also be sent to the members. The explanatory statement must be fair and, so far as possible, give all information reasonably necessary to enable the recipient to determine how to vote. Before summoning a meeting, the court has to be satisfied that the scheme has sufficient general support to have a prospect of success and that the proposed division of the members into one or more voting classes appears to be correct. At a meeting properly summoned, a majority in number representing 75 per cent in value of the members or each class of them (as the case may be), must agree to the compromise or arrangement. The second stage involves the detailed analysis by the court of the proposed scheme and the procedure that led to its approval. At this stage, the court has to be satisfied on a number of matters: that the approval of the scheme was reasonable (ie such that an intelligent and honest person, a member of the class concerned, acting in respect of his or her interests might reasonably approve), that there was sufficient class representation and whether those attending the meeting and the statutory majority acted bona fide, and that the scheme complies with the statutory provisions contained in Part 26 of the Companies Act 2006 and is in overall compliance with the law. The court has a wide discretion and it is not obliged to sanction a scheme even if the majority had approved it. The main advantage of a scheme of arrangement is that it is a concerted procedure that is binding on all members of each class able to vote on the scheme, if the approval of the relevant majority of each class is obtained and the scheme is sanctioned by the court. In addition, schemes can address a wide range of issues and are very flexible. Disadvantages include the fact that the statutory procedure can be burdensome and expensive.

---

[128] *Re NFU Development Trust Ltd* [1973] 1 All ER 135.

[129] These well-established principles are regularly cited, including in *re TDG plc* [2009] 1 BCLC 445; *re Halcrow Holdings Ltd* [2011] EWHC 3662 (Ch).

[130] *Re TDG plc* [2009] 1 BCLC 445; *re Halcrow Holdings Ltd* [2011] EWHC 3662 (Ch).

[131] eg, *Re Liberty International plc* [2010] 2 BCLC 665.   [132] Companies Act 2006, s 895(1).

We can now move on to consider examples of where a scheme of arrangement has been used in conjunction with a reduction of capital.

Re Uniq

This examination can usefully be conducted with reference first to a case study involving the decision in *Re Uniq plc*.[133] *Re Uniq* involved a listed company that found itself crippled by a huge deficit on its pension fund. Faced with the prospect of insolvency, the directors of the company proposed a scheme of arrangement to achieve the goal of divesting the business of the pension fund liability. The main steps in the scheme involved the shareholders in the company giving up 90.2 per cent of their equity in favour of a new company (Newco) and the assumption by Newco of the company's pension scheme liabilities. The intention was for Newco eventually to go into administration with pensioners being protected by the Pension Protection Fund in regard to the shortfall in the fund. Shareholders would give up most of their equity in exchange for the company being discharged from its obligations under the pension scheme, thus leaving them with one-tenth of their original shareholding but in a company unencumbered by the pension fund liability. The scheme had the approval of the pensions regulator, the Pension Protection Fund, and the trustee of the pension scheme.

As part of the restructuring of which the scheme was a part, Uniq's share capital needed to be reorganized, first by a subdivision of existing shares and a bonus issue of new shares paid up from the share premium account, and then by a reduction of capital in the form of a cancellation for no consideration of 100 out of every 101 ordinary shares held following the subdivision and bonus issue. This reduction of capital was necessary in order to give Newco its 90.2 per cent shareholding in the company. The company gave the usual form of undertaking for the protection of creditors who did not agree to the reduction to treat the reserve resulting from the cancellation as non-distributable for so long as any liabilities as at the date of the reduction remained undischarged.

Procedurally, the process of implementing the Uniq scheme of arrangement involved the convening by the court of a meeting of the members of the company under the Companies Act 2006, section 896. In order for the scheme to be approved by the court, section 899(1) requires the scheme to be approved by a majority in number representing 75 per cent in value of the members voting at the meeting. Of the 1,695 members holding 58,333,463 shares who voted at the meeting, 1,646 members holding 58,290,359 voted to approve the scheme. The turnout by number was 14.8 per cent. In sanctioning the scheme, Richards J noted that the court is concerned to see that the class to be bound by the scheme was fairly represented at the meeting. Depending on the circumstances, a low turn-out in terms of value or number could be a matter of concern. However, against the background of a history in which Uniq had an unusually high number of members with very small shareholdings, it was neither a surprise nor a matter of concern that the turn-out by members was not larger. As for the requirement for a compromise or arrangement, Richards J accepted that if members or creditors gave up all their rights and received no benefit, this element would not be satisfied. However, he also determined that it was to the wider context of the restructuring that regard had to be given in order to determine whether there was a fair compromise or arrangement. Whilst it was the case that looking in isolation at the terms of the scheme itself, the existing members would see their 100 per cent equity interest diluted to 9.8 per cent, without any benefit to Uniq or themselves, on completion of the restructuring a very substantial benefit would be conferred on Uniq and, in addition, the existing members, though significantly diluted, would retain an interest in a viable company. Richards J concluded that it would be artificial to confine the analysis to the terms of the scheme itself when the scheme formed an integral part of a restructuring which conferred substantial benefit on the members bound by the scheme.[134]

The convening of the court meeting to approve the Uniq scheme of arrangement was in addition to the meeting of the company required by the Companies Act, section 641 for the passing of a special resolution to approve the reduction of capital. The confirmation of the court of the resolution to reduce capital was also a distinct stage in the process separate from the court hearing to sanction the scheme.

Prior to the scheme of arrangement, Uniq's shares had been listed on the Official List of the London Stock Exchange. This listing was cancelled to accommodate the restructuring, and the shares were subsequently admitted to the Alternative Investment Market. Thereafter the company was acquired in a takeover by a rival business, the Greencore Group.

Cape Group

The other case study that has been selected to demonstrate the use of a scheme of arrangement in conjunction with a reduction of capital involves a group reorganization conducted by the Cape group of companies in 2011.[135] Whereas the Uniq case study had certain quite distinctive features, this example is more mainstream and is indicative of the relatively common use of a scheme of arrangement along with a reduction of capital to introduce a new holding company into a corporate group.

Under the Cape scheme, the shareholders in Old Cape became holders of the New Cape Shares and Old Cape became a subsidiary of New Cape. The mechanics of the exchange involved the cancellation of the Old Cape shares by way of a reduction of capital, giving rise to a reserve which was then used to pay up new ordinary shares in Old Cape that were issued to New Cape. The rights attaching to the New Cape shares were substantially the same as those attaching to the Old Cape shares and a New Cape shareholder in all material respects had the same voting rights and the same proportionate interest in the profits, net assets, and dividends of the Cape Group as he or she had as an Old Cape shareholder. The commercial drivers of the reorganization were that the directors had decided to move from AIM to the Official List and as part of the process for the transfer had closely examined the structure of the Cape Group. This led them to conclude that the geographic mix of the Cape Group's business had become increasingly international, that the future growth of the business would come primarily from operations in international markets, particularly the Pacific Rim and Far East regions, that certain tax incentives could be secured in Singapore, and that Cape and its shareholders would be better served through an international holding company structure that would best support the Group's operational and financial management. The Board determined that the most appropriate structure was the new Group holding company (New Cape) to be Jersey-incorporated and UK listed, with its tax residence in Singapore.

---

[134] Agreeing with the approach in *Re Bluebrook Ltd* [2010] 1 BCLC 338.

[135] This account in the text is derived from the Scheme Circular and Prospectus (May 2011) and related regulatory announcements. The Cape Group provides an especially fruitful source of examples of the use of schemes of arrangement in that it had previously used a creditors' scheme of arrangement to resolve uncertainties relating to future asbestos-related claims (for litigation arising in relation to that scheme, see *Re Cape plc* [2007] 2 BCLC 546).

After the scheme, there was a further reduction of capital, this time by New Cape, effected in accordance with Jersey law. The New Cape reduction of date created distributable reserves in the accounts of New Cape. This was achieved through the cancellation of the entire amount standing to the credit of New Cape's share premium account.

Exceptional Reduction of Capital Procedures

Reduction of capital following redenomination of shares

The Companies Act 2006 allows companies to redenominate their share capital.[136] The redenomination process may result in shares that are denominated in awkward fractions of the new currency and, in that case, companies may wish to adjust the share capital in order to achieve shares with nominal values that are in whole units of the new currency. Companies can achieve this result by increasing the nominal value of the shares (with a capitalization of reserves up to the amount by which the capital is increased).

The 2006 Act also introduced another procedure whereby a company can reduce its share capital (but not its overall undistributable reserves) in order to adjust the nominal value of redenominated shares to obtain more suitable values.[137] This special procedure requires a special resolution of the company but neither a solvency statement from the directors nor court approval is required. The amount by which a company's share capital is reduced must be transferred to a redenomination reserve, which may be applied in paying up fully paid bonus shares but which must otherwise be treated as if it were part of the company's share capital.[138] The amount by which a company is allowed to reduce its share capital under this procedure is limited to 10 per cent of the nominal value of the company's allotted share capital immediately after the reduction.[139] A reduction of capital in connection with redenomination must be notified to the registrar and, in the usual way, the notification must be accompanied by a statement of capital.[140]

Reduction of capital pursuant to an order of the court

Various sections of the Companies Act 2006 empower the court to grant remedial orders providing for the purchase by the company of the shares of any member and for a consequential reduction of the company's capital.[141]

Reduction of capital in respect of forfeited or acquired shares

A public company that forfeits shares for non-payment of calls or instalments pursuant to its articles or accepts shares surrendered in lieu of forfeiture must either dispose of such shares, or cancel them and diminish the amount of the share capital by their nominal value within three years.[142] The steps to cancel the forfeited or surrendered shares and

---

[136] Companies Act 2006, s 622.   [137] Companies Act 2006, s 626.   [138] Companies Act 2006, s 628.

[139] Companies Act 2006, s 626(4). See Second Company Law Directive, Art 37, which permits Member States to exclude from ordinary reduction procedures a reduction in the subscribed capital whose purpose is to include sums of money in a reserve provided that, following this operation, the amount of such reserve is not more than 10 per cent of the reduced subscribed capital.

[140] Companies Act 2006, s 627.

[141] Companies Act 2006, s 996(2)(e) (relief from unfairly prejudicial conduct), s 98(5) (relief in respect of re-registration of a public company as a private company), s 721(6) (relief in respect of a redemption or purchase of shares from capital by a private company), and s 759(5) (relief in respect of breach of the prohibition of public offers of securities by a private company).

[142] Companies Act 2006, s 662.

to diminish the share capital figure can be taken by the directors without recourse to the general reduction of capital procedures.[143] This dispensation also applies where a public company acquires any of its own fully paid shares otherwise than for valuable consideration or has a beneficial interest in shares acquired by a nominee or other person in circumstances where the company is required either to dispose of the shares or to cancel them.[144] However, where shares are bought back or redeemed in accordance with the main statutory procedures governing redeemable shares and share buy-backs, the consequential adjustments to share capital and other undistributable reserves are governed by their own dedicated statutory framework.[145]

---

[143] Companies Act 2006, s 662(4).   [144] Companies Act 2006, s 662.
[145] Companies Act 2006, Pt 18, chs 3–7. See further ch 8.

8

Share Buy-backs and Redeemable Shares

Introduction

The Companies Act 2006 contains a general rule prohibiting the acquisition by limited companies of their own shares[1] but the impact of this ban is attenuated by other provisions in the Act whereby they are permitted to purchase their own shares and also to issue redeemable shares.[2] The law has been progressively relaxed over the years so as to extend the range of financing options available to the corporate sector and to increase flexibility but the statutory powers whereby buy-backs and redeemable shares are permitted remain subject to restrictions that are intended to prevent abuse that would prejudice creditors or discriminate against groups of shareholders.

Arguments For and Against Allowing Companies Share Buy-back/Redeemable Share Issuance Powers[3]

To attract external investors

A company whose shares are not actively traded is a less attractive investment prospect to external investors because of the risk of being permanently locked into that investment. Whilst the other existing shareholders are the persons who are most likely to be interested in acquiring the shares of an investor who wants to leave the company, and indeed they may have pre-emption rights in respect of the shares under the company's articles, their personal circumstances may be such that they are unwilling or unable to commit more of their own resources to an investment in the company. The risk of being locked into an investment in shares that are not actively traded is lessened if the company is able to act as an alternative purchaser and, by being able to offer this possibility, smaller companies may find it easier to raise share capital from external sources than would otherwise be the case.

Redeemable shares offer the most comfort to external investors who are concerned about becoming locked into their investment; although investors are not absolutely guaranteed the return of their capital, since this will depend on the company having available funds at the time of redemption, by holding redeemable shares they are, broadly speaking, assured of an exit from the company provided it remains prosperous.[4]

---

[1] Companies Act 2006, s 658.

[2] The maintenance of capital rules do not apply to unlimited companies but they are subject to the distribution rules in Companies Act 2006, Pt 23. This means that unlimited companies can purchase their own shares but must finance this from distributable profits as defined by Pt 23.

[3] A Dhanani and R Roberts, *Corporate Share Repurchases: The Perceptions and Practices of UK Financial Managers and Corporate Investors* (Edinburgh: Institute of Chartered Accountants of Scotland, 2009).

[4] Arrangements whereby a company tries to guarantee that investors in its redeemable shares will obtain a capital payment when the shares are due to be redeemed even though the company itself may be insolvent (eg by arranging for a third party to buy the shares in that event) need to be examined closely for potential maintenance of capital and financial assistance concerns. See *Barclays Bank plc v British & Commonwealth Holdings plc* [1995] BCC 19 (affirmed [1995] BCC 1059, CA).

To facilitate exit

Being able to sell the shares back to the company also offers a way of unlocking the investment made by a proprietor of a small business who subsequently wishes to retire. The estate of a dead shareholder may similarly benefit from the company being able to purchase the shares. Where the management of a smaller company is paralyzed because of a dispute between its proprietors, for the company to buy one faction's shares may be a way of resolving the deadlock without recourse to litigation (probably a petition under section 994 of the Companies Act 2006 for relief from unfair prejudice).

To structure a temporary loss of control

By issuing redeemable shares the controllers of a company can raise share capital without a permanent dilution of their controlling stake.

To return value to shareholders

Buying back shares is one way of returning to shareholders surplus cash (sometimes termed 'free cash flow') that the company itself is unable to invest efficiently in profitable investment projects.[5] This argument for share buy-backs presupposes that corporate managers will do a good job of distinguishing between value-enhancing and non-value-enhancing investment opportunities. Miscalculations could increase dependency on debt, reduce corporate liquidity and even lead to underinvestment in long-term research and development.

In circumstances in which a company does have cash reserves that are genuinely surplus to requirements, a buy-back of shares can prove to be a particularly useful application of that surplus because it can have a positive impact on some of the performance ratios that are commonly used by analysts and investors to assess corporate performance. The performance of a listed company is commonly assessed by reference to its earnings per share, ie the profits which are attributable to equity shareholders divided by the number of equity shares in issue. Buying back shares will improve this figure provided the positive effect of the reduction in the number of shares is not outweighed by the negative effect on the company's profits of the loss of interest on the cash used to finance the buy-back. Certain companies, in particular property and investment companies, are also commonly measured by the yardstick of net assets per shares, ie the net assets divided by the number of equity shares in issue. Again, a buy-back of shares can improve this figure.

Although it was the 1981 companies legislation that first permitted UK companies to purchase their own shares, it was not until the 1990s that this method of returning value to shareholders came to be extensively used in UK market practice. This was a time when factors such as the ending of recession and the existence of a largely dormant takeover market combined to create a build-up of surplus cash in the corporate sector. New trends in techniques for returning value, which were strongly influenced by tax considerations,[6] brought share buy-backs into vogue. It has been estimated that by 2006 British companies spent £46 billion

[5] Other methods are dividends (see ch 9), formal reductions of capital, and schemes of arrangement (see ch 7). Generally, R Moore, B Ward, B Phillips, and S Stewart, 'Returning Value to Shareholders: Giving Something Back' (2012) 23(8) PLC 23; T Scott, 'Returning Cash to Shareholders. Options for Companies' (1997) 8(3) PLC 19.

[6] J Tiley, 'The Purchase by a Company of Its Own Shares' [1992] *British Tax Review* 21; S Edge, 'Do We Have an Imputation System on Not?' (1996) 375 *Tax Journal* 2; S Edge, 'The Background to the Introduction of Schedule 7' [1997] *British Tax Review* 221; PR Rau and T Vermaelen, 'Regulation, Taxes and Share Repurchases in the United Kingdom' (2002) 75 *Journal of Business* 245.

on share buy-backs compared to an annual spend of around £20 billion in the late 1990s.[7] The percentage of companies engaging in share repurchase programmes increased threefold between 1998 and 2007.[8] The difficult market conditions after the 2007–9 financial crisis led to a reversal of the trend, but share buy-backs have still continued to be an important financial management tool.[9]

Tax considerations for both the company itself and its shareholders are often an important factor in the use of this tool. The precise nature of the tax consequences for a selling shareholder will depend on whether the company buys directly or through an intermediary.[10] When a company buys back its own shares directly, the purchase price is usually divided into a capital element, which is subject to tax on chargeable gains, and a distribution element, which is subject to tax on income. A buy-back conducted through an intermediary is generally treated as a repayment of capital for tax purposes. For the company, stamp duty is payable on shares that it buys back.

In UK corporate finance practice, share buy-backs are not generally regarded as being interchangeable with dividends.[11] The different tax and other characteristics of buy-backs and dividend payments mean that they are perceived to play different roles.

To address principal-agent concerns

Value that is returned to shareholders by means of a share buy-back is, by definition, no longer available to the managers of the company to invest in opportunities that, in reality, are not value-enhancing and which appeal mostly because of managerial self-interest in building a larger and, at least in the short term, more prestigious operation. However, there is also the potential for share buy-backs to exacerbate principal-agent problems because of the way in which they can impact on performance ratios. Since these ratios are often used in remuneration packages as a basis for evaluation of managerial performance, there are potential incentives for self-interested managers to misuse share buy-back powers in order to maximize short-term share prices.

To give information signals

A buy-back of shares by a company can serve as a mechanism for delivering credible information signals to the market in that it can be used to demonstrate that its management considers its share price to be undervalued based on expected improvements in future cash flow and earnings. Credibility is assured because only successful companies can afford to use this mechanism. However, the reliability of the signal is dependent on the quality of the managerial judgment in question; this could be affected by managerial overconfidence in their company's future prospects or by their self-interest.

Signalling effects are also associated with dividend payout policies.[12] However, there are differences in the signals that may be conveyed by these alternative ways of returning value to shareholders. There are strong expectations around dividends with regard to the maintenance of a steady payout policy over time; accordingly, an increase in dividends is likely to be interpreted by the market as a signal of managerial confidence in their company's future

---

[7] Dhanani and Roberts, *Corporate Share Repurchases*, 1–2 (reviewing the empirical literature).
[8] Dhanani and Roberts, *Corporate Share Repurchases*, 1–2.
[9] Dhanani and Roberts, *Corporate Share Repurchases*, 1–2.
[10] Moore, Ward, Phillips, and Stewart, 'Returning Value to Shareholders.'
[11] Dhanani and Roberts, *Corporate Share Repurchases*, 52–3.   [12] See ch 9.

prospects. The same expectations do not surround share buy-backs; hence, less is likely to be read into the signal emitted by a buy-back programme with respect to future prospects.

To achieve a target capital structure

A company may choose to buy back its shares in order to achieve a target capital structure. For example, a company may want to eliminate a particular class of shares and replace it with another class of shares with special rights or with ordinary shares. Or, it may want to increase financial leverage by replacing expensive share capital with cheaper debt. Increasing financial leverage is not necessarily an unalloyed benefit.

The company will need to consider the ramifications of a buy-back programme for the percentage holdings of the remaining shareholders. A particular point to note is that if the company has a premium listing, it must ensure that it can still comply with the requirement of the *Listing Rules* that a sufficient number of shares must be distributed to the public, with 25 per cent of the shares generally taken to be sufficient for this purpose.[13]

To expand the range of financing options

Redeemable shares are a type of hybrid security: they are shares but the fact that they are to be repaid on or by a specified date is a feature that makes them akin to impermanent debt finance. As such, the power to issue redeemable shares adds to the range of financing options available to the corporate sector and thus enhances flexibility.

To buy back redeemable shares at a discounted price

Early repurchase of redeemable shares that are trading at a discount to their redemption price can enhance efficiency by enabling the issuer to retire those securities at a price that is lower than it would have to pay on redemption.

To facilitate the organization of employee share schemes

Another advantage claimed for allowing companies to purchase their own shares is that this can facilitate the operation of an employee share scheme by assuring employees of a purchaser for their shares when they leave the company. In larger companies it is common for employee share schemes to be operated through a trust and for the trustees to buy the shares of employees who are leaving the company, but for the company to be able to buy back the employee shares is an alternative that can be more straightforward and which can therefore make the establishment of employee share schemes less of a burden for smaller companies.

In 2013 certain modifications were made to the legislative framework governing share buy-backs for the purpose of improving the operation of internal share markets to support companies using direct share ownership.[14] These changes were part of a wider policy to promote employee share ownership, that policy being based on an assessment of the economic and social benefits achieved by employee owned companies.[15]

---

[13] *LR* 6.1.19. This rule is a requirement for admission to premium listing in respect of equity securities and it is provided as a continuing obligation that a listed company must comply with *LR* 6.1.19 at all times: *LR* 9.2.15. In limited circumstances, the FCA may accept a percentage of less than 25 per cent. See ch 13 for further discussion of free float requirements for premium and standard listed issuers.

[14] The Companies Act 2006 (Amendment of Part 18) Regulations 2013, SI 2013/999.

[15] BIS, *Employee Ownership & Share Buy Backs: Implementation of Nuttall Review—Recommendation V: Government Response to Consultation* (February 2013).

To achieve an informal reduction of capital

If left unregulated, a redemption or repurchase of shares could be used by a company in order to reduce its share capital without the need for court approval (where applicable) and in disregard of the obligation to observe the other formalities attending a reduction of capital under the Companies Act 2006. Historically, the potential for creditors to be prejudiced by an informal reduction of capital was a key objection to allowing companies to buy back their own shares. In *Trevor v Whitworth*[16] the House of Lords relied on infringement of the maintenance of capital principle as the main reason for coming to the conclusion that the purchase by a company of its own shares was unlawful. However, as doubts have grown about the value of legal capital as a creditor protection mechanism, objections to buy-backs that are rooted in this concern have receded and this has led to some relaxation of the regulatory framework governing buy-backs.

To defend against a takeover or to deal with dissident shareholders

A buy-back may be viewed as a useful defensive mechanism in a takeover situation by, for example, reducing the number of shares potentially available to a hostile bidder. The controllers of a company may also welcome the flexibility of buy-back powers that enable them to negotiate an exit for troublesome shareholders by buying them out at a favourable price. On the other hand, however, giving the management of a company threatened with a takeover free rein to buy back shares as a defensive tactic could enable management to entrench themselves in position and thereby impede the efficient functioning of the market for corporate control. The use of buy-back powers in order to deal with dissenting shareholders is also potentially open to abuse.

The argument that a company ought to be able to purchase its own shares in order to buy out shareholders whose continued presence in the company was undesirable was accepted in some nineteenth-century cases[17] but it found little favour in the House of Lords in *Trevor v Whitworth*. Lord Macnaghten stated:[18]

> But I would ask, Is it possible to suggest anything more dangerous to the welfare of companies and to the security of their creditors than such a doctrine? Who are the shareholders whose continuance in a company the company or its executive consider undesirable? Why, shareholders who quarrel with the policy of the board, and wish to turn the directors out; shareholders who ask questions which it may not be convenient to answer; shareholders who want information which the directors think it prudent to withhold. Can it be contended that when the policy of directors is assailed they may spend the capital of the company in keeping themselves in power, or in purchasing the retirement of inquisitive and troublesome critics?

The constitutional function of the directors in a conventionally structured company is to manage the company and it is beyond their powers to seek to control the ownership of its shares. Allowing a company to purchase its own shares could be open to abuse because directors could, by offering an exceptionally favourable price, use the power to secure their own control by getting rid of troublesome or disaffected shareholders who might otherwise have been tempted to make a takeover bid or to accept another's bid. The directors of a company might also be tempted to pay too much for the company's shares in order to favour a selling shareholder who has a special connection to the company, such as one of its original

---

[16] (1887) 12 App Cas 409, HL.   [17] eg *Re Dronfield Silkstone Coal Co* (1881) 17 Ch D 76, CA.
[18] (1887) 12 App Cas 409, HL, 435.

proprietors who is retiring from the company after many years of service. If a company were to pay an unjustifiably high price for the shares, this wealth transfer would be detrimental to its remaining shareholders and, potentially, its creditors.

To stabilize the share price

A company may want to have the power to buy its own shares in order to bolster or stabilize their market price. However, whilst this can be presented as an argument in favour of share buy-backs, allowing a company to be able to buy its own shares to bolster or stabilize the price at which they are trading in the market also raises concerns about market abuse. For a company to use its own money to bolster or stabilize its share price is open to the obvious objection that this practice could mislead the investing public about the value of the company's shares and could create a false market in those shares.[19] Yet, if the risk of market manipulation were the only argument against permitting companies to buy back their own shares, it would be doubtful whether this would justify a specific company law ban on the practice because market abuse is in any event regulated by UK and EU law. The UK's regulator of financial market conduct, the Financial Conduct Authority (FCA), can impose administrative sanctions on perpetrators of market abuse and also seek criminal sanctions.[20]

Consideration by Review Bodies

Following the Report of the Greene Committee in 1926,[21] section 18 of the Companies Act 1928 first allowed companies to issue redeemable preference shares subject to safeguards that were intended to preserve the amount of the company's share capital. The Jenkins Committee, which reviewed the position in 1962, compared the limited power allowed to British companies with the freedom enjoyed by US companies to repurchase shares, and acknowledged the usefulness of the US position with regard to such matters as employee share schemes and the unlocking of investment in small companies.[22] The Committee thought that if British companies were to be given a wider power to purchase their own shares it would be necessary to introduce stringent safeguards to protect creditors and shareholders but that it would be possible to devise effective safeguards and that they would not be unduly complicated. However, it refrained from recommending the general abrogation of the rule that a company could not purchase its own shares because it had received no evidence that British companies needed the power and because it identified serious tax disadvantages in selling shares back to the company rather than to a third party.

At the end of the 1970s, the problems in raising capital encountered by smaller companies were the subject of a review by a Committee under the chairmanship of Sir Harold Wilson. In its Interim Report on the *Financing of Small Firms* this Committee suggested that consideration should be given to permitting such companies to issue redeemable equity shares as a means of raising capital without parting permanently with family control.[23] During Parliamentary debates on the Bill which became the Companies Act 1980, it was indicated that the government attached high priority to relaxing the general prohibition on companies

---

[19] *General Property Co Ltd v Matheson's Trustees* (1888) 16 R 82 Ct of Sess.
[20] Financial Services and Markets Act 2000, Pt 8 (administrative penalties for market abuse) and Financial Services Act 2012, ss 89–90 (criminal sanctions for misleading statements and impressions).
[21] *The Report of the Committee on Company Law* (Cmd 2657, 1926) para 28.
[22] *Report of the Company Law Committee* (Cmnd 1749, 1962) paras 167–9.   [23] Cmnd 7503 (1979).

purchasing their own shares. This was then followed by the publication by the relevant government department of a consultative document on *The Purchase by a Company of its Own Shares*, which was written by Professor Gower.[24] In the consultative document, Professor Gower recommended that companies should be allowed to issue redeemable equity shares and that consideration should be given to the possibility of permitting public and private companies to repurchase their own shares.[25] He outlined safeguards intended to ensure that capital would be maintained despite repurchase or redemption of shares but, in relation to private companies, he further recommended that consideration be given to allowing them to reduce their capital by repurchasing or redeeming shares.

Powers broadly in line with those recommended for consideration by Professor Gower were enacted in the Companies Act 1981, later consolidated into the Companies Act 1985.

The next purely domestic step in the process of gradual relaxation of the rules relating to share buy-backs was taken in relation to treasury shares. At the time of the Gower review in 1980, the mood was against allowing companies to purchase own shares, hold them in 'treasury,' and then resell them. In 1998, however, the government returned to this issue and published a new consultative document seeking views on whether there should be a change in the law to permit treasury shares.[26] This time, the response was favourable and in 2003 the Companies Act 1985 was amended to introduce a limited power for companies to have treasury shares.[27] In principle, treasury shares give companies additional flexibility with regard to the management of their capital structure because the shares can be re-sold without having to go through the full range of formalities that apply to new share issues. However, in fact, the amending provisions that introduced treasury shares included a requirement for the resale of treasury shares to be subject to pre-emption rights in favour of existing shareholders, and this had the effect of reducing flexibility. Nevertheless, a significant practical benefit resulting from the introduction of treasury shares is that the shares can be used to satisfy entitlements under employee share schemes.[28]

Perhaps because it had been officially reviewed on several occasions in the relatively recent past, the law relating to share buy-backs and redeemable shares was not a particularly controversial area in the context of the general review of UK company law that preceded the Companies Act 2006. Chapters 3 to 7 of Part 18 of that Act, which contain the enabling provisions that empower limited companies to issue redeemable shares and to purchase their own shares, are largely restated versions of the previous law, with only limited substantive change. Certain detailed aspects of the statutory regime were modified in 2013 in order, primarily, to facilitate employee share ownership.[29] The changes related to the procedures for authorizing share buy-backs, the timing of payment for shares bought back, the reserves available for buy-backs, and the holding of treasury shares.

The European Dimension

Before turning to the detail of the Companies Act 2006, it is necessary also to mention the European dimension.

---

[24] Cmnd 7944 (1980).   [25] Cmnd 7944 (1980) para 67 (Conclusions).

[26] DTI, *Share Buybacks: A Consultative Document* (1998).

[27] The changes were introduced by the Companies (Acquisition of Own Shares) (Treasury Shares) Regulations 2003, SI 2003/1116.

[28] V Knapp, 'Treasury Shares: The Practicalities' (2004) 15(2) PLC 15.

[29] The Companies Act 2006 (Amendment of Part 18) Regulations 2013, SI 2013/999.

The Second Company Law Directive[30] does not require Member States to have laws permitting companies to issue redeemable shares or to repurchase shares but those Member States that do have such enabling provisions in their company laws must observe the conditions imposed by the Directive. The core provision is Article 21(1), which, as amended in 2006,[31] provides that own share acquisitions must be subject to the following conditions:

(a) authorization shall be given by the general meeting, which shall determine the terms and conditions of such acquisitions, and, in particular, the maximum number of shares to be acquired, the duration of the period for which the authorization is given, the maximum length of which shall be determined by national law without, however, exceeding five years, and, in the case of acquisition for value, the maximum and minimum consideration.

(b) the acquisitions, including shares previously acquired by the company and held by it, and shares acquired by a person acting in his own name but on the company's behalf, may not have the effect of reducing the net assets below the amount of distributable reserves; and

(c) only fully paid up shares may be included in the transaction.

Members of the administrative or management body must satisfy themselves that, at the time when each authorized acquisition is effected, the conditions referred to in points (b) and (c) are respected.

In addition, Article 21(1) gives Member States the option of applying any of the following conditions:

(i) that the nominal value or, in the absence thereof, the accountable par of the acquired shares, including shares previously acquired by the company and held by it, and shares acquired by a person acting in his own name but on the company's behalf, may not exceed a limit to be determined by Member States. This limit on the number of shares acquired and held in treasury may not be lower than 10 per cent of the subscribed capital;

(ii) that the power of the company to acquire its own shares, the maximum number of shares to be acquired, the duration of the period for which the power is given and the maximum or minimum consideration must be laid down in the statutes or in the instrument of incorporation of the company;

(iii) that the company must comply with appropriate reporting and notification requirements;

(iv) that certain companies, as determined by Member States, may be required to cancel the acquired shares provided that an amount equal to the nominal value of the shares cancelled must be included in a reserve which cannot be distributed to the shareholders, except in the event of a reduction in the subscribed capital. This reserve may be used only for the purposes of increasing the subscribed capital by the capitalization of reserves;

(v) that the acquisition shall not prejudice the satisfaction of creditors' claims.

---

[30] Now recast as Directive 2012/30/EU of the European Parliament and of the Council of 25 October 2012 on coordination of safeguards which, for the protection of the interests of members and others, are required by Member States of companies within the meaning of the second paragraph of Article 54 of the Treaty on the Functioning of the European Union, in respect of the formation of public limited liability companies and the maintenance and alteration of their capital, with a view to making such safeguards equivalent (Recast) [2012] L315/74 (Second Company Law Directive).

[31] By Directive 2006/68/EC, [2006] OJL 264.

Prior to the amendments made in 2006, the Second Company Law Directive had stipulated that the period of authorization granted by the general meeting for own share purchases could not exceed eighteen months and that the amount of shares bought back and held in treasury could not exceed 10 per cent of the subscribed capital. These conditions were relaxed because it came to be accepted that they were too rigid and that they inhibited useful share buy-back programmes.[32] A further change effected by the 2006 amendments was that the list of mandatory and additional optional conditions to which own share purchases can be made subject is now exhaustive.

Article 21 now also expressly provides that the powers conferred are without prejudice to the principle of equal treatment of all shareholders who are in the same position. It is also stipulated that Member States must for the purpose of implementation take into account the provisions of Directive 2003/6/EC of the European Parliament and of the Council of 28 January 2003 on insider dealing and market manipulation (market abuse) and associated delegated measures on exemptions for buy-back programmes and stabilization of financial instruments, and related matters.[33]

The 2006 changes to the Second Company Law Directive came too late to be reflected in the Companies Act 2006 as originally enacted but an amending power in that Act provided a mechanism for introducing them into UK law.[34] This mechanism has since been used.[35]

Excessive Deregulation?

There have been some calls for tighter controls on share buy-backs to be reintroduced. It has been argued, for instance, that share buy-backs move money from firms to investors in ways that often come at the expense of investment in research and development and can even depress the job market. Share buy-backs, it is said, fit with a model of 'impatient capital' and, as such, they compare unfavourably with dividends that reward stable shareholding. Doubts have been expressed about the quality of managerial decisions that their company's shares are undervalued by the market. Furthermore, it has been asserted that share buy-backs can still be viewed as a form of market manipulation, and even as a potential threat to financial stability.[36]

An outright ban on share buy-backs would be an extreme policy choice that would narrow the range of ways in which a company could return surplus value to investors in a tax-efficient manner and could lead to a resurgence of unwelcome empire-building type, non-value-enhancing investments by corporate managers. Moreover, given the propensity of the markets to find ingenious ways around bans, pushing practices underground probably would not succeed in stamping out many of the perceived problems in relation to share buy-backs in any event. This is not to deny the potential for buy-back powers to be misused and the need, therefore, for rigorous scrutiny of their use by investors, the market, and by supervisory authorities. Indeed there have been signs that some significant investor groups

---

[32] The Company Law SLIM Working Group on the Simplification of the First and Second Company Law Directives recommended these changes, which were then endorsed by a High Level Group that reviewed aspects of EC company law on behalf of the European Commission: European Commission, *Report of the High Level Group of Company Law Experts on a Regulatory Framework for Company Law in Europe* (Brussels, November 2002) 84–5.

[33] Second Company Law Directive, recital 13 and Art 21(1).

[34] Companies Act 2006, s 737.

[35] The Companies (Share Capital and Acquisition by Company of its Own Shares) Regulations 2009, SI 2009/2022, regs 4–5.

[36] The views reported here are developed in FINNOV, *Financing Innovation and Growth: Reforming a Dysfunctional System* (February 2012).

are becoming less favourably disposed towards share buy-back programmes.[37] However, in the absence of clear evidence that share buy-back activity has spiralled out of control, thereby exposing glaring weaknesses in the legal and regulatory framework, the case for heavy-handed intervention is not established.

General Statutory Rule in the Companies Act 2006 Against a Company Acquiring Its Own Shares

The thrust of *Trevor v Whitworth*[38] is now embodied in section 658 of the Companies Act 2006, which provides that a limited company must not acquire its own shares, whether by purchase, subscription, or otherwise. If a company purports to act in contravention of this rule it is liable to a fine and every officer of the company who is in default is liable to imprisonment or a fine, or both; and the purported acquisition is void. The general prohibition is, however, qualified by section 659 of the Companies Act 2006, which provides exceptions to the general rule as follows.

Under section 659 a limited company may acquire any of its own fully paid shares otherwise than for valuable consideration. This does not infringe the Second Company Law Directive because Article 22(1)(c) provides that Member States are not obliged to apply Article 21 to fully paid up shares acquired free of charge. Other exceptions to the general rule stated in section 659, and which are also sanctioned by the Second Company Law Directive, are:[39]

1. the acquisition of shares in a reduction of capital duly made;

2. the purchase of shares in pursuance of court orders made under certain sections of the Companies Act 2006; and

3. the forfeiture of shares, or the acceptance of shares surrendered in lieu, in pursuance of the articles, for failure to pay any sum payable in respect of the shares.

In *Acatos and Hutcheson plc v Watson*[40] the High Court was asked to rule on whether the purchase by a company of another company whose sole asset was a substantial holding of shares in the purchasing company would infringe the prohibition that is now contained in section 658 of the Companies Act 2006. Lightman J held that the proposed acquisition would not amount to a side-stepping of the prohibition which the court would prevent by lifting the veil between the purchaser and the target company. In reaching this conclusion, Lightman J followed three Australian cases that had adopted the same approach.[41] He noted that the opposite conclusion would enable companies to protect themselves from becoming the target of a takeover bid simply by acquiring some of the predator's shares, a result which he characterized as 'absurd.' Lightman J also drew support from what is now section 136 of the Companies Act 2006 (a prohibition on a subsidiary being a member of its holding company), which recognizes the possibility that a company may acquire shares in a company that later

---

[37] Pensions Investments and Research Consultants (PIRC), *Shareholder Voting Guidelines 2012* (moving towards a position of regarding buy-backs negatively and preferring dividends instead because of concern about the quality of information on which corporate management make buy-back decisions and also additional complexities especially in relation to remuneration schemes). PIRC is an independent body that offers advice to pension fund investors.

[38] (1887) 12 App Cas 409, HL.   [39] Companies Act 2006, s 659(2).   [40] [1995] BCC 446.

[41] *August Investments Pty Ltd v Poseidon Ltd* (1971) 2 SASR 71, SA SC-FC, noted H Leigh French, 'Exceptions to Self-Purchase of Shares' (1987) 8 *Company Lawyer* 88; *Dyason v JC Hutton Pty Ltd* (1935) 41 ALR 419, V SC; *Trade Practices Commission v Australian Iron & Steel Pty Ltd* (1990) 22 FCR 305.

becomes its holding company; in that event, the subsidiary may continue to hold the shares but may not exercise any votes attaching to them.

Also of note in this context is section 660 of the Companies Act 2006, which specifically regulates the subscription or acquisition of shares in a limited company by a nominee of that company. Subject to limited qualifications, where shares are issued to a nominee of a limited company or are acquired by a nominee from a third person as partly paid up, then, for all purposes, the shares are to be treated as held by the nominee on his or her own account and the company is to be regarded as having no beneficial interest in them.

In circumstances where a company is permitted to acquire its own shares, it must then observe any statutory limitations on what it can do with the shares so acquired. Relevant limitations are determined by reference to the method of acquisition.[42]

Share Buy-backs—Authorizations Required by the Companies Act 2006

A limited company having a share capital may purchase its own shares provided that it abides by the requirements of the legislation and subject to any restriction or limitation in its articles.[43] That the 2006 Act provides that companies can buy back shares unless their articles provide otherwise is a reversal of the position under the previous companies legislation, which was that specific constitutional authorization via the articles was required.

The Companies Act 2006 gives effect to the requirement in Article 21 of the Second Company Law Directive for buy-backs to be authorized by the general meeting. The details of the statutory shareholder authorization requirements are different depending on whether the buy-back is to be a 'market' or an 'off-market' purchase.

Market purchase

A market purchase by a company of its own shares means a purchase made on a recognized investment exchange (RIE) provided that the shares are subject to a marketing arrangement on that exchange.[44] The FCA is responsible for the recognition and supervision of recognized investment exchanges under the Financial Services and Markets Act 2000.[45] All FCA-regulated RIEs, other than those that are overseas investment exchanges, are recognized investment exchanges for the purposes of the buy-back requirements in the Companies Act 2006.[46] Officially listed shares (such as shares admitted to trading on the listed segment of the London Stock Exchange) are automatically treated as being subject to a marketing arrangement.[47] Otherwise, shares admitted to trading on a recognized investment exchange are subject to a marketing arrangement if the company has been afforded facilities for dealing in those shares to take place on the exchange without prior permission from the exchange and without limit as to the time during which those facilities are to be available.[48] This would encompass, for example, shares that are admitted to trading on the Alternative Investment Market, which is not a market for listed securities.

---

[42] Companies Act 2006, ss 662–9 deal with cancellation of shares in a public company held by or for the company.
[43] Companies Act 2006, s 690.   [44] Companies Act 2006, s 693(4).
[45] Financial Services and Markets Act 2000, Pt 18.   [46] Companies Act 2006, s 693(5).
[47] Companies Act 2006, s 693(3)(a).   [48] Companies Act 2006, s 693(3)(b).

Ordinary or special resolution?

Section 701 of the Companies Act 2006 provides that the shareholder authorization required in respect of an on-market purchase of shares is a resolution, which implies an ordinary resolution. In practice, listed companies which take power to purchase their own shares commonly do so by special resolution in order to comply with recommendations from the Association of British Insurers (ABI), the representative body of a major group of institutional investors.[49] An important feature of an on-market authority, whether in the form of an ordinary or a special resolution, is that it can be a general authority not linked to any particular purchase of shares.[50] The authority must, however (and as required by the Second Company Law Directive), specify limits with regard to the maximum number of shares authorized to be acquired and the maximum and minimum prices which may be paid for the shares.[51] Such prices may be fixed or may be determined by reference to a formula, provided this is without reference to any person's discretion or opinion.[52] The Companies Act 2006 does not go as far as to link purchase prices to the price at which shares are trading in the market (but, on this, see the regulatory requirements discussed later in this chapter). The legislation does mandate that the authorizing resolution must state the date on which it is to expire, which must be no later than five years after the date when the resolution is passed.[53] The ABI favours annual renewal of the authority. With regard to amount, the ABI has said that, assuming the company is trading normally, authority to purchase up to 5 per cent of the ordinary share capital is unlikely to cause concern but regard will be had to the effect on gearing, etc where larger amounts of capital are involved. There is reluctance among some institutional investors to accept own share purchase powers over share capital in excess of 10 per cent of the issued ordinary share capital; and a proposal to take the power to purchase to 15 per cent or more would cause significant concern.[54] As a consequence of these various requirements and investor expectations, in practice, it is usual for publicly quoted companies to seek a general authority to purchase up to 10 per cent at each annual general meeting (AGM). A further ABI expectation is that the company should undertake only to exercise the power if to do so will result in an increase in earnings per share (or asset value per share in the case of property companies or investment trusts) and is in the best interests of shareholders generally.

The Companies Act 2006 provides for a resolution authorizing a market purchase of shares to be varied, revoked, or renewed by ordinary resolution.[55] Provided this is permitted by the resolution, a company may, after the expiry of an authority, complete a purchase of shares arising from a contract entered into before the authority expired.[56]

Off-market purchase

A purchase of shares that is not a market purchase is an off-market purchase. The Companies Act 2006, as amended in 2013, requires off-market purchases of shares to be authorized by ordinary resolution.[57] Subject to an exception for private company buy-backs connected to

---

[49] The ABI has not published formal guidelines on this subject but its views are public and well-known. A statement of these views is available at <http://www.ivis.co.uk/PDF/3.2_Own_Share_Purchase.pdf> accessed July 2013. The ABI's stance on this matter is supported by PIRC.

[50] Companies Act 2006, s 701(2).   [51] Companies Act 2006, s 701(3).

[52] Companies Act 2006, s 701(7).   [53] Companies Act 2006, s 701(5).

[54] PIRC has stated that general authorities of up to 15 per cent are generally acceptable.

[55] Companies Act 2006, s 701(4).   [56] Companies Act 2006, s 701(6).

[57] Companies Act 2006, s 694, as amended by The Companies Act 2006 (Amendment of Part 18) Regulation 2013, SI 2013/999.

an employee share scheme,[58] the shareholders must approve specifically either the terms of the proposed contract by which the shares are to be purchased before it is entered into or the contract must provide that no shares may be purchased until its terms have been authorized by a special resolution of the company.[59] The contract may be a straightforward share purchase contract or a contract under which the company may (subject to any conditions) become entitled or obliged to purchase shares.[60] An example of such a contract would be an option contract under which the company is entitled to call for the shares in specified circumstances.

Apart from the special arrangements for employee share schemes, a resolution approving an off-market purchase of own shares will not be effective if any shareholder holding shares to which the resolution relates exercised the voting rights carried by those shares in voting on the resolution and the resolution would not have been passed if he or she had not done so.[61] Where the resolution is proposed as a written resolution, any member holding shares to which the resolution relates is not an eligible member.[62] In the case of a resolution passed at a shareholders' meeting, the contract (or a written memorandum of its terms if it is not in writing) must be available for inspection by members of the company both at the company's registered office for not less than fifteen days ending with the date of the meeting at which the resolution is passed and also at the meeting itself.[63] Where a private company uses the statutory written resolution regime to pass a resolution authorizing an off-market purchase of its own shares, the requirement for the contract (or its terms) to be available for inspection by members is necessarily varied to provide that details must have been supplied to each member before he or she signed the resolution.[64] The names of all of the selling shareholders must always be disclosed.[65]

Non-compliance with the publicity requirements in respect of the details of the contract renders any resolution which is passed invalid.[66] The disclosure requirements are aimed at preventing directors entering into arrangements to buy back favoured members' shares at especially favourable terms or otherwise abusing their powers. The requirement of equal treatment for shareholders is, for public companies, expressly backed by Article 21 and Article 46 of the Second Company Law Directive. However, it has been held that failure to comply with the requirement to make available the contract or a memorandum containing its terms is a formality for the benefit of shareholders only and is therefore capable of being waived if they all agree.[67]

A resolution passed by a public company authorizing an off-market purchase of shares must state when the authority conferred by the resolution is to expire and the expiry date must be not later than five years after the passing of the resolution.[68] Aside from the special arrangements for employee share schemes, a private company resolution authorizing an off-market purchase of shares may be of unlimited duration but, given that the contract terms must be authorized before it is entered into or the contract must be made conditional on the passing of an authorizing resolution, it is reasonable to expect that the time gap will usually be fairly short. A resolution authorizing an off-market purchase of shares can be varied, revoked, or renewed by a subsequent resolution.[69] Any variation in the terms of the

---

[58] Companies Act 2006, s 693A, introduced by The Companies Act 2006 (Amendment of Part 18) Regulation 2013, SI 2013/999.
[59] Companies Act 2006, s 694(2).   [60] Companies Act 2006, s 694(3).
[61] Companies Act 2006, s 695(3).   [62] Companies Act 2006, s 695(2).
[63] Companies Act 2006, s 696(2)(b).   [64] Companies Act 2006, s 696(2)(a).
[65] Companies Act 2006, s 696(3)–(4).   [66] Companies Act 2006, s 696(5).
[67] *Kinlan v Crimmin* [2007] BCC 106, citing *BDG Roof-Bond Ltd v Douglas* [2000] 1 BCLC 401.
[68] Companies Act 2006, s 694(5).   [69] Companies Act 2006, s 694(4).

contract by which the shares are to be purchased must be approved before it is agreed to by the company, and the rules on eligibility to vote on the resolution and with regard to the disclosure to members of the proposed variation track those for authorization of the original contract.[70]

The private company employee share scheme exception permits the authorization of multiple buy-backs connected to an employee share scheme.[71] The ordinary resolution giving authority for off-market purchases for the purposes of, or pursuant to, an employee share scheme may be general or limited, unconditional or conditional, and must specify the maximum number of shares that can be acquired, and maximum and minimum prices. Its maximum duration is five years. Restrictions on the exercise of voting rights do not apply.

Significance of procedural requirements

Generally speaking, the authorization and other procedural requirements in the Companies Act 2006 in respect of share buy-backs are mandatory.[72] This means that they must be complied with even in circumstances where all of the shareholders would be willing to waive them. The normal consequence of non-compliance is that the purported acquisition is void in accordance with section 658 of the Companies Act 2006.[73] It has been held that these requirements are to be viewed in this way because their purpose extends beyond protection of the existing shareholders and encompasses protection of creditors' interests, and possibly also wider public interests.[74] However, particular provisions are for the protection of shareholders only, and in respect of those provisions it is open to the shareholders acting unanimously to waive compliance.[75]

Other Statutory Restrictions on the Terms and Manner of Buy-backs

A company must not purchase its own shares where to do so would result in there being no member of the company holding shares other than redeemable shares or shares held as treasury shares.[76] The purpose of this requirement is to ensure that a company does not bring its existence to an end through buy-backs and later redemptions. Shares may not be bought back unless they are fully paid (so that the valuable asset represented by uncalled capital is not lost) and, subject to an exception in connection with private company employee share schemes, the shares must be paid for on purchase.[77] The requirement for shareholders to be paid off at once ensures that members cannot be pressurized into accepting terms under which they are required to sell and thus lose their rights as members immediately but are not compensated for this for some considerable time. However, having to find all of the purchase money up front rather than agreeing to deferred payment by instalments may pose a difficulty to smaller companies and thus may inhibit the use of the buy-back power. In response to concerns of this nature, the power was introduced in 2013 for private companies to pay

---

[70] Companies Act 2006, ss 697–9. [71] Companies Act 2006, s 693A.
[72] *Re RW Peak (Kings Lynn) Ltd* [1998] 1 BCLC 193.
[73] *Re RW Peak (Kings Lynn) Ltd* [1998] 1 BCLC 193, as explained in *Wright v Atlas Wright (Europe) Ltd* [1999] 2 BCLC 301 CA, 310–15 *per* Potter LJ. Note Companies Act 2006, s 696(5).
[74] *Wright v Atlas Wright (Europe) Ltd*, 204–5.
[75] *Kinlan v Crimmin* [2007] BCC 106 (sanctioning waiver in relation to what is now Companies Act 2006, s 696(2)); *Dashfield v Dashfield* [2008] BCC 222.
[76] Companies Act 2006, s 690.
[77] Companies Act 2006, s 691. See *Pena v Dale* [2004] 2 BCLC 508; *Kinlan v Crimmin* [2007] BCC 106.

for bought back shares by instalments where the buy-back is in connection with an employee share scheme.[78]

There is some support for the view that a company can pay for shares that it is buying back either in cash or by a transfer of assets.[79]

Accounting for a Share Buy-back

Share buy-backs have implications for shareholder funds. The purchase price can be met from distributable reserves, in which case, in accounting terms, the reduction in the company's cash or other assets represented by the purchase price will be matched by a reduction in distributable reserves.[80] Alternatively, the proceeds of a fresh issue of shares can be used provided that the issue was made for the purpose of financing the purchase.[81] Any premium payable on purchase must be paid out of distributable profits, save that where shares were issued at a premium, the company may pay a premium on redemption out of the proceeds of a fresh issue of shares up to an amount equal to the lesser of the aggregate of the premiums received by the company on the issue of the shares repurchased and the current amount of the company's share premium account (including any premium in respect of the new shares).[82]

When shares are purchased they must be treated as cancelled and the amount of the company's issued share capital must be diminished by the nominal value of those shares accordingly, save to the extent that those shares are to be held as treasury shares.[83] Where shares are cancelled as a result of a buy-back from distributable reserves, an amount equivalent to the nominal value of those shares must be credited to a capital redemption reserve, which is to be treated as if it were share capital with the one exception that it may be used to pay up fully paid bonus shares.[84] This requirement, which is relaxed in certain respects for private companies as discussed later in this chapter, ensures that the company's overall undistributable reserves remain intact and prevents buy-backs being used to effect informal reductions of capital. Where, or to the extent that, a buy-back is made from the proceeds of a fresh issue of shares made specifically for that purpose, it is necessary to credit the capital redemption reserve only with the amount (if any) by which the aggregate amount of the proceeds is less than the aggregate nominal value of the shares redeemed or purchased.[85] In effect, the new capital raised from the share issue takes the place of the amount repaid; creditors are not prejudiced because the fresh issue was made specifically for the purposes of the buy-back and not as an injection of new equity finance.

The accounting implications of these rules are illustrated by the following simplified examples (Table 8.1 and Table 8.2).

---

[78] Companies Act 2006, s 691(3), as inserted by The Companies Act 2006 (Amendment of Part 18) Regulations 2013, SI 2013/999.

[79] *BDG Roof-Bond Ltd v Douglas* [2000] 1 BCLC 401 but on the facts there was actually money consideration for the shares.

[80] Companies Act 2006, s 692(2)(a)(i). For this purpose, 'distributable profits' means profits out of which the company could lawfully make a distribution within the meaning given by Companies Act 2006, s 736. See further ch 9.

[81] Companies Act 2006, s 692(2)(a)(ii).   [82] Companies Act 2006, s 692(2)(ii).

[83] Companies Act 2006, s 706(b).   [84] Companies Act 2006, s 733.   [85] Companies Act 2006, s 733(3).

Table 8.1 A buy-back from distributable reserves of 1 million shares of nominal value £1 each for £1.3m:

	Before £000	Issue £000	Purchase £000	Maintain capital £000	After £000
Cash	3,800		(1,300)		2,500
Net assets	3,800		(1,300)		2,500
Capital and reserves					
Share capital: £1 ordinary shares	2,000			(1,000)	1,000
Share premium account	400				400
Capital redemption reserve				1,000	1,000
Share capital + undistributed reserves	2,400				2,400
P&L (income) reserve	1,400		(1,300)		100
	3,800		(1,300)	—	2,500

Table 8.2 As in the example above, save that there is an issue of 500,000 new shares at par of £1 each for the purposes of financing the purchase:

	Before £000	Issue £000	Purchase £000	Maintain capital £000	After £000
Cash	3,800	500	(1,300)		3,000
Net assets	3,800	500	(1,300)		3,000
Capital and reserves					
Share capital: £1 ordinary shares	2,000	500		(1,000)	1,500
Share premium account	400				400
Capital redemption reserve				500	500
Share capital + undistributed reserves	2,400	500	(500)		2,400
P&L (income) reserve	1,400		(800)		600
	3,800	500	(1,300)		3,000

Treasury Shares[86]

Treasury shares are own shares that are purchased by a company with the company then being entered in the register of members in respect of them for reasons of transparency.[87] In the UK powers for publicly quoted companies to hold shares in treasury were introduced in 2003. These powers were extended to unquoted public companies and private companies in 2013.[88] For own shares to be treated as treasury shares, the purchase must be made out of distributable profits or with cash where permitted in the case of private companies.[89] There is now no statutory limit on the number or value of shares held in treasury.

During the period that own shares are held in treasury, the company may not exercise any rights in respect of them, such as a right to attend or vote at meetings, and no dividends may be paid in respect of them.[90] However, bonus shares may be allotted in respect of them and where they are redeemable shares, the redemption obligation may be honoured.[91]

---

[86] G Morse, 'The Introduction of Treasury Shares into English Law and Practice' [2004] JBL 303.
[87] Companies Act 2006, s 724.
[88] Companies Act 2006, s 724, as amended by The Companies Act 2006 (Amendment of Part 18) Regulations 2013, SI 2013/999.
[89] Companies Act 2006, s 724(1), as amended.   [90] Companies Act 2006, s 726(2)–(3).
[91] Companies Act 2006, s 726(4).

A company that has treasury shares may deal with them by disposing of them[92] or cancelling them.[93] 'Disposal' in this context means selling the shares for a cash consideration or transferring them for the purposes of, or pursuant to, an employees' share scheme.[94] The proceeds on a disposal at a price that is equal to or less than the price paid for the treasury shares by the company are treated as a realized profit, but where the proceeds exceed the price that the company paid for them the excess must be credited to the share premium account.[95] When treasury shares are cancelled, the amount of the share capital is reduced accordingly by the nominal amount of the shares cancelled[96] and an equivalent amount must be transferred to the capital redemption reserve.[97] The potential to restore the distributable profits that were used to buy back the shares is one of the main advantages of treasury shares. Buying back shares and holding them in treasury for a limited period can serve as a mechanism for a company to manage the supply and demand in respect of its shares and to affect earnings per share ratios. Selling or transferring shares out of treasury is not an allotment of shares for the purposes of section 551 of the Companies Act 2006 and therefore does not end in the directors' authority to allot shares. However, statutory pre-emption rights under the Companies Act 2006, section 561 do apply, subject to exceptions. One important exception from pre-emption rights relates to employee share schemes: treasury shares may be used to satisfy entitlements under such schemes and statutory pre-emption rights do not apply in this situation.[98]

A premium listed company must also comply with requirements in the *Listing Rules* relating to treasury shares.[99]

Buy-back of Own Shares Out of Capital or from Cash: Private Companies Only

Private companies seeking to buy back small amounts of shares—the lower of £15,000 or the equivalent of 5 per cent of share capital in any financial year—are now permitted to do so without having to specify that the cash is from distributable profits, provided there is provision to this effect in the company's articles.[100] This 'de minimis' permission was introduced in 2013 and reflected a determination by the government that the thresholds should be low enough to pose little or no risk to shareholders or creditors but would still allow smaller companies in particular greater flexibility to finance share buy-backs.[101]

In addition, a more formal procedure enables private companies under certain conditions to reduce their capital by purchasing shares. These conditions are intended to protect creditors from the risks that lie in permitting companies to use their capital in this way. They are also designed to protect members of the company.

Under this procedure, recourse can only be had to the company's capital where there is a shortfall after the available profits and the proceeds of any fresh issue made for the purpose of the purchase have been applied.[102] The amount of capital that the company can use to make up the shortfall is referred to as the 'permissible capital payment'.[103] The available profits of the company for this purpose are determined first by reference to the company's accounts but the amount so

---

[92] Companies Act 2006, s 727. On notifications relating to disposal: Companies Act 2006, s 728.

[93] Companies Act 2006, s 729. On notifications relating to cancellation: Companies Act 2006, s 730.

[94] Companies Act 2006, s 727. On cash consideration: s 727(2).   [95] Companies Act 2006, s 731.

[96] Companies Act 2006, s 729(4).   [97] Companies Act 2006, s 733(4).

[98] Companies Act 2006, s 566.   [99] *LR* 12.6.

[100] Companies Act 2006, s 692(1)(b), as amended by The Companies Act 2006 (Amendment of Part 18) Regulations 2013, SI 2013/999.

[101] BIS, *Employee Ownership & Share Buy Backs.*   [102] Companies Act 2006, s 710.

[103] Companies Act 2006, s 710.

determined must then be reduced by the amount of any lawful distributions and other specified payments made by the company after the date of the relevant accounts.[104] If the permissible capital payment, together with the proceeds of any fresh issue of shares, is less than the nominal value of the shares purchased, the difference must be credited to the capital redemption reserve[105] but, if it is greater, the capital redemption reserve, share premium account, share capital account, or revaluation reserve may be reduced by the excess amount.[106] These rules can be illustrated by the following simplified example (Table 8.3, Table 8.4, and Table 8.5).

There are various procedural formalities associated with a payment out of capital under this private company procedure.[107] These are: a directors' statutory statement as to the solvency of the company, an auditor's report, a shareholders' special resolution, and public notice.[108] The directors' statement must specify the amount of the permissible capital payment and must state that, having made full inquiry into the affairs and prospects of the company, the directors have formed the opinion:

1 that immediately following the payment out of capital, there will be no grounds on which the company could then be found to be unable to pay its debts (taking into account contingent and prospective liabilities); and

2 that, prospectively, having regard to their intentions with regard to the management of the company and the amount and character of the financial resources which in their view will be available to the company throughout the year following the date on which the payment is made, the company will be able to continue to carry on its business as a going concern (and will accordingly be able to pay its debts as they fall due).[109]

There are criminal sanctions for making a statement without having reasonable grounds for the opinion expressed in it.[110] The directors' statement must have annexed to it a report

Table 8.3 A private company has the following balance sheet (Statement of financial position)

	£000
Cash	2,400
Net assets	2,400
Capital and reserves	
Share capital: £1 ordinary shares	2,000
P&L (income) reserve	400
	2,400

Assuming all conditions and formalities have been met, the company redeems 1 million shares for £1.3m and no fresh issue of shares is to be made.

Table 8.4 (a) What is the Permissible Capital Payment (PCP)?

	£000
Price of purchase	1,300
Less: proceeds of fresh issue	0
Less: balance on distributable reserves	(400)
PCP	900

---

[104] Companies Act 2006, ss 711–12.   [105] Companies Act 2006, s 734(2) and (4).
[106] Companies Act 2006, s 734(3) and (4).
[107] Companies Act 2006, s 713. The procedure is modified for buy-backs in connection with employee share schemes. The modified regime is considered separately later.
[108] Companies Act 2006, s 714.   [109] Companies Act 2006, s 714(2)–(3).   [110] Companies Act 2006, s 715.

Table 8.5 (b) The Balance Sheet (Statement of Financial Position) of the company after the transaction

	Before £000	Purchase £000	Maintain capital £000	After £000
Cash	2,400	(1,300)		(1,100)
Net assets	2,400	(1,300)		
Capital and reserves				
Share capital: £1 ordinary shares	2,000		(1,000)	1,000
Capital redemption reserve			100	100
Share capital + undistributed reserves	2,000	(900)		1,100
P&L (income) reserve	400	(400)		—
	2,400	(1,300)	—	1,100

from the company's auditor indicating that he or she has inquired into the company's affairs, checked that the permissible capital payment has been properly determined, and is not aware of anything to indicate that the directors' opinion is unreasonable in all the circumstances.[111] The directors' statement, and the accompanying auditor's report, must be made available to members prior to their vote on whether to approve the payment from capital.[112] The directors' statement and auditor's report must be kept available at the registered office for a specified period for inspection by any member or creditor.[113] Delivery of a copy of the statement and accompanying report to the registrar is also required.[114]

Under this procedure, the payment must be approved by a special resolution of the shareholders passed on or within the week immediately following after the date on which the directors made their statement.[115] This resolution is ineffective if any member of the company holding shares to which the resolution relates votes on it and the resolution would not have been passed if he or she had not done so.[116] The fact that the company has passed a special resolution for payment out of capital must be publicized by a notice in the *London Gazette*.[117] A notice to the same effect must also be published in an appropriate national newspaper unless the company gives such notice in writing to each of its creditors.[118]

Within five weeks of the passing of a special resolution approving a payment from capital for the purchase of shares, an application may be made to the court by any creditor of the company and by any member other than one who consented to or voted in favour of the resolution.[119] On the hearing of an application the court may adjourn the proceedings to give the parties an opportunity to come to an arrangement for the purchase of the interests of dissentient members or for the protection of dissentient creditors, as the case may be. Subject to that, on the hearing of the application the court is required to make an order on such terms and conditions as it thinks fit either confirming or cancelling the resolution. The court order can provide for the purchase by the company of the shares of any member and for the reduction accordingly of the company's capital. To allow for the possibility of an application to court being made, the payment out of capital must be made no earlier than five weeks after

---

[111] Companies Act 2006, s 714(6).   [112] Companies Act 2006, s 718.   [113] Companies Act 2006, s 720.
[114] Companies Act 2006, s 719(4).   [115] Companies Act 2006, s 716.
[116] Companies Act 2006, s 717(3). Where the resolution is passed by means of a written resolution, a member who holds shares to which the resolution relates is not an eligible member (s 717(2)).
[117] Companies Act 2006, s 719(1)   [118] Companies Act 2006, s 719(3).
[119] Companies Act 2006, s 721. The rest of this paragraph outlines the requirements of this section.

the date of the special resolution but it must also be no later than seven weeks after that date unless the court orders otherwise.[120]

As part of the reforms relating to the facilitation of employee share schemes, in 2013 a more streamlined regime was introduced whereby a private company can use capital to buy back shares in connection with an employee share scheme on the basis of a directors' solvency statement and shareholders' special resolution, but without the need for an auditor's report.[121] The use of the simplified regime is optional.

Section 76 of the Insolvency Act 1986 is relevant where a company is being wound up and it has previously made a payment out of capital to purchase its own shares. If (a) the aggregate amount of the company's assets and the amounts paid by way of contribution to its assets (apart from this section) is insufficient for the payment of its debts and liabilities and the expenses of the winding up, and (b) the winding up commenced within a year of the date on which the relevant payment was made, the person from whom the shares were purchased and the directors who signed the statutory statement as to the company's solvency are prima facie personally liable to contribute to the company's assets to enable that insufficiency to be met. The former member who sold his or her shares is liable to contribute an amount not exceeding so much of the relevant payment as was made by the company in respect of the shares. The directors are jointly and severally liable with that person to contribute that amount but a director can escape this liability by showing that he or she had reasonable grounds for forming the opinion as to the company's solvency set out in the statement.

Statutory Modification of Contractual Matters Relating to Share Buy-backs

The consequences of a company failing to complete its bargain to purchase shares are dealt with by section 735 of the Companies Act 2006. The company is not liable in damages in that event but this is without prejudice to any other right that the shareholder may have; the shareholder may thus seek specific performance of the contract, but the court must not grant this if the company shows that it is unable to meet the costs of redeeming or purchasing the shares in question out of distributable profits. The winding up of the company does not necessarily preclude enforcement of a contract to purchase shares, but payment of the sums due under any such contract ranks behind the ordinary debts and liabilities of the company and any sums due in satisfaction of preferred rights attaching to other shares.

The rights of a company under a contract to purchase its own shares cannot be assigned.[122]

FCA Regulatory Requirements Relating to Share Buy-backs

The purchase of its own securities by a company with a premium listing is regulated by the FCA *Listing Rules* as well as by the general law.[123] Included in the *Listing Rules* are provisions relating to the price paid for own shares.[124] The general requirement is that unless a tender offer is made to all holders of a class, purchases by a listed company of less than 15 per cent of any class of its equity shares (excluding treasury shares) pursuant to a general authority granted

---

[120] Companies Act 2006, s 723.

[121] Companies Act 2006, ss 720A–720B, as inserted by The Companies Act 2006 (Amendment of Part 18) Regulations 2013, SI 2013/999.

[122] Companies Act 2006, s 704.

[123] *LR* 12 For the interpretation of 'premium' listing, see ch 13. For AIM companies, see AIM Rules, in particular Rule 13 (related party transactions), Rule 17 (disclosure), and Rule 21 (restrictions on timing of deals).

[124] *LR* 12.2–12.4.

by shareholders, may only be made if the price to be paid is not more than the higher of (a) 5 per cent above the average market value of the company's equity shares for the five business days prior to the purchase and (b) the higher of the price of the last independent trade and the highest current independent bid on the trading venues where the purchase is carried out.[125] Purchases of 15 per cent or more of any class of equity shares (excluding treasury shares) must be by way of a tender offer to all shareholders of that class, unless the full terms of the buy-back have been specifically approved by the shareholders.[126] A tender offer is defined by the *Listing Rules* as an offer by a company to purchase all or part of a class of securities at a maximum or fixed price (that may be established by means of a formula) that is: (a) communicated to all holders of that class by means of a circular or advertisement in two national newspapers; (b) open to all holders of that class on the same terms for at least seven days; and (c) open for acceptance by all holders of that class pro rata to their existing holdings. Prior to 2012, the *Listing Rules* did not allow shareholders to sanction share buy-backs above 15 per cent otherwise than by means of a tender offer but this was removed when the Financial Services Authority (FSA) (which was the competent authority at that time) concluded that narrowing the options available to the shareholders in this way could not be justified.[127]

So far as timing is concerned, the *Listing Rules* generally prohibit buy-backs during prohibited periods (ie periods immediately prior to the announcement of financial results or periods when there exists inside information in relation to the company),[128] although there are some exceptions.[129] Additional requirements may apply where the vendor of the shares that are to be bought back is a related party.[130] The *Listing Rules* also require that the circular accompanying the buy-back resolution must include a statement of the directors' intentions about using the buy-back authority and, in particular, whether the company intends to cancel the shares or hold them in treasury.[131] In a case where a listed company is buying back 15 per cent or more other than by way of a tender offer, the circular must include an explanation of the potential impact of the proposed acquisition, including whether control may be concentrated following the transaction.[132] There are also additional matters that must be disclosed in the circular if the exercise in full of the authority sought would result in the purchase of 25 per cent or more of the company's issued equity shares.[133] A listed issuer must provide details of buy-backs through a regulatory information service as soon as possible after the purchase occurs[134] and must also take care to comply with notification and disclosure requirements under the *Disclosure and Transparency Rules*.[135]

Care must also be taken to ensure that a share buy-back programme does not give rise to concerns with regard to market abuse. There is a specific safe harbour in EU law for share buy-back programmes and, provided the conditions associated with this safe harbour are adhered to, the programme will not amount to market abuse.[136]

---

[125] *LR* 12.4.1.   [126] *LR* 12.4.2–12.42A.

[127] FSA, *Amendments to the Listing Rules, Prospectus Rules, Disclosure Rules and Transparency Rules* (CP12/2) paras 4.33–4.35.

[128] *LR* 9 Annex 1, the Model Code, para 1(e).

[129] *LR* 12.2. See also *LR* 12.6, which bans (subject to exceptions) sales or transfers of treasury shares during prohibited periods.

[130] *LR* 12.3.   [131] *LR* 13.7.1(a) and (c).   [132] *LR*, 13.7.1(g) and 13.7.1A.   [133] *LR*, 13.7.1(2).

[134] *LR*, 12.4.6.   [135] *DTR*, 5.5–5.6. These requirements are also applicable to AIM issuers.

[136] FSMA 2000, s 118A(5)(b); Commission Regulation (EC) 2273/2003 of 22 December 2003 implementing the Market Abuse Directive as regards exemptions for buy-back programmes and stabilization of financial instruments [2003] OJ L336/33. The Market Abuse Regulation that will replace the Market Abuse Directive will continue a carveout for stabilization in relation to buy-backs. The European Parliament endorsed the Council's political agreement on the Regulation in September 2013. The Market Abuse Regulation needs to be aligned with MiFID 2 proposals and is to be part of a package that will also contain a Directive on criminal sanctions for market abuse. The package will enter into force, along with the MiFID 2 proposals, once negotiations on those other measures have been successfully concluded.

Takeover Code Implications of Share Buy-backs

The Takeover Code maintained by the Panel on Takeovers and Mergers contains certain rules relating to the purchase by a company of its own shares. The Takeover Code is of relevance mainly in relation to offers for UK incorporated public companies, although its exact scope is wider.[137] The Code provides, in Rule 37.1, that a person who comes to exceed the 30 per cent threshold for a mandatory bid, as specified in Rule 9, as a result of the redemption or purchase by a company of its own securities will not normally incur an obligation to make a mandatory offer unless that person is a director, or the relationship of the person with any one or more of the directors is such that the person is, or is presumed to be, acting in concert with any of the directors. Where the directors are aware that a company's redemption or purchase of its own shares would otherwise give rise to an obligation to make a mandatory offer, the board should ensure that an appropriate resolution to approve a waiver of this obligation is put to independent shareholders prior to implementation of the relevant redemption or purchase and as a pre-condition to its implementation. The Panel must also be consulted in advance in any case where Rule 9 might be relevant. There are indications that institutional investors are not for the most part supportive of Rule 9 waivers in relation to buy-backs.

Rule 37.3 addresses the use of the buy-back power as a defensive measure by a target in a takeover situation. This reinforces the general prohibition in the Code on directors of a target company taking frustrating action without the approval of the shareholders in general meeting.[138] During the course of an offer, or even before the date of an offer if the board of the offeree company has reason to believe that a bona fide offer may be imminent, no redemption or purchase by the target company may be made unless it is approved by the shareholders in general meeting. Where it is felt that the redemption or purchase is in pursuance of a contract entered into earlier or another pre-existing obligation, the Panel must be consulted and its consent to proceed without a shareholders' meeting obtained.

The Authorizations Required for an Issue of Redeemable Shares

A limited company which has a share capital is permitted by section 684 of the Companies Act 2006 to issue redeemable shares. In the case of a private company there is no requirement for the articles to authorize the issue of redeemable shares, although articles may exclude or restrict this power.[139] The articles of a public company must authorize the issue of redeemable shares.[140] Subject to the articles (where relevant), section 684(1) allows for the issuance of shares which are to be redeemed or are liable to be redeemed at the option of the company or of the shareholder. Any class of shares may be issued as redeemable. However, a company must not issue redeemable shares at a time when there are no issued shares of the company that are not redeemable: in other words, a company may not create a situation in which it could redeem itself out of existence.[141] Stamp duty is not payable on a redemption of shares (unlike a buy-back).

Prior to the Companies Act 2006, there was uncertainty whether the details of the terms and manner of redemption had to be specified precisely in the articles or whether it was sufficient for the articles simply to state that these details were to be fixed by the directors at the time when the shares were actually issued. The latter interpretation was preferable from the viewpoint of flexibility in that it allowed for fine-tuning of the terms on which shares were to be issued to reflect the market conditions at the time of issue. However, it was unclear

---

[137] As discussed in ch 1.   [138] Takeover Code, Rule 21.   [139] Companies Act 2006, s 684(2).
[140] Companies Act 2006, s 684(3).   [141] Companies Act 2006, s 684(4).

whether it could be adopted (at least in relation to public companies) because of a reference in Article 43 of the Second Company Law Directive to the terms and manner of redemption being 'laid down' in the company's statutes or instrument of incorporation. Section 685 of the Companies Act 2006 resolves the issue in favour of a broadly flexible approach by permitting the directors to fix the terms, conditions, and manner of redemption provided that they are authorized to do so by the company's articles or by a resolution of the company. This provision applies to both public and private companies. Where the directors are so authorized, they must determine the terms, conditions, and manner of redemption before the shares are allotted and these details must be disclosed in a statement of capital.[142] Where the directors are not so authorized, the terms, conditions, and manner of redemption must be stated in the company's articles.[143]

Other Requirements of the Companies Act 2006 Relating to Redemption of Redeemable Shares

The statutory framework governing the financing of the redemption of redeemable shares follows the same pattern as that which applies in relation to share buy-backs. Thus redeemable shares may only be redeemed out of distributable profits or the proceeds of a fresh issue of shares made for the purpose of the redemption.[144] This is subject to the qualification that, in the circumstances considered earlier in relation to buy-backs, a private company may use its capital to redeem its shares.[145] Any redemption premium should usually be paid from distributable profits, but if the shares were issued at a premium the proceeds of a fresh issue can be applied for this purpose up to the aggregate of the premiums so received or the current amount of the company's share premium account, whichever is the lesser.[146] Only fully paid redeemable shares can be redeemed and the shares must be paid for on redemption unless the redemption terms provide for payment on a later date.[147] Redeemed shares must be cancelled, which has the effect of reducing the company's issued share capital; they may not be held in treasury.[148] Notice must be given to the registrar of companies of the redemption and cancellation of redeemable shares.[149]

If a company fails to redeem redeemable shares in accordance with their terms, the holder may seek specific performance but not damages.[150] The court must not grant an order for specific performance if the company shows that it is unable to meet the costs of the redemption from its distributable profits.[151]

Class Rights Issues Relating to Share Buy-backs and Redeemable Shares

Where a company's share capital comprises more than one class of shares, a proposal to buy back shares may amount to a variation of class rights. If so, an appropriate class consent must be obtained in addition to the corporate consents considered in this chapter. Likewise, an issue of redeemable shares may vary the class rights of existing preference shares which

---

[142] Companies Act 2006, s 685(3).   [143] Companies Act 2006, s 685(4).
[144] Companies Act 2006, s 687(2).
[145] Companies Act 2006, s 687(1). The 'de minimis' relaxation for purchases of small amounts under Companies Act 2006, s 692(1)(b) is not extended to redemptions.
[146] Companies Act 2006, s 687(3)–(4).   [147] Companies Act 2006, s 686.
[148] Companies Act 2006, s 688.   [149] Companies Act 2006, s 689.
[150] Companies Act 2006, s 735.   [151] Companies Act 2006, s 735.

are entitled to priority on any return of capital and, again therefore, class consents may be required.[152] The Association of British Insurers recommends that class meeting consent to a buy-back of ordinary shares should be obtained in any case where a company has preference shares. This is a general recommendation and is not limited to instances where the buy-back would amount to a variation in the rights attaching to the preference shares.

Share Buy-backs and Redeemable Shares and Protection of Minorities

It would be open to a shareholder who objects to any aspect of the capital reorganizations discussed in this chapter to seek relief under section 994 of the Companies Act 2006, on the ground that the action amounts to unfairly prejudicial conduct. An example of an unsuccessful claim arising from a proposal to buy back shares is provided by *Rutherford, Petitioner*,[153] a decision of the Scottish Court of Session (Outer House). The company proposed to buy back a 33 per cent interest in the company's shares. The purpose of this acquisition was to satisfy the view of most of the shareholders of the company that shareholdings should be widely spread and that there should be no dominant block of shares available to encourage individual shareholders to acquire a controlling interest. The petitioner averred that the company was proposing to pay too much for the shares because it was proposing to offer 64p per share even though the shares were trading in the market at 19p. The court held that a prima facie case to this effect was not established on the facts, concluding that the transactions in which the shares had traded at around 19p probably involved small blocks of shares and that the value of the dominant block of shares would be likely to be materially more valuable. In this context, it was held to be relevant that there was known to be an investment trust that was willing to pay up to 72p per share for a controlling interest in the company. Also, the proposed share purchase was designed to stabilize the management of the company which, the court concluded, might well elevate the price of the shares. The court held further that the petitioner would face problems in establishing the second claim, namely that the company was not in a position to fund the purchase and that interest payments on borrowings to finance the acquisition would exceed the company's annual profits. Thirdly, although the petitioner might further wish to allege that the purchase would have the effect of discouraging the investment trust which was willing to pay a premium for a controlling interest, the court thought that if this was what the majority of the shareholders wanted, it would be a fine question whether the petitioner's decreased chance of securing an offer from that bidder could be described as unfair. Taking all these factors into account in determining the balance of convenience, the court refused to grant the interdict (injunction) sought by the petitioner.

---

[152] On class rights generally, see ch 6.   [153] [1994] BCC 876.

9

Distributions to Shareholders

Investor Expectations

Established canons of corporate finance are that shareholders in widely-owned companies where dividends have been paid in the past are conservative in their dividend expectations: they expect to continue to receive regular dividends in respect of their shares, that those dividends will be smoothed over time, and that any increases will reflect underlying longer-term prospects for the business.[1] Empirical work has confirmed that these principles are still supported by market practice: dividend conservatism is prevalent and only firms that are confident about the prospects for sustainable earnings growth tend to consider increasing dividends.[2] One factor that has changed in recent years is that it has become more common for companies to return value to shareholders by means of share buy-backs. Substitution of repurchases for dividend increases has been identified in the US.[3] It is thought that a decrease in the overall number of firms paying dividends that was evident during the 1980s and 1990s[4] may have been linked to the availability of share buy-backs as an alternative payout mechanism.[5] In the UK, share buy-back programmes by large companies have also become common (a trend linked to changes in the applicable taxation rules).[6] Share buy-backs are more flexible than dividends because they have not become associated with raised expectations with regard to future payouts.[7] As such they can be a useful mechanism for returning to shareholders occasional cash surpluses that arise from time to time. However, in the UK share buy-back programmes generally have not taken the place of regular dividend payments.[8] Even in times of crisis, companies can be reluctant to cut or cancel dividends, as is

---

[1] J Lintner, 'Distribution of Incomes of Corporations Among Dividends, Retained Earnings, and Taxes' (1956) 46(2) *American Economic Review* 97. The Lintner 'smoothing' theory has generated a large body of literature, as surveyed in I Guttman, O Kadan, and E Kandel, 'Dividend Stickiness and Strategic Pooling' (2010) 23 *Review of Financial Studies* 4455; MT Leary and R Michaely, 'Determinants of Dividend Smoothing: Empirical Evidence' (2011) 24 *Review of Financial Studies* 3197. It continues to serve as a departure point for new research, eg, BM Lambrecht, 'A Lintner Model of Payout and Managerial Rents' (2012) 67 *Journal of Finance* 1761.

[2] A Brav, JR Graham, R Campbell, CR Harvey, and R Michaely, 'Payout Policy in the 21st Century' (2005) 77 *Journal of Financial Economics* 483. European managers broadly agree in that they try to smooth dividends from year to year and avoid reducing dividends: F Bancel, UR Mittoo, and N Bhattacharyya, 'Cross-Country Determinants of Payout Policy: A Survey of European Firms' (2004) 33 *Financial Management* 103.

[3] G Grullon and R Michaely, 'Dividends, Share Repurchases and the Substitution Hypothesis' (2002) 57(4) *Journal of Finance* 1649. But evidence suggests that a different position obtains elsewhere: A Dhanani and R Roberts, *Corporate Share Repurchases: The Perceptions and Practices of UK Financial Managers and Corporate Investors* (Edinburgh: Institute of Chartered Accountants of Scotland, 2009), discussed further in ch 8.

[4] Noted by E Fama and K French, 'Disappearing Dividends: Changing Firm Characteristics or Lower Propensity to Pay?' (2001) 60 *Journal of Financial Economics* 3. Nevertheless, the aggregate amount of dividends paid by industrial firms increased over the period, both in nominal and in real terms: H DeAngelo, L DeAngelo, and DJ Skinner, 'Are Dividends Disappearing? Dividend Concentration and the Consolidation of Earnings' (2004) 72 *Journal of Financial Economics* 425. Since 2000, a rebound of conventional dividend policies has been detected: B Julio and D Ikenberry, 'Reappearing Dividends' (2004) 16(4) *Journal of Applied Corporate Finance* 89.

[5] Brav et al, 'Payout Policy in the 21st Century'; F Allen and R Michaely, 'Payout Policy' in G Constantinides, M Harris, and R Stulz, (eds), *Handbook of the Economics of Finance Vol 1A* (North-Holland: Elsevier 2003) 337, 404–20.

[6] D Oswald and S Young, 'Cashing in on Share Buybacks' (November 2003) *Accountancy* 55.

[7] D Oswald and S Young, 'Cashing in on Share Buybacks' (in relation to the UK); Brav *et al*, 'Payout Policy in the 21st Century' (in relation to the US).

[8] Dhanani and Roberts, *Corporate Share Repurchases*.

evident from data on banks' dividend policies during the financial turmoil of 2007–9.[9] The dividends paid by Bank of America and Citigroup showed no slowdown until the third quarter of 2008. Bank of America then continued to pay dividends, at a slower rate, until the end of the fourth quarter of 2009. Citigroup did not cut its dividend until the fourth quarter of 2008, although it paid zero dividends from the second to the fourth quarter of 2009. Merrill Lynch almost doubled its dividend in the fourth quarter of 2008 compared to the previous year. Perhaps most strikingly of all, Lehmans increased its dividend from $95 million in the second quarter of 2008 to $118 million in the third quarter of 2008, which was just before it collapsed into bankruptcy in September 2008. In the EU, temporary restrictions on dividends were imposed as conditions of the State Aid provided by Member States to crisis-hit distressed financial institutions under arrangements overseen by the European Commission.[10]

Not paying a dividend makes a company an unattractive proposition for cautious investors in search of a steady income stream. Furthermore, for a company to switch from paying dividends to not doing so can create hardship for its existing shareholders who can find themselves effectively locked into an increasingly unattractive investment. As the Lloyds Banking Group noted in its 2011 Annual Report and Accounts, when its State Aid ban on dividend payments was in force 'We understand that the absence of dividends has created difficulties for many of our shareholders and we remain committed to recommencing progressive dividend payments as soon as we are able... Our Board is grateful for the support of our shareholders in 2011 and is very conscious that they—including most of our staff who themselves are shareholders—have suffered through the decline of the share price and the absence of a dividend.'[11]

Determinants of Dividend Policy[12]

Dividend policy—why companies choose to initiate dividend payouts, the factors that explain the level of payout, the reasons for increasing or cutting the payout level—has been described as one of the most thoroughly researched issues in modern finance.[13] Yet despite the intense attention it has received, there has yet to emerge a theory that is fully consistent with real-life dividend policy.[14] The following paragraphs outline key lines of inquiry in the literature exploring determinants of payout policy. It has been observed that how and why firms decide on a particular dividend policy is still not well understood despite an abundance of empirical evidence.[15]

Dividend policy and market value

A foundation of modern corporate finance theory is that in frictionless markets dividend policy should not affect the overall market value of a company's shares.[16] The theory is based

---

[9] The data on US investment banks that follows is taken from: VV Acharya, I Gujral, N Kulkarni, and HS Shin, 'Dividends and Bank Capital in the Financial Crisis of 2007–2009,' NBER Working Paper Series No 16896 (2012).

[10] European Commission, *The Effects of Temporary State Aid Rules Adopted in the Context of the Financial and Economic Crisis* (Commission Staff Working Paper, October 2011).

[11] At 11 and 14. For the classic account of the nature of the 'dividend puzzle': F Black, 'The Dividend Puzzle' (1976) 2 *The Journal of Portfolio Management* 5.

[12] HK Baker (ed), *Dividends and Dividend Policy* (Hoboken, New Jersey: John Wiley & Sons, 2009).

[13] WL Megginson, *Corporate Finance Theory* (Reading, Mass: Addison Wesley, 1997) 353. See also WL Megginson, SB Smart, and BM Lucey, *Introduction to Corporate Finance* (London: South-Western Cengate Learning, 2008) ch 13.

[14] MW Faulkender, TT Milbourn, and AV Thakor, 'Does Corporate Performance Determine Capital Structure and Dividend Policy?' (9 March 2006) <http://ssrn.com/abstract=686865>; Bancel, Mittoo, and Bhattacharyya, 'Cross-Country Determinants of Payout Policy.'

[15] R Michaely and MR Roberts, 'Corporate Dividend Policies: Lessons from Private Firms' (2012) 25 *Review of Financial Studies* 711.

[16] MH Miller and F Modigliani, 'Dividend Policy, Growth and the Valuation of Shares' (1961) 34 *Journal of Business* 411.

on the fact that shares give their holders the right to share in capital growth as well as in whatever income is distributed by the company from time to time. Shares will have a higher capital value where the company retains the profits and invests them in new profitable ventures than they would have if the company distributed those profits by way of dividend and then raised further capital to fund the new venture by an issue of new shares. An investor who wants cash can always sell his shares to realize a capital gain instead of relying on the company to pay him a dividend. The theory implies that dividend policy should be a simple matter of paying out the residual cash flow after decisions on investment opportunities have been made.

However, real markets are not frictionless and there are various practical difficulties with this theory. It ignores the transaction costs involved in buying and selling shares and the differing tax treatment of dividends and capital gains on the disposal of shares.[17] It assumes the existence of a liquid market for the shares which may not in fact exist. It also assumes that new investments will be perfectly reflected in the company's share price. However, although in theory, the effect of low dividends in the early years of a project should be counterbalanced by the expected higher dividends in future years where shares are valued on the basis of their expected future dividend yield, in practice, investors may view the future gains that may result from new projects funded from retained earnings as more risky than dividends paid here and now and may, as a result, undervalue the shares of a company that pays out a low level of dividends.[18] The theory also ignores principal-agent concerns and it excludes the possibility of investor irrationality: irrespective of the value maximizing arguments, shareholders may simply prefer to receive steady dividends than to have to sell part of their shareholding in order to generate cash.[19]

Once the restrictive assumptions on which the 'irrelevance' theory was first developed are relaxed, it becomes evident that dividend policy can affect the overall value of a company's shares.[20] Empirical data indicates that corporate managers do not behave as the 'irrelevance' theory would predict and that they will pass up positive investment opportunities or borrow to fund them before cutting dividends because of the adverse impact that taking that step will have on the share price.[21] Implicit within this finding is the recognition that maintaining the dividend level is a priority on a level with investment decisions rather than being secondary to them. The high commercial significance of maintaining a steady dividend explains why the dividend policies of publicly owned companies tend to be path dependent, with the level of payouts by a firm in any given period being constrained by its previous payout policy. In other words, once a company has initiated a particular dividend policy its choices thereafter are liable to be constrained by the pressure to cater to the preferences of the clientele of investors that it has attracted.[22]

Dividend policy, information asymmetries, and signalling

Dividends can perform an information function: paying healthy, consistent dividends in an environment shaped by conservatism is a way of indicating to investors who are not directly

---

[17] If income gains are taxed more heavily than capital gains a generous dividend policy can reduce shareholder wealth: MJ Brennan, 'Taxes, Market Valuation and Corporate Financial Policy' (1970) *National Tax Journal* 417; MH Miller, 'Behavioral Rationality in Finance: The Case of Dividends' (1986) 59(4.2) *Journal of Business* S451.

[18] MJ Gordon, 'Dividends, Earnings and Stock Prices' (1959) 41 *Review of Economics and Statistics* 99; S Keane, 'Dividends and the Resolution of Uncertainty' (1974) 1 *Journal of Business Finance and Accounting* 389.

[19] Allen and Michaely, 'Payout Policy' 399–404 consider investor irrationality as a factor affecting payout policy.

[20] Allen and Michaely, 'Payout Policy' 376–7.

[21] Brav et al, 'Payout Policy in the 21st Century.'

[22] The 'catering' theory of dividend policy indicates that managers rationally cater to investor (uninformed and perhaps time-varying) demands by paying dividends when investors favour payouts and not paying dividends when that accords with investor preferences: Baker and JA Wurgler, 'Catering Theory of Dividends' (2004) 59 *Journal of Finance* 1125.

involved in managing a publicly-owned company that its management has long-term confidence in the business and its prospects.[23] If managers choose to increase the level of dividend, that is liable to be interpreted not just as an indication of the company's past profitability but also as a sign of greater dividend-paying capacity in the future. Conversely, a dividend cut may be taken as an indicator of long-term problems within the company rather than as a temporary blip in profitability or liquidity.[24]

Viewed in this way, dividends act as a counterweight to the information asymmetries between managers and investors. Some academics have developed the idea of dividends as an information-conveying mechanism to suggest that managers may use dividend policy to signal the strength of their company and to distinguish it from competitors, the underlying reasoning being that weaker competitors will not be able to afford to take that step because of the longer-term expectations associated with paying a generous dividend in one period.[25]

However, there is also scholarship that casts doubt on whether signalling to investors is a significant determinant of corporate dividend policy.[26] One US study found that dividends were mainly paid by major companies that already enjoyed significant coverage from analysts and journalists.[27] Companies of such prominence are unlikely to have much need to use financial decisions to communicate to investors. The authors of the study concluded that it is 'possible that signalling motives may be important on the margin for some prominent dividend-paying firms' but that 'it is hard to envision plausible scenarios in which a material portion of aggregate dividends reflects signalling motives.'[28] Another study, which examined managers' opinions and the motives underlying their companies' dividend policy, found that managers regarded payout policy as performing an information-conveying function but that it was 'rarely thought of as a tool to separate a company from competitors.'[29]

Dividend policy, principal-agent problems and agency costs

The standard way of looking at the internal structure of a company from an economic perspective is to regard it as a 'nexus of contracts'[30] between the shareholders, who provide the capital, and the managers, who are engaged as agents[31] of the shareholders to manage the business on their behalf. Where the managers and the shareholders do not comprise broadly the same group of people, an agency conflict arises: the shareholders fund the business but do not manage it; the managers run the business but they lack the incentive to maximize profits

---

[23] S Bhattacharya, 'Imperfect Information, Dividend Policy and the "Bird in the Hand" Fallacy' (1979) *Bell Journal of Economics* 259. This is not a particularly recent phenomenon: JB Baskin and PJ Miranti, *A History of Corporate Finance* (CUP, 1997) 86–7 discussing dividends as a source of information in the period up to the early 18th century.

[24] JR Woolridge and C Ghosh, 'Dividend Cuts: Do They Always Signal Bad News' (Winter 1986) *Midland Corporate Finance Journal* 20; J Tirole, *The Theory of Corporate Finance* (Princeton NJ: Princeton University Press, 2006) 257.

[25] Bhattacharya, 'Imperfect Information'; MH Miller and K Rock, 'Dividend Policy under Asymmetric Information' (1985) 40 *Journal of Finance* 40, 1031; K John and J Williams, 'Dividends, Dilution, and Taxes: A Signaling Equilibrium' (1985) 40(4) *Journal of Finance* 1053. Allen and Michaely, 'Payout Policy' provides a review of the signalling literature. For a recent contribution from a behavioural finance perspective: M Baker and J Wurgler, 'Dividends as Reference Points: A Behavioral Signaling Approach,' NBER Working Paper Series No 18242 (2012).

[26] Allen and Michaely, 'Payout Policy.'

[27] DeAngelo, DeAngelo, and Skinner, 'Are Dividends Disappearing?'

[28] DeAngelo, DeAngelo, and Skinner, 'Are Dividends Disappearing?' 453.

[29] Brav et al, 'Payout Policy in the 21st Century.'

[30] FH Easterbrook and DR Fischel, 'The Corporate Contract' (1989) 89 *Columbia Law Review* 1416.

[31] In legal terms, the directors are the agents of the company, not of the shareholders: *Automatic Self-Cleansing Filter Syndicate Co Ltd v Cuninghame* [1906] 2 Ch 34, CA.

over the longer term and are liable instead to act in their own self-interest.[32] The agency conflict produces 'agency costs', meaning that, because of the divergence between shareholders' interests and managers' interests, investors will pay less for shares in companies where shareholding is widely dispersed and management is the responsibility of a few individuals. It follows that to improve the price which investors are willing to pay for its shares, the managers of a company should do all that they can to reduce agency costs.

Agency cost analysis suggests that companies should pay high dividends and, where necessary, raise finance from other sources: this will reduce agency costs because equity investors have the security of knowing that management will have had to expose their business record and their plans for the future to the scrutiny of lenders or to the market, and may have had to submit to restrictive covenants in order to secure the funds.[33] In Easterbrook's words: 'expected, continuing dividends compel firms to raise new money in order to carry out their activities. They therefore precipitate the monitoring and debt-equity adjustments that benefit stockholders.'[34]

There is some evidence to support the hypothesis that mitigating agency problems is significant as a determinant of dividend policy.[35] Even though it has been found that corporate managers do not regard dividend policy as a means of imposing discipline on themselves,[36] the fact that the probability of paying dividends increases with the amount of earned equity in the capital structure can be explained as a response to the agency problems that would loom large for high-earning companies if they retained earnings and thereby increased opportunities for managers to engage in activities that benefited themselves more than their shareholders.[37] However, it is also possible to find evidence that is inconsistent with this hypothesis.[38]

A recent line of scholarship on agency costs suggests two models in which dividend policy is associated with the quality of legal protection for shareholders: the 'outcome' model, which associates high dividends with high quality legal protections because shareholders are able to exert pressure on the managers to disgorge cash; and the 'substitute' model, which associates high dividends with low quality legal protections because managers want to build a good reputation with investors.[39] However, the significance of shareholder protection laws as a determinant of dividend policy is controversial.[40]

---

[32] On the problem of agency conflicts and agency costs generally, see M Jensen and W Meckling, 'Theory of the Firm: Managerial Behavior, Agency Costs and Ownership Structure' (1976) 3 *Journal of Financial Economics* 305; EF Fama, 'Agency Problems and the Theory of the Firm' (1980) 88 *Journal of Political Economy* 288.

[33] M Jensen, 'Agency Costs of Free Cash Flow, Corporate Finance and Takeovers' (May 1986) 76 *American Economic Review* 323; FH Easterbrook, 'Two Agency-Cost Explanations of Dividends' (1984) 74 *American Economic Review* 650; RC Clark, *Corporate Law* (Boston: Little, Brown, 1986) 598–9. A draconian proposal following this line of reasoning is that companies should be legally obliged to pay out all or a designated portion of earnings as dividends: K Brewster, 'The Corporation and Economic Federalism' in ES Mason (ed), *The Corporation in Modern Society* (Cambridge: CUP, 1959) 72. A more moderate proposal is that there should be greater mandatory disclosure of the way in which management arrives at the company's dividend policy: V Brudney, 'Dividends, Discretion and Disclosure' (1980) 66 *Virginia Law Review* 85.

[34] FH Easterbrook, 'Two Agency-Cost Explanations of Dividends.' See also R La Porta, F Lopez de Silanes, A Shleifer, and RW Vishny, 'Agency Problems and Dividend Policies Around the World' (2000) 55 *Journal of Finance* 1. For a review of the literature on agency problems-related explanations of dividends see Allen and Michaely, 'Payout Policy.' Cheffins has suggested that dividend policies contributed to the separation of ownership and control in Britain that occurred from the 1940s onwards: BR Cheffins, 'Dividends as a Substitute for Corporate Law: The Separation of Ownership and Control in the United Kingdom' (2006) 63 *Washington and Lee Law Review* 1273.

[35] H DeAngelo, L DeAngelo, and RM Stulz, 'Dividend Policy, Agency Costs, and Earned Equity,' (2006) 81 *Journal of Financial Economics* 227.

[36] Brav et al, 'Payout Policy in the 21st Century.'

[37] DeAngelo, DeAngelo, and Stulz, 'Dividend Policy, Agency Costs, and Earned Equity.'

[38] See the literature review in Faulkender, Thakor, and Milbourn, 'Does Corporate Performance Determine Capital Structure and Dividend Policy?' See also the survey of European managers' views by Bancel, Mittoo, and Bhattacharyya, 'Cross-Country Determinants of Payout Policy,' which finds little support for the agency theory.

[39] La Porta et al, 'Agency Problems and Dividend Policies Around the World.'

[40] Bancel, Mittoo, and Bhattacharyya, 'Cross-Country Determinants of Payout Policy' do not find a systematic relation between quality of legal systems and dividend policies.

Regulation of Dividend Policy Decisions

An overview of the regulatory response to agency problems relating to shareholders

The commercial necessity in companies with dispersed ownership of meeting investors' expectations with regard to dividends limits the opportunity for managerial abuse of the power to control dividend policy.[41] Failure to meet shareholders' expectations will have a negative effect on share price and may put the company into the frame as a potential takeover target. The finance director and others most closely associated with the policy may be criticized and their job security put at risk. Yet even though these market pressures are powerful, they do not entirely eliminate the risk of managerial abuse because it may be possible for directors to satisfy investor expectations by paying a reasonable dividend in circumstances where the company's performance and the investment opportunities available to it would warrant a different level of payout. This scenario suggests that there may be considerable leeway for directors to decide to retain profits to expand the company's business into new ventures for reasons that are more to do with the enhancement of their personal reputation resulting from the growth of the company than with the benefits that may ultimately flow to the shareholders from the company from those new investments.[42] Equally, directors may decide to pay out excessive dividends because of short-term personal considerations arising from their ownership of shares and share options in the company, rather than because they genuinely believe this to be in the company's interests.

Systems of company law and corporate governance employ various strategies to bolster market-based controls of the director-shareholder principal-agent problems that arise in classic form in the context of corporate distributions. One is to give shareholders a say in distribution decisions. Shareholder involvement in distribution decisions is not compulsory in the UK under general company law but the norm is for companies to include requirements to this effect in their internal constitutions.[43] The procedure for the declaration and payment of dividends is set out in the articles of association, which usually provide for final dividends to be declared by shareholders in general meeting on the recommendation of the directors and for interim dividends to be paid by the directors without reference to the shareholders for approval. It has been judicially noted that for a company to pay an endless stream of interim dividends, with no final dividend ever recommended by the directors and approved by the company in general meeting, could not be a proper exercise of the powers conferred by the articles.[44] Articles usually provide that shareholders cannot declare a dividend in excess of the amount recommended by the directors. Apart from contested takeover or other exceptional circumstances where tactical disputes over directors' dividend recommendations may arise between majority and minority shareholders,[45] shareholders can be expected generally to be disinclined to opt for a lesser amount than that recommended by the directors. This means that the shareholders' decision to approve final dividends can appear to be little more than a rubber stamp but the fact that the shareholders do at least have the opportunity formally

---

[41] DR Fischel, 'The Law and Economics of Dividend Policy' (1981) 67 *Virginia Law Review* 699, 715–6.

[42] V Brudney, 'Dividends, Discretion and Disclosure' (1980) 66 *Virginia Law Review* 85, 95; Fischel, 'The Law and Economics of Dividend Policy', 710–4; MC Jensen, 'Eclipse of the Public Corporation' (Sept–Oct 1989) *Harvard Business Review* 61.

[43] See Model Articles (plc), art 70; Model Articles (Ltd), art 30.

[44] *Re Paycheck Services 3 Ltd and others; Revenue and Customs Commissioners v Holland* [2011] 1 BCLC 141, SC, [104] *per* Lord Walker.

[45] As in the factual background to *Re Astec (BSR) plc* [1999] BCC 59 where a majority shareholder, which was seeking to acquire the remainder of the shares, opposed the board's dividend recommendation.

to review dividend recommendations and to require directors to justify them may have a disciplining effect. The importance that institutional investors attach to the standard mechanism for shareholder approval of the final dividend can be seen from guidance issued by the National Association of Pension Funds (NAPF), which states that if shareholder approval is not sought for the approval of the final dividend, investors may wish to consider submitting a shareholder resolution or voting against the company's report and accounts, except where companies can demonstrate that changing their practice to seek shareholder approval of the dividend would significantly delay payment, to the material disadvantage of shareholders.[46]

It would be open to companies to vest more direct control in shareholders via their articles—for example, by giving shareholders the power to exceed the amount of payout recommended by the directors—but this could be unwise as it could result in important managerial decisions that have ramifications for share prices being taken by an inexpert, ill-informed group. Moreover, its success in addressing principal-agent conflicts between shareholders and management could be outweighed by its adverse effects with regard to majority-minority shareholder agency issues: placing more power in the hands of shareholders could intensify the latter problems by, for example, enabling majority shareholders more easily to force through excessive dividend payouts that would then make it difficult for the company to pursue profitable business opportunities that would be beneficial for minority shareholders. In assessing the (de-)merits of a shareholder power 'grab', it should not be forgotten that leaving decision-making power to the directors, as a concentrated, focused, and expert group, does not mean that the shareholders are left powerless because, if dissatisfied they can, as a last resort, replace the directors. The Companies Act 2006 allows shareholders to vote directors out of office by an ordinary resolution.[47] This important provision helps to ensure that directors focus on shareholders' interests rather than their own.

Another strategy for controlling agency problems is the governance mechanism of appointing independent non-executive directors to the board. Non-executive directors have much greater access than the shareholders in general meeting to information about the company's financial position and prospects, and are much better placed to impose pressure on the executive directors and senior management to justify their dividend policy. The UK Corporate Governance Code, which is applicable to companies with a premium listing of equity in the UK,[48] provides as a main principle that a board should have the appropriate balance of skills, experience, independence, and knowledge, and as a supporting principle that the board should include an appropriate combination of executive and non-executive directors (and in particular independent non-executive directors).[49] There is also a specific Code provision that, except for smaller companies, at least half the board, excluding the chair, should comprise non-executive directors determined by the board to be independent.[50]

All directors, executive and non-executive, are constrained by the duties attaching to their office. If directors were to manipulate the dividend policy to serve private interests rather than those of the members generally, that would amount to a breach of their statutory duties to promote the success of the company and to avoid conflicts of interest.[51] Yet the level of the deterrent effect of directors' duties, which are owed to the company rather than to the shareholders directly is debatable, because of the existence of various factors that militate against the effective deployment of formal corporate enforcement tools. First, the masking effect of a policy of paying dividends which are sufficient to satisfy investor demands even though the company's business and prospects would justify higher levels, means that it may be difficult

---

[46] NAPF, *Corporate Governance Policy and Voting Guidelines* (2012) F.7.1.   [47] Companies Act 2006, s 168.
[48] *LR* 9.8.6(5)–(6) and 9.8.7.   [49] UK Corporate Governance Code, B1.
[50] UK Corporate Governance Code, B.1.2.   [51] Companies Act 2006, Pt 10, ch 2.

to detect and prove wrongdoing.[52] Secondly, even if an action did reach the courts, it is likely that, in the absence of evidence demonstrating a clear conflict of interests, the court would be reluctant to second-guess the directors' business judgment about dividend policy.[53] In general the reluctance of the courts to intervene in intra-corporate disputes of this nature is entirely appropriate given the complexity and commercial sensitivity of the issue but there is a risk that it could be taken too far leaving deserving claimants without redress.[54] Thirdly, there are procedural difficulties that active shareholders who are seeking to use litigation to test compliance with directors' duties may struggle to overcome. Since 2006, the derivative claim, which is the mechanism whereby a minority shareholder can pursue on behalf of the company a claim for breach of directors' duties, has been set out in statute[55] rather than in obscure and often difficult to understand case law but clarification of the law has not yet led to the transformation of the derivative claim into a principal mechanism of corporate govern-ance control in the UK. Despite the reforms, active shareholders may still be disinclined to bring a derivative claim for a range of reasons, including the availability of less burdensome options (such as exiting the company by a sale of the shares on the open market), free-rider concerns (if a claim succeeds judgment will be in favour of the company not the shareholder who pursued the claim on its behalf), the high hurdles that must be cleared in order to obtain permission from the court to proceed with a derivative claim, and complexities in civil pro-cedure relating to the funding of litigation and costs rules.

As an alternative to the bringing of a derivative claim for breach of directors' duties, there is also the possibility of mounting a legal challenge to a policy of paying low dividends (or, as the case may be, excessive dividends) on the grounds that it amounts to unfairly prejudicial conduct. Section 994 of the Companies Act 2006 allows a shareholder to petition the court for relief where the affairs of the company are being conducted in an unfairly prejudicial manner. To succeed in a section 994 petition, a shareholder must ordinarily show that there has been some breach of the terms on which he agreed (contractually or otherwise) that the affairs of the company should be conducted or some use of the rules in a manner which equity would regard as contrary to good faith.[56] It has been judicially stated that a useful question to ask in relation to unfair prejudice complaints is whether the exercise of the power or rights in question would involve a breach of an agreement or understanding between the parties which it would be unfair to allow a member to ignore.[57] Mere disappointment that invest-ment or involvement in a company has not turned out as had been hoped does not suffice.

The need to show breach of an agreement or an inequitable use of power restricts the scope for shareholders to use unfair prejudice petitions to complain about dividend policy. Shareholders in UK companies have no absolute entitlements to dividends. Their legal rights depend on the terms on which the shares were issued and the company's constitution. As discussed already, the standard constitutional position is that shareholders are only entitled to such dividends as may be declared by the shareholders in general meeting on the basis of a recommendation from the directors or as may be paid by the directors in the form of interim dividends. This means that even though a company's dividend policy may not be to the liking of the shareholders, it will not ordinarily be possible to show that it is in breach of an agree-ment. Dashed hopes or disappointed commercial expectations will not suffice to give rise to a

---

[52] *Re a Company, ex p Glossop* [1988] 1 WLR 1068, 1076. [53] *Burland v Earle* [1902] AC 83, PC.
[54] *Miles v Sydney Meat Preserving Co Ltd* (1912) 12 SR (NSW) 98, 103 *per* AH Simpson, CJ in E Fischel, 'The Law and Economics of Dividend Policy' 715–6; V Brudney, 'Dividends, Discretion and Disclosure' (1980) 66 *Virginia Law Review* 85, 103–5.
[55] Companies Act 2006, Pt 11.   [56] *O'Neill v Phillips* [1999] 1 WLR 1092, HL.
[57] *Grace v Biagioli* [2006] 2 BCLC 70, CA.

viable claim based on unfair prejudice; it must be established that the directors were in breach of duty and that this breach resulted in conduct that was both prejudicial and unfair.[58] In the public company context, any such special entitlements would need to be clearly spelt out and publicly disclosed because outside investors are entitled to proceed on the footing that the company's public documents provide a complete account of the shareholders' rights.[59] Special entitlements could arise in respect of particular shares, as in the case of preference shares that have a preferential right to dividends (but, even there, fulfilment of the special entitlements will usually depend on dividends being declared).

There may be more prospect of success on an unfair prejudice petition brought by a shareholder in a closely-held private company where the complaints relating to the way in which the affairs of the company have been conducted include the management of its dividend policy.[60] It may be possible in such a company to show that there was a side agreement or understanding between the parties involved in the business, perhaps driven by fiscal considerations, on how profits should be distributed and that there is unfair prejudice because that understanding has not been followed. Complaints about dividend policy now often feature in unfair prejudice cases involving private companies, and only a few examples need be given to illustrate the courts' approach.[61] *Irvine v Irvine*[62] involved a group of companies that had been run over many years by two brothers who were equal shareholders. After the death of one of them, his widow and a family trust, of which she was one of the trustees, petitioned for relief as minority shareholders on the grounds that the surviving brother had procured the payment to himself of excessive remuneration and that, as a result, the shareholders had received no or inadequate dividends. The evidence was that during the twenty-two years or so that the brothers ran the business, the entire annual profits had been extracted and divided between them, apart from amounts needed for tax, regulatory, and other immediate business concerns. There had been no dividend policy and dividends had been paid only in four years. Instead, profit extraction had been effected by whatever means the firm's accountants advised to be fiscally advantageous. The court agreed that the surviving brother had paid himself excessively and that, taking into account the historic policy of extracting all profits apart from the bare minimum needed for the business, this prevented the minority shareholders from receiving their proper share of the profits through dividend payments. Unfair prejudice having been so established, the majority shareholder was ordered to buy out the shares of the minority.

Another illustration is provided by *Croly v Good*.[63] In this case the petitioner had agreed to a 'remuneration strategy' under which he would draw £10,000 per month from the company, with these drawings being treated partly as remuneration and partly as dividends. The petitioner's unfair prejudice claim cited a range of complaints including that the refusal to declare dividends in respect of the shares meant that he became indebted to the company because the drawings corresponding to the amount of his dividends were charged to a loan account. The court agreed that it was an essential part of the remuneration strategy that dividends would be declared at the end of each year in order to clear as far as possible the amounts which had been drawn on account of dividend. Failure to declare such dividends was 'obviously

---

[58] *Re McCarthy Surfacing Ltd* [2009] 1 BCLC 622.

[59] *Re Blue Arrow plc* [1987] BCLC 585 at 590 *per* Vinelott J; *Re Leeds United Holdings plc* [1996] 2 BCLC 545 at 559 *per* Rattee J; *Re Astec (BSR) plc* [1998] 2 BCLC 556 at 588 *per* Jonathan Parker J.

[60] *Re a Company (No 00370 of 1987) ex parte Glossop* [1988] 1 WLR 1068; *Re Sam Weller & Sons Ltd* [1990] 1 Ch 682.

[61] In addition to the authorities mentioned in the text, other recent unfair prejudice cases that have involved complaints about dividend policy include *Fowler v Gruber* [2010] 1 BCLC 563; *Grace v Biagioli* [2006] 2 BCLC 70, CA.

[62] [2007] 1 BCLC 349.   [63] [2010] 2 BCLC 569.

prejudicial' to the petitioner's interest as a member, and it was unfair because it was a breach of what had been agreed.

Yet even in the private company context, the courts will not interfere lightly in decisions on dividend policy that are genuinely driven by commercial considerations rather than being distorted by individuals' personal interests. *Re Sunrise Radio Ltd* illustrates.[64] Despite having significant accumulated profits, Sunrise followed a policy of not paying dividends. The commercial explanation proffered for this policy was that the company was going for growth through the establishment and sale of subsidiary companies with a view to eventual sale or flotation. The court rejected the complaint that the directors had acted improperly or unfairly towards the petitioner in not declaring dividends. On the other hand, the misuse of share allotment powers to dilute the petitioner's stake in the company was held to constitute unfair prejudice.[65]

Dividend policy could conceivably form the basis for a shareholder petition under the Insolvency Act 1986 for the company to be wound up on the grounds that it is just and equitable to do so.[66] In one case it was said that if it were to be proved that directors had resolved to exercise their powers to recommend dividends to a general meeting, and thereby prevent the company in general meeting declaring any dividend greater than that recommended, with intent to keep moneys in the company so as to build a larger company in the future and without regard to the right of members to have profits distributed so far as was commercially possible, the directors' decision would be open to challenge; and that if it were proved that the board of directors had habitually so exercised its powers, that could justify the making of an order for winding up on the just and equitable ground.[67] However, winding up is a remedy of last resort, as no court will lightly pass a death sentence on a viable business.

There is a very detailed statutory framework now in the Companies Act 2006 governing the funds from which distributions can be made and the financial disclosure requirements that must be satisfied in respect of them. This form of regulation is mainly associated with creditor protection goals, and it is considered in more detail in that context later in this chapter, but it is relevant to note here that the detailed statutory framework also has a shareholder protection dimension in that it can operate so as to prevent excessive payouts being made to satisfy the preferences of controlling shareholders. Controlling shareholders are less commonly found in UK listed companies than elsewhere in the world (apart from the US) but they are not wholly unknown even within the top segment of the markets for publicly owned companies and they can certainly be found in unquoted and private companies.

An introduction to the regulatory response to agency problems in relation to creditors

Agency problems also arise as between creditors and the controllers of a company, whether they be its directors or its dominant shareholder(s), because excessive payouts are liable to undermine a company's financial position to the detriment of its creditors. However, the extent to which it is appropriate to emphasize creditor protection as part of the functions of company law is a matter for considerable debate. One reason for thinking that it is not appropriate to shape company law too much around the needs of creditors is that they (or at least those with commercial muscle) can protect themselves contractually. Loan agreements between sophisticated lenders and companies often contain covenants restricting dividends.

---

[64] [2010] 1 BCLC 367.   [65] See further ch 5 on share allotment.
[66] Insolvency Act 1986, s 122(1)(g). *Ebrahimi v Westbourne Galleries Ltd* [1973] AC 360, HL.
[67] *Re a Company, ex p Glossop* [1988] 1 WLR 1068, 1075.

Another reason for caution is that insolvency law is designed to address creditors' interests, including the interests of creditors who are unable to protect themselves contractually and, save perhaps for some specific rules that might apply in the period when companies are in serious financial difficulties and potentially heading towards insolvency, it is therefore duplicative and perhaps damaging to worthwhile economic activity for company law to take on that role as well. We return to these issues after we have considered in more detail the current company rules restricting distributions that have a strong creditor protection focus.

Statutory Regulation of Distributions

Part 23 of the Companies Act 2006 (sections 829 to 853) regulates distributions by public and private companies. In summary, Part 23 provides that a company can only lawfully make distributions out of profits available for the purpose. It defines distributable profits and requires the availability of distributable profits to be supported by the distributing company's financial statements. The requirements for public companies are stricter than those for private companies. So far as public companies are concerned, Part 23 gives effect to Article 17 of the Second Company Law Directive,[68] which restricts distributions by public companies. The UK, along with other EU Member States, has extended broadly the same rules to private companies.

It fell originally to the courts to develop distribution rules out of the principle of maintenance of capital but the detailed statutory code that now operates has been in place from 1980, although it has been amended from time to time since then.[69] The statutory code is without prejudice to the maintenance of capital principle, which continues therefore to play a role in this area. It is open to companies to supplement the statutory code in their internal constitutions. As we have seen, it is usual for articles of association to regulate the procedure for the declaration and payment of dividends.

What is a 'distribution'?

In Part 23 a distribution means 'every description of distribution of a company's assets to its members, whether in cash or otherwise' subject to four exceptions.[70] The exceptions are:

1. an issue of shares as fully or partly paid bonus shares;
2. the reduction of share capital by extinguishing or reducing the liability of any of the members on any of the company's shares in respect of share capital not paid up, or by paying off share capital;
3. the redemption or purchase of any of the company's own shares out of capital (including the proceeds of a fresh issue of shares) or out of unrealized profits in accordance with the provisions of the Act governing redemption and purchase of shares;
4. a distribution of assets to members of the company on its winding up.

---

[68] Now recast as Directive 2012/30/EU of the European Parliament and of the Council of 25 October 2012 on co-ordination of safeguards which, for the protection of the interests of members and others, are required by Member States of companies within the meaning of the second paragraph of Article 54 of the Treaty on the Functioning of the European Union, in respect of the formation of public limited companies and the maintenance and alteration of their capital with a view to making such safeguards equivalent (Recast) [2012] OJ L315/74 (Second Company Law Directive).

[69] EA French, 'The Evolution of the Dividend Law of England' in WT Baxter and S Davidson, *Studies in Accounting* 3rd edn (London: ICAEW, 1977); BS Yamey, 'Aspects of the Law Relating to Company Dividends' (1941) 4 MLR 273.

[70] Companies Act 2006, s 829.

All kinds of cash and non-cash (sometimes described as *in specie*) dividends are thus within the statutory code. This includes 'special' dividends, which in substance are simply interim dividends paid by the directors in accordance with the normal procedure in the articles.[71] The label 'special' is important in commercial terms because it signals that the dividend is meant to be a 'one-off', either as a stand-alone step or in combination with a restructuring of the share capital, and should not be seen as indicating the start of a more permanent increase in the level of payout. However, the label carries no significance so far as the application of the Part 23 statutory code is concerned: special dividends are subject to it as much as (and to no greater extent than) any other type of dividend. Special dividends can be used for one-off returns of value to shareholders: their advantages over other methods of returning value, such as buy-backs or reductions of capital, relate mainly to speed and simplicity; their disadvantages concern lack of optionality for investors, for example, with regard to tax treatment.[72]

The exception for distributions to members of its company on a winding up does not extend to payments to a member after the successful completion of a company voluntary arrangement.[73] This is so notwithstanding that such a payment carries no risk of prejudice to creditors' interests: the restrictions on distributions in the Companies Act 2006, Part 23 apply irrespective of whether on the particular facts of an individual case creditors' interests could be prejudiced.

While there is no doubt that all types of dividend are distributions, more complicated characterization questions can arise in relation to corporate actions that do not follow the procedure for dividends but which result in cash or other assets that belonged to the company ending up in the hands of shareholders. Examples of situations where these complex questions can arise are transfers of assets between companies in a corporate group and the payment of remuneration to directors who are also shareholders. Dispositions of property or payments to persons who happen to be shareholders of a company are not distributions by reason only of the fact of that relationship, even where the amount of the disposition or payment is in proportion to the amount of the shareholdings.[74] Accordingly, many transactions between companies and shareholders will unquestionably be outside the scope of the law relating to distributions. But some will be caught. In *Ridge Securities Ltd v IRC*[75] the distinction between permissible and impermissible (because caught by the law on distributions) transactions was explained in the following terms: 'The corporators may take assets out of the company by way of dividend or, with leave of the court, by way of reduction of capital, or in a winding up. They may of course acquire them for full consideration. They cannot take assets out of the company by way of voluntary disposition, however described, and, if they attempt to do so, the disposition is ultra vires the company.'

Difficulties arise where the company appears to have overpaid for what it received or to have been underpaid for what it delivered because this suggests the possibility of a disguised distribution. The courts disregard the form of a transaction where it is a sham but this power is used only in quite narrow circumstances.[76] Significantly, however, the courts have been willing to recharacterize some corporate transactions as distributions even where they are not shams. This is demonstrated by *Aveling Barford Ltd v Perion Ltd*[77] where an intra-group

---

[71] Special dividends are examined in H DeAngelo, L DeAngelo, and DJ Skinner, 'Special Dividends and the Evolution of Dividend Signaling' (2000) 57 *Journal of Financial Economics* 309.

[72] R Moore, B Ward, B Phillips, and S Stewart, 'Returning Value to Shareholders: Giving Something Back' (2012) 23(8) PLC 23.

[73] *Re TXU Europe Group Plc* [2012] BCC 363.

[74] *MacPherson v European Strategic Bureau* [2000] 2 BCLC 683 CA, 702 *per* Chadwick LJ.

[75] [1964] 1 All ER 275, 288 *per* Pennycuick J.

[76] *Snook v London and West Riding Investments Ltd* [1967] 2 QB 786, CA, 802 *per* Diplock LJ.

[77] [1989] BCLC 626.

sale of assets at less than their market value was held to be in law a sale rather than a sham but it was still an unlawful distribution because it infringed the rule that capital may not be returned to shareholders. Similarly, in *MacPherson v European Strategic Bureau Ltd*,[78] where a so-called payment for consultancy services was in issue, the Court of Appeal held that it was not necessary to categorize the provision as a sham but that it was an unlawful distribution because it was ultra vires the company to seek to distribute assets to shareholders without making proper provision for creditors.

The position was reviewed by the Supreme Court in *Progress Property Co Ltd v Moorgarth*.[79] This case involved the transfer of assets, namely a subsidiary company, in circumstances in which the vendor (V) and purchaser (P) companies both had the same controlling shareholder. The controlling shareholder then sold its shareholding in V. After the change of control, it was alleged by V that the transfer of the subsidiary had been at a gross undervalue and had therefore been ultra vires and unlawful as an unauthorized return of capital. It was accepted, however, that the director who had procured the sale had genuinely believed that the sale was at market value. Dismissing the appeal, the Supreme Court held the sale of the subsidiary was a genuine commercial sale and should not be recharacterized. In reaching this conclusion, the court made the following points:

- whether a transaction infringed the common law rule that the distribution of a company's assets to a shareholder, except in accordance with specific statutory procedures, was unlawful and ultra vires the company, was a matter of substance and not form;

- that the essential issue was how the transaction was to be characterized and the label attached to the transaction by the parties was not decisive;

- that where a transaction which had been negotiated at arm's length and in good faith between a company and a shareholder proved with hindsight to have been detrimental to the company, the court's real task was to inquire into the true purpose and substance of the impugned transaction by investigating all the relevant facts, which might include the states of mind of those orchestrating the corporate activity;

- that sometimes the states of mind of the directors were irrelevant, and what they did was enough by itself to establish the unlawful character of the transaction, however well-meaning the directors were who negotiated the transaction;

- that if the court concluded that there was a genuine arm's length transaction, then it would stand even if it might appear with hindsight to have been a bad bargain for the company but, if it was an improper attempt to extract value by the pretence of an arm's length sale, it would be held to be unlawful; and

- that either conclusion depended on a realistic assessment of all the relevant facts and was not simply a retrospective valuation exercise conducted in isolation from all other inquiries.

Where a transaction takes the form of a sale but is properly to be characterized as a distribution, questions then arise about the valuation of the distribution element for the purposes of statutory rules regulating distributions. These questions were given prominence by the decision in *Aveling Barford Ltd v Perion Ltd*.[80] The Companies Act 2006 introduced a new provision to resolve what had become known as the *Aveling Barford* problem; its operation

---

[78] [2000] 2 BCLC 683, CA.   [79] [2010] UKSC 55, [2011] 1 WLR 1.   [80] [1989] BCLC 626.

is examined later in this chapter after the general features of the statutory regime governing distributions are outlined.[81]

Profits available for distribution

The profits of a company that are available for distribution are defined in the Companies Act 2006 as its accumulated realized profits, so far as not previously utilized by distribution or capitalization, less its accumulated realized losses, so far as not previously written off in a reduction or reorganization of capital duly made.[82] No distinction is drawn between revenue profits and losses (profits and losses from trading) and capital profits and losses (profits and losses on the disposal of fixed assets) for this purpose. Losses incurred in previous years, so far as not previously written off, must be taken into account in determining the amount of distributable profits.[83] On the other hand, retained distributable profits from earlier years can be carried forward and used to pay dividends in years when the company makes a loss, so long as the loss is not so large as to wipe out the retained distributable reserves.

When fixed assets are revalued, increases in value are unrealized profits and they are not normally available for distribution.[84] Instead, they appear in the company's balance sheet (now also known as the 'Statement of financial position') as an undistributable reserve. A significant exception to this rule arises where a company makes a distribution of, or including, a non-cash asset. Any part of the amount at which the asset is shown in the relevant accounts which is an unrealized profit is to be treated as a realized profit for the purposes of determining the lawfulness of the distribution and complying with Companies Act accounting requirements.[85] Companies must pay dividends in cash unless dividends in kind are authorized by the articles.[86] Such authorization is commonly included.[87]

Depreciation charges in respect of assets are taken into account as realized losses in determining the profits available for distribution.[88] There is a special rule for depreciation charges in respect of revalued assets where the revaluation has given rise to an unrealized profit. The Companies Act 2006 allows the difference between the depreciation charge on the revalued amount and the depreciation charge on the original amount to be treated as a realized profit.[89]

Additional requirement for public companies

For public companies there is the further requirement that a distribution may only be made when the amount of its net assets is not less than the aggregate of its called up share capital and undistributable reserves and only if, and to the extent that, the distribution does not reduce the amount of those assets to less than that aggregate.[90] This additional requirement gives effect to Article 17(1) of the Second Company Law Directive, which states that 'no distribution to shareholders may be made when...the net assets as set out in the company's

---

[81] Companies Act 2006, s 845.   [82] Companies Act 2006, s 830(2).

[83] This reverses the common law position: *Lee v Neuchatel Asphalte Co* (1889) 41 Ch D 1, CA; *Ammonia Soda Co v Chamberlain* [1918] 1 Ch 266, CA.

[84] This reverses the common law position where unrealized profits on fixed assets could be distributed: *Dimbula Valley (Ceylon) Tea Co Ltd v Laurie* [1961] Ch 353.

[85] Companies Act 2006, s 846.   [86] *Wood v Odessa Waterworks Co* (1889) 42 Ch D 636.

[87] Model Articles (plc), art 76; Model Articles (Ltd), art 34.

[88] Companies Act 2006, s 841. Depreciation did not have to be charged under the common law rules: *Lee v Neuchatel Asphalte Co* (1889) 41 Ch D 1, CA.

[89] Companies Act 2006, s 841(5).   [90] Companies Act 2006, s 831.

annual accounts are, or following such a distribution would become, lower than the amount of the subscribed capital plus those reserves which may not be distributed under the law or the statutes.'

'Net assets' for this purpose means the aggregate of the company's assets less the aggregate of its liabilities.[91] A company's 'undistributable reserves' comprise: (1) the share premium account, (2) the capital redemption reserve, (3) the amount by which accumulated unrealized profits exceed accumulated unrealized losses, and (4) any other reserve which the company is prohibited from distributing by any enactment or by its articles.[92] The effect of this restriction can be illustrated by the following example.

> A company has net assets of £10 million, a share capital of £3 million, share premium account of £6 million, unrealized losses of £2 million, and distributable profits of £3 million. If the company is private, it can distribute the full amount of the distributable profits: £3 million. However, if the company is public, it must also meet the balance sheet test. Its undistributable reserves are its share capital (£3 million) and its share premium account (£6 million). The profits available for distribution are therefore only £1 million.

In effect, what the net asset test, as embodied in section 831, does is to require public companies to take unrealized losses into account in determining the maximum amount available for distribution.

The highly specialized circumstances in which section 831 gives rise to practical problems are addressed in detailed guidance issued by the accounting profession.[93] These circumstances tend to involve complex financial instruments that combine features of debt and equity, and which in accounting, but not company law, terms may fall to be treated as liabilities rather than as capital.

Relevant accounts

The amount of a distribution which may be made is to be determined by reference to the company's financial position as stated in its relevant accounts.[94] It is individual company accounts rather than group accounts that are relevant for this purpose.[95] The company's last annual accounts will usually constitute the 'relevant accounts'.[96] These accounts must have been properly prepared in accordance with the requirements of the Companies Act 2006 or have been so prepared but for immaterial matters.[97] As such, the accounts must give a true and fair view of the company's financial position.[98] Prescribed procedures with regard to the circulation of the accounts to members must be followed.[99] If the auditors have qualified their report on the accounts, they must also state in writing whether they consider the matter in respect of which the report is qualified to be material for determining the legality of the distribution.[100] If the last annual accounts do not show adequate reserves to cover a proposed distribution, the company can produce interim accounts and justify the distribution by reference to those accounts.[101] Generally, the interim accounts must enable a reasonable judgment to be made as to the company's financial position[102] but there are more

---

[91] Companies Act 2006, s 831(2).　　　[92] Companies Act 2006, s 831(4).

[93] ICAEW & ICAS, *Guidance on the Determination of Realised Profits and Losses in the Context of Distributions under the Companies Act 2006* (TECH 02/10) Pt 6 (Issues arising from IAS 32 and Pt 7 (employee share schemes)). Hereafter TECH 02/10.

[94] Companies Act 2006, s 836(1).　　　[95] Companies Act 2006, s 837(1).

[96] Companies Act 2006, s 836(2).　　　[97] Companies Act 2006, s 837(2).　　　[98] Companies Act 2006, s 393.

[99] Companies Act 2006, s 423.　　　[100] Companies Act 2006, s 837(4).

[101] Companies Act 2006, s 836(2).　　　[102] Companies Act 2006, s 838(1).

detailed requirements in respect of interim accounts prepared for a proposed distribution by a public company.[103]

Choice of accounting regulatory framework

A company's individual accounts by reference to which a proposed dividend is to be justified may be drawn up in accordance with either the UK's accounting rules (UK Generally Accepted Accounting Principles or UK GAAP) or with the International Financial Reporting Standards (IFRS).[104] This optionality is in contrast to the position with regard to consolidated accounts, where it is mandatory for EU companies that have their securities admitted to trading on an EU regulated market to use IFRS.[105] Notwithstanding a trend for convergence of UK GAAP towards IFRS,[106] certain aspects of IFRS may lead to a different result from UK GAAP so far as the determination of accounting profits is concerned, which has potentially adverse ramifications for the determination of profits that, as a matter of company law, are available for distribution. Possible threats to dividend-paying capacity presented by IFRS are a disincentive to switching to that system in respect of individual accounts even though, for companies that are subject to mandatory obligations regarding use of IFRS for consolidated accounts, it is clearly not ideal to maintain two different systems for financial records. So far as the position as between different companies within a group is concerned, there is a prima facie rule to the effect that financial reporting within a corporate group must be consistent, ie the individual accounts must all be prepared using the same financial reporting framework,[107] but this does not apply where there are 'good reasons for not doing so.'[108] Inconsistencies within the group would thus require justification.

Although section 395 of the Companies Act 2006 gives companies the option of using UK GAAP or IFRS, it has been suggested that accounts drawn up under IFRS may not satisfy the 'true and fair' view requirement of section 393 of the Act. The reasoning is that IFRS aim at achieving a fair presentation[109] and do not have 'any clear subservience to the true and fair concept.'[110] Dividends that are declared on the basis of accounts that do not give a true and fair view would be unlawful because they would not be justified by reference to 'relevant accounts.'[111] The Financial Reporting Council (FRC), which is the body responsible for accounting matters in the UK, however, is of the view that fair presentation under IFRS is equivalent to a true and fair view and in 2013 it published a statement, jointly with the Department for Business, Innovation and Skills (BIS) to confirm that all accounts prepared in accordance with UK standards or IFRS are compliant with UK and EU law.[112]

---

[103] Companies Act 2006, s 838(2)–(6). [104] Companies Act 2006, s 395.

[105] Regulation (EC) 1606/2002 of the European Parliament and of the Council of 19 July 2002 on the application of international accounting standards [2002] OJ L243/1. In the UK, AIM quoted companies are also required to produce their consolidated accounts under IFRS even though AIM is not a regulated market.

[106] In 2012 and 2013 the Financial Reporting Council (FRC), the body responsible for UK GAAP revised financial reporting standards in the UK and Republic of Ireland. The revisions fundamentally reformed financial reporting, replacing almost all extant standards with three Financial Reporting Standards: FRS 100 *Application of Financial Reporting Requirements*, FRS 101 *Reduced Disclosure Framework*, and FRS 102 *The Financial Reporting Standard Applicable in the UK and Republic of Ireland*. New UK GAAP will be effective from January 2015. FRSSE (*Financial Reporting Standard for Smaller Entities*), adopted in 2008, has also been updated and the new version will be effective from January 2015.

[107] Companies Act 2006, s 407(1). [108] Companies Act 2006, s 407(1). [109] IAS 1, para 15.

[110] G Bompas QC, *Opinion* (June 2013). [111] Companies Act 2006, s 836.

[112] FRC, *True and Fair* (July 2011); FRC, 'Accounting standards are part of legally binding corporate reporting framework,' 3 October 2013, referring to a definitive legal Opinion from Michael Moore QC.

Accounting profits and profits available for distribution

The controversy about the suitability of IFRS accounts for the determination of profits available for distribution is related to the fact that accounting profits and distributable profits do not necessarily equate to each other. One potential source of divergence between accounting and realized profits that has become more significant with the move to IFRS is that modern accounting frameworks increasingly permit reporting entities to account at fair value (which is, broadly, current market value) for certain assets. Where assets are recorded at fair value, changes in their value may be taken through the profit and loss account/income statement but these fluctuations may not always be 'realized,' as that concept is understood for the purposes of the legal rules. The legal rules give prominence to the accounting concept of prudence, which implies conservatism in the recognition of profits so that assets and income are not overstated (and also that liabilities are not understated), but the concept has become less significant for accounting purposes. At a fundamental level, there is a deepening divergence between the underlying aims of accounting regulation, which are to provide financial statements that provide information that is useful to investment decisions, and the distribution rules, which are concerned with capital maintenance and creditor protection. This divergence means that the numbers yielded by application of the accounting requirements may be increasingly inappropriate for the purposes of rules that are intended to protect creditors. In some circumstances, moreover, changes in accounting may lead to significant changes in the measurement of a company's assets or liabilities that could have adverse ramifications for dividend-paying capacity. This was an issue of real concern to many companies in 2005, when the accounting treatment of pension fund deficits was revised.[113] That companies could be constrained from paying dividends, not because their economic performance has declined but simply because of developments in the accounting measurement of that performance, is controversial and it has led to growing pressure to break the link between accounts and dividend-paying capacity in a way that instead determines capacity by reference to solvency, though no generally agreed consensus has emerged as yet on the details of how to do so.[114]

Generally accepted principles with respect to the determination of realized profits or losses

Section 853(4) of the Companies Act 2006 provides that references to 'realised profits' and 'realised losses' in relation to a company's accounts are to such profits or losses of the company as fall to be treated as realized in accordance with principles generally accepted at the time when the accounts are prepared, with respect to the determination for accounting purposes of realized profits or losses. In the UK, a leading role in establishing these 'generally accepted principles' is played by the Institute of Chartered Accountants in England and Wales (ICAEW) and the Institute of Chartered Accountants of Scotland (ICAS). The Institutes jointly provide detailed guidance (known now as TECH 02/10) on the determination of realized profits and losses in the context of distributions under the Companies

---

[113] Under the then extant UK GAAP, FRS 17, *Retirement Benefits*, which came fully into force in 2005. IAS 19, *Employee Benefits* is the IRFS equivalent. A prominent casualty was British Airways, which was unable to pay a dividend in 2005 despite an increase in operating profit, because its £1.4bn pension deficit effectively wiped out its distributable reserves.

[114] E Ferran, 'The Place for Creditor Protection on the Agenda for Modernization of Company Law in the European Union' (2006) 2 *European Company and Financial Law Review* 178. The Federation of European Accountants (FEE) has produced a thoughtful paper that suggests a solvency-based test: FEE, *Discussion Paper on Alternatives to Capital Maintenance Regimes* (September 2007). This paper is discussed further at the end of the chapter.

Act 2006.[115] TECH 02/10 notes that it is generally accepted that profits are to be treated as realized only when realized in the form of 'cash or of other assets the ultimate cash realization of which can be assessed with reasonable certainty.'[116] It acknowledges that in this context, 'realized' may encompass profits relating to assets that are readily realizable, which would embrace profits and losses resulting from the recognition of changes in fair values, in accordance with relevant accounting standards, to the extent that they are readily convertible to cash.[117] In assessing whether a company has a realized profit, transactions and arrangements should not be looked at in isolation: a realized profit will arise only where the overall commercial effect on the company is such that it meets the definition of realized profit set out in the guidance.[118] An unrealized profit becomes realized when the relevant criteria set out in the guidance are met (eg, a revaluation surplus becomes realized when the related asset is sold for 'qualifying consideration'); and a profit previously regarded as realized becomes unrealized when the criteria set out in the guidance cease to be met.[119]

The most obvious example of a realized profit is a profit arising from a transaction where the consideration received by the company is 'qualifying consideration.'[120] Under TECH 02/10 qualifying consideration comprises:[121]

(a) cash;

(b) an asset that is readily convertible to cash;

(c) the release, or the settlement or assumption by another party, of all or part of a liability of the company,

(d) an amount receivable in any of the above forms of consideration where:

   (i) the debtor is capable of settling the receivable within a reasonable period of time; and

   (ii) there is a reasonable certainty that the debtor will be capable of settling when called upon to do so; and

   (iii) there is an expectation that the receivable will be settled; or

(e) an amount receivable from a shareholder where and to the extent that:

   (i) the company intends to make a distribution to the shareholder of an amount equal to or less than its receivable from that shareholder; and

   (ii) the company intends to settle such distribution by off-setting against the amount receivable (in whole or in part); and

   (iii) (i) and (ii) are linked as defined in the guidance.

An asset, or change in the fair value of an asset or liability, is considered to be 'readily convertible to cash' if:[122]

(a) a value can be determined at which a transaction in the asset or liability could occur, at the date of determination, in its state at that date, without negotiation and/or marketing, to either convert the asset, liability or change in fair value into cash, or to close out the asset, liability or change in fair value; and

(b) in determining the value, information such as prices, rates or other factors that market participants would consider in setting a price is observable; and

---

[115] TECH 02/10.   [116] TECH 02/10, para 3.3.   [117] TECH 02/10, para 3.3.
[118] TECH 02/10, para 3.5.   [119] TECH 02/10, para 3.6.   [120] TECH 02/10, para 3.9(a).
[121] TECH 02/10, para 3.11.   [122] TECH 02/10, para 3.12 and section 4.

(c) the company's circumstances must not prevent immediate conversion to cash or close out of the asset, liability or change in fair value; for example, the company must be able to dispose of, or close out the asset, liability or the change in fair value, without any intention or need to liquidate or curtail materially the scale of its operations, or to undertake a transaction on adverse terms.

Whereas TECH 02/10 is quite lengthy on what a profit is and when it is to be regarded as realized, the definition of a realized loss is more succinct: the main stipulation provides that losses should be regarded as realized losses except to the extent that the law, accounting standards, or TECH 02/10 provide otherwise.[123]

Dividend payment procedure

The declaration of a final dividend is a standard part of the business at the AGMs of companies. If, between the date when the notices are dispatched and the holding of the meeting, it is discovered that the last annual accounts were not properly prepared then, unless the irregularity is immaterial, the dividend cannot lawfully be declared because, unless the accounts have been properly prepared, they cannot be 'relevant accounts' for the purposes of Part 23 of the Companies Act 2006.[124] The shareholders cannot sue the company for a dividend that has been recommended but not declared, because a final dividend does not become a debt payable to shareholders until it has been declared.[125] Furthermore, if the resolution declaring a final dividend specifies that it is payable on a future date, the dividend becomes due and payable only on that later date. The board's decision to pay an interim dividend does not give rise to a debt and that decision can therefore be reversed at any time before payment.[126] Historically, dividends relating to an accounting period, but declared after the balance sheet date, used to be recognized as a liability even if the approval of that dividend took place after the balance sheet date. However, the current position is that dividends are generally recorded in the accounts only when they become a legal obligation of the payer.[127] Accordingly, a final dividend that is based on Year 1 accounts and approved by the shareholders during Year 2 will be provided for in the Year 2 accounts.

Shares in quoted companies are traded either cum-dividend or ex-dividend. If a share is acquired at a cum-dividend price that means that the purchaser is entitled to the dividend. Conversely, an ex-dividend price means that the vendor keeps the dividend. In the absence of any contrary provision in the company's articles, it is the person who is the registered holder of the share on the date of the declaration of a final dividend or payment of an interim dividend who is entitled to the dividend.[128] However, articles commonly authorize the board to select a date (the record date) for the payment of dividends. Shareholders on the register on the selected date receive the dividend, which means that the share price goes ex-dividend on that date. For companies listed on the London Stock Exchange, including overseas issuers with a premium listing, ex-dividend dates normally fall on Wednesdays, with the associated record date falling two business days later, usually on a Friday.[129] The Exchange recommends

---

[123] TECH 02/10, para 3.10.   [124] Companies Act 2006, ss 837–839.
[125] *Bond v Barrow Haematite Steel Co* [1902] 1 Ch 353; *Re Accrington Corp Steam Tramways Co* [1909] 2 Ch 40.
[126] *Lagunas Nitrate Co v Schroeder & Co and Schmidt* (1901) 85 LT 22.
[127] IAS 10.
[128] *Re Wakley, Wakley v Vachell* [1920] 2 Ch 205, CA; *Godfrey Phillips Ltd v Investment Trust Corp Ltd* [1953] Ch 449.
[129] London Stock Exchange, *Dividend Procedure Timetable* (2013).

that companies should aim to pay straightforward cash dividends within thirty business days of the record date.

Dividends are paid on the nominal value of the shares unless the articles otherwise provide.[130] The effect of this is that the holder of a partly paid share of a particular class would receive the same amount of dividend as the holder of a fully paid share of that class. Companies can change the position in their articles. The Model Articles for public companies provide that dividends are to be calculated and paid on the amounts paid up on shares rather than their nominal value.[131] However, the point is largely theoretical because shares in such companies normally trade on a fully paid basis. The Model Articles for private companies envisage that all shares will be fully paid up,[132] which, in turn, paves the way for the default provision that dividends are to be paid by reference to the number of shares held.[133]

Unlawful Distributions

When is a distribution unlawful?

A dividend or other distribution may be unlawful because it is not covered by distributable reserves or because of a failure to comply with the requirements of the companies legislation for the distribution to be justified by reference to properly prepared company accounts that give a true and fair view of the financial position of the individual distributing company. A company's power to pay dividends (or make other distributions) is linked to and controlled by the very detailed codes for accounts[134] and failure to comply with the statutory requirements is not a mere procedural irregularity that the courts will readily overlook. In *Precision Dippings Ltd v Precision Dippings Marketing Ltd*[135] the legality of a dividend paid by a subsidiary to its parent company was challenged on the grounds that a statutory requirement to obtain a statement from the auditors on the materiality of a qualification in the accounts in relation to the dividend had not been satisfied. The claim was thus not that the dividend *had* been paid otherwise than from distributable reserves; rather it was that the company had failed to do all that it was required to do by the companies legislation to demonstrate that the dividend was permissible. The Court of Appeal rejected the argument that the company's failing was a mere procedural irregularity. Dillon LJ, giving the judgment of the court, stated that the relevant provisions of the companies legislation constituted a major protection to creditors and that the shareholders were not free to waive or dispense with those requirements. The Court of Appeal left open the question of whether anything could be done to restore the situation in a solvent company, for example, the production of an auditor's statement after the event, because that situation did not arise on the facts. In *Bairstow v Queens Moat House plc*[136] the Court of Appeal returned to the issue of distributions that could not be justified by reference to the relevant accounts. In this case, over several years, the company paid dividends that exceeded its distributable reserves, as disclosed in its relevant individual accounts. For some of the years in dispute, the accounts were also defective because they failed to give a true and fair view of the financial position. However, there were significant distributable reserves in the corporate group as a whole. This led counsel for the directors to argue that any breaches of the companies legislation could be regarded as technical, that they could be waived by the shareholders, and that the action of the parent company in declaring dividends in excess of its own distributable reserves must be taken to have amounted to the

---

[130] *Oakbank Oil Co Ltd v Crum* (1882) 8 App Cas 65, HL.   [131] Model Articles (plc), art 71.
[132] Model Articles (Ltd), art 21.   [133] Model Articles (Ltd), art 30.
[134] *Bairstow v Queens Moat House plc* [2001] 2 BCLC 531, CA, para 31 *per* Robert Walker LJ.
[135] [1986] Ch 447, CA.   [136] [2001] 2 BCLC 531, CA.

informal declaration of sufficient dividends from its wholly-owned subsidiaries. These arguments were rejected: the failure was not a procedural irregularity; it could not be waived; and the directors could not go behind the individual accounts that they had prepared and laid before the general meeting.

In drawing up accounts, the directors of a company will likely be called upon to make a number of judgment calls. For example, in the case of Companies Act accounts, the Accounting Regulations require provisions for liabilities, which are defined as amounts retained as reasonably necessary for the purpose of providing for any liability, the nature of which is clearly defined and which is either likely to be incurred or certain to be incurred but uncertain as to the amount or as to the date on which it will arise.[137] This requires directors to come to a reasonable judgment based on facts as reasonably perceived or that would have been ascertained by reasonable inquiry; if it is reasonable for the directors not to cause the company to make provision for such liabilities, dividends paid on the basis of those accounts will not be unlawful by reason only of the failure to make provision.[138]

Other restrictions on dividends

Notwithstanding that a company's relevant accounts are in order and it is evident from them that the company has healthy distributable reserves, it is not necessarily the case that the directors can safely proceed to pay or recommend the payment of a dividend. The Companies Act 2006 makes it clear that the statutory regime is not exhaustive and that other rules of law restricting distributions are also applicable.[139] So too are provisions of a company's articles restricting distributions.[140] If, for instance, the company's financial position has deteriorated significantly since the accounts were prepared, there is a possibility that the payment of a dividend in those circumstances could infringe the still extant common law principle not to make distributions from capital or could be held to be a fraud on the company's creditors. Directors will thus need to check that the proposed dividend is still permissible taking into account changes in the company's financial position since the relevant accounts were published. Their decision will need to be made within the framework of the general duties that they owe to their company. One particular change of circumstances that may require directors to focus on the maintenance of capital principle and their general duties is the introduction of a new accounting standard or the adoption of IFRS.[141] Whilst a change in accounting policies will not retrospectively invalidate dividends already accounted for, where the directors are considering the payment of an interim dividend in respect of a financial year, and a new accounting standard may, for example, lead to items being recognized as liabilities in the accounts for that year, the directors must have regard to the effect of these liabilities on the expected level of profits available for distribution at the end of the financial year when determining the lawfulness of the interim dividend. TECH 02/10 provides the following example:

> For a company adopting IFRS for its individual accounts in 2010 the position is as follows:
> - any final dividend for 2009 will not be provided in the 2009 UK GAAP accounts and will first be accounted for in the 2010 accounts. Such a dividend would therefore have to have regard to

---

[137] Companies Act 2006, s 396; The Small Companies and Groups (Accounts and Directors' Report) Regulations 2008, SI 2008/409, sch 7, pt 1; The Large and Medium-sized Companies and Groups (Accounts and Reports) Regulations 2008, SI 2008/410, sch 9, pt 1.

[138] *Re Paycheck Services 3 Ltd and others; Revenue and Customs Commissioners v Holland* [2008] 2 BCLC 613. This case went up to the Supreme Court ([2010] UKSC 51, [2011] 1 BCLC 141, SC) but on this particular point there was no appeal from the first instance decision.

[139] Companies Act 2006, s 851.   [140] Companies Act 2006, s 852.

[141] This paragraph draws heavily on TECH 02/10, para 3.32.

the effect of adoption of IFRSs even though the 'relevant accounts' may still be those for 2009 prepared under UK GAAP;
- any interim dividend paid during 2010 would have to have regard to the effect of adoption of IFRSs even though the 'relevant accounts' may still be those for 2009 prepared under UK GAAP; and
- the 2010 accounts prepared under IFRSs would be the relevant accounts for the purposes of the final dividend approved by shareholders in 2011. The effect of a change in accounting policy known to be adopted in 2011 needs to be taken into account in determining the dividend to be approved by shareholders in 2011. The dividend will be recognised in the 2011 accounts.

Liability consequences of unlawful dividends

The payment of unlawful dividends has serious consequences for the directors and potentially also for the recipient shareholders.

Directors' liability

Directors have traditionally been regarded as stewards of the company's property and trustee-like responsibilities have been held to attach to them in this role.[142] At common law it was regarded as a breach of the trustee-like obligations of directors to pay a dividend out of capital.[143] The common law liability of directors to account for dividends paid from capital is sometimes referred to as the principle in *Flitcroft's Case*. The principle in *Flitcroft's Case* has been held to apply also to failures to comply with requirements of the companies legislation with regard to distributions being based on accounts that give a true and fair view of the company's financial position.[144] The principle has also been held to be applicable to solvent as well as to insolvent companies, with the reasoning underlying this being that the regulatory regime for distributions is intended to protect shareholders as well as creditors.[145]

In some of the older cases, the liability of directors to account for unlawful dividends was expressed in very strict terms: 'as soon as the conclusion is arrived at that the company's money has been applied by the directors for purposes which the company cannot sanction it follows that the directors are liable to repay the money, however honestly they may have acted.'[146] However, a more forgiving standard whereby directors would not be held liable where they acted under an honest and reasonable belief that the facts justified the payment was applied in some other cases.[147] In *Re Paycheck Services 3 Ltd; Revenue and Customs Commissioners v Holland*[148] Lord Hope acknowledged that there were two lines of authority as to whether the liability for the payment of unlawful dividends is strict or depends on fault.[149] In his Lordship's view the trend of modern authority supported the view that a

---

[142] *Bairstow v Queens Moat House plc* [2001] 2 BCLC 531, CA, para 53. It is only in some respects that the position of a director is equated to that of a trustee. See LS Sealy, 'The Director as Trustee' [1967] CLJ 83.

[143] *Re Exchange Banking Co, Flitcroft's Case* (1882) 21 Ch D 519, CA; *Re Sharpe* [1892] 1 Ch 154, CA.

[144] *Precision Dippings Ltd v Precision Dippings Marketing Ltd* [1986] Ch 447, CA.

[145] *Bairstow v Queens Moat House plc* [2001] 2 BCLC 531, CA, para 44 *per* Robert Walker LJ.

[146] *Re Sharpe* [1892] 1 Ch 154, CA, 165–6 *per* Lindley LJ.

[147] *Dovey v Cory* [1901] AC 477, HL, where a director escaped liability for an unlawful dividend because he had no reason to doubt the company officials on whom he relied. The cases supporting the strict approach and the approach whereby honest and reasonable directors escape liability are reviewed by Vaughan Williams J at first instance in *Re Kingston Cotton Mill Co (No 2)* [1896] 1 Ch 331, affirmed [1896] 2 Ch 279, CA.

[148] [2011] 1 BCLC 141.   [149] [45].

director who causes a misapplication of a company's assets is in principle strictly liable to make good the misapplication; but it was not necessary to express a definite view on this issue in the particular case.[150] Remarks of Lord Walker in *Progress Property Co Ltd v Moorgarth Group Ltd*[151] point in the same direction ('Sometimes their [directors'] states of mind are totally irrelevant. A distribution described as a dividend but actually paid out of capital is unlawful, however technical the error and however well-meaning the directors who paid it'[152]) but, again, did not amount to a definitive ruling on the point.

Directors' duties have been partially codified by the Companies Act 2006. There is no statutory duty that is the direct equivalent of directors' trustee-like duties of stewardship developed in cases such as *Flitcroft's Case*. Since the statutory duties operate only in place of those they replace, the pre-codification authorities on stewardship and breach of trust still apply. In addition, the payment of unlawful dividends may breach the duty in section 171 of the Companies Act 2006 to exercise powers only for the purposes for which they were conferred, and the statutory duty of care and skill under section 174 of that Act.

A director who has been held to be in breach of duty can apply to the court to be relieved of liability on the grounds that he acted honestly and reasonably, and that having regard to all the circumstances of the case (including those connected with his own circumstances), he ought fairly to be excused.[153] This relieving provision is a safety valve that can mitigate the harshness of a strict liability standard. Yet for a careful director who has mistakenly authorized an impermissible dividend by, for example, being caught out by a technical irregularity, a finding that he or she was not in breach of duty at all because the standard is fault based would be far preferable to having to rely on the exercise of judicial discretion to grant relief. Moreover, when he or she learns that there are relatively few reported cases in which directors have succeeded in claiming this relief, the prudent director is very likely to conclude that this possibility offers only limited practical reassurance.[154] Directors who are guilty of technical non-compliance may alternatively take some comfort from a ruling that a dividend that is paid on the basis of proper accounts that give a true and fair view but which exceeds available distributable reserves is unlawful only to the extent of the excess and the liability of the directors is therefore limited to that amount.[155] However, this decision is not altogether easy to reconcile with authorities that have stressed the need for the paperwork relating to distributions to be in perfect order and to demonstrate clearly that the distribution is covered by available reserves.

Shareholder liability

Shareholders who receive an unlawful distribution may be liable to repay it. There is statutory liability under section 847 of the Companies Act 2006, which applies where a distribution, or part of one, is made in contravention of the Act. If, at the time of the distribution, the member knows or has reasonable grounds for believing that it is so made, he is liable to repay it (or that part of it, as the case may be) to the company. It used to be thought that statutory liability required more than fact-based knowledge but in *It's a Wrap (UK) Ltd v Gula*[156] the Court of

---

[150] [46]–[47].   [151] [2011] BCC 196, [28].

[152] [28]. And see also *Bairstow v Queens Moat Houses plc* [2001] 2 BCLC 531, CA.

[153] Companies Act 2006, s 1157. Note also Insolvency Act 1986, s 212 under which the court has a limited discretion to limit the amount that the director in breach of duty has to pay to a sum less than the full amount of the wrongly paid dividends. The width of this discretion is not settled: compare *Holland* [49] (Lord Hope) and [124] (Lord Walker).

[154] E Ferran, 'Directors' Liability for Unlawful Dividends' [2011] *Cambridge Law Journal* 321.

[155] *Re Marini Ltd* [2004] BCC 172.

[156] [2006] BCC 626, noted J Payne, 'Recipient Liability for Unlawful Dividends' [2007] LMCLQ 7.

Appeal held that it was not a precondition of statutory liability that the recipient shareholder must be shown to have had knowledge or reasonable grounds for belief that the distribution contravened the law. The Court of Appeal interpreted the statutory liability in the light of Article 18 of the Second Company Law Directive, to which it gave effect. According to the court, on its true interpretation, Article 18 (previously Article 16) meant that a shareholder was liable to return a distribution if he knew or could not have been unaware that it was paid in circumstances amounting to a contravention of the Second Directive, whether or not he knew of those legal restrictions.

Statutory liability is without prejudice to any other liability that may arise. A shareholder who receives an unlawful dividend may also incur personal liability in equity for knowing receipt of property that has been disposed of in breach of duty.[157] Recipient liability thus depends on a breach of duty by the directors, and on the recipient being aware of the factual circumstances amounting to the breach of trust but the recipient does not need to be aware of the law.[158] According to a leading case on recipient liability, the test for knowledge in such a claim is whether the defendant's knowledge made it unconscionable for him to retain the benefit of the receipt.[159] However, in *It's a Wrap (UK) Ltd v Gula* Arden LJ noted that the authorities under the general law on distributions established that liability attached where the shareholder knew or ought to have known of the factual circumstances that made the distribution unlawful rather than where the shareholder had acted unconscionably.[160]

The statutory and equitable regimes overlap to a significant extent but there are some differences between them.[161] For instance, statutory liability is based simply on the fact that there has been a contravention of the 2006 Act and it need not be shown that the directors were in breach of duty; in this respect the statutory liability regime is more stringent. On the other hand, statutory liability is limited to contraventions of the Act: where a dividend is permissible according to the properly prepared, relevant accounts but a post-accounts downturn in the company's financial position has rendered it unlawful as infringing common law maintenance of capital principles, only recipient liability in equity appears to be relevant. In addition, as Arden LJ noted in *It's a Wrap*, section 847 offers no defence for the member who acts on advice, whereas, under the general law, a shareholder may be able to claim that he did not have the requisite knowledge where he acted on advice.

The knowledge requirements in both the statutory and equitable regimes will make it hard for a company to recover improperly paid dividends from outside shareholders but controlling shareholders and director-shareholders are more at risk. In the *Precision Dippings* case, for example, recovery was achieved in respect of an unlawful dividend paid by a subsidiary to its parent and in *It's a Wrap Ltd v Gula* unlawful dividends were recovered from persons who were both directors and shareholders. It has been argued that restitutionary strict liability, coupled with a change of position defence, would be a preferable mechanism for the recovery of unlawful dividends to personal equitable liability which is fault based, but the extension of restitutionary liability into this field is controversial.[162] Looking at the issue from a European

---

[157] *Precision Dippings Ltd v Precision Dippings Marketing Ltd* [1986] Ch 447, CA.
[158] *Precision Dippings Ltd v Precision Dippings Marketing Ltd* [1986] Ch 447, CA; *It's a Wrap (UK) Ltd v Gula* [2006] 1 BCLC 143, CA, para 12 *per* Arden LJ.
[159] *Bank of Credit and Commerce International (Overseas) Ltd (in liquidation) v Akindele* [2001] Ch 437, CA.
[160] Citing in particular *Moxham v Grant* [1900] 1 QB 88, 69 LJQB 97, 7 Mans 65.
[161] For an account of differences see *It's a Wrap (UK) Ltd v Gula* [2006] 1 BCLC 143, CA, para 12 *per* Arden LJ.
[162] Arguments in favour are suggested by J Payne, 'Unjust Enrichment, Trusts and Recipient Liability of Unlawful Dividends' (2003) 119 LQR 583 but a contrary view is expressed in CH Tham, 'Unjust Enrichment and Unlawful Dividends: a Step Too Far?' [2005] CLJ 177. In *Bank of Credit and Commerce International (Overseas) Ltd (in liquidation) v Akindele* [2001] Ch 437, 456 Nourse LJ expressed the view that shifting the burden onto recipients to defend receipts either by a change of position or in some other way could be commercially unworkable and contrary

standpoint, there is an argument for saying that since the EU standard, as set by the Second Company Law Directive, is good faith/fault based there is good reason for the UK not to adopt a more stringent standard in its overlapping common law or equitable remedies (especially as in *It's a Wrap* Arden LJ noted that the statutory remedy giving effect to the Second Company Law Directive is already more absolute and stringent than that available under the general law). Current government policy is not to gold-plate directives unless there are exceptional circumstances, justified by a cost benefit analysis and consultation with stakeholders.[163] Of course, an anti-gold plating presumption with respect to implementing legislation does not relate directly to the possibility of a more stringent liability standard being developed by the courts through the application of principles in the law of restitution but it suggests a policy reason for questioning the merits of doing so.

Directors' claims against recipient shareholders

Shareholders who benefit from an unlawful dividend may be in line to receive an unmeritorious windfall if the amount of the unlawful dividend is restored to the company by the directors and then distributed again lawfully to the same people. The Court of Appeal in *Bairstow v Queens Moat House plc*[164] briefly considered this 'double recovery' argument but denied its relevance to the question of whether the directors were liable in the first place. However, earlier authority recognizes that directors who are held personally liable in respect of an unlawful dividend may be able to seek an indemnity from those shareholders who received the payment with notice of the facts.[165]

Other Issues

Scrip dividends

The articles of association of a company may permit shareholders to elect to take additional fully paid ordinary shares in the company in whole or in part in lieu of a cash dividend. A dividend in this form is known as a 'scrip dividend.' Scrip dividends enable shareholders to acquire additional shares without incurring dealing costs. Conceptually, a scrip dividend can be characterized either as a reinvestment of the cash amount of a dividend or as a bonus issue of shares. The reinvestment characterization is appropriate where shareholders make their election after the dividend has been declared. Because the electing shareholders release the company from the obligation to pay cash, the shares are allotted for cash for the purposes of the Companies Act 2006, with the consequence that the statutory pre-emption requirements are relevant.[166] For accounting purposes, the new shares are deemed to be paid up out of distributable reserves. The bonus issue characterization is appropriate where the shareholders' election is in place before the declaration of a dividend. There are advantages for the company in structuring its scrip dividends election procedures so that the elections precede the dividend. Shares allotted in satisfaction of elections timed in this way are not allotted for cash and therefore the statutory pre-emption requirements do not apply. Also, for accounting purposes, the shares are bonus shares and can be paid up from undistributable reserves, such

---

to established principles whereby persons dealing with companies generally are not affected by irregularities that are internal to the corporate operations.

[163] HM Government, *Reducing Regulation Made Simple: Less Regulation, Better Regulation and Regulation as a Last Resort* (December 2010).

[164] [2001] 2 BCLC 531, CA.   [165] *Moxham v Grant* [1896] 1 Ch 685.

[166] Companies Act 2006, s 561. See further ch 5.

as the share premium account, thereby preserving the distributable reserves for subsequent dividend payments.

Dividend reinvestment plans

Dividend reinvestment plans are like scrip dividends to the extent that they are a means whereby shareholders can acquire additional shares without having to pay the normal dealing costs, although an administration fee is usually charged. However, in a typically structured dividend reinvestment plan, the company does not allot new shares to shareholders who wish to take advantage of the scheme but, instead, it arranges for their dividends to be invested in existing shares in the company that are trading in the market. Since there is no allotment of new shares, no issues with regard to pre-emption rights arise and the share purchases do not have any effect on the company's capital as recorded in its accounts. The fact that there is no dilution of the existing share capital means that there is no impact on the company's earnings-per-share or dividend-per-share ratios as there would be where there is extensive take up of scrip dividend alternatives.

Intra-group distributions

The operation of the law relating to distributions within a corporate group calls for special consideration under a number of headings.

Intra-group transactions and principles of realization

Whether an intra-group transaction gives rise to a realized profit is an issue that is considered at some length in the guidance issued by the Accountancy Institutes.[167] TECH 02/10 emphasizes substance over form: 'in assessing whether a company has a realized profit, transactions and arrangements should not be looked at in isolation.'[168] A group or series of transactions or arrangements should be viewed as a whole, particularly if they are artificial, linked (whether legally or otherwise), or circular or any combination of these.[169] A circular or artificial transaction—where, for example, an asset is purchased by a subsidiary from its parent to create a profit in the parent but there is an agreement or understanding regarding the repurchase of the asset by the parent or the parent directly or indirectly provides the funds for the purchase—may result in there being no realized profit in the hands of its parent.[170] An investment by a parent in a subsidiary which has paid a dividend in the form of qualifying consideration does not in itself preclude that dividend from continuing to be treated as a realized profit by the parent.[171] However, if a subsidiary pays a dividend to a parent which directly or indirectly provides the funds for the dividend or reinvests the proceeds in the subsidiary the dividend may not represent a realized profit for the parent because of the need to look at the various steps in the round rather than in isolation.[172]

A further complication is that it is also necessary to consider the effect of an upstream dividend on the value of the investment in the subsidiary. An intra-group dividend that is in the form of qualifying consideration may not constitute a realized profit in the hands of its parent company if the effect of the dividend is to cause a diminution in the value of the parent company's investment in the subsidiary below its book amount. Under UK GAAP the

---

[167] Generally, TECH 02/10, part 9.   [168] TECH 02/10, para 3.5   [169] TECH 02/10, para 3.5A.
[170] TECH 02/10 para 9.28.   [171] TECH 02/10, para 9.19.   [172] TECH 02/10, para 9.19.

impairment in value caused by an intra-group dividend is a matter of judgment, which must
be applied on each occasion. Under IFRS the position up to 2008 was more rigid because
a dividend paid out of pre-acquisition profits had to be credited against the cost of investment.[173] This created a problem of 'dividend blocks' within a corporate group. In 2008, the
International Accounting Standards Board issued an amendment to the relevant Standard,
which removed this requirement and potential source of difficulty.[174]

Intra-group transfers of assets at an undervalue

Transactions whereby assets are moved round corporate groups at their book value instead of
their greater market value are commonplace. However, such transactions need to be structured
with care so as to ensure that they do not infringe the statutory and common law principles
relating to distributions. There is no doubt that a transaction in which assets are transferred
by a subsidiary to its parent at less than their market value is potentially within the scope of
the law on distributions.[175] Furthermore, it is clear from *Aveling Barford Ltd v Perion Ltd*,[176]
which involved a sale at an undervalue between companies that had the same controlling
shareholder, that undervalue transactions between sister companies can also be distributions.

Where a company which does not have any distributable profits makes a distribution by
way of a transfer of assets at an undervalue to an associated company, the transaction is an
unlawful distribution contrary to Part 23 of the Companies Act 2006 and also an infringement of the common law maintenance of capital principle. This was the situation in the
Aveling Barford decision itself, where the transferor company had an accumulated deficit on
its profit and loss account/income statement and therefore was not in a position to make any
distribution to its shareholders. The *Aveling Barford* case did not decide anything about the
situation where a company has some positive distributable reserves but those reserves fall
short of the difference between the consideration for which an asset is transferred (typically
its book value) and its market value. Nevertheless, the decision led to considerable uncertainty in practice about the lawfulness of such transactions. The concern focused essentially
on the determination of the 'amount' of the distribution and the need for the distribution to
be justified by reference to relevant accounts, as stipulated in section 836 of the Companies
Act 2006: if the requisite amount was held to be the difference between the book and the
market value of the asset, the transfer at book value would infringe the distribution rules
to the extent not covered by distributable reserves (although the transferor would have the
option of conducting a formal revaluation exercise to record the unrealized profit, which
could then be added to distributable reserves under the exception for *in specie* dividends);[177]
but if the 'amount' was held to be just the difference between the consideration and book
value (which, in the ordinary case, would be zero) no revaluation would be required and
the transfer would be lawful. Section 845 of the Companies Act 2006 resolves the issue by
providing that the amount of a distribution arising from a sale, transfer, or other disposition
of assets by a company with profits available for distribution is zero so long as the amount or
value of the consideration for the disposal is not less than the book value of the asset. If the

---

[173] IAS 27.

[174] IAS 27 was reissued in January 2008 and applies to annual periods beginning on or after 1 July 2009. IAS 27 is
superseded by IAS 27 *Separate Financial Statements* and IFRS 10 *Consolidated Financial Statements* with effect from
annual periods beginning on or after 1 January 2013.

[175] *Ridge Securities Ltd v IRC* [1964] 1 All ER 275, 288. See also *Progress Property Co Ltd v Moorgarth* [2010] UKSC
55, [2011] 1 WLR 1.

[176] [1989] BCLC 626. See also *Progress Property Co Ltd v Moorgarth* [2010] UKSC 55, [2011] 1 WLR 1.

[177] Companies Act 2006, s 846.

asset is transferred for a consideration less than its book value, the amount of the distribution is equal to that shortfall, which will therefore need to be covered by distributable profits.[178]

Further Reform?

The Companies Act 2006 restated the law in the UK relating to distributions and helpfully clarified some aspects of it (in particular, addressing the *Aveling Barford* problem). However, it did not effect radical change. As discussed already in chapter 7, there is now considerable discussion in Europe about the merits of abandoning rules that make certain reserves undistributable in favour of a regulatory approach that uses solvency tests to determine whether or not a distribution is permissible. This change would move the European position more into line with that of developed economies elsewhere in the world, and would address the increasingly awkward problems flowing from the determination of the lawfulness of distributions being linked to accounts that are drawn up under regulatory frameworks intended to serve different purposes. For the moment, the Second Company Law Directive precludes the full adoption of a solvency-based approach for public companies as a complete alternative to the existing regime.[179] The possibility of introducing an alternative solvency-based regime has been explored on a number of occasions by the European Commission, but it is not mentioned in its 2012 Company Law Action Plan and thus appears to have been relegated to the back burner.[180]

There are a number of underlying factors that go towards explaining why modernization of the law on distributions in Europe has not made more progress. Some of the reasons for hesitation surfaced in the UK in the debates leading up to the Companies Act 2006. Since the Second Company Law Directive applies only to public companies, in principle it was open to introduce a solvency-based regime for dividends and other distributions by private companies in that legislation. That possibility was discussed in the Parliamentary debates on the Bill but it was not ultimately pursued. One concern was that a solvency-based system appears to give more discretion to directors and places considerable faith in the deterrent effect of the sanctions that would apply to directors who deliberately or negligently authorized distributions that were not supported by the company's financial position. It is not altogether obvious that the strong and effective sanctioning system that is a prerequisite to reform is in place, either domestically or at EU level. For instance, whilst the UK wrongful trading regime in the Insolvency Act 1986, section 214 has been held out as a possible template for a European directors' liability rule to accompany an alternative solvency-based distributions regime,[181] in fact the practical impact of section 214 in the UK has been quite muted.[182] How to accommodate

---

[178] TECH 02/10, App 1 provides worked examples.

[179] Strictly interpreted, the Second Directive relates only to nominal share capital and it would therefore be possible for the UK to introduce for plcs a solvency-based system for distribution of share premiums. However, piecemeal reform holds little appeal.

[180] COM(2012) 740. The Commission's enthusiasm for reform in this area appeared to wane after a feasibility study conducted by KPMG found little need for change: KPMG, *Feasibility Study on Alternatives to the Capital Maintenance Regime* (2008).

[181] High Level Group of Company Law Experts, *A Modern Regulatory Framework for Company Law in Europe* (2002); European Commission, *Modernising Company Law and Enhancing Corporate Governance in the European Union—A Plan to Move Forward* (COM(2003) 284).

[182] R Williams, 'Reappraising the Wrongful Trading Remedy' (forthcoming). In 2013 the European Commission launched a consultation on a new European approach to business failure and insolvency. This consultation included questions about directors' duties and liability (the Commission noted that problems have been identified in relation to the enforcement of directors' duties after the company has entered insolvency proceedings. Liquidators may lack incentives to pursue claims against directors; moreover, the costs and duration of court proceedings may deter liquidators from bringing liability claims), cross-border gaps in liability, and disqualification regimes.

long-term liabilities within a solvency-based system is another concern: when the issue was considered in Parliament in the context of proposals to introduce a solvency-based regime for distributions by private companies, the government spokesperson was concerned that a solvency test that required directors to consider their company's solvency in the next year might be inadequate because it would leave no clear statutory rules to prevent the dissipation of assets needed for long-term obligations such as pensions.[183]

Yet models that seek to address fears that a solvency-based approach to distributions would intensify the problem of short-termism in corporate governance do exist, and can be found even within the Companies Act 2006 itself. Indeed, notwithstanding the concerns about solvency statements that surfaced in the distributions context, that legislation actually extended the circumstances in which a private company can adjust its capital structure through solvency-based mechanisms.[184] At the European level, a number of different models have been suggested.[185] One prominent example is the detailed blueprint that has been set out by the Federation of European Accountants (FEE).[186] FEE specifically addressed the question of what the directors' declaration of solvency would need to cover. It suggested both a 'snapshot' test and a 'forward looking' test, which it described in the following terms:

> The snapshot test would help determine whether the proposed distribution would lead to a financial situation where liabilities exceeded assets, thus precluding the making of such distribution. This test would protect the interests of creditors since they are directly affected by the company's ability or otherwise to meet its long-term liabilities. A minimum requirement of the solvency-based system should be that distribution should not lead to a situation where liabilities exceeded assets under the measurement basis adopted. We consider that there are different options regarding the question of which values should be taken from the balance sheet or should be used for a net asset test:
>
> Balance sheet test: values are directly derived from the balance sheet as drawn up under national GAAP or IFRS; and
>
> Net asset test: the company could discharge its debts, ie, the directors would need to compare the value of the company's assets and the amount of the company's liabilities at that date with assets stated at no more than fair value or value in use.

> The forward looking test would supplement the findings from the snapshot test. This test should be based on the financial position of the company and enhanced by a liquidity plan which included payments and receipts that are expected as sufficiently certain within the selected time horizon. The test could take a number of different forms:
>
> A simple cash flow test covering only cash receipts and payments over a certain period of time;
>
> A broader liquidity test, in addition, covering receivables and obligations that led to receipts and payments over a certain period of time; and
>
> A working capital test (including all short term assets and liabilities, such as inventories).

FEE recognized that a crucial element of the forward looking test would be the time horizon used in its calculation. It commented:

> The uncertainty of matters occurring or of the effects of payments in the future increases with the extension of the time horizon. However, a very short period may be of less or no protection

---

[183] *Hansard*, HL, vol 682, cols 188–189 (16 May 2006) *per* Lord Sainsbury.

[184] Ch 7 discussing the out-of-court solvency-based procedure for private company reductions of capital.

[185] Including J Rickford (ed), 'Reforming Capital. Report of the Interdisciplinary Group on Capital Maintenance' [2004] *European Business Law Review* 979. For a general review of various models, see JMN Grade and M Wauters, 'Reforming Legal Capital: Harmonisation or Fragmentation of Creditor Protection' in K Goens and KJ Hopt (eds), *The European Company Law Action Plan Revisited* (Leuven: Leuven University Press, 2010) 25.

[186] FEE, *Discussion Paper*.

for creditors of the company since they may also be directly interested in the company's ability to pay its debts later on in the future. FEE's view is that the proper length of the time horizon used for the forward looking test cannot be determined with a 'one size fits all' approach, but would have to be decided on a case by case basis. However a minimum time horizon could be put in place at EU level or Member State level. Should the EC set a minimum time horizon, this time horizon should be one year (which FEE considers the minimum level of protection for creditors). Individual Member States may set longer (than one year) minimum time horizons.

Yet the real obstacles to change may be less to do with technical design challenges than with the strength of path dependencies. The existing rules on distributions 'work' in the sense that they are 'deeply embedded in extensive case law and mountains of doctrine'[187] and experienced practitioners know their way round their complications and pitfalls. Particularly in an area where reform depends on securing cross-border agreement on matters that are influenced by distinctive features of national economies, such as historical differences with regard to the extent of the corporate sector's reliance on conservative bank-based financing as opposed to more dynamic capital market-based financing, challenging the status quo is not easy.

Battles over European Commission proposals for the adoption of a Statute for a European private company tend to support this assessment. The Commission's proposal, published in 2008, provided for relatively light touch capital rules for a European private company, including a minimum capital of just €1 and a distributions regime based on a balance sheet test (excess of assets over liabilities), plus, if required by the company's articles, a one-year solvency certificate from the directors.[188] The proposal has not made headway because of disagreements within the Council over a number of features, including those relating to capital.[189] An unsuccessful Council Presidency compromise text would have ratcheted up the control on distributions by, in effect, mimicking the Second Company Law Directive's net profits tests in addition to a balance sheet requirement. In its 2012 Company Law Action Plan the Commission lamented the fact that it was becoming increasingly difficult to reach agreement at EU level on the adoption of company law initiatives, citing the lack of progress on the European Private Company Statute to illustrate the problem and noting the public consultation had demonstrated stakeholders' hesitation about continuing the negotiations on that proposal.[190]

---

[187] KJ Hopt, 'The European Company Law Action Plan Revisited: An Introduction' in K Goens and KJ Hopt (eds), *The European Company Law Action Plan Revisited*, 9, 13.

[188] COM(2008) 396.

[189] A Presidency compromise text (10611/11) failed to secure the required unanimity: Council Meeting on Competitiveness (Internal Market, Industry Research and Space) 30/31 May 2011 (10547/11). The focus of concerns relating to capital is the minimum capital requirement: see further ch 4.

[190] COM(2012) 740. In June 2012 the European Parliament passed a resolution (TA2012/0259) on the future of European law calling on the Commission to address a range of matters including overcoming the impasse in Council on the private company statute.

10

Financial Assistance

Prohibition on the Giving of Financial Assistance—Some Preliminary Issues

What is 'financial assistance' law?

The law on financial assistance is concerned with actions whereby a company financially supports the acquisition of its shares. In *Chaston v SWP Group plc*[1] Arden LJ used the phrase 'smoothed the path to the acquisition of shares' to describe a payment that was held to constitute financial assistance[2] and this phrase usefully encapsulates the essence of the law. The giving of financial assistance by public companies or their subsidiaries is generally prohibited, although there are certain exceptions. Since the coming into force of the Companies Act 2006, private companies are no longer caught by the ban (except where they are subsidiaries of public companies).

Legislative history

The giving of financial assistance was first made a specific statutory[3] offence by section 16 of the Companies Act 1928.[4] This was re-enacted without change as section 45 of the Companies Act 1929.[5] Loopholes emerged in the drafting of that section[6] and it was redrafted in the Companies Act 1947 and then consolidated as section 54 of the Companies Act 1948. New companies legislation in the 1980s provided an opportunity to recast the prohibition on financial assistance and to clarify some of the difficulties that had been thrown up by cases and by the experience of the operation of section 54 of the Companies Act 1948 in practice.[7] A minor amendment was made in the Companies Act 1980 followed by a more wide-ranging revision in the Companies Act 1981. The Companies Act 1981 was later consolidated into the Companies Act 1985, with section 151 of that Act containing the basic prohibition and subsequent sections elaborating on its scope.

From the 1980s legislation onwards, the legislative history of the prohibition on financial assistance has been influenced by the Second Company Law Directive.[8] The Second

---

[1] [2003] 1 BCLC 675, CA.   [2] At [38].

[3] In *R v Lorang* (1931) 22 Cr App Rep 167, CCA this provision was described as declaratory and not as a new offence.

[4] On the statutory history of the ban generally: GR Bretten, 'Financial Assistance in Share Transactions' (1968) 32 Conv 6; GK Morse, 'Financial Assistance by a Company for the Purchase of its Own Shares' [1983] JBL 105; BG Pettet, 'Developments in the Law of Financial Assistance for the Purchase of Shares' (1988) 3 *Journal of International Banking Law* 96.

[5] It provided that: 'It shall not be lawful for a company to give, whether directly or indirectly, and whether by means of a loan, guarantee, the provision of security or otherwise, any financial assistance for the purpose of or in connection with a purchase made or to be made by any person of any shares in the company.'

[6] *Re VGM Holdings Ltd* [1942] 1 Ch 235, CA where it was held than the ban on financial assistance for the purchase of shares did not apply where the company provided financial assistance for the subscription of its shares. As a matter of construction the word 'purchase' could not be extended to include 'subscription.'

[7] Such as the views of members of the Court of Appeal in *Belmont Finance Corp v Williams Furniture Ltd (No 2)* [1980] 1 All ER 393, CA on transactions for full value and on transactions entered into for mixed purposes that including the giving of financial assistance.

[8] Directive 2012/30/EU on coordination of safeguards which, for the protection of the interests of members and others, are required by Member States of companies within the meaning of the second paragraph of Article 54 of

Company Law Directive seeks to coordinate on a Community-wide basis the requirements for the formation of public companies and the maintenance and alteration of their capital. As an aspect of this, Article 25(1) of the Second Directive now provides that a public company can, 'advance funds, or make loans, or provide security with a view to the acquisition of its shares by a third party' but only subject to a number of conditions that aim at safeguarding creditor and minority shareholder interests. This formulation, which dates from amendments to the Second Directive in 2006,[9] recasts in more permissive terms what was previously a ban subject to certain exceptions. However, the conditions under which financial assistance can be given remain onerous, time-consuming, and even, it has been said, 'unworkable in the context of most corporate transactions where financial assistance is an issue.'[10] Wymeersch notes that, despite the reforms, the EU requirements 'remain based on the largely false premise that financial assistance is an unacceptable practice.'[11] One measure of the weak impact of the amendments is that the UK, taking advantage of the optionality of EU law on this matter, has not implemented them into its domestic law.[12]

At the domestic level, financial assistance law received attention in the review of company law that preceded the Companies Act 2006.[13] By removing private companies from the scope of the ban, that Act takes to its endpoint the policy, supported by the Jenkins Committee in 1962 and implemented to some extent in the Companies Act 1981, of having a more relaxed approach in relation to the giving of financial assistance by private companies.[14] However, the options for change so far as public companies were concerned were constrained by the need to comply with the Community obligation to implement the Second Directive Article 25.

The Companies Act 2006 made few significant substantive changes to financial assistance law in relation to public companies and many of the difficulties and uncertainties that emerged in relation to the Companies Act 1985 thus continue to affect the law. Although some proposed redrafting of controversial sections was considered, suggested revisions failed to attract government support because of doubt as to whether they would actually improve the position.[15]

---

the Treaty on the Functioning of the European Union, in respect of the formation of public limited companies and the maintenance and alteration of their capital with a view to making such safeguards equivalent [2012] OJ L315/74 (Second Company Law Directive).

[9] By Directive 2006/68/EC of the European Parliament and of the Council of 6 September 2006 amending Council Directive 77/91/EEC as regards the formation of public limited liability companies and the maintenance and alteration of their capital [2006] OJ 2006 L264/32.

[10] Department of Trade and Industry, *Directive Proposals on Company Reporting, Capital Maintenance and Transfer of the Registered Office of a Company: A Consultative Document* (London, March 2005) para 3.4.2. Arguing for further modifications that could render the financial assistance regime more flexible without eliminating it altogether: G Strampelli, 'Rendering (Once More) the Financial Assistance Regime More Flexible' (2012) 4 *European Company and Financial Review* 530.

[11] E Wymeersch, 'The Directive Amending the Second Company Law Directive' in P Balzarini, G Carcano, and M Ventoruzzo (eds), *La Società per Azioni Oggi* (Milan: , Giuffrè, 2007) 333.

[12] At the time of the White Paper that preceded the Companies Act 2006, the Government indicated that rather than making technical changes it preferred to give priority to pressing for fundamental reform of the Second Company Law Directive: Cm 6456 (2005) 43. This was before Directive 2006/68/EC. That Directive dashed hopes for extensive reform.

[13] In particular Company Law Review Steering Group, *Modern Company Law for a Competitive Economy: Developing the Framework* (URN 00/656) paras 7.18–7.25.

[14] The Companies Act 1981 introduced the private company 'whitewash' regime whereby private companies were permitted to give financial assistance provided certain conditions (including a special resolution of the shareholders and a directors' statement of solvency) were fulfilled. A regime broadly to this effect had been recommended by the Jenkins Committee: *Report of the Company Law Committee* (Cmnd 1749, 1962) paras 178–9 and 187.

[15] *Hansard*, vol 680, GC col 24 (20 March 2006) and *Hansard*, HC vol 682, col 182 (16 May 2006).

Who is protected by the ban?

The ban on the giving of financial assistance is intended to protect company funds and the interests of shareholders in bid situations as well as the interests of creditors.[16] In the *Chaston* case[17] Arden LJ explained:

> The general mischief, however, remains the same, namely that the resources of the target company and its subsidiaries should not be used directly or indirectly to assist the purchaser financially to make the acquisition. This may prejudice the interests of the creditors of the target or its group, and the interests of any shareholders who do not accept the offer to acquire their shares or to whom the offer is not made.

Why is the Giving of Financial Assistance Banned?

Objections to leveraged takeovers/buyouts

In *Re VGM Holdings Ltd*[18] Lord Greene MR explained the practices against which the ban on the giving of financial assistance is directed in the following terms:

> Those whose memories enable them to recall what had been happening for several years after the last war will remember that a very common form of transaction in connection with companies was one by which persons—call them financiers, speculators, or what you will—finding a company with a substantial cash balance or easily realisable assets, such as war loan, bought up the whole, or the greater part, of the shares for cash, and so arranged matters that the purchase money which they then became bound to provide was advanced to them by the company whose shares they were acquiring, either out of its cash balance or by realization of its liquid investments. That type of transaction was a common one, and it gave rise to great dissatisfaction and, in some cases, great scandals.

This passage echoed comments that had appeared in the report of the Greene Committee, which had recommended that such practices should be against the law.[19]

Reporting in 1962, the Jenkins Committee on the reform of company law[20] also gave an example of the type of abuse that the prohibition of the giving of financial assistance was intended to correct:

> If people who cannot provide the funds necessary to acquire control of a company from their own resources, or by borrowing on their own credit, gain control of a company with large assets on the understanding that they will use the funds of the company to pay for their shares it seems to us all too likely that in many cases the company will be made to part with its funds either on inadequate security or for an illusory consideration.

In *Wallersteiner v Moir*[21] Lord Denning MR summed up the perceived abuse succinctly, describing it simply as a 'cheat.'

Market manipulation

In some circumstances, the effect of giving financial assistance may be to boost the price of the shares of the company giving the assistance. An obvious example of this arises in a takeover

---

[16] *Wallersteiner v Moir* [1974] 3 All ER 217, CA, 255 *per* Scarman LJ and 239 *per* Lord Denning MR.
[17] [2003] 1 BCLC 675, CA, [31].   [18] [1942] Ch 235, CA, 239.
[19] *Report of the Company Law Amendment Committee* (Cmd 2657, 1926) para 30.
[20] *Report of the Company Law Committee* (Cmnd 1749, 1962) para 173.   [21] [1974] 3 All ER 217, CA, 222.

situation where the consideration for the offer to the shareholders of the target takes the form of shares in the bidder and, to ensure that the price of those shares remains attractive, the bidder organizes a share-support operation in which purchasers of its shares are indemnified against any losses they may suffer as a result of their purchases. Looked at from this angle, the ban on the giving of financial assistance is closely connected to the rule whereby companies are prohibited from trading in their own shares.[22] The Greene Committee referred to the practice of 'share trafficking' when recommending that financial assistance should be prohibited.[23] In *Darvall v North Sydney Brick & Tile Co Ltd*,[24] an Australian case, Kirby P expressly stated that the purposes of the prohibition on financial assistance 'include the avoidance of the manipulation of the value of shares by companies and their officers dealing in such shares.'

Unconstitutional conduct by management

Another reason for banning financial assistance is to prevent the management of a company from interfering with the normal market in the company's shares by providing support from the company's resources to selected purchasers. In this respect, the ban on financial assistance again complements the ban on a company purchasing its own shares, one purpose of which is to prevent the management of a company from seeking to influence the outcome of a takeover bid by purchasing its own shares.[25]

Maintenance of capital and 'detriment'

Financial assistance law overlaps with the maintenance of capital principle,[26] as can be seen by considering the example of an issuing company that uses its existing capital to provide funds to investors to subscribe for a new issue of its shares; in these circumstances the appearance of an injection of fresh equity is simply illusory. However, whilst it is conventional to deal with financial assistance as part of the maintenance of capital/legal capital principle, the scope of the ban on the giving of financial assistance extends far beyond actions that would also infringe the maintenance of capital principle. For example, it covers actions whereby a company uses its distributable reserves to support share acquisitions and is not limited to misuse of capital or other undistributable reserves. It can even extend to certain actions that do not deplete the assets of the company that provides the assistance: actual financial detriment is not necessarily required.[27] Where a company makes a gift to enable someone to

---

[22] GR Bretten, 'Financial Assistance in Share Transactions' (1968) 32 Conv 6.

[23] *Report of the Company Law Amendment Committee* (Cmd 2657, 1926) para 30.

[24] (1989) 15 ACLR 230, NSW CA, 256 *per* Kirby J.   [25] *Trevor v Whitworth* (1887) 12 App Cas 409, HL.

[26] C Proctor, 'Financial Assistance: New Proposals and New Perspectives' (2007) 28 *Company Lawyer* 3.

[27] *Chaston v SWP Group plc* [2003] 1 BCLC 675, CA, [37] *per* Arden LJ. Accordingly, Lord Denning MR's description of financial assistance in *Wallersteiner v Moir* [1974] 3 All ER 217, CA, 239 ('You look to the company's money and see what has become of it. You look to the company's shares and see into whose hands they have got. You will then soon see if the company's money has been used to finance the purchase') should be read as merely one example of financial assistance and not as illustrative of the whole category: see JH Farrar and NV Lowe, 'Fraud, Representative Actions and the Gagging Writ' (1975) 38 MLR 455.

In Australia there was a competing line of authority on whether 'impoverishment' was a necessary element of financial assistance legislation based on the English model (which has since been overridden by more modern Australian legislation) but it has been stated judicially that the better view was that impoverishment was not a necessary element of the contravention: *Re HIH Insurance Ltd (in prov liquidation) and HIH Casualty and General Insurance Ltd (in prov liquidation); Australian Securities and Investments Commission v Adler* [2002] NSWSC 171, (2002) 41 ACSR 72, NSW Sup Ct EqD, para 363. In Singapore it has been said in relation to companies legislation based on the English model that the test is whether in the ordinary commercial sense the assets of the company have purchase its shares, there is a clear immediate reduction in its resources. However, unlawful financial assistance can come in many forms and is not confined to simple situations where the company makes a gift of the money which is to be used to buy its shares. Also included within the prohibition are loans, security, guarantees, and indemnities. These types of unlawful financial assistance do not necessarily involve any reduction in the company's assets at the time when they are given. For instance, a loan does not involve any diminution in the lender's assets provided the borrower's credit is good and no provision against the likelihood of default has to be made. A contingent obligation, such as a guarantee, does not reduce the assets of the company unless some provision has to be made against the obligation being enforced.[28] The granting of a security does not diminish or deplete the value of a company's assets and merely restricts the company from using the proceeds of the secured assets otherwise than in satisfaction of the secured debt.[29]

Is the Ban on the Giving of Financial Assistance Justified?[30]

Technical problems

The law on financial assistance is notorious for being riddled with costly uncertainty, which results in the corporate sector spending a large amount each year for legal advice on its potential impact on transactions. Whereas the costs associated specifically with financial assistance may be a drop in the ocean in the context of multi-billion pound mega-transactions involving publicly quoted companies, they will weigh more heavily in smaller deals. Accordingly, it is not surprising that cost considerations were prominent in the decision to abolish the ban on the giving of financial assistance by private companies in the Companies Act 2006.[31] Underlying the decision to take this more radical step, as opposed to trying to address the problem by improving the drafting of the relevant provisions, was the recognition that, to the extent that the ban sought to achieve worthwhile policy objectives by curbing harmful practices, it was possible to control perceived abuses in other, more cost-effective, ways.

Policy concerns

Financial assistance law is intended to protect the interests of creditors and also to protect shareholders in takeover situations from abusive conduct by controllers.[32] On the surface, these are uncontroversial objectives that are familiar to any company lawyer. However, company law has a variety of goals and the aim of protecting people who deal with companies

---

been used or put at risk in connection with the acquisition of its own shares: *PP v Lew Syn Pau and Wong Sheung Sze* [2006] SGHC 146, para 107.

Also BG Pettet, 'Developments in the Law of Financial Assistance for the Purchase of Shares', 100.

[28] *Milburn v Pivot Ltd* (1997) 15 ACLC 1520 Fed Ct of Aust, 1546 *per* Goldberg J; *Lipschitz No v UDC Bank Ltd* [1979] 1 SA 789, Sup Ct of SA, 800–1 *per* Miller JA.

[29] *Re MC Bacon Ltd* [1990] BCLC 324. This case concerned Insolvency Act 1986, s 238 (transactions at an undervalue). See also *Lipschitz No v UDC Bank Ltd* [1979] 1 SA 789, Sup Ct of SA, 800–1 *per* Miller JA.

[30] This section draws upon the following articles: E Ferran, 'Financial Assistance: Shifting Policy Perceptions but Static Law' [2004] CLJ 225; E Ferran, 'Simplification of European Company Law on Financial Assistance' [2005] *European Business Organization Law Review* 93; E Ferran, 'The Place for Creditor Protection on the Agenda for Modernisation of Company Law in the European Union' [2006] *European Company and Financial Law Review* 178; E Ferran, 'Regulation of Private Equity-Backed Leveraged Buyout Activity in Europe' (May 2007). ECGI—Law Working Paper No 84/2007 <http://ssrn.com/abstract=989748> accessed July 2013.

[31] *White Paper* (Cm 6456, 2005) 41.

[32] *Chaston v SWP Group plc* [2003] 1 BCLC 675, CA [31].

is not necessarily worthy of priority over all others. Contemporary thinking about the aims and objectives of company law have shifted away from prioritizing the protection of people who deal with companies (who can often protect themselves) to facilitating business activities so as to promote economic growth. From this perspective, financial assistance law is open to criticism for placing too much emphasis on protective functions and for making questionable policy choices on what constitutes 'abuse' from which protection is needed. In relation to creditors, for instance, the criticisms of the capital maintenance regime considered in chapter 7 apply in this context but with enhanced force because, whereas the general regime controls distributions of assets representing capital and other undistributable reserves, financial assistance law goes further and prohibits the distribution of any assets to support the acquisition of shares. Indeed, financial assistance law extends even beyond this because certain forms of prohibited financial assistance do not require any depletion of assets at all.

As for what financial assistance protects against, the bristling hostility of the post-Second World War judiciary to leveraged financing of company acquisitions is somewhat at odds with the contemporary environment in which leveraged buyouts are commonplace and the mood has shifted from viewing them as invariably questionable transactions in which sharp operators play the market for corporate control with other peoples' money to seeing them in a more nuanced way as transactions that undoubtedly present some classic agency problems—managers who are liable to promote their own interests over those of the general body of shareholders; majority shareholders who are poised to exploit minorities; and controllers who may load their company with a heavy additional debt burden that could threaten the interests of the existing creditors and of employees—but which can also be economically worthwhile, value-producing activities. This is not to say that hostility to the leveraged buyout model has completely faded away, and it can resurface particularly in times of crisis. This point was vividly demonstrated in the aftermath of the financial crisis of 2007–9. Investment and commercial banks were the eye of that storm, but even though private equity and hedge funds, the major actors in the leveraged buyouts market, played a much more marginal role they nevertheless found themselves on the receiving end of a regulatory backlash that was fuelled by concerns that had built up in the pre-crisis boom period about industry practices, including 'asset stripping' of portfolio companies to service acquisition finance.[33] However, it is noticeable that lawmakers did not look to a reinforced ban on the giving of financial assistance in order to crack down on perceived abuses: more nuanced regulatory tools have been deployed.[34]

There are difficult questions about the range of regulatory and governance strategies that can best address the agency problems inherent in highly leveraged transactions. This was recognized in the debate that preceded the Companies Act 2006: the decision to abolish financial assistance law completely for private companies was taken not because British policymakers decided that there was no need for some protective regulatory intervention to achieve the goals that underpin financial assistance law but rather because they concluded that general company law on directors' duties and minority protection, takeover regulations, and insolvency laws could be relied upon instead to perform that function. Insolvency laws

---

[33] E Ferran, 'After the Crisis: The Regulation of Hedge Funds and Private Equity in the EU' (2011) 12 *European Business Organization Law Review* 379.

[34] Directive 2011/61/EU of the European Parliament and of the Council of 8 June 2011 on Alternative Investment Fund Managers and amending Directives 2003/41/EC and 2009/65/EC and Regulations (EC) No 1060/2009 and (EU) No 1095/2010, [2011] OJ L174/1, Art 33 (restricting alternative investment fund managers from supporting distributions, capital reductions, share redemptions, and buy-backs by portfolio companies in the two years following the acquisition of control).

that allow for the unwinding of undervalue transactions made by companies in financial difficulties have particular significance in this context.[35] Whilst there is room for a difference of views on the effectiveness of these various strategies, all of them appear to be superior to financial assistance law, which is too blunt an instrument to address properly the various complex and multi-faceted concerns raised by such transactions.

The ban on financial assistance law is also an unnecessary appendage so far as it relates to concerns about market manipulation. These days, ensuring a clean and orderly securities market is rightly seen to be the province of securities regulation rather than company law. The Financial Services and Markets Act 2000 and the Financial Services Act 2012 provide for draconian sanctions against those who engage in market abuse, including the possibility of unlimited administrative fines and criminal penalties.[36]

A further criticism of financial assistance law is that it often fails to achieve its goals (though this may be no bad thing in so far as a more effective ban could prevent worthwhile transactions from taking place). On the face of it, a rule that prohibits public companies from giving financial assistance for the acquisition of their shares, appears to strike at the heart of leveraged buyouts because the economic structure of these transactions depends on being able to use the acquired company's assets as security for the debt financing incurred to effect the acquisition and that is precisely what the ban appears to prohibit. Yet the European buyout market has flourished in recent years in spite of the pan-European ban on the giving of financial assistance.[37] How has this come about? The answer is simple: it has happened because the market has worked out ways round the law, with the consequence that financial assistance law has been reduced to the level of a hindrance rather than an insurmountable hurdle.

This is not to say, however, that financial assistance law has been made practically irrelevant and that there is no real need therefore to continue to press for its reform. An emerging trend that is disquieting is of financial assistance law being used opportunistically by parties seeking to escape from obligations or to reverse the consequences of transactions they have undertaken, although in a number of cases the English courts have given short shrift to unmeritorious claims of this sort.[38] There is also concern about the potential for financial assistance law to be exploited in hostile takeover situations by the commencement of litigation as a tactical ploy, not necessarily with a view to winning the case but simply to hold up the transaction for long enough to undermine its commercial rationale.[39] Financial assistance is

---

[35] Insolvency Act 1986, s 238 (undervalue transactions). DG Baird, 'Legal Approaches to Restricting Distributions to Shareholders: The Role of Fraudulent Transfer Law' (2006) 7 *European Business Organization Law Review* 199. Baird suggests a similarity between the prohibition on financial assistance and the operation of US fraudulent conveyance law in connection with LBOs (at 201, note 6).

[36] Financial Services and Markets Act 2000, s 123; Financial Services Act 2012, ss 89–90.

[37] L Enriques, 'EC Company Law Directives and Regulations: How Trivial Are They?' (2006) 7 *University of Pennsylvania Journal of International Economic Law* 1.

[38] *Chaston v SWP Group plc* [2003] 1 BCLC 675, CA is an example of an unmeritorious case succeeding (purchaser benefited from due diligence reports for which subsidiary of the target company paid but later sued successfully for breach of duty the former director of the subsidiary who had authorized the payment). See also *Re Hill and Tyler Ltd, Harlow v Loveday* [2005] 1 BCLC 41. But cf *Dyment v Boyden* [2004] 2 BCLC 423, affirmed [2005] 1 BCLC 163, [2005] BCC 79, CA (company could not get out of obligations under a lease by claiming it was unlawful financial assistance); *Anglo Petroleum Ltd v TFB (Mortgages) Ltd* [2007] BCC 407, CA (parties could not escape liabilities under a guarantee and security by pleading financial assistance law); and *Corporate Development Partners LLC v E-Relationship Marketing Ltd* [2009] BCC 295 (commitment to pay an introduction fee was not financial assistance and was therefore enforceable).

[39] Ferran, 'Regulation of Private Equity-Backed Leveraged Buyout Activity in Europe' discusses the Gas Natural hostile bid for Endesa, where a suit was filed in the Spanish courts on grounds that included alleged contravention of the financial assistance prohibition, which led to the whole transaction being frozen by a preventive order for a considerable period of time.

a good choice as a spoiler because the uncertainties surrounding it mean that it is likely to take the court a considerable amount of time to come to a conclusion.

Had the options for change in relation to public companies not been constrained by the Second Company Law Directive, it is very likely that in the debate that preceded the Companies Act 2006 the policy arguments would have been found persuasive in relation to public companies as well as private companies, with the consequence that financial assistance law would have been abolished outright for all companies, or at least reduced in scope and effect to a shadow of its former self.

Outline of the Legal Framework

The statutory provisions on financial assistance are now found in chapter 2 of Part 18 of the Companies Act 2006. Apart from changes resulting from the decision to exclude private companies (other than subsidiaries of public companies) from the scope of the law on financial assistance, there are few differences of substance between the Companies Act 2006 and the predecessor 1985 Act. Cases that interpreted and applied the version of financial assistance law that was contained in the Companies Act 1985 therefore continue to be relevant. It can also be useful to refer back to older cases that related to former legislation, in particular the Companies Act 1948 and foreign statutes that used the 1948 Act as a precedent, but those authorities have to be read with some caution because of developments in the statutory framework since they were decided.

'Definition' of Financial Assistance

We now turn to a more detailed examination of the law. An obvious place to start this more detailed analysis is with the meaning of financial assistance. Perhaps surprisingly, the phrase 'financial assistance' is not defined by the legislation. Instead the Companies Act 2006 (following the same approach as predecessor legislation) merely lists the forms of financial assistance that are within the scope of the ban.[40] It has been suggested judicially that the legislature has thought it wise not to lay down a precise definition of financial assistance because of the risk that clever people would devise ways of defeating the purpose of the section while keeping within the letter of the law.[41]

'Financial assistance' is not a technical term

It has been said repeatedly in the relevant cases that the phrase 'financial assistance' does not have a technical meaning and that the frame of reference is the language of ordinary commerce. A statement by Hoffmann J in *Charterhouse Investment Trust Ltd v Tempest Diesels Ltd*[42] (a case on section 54 of the Companies Act 1948) is frequently cited:

> The words have no technical meaning and their frame of reference is in my judgment the language of ordinary commerce. One must examine the commercial realities of the transaction and decide whether it can properly be described as the giving of financial assistance by the company,

---

[40] In *Barclays Bank plc v British & Commonwealth Holdings plc* [1995] BCC 19, 37 Harman J said that 'Companies Act 1985, s 152 [now Companies Act 2006, s 677] supplied the definition of "financial assistance" that was missing from the earlier legislation' but this view is not generally accepted.

[41] *Anglo Petroleum Ltd v TFB (Mortgages) Ltd* [2007] BCC 407, [26] *per* Toulson LJ.

[42] (1985) 1 BCC 99, 544, 99,552.

bearing in mind that the section is a penal one and should not be strained to cover transactions which are not fairly within it.[43]

In *Barclays Bank plc v British & Commonwealth Holdings plc*[44] the Court of Appeal emphasized that the assistance has to be financial in nature. An example of assistance that is not financial in nature is where a company permits a potential purchaser of its shares to inspect its books and records.[45] Another example is of covenants given by a target company to reassure the purchaser of its shares where it is not anticipated at the time of the covenants that there would be any liability thereunder.[46] However, the concept of financial assistance is not limited to financial support that helps directly or indirectly to pay for the shares; it embraces inducements to acquire shares and there is no necessity for the financial assistance to impact directly on the price of the target shares.[47] As noted earlier, even though the assistance must be financial, for most forms of proscribed financial assistance there is no requirement for the giving of it to deplete the assets of the company. With regard to timing, it is at the point when a company undertakes an obligation, rather than when it comes to be performed, that the existence or otherwise of financial assistance is to be tested.[48]

Recent cases applying the test of commercial substance and reality

Chaston v SWP Group plc[49] arose out of the acquisition of Dunstable Rubber Company Holdings Ltd by SWP Group plc, a listed company. The acquisition did not turn out well from the purchaser's viewpoint. At the time of the acquisition, Robert Chaston was a director of a subsidiary of the target company. The claim brought against Mr Chaston was that he had breached his fiduciary duties to the subsidiary by procuring, or conniving in, the giving of financial assistance for the purpose of the acquisition by the purchaser of the shares in its parent company. The alleged financial assistance was the incurring of liability by the subsidiary to pay the accountants' fees for the short and long form reports in respect of the transaction and/or the payment of those fees. The purchaser brought the claim as assignee from its subsidiary of all the claims it might have had against Mr Chaston. The Court of Appeal held that the payment of the fees by the subsidiary of the target passed the commercial substance and reality test for 'financial assistance': the vendor and the purchaser were relieved from any obligation to pay for the service provided by the accountants and the payment of the fees smoothed the path to the acquisition of the shares.

On the other hand, the commercial substance and reality test was not passed in *MT Realisations Ltd (in liquidation) v Digital Equipment Co Ltd*.[50] This case concerned a transaction in which the purchaser acquired the share capital of the target, MT Realisations (MTR), for a nominal amount which, it was accepted, was a fair price for the shares. In a separate agreement the purchaser also agreed to pay the vendor £6.5 million in consideration of the assignment of an £8 million inter-company loan repayable on demand by MTR and associated security interests. The loan assignment agreement provided for the purchase price for

---

[43] See also *Barclays Bank plc v British & Commonwealth Holdings plc* [1996] 1 BCLC 1, CA; *Chaston v SWP Group plc* [2003] 1 BCLC 675, CA; *MacNiven v Westmoreland Investments Ltd* [2003] 1 AC 311, HL; *MT Realisations Ltd (in liquidation) v Digital Equipment Co Ltd* [2003] 2 BCLC 117, CA; *Anglo Petroleum Ltd v TFB (Mortgages) Ltd* [2007] BCC 407.

[44] [1995] BCC 1059, CA.   [45] *Burton v Palmer* (1980) 5 ACLR 481, NSW SC, 489 *per* Mahoney J.

[46] *Chaston v SWP Group plc* [2003] 1 BCLC 675, CA, [43] *per* Arden LJ.

[47] *Chaston v SWP Group plc* [2003] 1 BCLC 675, CA, especially [45] *per* Arden LJ. In so far as Laddie J at first instance in *MT Realisations Ltd (in liquidation) v Digital Equipment Co Ltd* [2002] 2 BCLC 688, Ch D took the opposite view, Arden LJ disagreed.

[48] This was common ground between the counsel involved in *Parlett v Guppys (Bridport) Ltd* [1996] BCC 299, CA.

[49] [2003] 1 BCLC 675, CA.   [50] [2003] 2 BCLC 117, CA.

the loan to be paid in instalments by the purchaser. The commercial effect of the loan assignment was to relieve the vendor of any credit exposure to its former subsidiary. In allowing the purchaser to pay for the assignment by instalments, the vendor instead assumed a new credit risk in relation to the purchaser. This structure was presumably helpful to the purchaser in that it meant that, at the time of completion, it did not have to raise finance to cover the full costs of the transaction. Subsequently, the purchaser was unable to meet its obligations to pay instalments due under the loan assignment. The arrangement was restructured at that point to provide for the set-off of any sums due from the vendor to MTR against the outstanding instalments of the purchase price due to be paid to the vendor by the purchaser under the loan assignment. When MTR later went into liquidation, its liquidator argued that the post-acquisition rescheduling of the purchaser's obligations under the loan assignment was prohibited financial assistance.

The Court of Appeal held that there was no financial assistance. Looked at commercially, there was no financial assistance in the rescheduling arrangement. Financial assistance did not exist in a vacuum, something had to be given to someone that they did not have already. The rescheduling did not give the purchaser any new rights against MTR and therefore no financial assistance had been given. Under the loan assignment the purchaser had already acquired an on-demand loan repayable by MTR and associated security. The purchaser could have required MTR to pay over any sums it received from the vendor (if need be, enforcing its security rights to recover its legal entitlement) and then used those sums to meet its own payment obligations under the loan assignment. The arrangement for sums due to MTR from the vendor to be set off against sums due to the vendor by the purchaser simply short-circuited the process. As a matter of commercial substance, the purchaser was exercising a pre-existing legal entitlement and was not receiving any form of financial assistance from the acquired company.

This test of discovering the commercial substance and reality of the facts was also taken as the starting point by the Court of Appeal in *Anglo Petroleum v TFB (Mortgages) Ltd*,[51] another case involving a post-acquisition financial restructuring that included new borrowings by the company that had been taken over, which were secured by charges and a personal guarantee. When the lender sought to obtain repayment and/or to enforce the security and guarantee, the target company and the guarantor advanced various arguments to the effect that the financing and related security arrangements were illegal and unenforceable because they infringed the ban on financial assistance. The Court of Appeal held that, while these arguments were 'ingenious,' the commercial reality was that the target company and guarantor were seeking to avoid their liabilities to the funder for what was in essence a straightforward commercial loan by a strained reading of the statute.

The *Anglo Petroleum* decision suggests that the courts will take a robust attitude towards what they perceive to be unmeritorious attempts to exploit financial assistance law in order to escape liability. A number of other recent cases are to similar effect.[52] They are in contrast to the first instance decision in *Re Hill and Tyler Ltd, Harlow v Loveday*,[53] where the financing for the acquisition of shares included financial assistance in the form of a loan provided by the target company. The target company had raised the money for the loan by entering into a financing arrangement secured by a charge on its assets. It was held that as a matter of

---

[51] [2007] BCC 407, CA.
[52] *Dyment v Boyden* [2004] 2 BCLC 423, affirmed [2005] 1 BCLC 163 CA (company could not get out of obligations under a lease by claiming it was unlawful financial assistance); *Corporate Development Partners LLC v E-Relationship Marketing Ltd* [2009] BCC 295 (commitment to pay an introduction fee was not financial assistance and was therefore enforceable).
[53] [2005] 1 BCLC 41.

commercial reality and applying the concept of 'smoothing the path,' the charge constituted financial assistance in circumstances where all the parties knew that the borrowed funds were to be used to finance the acquisition of shares. The court expressed the view that but for the use of the private company 'whitewash' procedure (a procedure under the Companies Act 1985 that enabled private companies in certain circumstances to give financial assistance that would otherwise have been prohibited),[54] the charge would have been illegal and unenforceable. This controversial decision was distinguished in the *Anglo Petroleum* case where the Court of Appeal determined that it was unnecessary to express any view as to its correctness.

Re Uniq plc[55] involved a scheme of arrangement that was part of a complicated corporate restructuring designed to address a crippling pension scheme deficit. Under the scheme, Newco was to become the 90.2 per cent shareholder in Uniq; Newco was to assume the pension scheme liabilities, thereby releasing Uniq and its subsidiaries from their obligations to the pension scheme; Newco was to be put into administration; and the pension scheme liabilities assumed by Newco would be eligible for compensation under the Pension Protection Fund. The funds needed by Newco to pay up the 90.2 per cent holding of Uniq shares were to be provided to it by means of payments from companies within the existing Uniq group. The potential for these payments to contravene the ban on the giving of financial assistance was therefore clear, even though this was self-evidently not a case in which a company was paying out money in return for nothing, or very little, in return. Richards J acknowledged the commercial realities of the situation in his remark that if a company made a payment for full consideration received by it or its subsidiary and with the genuine purpose of advancing its own interests and not in order to provide financial assistance, it could well be said that it was not, in the ordinary language of commerce, financial assistance, notwithstanding that it knew that the recipient would use the money paid to fund the acquisition of shares in the company or its holding company. However, Richards J considered that this robust view could be considered 'controversial' in view of some of the earlier authorities, and that it was better therefore to consider whether each of the specific payments fell within any of the categories of financial assistance set out in the legislation. Some did; some did not; in particular, and in line with previous authority, it was held that the repayment of an on demand loan was not capable of constituting financial assistance as it was simply the performance of an unconnected obligation.

Forms of financial assistance that are prohibited

The forms of financial assistance that are prohibited are set out in section 677 of the Companies Act 2006. They are as follows.

Financial assistance given by way of gift[56]

Any gift, irrespective of its size, either in absolute terms or as a percentage of the donor company's total assets, falls within this category. There is no *de minimis* exception.

A gift is normally taken to mean a gratuitous transfer of the ownership of property.[57] In *R v Braithwaite*,[58] a case concerned with the interpretation of the Prevention of Corruption

---

[54] This procedure is now abolished as it is no longer necessary.   [55] [2012] 1 BCLC 783.
[56] Companies Act 2006, s 677(1)(a).
[57] *Customs and Excise Commissioners v Telemed Ltd* [1989] VATTR 238, 243 (appeal dismissed [1992] STC 89).
[58] [1983] 1 WLR 385, CA

Act 1906, Lord Lane CJ said:[59] 'The word 'gift' is the other side of the coin, that is to say it comes into play where there is no consideration and no bargain. Consideration deals with the situation where there is a contract or a bargain and something moving the other way.' However, in relation to the category of 'gift' in section 677(1)(a) of the Companies Act 2006, it has been held that an arrangement in which the amount payable by a company was greater than the value of the assets it was to acquire constituted a gift, to the extent of the overpayment.[60] This case was considered by the Court of Appeal in *Barclays Bank plc v British & Commonwealth Holdings plc*[61] where Aldous LJ, delivering a judgment with which the other members of the court agreed, said that overpayments could be gifts depending on the circumstances of the case, and appeared to accept that in this context it was appropriate to look at the 'reality' of transactions rather than their form.

Charterhouse Trust Ltd v Tempest Diesels Ltd[62] concerned the reorganization of a corporate group prior to the disposal of one of the subsidiaries in the group. As part of this reorganization the subsidiary in question agreed to surrender certain tax losses. Hoffmann J held that the agreement to surrender tax losses had to be considered in conjunction with the transaction as a whole to determine where the net balance of financial advantage lay and that it could constitute the giving of financial assistance if it amounted to a net transfer of value which reduced the price that the purchaser had to pay for the subsidiary company. This case was decided under section 54 of the Companies Act 1948, which did not contain a list of the forms of financial assistance that were prohibited. This type of transaction could fall within the gift category provided it is construed in the extended sense as including arrangements in which the company gives more than it receives in return and is not limited to wholly gratuitous transactions.

It may even be possible to regard an issue of shares at a price that it is less than could otherwise have been achieved as a gift in this extended sense.[63] However, this would seem to be straining the category somewhat. It is not a gift within section 677(1)(a) of the Companies Act 2006 for a company to agree to issue warrants or options in return for a directorship.[64]

Financial assistance given by way of guarantee or security[65]

A company may be asked personally to guarantee borrowings that an acquirer of its shares has incurred in order to acquire the shares or it may be asked to grant security over the company's assets for that borrowing. Both of these transactions are straightforward examples of unlawful financial assistance within this category, as *Re Hill and Tyler Ltd, Harlow v Loveday*[66] illustrates. In this case, the purchaser borrowed money from a number of sources in order to acquire shares in the target. One of the sources was a director of the target company. The loan provided by the director was secured by a written guarantee and a charge given by the target company. There was no dispute that this guarantee and charge constituted financial assistance falling within the Act. More controversially, it was held that a charge given by the target company to secure funding obtained by it for the purposes of loaning it on to the purchaser to pay for the shares was also unlawful financial assistance within this category in circumstances where all the parties were aware of how the borrowed funds were to be used.

However, it is important to note that the mere fact that the arrangements for the acquisition of shares include the giving of security by the target in respect of its own indebtedness

---

[59] At 391.   [60] *Plaut v Steiner* (1989) 5 BCC 352.
[61] [1995] BCC 1059, CA.   [62] (1983–85) 1 BCC 99,544.
[63] On the possibility of a low subscription price for new shares being a form of financial assistance, see also *Milburn v Pivot Ltd* (1997) 15 ACLC 1520 Fed Ct of Aust.
[64] *Oxus Gold plc (formerly Oxus Mining plc) v Templeton Insurance Ltd* [2006] EWHC 864 (Ch), [184].
[65] Companies Act 2006, s 677(1)(b)(i).   [66] [2005] 1 BCLC 41.

does not lead inevitably to the conclusion that there is unlawful financial assistance within the Act. The security may be outside the scope of the Act because, applying the commercial reality test, there is no financial assistance or because the required causal link between the financial assistance and the purpose for which it is given (considered later in this chapter) is not present. The particular factual circumstances therefore require close examination. This can be illustrated by reference to *Anglo Petroleum v TFB (Mortgages) Ltd*.[67] In this case the target company was indebted to its parent in the sum of £30 million. That indebtedness was apparently repayable on demand and carried interest at a commercial rate. The target entered into a compromise agreement with its parent in which it agreed a repayment schedule in respect of a portion of its outstanding indebtedness and to grant security over its assets in respect of that indebtedness. In return, the parent released and discharged the target from repayment of the balance of the outstanding inter-company debt. On the same day the target was sold to the purchaser. A subsequent attempt to characterize the security as unlawful financial assistance failed since, as a matter of commercial reality, the security was the price the target had to pay for obtaining a reduction in its debt and was not financial assistance.

Financial assistance given by way of indemnity[68]

The term 'indemnity' is used in a technical sense in section 677 of the Companies Act 2006 and means a contract by one party to keep the other harmless against loss.[69] For a company, as part of a share-support operation, to undertake to make good any losses which investors in its shares may suffer as a result of having bought them would infringe this aspect of the ban on the giving of financial assistance.

A situation where indemnities are commonly given by companies to persons who acquire, or who may acquire, their shares is in the context of underwriting agreements. This type of indemnity differs from that considered in the previous paragraph in that it is an indemnity in respect of losses that the underwriter may incur arising from the underwriting process but not in respect of a fall in the share price, which is precisely the risk that the underwriter undertakes to bear. Section s 677(1)(b)(i) of the Companies Act 2006 expressly excludes indemnities that are in respect of the indemnifier's own loss or default, but indemnities in underwriting agreements may be more extensive. Where this is the case, there is a risk of the indemnity being challenged on financial assistance grounds. Again, however, it is important not to jump to the conclusion that an indemnity in an underwriting agreement that is not limited to the indemnifier's own loss or default is unlawful financial assistance. It may not be financial assistance at all because, as a matter of commercial reality, it is simply an element of the legitimate bargain that a company enters into as part of the process of raising capital by issuing shares to the market.

Financial assistance given by way of release or waiver[70]

The terms 'release' or 'waiver' relate to circumstances where a company relinquishes, or forbears from enforcing, rights that it has against another party. It is unclear whether contractual variations are within the scope of this category, although variation of a bilateral contract by mutual agreement of the parties is sometimes described as a waiver. Even if contractual variations can be regarded as waivers for this purpose, it may be that in many instances the

---

[67] [2007] BCC 407, CA.   [68] Companies Act 2006, s 677(1)(b)(i).
[69] *Yeoman Credit Ltd v Latter* [1961] 1 WLR 828, CA, 830 *per* Pearce LJ adopted in *Barclays Bank plc v British & Commonwealth Holdings plc* [1995] BCC 1059, CA.
[70] Companies Act 2006, s 677(1)(b)(ii).

new mix of benefits and burdens assumed by the parties to a varied contract will be such that it is not possible to conclude that, as a matter of commercial reality, a company has given assistance of a financial nature.

Financial assistance given by way of loan[71]

For a company to lend money to finance the acquisition of its own shares is among the most blatant forms of financial assistance and where there is clear evidence that this has occurred the point is unlikely to be disputed.[72]

The usual meaning of the term 'loan' is that it is an advance of money on terms providing for repayment.[73] An arrangement whereby a company pays off a debt that has been incurred by a purchaser of its shares to a third party on terms providing for the purchaser later to reimburse the company is not a loan within this interpretation. A loan is also to be distinguished from a transaction whereby a company buys goods on credit. Provided the form of the transaction is not a sham and its terms are consistent with the label which the parties have attached to it, buying goods on credit, or against a post-dated debt, does not give rise to a lender-borrower relationship.[74]

Financial assistance given by way of any other agreement under which the obligations of the person giving the assistance are to be fulfilled at a time when, in accordance with the agreement, any obligation of another party to the agreement remains unfulfilled[75]

This is the category that would apply to such things as a tripartite arrangement whereby a company pays off the debts incurred by a purchaser of its shares against an undertaking from that person to repay at some later stage, or transactions whereby a company sells assets for deferred consideration or buys assets and pays for them in advance. If the purchaser of assets from a company were to issue loan notes or other debt securities in circumstances where there was an active market for those securities so that they could readily be converted into cash, it is conceivable that this would be regarded as falling outside the scope of the ban because the consideration which the company has received is as good as cash. The position would be different where the securities which are issued are not liquid, because there would then be a risk of the issuer being unable to meet its obligations.[76]

Financial assistance given by way of novation of, or assignment of rights arising under, a loan or such other agreement[77]

When a contract is novated, the original agreement is discharged and is replaced by a new agreement between different parties. Novation acts as a mechanism whereby the burden of a

---

[71] Companies Act 2006, s 677(1)(c)(i).   [72] *Re Hill and Tyler Ltd, Harlow v Loveday* [2005] 1 BCLC 41.

[73] *Chow Yoong Hong v Choong Fah Rubber Manufactory* [1962] AC 209, PC, 216 *per* Lord Devlin; *Vigier v IRC* [1964] 1 WLR 1073, HL, 1084 *per* Lord Upjohn; *Champagne-Perrier SA v HH Finch Ltd* [1982] 3 All ER 713; *Potts v IRC* [1951] AC 443, HL.

[74] *Chow Yoong Hong v Choong Fah Rubber Manufactory* [1962] AC 209, PC; *IRC v Port of London Authority* [1923] AC 507, HL.

[75] Companies Act 2006, s 677(1)(c)(i).

[76] WJL Knight, *The Acquisition of Private Companies and Business Assets* 7th edn (London: FT Law & Tax, 1997) 61 discusses this example.

[77] Companies Act 2006, s 677(1)(c)(ii). 'Such other agreement' is a reference back to the second limb of s 677(1)(c)(i).

contract can be transferred to another party. This is in contrast to assignment, which can be used to transfer rights but not liabilities.

Any other financial assistance given by a company the net assets of which are thereby reduced to a material extent [78]

This is a 'catch all' category for forms of financial assistance that reduce the assisting company's net assets to a material extent. It is pertinent to undervalue transactions and to arrangements under which companies pay fees in return for services. It was the form of financial assistance that was relevant in *Chaston v SWP Group plc*[79] where the company paid for the accountant's reports. The category is potentially applicable to break fees, which are arrangements between a bidder and a target whereby a fee is payable by the target if a specified event occurs that prevents the takeover from going ahead.[80]

'Net assets' here means the aggregate amount of the company assets less the aggregate amount of its liabilities.[81] It is market, rather than book, values that are relevant.[82] There is no statutory definition of materiality in this context.[83] The materiality test is open to at least two distinct interpretations. One approach is to focus on the size of the reduction in percentage terms and to regard it as immaterial if it falls below a certain minimum threshold. The other approach is to look at the total amount involved and to regard it as material if it is a large number, even though it may represent a tiny reduction in the company's net assets based on a percentage test. Which (if either) of these alternative approaches is correct is not clear from the wording of the legislation. It is even possible that some form of combined method—in which the percentage reduction and the amount in absolute terms both feature as relevant considerations—could be held to apply. In *Parlett v Guppys Bridport Ltd*[84] it was said to be a question of degree and that there was no rule of thumb as to materiality.[85] Extinguishing the assets will clearly suffice.[86] Notwithstanding the reluctance of the courts to endorse a rule of thumb, a practice has grown up of regarding agreements to pay fees capped at 1 per cent of the payer's value as generally immaterial.[87] This practice has acquired a degree of regulatory endorsement in that whilst the UK Takeover Code generally prohibits inducement (break) fees where an offeror has announced a firm intention to make an offer which was not recommended by the board of the offeree company at the time of that announcement and remains not recommended, the Panel will normally consent to the offeree company entering into an inducement fee arrangement with a competing offeror at the time of the announcement of its firm intention to make a competing offer, provided that certain conditions are fulfilled, including that the aggregate value of the inducement fee or fees that may be payable by the offeree

---

[78] Companies Act 2006, s 677(1)(d)(i).   [79] [2003] 1 BCLC 675, CA.

[80] *Paros Plc v Worldlink Group Plc* [2012] EWHC 394. See also *LR* 10.2.6A-10.2.7.

[81] Companies Act 2006, s 677(2).

[82] This interpretation is based on a comparison between Companies Act 2006, ss 677(2) and 682(3)–(4). In *Parlett v Guppys (Bridport) Ltd* [1996] BCC 299, CA, it was common ground between counsel that it was market values that were relevant for the purposes of what is now Companies Act 1986, s 677(2). But Nourse LJ commented (at 305) that whilst it was easy to speak in the abstract about the difference between actual assets and liabilities and assets and liabilities as stated in accounting records, it was less easy to disassociate an actual asset or liability from the notion of what is or ought to be in the accounting records.

[83] *Paros Plc v Worldlink Group Plc* [2012] EWHC 394, [70], acknowledging the support in the literature for 1 per cent as a materiality threshold but noting the lack of definitive authority. That the fee payment in *Chaston* satisfied the materiality requirement was conceded by counsel: [2003] 1 BCLC 675, CA, [12].

[84] [1996] 2 BCLC 34, CA.   [85] At 35 *per* Nourse LJ.

[86] *MacPherson v European Strategic Bureau Ltd* [2000] 2 BCLC 683, CA.

[87] As acknowledged in *Paros Plc v Worldlink Group Plc* [2012] EWHC 394, [70].

company is de minimis, ie normally no more than 1 per cent of the value of the offeree company.[88] A break fee of more than 1 per cent undertaken by a premium listed company would be a Class 1 transaction under the *Listing Rules* and, as such, would require shareholder approval.[89]

This is the one form of financial assistance where 'detriment', ie a depletion of the assets of the assisting company, is essential.[90]

Any other financial assistance given by a company which has no net assets [91]

This is also a catch-all category of financial assistance that is applicable only to companies that have no net assets. It differs from the previous category in that any financial assistance, even of a *de minimis* amount, is prohibited where a company has negative net assets.[92] Furthermore, detriment is not required—indeed, something that is positively beneficial to the assisting company, such as a loan by it on highly favourable terms, could constitute unlawful financial assistance in this category.[93]

Circumstances in which the Giving of Financial Assistance is Prohibited

We now arrive at the heart of the ban on the giving of financial assistance. This is contained in section 678 of the Companies Act 2006[94] and is as follows:

(1) Where a person is acquiring or proposing to acquire shares in a public company, it is not lawful for that company, or a company that is a subsidiary of that company, to give financial assistance directly or indirectly for the purpose of the acquisition before or at the same time as the acquisition takes place.

. . .

(3) Where—
    (a) a person has acquired shares in a company, and
    (b) a liability has been incurred (by that or another person) for the purpose of the acquisition, it is not lawful for that company, or a company that is a subsidiary of that company, to give financial assistance directly or indirectly for the purpose of reducing or discharging the liability if, at the time the assistance is given, the company in which the shares were acquired is a public company.

Elements of these two provisions may be separated out for particular consideration.

An acquisition

The choice of the word 'acquisition' gives breadth to the scope of the ban because it ensures that it extends to issues of shares for non-cash consideration. This was not the case under section 54 of the Companies Act 1948, which referred to the purchase of, or subscription for,

---

[88] Takeover Code, Rule 21.2, note 2.   [89] *LR* 10.2.7.
[90] *Chaston v SWP Group plc* [2003] 1 BCLC 675, CA, [41] *per* Arden LJ.
[91] Companies Act 2006, s 677(1)(d)(ii).   [92] *Paros Plc v Worldlink Group Plc* [2012] EWHC 394.
[93] *Chaston v SWP Group plc* [2003] 1 BCLC 675, CA [41].
[94] Note also Companies Act 2006, s 679, which relates to financial assistance given by a public company subsidiary of a private company.

shares because the term 'subscription' has been held to mean taking shares for cash.[95] A purchase of shares for non-cash consideration is also an acquisition.[96]

Must an acquisition take place at some point in order for the prohibition to bite? On the one hand, it is possible to argue that financial assistance given in circumstances where an acquisition never takes place is not financial assistance given 'before' an acquisition, so it does not come within the scope of section 678(1) of the Companies Act 2006 (and section 678(3) being concerned with post-acquisition financial assistance is clearly inapplicable). On the other hand, the reference in section 678(1) to a 'proposed' acquisition of shares is a strong indication that it is not essential for an acquisition of shares ever to take place. The latter interpretation of the statute appears to have been adopted, without discussion of the point, in *Cox v Cox*,[97] where payments made by a company to a shareholder, who was in the process of divorcing her husband, another shareholder, were held to be unlawful pre-acquisition financial assistance in relation to the acquisition of the wife's shares by the husband notwithstanding that he had yet to acquire the shares by the time of the proceedings. This is also the view that underpins the legal analysis of break fees, which are fees that become payable in the event of a bid being aborted. In *Paros Plc v Worldlink Group Plc*[98] it was held definitively with respect to a break fee arrangement that the ban on the giving of financial assistance applied to cases where a person was proposing to acquire shares in the company, just as much as where he actually acquired them.

The ban relates only to an acquisition of shares

In *NZI Bank Ltd v Euro-National Corp Ltd*[99] it was held by the New Zealand Court of Appeal that providing money to acquire share options was not within the ban on the giving of financial assistance in the form of money for the acquisition of shares imposed by section 62 of the New Zealand Companies Act 1955. Section 62 of the 1955 Act was based on section 54 of the English Companies Act 1948 and the wording of section 62 is sufficiently close to that of section 678 of the Companies Act 2006 to give this case some persuasive authority in relation to the interpretation of section 678. This line of reasoning suggests that financial assistance given in relation to the acquisition of debt securities that are convertible into shares should also fall outside the statutory ban. This is subject to the qualification that the court may look through formalities to substance where a structure has been adopted in order to evade the application of a statute or where, as a matter of statutory interpretation, a particular statute requires or permits it to do so.[100]

The ban applies only to public companies and their subsidiaries

As mentioned earlier in this chapter, the one big difference between section 678 of the Companies Act 2006 and its predecessor, section 151 of the Companies Act 1985, is that the ban now applies only in relation to public companies and their subsidiaries. This point is now given closer examination.

---

[95]   *Government Stock and Other Securities Investment Co Ltd v Christopher* [1956] 1 All ER 490.
[96]   *Plaut v Steiner* (1989) 5 BCC 352, decided under the Companies Act 1985, s 151, involved a share-for-share exchange.
[97]   [2006] EWHC 1077 (Ch).   [98]   [2012] EWHC 394.   [99]   [1992] 3 NZLR 528, NZ CA.
[100]   *Barclays Bank plc v British & Commonwealth Holdings plc* [1995] BCC 1059, CA suggests that the courts can look to substance rather than form in applying the statutory provisions relating to financial assistance. See further J Vella, 'Departing from the Legal Substance of Transactions in the Corporate Field: the Ramsay Approach Beyond the Tax Sphere' [2007] *Journal of Corporate Law Studies* 243.

The status of the company whose shares are acquired

Under section 678 of the Companies Act 2006 the company whose shares are acquired must be a public company at the time when the assistance is given. This is straightforward in relation to pre-acquisition financial assistance and financial assistance that is contemporaneous with an acquisition (ie the situations covered by section 678(1)) but needed to be specifically addressed in relation to post-acquisition financial assistance (ie the situations covered by section 678(3)). The drafting of section 678(3) ensures that the ban on financial assistance does not affect refinancing activity relating to a public company that has been taken over, so long as the acquired company is re-registered as a private company before the refinancing takes place. This carveout is of considerable practical importance as it enables participants in leveraged buyouts to achieve desired financial restructurings of acquired companies free of the constraints imposed by financial assistance law.

Under section 679 of the Companies Act 2006 there is a ban on financially assisting the acquisition of shares in a *private* company where the company providing the assistance is a public company subsidiary of that private company. This section largely mirrors section 678.

The status of the company providing the assistance

To come within section 678 of the Companies Act 2006, the company providing the assistance must be either a public company whose shares are acquired or a public or private company that is a subsidiary of the public company whose shares are acquired. To this extent, the ban on the giving of financial assistance continues to apply to private companies. (For the purposes of section 679 of the 2006 Act, the assisting company must be a public company subsidiary of the private company whose shares are acquired.)

Section 678 (and section 679) of the Companies Act 2006 specify that the ban applies only to subsidiaries that are companies, thereby excluding foreign subsidiaries from their scope. This is a departure from the wording in section 151 of the Companies Act 1985, which, literally interpreted, did cover foreign subsidiaries, although case law established that a literal interpretation of the statute should not be adopted.[101] The revised drafting in the Companies Act 2006 in effect codifies the case law on the point. Whether a foreign subsidiary can lawfully give financial assistance will depend on the law of its place of incorporation. In some circumstances, the foreign subsidiary's actions may have implications for UK companies within the group: the hiving down of an asset by a British company to a foreign subsidiary in order to enable it to be made available to finance a contemplated acquisition of shares in the British company could be caught by section 678 (or section 679 as the case may be) as indirect provision of financial assistance by the British company.[102]

The acquirer of the shares

The ban applies to acquisitions of shares by natural persons or legal persons such as companies. Does it include acquisitions by the assisting company itself with the consequence that the ban is applicable in relation to share buy-backs (subject to any available exception)?[103]

---

[101] *Arab Bank plc v Merchantile Holdings Ltd* [1994] Ch 71.   [102] As Millett J noted in the *Arab Bank* case.

[103] Companies Act 2006, s 681(2)(d). The existence of this exception could be taken to indicate that the legislature must have considered that an acquisition by a company of its own shares could, if not specifically excluded, fall within the scope of the ban on the giving of financial assistance. On the other hand, however, it could have been included simply for the avoidance of doubt (as can also be said about other exceptions in s 681).

This is a controversial point on which different views are tenable. It may be that, as a matter of commercial reality, it is not financial assistance for a person to meet its own obligations from its own resources but, based on the current authorities, it is hard to be definite on this point. In *Chaston v SWP Group plc*[104] Arden LJ appeared to favour the view that an acquisition by a company of its own shares is potentially caught. However, in the Parliamentary debate on the Bill that became the Companies Act 2006, the government spokesperson said that, in the government's view, the references to 'person' did not include the company itself and indicated that it did not read the relevant passage in Arden LJ's judgment as being inconsistent with that view.[105] The spokesperson further suggested that to include the company within the scope of person to whom the company could not give financial assistance would be 'at odds' with the Second Company Law Directive, which envisages a person being a third party and not the company itself. Whilst some weight can be placed on the statement in Parliament,[106] it should be noted that the reference to the Second Company Law Directive is not wholly persuasive as Article 25 does not appear to be a maximum harmonization measure and it is therefore open to Member States to enact in their domestic legislation a version of financial assistance law that goes further than the minimum necessary to implement the Directive.

Must the acquirer be known to the company providing the assistance at the time when the assistance is given?

This question could, for example, arise in circumstances where the management of a company decides that its business would be more effectively conducted if it were part of a larger group and engages an investment bank or other professional adviser to find a buyer for the company's shares. Agreements to pay fees are capable of falling within one of the categories of financial assistance mentioned in section 677.[107] Can it be said that the ban on the giving of financial assistance does not apply because, at the time when the company agrees to pay the fee,[108] the company is unaware of the identity of any acquirer, or aspiring acquirer, of its shares? The answer to this question is not clear from the statute but some arguments may be advanced. The mere fact that there is no specifically identified purchaser by itself does not appear to take the situation outside the scope of the ban, which, as section 678(1)[109] indicates, extends to proposed acquisitions (which may never in fact take place). However, depending on the particular circumstances, it may be possible to argue that the agreement to pay the fees is too remote from any actual or proposed acquisition of shares to be capable of being regarded, as a matter of commercial reality, as financial assistance for the acquisition of shares. It may also be possible to argue that the company's actions were not causally linked in the way required by section 678 because they were not 'for the purpose' of an acquisition or proposed acquisition, though again this will depend on a close examination of the specific facts.

---

[104] [2003] 1 BCLC 675, CA.

[105] *Hansard*, Standing Committee D, Session 2005–06, cols 856–7 (20 July 2006) *per* Vera Baird MP.

[106] Following the decision in *Pepper v Hart* [1993] AC 593, HL, if primary legislation is ambiguous or obscure, the courts may in certain circumstances take account of statements made in Parliament by Ministers or other promoters of a Bill in construing that legislation.

[107] ie any other financial assistance that reduces net assets to a material extent or by a company that has no net assets (Companies Act 2006, s 677(1)(d)).

[108] This, rather than the time when the money is actually paid, is the relevant time: *Parlett v Guppys (Bridport) Ltd* [1996] BCC 299, CA where this was common ground between the counsel in the case.

[109] As does Companies Act 2006, s 679(1).

The assisted person—direct and indirect financial assistance

Unlawful financial assistance can be given directly, such as where the company whose shares are acquired, lends money to the purchaser to fund the acquisition, or indirectly, such as where the purchaser raises the purchase money from bank borrowings that are guaranteed by the company. The payment of the fees of professional advisers who advise on a share acquisition, such as the accountants in *Chaston v SWP Group plc*,[110] is another example of indirect financial assistance because the company's assumption of responsibility to pay the fees relieves the principals to the transaction of any obligation in that respect.

There can thus be no doubt that the fact that the vendor rather than the purchaser is the recipient of some action by a company does not preclude a finding that that action constitutes unlawful financial assistance.[111] Where, however, the action benefits only the vendor and is of no help whatsoever to the purchaser—for example, where the target company pays the fees of advisers engaged to figure out how to sell the company at the most favourable price—it is open to question whether this is capable of being regarded as financial assistance within the scope of the Act. As Arden LJ noted in *Chaston v SWP Group plc*,[112] the general mischief that underlies financial assistance law is 'that the resources of the target company and its subsidiaries should not be used directly or indirectly *to assist the purchaser financially to make the acquisition*' (emphasis added). Where the vendor is the exclusive beneficiary of some action (and perhaps it has worked to the purchaser's disadvantage by making the acquisition more expensive to complete), this mischief is not present. However, on the current state of the authorities it is not possible to reach a confident conclusion that the purchaser must be assisted in some way (directly or indirectly) for the prohibition to bite.

In *Armour Hick Northern Ltd v Armour Hick Trust Ltd*[113] a subsidiary paid off a debt due from its immediate holding company to a major shareholder and that shareholder then sold its shares in the holding company to its other existing shareholders. It was held that the subsidiary's action was financial assistance to the vendor shareholder for the purpose of or in connection with the share purchase by the remaining shareholders because it was a voluntary payment without which the vendor shareholder would not have proceeded with the sale. This case was decided in relation to section 54 of the Companies Act 1948, which banned financial assistance in 'connection with' as well as 'for the purpose of' a purchase of shares, but it continues to be cited as good authority for the proposition that financial assistance given to a vendor is within the scope of the ban, as currently formulated.[114] Since it was found that the acquisition would not have gone ahead but for the payment made by the subsidiary, it is possible to regard the *Armour Hick* case as being consistent with the proposition that the purchaser must benefit in some way from the action that is alleged to be unlawful financial assistance. As Rimer J noted in *Corporate Development Partners LLC v E-Relationship Marketing Ltd*,[115] the offending assistance given to the vendor 'was plainly directed at enabling the acquisition to happen.' However, a wider interpretation, namely, that any assistance to the vendor is caught irrespective of its impact on the purchaser, is also tenable. In practice, a cautious approach is warranted, given the draconian consequences of contravention of the ban on the giving of financial assistance.

---

[110] [2003] 1 BCLC 675, CA.

[111] *Armour Hick Northern Ltd v Whitehouse* [1980] 3 All ER 833, [1980] 1 WLR 1520.

[112] [2003] 1 BCLC 675, CA, [31].   [113] [1980] 3 All ER 833, [1980] 1 WLR 1520.

[114] eg *Chaston v SWP Group plc* [2003] 1 BCLC 675, CA; *Anglo Petroleum Ltd v TFB (Mortgages) Ltd* [2007] BCC 407, CA.

[115] [2007] EWHC 436 (Ch), [35].

The Purpose(s) for which Financial Assistance is Given

The causal link

The ban only applies to financial assistance given *for the purpose of* an acquisition (section 678(1)) or *for the purpose of* reducing or discharging a liability incurred *for the purpose of* an acquisition (section 678(3)).[116] 'Purpose' thus acts as the causal link between the financial assistance and the acquisition: simply coming within one of the categories of financial assistance mentioned in section 677 is not on its own enough and such assistance will only constitute a breach of section 678 if it is also assistance for a specified purpose. In relation to section 678(3), a person incurs a liability, inter alia, if they change their financial position by making any agreement (enforceable or unenforceable) either on their own account or with any other person, or by any other means, and a company reduces or discharges such a liability by the giving of financial assistance if it is given wholly or partly for the purpose of restoring that person's financial position to what it was before the acquisition took place.[117]

In *Dyment v Boyden*[118] a partnership within a corporate shell was dissolved with one shareholder acquiring the holdings of the two other shareholders in the company and, in return, the departing shareholders taking exclusive ownership of the business premises that were then leased to the company at a rent of £66,000 per annum. Sometime later, the shareholder who had remained with the company claimed that the real market rent for the property was £37,000 per annum, not £66,000 per annum; that the difference of £29,000 per annum amounted to unlawful financial assistance given by the company; and that the lease was unenforceable with the result that no rent was ever properly payable under it. It was agreed that the additional £29,000 had the effect of reducing the company's net assets to a material extent. The Court of Appeal upheld the first instance decision that this arrangement was not unlawful financial assistance. Although it was an implied term of the agreement dissolving the partnership that the applicant should procure the company to enter into the lease, it could not properly be said that the obligation to procure the company's acceptance of the lease was undertaken for the purpose of the acquisition of the shares or that the company, by subsequently entering into the lease, had discharged a liability contrary to the Act. Applying the test of commercial substance and reality, the company's acceptance of the lease, although connected with the acquisition of the shares, could not fairly be said to have been 'for the purpose' of that acquisition, since the reality was that the company entered into the lease in order to obtain the premises that it needed in order to continue in business, and had agreed to pay an excessive rent because the owners of the freehold were in a position to exact a ransom for that property.

The causal link was also held to be missing in *Corporate Development Partners LLC v E-Relationship Marketing Ltd*.[119] In this case the defendant engaged the claimant to work on identifying possible target companies for it to acquire but, as things turned out, the defendant was itself taken over by another company to which it had been introduced by the claimant. In the period between the parties to the takeover being introduced to each other and the completion of that takeover, the consultancy agreement between the claimant and defendant was renegotiated and the revised agreement included provision for the defendant to pay a specified fee in the event of that takeover going ahead. The defendant subsequently attempted to use financial assistance law to escape its obligation to pay the fee, arguing that (a) the introduction effected by the claimant facilitated, or smoothed the path towards, an acquisition of

---

[116] Likewise, Companies Act 2006, s 679.   [117] Companies Act 2006, s 683(2).
[118] [2005] 1 BCLC 163, CA.
[119] [2007] EWHC 436 (Ch). The relevant causal link of purpose was also lacking in *Re Uniq*: [40].

its shares; (b) the payment commitment in the revised agreement was by way of a reward for that introduction; and (c) therefore the commitment—or payment if ultimately made—itself facilitated the acquisition and so amounted to the giving of unlawful financial assistance for the purpose of the acquisition. The Court held that the third proposition was wrong on its facts. Rimer J explained:[120]

> Since CDP was playing no role in the negotiation of the acquisition—and was neither intended nor required to—the commitment to pay it the transaction fee was not going to, was not intended to and did not in fact assist or advance the acquisition at all. The payment commitment was not a condition of the takeover; it would not serve to reduce Red Eye's acquisition obligations by a single penny; and it was neither intended to, nor did it, smooth the path towards any ultimate acquisition. No doubt the reason for the commitment was because CDP had earlier introduced a party who might thereafter acquire E-RM; and it was intended to be by way of a financial reward to CDP for that introduction. But, for reasons given, the commitment was not entered into 'for the purpose' of such an acquisition.

Reference can also be made to the decision of the Court of Appeal in *Barclays Bank plc v British and Commonwealth Holdings plc*.[121] In that case the company, as part of a scheme whereby a shareholder took redeemable shares from it with an option to sell the shares to a third party if the company failed to redeem on the due date, covenanted with that third party to maintain a certain asset value. The company failed both to redeem the shares and to maintain that value. The shareholder exercised his option to sell and the third party sued the company for damages for breach of the covenant. One of the questions for the Court of Appeal was whether this covenant amounted to financial assistance for the acquisition of the shares, either by the shareholder or the third party. The Court of Appeal, upholding the decision of Harman J, held that the purpose of the covenant was to reassure the shareholder and that the covenant was a bona fide undertaking, the performance of which did not involve any financial assistance. This is not to say, however, that inducements, incentives, and concurrent benefits provided by target companies as part of a transaction in which their shares are acquired will necessarily always fail to satisfy the requirement for a causal link based on the purpose for which they are given.[122] Whether the required link exists depends on a close, fact-specific examination in each case.[123]

Mixed purposes

The purpose of assisting the acquisition of the shares or reducing or discharging a liability incurred for the purpose of an acquisition of shares need only be one of the purposes for which the financial assistance was given.[124] However, where there are mixed purposes, the financial assistance may be taken outside the scope of the prohibition if that purpose is subsidiary to another 'principal' purpose[125] or is incidental to another 'larger' purpose,[126] provided that,

---

[120] At [35].   [121] [1996] 1 BCLC 1, CA.

[122] *Chaston v SWP Group plc* [2003] 1 BCLC 675, CA, [43] *per* Arden LJ. In so far as the decision at first instance in *MT Realisations Ltd v Digital Equipment Co Ltd* [2002] 2 BCLC 688 suggests that an incentive that is part of a transaction for the acquisition of shares is not given for the purpose of the acquisition ([30]–[31] in particular) it must be treated with caution. The Court of Appeal upheld the decision but on different grounds: [2003] 2 BCLC 117, CA.

[123] Laddie J held that the purchaser's assumption of obligations to pay for the assignment of the loan (which the subsequent rescheduling agreement addressed) was not a liability incurred for the purpose of the acquisition of the shares. Although it was undoubtedly true that the loan assignment would not have gone through without the assignment of the shares, the loan assignment was properly to be characterized as something distinct from the acquisition, ie as an incentive connected to, but not for the purpose of, the sale of the shares.

[124] *Chaston v SWP Group plc* [2003] 1 BCLC 675, CA.   [125] Companies Act 2006, s 678(2). See also s 679(2).

[126] Companies Act 2006, s 678(4). See also s 679(4).

in either case, the assistance is given in good faith in the interests of the assisting company. Discussion of the scope of the principal or larger purpose exception is dominated by the difficult decision of the judicial House of Lords (now the Supreme Court) in *Brady v Brady*.[127]

Brady v Brady

This case concerned an arrangement that was put in place to break a deadlock in a group of family-run private companies where the businesses had become paralyzed because of disputes between family members. The solution was to divide the businesses, which necessitated a complex series of transactions including the transfer of a significant portion of the company's assets in order to meet liabilities incurred in purchasing that company's shares. The transfer was undoubtedly financial assistance given for a requisite purpose and the issue before the courts was whether it could it be saved by the principal purpose or larger purpose exception. At first instance it was held that the giving of the financial assistance to reduce or discharge a liability related to the acquisition of shares was incidental to the larger purpose of the arrangement and fell within the exception. The Court of Appeal also thought that there were mixed purposes and that the principal purpose was not to facilitate the acquisition of shares but to enable the businesses to continue by ending the deadlock between the two principal shareholders but it held that the exception did not apply because the assistance had not been given in good faith in the interests of the company.[128] In the House of Lords, it was held that the good faith requirement was satisfied but that there was no principal or larger purpose that could be relied upon to save the transaction.

Lord Oliver (with whom the other members of the House of Lords agreed) said:[129]

> …'purpose' is, in some contexts, a word of wide content but in construing it in the context of the fasciculus of sections regulating the provision of finance by a company in connection with the purchase of its own shares there has always to be borne in mind the mischief against which section 151 [now s 678] is aimed. In particular, if the section is not, effectively, to be deprived of any useful application, it is important to distinguish between a purpose and the reason why a purpose is formed. The ultimate reason for forming a purpose of financing an acquisition may, and in most cases probably will, be more important to those making the decision than the immediate transaction itself. But…'reason' [is not] the same as 'purpose.' If one postulates the case of a bidder for
>
> control of a public company financing his bid from the company's own funds—the obvious mischief at which the section is aimed—the immediate purpose which it is sought to achieve is that of completing the purchase and vesting control of the company in the bidder. The reasons why that course is considered desirable may be many and varied. The company may have fallen on hard times so that a change of management is considered necessary to avert disasters. It may merely be thought, and no doubt would be thought by the purchaser and the directors whom he nominates once he has control, that the business of the company would be more profitable under his management than it was heretofore. These may be excellent reasons but they cannot, in my judgment, constitute a 'larger purpose' of which the provision of assistance is merely an incident. The purpose and the only purpose of the financial assistance is and remains that of enabling the shares to be acquired and the financial or commercial advantages flowing from the acquisition, whilst they may form the reason for forming the purpose of providing assistance,

---

[127] [1989] AC 755, HL. The decision has attracted considerable comment, much of it critical. See eg BG Pettet, 'Developments in the Law of Financial Assistance for the Purchase of Shares'; R Greaves and B Hannigan, 'Gratuitous Transfers and Financial Assistance after *Brady*' (1989) 10 *Company Lawyer* 135; K Polack, 'Companies Act 1985—Scope of Section 153' [1988] CLJ 359.

[128] [1988] BCLC 20, CA.   [129] [1989] AC 755, HL, 779–80.

are a by-product of it rather than an independent purpose of which the assistance can properly be considered an incident.

This passage has become notorious among company lawyers because it has not proved easy to identify what counts as a principal or larger purpose as opposed to a 'mere' good reason for entering into a particular arrangement. Perhaps the most that can be said with certainty is that the House of Lords sent out a very strong signal that the term 'purpose' here is to be narrowly interpreted and therefore it should not be lightly assumed that a purpose-based exception is available.

Reversing Brady

For many years there have been calls for the purpose exception to be reformulated so as to remove its very narrow scope, as interpreted in the *Brady* case. During the 1990s it did appear to be the government's intention to reverse the effects of the *Brady* judgment by introducing a predominant reason test in place of the larger/principal purpose exception. Yet, when the opportunity to rewrite the exception in the Companies Act 2006 was presented, the government declined to do so. The explanation for this apparent volte-face emerged in discussion in Parliament on the Bill that became the Companies Act 2006: it was not that the government had changed its mind on the desirability of reversing the effect of the *Brady* case but rather that it had had second thoughts on whether it had yet hit upon a form of words that would achieve the desired effect. The government signalled that it remained prepared to consider a reworking of the provisions so as to have the intended effect of removing the very narrow scope of the purpose exceptions as interpreted in *Brady*, and indicated that new provisions could refer to concepts along the current lines or might be framed on an entirely different basis so long as they remained consistent with the implementation of Article 25 of the Second Company Law Directive.[130]

Examples of a larger or principal purpose

For now, it remains necessary therefore to grapple with thorny questions on the scope of the purpose-based exception for which few definite answers are available.

An example of a principal purpose was given by Lord Oliver in *Brady v Brady*:[131]

> The [principal purpose exception] envisages a principal and, by implication, a subsidiary purpose. The inquiry here is whether the assistance given was principally in order to relieve the purchaser of shares in the company of his indebtedness resulting from the acquisition or whether it was principally for some other purpose—for instance, the acquisition from the purchaser of some asset which the company requires for its business.

Re Uniq[132] provides an example of a case in which the principal purpose exemption might have operated. As mentioned earlier, this case involved the making of loans by companies within a corporate group to facilitate the insertion of a new holding company. The court was satisfied that the purpose of the companies in making loans was to provide funds to secure the release from crippling pension fund liabilities. This was the case, according to Richards J, notwithstanding that it was known and intended that the funds would be used by Newco to pay up the new shares. Furthermore, even if payment for shares could properly be regarded

---

[130] *Hansard*, vol 680, GC col 24 (20 March 2006) and *Hansard*, HC vol 682, col 182 (16 May 2006).
[131] [1989] AC 755, HL, 779.   [132] [2012] 1 BCLC 783.

as *a* purpose of the loans and payments, the court declared itself satisfied that the principal purpose was to obtain the release.

An example of an operative larger purpose is more difficult to formulate.[133] Even Lord Oliver in the *Brady* case acknowledged that the concept of a larger corporate purpose was not easy to grasp.[134] One situation that may yield an example is the case of a subsidiary company that provides funds to its parent company some years after its acquisition to effect a more efficient deployment of assets within the group or to improve the group's financial position. Should the parent use the funds so provided to repay a debt that was incurred for the purpose of acquiring the subsidiary, it is possible that the purpose of achieving that greater efficiency could be viewed as an operative larger purpose. What would distinguish these facts from those in *Brady*? A discernible difference between the two situations can be found by focusing attention on *corporate* purpose, as opposed to the purpose of individual shareholders or directors. A larger *corporate* purpose may have been what was lacking in the *Brady* case where the driving factor was the desire of the shareholders to ensure the survival of the businesses. This contrasts with the example of an intra-group transaction for which there may exist many legitimate corporate purposes that a company seeks to achieve by its participation.[135]

Good faith

The purpose exception is available only where there is an operative principal or larger purpose *and* the assistance is given in good faith in the interests of the company. In the *Brady* case Lord Oliver held that this phrase was a single, composite expression and that it postulated a requirement that those responsible for procuring the company to provide the assistance must act in the genuine belief that it is being done in the company's interest.[136] In the Court of Appeal[137] Nourse LJ had placed particular emphasis on how the scheme would affect the company's creditors and regarded it as fatal to the claim to rely on the exception that there was no evidence that the directors had considered the interests of the creditors; whilst the directors had acted in the interests of the shareholders, in not considering the creditors they had failed to act in the interests of the company. Lord Oliver disagreed with Nourse LJ's treatment of the evidence but accepted that the interests of the creditors had to be considered at the time when the financial assistance was given: the directors had to satisfy themselves at that time that the giving of the financial assistance would not impair the company's power to pay its debts as they fell due. In a case decided shortly after *Brady*,[138] it was held that where a company would have been insolvent if it had given the financial assistance, the good faith test could not be satisfied.

Unconditional Exceptions

Section 681 of the Companies Act 2006 lists a number of specific matters that are not within the scope of the ban on the giving of financial assistance. This list of 'unconditional exceptions'

[133] Greaves and Hannigan, 'Gratuitous Transfers and Financial Assistance after *Brady*', 139: 'it is difficult to envisage a situation where the section will be applicable'; Polack, 'Companies Act 1985—Scope of Section 153,' 361: 'It may be that Lord Oliver's analysis has rendered [the larger purpose] ... exception virtually unattainable.'

[134] [1989] AC 755 HL, 779.

[135] This suggestion derives some support from the Irish case *CH (Ireland) Ltd v Credit Suisse Canada* [1999] 4 IR 542, HC, where it was held that the principal purpose for the giving of a guarantee was to secure continued financial assistance for the guarantor's corporate group rather than to provide financial assistance. As so interpreted, the facts disclosed a legitimate corporate purpose. However, other aspects of the arrangements between the parties amounted to unlawful financial assistance.

[136] [1989] AC 755, HL, 777–8.   [137] [1988] BCLC 20, CA.   [138] *Plaut v Steiner* (1989) 5 BCC 352.

is largely for the avoidance of doubt.[139] A common theme underlying many of the exceptions in this section is that they relate to matters that are regulated by other provisions of the Companies Act 2006 or the Insolvency Act 1986, and regulatory duplication or inconsistency is thus avoided.

Distributions

In *Re Wellington Publishing Co Ltd*[140] it was held that the payment of a dividend was not something which would ordinarily be regarded as the giving of financial assistance within the meaning of the New Zealand equivalent of section 54 of the English Companies Act 1948. Section 681(2)(a) of the Companies Act 2006 puts this beyond doubt by providing an exception for any distribution of a company's assets by way of dividend lawfully made or distribution made in the course of the company's winding up. This important exception facilitates the extraction of liquid funds from companies.

Bonus issues

Literally interpreted, an allotment of bonus shares could be an 'acquisition' but it would be outside the mischief that the ban on the giving of financial assistance is meant to address for bonus share issues to be included. Section 681(2)(b) provides an exception.

Other unconditional exceptions

The other matters listed in section 681 as following outside the scope of the ban are:

(1) any reduction of capital under chapter 10 of Part 17 of the Companies Act 2006;

(2) a redemption of shares under chapter 3 of Part 18 of the Companies Act 2006;

(3) a purchase of its own shares by a company under chapter 4 of Part 18 of the Companies Act 2006;

(4) anything done in pursuance of an order of the court under Part 26 of the Companies Act 2006 (order sanctioning compromise or arrangement with members or creditors); and

(5) anything done under an arrangement made in pursuance of section 110 of the Insolvency Act 1986 or the equivalent provision of the Insolvency (Northern Ireland) Order 1989;[141] and

(6) anything done under an arrangement made between a company and its creditors which is binding on the creditors by virtue of Part 1 of the Insolvency Act 1986 (voluntary arrangements) or the Northern Irish equivalent.[142]

Conditional Exceptions

Section 682 of the Companies Act 2006 provides 'conditional exceptions' for loans in the ordinary course of a lending business and for certain arrangements to support the acquisition of shares by employees. These exceptions apply in favour of private companies as well as

[139] *Hansard*, Standing Committee A, Session 1980–81, col 301 (30 June 1981).
[140] [1973] 1 NZLR 133, NZ SC.   [141] SI 1989/2405 (NI 19), art 96.
[142] Insolvency (Northern Ireland) Order 1989, SI 1989/2405 (NI 19), Pt 2.

public companies but they operate more restrictively in relation to public companies. Since a private company is within the scope of financial assistance law only in relation to the giving of financial assistance for the acquisition of shares in a public company of which it is a subsidiary, the circumstances in which a private company will need to rely on these exceptions are limited.

The restrictive condition that must be satisfied where a public company seeks to rely on one of the these exceptions is that the financial assistance must not reduce the assisting company's net assets or, to the extent that it does, the financial assistance must be provided out of distributable profits.[143] For this purpose, net assets are calculated by looking at the amount by which the aggregate of the company's assets exceeds the aggregate of its liabilities, taking the amount of both assets and liabilities to be as stated in the company's accounting records immediately before the financial assistance is given.[144] In other words, it is book values as opposed to market values that must be considered. The term 'liabilities' includes an amount retained as reasonably necessary for the purpose of providing for any liability or loss which is either likely to be incurred, or certain to be incurred but uncertain as to amount, or as to the date on which it will arise.[145]

Prima facie a loan would not reduce the net assets of the lender company provided the borrower's credit is good and no provision against default has to be made. Similarly, with contingent liabilities such as guarantees and indemnities, if the contingency is so remote that in accounting terms it would be valued at nil, there will be no immediate reduction in net assets.

Exception for money-lending businesses

The Second Company Law Directive, Article 25(6) provides a carveout for 'transactions concluded by banks and other financial institutions in the normal course of business' provided those transactions do not reduce net assets below undistributable reserves. The domestic equivalent of this exception is section 682(2)(a) of the Companies Act 2006, which provides that the ban on the giving of financial assistance does not apply to the lending of money by a company in the ordinary course of business where the lending of money is part of the ordinary business of the company. Section 54 of the Companies Act 1948 had a similarly worded exemption which was considered by the Privy Council in *Steen v Law*[146] and given quite a narrow scope. Viscount Radcliffe, delivering the judgment of the Judicial Committee, commented that the exemption had to be read as:

> ...protecting a company engaged in money lending as part of its ordinary business from an infraction of the law, even though moneys borrowed from it are used and, perhaps, used to its knowledge, in the purchase of its own shares. Even so, the qualification is imposed that, to escape liability, the loan transaction must be made in the ordinary course of its business. Nothing, therefore, is protected except what is consistent with the normal course of its business and is lending which the company ordinarily practices...it is, on the other hand, virtually impossible to see how loans, big or small, deliberately made by a company for the direct purpose of financing a purchase of its shares could ever be described as made in the ordinary course of business.

It is thus not sufficient that the company's ordinary business involves lending money; the particular loan must also be within the ordinary course of its business and, if it is a loan made specifically to finance an acquisition of its own shares, there is every likelihood that it will

---

[143] Companies Act 2006, s 682(1)(b).   [144] Companies Act 2006, s 682(4)(a).
[145] Companies Act 2006, s 682(4)(b).   [146] [1964] AC 287, PC.

fail this test. Thus, in *Fowlie v Slater*[147] loans deliberately made by an investment bank for the purpose of financing the purchase of shares in its holding company were held to be special loans for special purposes. They could not be regarded as being within the ordinary course of business of the investment bank and, accordingly, they did not come within the exception.

At the time of writing the scope of an equivalent provision in the Irish companies legislation is due to be tested in criminal prosecutions in Ireland arising from the 2007–9 financial crisis. It is alleged that the management of the failed bank, Anglo Irish, organized the financing for the acquisition of a significant stake in the bank in order to avoid the negative effect that such a large disposal via normal channels would have on the bank's share price generally. However, the trials are not due to start until January 2014 and are expected to be lengthy.[148]

Exception for employee share purchases

A number of overlapping exemptions are intended to allow companies to support employee share schemes and other acquisitions of shares by employees. Again, these exemptions exist against the background of a specific exemption in the Second Company Law Directive: Article 25(6) provides that the prohibition does not apply to transactions effected with a view to the acquisition of shares by or for the company's employees or the employees of an associate company, but those transactions must not reduce net assets below undistributable reserves.

The first exception, in section 682(2)(b) of the Companies Act 2006 relates to the provision by a company, in good faith in the interests of the company or its holding company, of financial assistance for the purposes of an employee share scheme.[149] This provision was first inserted into the companies legislation by the Companies Act 1989 in order to replace a more restrictively worded exception. *NZI Bank Ltd v Euro-National Corporation Ltd*[150] involved an attempt to take advantage of the employee share scheme exception to the ban on the giving of financial assistance in the New Zealand companies legislation. The employee share scheme was to act as the conduit for the provision of financial assistance to certain major shareholders in the company, the aim of this being to avoid the likely effect on the company's share price if they sold their shares. The New Zealand Court of Appeal held that it was necessary to examine what the directors were in truth endeavouring to achieve in setting up the employee share scheme so as to ensure that the exception was not being used to cover a financial engineering purpose for which it was never designed. It seems likely that the English courts would adopt a similarly inquiring approach in order to prevent manipulation or abuse of the exemption.

Section 682(2)(c) of the Companies Act 2006 authorizes the provision of financial assistance by a company for the purpose of, or in connection with, anything done by the company (or another company in the same group) for the purpose of enabling or facilitating transactions in shares in the first-mentioned company between, and involving the acquisition of beneficial ownership of, those shares by bona fide employees or former employees of that company (or another company in the same group) or their dependants, ie their spouses, civil partners, widows, widowers, surviving civil partners, and minor children and step children. For this purpose a company is in the same group as another company if it is a holding company or a subsidiary of that company, or a subsidiary of a holding company of that company.[151] The gist of this is clear: it is intended to allow companies to support internal share-dealing schemes. But the dual requirement—that only present or

---

147 Unreported but noted by K Walmsley, 'Lending in the "Ordinary Course of Business"' (1979) 129 NLJ 801.
148 C Lally, 'Judge Warns of Length of Anglo Trial for Jurors' *The Irish Times*, 7 March 2013, 2.
149 Employee share schemes are defined by Companies Act 2006, s 1165.
150 [1992] 3 NZLR 528, NZ CA.   151 Companies Act 2006, s 682(5).

former employees (or connected persons) should be the beneficial participants and should be the only parties to transactions—appears to exclude common types of schemes where one of the parties to transactions can be a trust established for the benefit of employees and connected persons.

Section 682(2)(d) of the Companies Act 2006 relates to the making by a company of loans to persons other than directors employed in good faith by the company with a view to enabling those persons to acquire fully paid shares in the company or a holding company to be held by them by way of beneficial ownership. It has been held, in relation to an the equivalent section in New South Wales legislation, that this exception only applies if the sole or major purpose is to allow the employees to purchase shares. If the major purpose is to facilitate the change of control of a company then the exception does not apply.[152]

Criminal Sanctions for Unlawful Financial Assistance

A company commits an offence if it gives unlawful financial assistance and is liable to a fine.[153] Since the persons who are intended to be protected by the ban on the giving of financial assistance include the company that provides the assistance, the company's inclusion in the category of perpetrators of the crime requires comment. The general question of when to impose corporate liability on a company was considered carefully in the Review that preceded the Companies Act 2006. The Review Steering Group suggested a presumption against imposing liability on the company where both (a) the act was capable of seriously damaging the company, and (b) making the responsible individuals criminally liable was likely to be a sufficient deterrent.[154] However, during the passage of the Bill that became the Companies Act 2006 the government indicated that it had chosen to adopt a different approach:

> The general principle adopted as to whether a company should be liable for a breach of the requirements of Companies Acts is that where the only victims of the offence are the company or its members, the company should not be liable for the offence. On the other hand, where members or the company are potential victims, but not the only ones, then the company should be potentially liable for a breach. All the offences in the Companies Acts, both those in the Bill and those that remain in the 1985 Act, have been reviewed in the light of this principle.[155]

Since the prohibition on the giving of financial assistance is intended to protect creditors as well as shareholders and the company, it is therefore an example of conduct for which corporate criminal liability was not ruled out under the general principle.

Every officer of the company who is in default is also guilty of a criminal offence for which the penalty is imprisonment, up to a maximum of two years, or a fine or both.[156] The Review Steering Group considered decriminalizing some offences by directors, including the giving of financial assistance, and giving greater emphasis to administrative penalties.[157] Consultation elicited mixed views and in the end the Group recommended retention of criminal sanctions for financial assistance because it was not convinced that an approach

---

[152] *Saltergate Insurance Co Ltd v Knight* [1982] 1 NSWLR 369.

[153] Companies Act 2006, s 680. According to s 680(2), any person who commits the offence is also liable to be imprisoned but clearly this does not make sense in relation to a company. cf Companies Act 1985, s 151 where the drafting was different and the point did not arise.

[154] Company Law Review Steering Group, *Modern Company Law for a Competitive Economy: Final Report* (URN 01/942) para 15.36.

[155] Explanatory Notes on the Companies Act 2006, paras 1433–5.   [156] Companies Act 2006, s 680.

[157] Company Law Review Steering Group, *Modern Company Law for a Competitive Economy: Completing the Structure* (URN 00/1335) para 13.42.

based on civil penalties and the market abuse provisions of the Financial Services and Market Act 2000 would work.[158] According to the government spokesperson in the Parliamentary debate on the Bill that became the Companies Act 2006, it was appropriate to retain criminal sanctions for financial assistance because offences were less likely to be committed if they were backed up by criminal penalties. In the government's view, criminal sanctions were appropriate, proportionate, and essential for effective enforcement of breaches, but the underlying threat of prosecution enabled authorities to exercise a progressive approach to enforcement that secured compliance without prosecution.[159]

Civil Consequences of Unlawful Financial Assistance

The Companies Act 2006 does not refer to the civil consequences of unlawful financial assistance. These consequences are derived from case law and to examine them fully would take this discussion beyond the scope of this book and into an analysis of complex issues in the fields of equity, contract, and restitution where aspects of the law are still developing. It is not proposed here to attempt to give an exhaustive account of all of the remedies available in respect of, and other civil consequences of, transactions that are tainted by unlawful financial assistance. Instead, it suffices for the purposes of this book to indicate the main areas of concern and the issues that arise in relation to them.

The invalidity of the financial assistance transaction

Any security, guarantee, or other transaction constituting unlawful financial assistance is illegal and any obligations undertaken by the company providing the financial assistance are unenforceable.[160] An undertaking can be viewed as financial assistance even though it is without legal effect because, as Fisher J explained in *Heald v O'Connor*:[161]

> By the provision of a security…the company undoubtedly gives financial assistance to the purchaser of the shares whether the security is valid or not. All that is necessary to make the financial assistance effective is that the lender should believe the security to be valid and on the strength of it make the loan.

If all that has happened is that the company has undertaken some commitment which amounts to the giving of unlawful financial assistance, a declaration that the commitment is unenforceable may be the only remedy that the company needs. However, the position is more complicated if the company seeks to recover money or other property that it has parted with in purported performance of its contractual obligations. Although a person who parts with money or other property in the mistaken belief that he or she is contractually obliged to do so is normally entitled to a restitutionary claim, the general rule is that illegality operates as a defence to a restitutionary claim.[162] An exception to this rule allows the less guilty party to recover in certain circumstances. This exception has been held to apply where a contract is rendered illegal by a statute in order to protect a class of persons and the claimant is within the protected class. In one case it was held that a company providing financial assistance was not

---

[158] Company Law Review Steering Group, *Final Report*, para 15.18.
[159] *Hansard*, Standing Committee D, Session 2005–06, cols 858–60 (20 July 2006) *per* Vera Baird MP.
[160] *Brady v Brady* [1989] AC 755, HL; *Selangor United Rubber Estates Ltd v Cradock* [1968] 2 All ER 1073, 1154; *Heald v O'Connor* [1971] 2 All ER 1105; *Dressy Frocks Pty Ltd v Bock* (1951) 51 SR (NSW) 390; *EH Dey Pty Ltd (in liquidation) v Dey* [1966] VR 464, Vic SC; *Shearer Transport Co Pty Ltd v McGrath* [1956] VLR 316, Vic SC. *Re Hill and Tyler Ltd, Harlow v Loveday* [2005] 1 BCLC 41, [65]–[70]; *Paros Plc v Worldlink Group Plc* [2012] EWHC 394.
[161] [1971] 2 All ER 1105, 1109.
[162] G Virgo, *The Principles of the Law of Restitution* 2nd edn (Oxford: OUP, 2006) 168–9.

within the protected class and thus could not have a personal claim in respect of money that it had lent pursuant to a loan that constituted unlawful financial assistance.[163] The inclusion of the assisting company among the perpetrators of the crime of giving unlawful financial assistance has particular significance in this context.[164]

Validity of the acquisition of the shares

In *Carney v Herbert*[165] it was not disputed that unlawful financial assistance in the form of mortgages had been given in relation to the sale of shares. The issue was whether this illegality tainted the whole transaction or whether the illegal mortgages could be severed so as to leave the sale of the shares intact. The Privy Council held that severance was possible. Lord Brightman, giving the judgment of the Judicial Committee, stated:[166]

> Subject to a caveat that it is undesirable, if not impossible, to lay down any principles which will cover all problems in this field, their Lordships venture to suggest that, as a general rule, where parties enter into a lawful contract of, for example, sale and purchase, and there is an ancillary provision which is illegal but exists for the exclusive benefit of the plaintiff, the court may and probably will, if the justice of the case so requires, and there is no public policy objection, permit the plaintiff if he so wishes to enforce the contract without the illegal provision.

In *Neilson v Stewart*[167] this dictum was quoted by Lord Jauncey in the House of Lords as authority for the proposition that a share transfer would normally be severable from surrounding unlawful financial assistance.[168]

Claims against directors

In *Wallersteiner v Moir*[169] Lord Denning MR said: 'Every director who is a party to a breach of [the ban on the giving of financial assistance] is guilty of a misfeasance and breach of trust; and is liable to recoup to the company any loss occasioned to it by the default.' In *Steen v Law*[170] the Privy Council was of the view that where directors had given unlawful financial assistance in breach of their duty to the company, it was not a defence to plead merely that they acted in ignorance of the law. Numerous other cases on directors' duties prior to the Companies Act 2006 regarded participation in the giving of unlawful financial assistance by directors as a breach of trust or of fiduciary duty.[171]

General duties of directors were codified by the Companies Act 2006. Under the statutory scheme, a director who is party to a breach of the prohibition on the giving of financial assistance could be held to be in breach of the duty in section 171 of the Companies Act 2006 to act in accordance with the company's constitution and only exercise powers for the

---

[163] *Selangor United Rubber Estates Ltd v Cradock* [1968] 2 All ER 1073. The facts and decision in the *Selangor* case are analyzed in detail by MR Chesterman and AS Grabiner, 'Sorting Out A Company Fraud' (1969) 32 MLR 328.

[164] GR Bretten, 'Financial Assistance in Share Transactions' (1968) 32 Conv 6, 12–5; R Barrett, 'Financial Assistance and Share Acquisitions' (1974) 48 ALJ 6, 8–11.

[165] [1985] 1 AC 301, PC.   [166] [1985] 1 AC 301, PC, 317.   [167] [1991] BCC 713, HL.

[168] Earlier cases supporting the possibility of severance, at least in some circumstances, are *Spink (Bournemouth) Ltd v Spink* [1936] Ch 544; *South Western Mineral Water Co Ltd v Ashmore* [1967] 2 All ER 953; *Lawlor v Gray* (1980) 130 NLJ 317, CA. See also the obiter discussion in *Re Hill and Tyler Ltd, Harlow v Loveday* [2005] 1 BCLC 41, [79].

[169] [1974] 3 All ER 217, CA, 239. See also at 249 *per* Buckley LJ and 255 *per* Scarman LJ; *Steen v Law* [1964] AC 287, PC.

[170] [1964] AC 287, PC.

[171] See eg *Belmont Finance Corp v Williams Furniture Ltd (No 2)* [1980] All ER 393, CA; *Karak Rubber Co v Burden (No 2)* [1972] 1 WLR 602; *Selangor United Rubber Estates Ltd v Cradock (No 3)* [1968] 1 WLR 1555; *Curtis's Furnishing Store Ltd v Freedman* [1966] 1 WLR 1219; *Steen v Law* [1964] AC 287, PC.

purposes for which they are conferred. In addition, since the codification was not intended to be exhaustive, such a director could also be held to be in breach of the duty of the stewardship in respect of the company's assets that was established by case law. A director who is technically in breach of duty but not morally culpable may seek relief from the court on the grounds that he acted honestly and reasonably and having regard to all the circumstances of the case ought fairly to be excused.[172]

Liability of other parties

Third parties, such as lending banks, that are implicated in a scheme involving unlawful financial assistance (accessories) or who receive money or property from the company by reason of it (recipients) may also be personally liable to the company. Detailed analysis of the circumstances in which a company may have a claim against third parties shifts the focus from the relatively narrow confines of financial assistance law into much broader fields of equity and restitution that are not explored in detail here. However, an outline is called for because these potential civil liabilities add significantly to the legal risks faced by lending institutions and other professionals involved in corporate finance transactions that raise financial assistance concerns.[173]

Accessory liability

Traditionally called liability for 'knowing assistance,' anyone who assists the directors to misapply company funds in the giving of unlawful financial assistance may be held personally liable to compensate the company.[174] The degree of knowledge needed to trigger this liability is a thorny question that has divided judicial opinion over many years.[175] In *Royal Brunei Airlines Sdn Bhd v Tan*[176] the Privy Council delivered a powerful restatement of the law. Lord Nicholls, giving the judgment, said, first, that the breach of trust or fiduciary obligation need not itself be either dishonest or fraudulent. So, in a case involving the giving of unlawful financial assistance by directors, it does not matter whether the directors are themselves acting fraudulently. Secondly, Lord Nicholls decided that to couch accessory liability in terms of knowledge was unhelpful and preferred the test of dishonestly procuring or assisting in the breach of trust or fiduciary obligation. Honesty in this context, said Lord Nicholls, was an objective standard and meant not acting as an honest person would act in the circumstances. However, the court would look at all the circumstances known to the accessory at the time, not to what a reasonable person would have known or appreciated, and regard could be had to the personal attributes of the accessory, such as his experience and intelligence, and the reason why he acted as he did. This was followed by the House of Lords in *Twinsectra Ltd v Yardley*[177] but, unfortunately, the majority of the House of Lords again muddied the waters by saying that a defendant would not be held to be dishonest unless it was established that his conduct had been dishonest by the ordinary

---

[172] Companies Act 2006, s 1157. Note also the possibility of relief under Insolvency Act 1986, s 212 but the scope of the court's discretion under this provision is uncertain.

[173] D Hayton, 'Suing Third Parties Involved in Fraud: Some Key Issues' (2012) 26 *Trust Law International* 197.

[174] *Belmont Finance Corp v Williams Furniture (No 2)* [1980] All ER 393, CA.

[175] *Baden Delvaux v Société Générale pour Favoriser le Développement du Commerce et de l'Industrie en France SA (Note)* [1993] 1 WLR 509; *Agip (Africa) Ltd v Jackson* [1991] Ch 547, CA; *Eagle Trust plc v SBC Securities Ltd* [1993] 1 WLR 484; *Cowan de Groot Properties Ltd v Eagle Trust plc* [1992] 4 All ER 488; *Polly Peck International plc v Nadir (No 2)* [1992] 4 All ER 700, CA.

[176] [1995] AC 378, PC.   [177] [2002] 2 AC 164, HL.

standards of reasonable and honest people and that he himself had realized that by those standards his conduct was dishonest even though he might not have so regarded it himself. The second limb of this formulation attracted criticism because it appeared to suggest that a defendant who had a subjective belief that his conduct was not dishonest by ordinary standards would escape liability.[178] The Privy Council returned to the issue in *Barlow Clowes International Ltd (in liquidation) v Eurotrust International Ltd*[179] where the majority view in *Twinsectra* was 'explained' as not having this meaning: in considering whether a defendant's state of mind was dishonest, an inquiry into the defendant's view about standards of honesty was required; the defendant's knowledge of a transaction had to be such as to render his participation contrary to normally acceptable standards of honest conduct but there was no requirement that he should have had reflections about what those normally acceptable standards were. Some commentators suggested that the Privy Council in the *Eurotrust* case in fact went beyond explaining the second limb in *Twinsectra* and actually excluded it.[180] Subsequent cases have generally applied the *Eurotrust* interpretation. The recent cases broadly confirm a move away from subjective dishonesty in civil claims based on dishonest assistance in a breach of trust.[181]

Recipient liability

Anyone who receives the funds of the company misapplied by the directors with knowledge of the breach may be held personally liable to the company. The degree of knowledge needed to trigger this liability, which is traditionally described as liability for knowing receipt, has also generated a considerable amount of case law and academic commentary.[182] The position was comprehensively reviewed by the Court of Appeal in *Bank of Credit and Commerce International (Overseas) Ltd v Akindele*.[183] The Court of Appeal in this case considered that there should be a single test to determine the requisite knowledge for liability for knowing receipt. That was whether the recipient's state of knowledge was such as to make it unconscionable for him to retain the benefit of receipt. Such a test, said the court, would still involve difficulties of application but would simplify the issue and enable the courts to give common-sense decisions in a commercial context.[184]

---

[178] TM Yeo and H Tijo, 'Knowing What is Dishonesty' (2002) 118 LQR 502.   [179] [2006] 1 WLR 1276, PC.

[180] M Conaglen and A Goymour, 'Dishonesty in the Context of Assistance—Again' [2006] CLJ 18; TM Yeo, 'Dishonest Assistance: Restatement From The Privy Council' (2006) 122 LQR 171. But see Sir Anthony Clarke, 'Claims Against Professionals: Negligence, Dishonesty and Fraud' [2006] 22 *Professional Negligence* 70. Other comments on the *Eurotrust* re-statement of the position include D Ryan, 'Royal Brunei Dishonesty: Clarity at Last' [2006] *Conveyancer and Property Lawyer* 188; N Kiri, 'Recipient and Accessory Liability—Where Do We Stand Now?' (2006) 21 *Journal of International Banking Law and Regulation* 611; JE Penner, 'Dishonest Assistance Revisited: Barlow Clowes International Ltd (In Liquidation) And Others v Eurotrust International Ltd' (2006) 20 *Trust Law International* 122.

[181] Hayton, 'Suing Third Parties Involved in Fraud.' *Starglade Properties Ltd v Nash* [2010] EWCA Civ 1314.

[182] The cases include *Belmont Finance Corp v Williams Furniture (No 2)* [1980] All ER 393, CA; *Selangor United Rubber Estates v Cradock (No 3)* [1968] 1 WLR 1555; *Karak Rubber Co v Burden (No 2)* [1972] 1 WLR 602; *Re Montagu's ST* [1987] Ch 264; *Polly Peck International plc v Nadir (No 2)* [1992] 4 All ER 769, CA; *El Ajou v Dollar Land Holdings plc* [1993] BCLC 735. Pre-*Akindele* commentary on knowing receipt liability includes the following chapters of WR Cornish, R Nolan, J O'Sullivan, and G Virgo (eds), *Restitution Past, Present and Future* (Oxford: Hart, 1998): Sir Peter Millett, 'Restitution and Constructive Trusts' 199; AJ Oakley, 'Restitution and Constructive Trusts: A Commentary' 219; Lord Nicholls, 'Knowing Receipt: The Need for a New Landmark' 231; and C Harpum, 'Knowing Receipt: The Need for a New Landmark: Some Reflections' 247.

[183] [2000] 4 All ER 221, CA.

[184] Commentary on the decision in *Akindele* includes S Barkehall Thomas, '"Goodbye" Knowing Receipt. "Hello" Unconscientious Receipt' (2001) 21 OJLS 239; J Stevens, 'No New Landmark—An Unconscionable Mess in Knowing Receipt' (2001) 9 *Restitution Law Review* 99. See also PBH Birks, 'Knowing Receipt: Re Montagu's Settlement Trusts Revisited' (2001) 1 (2) *Global Jurist Advances*, article 2.

The tort of conspiracy

A combination between a number of persons to procure a company to give unlawful financial assistance amounts to a conspiracy to effect an unlawful purpose. It has been held that the company that provides the financial assistance is not barred by reason of the fact that it is technically a party to the illegality from suing the conspirators in tort for compensation for loss suffered as a result of any such conspiracy.[185]

Unjust enrichment

The possibility of a strict liability claim against third parties based on unjust enrichment is supported by dicta by Lord Nicolls in *Criterion Properties plc v Stratford UK Properties LLC*[186] that where a benefit has been conferred on B by Company A as a result of its directors acting for an improper purpose and without authority then 'irrespective of whether B still has the assets in question, A will have a personal claim against B for unjust enrichment subject always to a defence of change of position.' Hayton notes that whilst much has been written for or against extending strict liability, the orthodox position is that liability in equity depends on the defendant being at fault in some way.[187]

Disqualification

A person who is guilty of an indictable offence in connection with the management of a company is liable to be disqualified under section 2 of the Company Directors Disqualification Act 1986. Giving unlawful financial assistance is an indictable offence.[188] A director's failure to recognize that actions taken by the company amounted to the giving of unlawful financial assistance is also a factor that can be taken into account in disqualification proceedings on grounds of unfitness under section 6 of the Company Directors Disqualification Act 1986.[189]

---

[185] *Belmont Finance Corp v Williams Furniture Ltd* [1979] Ch 250, CA.

[186] [2004] UKHL 28, [2004] 1 WLR 1846, [4] *per* Lord Nicholls. Considered in *Relfo Ltd v Varsani* [2012] EWHC 2168 (Ch), [86]–[90]

[187] Hayton, 'Suing Third Parties Involved in Fraud.'   [188] Companies Act 2006, s 680.

[189] *Re Continental Assurance Co of London plc, Secretary of State for Trade and Industry v Burrows* [1997] 1 BCLC 48.

PART III

DEBT CORPORATE FINANCE

11

Debt Corporate Finance—General Considerations

Scope of this Part

Companies can raise debt finance by issuing debt securities (bonds) directly into the capital markets or by borrowing from banks or other lenders. Other financing mechanisms, such as invoice financing, factoring, and invoice discounting, can also be used to smooth out cash flow by providing short-term working capital in return for an assignment of receivables.[1] Most of the debt finance for small and medium-sized enterprises (SMEs) in the UK is provided by the banking sector.[2] Small quoted companies (SQCs) also depend heavily on the banks because their size and lack of credit ratings, in practice, tend to rule out access to the bond markets at reasonable rates.[3] Large companies have more choices available to them.[4] Whether bank-based or market-based financing is better at financing industrial expansion and achieving the efficient allocation of capital resources is much debated but the evidence is inconclusive.[5]

This chapter examines general issues relating to unsecured debt corporate finance.[6] It concentrates mainly on traditional types of bank lending (overdrafts and term loans) but many of the issues discussed are relevant also to corporate bonds. Chapter 12 deals with issues that arise when debt finance is made available to companies on a secured basis. Also relevant is chapter 15 on corporate bonds.

Unsecured Lending—Overview

The terms on which a loan is made available depend on agreement between borrower and lender. Provided they refrain from agreeing to something that is illegal, conceptually

---

[1] Invoice financing comes in two forms: factoring and invoice discounting. Both services normally provide finance against debtor balances outstanding. Factoring provides the additional advantage of a full sales ledger and collections service under which the Factor takes on the responsibility for the sales ledger. Under an Invoice Discounting service the company continues to administer the sales ledger and the service is usually undisclosed to customers. These definitions are taken from the website of the Factors and Discounters Association <http://www.factors.org.uk> (accessed October 2013). See also, A Hewitt, 'Asset Finance' (2003) 43(2) *Bank of England Quarterly Bulletin* 207. These invoice financing arrangements do not create a security interest over the receivables: *Hallmark Cards v Yun Choy* [2011] HKCFI 395, Hong Kong High Court.

[2] Competition Commission, *The Supply of Banking Services by Clearing Banks to Small and Medium-sized Enterprises* (2002). See further ch 3 on sources of finance for smaller companies.

[3] P Brierley and M Young, 'The Financing of Smaller Quoted Companies: a Survey' (2004) 44(2) *Bank of England Quarterly Bulletin* 160.

[4] By way of comparison, a US study found debt financing to be the predominant source of new external funds for US corporations: firms with the highest credit quality borrow from public sources, firms with medium credit quality borrow from banks, and firms with the lowest credit quality borrow from non-bank private lenders: DJ Denis and VT Mihov, 'The Choice Among Bank Debt, Non-bank Private Debt, and Public Debt: Evidence From New Corporate Borrowings' (2003) 70 *Journal of Financial Economics* 3.

[5] T Beck and R Levine, 'Industry Growth and Capital Allocation: Does Having a Market- or Bank-based System Matter?' (2002) 64 *Journal of Financial Economics* 147.

[6] Sections of this chapter are derived from E Ferran, 'The Place for Creditor Protection on the Agenda for Modernisation of Company Law in the European Union' [2006] *European Company and Financial Law Review* 178.

impossible,[7] or contrary to public policy, the law will give contractual effect to whatever bargain the parties arrive at. This provides great scope for variety and innovation in the corporate debt sector. Studies of the negotiation process associated with determining the contents of documentation in the bank loan market in several countries with Anglo-American financing systems indicate that the process can be intensely contentious and that a range of borrower-specific considerations (such as size, internal governance structure, ownership, management reputation, and business risk) and contract-specific characteristics (such as term and size of loan) act as determinants of the terms in any particular case.[8] Individual loan officers have considerable discretion to depart from standard form precedents to suit particular circumstances.[9]

The main terms of a loan are those governing the principal (the amount, the basis on which it is to be made available to the borrower, and the mechanisms for repayment) and the interest charges. A company may secure lending facilities on which it can draw from time to time, an agreed overdraft facility being a familiar example of this type of lending arrangement,[10] or it may borrow a principal amount all at once or in agreed instalments. Interest will usually be charged on amounts borrowed and the company may also be required to pay commitment or negotiation fees in respect of lending facilities that have been made available. Interest rates may be fixed for the period of the loan or may be liable to be adjusted from time to time. An alternative to interest charges is for a company to borrow less than the stated principal amount of a loan on terms that oblige it to repay the full principal amount. In this case, the discount between the amount borrowed and the principal amount of the loan represents the return to the lender.[11]

The principal amount of a loan may be denominated in one currency or it may be divided into a number of portions, each of which is denominated in a different currency. The principal may be repayable on demand or may be lent to the company for a set term but with provision for early repayment and for termination by the lender upon the occurrence of specified events of default. The principal may be required to be repaid in one lump sum or the agreement may provide for repayment by instalments.

In addition to the core operative terms governing principal and interest, loan agreements commonly contain covenants by which the company undertakes to meet performance targets, to refrain from certain activities, and to provide the lender with information about its affairs. Covenants enable the lender to monitor the company while the debt is outstanding. Failure to comply with covenants will usually be an event of default that entitles the lender to, among other

---

[7] But 'the courts should be very slow to declare a practice of the commercial community to be conceptually impossible': *Re Bank of Credit and Commerce International SA (No 8)* [1998] AC 214, HL, 228 *per* Lord Hoffmann. See also *Re Lehman Brothers International (Europe)* [2012] EWHC 2997 (Ch), [34].

[8] P Mather, 'The Determinants of Financial Covenants in Bank-Loan Contracts' [2004] *Journal of International Banking Law and Regulation* 33; JFS Day and PJ Taylor, 'Evidence on Practices of UK Bankers in Contracting for Medium-Term Debt' [1995] *Journal of International Banking Law* 394; JFS Day and PJ Taylor, 'Bankers' Perspectives on the Role of Covenants in Debt Contracts' [1996] *Journal of International Banking Law* 201–5; JFS Day and PJ Taylor, 'Loan Contracting by UK Corporate Borrowers' [1996] *Journal of International Banking Law* 318; JFS Day and PJ Taylor, 'Loan Documentation in the Market for UK Corporate Debt: Current Practice and Future Prospects' [1997] *Journal of International Banking Law* 7; RN Nash, JM Netter, and AB Poulsen, 'Determinants of Contractual Relations Between Shareholders and Bondholders: Investment Opportunities and Restrictive Covenants' (2003) 9 *Journal of Corporate Finance* 201.

[9] P Mather, 'The Determinants of Financial Covenants in Bank-Loan Contracts' [2004] *Journal of International Banking Law and Regulation* 33, 36.

[10] A more complex example is a revolving loan that enables the borrower to borrow, repay, and re-borrow up to a maximum amount. A revolving loan differs from an overdraft in that it is not current account financing (and is not repayable on demand as an overdraft normally is). An ordinary term loan may allow for early repayment but will not provide for re-borrowing.

[11] WL Megginson, *Corporate Finance Theory* (Addison-Wesley, 1997) 404–5.

things, terminate the loan. Other typical terms in loan agreements include conditions that must be satisfied before the company can obtain the money (or 'draw down' the funds, as this process is often referred to) and representations and warranties about the company and its affairs.

An individual bank or other lender may be unwilling to accept the whole of the risk involved in lending a very large sum of money to a company. In that event, provided the company is sufficiently creditworthy, it may still be able to obtain the required funds by entering into a syndicated loan agreement (secured or unsecured) with a number of financial institutions under which each participant in the syndicate contributes a part of the loan and shares the rights in respect of such lending.[12] It is normally only the largest corporate borrowers that require syndicated loans. Sovereign states and other public authorities also enter into syndicated loans. In recent years the syndicated loan market (now increasingly known as the 'leveraged loan' market) has played a major role in providing the debt finance for leveraged buyout activity by private equity firms.[13] The emergence of sophisticated mechanisms for trading syndicated debt in the secondary market has facilitated this development.[14]

A company may also borrow from its directors or other insiders. This form of lending is most likely to be encountered in smaller or family-owned concerns where the directors and shareholders have a particularly strong personal interest in the company's affairs. Insider loans can give rise to particular points of note or concern. At one end of the spectrum, an insider loan may be made on much softer terms than would be available from a commercial lender—for example, the loan may be interest free or may be made on the basis that the lender is to be subordinated to some or all of the company's other creditors. The legal validity of contractual subordination of debts in the event of insolvency of the debtor,[15] which was once a matter of some uncertainty, is now clearly established.[16] At the other extreme, an insider may seek to exploit his position by requiring the company to accept exceptionally harsh or onerous terms, perhaps with a view to masking what is really an unlawful gift from capital by describing it as an 'interest charge'.[17]

Overdrafts

An overdraft is a form of debt financing provided through a customer's current account. An overdraft arises when a company draws on its current account to such an extent that a negative balance is produced. If the drawing that overdraws the account is met by the bank,

---

[12] *Saltri III v MD Mezzanine SA SICAR* [2012] EWHC 3025 (Comm), [2013] 1 All ER (Comm) 661, [23]. On syndicated loans generally, see PR Wood, *International Loans, Bonds, Guarantees, Legal Opinions* 2nd edn (London: Sweet & Maxwell, 2007); R Cranston, *Principles of Banking Law* 2nd edn (Oxford: OUP, 2002) ch 2, V.

[13] U Axelson, T Jenkinson, PR Strömberg, and MS Weisbach, 'Leverage and Pricing in Buyouts: An Empirical Analysis,' Swedish Institute for Financial Research Conference on The Economics of the Private Equity Market (August 2007) <http://ssrn.com/abstract=1027127> accessed July 2013.

[14] S Drucker and M Puri, 'On Loan Sales, Loan Contracting, and Lending Relationships' (March 2007) <http://ssrn.com/abstract=920877> <http://www.lma.eu.com> accessed July 2013. The Loan Market Association (LMA) was established in December 1996 with the objective of fostering an environment that would facilitate the development of a secondary market for loans. It has supplied standard form documentation for secondary market trading activities.

[15] The validity of contractual subordination where the debtor is not insolvent is uncontroversial: *Nakanishi Marine v Gora Shipping* [2012] EWHC 3383 (Comm), [23]–[32]; *Gemini (Eclipse 2006-3) v Danske Bank* [2012] EWHC 3103 (Comm).

[16] *Re SSSL Realisations (2002) Ltd* [2006] Ch 610, CA. At [66] Chadwick LJ commented: 'It seems to me commercially important that, if group companies enter into subordination agreements of this nature with their creditors while solvent, they and the creditors should be held to the bargain when the event for which the agreement was intended to provide (insolvency) occurs.' See also *Re Kaupthing Singer & Friedlander* [2010] EWHC 316 (Ch), [10].

[17] See eg *Ridge Securities Ltd v IRC* [1964] 1 All ER 275. R La Porta, F Lopez de Silanes, and G Zamarripa, 'Related Lending' (2003) 118(1) *Quarterly Journal of Economics* 231 report that a study of bank lending to firms in Mexico found evidence to support the view that related lending is a manifestation of looting. -

the bank becomes the creditor of the company for the amount so overdrawn. An arrangement to overdraw up to a specified maximum amount would usually be agreed in advance between a company and its bank, and the company may be required to pay a commitment fee for this facility. There is no implied term in the banker–customer relationship that permits a customer to overdraw, with the consequence that, in the absence of agreement to the contrary, the bank is not bound to meet any drawing which is not covered by funds in the account.[18] If a customer makes an unauthorized drawing, this can be viewed conceptually as requesting overdraft facilities[19] and, if the bank meets the drawing, this constitutes an acceptance of the customer's request and the customer is taken to have agreed to accept the bank's relevant standard terms, unless the parties have otherwise agreed and unless the terms are unreasonable or extortionate or contrary to all approved banking practice.[20] By honouring a cheque drawn on an overdrawn account, a bank is lending the sum in question to its customer and, as agent of the customer, paying that sum to the person in whose favour the cheque is drawn.[21]

Just as a bank must pay any sums standing to the credit of a current account to the company whenever it demands it,[22] an overdraft is normally repayable on demand,[23] unless the bank is obliged to provide an overdraft facility for the whole of a fixed term.[24] Whatever its legal rights, as a matter of practice a bank would almost certainly exercise a degree of caution in demanding repayment of an overdraft in order to protect its commercial reputation:

> …it is obvious that neither party would have it in contemplation that when the bank had granted the overdraft it would immediately, without notice, proceed to sue for the money; and the truth is that whether there were any legal obligation to abstain from so doing or not, it is obvious that, having regard to the course of business, if a bank which had agreed to give an overdraft were to act in such a fashion, the results to its business would be of the most serious nature.[25]

What is meant by 'on demand'?[26] According to the English cases all that the bank is required to do is to give the company time to effect the mechanics of payment, such as by arranging

---

[18] *Cunliffe Brooks & Co v Blackburn Benefit Society* (1884) 9 App Cas 857, HL, 864 *per* Lord Blackburn; *Barclays Bank Ltd v WJ Simms Son & Cooke (Southern) Ltd* [1980] 1 QBD 699. An agreement to grant an overdraft may be inferred from a course of conduct: *Cumming v Shand* (1860) 5 H&N 95, 157 ER 1114.

[19] *Barclays Bank Ltd v WJ Simms Son & Cooke (Southern) Ltd* [1980] 1 QBD 699; *Cuthbert v Robarts Lubbock & Co* [1909] 2 Ch 226, CA, 233 *per* Cozens Hardy MR.

[20] *Barclays Bank Ltd v WJ Simms Son & Cooke (Southern) Ltd* [1980] 1 QBD 699; *Office of Fair Trading v Abbey National* [2008] EWHC 875 (Comm), [2008] 2 All ER (Comm) 625, [55], [64]–[65] (this point was not subject to any appeal and was in fact confirmed by the Supreme Court, see *Office of Fair Trading v Abbey National* [2009] UKSC 6; [2010] 1 AC 696, [100]).

[21] *Coutts & Co v Stock* [2000] 2 All ER 56.

[22] *Walker v Bradford Old Bank* (1884) 12 QBD 511, 516 *per* Smith J; *Joachimson v Swiss Banking Corp* [1921] 3 KB 110, CA.

[23] *Williams and Glyn's Bank v Barnes* [1981] Com LR 205, (1977–86) 10 *Legal Decisions Affecting Bankers* 220. The parties can agree otherwise but whether they have done so is a question of construction and it is not inconsistent for a bank to grant a facility that it is envisaged will endure for some time but with a term allowing it to call for repayment on demand: *Lloyds Bank plc v Lampert* [1999] BCC 507, CA; *Hall v Royal Bank of Scotland* [2009] EWHC 3163 (QB); *Carey Group v AIB Group (UK)* [2011] EWHC 567 (Ch), [2012] Ch 304. On the emergence in practice of committed one-year overdraft facilities see Competition Commission, *The Supply of Banking Services by Clearing Banks to Small and Medium-sized Enterprises* (2002) para 3.92.

[24] *Carey Group v AIB Group (UK)* [2011] EWHC 567 (Ch), [2012] Ch 304, [38].

[25] *Rouse v Bradford Banking Co* [1894] AC 586, HL, 596 *per* Lord Herschell LC.

[26] At common law, a loan made where no time for repayment is specified, or where the loan is stated to be payable 'on demand,' creates an immediate debt by which the money is repayable immediately without the creditor first making a demand for payment. A loan payable 'on demand' in this sense is to be distinguished from a loan only repayable on condition that a demand is made first. In the latter case, but not the former, the making of the demand is a condition precedent to liability to repay, and the cause of action does not arise until the demand has been made. Where the parties do not expressly fix a time for repayment, or agree that the repayment is to be conditional upon the making of a demand, implications as to such matters may be made or inferred in appropriate circumstances: *Central City v Montevento Holdings* [2011] WASCA 5, Western Australia CA, [36]–[38].

for the transfer of funds from one account to another. The bank is not obliged to give the customer time to raise funds that it does not have at the time when the demand is made. In *Cripps (Pharmaceutical) Ltd v Wickenden*[27] the bank was held to be within its rights when it appointed a receiver to enforce its rights less than two hours after it had demanded repayment in circumstances where it was clear that the company did not have the money to pay. A delay of just one hour between the making of the demand and the sending in of the receivers has also been held to be justifiable.[28]

With regard to interest charges on an overdraft,[29] it is usual for the interest to be calculated on the daily balance and then debited to the account on a periodic basis.[30] Once the interest has been debited to the account it is capitalized and thereafter interest is charged on an amount including the capitalized interest. The practice of charging compound interest on overdrafts is well established as a general banking usage, which will be implied into all contracts between banks and customers unless there is express provision to the contrary.[31] Banks can be expected usually to make express provision for compound interest charges and the practice of having the position clearly spelt out has received judicial endorsement: '[Banks] should make express provisions for compound interest in their contracts. Since the repeal of the Usury Acts there has been nothing to stop them.'[32]

When money is paid into a bank account that is overdrawn, unless the parties have reached a contrary agreement, it is treated as discharging the earlier debit items. Applying this rule to the following facts:

- 1 January, company's current account has a debit balance of £200,000
- 15 January, the company draws on the overdraft facility for a further £150,000
- 30 January, £250,000 is paid into the account

The position is that, first, the whole of the £200,000 that was outstanding on 1 January is to be regarded as having been repaid and, secondly, £50,000 of the amount borrowed on 15 January is also to be treated as having been repaid; the balance of the amount borrowed on 15 January remains outstanding. This rule of appropriation of payments was established in *Devaynes v Noble, Clayton's Case*[33] and it is commonly referred to as the rule in *Clayton's Case*. It can be relevant where, for example, a bank takes security for an existing overdrawn account and the company then continues to draw on, and make payments into, that account because

---

[27] [1973] 1 WLR 944.

[28] *Bank of Baroda v Panessar* [1986] 3 All ER 751, noted JD Kay, '"On Demand" Liabilities' [1986] *Journal of International Banking Law* 241 where reference is made to a number of Commonwealth cases which appear to be more generous to the borrower by allowing it a reasonable time to repay; *Sheppard & Cooper Ltd v TSB Bank plc* [1996] 2 All ER 654.

[29] The basis on which a bank may charge for an overdraft is a matter for negotiation, as to the rate of interest, the length of the clearance cycle, and any other terms. A bank can, however, be expected to have standard terms of trading on such matters as the length of the clearance cycle, which apply in the absence of specific negotiation. A customer who seeks and obtains an overdraft facility can be taken to have agreed those standard terms unless a different agreement is made or unless the term so implied is extortionate or contrary to all approved banking practice: *Emerald Meats (London) v AIB Group (UK)* [2002] EWCA Civ 460, [14].

[30] *Reddie v Williamson* (1863) 1 Macph 228; *Parr's Banking Co Ltd v Yates* [1898] 2 QB 460, CA; *Yourell v Hibernian Bank Ltd* [1918] AC 372, HL, 385 *per* Lord Atkinson; *IRC v Holder* [1931] 2 KB 81, CA, 96 *per* Lord Hanworth MR and 98 *per* Romer LJ; *Paton v IRC* [1938] AC 341, HL.

[31] *National Bank of Greece SA v Pinios Shipping Co (No 1)* [1990] 1 AC 637, CA and HL. In *Financial Institutions Services v Negril Negril Holdings* [2004] UKPC 40, the Privy Council held that the bank in question was entitled to interest at a reasonable commercial rate on the overdrawn balances from time to time due, but with unpaid interest added to the overdrawn accounts at monthly intervals. This solution could be justified either by the implication of a contractual term, or as a requirement imposed by the court in granting relief of a restitutionary nature.

[32] *National Bank of Greece SA v Pinios Shipping Co (No 1)* [1990] 1 AC 637, CA and HL 659 *per* Lloyd LJ. Although the Court of Appeal's decision was reversed by the House of Lords, this comment is unaffected.

[33] (1816) 1 Mer 572, 35 ER 781.

under the insolvency legislation a security can be held to be invalid if it is given in respect of moneys previously advanced to the borrower. Unless displaced by agreement between the parties, the rule in *Clayton's Case* will determine whether the balance outstanding on the account at the time when the insolvency legislation falls to be applied represents new money advanced after the security was granted, in which case the security will be valid, or old money which had been lent to the company before the security was created, in which case the security may be invalid.[34] Studies of different segments of the corporate sector establish that overdraft facilities are common but that active usage is less prevalent and that sometimes they are put in place only as a contingency. A Bank of England survey of SQCs, for instance, found that only 24 per cent of the firms with overdraft facilities were using at least half of them and some 42 per cent claimed to be making no use of them.[35] Among SMEs, in recent years there has been a shift away from overdraft financing in favour of term loans.[36] Alternative forms of asset finance, including invoice financing, leasing and hire purchase, and asset-based lending (which involve financiers taking ownership of assets and selling them to firms on credit terms) have also grown in significance.[37] British banks are sometimes criticized for favouring overdraft financing at the expense of longer-term, more stable financial support for the corporate sector, especially SMEs. However, it is debatable how far the incidence of overdraft financing reflects the preferences of those who run businesses, who may be attracted to overdraft financing because it is simple, flexible, and does not require them to surrender equity, and how far it is a function of a limited range of financing options that are offered by banks to smaller businesses and a preference among banks for on-demand financing.[38]

Term Loans

Term loans are, as the name implies, loans for a specified period requiring payment at or by the end of the period; such repayment may be of the entire sum borrowed or, and more usually in practice, according to an agreed repayment schedule.[39] A distinction is often drawn in practice between short-term loans (used to mean loans of up to one year), medium-term loans (between one and five years), and long-term loans (between five and ten years, or perhaps even longer).[40]

---

[34] See Insolvency Act 1986, s 245 and the application of the rule in *Clayton's Case* in *Re Yeovil Glove Co Ltd* [1965] Ch 148, CA. See also *ASB Bank v South Canterbury Finance* [2011] NZCA 368, [2011] 3 NZLR 798 where the court held that the application of the rules in *Hopkinson v Rolt* (1861) 9 HL Cas 514 and *Clayton's Case* can have the effect that when a bank has lent money under a charge securing further advances, payment by the debtor credited to the secured account will reduce the debt, and subsequent advances, although extending no further than the original loan, will not take priority over a subsequent charge holder of which the bank has notice when the further advances are made. The rule in *Hopkinson v Rolt* may, however, give way to agreement between the parties: *Naxatu v Perpetual Trustee Company* [2012] FCAFC 163, [93].

[35] P Brierley and M Young, 'The Financing of Smaller Quoted Companies: a Survey' (2004) 44(2) *Bank of England Quarterly Bulletin* 160, 163. See also A Kearns and J Young, Provision of Finance to Smaller Quoted Companies: Some Evidence from Survey Responses and Liaison Meetings' (2002) 42(1) *Bank of England Quarterly Bulletin* 26.

[36] *Competition in UK Banking: A Report to the Chancellor of the Exchequer* (Cruickshank Report, 2000) para 5.26.

[37] A Hewitt, 'Asset Finance' (2003) 43(2) *Bank of England Quarterly Bulletin* 207.

[38] J Charkham, *Keeping Good Company* (Oxford: OUP, 1995) 297–8; A Hughes, 'The "Problems" of Finance for Smaller Businesses' in N Dimsdale and M Prevezer (eds), *Capital Markets and Corporate Governance* (Oxford: Clarendon Press, 1994) 209; A Hughes, 'Finance for SMEs: A UK Perspective' (1997) 9 *Small Business Economics* 151.

[39] *Danske Bank v Durkan New Homes* [2009] IEHC 278, [22].

[40] Terminological practice differs: eg P Brierley and M Young, 'The Financing of Smaller Quoted Companies: a Survey' (2004) 44(2) *Bank of England Quarterly Bulletin* 160, 163 use 'short term' to mean less than five years by original maturity, 'medium term' to mean six to ten years by original maturity and 'long term' to mean in excess of ten years.

Principal

The core operative term of a term loan agreement is the one specifying the principal amount of the loan; the currency, or currencies, in which it is denominated; and the way in which it is to be made available to the borrower. The full amount of the loan may be made available to the borrower at one time or the agreement may provide for the borrower to be entitled to draw down successive tranches of the loan at, or by, specified times. The period during which the borrower is entitled to draw down (the 'availability period') may be limited so that, at the end of the period, the lender is no longer obliged to lend and any undrawn portion of the loan is no longer available to the borrower. With regard to repayment, the agreement may provide for repayment of the whole loan at one time (commonly known as bullet repayment) or for repayment in instalments over a period of time (sometimes described as amortized repayment). Where there is an instalment repayment obligation with a final instalment that is larger than earlier ones, this is sometimes described as a 'balloon' repayment. An instalment repayment obligation is a mechanism that can allow a lender to detect early signs of a borrower's financial difficulties.[41] The borrower may be granted an option to repay early and in any well-drafted agreement the lender will be entitled to demand early repayment in the event of the occurrence of any one of a number of specified events of default.[42] Can the lender insert a term to the effect that the principal amount is to be repayable on demand? It has been held that a provision for on-demand repayment is not incompatible with the nature of a facility which it is envisaged by the lender and borrower will last for some time.[43] Where the lender is legally committed to a loan of a certain term (as opposed to the duration being merely a matter of looser expectations between the parties) it is a question of construction whether a provision for repayment on demand is repugnant to the lending agreement as a whole,[44] although the court will not lightly find that an important provision in a banking facility, such as for repayment on demand, is repugnant.[45] The alternative, and more conventional, mechanism in term loans for the protection of lenders' interests is through events of default, whose occurrence would trigger rights to accelerate repayment.

If a lender refuses to lend in breach of contract, the borrowing company is entitled to damages. If the company can secure broadly the same lending terms from another lender, the damages may be little more than nominal[46] but if, say, the first lender had agreed to an exceptionally low rate of interest, the damages could be more substantial. In *South African Territories v Wallington*[47] the House of Lords refused to grant specific performance of a contract to lend money to a company. This ruling is consistent with the general rule that specific performance will not be ordered where damages are an adequate remedy,[48] but in some

---

[41] WL Megginson, *Corporate Finance Theory* (Addison-Wesley, 1997) 405.

[42] There is nothing about a term loan which excludes events being defined within it whereby during its term the loan may be recalled: *Danske Bank v Durkan New Homes* [2009] IEHC 278, [22].

[43] *Lloyd's Bank plc v Lampert* [1999] BCC 507; *Bank of Ireland v AMCD (Property Holdings)* [2001] 2 All ER (Comm) 894; *Danske Bank v Durkan New Homes* [2009] IEHC 278; *SRM Global Master Fund v Her Majesty's Treasury* [2009] EWHC 227 (Admin), [2009] BCC 251, [139] ('It is settled law that where a facility letter provides that a loan is "repayable on demand," that provision prevails even though there are other provisions in the facility agreement indicating that the bank intends to make the facility available until a specific date…').

[44] *Williams & Glyn's Bank Ltd v Barnes* [1981] Com LR 205; *Titford Property Co Ltd v Cannon Street Acceptances Ltd* (unreported, 25 May 1975).

[45] *Carey Group v AIB Group (UK)* [2011] EWHC 567 (Ch), [2012] Ch 304, [39].

[46] The costs of negotiating a substitute loan may be recoverable: *Prehn v Royal Bank of Liverpool* (1870) LR 5 Exch 92.

[47] [1898] AC 309, HL. Also *Western Wagon and Property Co v West* [1892] 1 Ch 271, 275 *per* Chitty J; *Rogers v Challis* (1859) 27 Beav 175, 54 ER 68; *Sichel v Mosenthal* (1862) 30 Beav 371, 54 ER 932.

[48] G Jones and W Goodhart, *Specific Performance* 2nd edn (London: Butterworths, 1996) 154–61 where the general principle is described as 'arguably too harsh' (at 155) and various recognized exceptions are discussed. See

circumstances loan agreements can be the subject of specific performance.[49] The decision in *Wallington* must now also be read in conjunction with section 740 of the Companies Act 2006. This provision, which was first introduced into the companies legislation after the *Wallington* decision,[50] provides that a contract with a company to take up and pay for debentures of a company may be enforced by an order for specific performance. The term 'debenture' has no hard and fast meaning,[51] although a commonly cited description is that it encompasses any document which creates or acknowledges a debt.[52] It is debatable whether a loan agreement can be said to create or acknowledge a debt because in normal circumstances the debt is not actually created until after the agreement is concluded and the money is advanced. Another view is that an instrument containing a promise to pay can be a debenture.[53] This description would catch a loan agreement since it contains a promise by the borrower to repay the principal and also, usually, a promise to pay interest at specified intervals. However, it is suggested that for the purposes of section 740 of the Companies Act 2006, the term 'debenture' should be more narrowly interpreted and should be limited to debt securities issued directly to investors and which can be traded by them.[54] This interpretation is based on the reference in that section to taking up and paying for debentures. Those words are apt to describe an investor's decision to acquire debt securities issued to the market but they do not easily fit a promise in a loan agreement to lend money. Also the context of the Part of the Companies Act 2006 in which section 740 appears suggests that it is concerned only with debt securities issued to investors and not with loan agreements negotiated between companies and banks or other lenders.[55]

It is unlikely that a borrower would not draw down the loan having gone to the trouble of arranging it. Should this occur, it will be a matter of construction to determine whether the borrower was obliged to draw down or had simply acquired an option to do so. Even if the borrower is in breach of contract, in accordance with the general principle that specific performance of contracts to lend money will not be ordered, the lender's remedy will lie only in damages and these are likely to be minimal.[56]

---

also ICF Spry, *The Principles of Equitable Remedies: Specific Performance, Injunctions, Rectification and Equitable Damages* 8th edn (Thomson Reuters Australia, 2009) ch 3; *Loan Investment Corporation of Australasia v Bonner* [1970] NZLR 724, PC, 741–2 *per* Sir Garwick Berwick (dissenting) where the possibility of an order for specific performance of an obligation to lend being granted in exceptional circumstances was envisaged.

[49] *Georges v Wieland* [2009] NSWSC 733.　　　[50] As Companies Act 1907, s 16.

[51] Companies Act 2006, s 738 lists various instruments which are debentures but does not contain an exhaustive definition of the term. This section does make clear that the term 'debenture' is not confined to secured loans. The courts have frequently acknowledged the absence of a precise definition: see eg *British India Steam Navigation Co v Commissioners of Inland Revenue* [1881] 7 QBD 165; *Knightsbridge Estates Trust Ltd v Byrne* [1940] AC 613 HL, 621 *per* Viscount Maugham; *NV Slavenburg's Bank v Intercontinental Natural Resources Ltd* [1980] 1 All ER 955, 976. The absence of a precise definition has given rise to few practical problems: *Re SH & Co (Realisations) 1990 Ltd* [1993] BCC 60, 67 quoting LBC Gower, *Principles of Modern Company Law* 5th edn (London: Sweet & Maxwell, 1992) 379.

[52] *Levy v Abercorris Slate and Slab Co* (1887) 37 Ch D 260. See also *Edmonds v Blaina Furnaces Co* (1887) 36 Ch D 215; *Lemon v Austin Friars Investment Trust Ltd* [1926] 1 Ch 1, CA; *Knightsbridge Estates Trust v Byrne* [1940] AC 613, HL; *R v Findlater* [1939] 1 KB 594, CCA.

[53] *British India Steam Navigation Co v Commissioners of Inland Revenue* [1881] 7 QBD 165, 173 *per* Lindley J. The court was required to determine whether the instrument was a debenture or a promissory note for stamping purposes.

[54] Tradability by itself does not provide the key to distinguishing between what is and is not within the scope of the term 'debenture' for the purposes of Companies Act 2006, s 740 since there are secondary markets in lenders' participations in loan agreements. On the secondary market in loan participations: J Barratt, 'Distressed Debt—The Sale of Loan Assets' [1998] *Journal of International Banking Law* 50; S Drucker and M Puri, 'On Loan Sales, Loan Contracting, and Lending Relationships.'

[55] Contrast A Berg, 'Syndicated Lending and the FSA' (1991) 10(1) *International Financial Law Review* 27.

[56] *Rogers v Challis* (1859) 27 Beav 175, 54 ER 68.

In the absence of any provision to the contrary, it is unclear whether a borrower can make early repayments of borrowed money[57] but express provisions regarding early repayment are commonly included. These provisions typically require the borrower to give notice of an intended early repayment and to make the repayment on a specified date, such as the last day of an interest period. Restrictions on early repayment are usually closely linked to the lender's own financing commitments. It is usual to provide that any amount pre-paid is to be applied to the repayment instalments in inverse order to their maturity. This has the effect of shortening the life of the loan.

Interest

In the absence of express agreement to the contrary or some course of dealing or custom to such effect, interest is not payable on a bank loan.[58] This point is of limited practical signifi-cance since loan agreements almost invariably make express provision for interest charges. Since the Usury Laws Repeal Act 1954, there is no statutory control with regard to interest rates charged to companies. The rate of interest may be fixed for the term of the loan or may be variable (or 'floating') over the life of the loan. It is theoretically possible to provide for inter-est to be variable entirely at the discretion of the lender, but borrowers with sufficient nego-tiating strength would be likely to resist agreeing to this degree of uncertainty. Floating-rate loan agreements commonly provide for the interest rate to be adjusted at specified intervals by reference to a formula which is intended to maintain the lender's return on the loan.

The money that a bank lends to its borrowing customers may be its own money (share capi-tal and reserves) or it may be money which it has borrowed either from depositors (the rela-tionship between banks and depositing customers being one of debtor and creditor) or from other lenders. Banks can borrow in the inter-bank market by taking in short-term deposits. Such deposits are made for short specific periods, typically three or six months, and they bear interest at a fixed rate. LIBOR, the London Inter-Bank Offered Rate, is a benchmark giving an indication of the average rate at which a LIBOR contributor bank can obtain unsecured fund-ing in the London inter-bank market for a given period, in a given currency.[59] This is just one of the interest bases that may be used for calculating floating interest rates in loan agreements but it suffices for the purposes of illustration. Where a bank takes deposits in the inter-bank mar-ket and then makes a term loan to a borrower, there is an obvious mismatch between the bank's obligation to repay the deposit, in three or six months' time, and its rights to claim repayment in what may be many years' time: it has borrowed short to lend long. One of the ways of man-aging the consequences of this mismatch is for the bank to adjust the rate of interest that the borrower is required to pay to reflect LIBOR on each occasion when it is required to refinance

---

[57] The Australian courts have held that a borrower does not have the right to repay early unless this is provided for expressly: *Hyde Management Services (Pty) Ltd v FAI Insurances* (1979–80) 144 CLR 541, H Ct of Aust; *Gladstone & District Leagues Club v Hutson* [2007] QSC 10. It has also been held in England that an issuer of debt securities cannot redeem them early unless the terms of issue provide for this: *Hooper v Western Counties and South Wales Telephone Co Ltd* (1892) 68 LT 78.

[58] *Chatham & Dover Rly v South East Rly* [1893] AC 429, HL.

[59] The British Bankers Association (BBA) publishes a daily LIBOR rate (for details of how it is calculated and the publication process see <http://www.bba.org.uk/media/article/understanding-bba-libor> (accessed October 2013)). According to the BBA, BBA LIBOR is the most widely used 'benchmark' or reference rate for short-term interest rates. It is, claims the BBA, the primary benchmark for short-term interest rates globally. It is used as the basis for settlement of interest rate contracts on many of the world's major futures and options exchanges as well as many loan agreements throughout global markets, including mortgage agreements. Following the revelation that the LIBOR process was open to misuse, the rate-setting procedure is in the process of being reformed and NYSE Euronext Rates Administration Limited is expected to take over from the BBA the administration of LIBOR from early 2014 (for details, see <http://www.bbalibor.com> (accessed October 2013)).

in the inter-bank market. To achieve this, the agreement should provide for the borrower to pay interest at a rate equivalent to LIBOR from time to time plus an additional margin which is set at the outset and which is the bank's return on the transaction. This structure enables the bank to pass its funding costs through to the borrower. If a lender is in financial difficulty, for example, because it is obliged to pay higher rates on interest to the money market, then it is likely to have to pass those increased costs on to its borrowers. It follows that if it encounters financial difficulties, it may feel obliged to raise the interest rates paid by its borrowers. If in such circumstances the rate of interest charged to a borrower is increased, it is impossible to say that the discretion to set the rate of interest is being exercised for an improper purpose, capriciously, arbitrarily, or in a way in which no reasonable lender would reasonably do.[60]

There are various ways in which a lender may seek to protect its interests against the possibility of a borrower company failing to make an interest payment when it is due. Failure to pay any sum, representing either interest or principal, which is due and payable is the first event of default in a typical loan agreement. Such an agreement will typically provide that, upon the occurrence of an event of default, the lender is entitled to terminate the agreement; to demand repayment of principal, interest, and any other sums payable pursuant to the agreement; and to cancel any facilities that remain outstanding. The occurrence of an event of default thus does not, in the usual case, terminate the agreement automatically but it gives the lender an option to do so.[61] The courts have a jurisdiction to hold unenforceable a contractual term that amounts to a penalty clause intended to punish the party in breach.[62] A penalty clause is a clause which, without commercial justification, provides for payment or forfeiture of a sum of money, or transfer of property by one party to the other, in the event of a breach of contract,[63] the clause being designed to secure performance of the contract rather than to compensate the payee for the loss occasioned through the breach. The policy of the rule is aimed at a party stipulating to be paid more than his actual loss in circumstances in which he can fairly be compensated for such loss by being left to his remedy in damages.[64] However, it is clear that a contractual provision that entitles the lender to terminate the agreement if the borrower fails to make an interest payment when due is not a penalty clause.[65] Further, the doctrine concerning penalties does not apply to a contractual provision that provides for a standard interest rate and also provides that while the borrower is not in default the lender will accept interest at a concessional rate which is lower than the standard interest.[66]

The onus of showing that a contractual provision is a penalty clause lies with the party who is sued upon it.[67] Whether or not a contractual provision is liable to be struck down as a

---

[60] *Paragon Finance v Nash* [2001] EWCA Civ 1466, [2002] 1 WLR 685.

[61] This is in accordance with established general contractual principles: *Decro-Wall International SA v Practitioners in Marketing Ltd* [1971] 1 WLR 361, CA; *Photo Production Ltd v Securicor Transport Ltd* [1980] AC 827, HL.

[62] The public policy that the court will not enforce a penalty clause so as to permit a party to a contract to recover in an action a sum greater than the measure of damages to which he would be entitled at common law, though well established at law, is anomalous and appears to be sui generis, as the court has no jurisdiction to re-write the terms of a contract because it thinks them unduly onerous to one of the parties: *Ip Ming Kin v Wong Siu Lan* [2013] HKCA 252, [35], Hong Kong CA.

[63] A sum of money payable under a contract on the occurrence of an event other than a breach of a contractual duty owed by the paying to the receiving party is not a penalty: *Berg v Blackburn Rovers Football Club & Athletic* [2013] EWHC 1070 (Ch), [33].

[64] *Imam-Sadeque v Bluebay Asset Management (Services)* [2012] EWHC 3511 (QB), [190] and [202]; *Makdessi v Cavendish Square Holdings* [2013] EWCA Civ 1539, [46]. The law as to penalties applies to a clause which (a) disentitles the contract breaker to receive a sum which would otherwise be due to him; or (b) requires a transfer of property from the guilty to the innocent party either for nothing or at an undervalue.

[65] *Keene v Biscoe* (1878) 8 Ch D 201; *Wallingford v Mutual Society* (1880) 5 App Case 685, HL; *Oresundsvarvet Aktiebolag v Marcos Diamantis Lemos, The Angelic Star* [1988] 1 Lloyd's Rep 122, CA.

[66] *Kellas-Sharpe v PSAL* [2012] QCA 371, Queensland CA.

[67] *Ip Ming Kin v Wong Siu Lan* [2013] HKCA 252, [38], Hong Kong CA.

penalty is to be determined as a matter of construction viewed as at the date of the contract.[68] The rules on penalty clauses require examination in relation to provisions that seek to impose a higher rate of interest if the borrower defaults on making a payment when due.[69] A penalty clause is to be distinguished from a provision for liquidated damages, which is valid.[70] Into which category a particular agreement falls is a question of construction and the label attached by the parties is not conclusive.[71] In the leading case on penalties it was said that one of the indicia of a penalty was where the breach consisted only in not paying a sum of money and the sum stipulated was greater than the sum that ought to have been paid.[72] Concern that this could catch a provision for default interest led to the development of structures that achieved the same economic effect as default interest but adopted a different legal form. Such arrangements were held to be legally effective in a number of cases. Thus it was held that a provision specifying a high rate of interest and providing for it to be reduced to a lower rate in the event of punctual payment was effective even though there is no difference in substance between this and a default interest clause.[73] Another rather technical and fine distinction was upheld in *General Credit and Discount Co v Glegg*.[74] In this case the terms of an interest-bearing loan provided for repayment by instalments. If default was made in the payment of any instalment at the due date there was also to be paid a 'commission' of 1 per cent upon what ought to have been paid for every month or part of a month from the due date to the date of payment of such instalment. This arrangement was held to be a distinct, separate, substantive contract to pay something in the event of default and not an agreement in the nature of a penalty. The Court gave effect to the agreement as drafted and did not treat the commission simply as a device intended to allow the lender to increase the rate of interest on default.

A robust review of the effect of default interest clauses under English law finally took place in *Lordsvale Finance plc v Bank of Zambia*.[75] The Court held that a provision for default interest was not an invalid penalty where it operated only with effect from the event of default, provided that the increase in the interest rate was no more than sufficient to compensate the lender for its additional funding costs and the increased credit risk involved in lending to a defaulting borrower. Apparently inconsistent older cases[76] were

---

[68] *Cadogan Petroleum Holdings v Global Process Systems* [2013] EWHC 214 (Comm), [34].

[69] The court must take account of all the terms of the bargain, and of the circumstances of the contracting parties. What must be justifiable is the clause itself, but it is not to be looked at in isolation from the other terms of the contract. It is to be judged as one of the bundle of obligations undertaken by both parties to the contract, which must be looked at as a whole. The relative sophistication and bargaining power of the parties are also relevant considerations. The fact that the parties are of equal bargaining power does not itself displace the doctrine. But the court should be reluctant to hold that there is no commercial justification for a term which has been freely negotiated by sophisticated parties with equal bargaining power and access to legal advice: *Imam-Sadeque v Bluebay Asset Management (Services)* [2012] EWHC 3511 (QB), [199]. It has been held in Australia that '[t]he critical question is whether the burden imposed by the clause is extravagant and unconscionable. The factors to consider include the circumstances of the parties at the date of the contract, their perceptions at that time regarding their respective positions should breach of contract occur at a later and perhaps distant time, and their understanding of the likely imposition generated by the clause': *Cedar Meats v Five Star Lamb* [2013] VSC 164, [102] (footnotes omitted).

[70] Note the modern approach dictates that (a) undue significance is not given to the discrepancy between the amount payable under the clause and the loss that might be sustained on breach – the significance of the discrepancy may depend on how closely the justification relates to the nature or extent of the loss; (b) no presumptions are treated as irrebuttable; (c) proper account is taken of the desirability of upholding bargains freely entered into and of any commercial justification for allegedly penal clauses, before deciding that the predominant function of the clause is deterrent and that it is penal. *Makdessi v Cavendish Square Holdings* [2013] EWCA Civ 1539, [214].

[71] *Dunlop Pneumatic Tyre Co Ltd v New Garage and Motor Co Ltd* [1915] AC 79, HL.

[72] *Dunlop Pneumatic Tyre Co Ltd v New Garage and Motor Co Ltd* [1915] AC 79, 87, HL, *per* Lord Dunedin.

[73] *Wallingford v Mutual Society* (1880) 5 App Cas 685, HL, 702 *per* Lord Hatherley; *Herbert v Salisbury and Yeovil Rly Co* (1866) 2 LR Eq 221, 224 *per* Lord Romilly MR.

[74] (1883) 22 Ch D 549.   [75] [1996] QB 752.

[76] *Holles v Vyse* (1693) 2 Vern 289, 23 ER 787; *Hunter v Seton* (1802) 7 Ves 265, 32 ER 108. In *Herbert v Salisbury and Yeovil Rly Co* (1866) 2 LR Eq 221, 224 Lord Romilly MR said: 'but if the mortgage interest is at 4 per cent, and there is an agreement that if it is not paid punctually 5 or 6 per cent interest shall be paid, that is in the nature of a penalty which this Court will relieve against.'

distinguished on the grounds that they concerned default interest clauses that operated retrospectively as well as prospectively from the date of default. The *Lordsvale* decision clarifies English law and brings it into line with that in the US, Canada, and Australia.[77] The *Lordsvale* decision is part of a trend in the modern authorities, which is to the effect that the courts will not lightly hold a clause in a commercial document involving sophisticated parties who can be expected to look after themselves to be a penalty.[78] Even though a stipulated amount exceeds what would otherwise be payable under a contract, it will not be penal so long as its contractual purpose is compensatory rather than deterrent.[79] What is objectionable is a clause the predominant function of which is to deter breach in contradistinction to any function it has by way of compensation. Thus the fact that the provision will have some coercive effect in encouraging performance of the contract is not sufficient to render it unenforceable.[80]

Conditions precedent[81]

A loan agreement may require the borrower to satisfy various conditions before it can draw down the funds. For example, the company may be required to supply the lender with copies of its constitutional documents and relevant board resolutions to enable the lender to check that the loan is duly authorized. This practice may not now be strictly necessary where the borrower is incorporated under the British companies legislation, given that lenders are largely protected against the lack of authorization by the provisions of the companies legislation[82] that operate in conjunction with established agency principles and with the rule of company law known as the internal management rule, which protects outsiders against internal irregularities (for example, the lack of a quorum at relevant board meetings) unless they are put on notice to the contrary.[83] However, there is still something to be said for maintaining a policy of checking in advance that the loan is duly authorized because of the greater certainty that this affords; whilst the statutory protections given to persons who deal with companies are now very extensive, there would be a risk that a borrower or its liquidator (insolvency being a particular situation in which a borrower may be especially keen to escape from its obligations) might seek to challenge their application in a particular case, thereby delaying repayment. Another common condition precedent is for the borrower to be

---

[77] *Lordsvale Finance plc v Bank of Zambia* [1996] QB 752, 765–7.

[78] *Philips Hong Kong v A-G of Hong Kong* (1993) 61 BLR 49; *United International Pictures v Cine Bes Filmcilik VE Yapimcilik* [2004] 1 CLC 491, CA; *Murray v Leisureplay plc* [2005] IRLR 946, CA.

[79] *Lordsvale Finance plc v Bank of Zambia* [1996] QB 752, 762, a passage cited with approval in *United International Pictures v Cine Bes Filmcilik VE Yapimcilik* [2004] 1 CLC 401 CA, [13] *per* Mance LJ and in *Murray v Leisureplay plc* [2005] IRLR 946, CA, [13] *per* Arden LJ, [106] *per* Clarke LJ, and [100] *per* Buxton LJ. See also *Euro London Appointments Ltd v Claessens International Ltd* [2006] 2 Lloyd's Rep 436, CA. In *Fernhill Properties (Northern Ireland) v Mulgrew* [2010] NICh 20, the court held a default interest of 15 per cent to be a penalty designed to deter a purchaser from defaulting on completion, but in *Slocom Trading v Tatik* [2013] EWHC 1201 (Ch) the court had no issue with enforcing a loan agreement providing for a default interest of 15 per cent compounded monthly.

[80] *Imam-Sadeque v Bluebay Asset Management (Services)* [2012] EWHC 3511 (QB), [189].

[81] It has been said that '[c]onditions precedent describe an act or event that must occur as a prerequisite to the duty to perform. The use of certain language may be indicative that the parties intended to create a condition precedent…Although no particular words are necessary for the existence of a condition, such terms as "if", "provided that," "on condition that," or some other phrase that conditions performance usually connote an intent for a condition rather than a promise. While there is no requirement that such phrases be utilized, their absence is probative of the parties' intention that a promise be made rather than a condition imposed, so that the terms will be construed as a covenant': *Global Energy Finance LLC v Peabody Energy Corp.*, 2010 Del. Super. LEXIS 430 (Del. Super. Ct. 14 Oct. 2010) (citation omitted).

[82] Companies Act 2006, ss 39–40.

[83] *Royal British Bank v Turquand* (1865) 6 E&B 327, 119 ER 327; *Mahoney v East Holyford Mining Co* (1875) LR 7 HL 869.

required to confirm that no events of default have occurred and that the representations and warranties are true and accurate.

The lender is only obliged to make the funds available when the borrower has fulfilled the specified conditions precedent. Can the lender withdraw completely from the agreement before the borrower has had an opportunity to satisfy those requirements? This will depend on the construction of the agreement.[84] The cases indicate that the effect of including conditions precedent in an agreement can, depending on the drafting, include the following: (a) the agreement is not fully binding until the conditions are fulfilled and until then either party can withdraw with impunity;[85] (b) the main agreement is not binding but, so long as the events constituting the conditions precedent can still occur, one (or both) of the parties cannot withdraw;[86] (c) the main agreement is not binding but neither party must do anything to prevent the occurrence of the events[87] or one of the parties undertakes to make reasonable endeavours to bring about the events.[88]

Representations and warranties

Loan agreements commonly contain representations and warranties covering such matters as:

(1) the capacity of the company and the authority of its directors and officers to enter into the loan agreement;

(2) compliance with applicable laws and regulations;

(3) compliance with other contractual obligations of the company—the lender will be concerned to ensure that this loan will not, for example, trigger default under another loan agreement in which the company has covenanted to limit the amount of its borrowings;

(4) the accuracy of the information about the borrower that was supplied to the lender during the course of the negotiations, including confirmation that no facts or circumstances have been omitted so as to render the information that was supplied misleading;

(5) the financial position of the borrower—representations and warranties on this matter would commonly take the form of a statement from the borrower to the effect that its last audited accounts represent a true and fair view of its financial position and that there has been no material adverse change since they were prepared;[89]

(6) claims against the borrower, ie whether any litigation is pending or threatened which might have a material adverse effect on the borrower or on its ability to perform its obligations under the loan agreement;

---

[84] *Total Gas Marketing Ltd v Arco British Ltd* [1998] 2 Lloyd's Rep 209, HL; R Cranston, *Principles of Banking Law* 2nd edn (Oxford: OUP, 2002) 312–3.

[85] *Pym v Campbell* (1856) 6 E&B 370, 119 ER 903.   [86] *Smith v Butler* [1900] 1 QB 694, CA.

[87] *Mackay v Dick* (1881) 6 App Cas 251, HL.   [88] *Hargreaves Transport Ltd v Lynch* [1969] 1 WLR 215, CA.

[89] The interpretation of a 'material adverse change' clause depends on the terms of the clause construed according to well-established principles. Where the borrower represents that there has been no material adverse change in its financial position since the date of the loan agreement, the assessment of the financial position of the borrower should normally begin with its financial information at the relevant times, and a lender seeking to demonstrate a material adverse change should show an adverse change over the period in question by reference to that information. However, the enquiry is not necessarily limited to the financial information if there is other compelling evidence. Unless the adverse change in its financial condition significantly affects the borrower's ability to perform its obligations, and in particular its ability to repay the loan, it is not a material change. A lender cannot trigger such a clause on the basis of circumstances of which it was aware at the time of the agreement. Finally, it is up to the lender to prove the breach: *Grupo Hotelero Urvasco v Carey Value Added* [2013] EWHC 1039 (Comm), [364].

(7) whether any event of default has occurred;

(8) the existing security arrangements into which the borrower has entered, including hire purchase agreements, conditional sales, factoring agreements and guarantees;

(9) the location of the borrower's centre of main interests in a particular jurisdiction.

If the borrower is a holding company, representations and warranties may also relate to the other companies in its group.

Representations and warranties perform an investigative function.[90] In the negotiations leading up to the signing of the loan agreement the borrower will need to disclose any information that is inconsistent with the representations and warranties that are to be included in the agreement or risk being held liable thereafter for breach. This helps to extend the lender's knowledge and understanding of the borrowing entity. The representations and warranties that are finally agreed seek to encapsulate the factual circumstances in reliance on which the lender makes its decision to lend. As such, the truth of the matters contained in the representations and warranties is likely to remain important to a lender throughout the life of a loan and for this reason it may require the borrower to repeat the representations and warranties at specified intervals. A situation in which a lender would be likely to attach particular importance to the repetition of representations and warranties is where the loan is to be available to the borrower in instalments: the lender may require the borrower to repeat the representations and warranties before each drawing is made. Repetition can be required at more frequent intervals, for example, at the beginning of each interest period. The way in which repetition will normally be effected is by a provision in the loan agreement to the effect that there is deemed repetition at the specified intervals. Representations and warranties that are required to be repeated at specified intervals are sometimes described as 'evergreen.'

Under the general law relating to liability for statements, the term 'representation' is used to denote a statement of fact that induces an innocent party to enter into a contract and which, if it is later discovered to have been untrue, gives the innocent party a remedy for misrepresentation. A 'warranty' is a contractual statement that, if untrue, allows the innocent party to sue for breach of contract; generally,[91] 'warranty' is used in contradistinction to 'condition' to describe a term that, if breached, allows for a claim for damages but does not entitle the innocent party to terminate the agreement. The need for detailed analysis of these technicalities is avoided in well-drafted loan agreements which stipulate expressly the consequences of making a representation or warranty which is incorrect or, allowing some leeway to the borrower, which is incorrect in any material respect. If the making of an inaccurate representation or warranty constitutes an event of default, this will entitle the lender to call for repayment of the whole loan at once and to sue in debt for the amount due under the agreement if the borrower refuses to pay.

Covenants

The function of the covenants in a loan agreement is to seek to restrict the borrower in the conduct of its business and thus to give the lender some control over the way in which that business is managed. They aim to ensure that the borrower's credit rating does not decline

---

[90] PR Wood, *International Loans, Bonds, Guarantees, Legal Opinions* 2nd edn (London: Sweet & Maxwell, 2007) ch 4.

[91] The term 'warranty' can also be used to describe an agreement which is collateral to another contract between the same parties. Breach of a collateral warranty may lead to an action for damages or may be a ground on which the court refuses specific performance of the main contract: *Brewer v Mann* [2012] EWCA Civ 246. See generally KW Wedderburn, 'Collateral Contracts' [1959] CLJ 58.

whilst the loan is outstanding. Covenants divide, broadly, into things that the borrower promises to do (positive covenants) and things that it promises to refrain from doing (negative covenants).[92] The underlying aim is to ensure that the borrower remains able to fulfil its obligations under the loan and does not engage in conduct that would prejudice that ability. The inclusion of a range of financial covenants is a common feature of lending in the UK and Ireland.[93] Continental European lending practices have been less dependent on financial covenants historically but recent reviews indicate a trend towards greater use.[94] This occurrence is attributed to market integration and globalization pressures that are moving business practices towards Anglo-American models.[95]

Covenants commonly found in loan agreements include:

(1) *Provision of information.* The borrower must supply the lender with copies of its annual audited accounts and interim financial statements (including consolidated accounts where relevant), any communications sent to the borrower's shareholders, and any other information that the lender reasonably requires.

(2) *Events of default.* The borrower must notify the lender of the occurrence of an event of default or of any other event which, with the giving of notice or passage of time, would constitute an event of default.

(3) *Working capital.* The borrower must ensure that its current assets exceed its current liabilities (or, where relevant, group assets and liabilities) by a specified multiple and that the ratio of current assets to current liabilities does not fall below a specified minimum.

(4) *Tangible net worth.* The borrower must ensure that its (or, where relevant, its group's) paid up share capital and reserves exceed a specified figure and that the ratio between total liabilities and total net worth (consolidated where appropriate) does not fall below a specified minimum.

(5) *Distributions.* The borrower must ensure that dividends and other distributions to shareholders do not exceed a specified percentage of the company's net profits.

(6) *Disposal of assets or change of business.* The borrower must not dispose of any substantial part of its undertaking or, except in the ordinary course of business, assets unless it has the lender's consent; similarly it must not, without the lender's consent, change the scope or nature of its business in a way that would have a material adverse effect on its business, assets, or financial condition; if the borrower is a holding company, it may be required to undertake to procure, so far as it is able to do so,[96] that other

---

[92] WL Megginson, *Corporate Finance Theory* (Addison-Wesley, 1997) 407. WW Bratton, 'Bond Covenants and Creditor Protection: Economics and Law, Theory and Practice, Substance and Process' (2006) 7 *European Business Organization Law Review* 39.

[93] J Day, P Ormrod, and P Taylor, 'Implications for Lending Decisions and Debt Contracting of the Adoption of International Financial Reporting Standards' [2004] *Journal of International Banking Law and Regulation* 475.

[94] J Day, P Ormrod, and P Taylor, 'Implications for Lending Decisions and Debt Contracting of the Adoption of International Financial Reporting Standards' [2004] Journal of International Banking Law and Regulation 475. Historically, German banks have tended to rely on contractual provisions giving them the right to ask for further security/collateral or to accelerate the maturity of a loan agreement if the financial condition of the debtor's business worsens substantially. It is consistent with British evidence to suggest that lenders are more relaxed about the degree of covenant protection they look for when their lending is secured: P Brierley and M Young, 'The Financing of Smaller Quoted Companies: a Survey' (2004) 44(2) *Bank of England Quarterly Bulletin* 160.

[95] J Day, P Ormrod, and P Taylor, 'Implications for Lending Decisions and Debt Contracting of the Adoption of International Financial Reporting Standards' [2004] *Journal of International Banking Law and Regulation* 475.

[96] The extent of parent company control over the conduct of its subsidiaries' affairs and the dangers involved in having too much control (ie potential de facto or shadow directorship liability) are considered in ch 2.

companies within its group also abide by this covenant but the covenant may be qualified so as to permit some intra-group transfers of assets.

(7) *Creation of security.* The borrower must not create any further security over the whole or any part of its undertaking or assets without the consent of the lender (and, where relevant, the borrower may be required to undertake to procure, so far as it can do so, that other companies in its group will also abide by this covenant); the covenant may extend to increasing the amount secured by existing securities, entering into hire purchase, conditional sales, factoring and similar agreements, and to the giving of guarantees.

(8) *Obligations to rank pari passu.* The borrower must ensure that its obligations under the loan facility are unconditional and unsubordinated and will at all times rank at least pari passu with all its other unsecured and unsubordinated obligations (except for such obligations mandatorily preferred by law).[97]

The covenants that are actually included in a particular financing arrangement will depend on a number of factors including the negotiating strength of the borrowing company, the amounts involved (a lender which is advancing a relatively small amount may attach less importance to covenants than a lender which is taking a large exposure), the rate of interest (a high interest rate may compensate the lender for fewer covenants), the intended duration of the loan, whether it is to be secured or unsecured, and whether it is a bank loan or an issue of securities.[98] As noted earlier in this chapter, the process of agreeing the terms of a loan can be very contentious and it is typically the covenants that are the most heavily negotiated part of the documentation.[99] There are dangers (for the lender as well as the borrower) in having very restrictive covenants, as these could damage a borrowing company's potential for economic growth by preventing it from pursuing worthwhile investment and financing opportunities; in an extreme case, onerous covenants could even hinder efforts to rescue a borrowing company that is in serious financial difficulties.[100] Under the costly contracting hypothesis developed by Smith and Warner, companies will search for an optimal financing structure by comparing the benefits of affording control to lenders, via covenants, against the reduction of flexibility for the borrowing company so as to arrive at a value-maximizing set of borrowing terms.[101] Studies support the proposition that there is a trade-off between the costs imposed on borrowers when covenants are imposed and the benefits of restrictive

---

[97] *DBS Bank v Tam Chee Chong* [2011] SGCA 47, [2011] 4 SLR 948, [52]: 'A pari passu undertaking has the function of preventing a creditor from applying undue pressure on the debtor to pay its overdue debts to the former. Unlike a negative pledge, which is directed against the giving of security, a pari passu undertaking is directed against the payment of moneys to creditors. Further, unlike a negative pledge, a pari passu undertaking is a positive obligation to treat all creditors on a pari passu basis at all times, and it is inherent in such an undertaking that the borrower will not prefer one creditor to another creditor. Accordingly, the inducement by one creditor of a breach of the debtor's obligation under a pari passu undertaking will have the same effect in law as the inducement of a breach of the debtor's obligation under a negative pledge, ie, it will amount to an interference with contractual relations.'

[98] WW Bratton, 'Bond Covenants and Creditor Protection: Economics and Law, Theory and Practice, Substance and Process' (2006) 7 *European Business Organization Law Review* 39 looks at US experience in using contractual covenant protection for creditors.

[99] See also RJ Lister, 'Debenture Covenants and Corporate Value' (1985) 6 *Company Lawyer* 209.

[100] PR Wood, *International Loans, Bonds, Guarantees, Legal Opinions* 2nd edn (London: Sweet & Maxwell, 2007) ch 5; J Day and P Taylor, 'Evidence on the Practice of UK Bankers in Contracting for Medium-Term Debt' [1995] *Journal of International Banking Law* 394; J Day and P Taylor, 'Bankers' Perspectives on the Role of Covenants in Debt Contracts' [1996] *Journal of International Banking Law* 201. Wider considerations arising from market and economic conditions may also over time cause lenders to vary their perception of the importance of particular covenants: WW Bratton, 'Corporate Debt Relationships: Legal Theory in a Time of Restructuring' [1989] *Duke Law Journal* 135.

[101] CW Smith and JB Warner, 'On Financial Contracting: An Analysis of Bond Covenants' (1979) 7 *Journal of Financial Economics* 117.

covenants that reduce the scope for controllers of companies to behave opportunistically at creditors' expense.[102] There is evidence that the price impact of including covenants restricting investments and distributions can be economically significant.[103]

The potential problems that could result from very tight covenants arise most sharply in the context of bond issues because if bond covenants prove to be too restrictive, the process of obtaining a relaxation may be particularly cumbersome, time-consuming, and expensive, as it may require the convening of a special meeting of the holders of the securities for that purpose. It is easy to see why the process of renegotiating a loan agreement involving just a small number of parties is likely to be much more straightforward. Concern about potential future renegotiation difficulties is a factor that helps to explain why covenants in publicly issued bonds tend to be lighter than in privately negotiated debt financing arrangements[104] and to have more of a predictable, standardized character.[105] Bond issue covenants are considered further in chapter 15.

A boom in leveraged buyout activity in the 2000s led to the emergence of 'covenant lite' loan deals in which borrowers were not required to give significant covenants to maintain financial ratios and which had other borrower-friendly features such as clauses to the effect that a breach of covenant would not constitute an event of default unless it was repeated. This trend reached a high-water mark in the summer of 2007 but thereafter changing market conditions (commonly referred to as a 'credit crunch') led to indications that the tide was turning away from loan financing on bond-like covenant lite terms.[106]

Reporting covenants

Reporting covenants that require the borrower to supply the lender with copies of accounts and other information are important to the lender because they facilitate the task of monitoring the company's affairs on an ongoing basis. Information covenants supplement the disclosure of financial information and audit requirements of the companies legislation and securities regulation in that they are likely to be more extensive than those requirements and may require information to be updated more regularly or more promptly. It is clearly vital for a lender to have early notice of the occurrence of an event of default so that it can consider its position and it is not unreasonable to require the borrower to notify the lender when it is in default. A requirement to notify the lender of impending events of default may create some uncertainty.

---

[102] Examples include S Chava, P Kumar, and A Warga, 'Managerial Moral Hazard and Bond Covenants' (26 May 2007) <http://ssrn.com/abstract=989342> accessed July 2103; MH Bradley and MR Roberts, 'The Structure and Pricing of Corporate Debt Covenants' (13 May 2004) <http://ssrn.com/abstract=466240> accessed July 2013; BE Adler and M Kahan, 'The Technology of Creditor Protection' (2013) 161 *University of Pennsylvania Law Review* 1773; EB Rock, 'Adapting to the New Shareholder-Centric Reality' (2013) 161 *University of Pennsylvania Law Review* 1907; G Triantis, 'Exploring the Limits of Contract Design in Debt Financing' (2013) 161 *University of Pennsylvania Law Review* 2041.

[103] Examples include S Chava, P Kumar, and A Warga, 'Managerial Moral Hazard and Bond Covenants' (26 May 2007) <http://ssrn.com/abstract=989342> accessed July 2103; MH Bradley and MR Roberts, 'The Structure and Pricing of Corporate Debt Covenants' (13 May 2004) <http://ssrn.com/abstract=466240> accessed July 2013; BE Adler and M Kahan, 'The Technology of Creditor Protection' (2013) 161 *University of Pennsylvania Law Review* 1773; EB Rock, 'Adapting to the New Shareholder-Centric Reality' (2013) 161 *University of Pennsylvania Law Review* 1907; G Triantis, 'Exploring the Limits of Contract Design in Debt Financing' (2013) 161 *University of Pennsylvania Law Review* 2041.

[104] eg M Kahan and D Yermack, 'Investment Opportunities and the Design of Debt Securities' (1998) 14 *Journal of Law, Economics and Organization* 136 is a study finding that high-growth companies tended to prefer conversion rights to covenants in their public market bond issues.

[105] I Ramsay and BK Sidhu, 'Accounting and Non-accounting Based Information Market for Debt: Evidence from Australian Private Debt Contracts' (1998) 38 *Accounting and Finance* 197.

[106] M Hitching and D O'Brien. 'Leveraged Lending Terms: a Less Brave New World?' (2007) 18(10) *Practical Law for Companies* 9.

Financial covenants

Financial covenants seek to ensure that the borrower's solvency will be maintained and that the borrower will not become too heavily dependent on debt finance: the thinking is that it will be able to pay its debts as they fall due (cash-flow solvency) because its current assets comfortably exceed its current liabilities (the working capital covenant) and it will also be solvent in a balance sheet sense because its total assets easily exceed its total liabilities (the tangible net worth covenant). The effect of financial covenants may be to oblige a company to seek new equity capital for a new venture that it wants to pursue. The lender can argue that this is reasonable on the grounds that, if the venture were to be financed by additional borrowed funds, this would dilute the value of each lender's claim in the event of failure putting the company's solvency at risk, but lenders would not reap the benefits of success since they do not share in capital growth.[107] Conversely it can be argued that overreliance on debt can result in companies rejecting potentially profitable opportunities because substantial benefits from those opportunities will accrue to lenders rather than to shareholders;[108] looked at in this way, covenants restricting borrowing may reduce the incentive to underinvest.[109]

Covenants restricting dividends are less common in European loan agreements than in US equivalents; one study found that dividend restrictions in debt contracts are an important factor for 42 per cent of US managers and for only 8 per cent of European managers.[110] Article 17 of the Second Company Law Directive imposes payout restrictions under the general law.[111] There is some suggestion that the lack of covenants restricting dividends in British[112] and German[113] loan documentation can be explained in terms of lenders being content with the position under the general law and seeing no need to follow US market practice, where dividend covenants are more common[114] but there are, broadly speaking, no such payout constraints under the general law.[115] How far the Second Directive can be regarded as playing

---

[107] DR Fischel, 'The Economics of Lender Liability' (1989) 99 *Yale Law Journal* 131.

[108] SC Myers, 'Determinants of Corporate Borrowing' (1977) 5 *Journal of Financial Economics* 147; R Sappideen, 'Fiduciary Obligations to Corporate Creditors' [1991] JBL 365.

[109] CW Smith and JB Warner, 'On Financial Contracting: An Analysis of Bond Covenants' (1979) 7 *Journal of Financial Economics* 117, 124.

[110] F Bancel, UR Mittoo, and N Bhattacharyya, 'Cross-Country Determinants of Payout Policy: A Survey of European Firms' (2004) 33 *Financial Management* 103.

[111] Directive 2012/30/EU of the European Parliament and of the Council of 25 October 2012 on coordination of safeguards which, for the protection of the interests of members and others, are required by Member States of companies within the meaning of the second paragraph of Article 54 of the Treaty on the Functioning of the European Union, in respect of the formation of public limited liability companies and the maintenance and alteration of their capital, with a view to making such safeguards equivalent (Recast) [2012] L315/74. Art 17 limits distributions to net profits accumulated since the company's incorporation and imposes the further restriction that distributions must not reduce net assets to an amount that is lower than subscribed capital and undistributable reserves.

[112] JFS Day and PJ Taylor, 'The Role of Debt Contracts in UK Corporate Governance' (1998) 2 *Journal of Management and Governance* 171.

[113] C Leuz, D Deller, and M Stubenrath, 'An International Comparison of Accounting-Based Pay-Out Restrictions in the United States, United Kingdom and Germany' (1998) 28 *Accounting and Business Research* 111; C Leuz, 'The Role of Accrual Accounting in Restricting Dividends to Shareholders' (1998) 7 *European Accounting Review* 579, 580; C Leuz and J Wüstemann, 'The Role of Accounting in the German Financial System,' in P Krahnen and RH Schmidt (eds), *The German Financial System* (OUP, 2004) 450–81.

[114] A Kalay, 'Stockholder-Bondholder Conflict and Dividend Constraints' (1982) 10 *Journal of Financial Economics* 211; WW Bratton, 'Bond Covenants and Creditor Protection: Economics and Law, Theory and Practice, Substance and Process' (2006) 7 *European Business Organization Law Review* 39.

[115] C Leuz, D Deller, and M Stubenrath, 'An International Comparison of Accounting-Based Pay-Out Restrictions in the United States, United Kingdom and Germany' (1998) 28 *Accounting and Business Research* 111. The idea that regulation can substitute for covenants is explored in a range of different contexts: eg EL Black, TA Carnes, M Mosebach, and SE Moyer, 'Regulatory Monitoring as a Substitute for Debt Covenants' (2004) 37 *Journal of Accounting and Economics* 367 is a study examining whether banks substituted regulatory monitoring for covenants by investigating debt issues of 105 banks between 1979 and 1984, a period when monitoring increased.

a useful role because it mimics lenders' preference is a controversial issue. It is relevant to note that contractual debt financing terms can differ from case to case as a result of context-specific considerations, unlike legal capital rules that provide one rigid, universally applicable model which cannot be adapted to different circumstances. The degree of flexibility and adaptability within contractual processes gives credence to the view that situations where the debt financing terms that are actually agreed in practice will bear close resemblance to the legal model are likely to be infrequent.[116]

An argument in favour of constraints on dividends is that they can encourage new investment by the company,[117] so that although shareholders may appear to lose out in the short term (in that the company's freedom to determine whether to distribute profits or to retain them for investment is restricted), such a covenant can operate to their benefit in the longer term where it results in enhanced capital growth. Balanced against this is the suggestion that if a covenant is unduly onerous so that management is required to retain more of the company's profits than it can prudently invest, this could result in investments being made in risky ventures with potentially adverse consequences for both lenders and shareholders.[118] Where a company has surplus retentions, it may be possible to use these to make early repayment of expensive or restrictive debt to the extent that this is permitted by the relevant debt financing terms.[119]

Disposals of assets covenant

A covenant restricting disposals of assets is intended to prevent asset-stripping, such as where property is sold by the borrowing company at a nominal price. Even disposals of assets at a fair market price could prejudice the lender because piecemeal sales of assets may generate significantly lower proceeds than a sale of all of the assets and undertaking of the business as a going concern. Where the borrower is a holding company, a transfer of assets between wholly-owned subsidiaries, even at a nominal value, does not prejudice the lender since the value remains within the group throughout. A transfer from the holding company borrower to another company in its group is, however, potentially prejudicial because it means that assets that would previously have been available to repay the borrower's creditors will be claimed first by the creditors of the transferee subsidiary. A transfer from a wholly-owned subsidiary to another group company that is not wholly owned could also be problematic in that the other shareholders in the transferee company or undertaking will acquire an interest in the assets which ranks equally with that of the borrowing holding company. In effect, creditors of the holding company will be structurally subordinated. Hence, if the covenant is qualified so as to permit intra-group transfers, this will usually exclude transfers by the borrower itself and may also exclude or restrict transfers otherwise than between wholly-owned subsidiaries. A disposals covenant must necessarily be qualified so as to permit disposals of assets in the ordinary course of business. Disposals of insubstantial parts of the borrower's business and undertaking may also be permitted, although the introduction of a substance test may sow the seeds of potential future difficulties in interpretation and application.

---

[116] L Enriques and J Macey, 'Creditors Versus Capital Formation: The Case Against the European Legal Capital Rules' (2001) 86 *Cornell Law Review* 1165, 1193.

[117] A Kalay, 'Stockholder—Bondholder Conflict and Dividend Constraints' (1982) 10 *Journal of Financial Economics* 211.

[118] RJ Lister, 'Debenture Covenants and Corporate Value' (1985) 6 *Company Lawyer* 209, 213; R Sappideen, 'Fiduciary Obligations to Corporate Creditors' [1991] JBL 365, 378.

[119] In the case of debt securities, the borrower may be required to make payments into a sinking fund which is to be used to buy back securities before they mature.

Change of business covenant

A covenant requiring the borrower not to change its business or operations helps to preserve the identity of the borrower throughout the term of the loan. However, where, as is common, the covenant is qualified so as to restrict only changes that would have 'a material adverse effect' on its business, assets, or financial condition, interpretative uncertainties may complicate the process of monitoring compliance with this covenant.[120]

Negative pledge covenant

The purpose of a covenant whereby the company undertakes not to create new security interests or to increase the amount secured by existing securities is to ensure that the priority position of the lender does not change whilst the loan is outstanding. The lender does not want to find itself postponed to subsequent creditors and thereby subject to the risk that the borrower's assets will be exhausted before its turn to be paid. A covenant to this effect is commonly described as a 'negative pledge' covenant. Forms of negative pledge covenants can be found in both unsecured and secured loans but in this chapter the focus is solely on unsecured lending.[121] A typical clause would seek to prohibit quasi-securities (such as credit sales) as well as conventional security interests but the lender's attempts to produce an all-embracing clause may be defeated by the ingenuity of other corporate financiers who subsequently devise arrangements that perform the same economic function as a secured loan but which adopt a legal form that is not anticipated by the negative pledge covenant.

As with any other covenant, breach of a negative pledge covenant will be a breach of contract entitling the lender to contractual remedies. In a well-drafted loan agreement, the breach is likely to be an express event of default entitling the lender to terminate the agreement and to demand repayment of the principal and of any other sums that are outstanding. It is possible for a lender to seek an injunction to prevent a company from granting security in breach of a negative pledge covenant but practical difficulties in detecting whether or when a company proposes to do this are likely to preclude extensive successful recourse to this remedy.[122] Another equitable remedy is for the court to appoint a receiver but this remedy is generally only available to secured lenders, although the possibility of exercising this power in favour of an unsecured lender in the event of breach of a negative pledge in its favour was left open in one Australian decision.[123]

Does the breach of a negative pledge covenant by the granting of a subsequent security have any legal implications for the creditor in whose favour the offending security is created? In a broad sense, the answer to this question is yes, because a company that is in a position where it is prepared to break the terms of its existing financial facilities in this way is, inferentially, a company that is very likely to be in financial difficulties. The lender in whose favour the relevant security is created, in common with the company's other creditors, may thus soon

---

[120] In *Re IBP, Inc Shareholders' Litigation* [2001] WL 675339 (Del Ch 2001) the Delaware Court of Chancery held in the context of a merger agreement that a material adverse change (MAC) event was something that produced 'a significant diminution of the value of the business entity as a whole.' However, this 'well meaning effort' to deal with ambiguity has attracted criticism: RJ Gilson and A Schwartz, 'Understanding MACs: Moral Hazard in Acquisitions' (2005) 21 *Journal of Law, Economics and Organization* 330. See also *Cukurova Finance International v Alfa Telecom Turkey* [2013] UKPC 2, and *Torre Asset Funding v The Royal Bank of Scotland* [2013] EWHC 2670 (Ch).
[121] See ch 12 for negative pledges in secured lending.
[122] An injunction for this purpose was granted in *Pullen v Abelcheck Pty Ltd* (1990) 20 NSWLR 732, discussed in JRC Arkins, ' "OK—So You've Promised, Right?" The Negative Pledge Clause and the "Security" it Provides' [2000] *Journal of International Banking Law* 198.
[123] *Bond Brewing Holdings Ltd v National Australia Bank Ltd* (1989–90) 1 ACSR 445, Vic SC, App D and (1980–90) 1 ACSR 722, High Ct of Aust (refusing leave to appeal).

find itself embroiled in the consequences of having advanced credit to an insolvent company. In particular, should the company enter into the insolvency procedures of administration or liquidation,[124] the security may be vulnerable under those provisions of the Insolvency Act 1986 that invalidate, or authorize the court to invalidate, security that was created in the twilight period of a company's solvency.[125]

A specific technical issue is whether the original unsecured lender in whose favour the negative pledge covenant was given may have a claim against the subsequent lender whose security[126] was created in breach of the covenant. The point of departure here is the privity of contract rule, which is to the effect that contracts cannot give rights to, or impose burdens on, persons who are not parties to them.[127] This rule is subject to various exceptions and qualifications, but the one that is particularly relevant in this context is the equitable principle in *de Mattos v Gibson*.[128] This principle is that where a person acquires property or an interest in property with knowledge of a previous contract affecting that property, he can be restrained by injunction from acting in a manner that is inconsistent with that contract.[129] The basis of this principle, its limits, and even whether it remains good law are issues on which the cases provide scope for different interpretations and for this reason it is unsurprising to discover that these are matters that have been extensively discussed by academic commentators.[130] One point on which there is broad agreement is that, even if it does survive as an extant legal principle, *de Mattos v Gibson* is subject to restrictive conditions that severely limit its application. In particular, it only operates against persons who know of the existence of the earlier covenant and knowledge in this context means actual knowledge of the prior rights.[131] Constructive knowledge—which can arise from the public filing of information—does not suffice and, in any case, negative pledge clauses in unsecured loan agreements are not subject to any general disclosure or registration requirement under British law that would fix the public with deemed knowledge of their terms. Thus, whilst there could be particular situations in which an original lender is able to prove that the security holder became aware of the existence of a prior negative pledge as part of the process of negotiating the terms of its secured financing, in many instances claims based on *de Mattos v Gibson* will fall at the first hurdle because relevant knowledge cannot be shown.

---

[124] Where a company's existing facilities contain cross-default clauses, the creation of security in breach of a negative pledge covenant in one agreement may mean that it is in default under all of them and therefore that all of its lenders can call for repayment. The domino effect of a cross-default clause thus increases the likelihood of the company being unable to pay its debts as they fall due, and that will form the basis for the making of an administration order or a winding-up order under the Insolvency Act 1986. Cross-default clauses are discussed further later in this chapter.

[125] Especially Insolvency Act 1986, ss 245 (avoidance of certain floating charges) and 239 (preferences).

[126] Here this term is used loosely to include interests that perform the same economic function as a security but which are in a different legal form.

[127] Law Commission, *Privity of Contract: Contracts for the Benefit of Third Parties* (Report No 242, 1996) provides a general review of the law in this area.

[128] (1858) De G&J 276, 282, [1843–60] All ER Rep 803, 805 *per* Knight-Bruce LJ. But the principle is not a panacea for outflanking the doctrine of privity of contract: *Law Debenture Corp v Ural Caspian Ltd* [1993] 2 All ER 355, 362 *per* Hoffmann LJ (sitting as an additional judge of the High Court). This decision was reversed on appeal ([1995] 1 All ER 157, CA) but on grounds that are not relevant to this point.

[129] *Law Debenture Corp v Ural Caspian Ltd* [1993] 2 All ER 355, 362 *per* Hoffmann LJ.

[130] S Worthington, *Proprietary Interests in Commercial Transactions* (Oxford: Clarendon Press, 1996) ch 5 provides a detailed and careful review of the authorities and the different interpretations that have been ascribed to them by numerous commentators.

[131] *Swiss Bank Corp v Lloyds Bank Ltd* [1979] 1 Ch 548, 575 *per* Browne-Wilkinson J (varied on appeal but on other grounds [1982] AC 584, CA and HL). In the context of the economic tort of inducing breach of contract, actual knowledge can embrace a conscious decision not to inquire into the existence of a fact (turning a blind eye): *OBG v Allan; Douglas v Hello! Ltd; Mainstream Properties Ltd v Young* [2007] 2 WLR 920, HL. The *de Mattos v Gibson* principle can be viewed as the equitable counterpart of the tort of inducing breach of contract (see *Swiss Bank Corp v Lloyds Bank Ltd* [1979] 1 Ch 548, 573).

Even if the knowledge hurdle can be cleared, there remain formidable barriers to success in a claim by an unsecured holder of a negative pledge covenant that is based on *de Mattos v Gibson*. The principle operates where a person acquires property and *thereafter* seeks to deal with it in a manner that is inconsistent with an earlier contractual promise that was known about at the time of the acquisition. This wording is not apt to cover situations where security is created in breach of a negative pledge because, there, it is the very acquisition of the security interest in the property, rather than subsequent dealings with it, that infringes the earlier covenant. Following this line of analysis, breach of a negative pledge covenant may lie outside the scope of the *de Mattos v Gibson* principle altogether.

In support of this viewpoint, it can be argued that the underlying purpose of the *de Mattos v Gibson* principle is to give bite to an undertaking by an acquirer of property to respect existing third-party claims on that property; where security is taken in breach of an earlier negative pledge it is self-evidently not part of the bargain that the acquirer will abide by existing restrictions.[132]

As an alternative to the equitable *de Mattos v Gibson* principle, the lender whose negative pledge covenant has been breached has the possibility of a tort claim against the taker of the security.[133] To succeed in a claim based on the economic tort of inducing a breach of contract, the claimant must demonstrate that the defendant intentionally violated its contractual rights.[134] An inherent element of intentional violation is that the defendant must know that it is inducing a breach of contract.[135] Actual knowledge is required but this can embrace a conscious decision not to inquire into the existence of a fact or, putting it another way, turning a blind eye to the obvious.[136] In determining intention, the breach of contract must be the ends or the means to an end and not just a foreseeable consequence of certain actions.[137] Whether a lender that has provided a facility on the basis of a negative pledge which is later broken will be able to establish the elements of the tort will depend heavily on what it can discover about the disclosure process that preceded the subsequent secured loan agreement.[138]

It is sometimes the case that negative pledge lenders attempt 'self-help' by including in their loan agreements a clause to the effect that the loan will become secured in the event

---

[132] This places *de Mattos v Gibson* under the broader heading of prevention of unjust enrichment. For further development of this idea see S Worthington, *Proprietary Interests in Commercial Transactions* (Oxford: Clarendon Press, 1996) 102–5 and the sources cited there.

[133] Although *Swiss Bank Corp v Lloyds Bank Ltd* [1979] 1 Ch 548 may suggest that the *de Mattos v Gibson* principle is simply concerned with the granting of an equitable remedy to prevent the commission of a tort, it is also possible to regard that principle and tort claims as distinct: AP Bell, *Modern Law of Personal Property in England and Wales* (London: Butterworths, 1989) 210–6.

[134] *Lumley v Gye* [1843–60] All ER Rep 208; *OBG v Allan* [2007] UKHL 21, [2008] 1 AC 1. There is also the possibility of pursuing claims based on other economic torts such as conspiracy. See further J Stone, 'Negative Pledges and the Tort of Interference with Contractual Relations' [1991] *Journal of International Banking Law* 310.

[135] *OBG v Allan* [2007] UKHL 21, [2008] 1 AC 1; *Torquay Hotel Co Ltd v Cousins* [1969] 1 All ER 522, CA.

[136] *Torquay Hotel Co Ltd v Cousins* [1969] 1 All ER 522, CA, 530 *per* Lord Denning MR; *Emerald Construction Co Ltd v Lowthian* [1966] 1 WLR 691, CA, 700–1 *per* Lord Denning MR. In *OBG v Allan* Lord Hoffmann referred to Lord Denning's views in *Emerald* and said that it was in accordance with the general principle of law that a conscious decision not to inquire into the existence of a fact is in many cases treated as equivalent to knowledge of that fact. Lord Hoffmann emphasized that it is not the same as negligence or even gross negligence.

[137] *OBG v Allan* [2007] UKHL 21, [2008] 1 AC 1.

[138] *DBS Bank v Tam Chee Chong* [2011] SGCA 47, [2011] 4 SLR 948, [50]: 'A negative pledge is an undertaking by a borrower or debtor to a lender or creditor not to give security to any other present or future lender or creditor. It is a device usually employed by a borrower who has commercial bargaining power not to encumber any of its assets where its business or operations are financed by more than one lender so that it can deal with its assets freely in its own commercial interests. A negative pledge clause fulfils the function of contractually preventing any creditor from trying to obtain security over the assets of the debtor at any time, and particularly when the debtor is in deep financial distress and the creditor wants its overdue debts paid before the claims of other creditors. In such cases, a creditor who induces the debtor to breach the latter's negative pledges to other creditors may be liable for the tort of interfering with the contractual relations of the debtor with those creditors...'

of breach of the negative pledge. The legal effectiveness of this form of self-help is doubtful. First, a provision for automatic security may fail to result in a valid security because it does not define the subject matter of the security with sufficient certainty.[139] Secondly, the security that springs into effect on breach of the negative pledge may not achieve the desired priority effect, ie to rank ahead of the security created in breach of the negative pledge. According to the conventional view, an agreement that provides for security to take effect on fulfilment of a contingency (the contingency in this case being breach of the negative pledge) does not give rise to a security until that contingency is fulfilled.[140] Therefore, in order to win any priority battle that is governed by a 'first in time' rule, careful drafting is needed to ensure that the security comes into effect immediately prior to the creation of the security in breach of the negative pledge. There is some doubt as to whether drafting can in fact achieve this effect.[141] In *Smith (Administrator of Cosslett (Contractors) Ltd) v Bridgend County Borough Council*[142] Lord Scott suggested that a charge expressed to come into existence on the occurrence of an uncertain future event could, even prior to fulfilment of the contingency, count as a charge for some of the requirements relating to company charges[143] but the majority of the House agreed with Lord Hoffmann, whose speech did not make reference to this point. In *Re Spectrum Plus Ltd*[144] Lord Scott again mentioned the issue and suggested that a fixed charge expressed to come into existence on a future event in relation to a specified class of assets would in principle be categorized prior to the fulfilment of the contingency as a floating charge[145] but this remark was peripheral to the decision in the case. In neither case did Lord Scott consider previous authority to the effect that a contingent security is not a security until the contingency is fulfilled. In the absence of a full examination of the issues in a case decided squarely on the basis of the legal effect of a contingent security, the conventional view, based on clear authority, still stands.

The third problem with which a lender that is seeking to rely on a security arising automatically on breach of a negative pledge covenant must contend arises from registration requirements relating to company charges. Most forms of security must be registered within twenty-one days of creation in order to preserve their validity against other secured creditors and against the borrowing company, should it enter into the formal insolvency proceedings of administration or liquidation.[146] Under the conventional view of contingent securities, the period for registration runs from the fulfilment of the contingency and there is therefore an onus of considerable vigilance on the lender.[147] Lord Scott's alternative view would mean that the time period would run from the date of the original loan agreement but that would rather defeat the purpose of the lending being on an unsecured basis.

There are other problems too. It is not clear whether a contingent security has to be supported by fresh consideration provided at the time when the contingency is fulfilled.[148] Furthermore, the implications of the potential mismatch between the appearance that the loan is still unsecured and the reality that it has become secured are unexplored. All in

---

[139] *National Provincial Bank v Charnley* [1924] 1 KB 431, CA.

[140] *Re Gregory Love Ltd* [1916] 1 Ch 203; *Roberts v Investwell* [2012] NSWCA 134.

[141] *Fire Nymph Products Ltd v The Heating Centre Pty Ltd* (1991–92) 7 ACSR 365, NSW CA recognizes that it is possible to achieve this order of events. This was a case involving automatic crystallization of a floating charge but the reasoning may be equally applicable to unsecured negative pledge lending, although this has been doubted: JRC Arkins, ' "OK—So You've Promised, Right?" The Negative Pledge Clause and the "Security" it Provides' [2000] *Journal of International Banking Law* 198. On the priority of competing securities, see ch 12.

[142] [2002] 1 AC 336, HL.   [143] At [63].

[144] *Re Spectrum Plus Ltd; National Westminster Bank plc v Spectrum Plus Ltd* [2005] 2 AC 680, HL.   [145] At [107].

[146] Companies Act 2006, s 874.   [147] *Re Jackson and Bassford Ltd* [1906] 2 Ch 467, 476–7.

[148] J Maxton, 'Negative Pledges and Equitable Principles' [1993] JBL 458 argues that fresh consideration is needed but cf J Stone, 'The "Affirmative" Negative Pledge' [1991] *Journal of International Banking Law* 364.

all, the irresistible conclusion is that self-help through the mechanism of a provision for automatic security on breach of a negative pledge is highly unreliable. The negative pledge unsecured lender should accept at the negotiation stage that, for practical purposes, its remedies for default will lie only against the defaulting company, and should price its risk accordingly.[149]

Implied covenants

In addition to the terms expressly agreed by the parties, in theory terms may also be implied into their contractual relationship. Terms may be implied in fact, in specific contexts terms in law (for example, in relation to contracts for the sale of goods under the Sale of Goods Act 1979), or as a matter of custom. The question of implication of terms only arises when the instrument does not expressly provide for what is to happen when some particular (often unforeseen) event occurs.[150] Recent jurisprudence suggests that 'the test which the court has to apply is: would [the implied] term spell out in express words what the agreement read against the relevant background would reasonably be understood to mean?'[151] As it is not the court's function to rewrite the parties' bargain but to give effect to it as they must have intended, judges have stressed the need for a court not to imply a term merely because it is fair or reasonable to do so but only where it is necessary to do so to give the contract its intended meaning;[152] terms are implied only where it is necessary to give business efficacy to the particular contract in question[153] at the time the parties contract, not in the light of the particular circumstances which arise later.[154] Accordingly, it is impossible for the court to imply a term that is inconsistent with an express term. The detailed and extensive drafting of a typical loan agreement will usually leave little scope for the implication of terms. Further, given that the default position is that nothing is to be implied in the instrument,[155] there is real difficulty in seeking to imply a term into a detailed standard form contract because the strong presumption is likely to be that the detailed terms of the contract are complete.[156]

An interesting development is the possibility of an implied covenant of good faith and fair dealing in contractual matters under English law. There is a traditional English hostility

---

[149] A McKnight, 'Restrictions on Dealing with Assets in Financing Documents: Their Role, Meaning and Effect' [2002] *Journal of International Banking Law* 193.

[150] *Forstater v Python (Monty) Pictures* [2013] EWHC 1873 (Ch), [134].

[151] *Consolidated Finance v McCluskey* [2012] EWCA Civ 1325, [22]; *Dear v Jackson* [2013] EWCA Civ 89, [15]–[18]. Although its correctness is open to doubt, there is some authority to the effect that the reasonable observer, having all the background knowledge which would reasonably have been available to the parties in the situation in which they were at the time of the contract, must be endowed with knowledge as to the established legal effect of the contract, even if the parties were themselves not so aware, and that when considering the implication of a term, it was permissible to assume that the reasonable observer had knowledge that the parties did not in fact have, certainly if that knowledge is as to established and well-known legal principles: *Barden v Commodities Research Unit* [2013] EWHC 1633 (Ch), [42].

[152] *Liverpool City Council v Irwin* [1977] AC 239, HL; *Wuhan Ocean Economic and Technical Cooperation Company v Schiffahrts-Gesellschaft 'Hansa Murcia' mbH & Co KG* [2012] EWHC 3104 (Comm); [2013] 1 All ER (Comm) 1277; *Forstater v Python (Monty) Pictures* [2013] EWHC 1873 (Ch), para 134.

[153] *Societe Generale, London Branch v Geys* [2012] UKSC 63; [2013] 1 All ER 1061, [55]. The court has warned of the danger of detaching the phrase 'necessary to give business efficacy' from the basic process of construction of the instrument. It is frequently the case that a contract may work perfectly well in the sense that both parties can perform their express obligations, but the consequences would contradict what a reasonable person would understand the contract to mean: *Grainmarket Asset Management v PGF II* [2013] EWHC 1879 (Ch), [40].

[154] *Telfer v Sakellarios* [2013] EWHC 1556 (Comm), [71].

[155] *Forstater v Python (Monty) Pictures* [2013] EWHC 1873 (Ch), [134].

[156] *Greatship (India) v Oceanografia SA de CV (The Greatship Dhriti)* [2012] EWHC 3468 (Comm), [2013] 1 All ER (Comm) 1244, [41]; *Wimpole Theatre (a firm) v JJ Goodman* [2012] EWHC 1600 (QB) at [44] ('The barrier to the implication of an unexpressed term into a written agreement is high').

towards a doctrine of good faith.[157] This hostility is rapidly becoming out of date. Although there is no general doctrine of good faith in English contract law, a duty of good faith is implied by law as an incident of certain categories of contract.[158] Moreover, while English law has not reached the stage where it is ready to recognize a requirement of good faith as a duty implied by law, even as a default rule, into all commercial contracts, there seems to be no difficulty, following the established methodology of English law for the implication of terms in fact, in implying such a duty in any ordinary commercial contract based on the presumed intention of the parties. What good faith requires is sensitive to context. That includes the core value of honesty. In any situation it is dishonest to deceive another person by making a statement of fact intending that other person to rely on it while knowing the statement to be untrue. Frequently, however, the requirements of honesty go further. For example, if A gives information to B knowing that B is likely to rely on the information and A believes the information to be true at the time it is given but afterwards discovers that the information was, or has since become, false, it may be dishonest for A to keep silent and not to disclose the true position to B. Another example of conduct falling short of a lie which may, depending on the context, be dishonest is deliberately avoiding giving an answer, or giving an answer which is evasive, in response to a request for information. Although its requirements are sensitive to context, the test of good faith is objective in the sense that it depends not on either party's perception of whether particular conduct is improper but on whether in the particular context the conduct would be regarded as commercially unacceptable by reasonable and honest people.[159]

Events of default

A well-drafted loan agreement will entitle the lender to accelerate the loan upon the occurrence of any one of a number of specified 'events of default.'[160] Common events of default include:

(1) the borrower's failure to pay any sum due and payable pursuant to the agreement;

(2) the borrower's breach of any other obligation or undertaking under the agreement;

(3) any representation or warranty proving to be incorrect (or, less severe, incorrect in a material respect);

(4) cross default: the borrower's failure to pay or meet any other indebtedness or financial obligation when due;

---

[157] *Walford v Miles* [1992] 2 AC 128, HL; *Ng Giap Hon v Westcomb Securities* [2009] SGCA 19, [2009] 3 SLR 518, Singapore CA; *Tang v Grant Thornton International* [2012] EWHC 3198 (Ch), [2013] 1 All ER (Comm) 1226, [57] ('Agreements to agree and agreements to negotiate in good faith, without more, must be taken to be unenforceable: good faith is too open-ended a concept or criterion to provide a sufficient definition of what such an agreement must as a minimum involve and when it can objectively be determined to be properly concluded.'). The US courts have closed the doors to good faith claims in bond contracts: WW Bratton, 'Bond Covenants and Creditor Protection: Economics and Law, Theory and Practice, Substance and Process' (2006) 7 *European Business Organization Law Review* 39.

[158] *Mid Essex Hospital Services NHS Trust v Compass Group UK and Ireland* [2013] EWCA Civ 200, [105].

[159] *Yam Seng v International Trade Corporation* [2013] EWHC 111 (QB), [2013] 1 All ER (Comm) 1321, [119]–[145]. Note that in *Hamsard 3147 (t/a Mini Mode Childrenswear) v Boots UK* [2013] EWHC 3251 (Pat), [86], the court refused to treat *Yam Seng* as an authority for the proposition that in commercial contracts it may be taken to be the presumed intention of the parties that there is a general obligation of good faith because while there will generally be an implied term not to do anything to frustrate the purpose of the contract, there cannot be a routinely implied positive obligation upon a contracting party to subordinate its own commercial interests to those of the other contracting party. See also *HSBC Institutional Trust Services (Singapore) (trustee of Starhill Global Real Estate Investment Trust) v Toshin Development Singapore* [2012] SGCA 48, Singapore CA; *TSG Building Services v South Anglia Housing* [2013] EWHC 1151 (TCC).

[160] R Youard, 'Default in International Loan Agreements I and II' [1986] JBL 276 and [1986] JBL 378.

(5) the commencement of the winding up of the borrower or of other insolvency or reorganization procedures;

(6) distress or execution being levied against any assets of the borrower;

(7) cessation of business by the borrower.

Where the borrower is a holding company, events of default may also relate to subsidiaries and subsidiary undertakings within its group. Grace periods of a number of days may be allowed to the borrower in respect of some or all of the events of default to give the borrower an opportunity to rectify the position before the lender can call in the loan, a concession that will be important to the borrower in relation to trivial or technical breaches.

When a borrower defaults, the lender, if the loan is typically drafted, will have an option whether to declare the loan due and this will not be an automatic consequence of the default.[161] Youard has explained why automatic acceleration would generally be unusual:[162]

> ...since the events of default (other than non-payment) simply amount to an informed guess by the parties at the time the loan is negotiated as to the events which might occur over the next (say) 10 years, and which would entitle the lender to call for immediate repayment, it would in normal circumstances be wholly inappropriate for the occurrence of those events to give rise to automatic acceleration.

The cross-default clause is especially noteworthy. Under this provision the lender is entitled to call in the loan in circumstances where the borrowing company has defaulted on its obligations *to someone else* even though (apart from the cross-default clause) the borrower may have met all of its obligations to this particular lender. The rationale of the cross-default clause is that any default is a sign of trouble in response to which the lender will want to be entitled to accelerate its claim to prevent other creditors stealing a march over it with regard to enforcement or with regard to renegotiation of terms. When a borrower is negotiating the events of default in one loan agreement, it will need to bear in mind that it may in the future enter into other loan agreements containing cross-default clauses, so that accepting very strict events of default on one occasion (for example, no grace periods or no qualifications with regard to 'materiality') could be sowing the seeds of a later catastrophe because of the 'domino' effect of cross default. Also, the terms of any cross-default clause itself will need to be considered closely: if all of the borrower's obligations are included, it may find itself almost always technically in default and it may therefore press for a more limited clause that, perhaps, limits the cross default to failure to pay amounts exceeding a specified threshold figure or which is confined only to particular types of indebtedness.

Sometimes lenders also require cross-default clauses between multiple facilities with a borrower. In one instance, the court explained the legitimate use of cross-default clauses thus:[163]

> ...there were multiple facilities offered to various costs centres all of which were supported by multiple securities. In such a case there are sound commercial reasons for the cross default clause.

---

[161] In the event of any ambiguity, the courts will favour the interpretation that the lender has an option to accelerate and that this is not an automatic consequence of default: *Government Stock and Other Securities Investment Co v Manila Rly Co* [1897] AC 81, HL. For interpretation of the contractual procedure to be followed upon the occurrence (or apparent occurrence) of an event of default in a bond issue, see *Law Debenture Trust Corp plc v Acciona SA* [2004] EWHC 270 (Ch); *Concord Trust v Law Debenture Trust Corp plc* [2005] 1 WLR 1591, HL; *Law Debenture Trust Corp plc v Elektrim Finance BV* [2005] EWHC 1999 (Ch); *Law Debenture Trust Corp plc v Concord Trust* [2007] EWHC 2255 (Ch). P Rawlings, 'The Changing Role of the Trustee in International Bond Issues' [2007] JBL 43; S Wright, 'Making Lenders Liable for Damage Caused by "Wrongful Acceleration" of Loans' (2006) 27 *Company Lawyer* 123.

[162] R Youard, 'Default in International Loan Agreements I and II' [1986] JBL 276, 278.

[163] *Rahman v HSBC Bank* [2012] EWHC 11 (Ch), [278]–[279].

Suppose property A is security for a 15 year term and a 5 year term. At the end of the 5 year term no repayment is made and Property A is sold realising more than enough to satisfy the sums due under the 5 year term. In the absence of a cross default clause there is, to put it no higher, doubt as to whether the mortgagee can retain the surplus as security for sums due in respect of the 15 year term. No such problems arise if there is a cross default clause…[I]t is not unfair that a cost centre should be able to maintain its 15 year interest only [residential investment property] loans for the full 15 years only so long as it honours the terms of its 5 year interest only [commercial investment property] loans and repays them when they fall due.

Lenders tend to favour cross-default clauses that are drafted so as to come into effect when the relevant other indebtedness has become due or '*is capable of being declared due.*' The italicized words relate back to the fact that default does not, in normal practice, cause automatic acceleration of a loan. When a borrowing company defaults on one loan, instead of demanding repayment, the lender may seek to impose harsher terms on the borrower, with the threat of acceleration hovering in the background should the borrower fail to comply. If the borrower's other lenders have accepted cross-default clauses that only come into effect when borrowings become 'due,' those lenders are in a weaker negotiating position (unless there have been separate defaults apart from the cross-default clause) because they cannot threaten to call in their loans under the cross-default clause as so drafted, and this may defeat the purpose of the clause which was to ensure equality among creditors.

In large-scale commercial lending where both parties have equal bargaining power, the enforcement of cross-default clauses is unlikely to be unfair within section 140A of the Consumer Credit Act 1974.[164]

Debt Finance and Corporate Governance[165]

Although a single theory to explain corporate capital structures has not yet emerged, debt finance features prominently in the two models that dominate the literature: the trade-off theory[166] and the pecking order theory.[167] The dependence of the corporate sector on debt means that providers of debt finance are in a position to play a significant role in corporate governance by imposing constraints on managers.[168] They have the power to supply or to withhold finance and to stipulate the terms on which it is to be made available. In particular, covenants allow debt financiers a say in the way that borrowing companies conduct their affairs and events of default clauses provide them with the leverage to renegotiate for yet more stringent control of borrowers in financial difficulties. Should a company become unable to pay its debts, providers of debt finance move into a central corporate governance position because, in effect, they replace the shareholders as residual claimants on the firm's assets.[169] Corporate managers can send out positive signals by voluntarily committing to the discipline

---

[164] *Rahman v HSBC Bank* [2012] EWHC 11 (Ch).

[165] See generally GG Triantis and RJ Daniels, 'The Role of Debt in Interactive Corporate Governance' (1995) 83 *California Law Review* 1073; BR Cheffins, *Company Law Theory, Structure and Operation* (Oxford: OUP, 1997) 75–9.

[166] That firms identify optimal leverage by weighing the costs (bankruptcy costs) and benefits (tax treatment) of additional debt: EF Fama and KR French, 'Financing Decisions: Who Issues Stock?' (2005) 76 *Journal of Financial Economics* 549, 549–50.

[167] That asymmetric information problems and transaction costs involved in the issuance of equity securities lead firms to finance new investments first with retained earnings, then with debt, and only finally with outside equity: SC Myers, 'The Capital Structure Puzzle' (1984) 39 *Journal of Finance* 575.

[168] GG Triantis and RJ Daniels, 'The Role of Debt in Interactive Corporate Governance' (1995) 83 *California Law Review* 1073.

[169] J Armour, B Cheffins, and DA Skeel, 'Corporate Ownership Structure and the Evolution of Bankruptcy Law: Lessons from the United Kingdom' (2002) 55 *Vanderbilt Law Review* 1699, 1722; DG Baird, 'The Uneasy Case for Corporate Reorganizations' (1986) 15 *Journal of Legal Studies* 127, 129–31.

of legally enforceable debt servicing obligations and monitoring covenants.[170] Debt can thus mitigate the effects of agency and information problems within companies, although its constraining effect depends on the type of debt[171] and the intensity of monitoring activity by lenders.[172]

The contractual framework for monitoring by banks emerges from a process of contractual negotiation and is therefore liable to be affected by a range of variables, including the maturity and track record of the borrower, the size and duration of the financing, whether the financing is to be secured or unsecured, and broader competitive pressures. For instance, a small or recently formed company that has limited access to external sources of debt finance apart from banks may have no commercial alternative but to accept short-term loans or loans which are subject to detailed restrictive covenants.[173] Thus it has been said that: 'Bank power tends to be inversely related to borrower size, because the latter is closely correlated with credit rating and available borrowing options.'[174] Bond market financing, which in practice is only accessible to larger companies, tends to be more standardized and covenants, which provide the basis for monitoring, tend to be quite limited in scope.

The actual process of monitoring has been described as 'the ongoing acquisition, processing, interpretation, and verification of information about the firm.'[175] The relationship between borrowing companies and their banks tends to be closer than that which exists between issuers and holders of their debt securities, giving banks informational advantages that should make them more efficient monitors.[176] The superiority of banks as monitors is further reinforced by the fact that even though bond issues often have trustees to represent the collective interests of the bondholders, standard documentation limits trustees' monitoring obligations by permitting them to assume that issuers are complying with their obligations and that there is no event of default, unless they have actual knowledge or express notice to the contrary.[177] Until a trustee has such knowledge or notice, normal monitoring practice involves simply receiving annual directors' certificates as to compliance with covenants and other bond issue terms, and reviewing issuers' annual accounts and other documents sent out to shareholders or creditors.[178] Even where an event of default has occurred, a trustee is usually permitted to refrain from taking action unless it has been indemnified by or on behalf of the holders against any resultant costs and liabilities.[179]

---

[170] H Leland and D Pyle, 'Informational Asymmetries, Financial Structure, and Financial Intermediation' (1977) 32 *Journal of Finance* 371; SA Ross, 'The Determination of Financial Structure: the Incentive-signaling Approach' (1977) 8 *Bell Journal of Economics* 23.

[171] O Hart, *Firms, Contracts and Financial Structures* (Oxford: Clarendon Press, 1995) ch 5.

[172] CR Harvey, KV Linsc, and AH Roper 'The Effect of Capital Structure when Expected Agency Costs are Extreme' (2004) 74 *Journal of Financial Economics* 3.

[173] M Middleton, M Cowling, J Samuels, and R Sugden, 'Small Firms and Clearing Banks' in N Dimsdale and M Prevezer (eds), *Capital Markets and Corporate Governance* (Oxford: Clarendon Press, 1994) 141.

[174] ES Herman, *Corporate Control, Corporate Power* (Cambridge: CUP, 1981) 122. See also D Lomax, 'The Role of the Banks' in N Dimsdale and M Prevezer (eds), *Capital Markets and Corporate Governance* (Oxford: Clarendon Press, 1994) 161, 173–7 outlining differences in a clearing bank's relationships with small and larger businesses.

[175] GG Triantis and RJ Daniels, 'The Role of Debt in Interactive Corporate Governance' (1995) 83 *California Law Review* 1073, 1079.

[176] GG Triantis and RJ Daniels, 'The Role of Debt in Interactive Corporate Governance' (1995) 83 *California Law Review* 1073, 1088–90.

[177] Financial Markets Law Committee, 'Trustee Exemption Clauses,' Issue No 62 (May 2004) ch 3, available at <http://www.fmlc.org/Documents/trustee_exemption_clauses_issue62.pdf> (accessed August 2013). This report fed into a project by the Law Commission (the law reform body for England and Wales), which consulted on trustee exemption clauses in 2003 and then reported on the matter in 2006: *Trustee Exemption Clauses* (Law Com Rep No 301, 2006). In its Report the Law Commission stepped back from recommending statutory intervention.

[178] Financial Markets Law Committee, 'Trustee Exemption Clauses,' Issue No 62 (May 2004), available at <http://www.fmlc.org/Documents/trustee_exemption_clauses_issue62.pdf> (accessed August 2013).

[179] Financial Markets Law Committee, 'Trustee Exemption Clauses,' Issue No 62 (May 2004), available at <http://www.fmlc.org/Documents/trustee_exemption_clauses_issue62.pdf> (accessed August 2013).

Naturally, the level of bank monitoring is driven by each bank's self-interest and is not an exercise in altruism, but its disciplining effect can yield benefits for other creditors, shareholders, and wider groups of stakeholders. This suggests that the policy framework should, broadly speaking, encourage diligent bank monitoring because of its positive externalities. On the other hand, there is the obvious danger that, as Triantis and Daniels put it, 'the bank also has incentives to use its considerable monitoring advantage and its leverage over firm decisions to enhance its position at the expense of other stakeholders.'[180] This indicates the need, in policy terms, for boundaries so as to limit the scope for banks to exploit their informational advantages. English law uses a range of mechanisms to rein in the potential for inter-stakeholder conflicts of this sort.[181] In particular, where monitoring shades into actually telling companies how to run their affairs, a bank runs the risk of being held liable as a de facto or a shadow director.[182] A de facto director is someone who fits within the definition of a director in the sense of occupying the position of a director, even though not formally appointed as such, and a person in that position is subject to the range of duties that apply to directors who have been formally appointed.[183] The concept of de facto director is confined to those who willingly or voluntarily take upon themselves the role, either by usurping the office or by continuing to act once their formal role has ceased. It does not extend to a person who does not willingly adopt the role of director.[184] '[A] single decisive test could not be formulated to determine whether a person was a de facto director and that all relevant circumstances must be taken into account.'[185] But in order to establish that a person is a de facto director of a company, it is necessary to plead and prove that he

---

[180] GG Triantis and RJ Daniels, 'The Role of Debt in Interactive Corporate Governance' (1995) 83 *California Law Review* 1073, 1091.

[181] As well as the potential directorial liability discussed in the text, other important constraints are provided by provisions of the insolvency legislation which allow for the invalidation of certain transactions in the period immediately before insolvency, which could be infringed, for instance, where, because of close relationships between a company and selected lenders, certain debts are repaid ahead of others or unsecured debts are converted into secured debts (Insolvency Act 1986, ss 238–9).

[182] The two categories are not necessarily mutually exclusive: *Secretary of State for Trade and Industry v Aviss* [2007] BCC 288, [88]–[89] commenting on *Re Hydrodam Ltd* [1994] 2 BCLC 180; *Revenue and Customs Commissioners v Holland* [2010] UKSC 51, [2010] 1 WLR 2793, [110]. The functions of a shadow director are different from those of a de facto director but the point being made in *Aviss* is that a person can be both simultaneously. It is now clear that (a) the same sort of evidential indicia are likely to be relevant to establishing both shadow and de facto directorship and (b) a person may act as both, the one in fact shading into the other: *Secretary of State for Business Innovation and Skills v Chohan* [2013] EWHC 680 (Ch), [46]. An example might be a controlling shareholder who attended board meetings with the de jure directors, but told them what to do on all subjects: *McKillen v Misland (Cyprus) Investments* [2012] EWHC 521 (Ch), [32]. While the concepts of de facto director and shadow director are not fundamentally different and the distinction has been eroded, it does not mean that the distinction has disappeared. For the most part, it remains. The fact that persons in both categories will have a real influence in the corporate governance of the company does not mean that it need only be shown that a person has such influence for him or her to be both a de facto and a shadow director: *McKillen v Misland (Cyprus) Investments* [2012] EWHC 521 (Ch), [34]. It may also be necessary to distinguish between the two categories in determining the extent of their culpability: *Secretary of State for Business Innovation and Skills v Chohan* [2013] EWHC 680 (Ch), [47]. But it has been said that '[t]he distinction between shadow and de facto directors [has become] impossible to maintain as in both instances their real influence in the affairs of a company may be a measure of the actual role they have in it': *Grimaldi v Chameleon Mining NL (No 2)* [2012] FCAFC 6, [61]. Note that the identification of the hat which the individual was wearing in his or her dealings with and for the company is crucial in determining whether he or she is a de facto or shadow director. Hat identification is an important legal qualification to the general principle that one must look at what the putative director actually does rather than how he or she is described when deciding whether to impose fiduciary duties upon him or her: *Smithton v Naggar* [2013] EWHC 1961 (Ch), [61] and [67]. See also D Noonan and S Watson, 'The Nature of Shadow Directorship: Ad Hoc Statutory Liability or Core Company Law Principle' [2006] JBL 763.

[183] *Ultraframe (UK) Ltd v Fielding* [2005] EWHC 1638, [1254].

[184] *Delegat v Norman* [2012] NZHC 2358, [31].

[185] *McKillen v Misland (Cyprus) Investments* [2012] EWHC 521 (Ch), [26]. In so far as earlier cases suggested that the de facto director needed to have held himself out to third parties as being a director of the company, or to have been held out by the management of the company as being a director, that is now relegated to being one of a number of factors to consider rather than an essential element in the test: *Smithton v Naggar* [2013] EWHC 1961 (Ch), [53].

undertook functions in relation to the company that could properly be discharged only by a director. There needs to be clear evidence that the person was either the sole person directing the affairs of the company or if there were others who were true directors that he was acting on an equal footing with the others in directing the affairs of the company. If it is unclear whether the acts of the person are referable to an assumed directorship or to some other capacity, such as shareholder or consultant, the person must be entitled to the benefit of the doubt.[186] Generally, the risk of monitoring activity escalating to a level that would put a bank into the category of de facto director is not significant. Where (as sometimes happens) a bank has the right to appoint a director to the board of a borrowing company, the individual appointed would, of course, be subject to directors' duties but the bank, as nominator, would not be vicariously responsible for that individual's actions nor, in the absence of fraud or bad faith, would it have direct personal responsibility to ensure that the duties are properly discharged.[187]

A shadow director means a person in accordance with whose directions or instructions the directors of the company are accustomed to act.[188] A shadow director is someone who has real influence in the affairs of a company.[189] It is not necessary that such influence should be exercised over the whole field of its corporate activities[190] but there must be proof of a pattern of consistent conduct in which the actual directors (or at least the majority of them) act on the instructions or directions of the alleged shadow director.[191] However, there may be circumstances in which the evidence establishes that a person who has given instructions and/or advice to the directors upon which they have acted was doing so in an appropriate capacity which does not carry with it the suggestion that they were, in giving such instructions or advice, acting as a shadow director. If the acts alleged to demonstrate that a person was acting as a shadow director are referable to another role or interest, that person is unlikely to be a shadow director. For instance, if someone in the capacity of a company secretary had given directions or instructions as to the administrative requirements of the company, for example, in relation to matters such as filing annual returns, he could not be regarded as acting as a shadow director if the board of directors complied with the instructions and/or advice in that regard.[192]

Certain statutory duties apply to shadow directors,[193] including the possibility of being held personally liable to make good losses incurred through wrongful trading.[194] A shadow

---

[186] *Delegat v Norman* [2012] NZHC 2358, [32]; *Secretary of State for Business Innovation and Skills v Chohan* [2013] EWHC 680 (Ch), [38]–[41].

[187] *Kuwait Asia Bank EC v National Mutual Life Nominees Ltd* [1991] 1 AC 187, PC.

[188] Companies Act 2006, s 251, Insolvency Act 1986, s 251, and Company Directors Disqualification Act 1986, s 22. *Secretary of State for Trade and Industry v Deverell* [2001] Ch 340, CA; *Secretary of State for Trade and Industry v Becker* [2003] 1 BCLC 555; *Vivendi v Richards* [2013] EWHC 3006 (Ch) at [133] ('The definition of "shadow director" can be traced back to the Companies (Particulars as to Directors) Act 1917. At that time, the Companies Act 1908 required details of directors to be given in a company's annual returns…and register of directors…; an overseas company with a United Kingdom presence had, moreover, to file details of its directors at Companies House…Section 3 of the 1917 Act extended the definition of "director" applicable in relation to these provisions so that it included "any person in accordance with whose directions or instructions the directors of a company are accustomed to act." The same form of words was used in the Companies Act 1928 to impose criminal liability on a person who would now be termed a "shadow director" if he failed to cooperate with a liquidator, and the concept was also used in the Companies Acts of 1948 and 1967. It was not, however, until 1980 that the expression "shadow director" first featured in the legislation. Section 63 of the Companies Act 1980 provided for a "shadow director" to be treated as a director for the purposes of Part IV of the Act (which dealt with duties of directors and conflicts of interest).').

[189] *Secretary of State for Trade and Industry v Deverell* [2001] Ch 340, CA, [35] *per* Morritt LJ.

[190] *Secretary of State for Trade and Industry v Deverell* [2001] Ch 340, CA.

[191] *Secretary of State for Trade and Industry v Becker* [2003] 1 BCLC 555.

[192] *Pyne v Van Deventer* [2012] IEHC 263.   [193] Companies Act 2006, s 170(5).

[194] Under Insolvency Act 1986, s 214.

director may also owe some fiduciary duties.[195] A number of cases have considered the possibility that lenders might fall to be regarded as shadow directors[196] but the position that has emerged is that a bank must step outside the ordinary bank–customer relationship to be at risk of being held to be a shadow director.[197] Merely having a nominee director on a board does not make the appointor a shadow director.[198] It is established that a bank is entitled to keep a close eye on what is done with its money, and to impose conditions on its support for the company.[199] This does not mean that the bank is running the company or emasculating the powers of the directors, even if (given their situation) the directors feel that they have little practical choice but to accede to its requests.[200] When a bank follows the usual practice of requiring the borrower to give warranties about its present circumstances and covenants as to the conduct of its affairs and imposes conditions precedent before the funds can be accessed, and thereafter monitors compliance, it is not giving 'directions' or 'instructions' but is simply attaching terms and conditions to the provision and continuation of its financial support which, technically, the company is free to accept or reject. A person or company is not a shadow director merely because that party imposes conditions on his or her commercial dealings with the company with which the directors feel obliged to comply. A lender who is entitled to demand repayment of a loan and appoint a receiver can say, for example, that it will stay its hand only if the borrowing company sells certain assets. The reason that third parties having commercial dealings with a company who are able to insist on certain terms if their support for the company is to continue, and are successful in procuring the company's compliance with those terms over an extended period, are not thereby to be treated as shadow directors, is because to insist on such terms as a commercial dealing between a third party and the company is not ipso facto to give an instruction or express a wish as to how the directors are to exercise their powers. Unless something more intrudes, the directors are free and would be expected to exercise their own judgment as to whether it is in the interests of the company to comply with the terms upon which the third party insists, or to reject those terms. If, in the exercise of their own judgment, they habitually comply with the third party's terms, it does not follow that the third party has given instructions or expressed a wish as to how they should exercise their functions as directors.[201]

Keeping on the right side of the line in the context of corporate rescue situations is especially challenging but also especially important because it is then that the potential for wrongful trading liability looms large as a legal risk.[202] In the UK, a movement away from debt collection to more monitoring and intervention to effect corporate turnaround has been identified.[203] This trend has been fostered by legislative changes designed to promote a

---

[195] *Vivendi v Richards* [2013] EWHC 3006 (Ch), [143] ('a shadow director will typically owe [fiduciary] duties in relation at least to the directions or instructions that he gives to the de jure directors. More particularly,…a shadow director will normally owe the duty of good faith (or loyalty)…when giving such directions or instructions. A shadow director can…reasonably be expected to act in the company's interests rather than his own separate interests when giving such directions and instructions').

[196] *Re a Company No 005009 of 1987* (1988) 4 BCC 424; *Re PTZFM Ltd* [1995] 2 BCLC 354; *Ultraframe (UK) Ltd v Fielding* [2005] EWHC 1638, [1254]; *Krtolica v Westpac Banking Corporation* [2008] NZHC 1.

[197] That the case law would evolve in this direction was predicted by a leading judge, writing extra judicially: Sir Peter Millett, 'Shadow Directorship—A Real or Imagined Threat to the Banks' [1991] *Insolvency Practitioner* 14.

[198] *Lord v Sinai Securities Ltd and ors* [2005] 1 BCLC 295.

[199] *Ultraframe (UK) Ltd v Fielding* [2005] EWHC 1638, [1268]. This was a submission by Counsel accepted 'in broad terms' by Lewison J.

[200] *Ultraframe (UK) Ltd v Fielding* [2005] EWHC 1638, [1268].

[201] *Buzzle Operations v Apple Computer Australia* [2011] NSWCA 109, [242]–[243]; *Pyne v Van Deventer* [2012] IEHC 263.

[202] D Milman, 'Strategies for Regulating Managerial Performance in the "Twilight Zone"—Familiar Dilemmas: New Considerations' [2004] JBL 493, 495–6.

[203] V Finch, 'Doctoring in the Shadows of Insolvency' [2005] JBL 690.

'rescue culture.'[204] Finch reports that the change in the focus of insolvency-related processes has brought a burgeoning group of turnaround specialists onto the scene to assist banks and companies in effecting turnarounds.[205] The development of a stronger rescue culture and of a healthy market for the supply of specialist turnaround services could be taken to indicate that the risk of shadow directorship liability is not excessive and that it may in fact be set at a level that fits reasonably well within a policy framework that aims to provide incentives for bank monitoring and early reaction to emerging problems but, at the same time, to curb opportunities for inter-stakeholder conflicts.[206]

---

[204] V Finch, 'Control and Co-ordination in Corporate Rescue' (2005) 25 *Legal Studies* 374; S Frisby, 'In Search of a Rescue Regime: The Enterprise Act 2002' (2004) 67 MLR 247; V Finch, 'The Recasting of Insolvency Law' (2005) 68 MLR 713.

[205] V Finch, 'Doctoring in the Shadows of Insolvency' [2005] JBL 690, 692.

[206] V Finch, 'Doctoring in the Shadows of Insolvency' [2005] JBL 690, 728–30.

12

Secured Debt

Advantages of Being a Secured Creditor

This chapter is concerned with forms of real security that companies can give to lenders. A lender with a real security has control over the assets which form the security and is entitled to enforce its claims against those assets in the event of the company failing to meet its obligations to service and repay the debt. A lender can also take guarantees in respect of the company's indebtedness from third parties (for example, from its directors or its parent company). Guarantees are sometimes described as personal security[1] but in this chapter the term 'security' denotes a proprietary claim, ie a claim which involves rights in relation to a thing.[2] A guarantee is not a security as so defined because the creditor has only a personal claim against the guarantor.[3]

If a company becomes insolvent, its secured creditors are, generally speaking, in a much stronger position than its unsecured creditors. In insolvency, unsecured debts are governed by the *pari passu* rule,[4] which means that if there are insufficient assets to meet all of the claims, they must abate rateably among themselves. The result of the application of the *pari passu* rule is that the company's pool of assets is distributed to its unsecured creditors in proportion to the size of their respective claims, and each of the creditors must bear a proportionate share of the shortfall. The *pari passu* rule is subject to various qualifications and exceptions.[5] For the purposes of this chapter, the most important qualification is that the rule has no application in relation to secured debts because proprietary rights acquired before insolvency are respected and not subjected to the collective procedures of insolvency law.[6] Avoiding the *pari passu* rule and ensuring priority over unsecured creditors in the event of insolvency are compelling reasons for taking security.[7] This remains so even though insolvency legislation has intervened in certain respects so as to redistribute assets that are subject to a security back to unsecured creditors: such legislation erodes the advantages of being a secured creditor but it does not destroy them completely.[8] Redistributive insolvency legislation creates incentives for lenders to obtain forms of security that do not fall within its scope.[9]

---

[1] cf *Estate of Imorette Palmer v Cornerstone Investments & Finance Company (Jamaica)* [2007] UKPC 49.

[2] EI Sykes and S Walker, *The Law of Securities* 5th edn (Sydney: Law Book Company, 1993) 9.

[3] Unless, of course, the guarantor has given the creditor a mortgage, charge, or other form of security interest.

[4] eg Insolvency Act 1986, s 107.

[5] In particular, the Insolvency Act 1986 creates a category of preferential debts which are to be paid before ordinary unsecured debts (and also before debts secured by a floating charge). See generally F Oditah, 'Assets and the Treatment of Claims in Insolvency' (1992) 108 LQR 459.

[6] *Sowman v David Samuel Trust Ltd* [1978] 1 WLR 22; *Re Potters Oils Ltd* [1986] 1 WLR 201. The importance of property rights in an insolvency context are discussed generally by RM Goode, 'Ownership and Obligations in Transactions' (1987) 103 LQR 433, 434–53.

[7] *Insolvency Law and Practice* (Cmnd 8558, 1982) ch 34 (Report of the Review Committee under the Chairmanship of Sir Kenneth Cork).

[8] J Armour, 'Should We Redistribute in Insolvency?' in J Getzler and J Payne (eds), *Company Charges: Spectrum and Beyond* (Oxford: OUP, 2006) ch 9 discusses the redistributive effects of Insolvency Act 1986, ss 40, 175, 386 (preferential claims which are elevated above those of the holders of a floating charge), and 176A (which requires a prescribed part of the assets subject to a floating charge to be set aside for unsecured creditors).

[9] The story of charges on book debts, which is discussed later in this chapter, can be summed up as an attempt by lenders to create fixed charges so as to fall outside the ambit of redistributive insolvency legislation affecting floating charges.

More options are available to a secured creditor in the event of default by a borrower than are open to unsecured creditors. In a well-drafted loan agreement an unauthorized disposal of assets in breach of a covenant prohibiting or restricting disposals will be an event of default that entitles the lender, whether secured or unsecured, to accelerate the loan and demand repayment. However, if the loan is secured and the assets disposed of were part of the subject matter of the security, the secured creditor may be able, subject to the protections afforded to persons who acquire property in good faith, for value, and without notice of competing interests, to follow the assets into the hands of the person who received them or to claim the proceeds of the disposal. An unsecured creditor does not have these rights.[10] In the event of default, a secured creditor may appoint a receiver to realize the security where the security provides for this or may petition the court for the appointment of a receiver (although such applications are now rare as lenders are normally adequately protected by their contractual powers of appointment). The court will not normally appoint a receiver on the application of an unsecured creditor.[11] Statute has recently intervened to limit the secured creditor's right to appoint a receiver—apart from certain special cases, the holder of a floating charge created on or after 15 September 2003 cannot appoint an *administrative* receiver,[12] ie a receiver or manager of the whole (or substantially the whole) of the company's property,[13] though the floating charge holder remains free to appoint an ordinary receiver. A secured creditor who before September 2003 could have appointed an administrative receiver, can now appoint an administrator[14] but administration, unlike receivership, is a collective insolvency procedure for the benefit of all creditors.[15]

Economic Perspectives on Secured Debt[16]

There is at least the potential for a trade-off between the granting of security and the rates at which a company can borrow.[17] Because security puts its holder in an advantageous position in insolvency, it may enable the company to borrow from a particular lender which would otherwise have been unwilling to sanction the loan or, at least, to borrow at cheaper rates than that lender would otherwise have been willing to offer.[18] Improvements in interest charges may also be secured because of the monitoring costs savings of secured debt: instead of having to monitor the whole of the company's business through covenants, a secured creditor can simply check that the assets which are subject to its security have

---

[10] Apart from covenants or other contractual restrictions, an unsecured creditor has no standing to object to the way in which a borrower deals with its assets: *Re Ehrmann Bros Ltd* [1906] 2 Ch 697, CA.

[11] *Harris v Beauchamp Bros* [1894] 1 QB 802, CA.

[12] *Feetum v Levy* [2005] EWCA Civ 1601, [2006] Ch 585.

[13] Defined by Insolvency Act 1986, s 29.

[14] Insolvency Act 1986, Sch B1, para 14.

[15] Ways in which this change in the law puts the charge holder into a less advantageous position include the following: the administrator has to act in the interests of the creditors as a whole rather than primarily in the interests of the charge holder; satisfying the charge holder's security ranks last in the hierarchy of objectives of an administration; and the new administration regime is more formal and elaborate than a receivership, and consequently slower and more expensive.

[16] JL Westbrook, 'The Control of Wealth in Bankruptcy' (2004) 82 *Texas Law Review* 795, 838–43 reviews the two decades of literature on this topic published in the US law reviews.

[17] However, empirical data does not unambiguously support the conclusion that loan interest margins and security are negatively correlated: SA Davydenko and JR Franks, 'Do Bankruptcy Codes Matter? A Study of Defaults in France, Germany and the UK', ECGI Finance Working Paper No 89 (2005).

[18] In a perfectly competitive market, interest rates would rise with the degree of risk associated with a project. But information imbalances create market imperfections and the theory of credit rationing (J Stiglitz and A Weiss, 'Credit Rationing in Markets with Imperfect Information' (1981) 71 *American Economic Review* 393) suggests that for a given interest rate, debt may not be provided to all borrowers who want it: 'Competition in UK Banking: A Report to the Chancellor of the Exchequer' (Cruickshank Report, 2000) para 5.8.

not been dissipated.[19] However, other unsecured creditors may demand higher interest to compensate them for the risk of being postponed to the secured debt in the event of the borrowing company's insolvency.[20] Likewise, reductions in monitoring costs so far as secured creditors are concerned have to be set against possible increases in unsecured creditors' monitoring costs; as one commentator has explained: 'the existence of security raises the expected cost of default for unsecured creditors by reducing the available asset pool and thus creates incentives for these parties to monitor more extensively.'[21]

Overall, secured debt will only be worthwhile where the additional price that unsecured creditors charge for lending to a company that has given security over its assets does not eclipse the savings that flow from the lower price charged on secured debt.[22] The existence of security can yield positive externalities for unsecured creditors because it prevents the borrowing company from disposing of its existing major assets and embarking on new and more risky ventures[23] and puts in place a focused monitor.[24] The presence of a powerfully secured lender may also facilitate efficient enforcement[25] or restructuring in times of financial distress.[26] In some instances, security may be given in return for an injection of debt finance that enables the company to stay afloat and avoid costly insolvency.[27] Such considerations suggest that the lower monitoring costs of secured creditors may not be entirely cancelled out by the higher monitoring costs incurred by unsecured creditors, with the result that raising part of its debt on a secured basis may have a beneficial overall effect on a company's cost of capital.

The efficiency case for secured debt, though much debated, remains, as Westbrook has said, incomplete and inconclusive.[28] Whilst it is true that in a perfect market, unsecured creditors would, after taking due account of positive externalities, accurately adjust the price of their debt to compensate for the additional risks inherent in lending to a borrower that has granted security over its assets, there are situations, such as involuntary credit or credit provided by unsophisticated lenders that lack the skills to price risk correctly, in which price adjustment

[19] TH Jackson and AT Kronman, 'Secured Financing and Priorities Among Creditors' (1979) 88 *Yale Law Journal* 1143. But where the security is a floating charge this analysis breaks down because the essence of the floating charge is that it allows the debtor to continue to deal with its assets as if they were not subject to a security.

[20] A Schwartz, 'Security Interests and Bankruptcy Priorities: A Review of Current Theories' (1981) 10 *Journal of Legal Studies* 1; A Schwartz, 'The Continuing Puzzle of Secured Debt' (1984) 37 *Vanderbilt Law Review* 1051.

[21] A Schwartz, 'Security Interests and Bankruptcy Priorities: A Review of Current Theories' (1981) 10 *Journal of Legal Studies* 1, 10. For variations on the 'monitoring' explanation of secured debt: S Levmore, 'Monitors and Freeriders in Commercial and Corporate Settings' (1982) 92 *Yale Law Journal* 49; RE Scott, 'A Relational Theory of Secured Financing' (1986) 86 *Columbia Law Review* 901, 925 et seq.

[22] JJ White, 'Efficiency Justifications for Personal Property Security' (1984) *Vanderbilt Law Review* 473; FH Buckley, 'The Bankruptcy Priority Puzzle' (1986) 72 *Virginia Law Review* 1393; H Kripke, 'Law and Economics: Measuring the Economic Efficiency of Commercial Law in a Vacuum of Fact' (1985) 133 *University of Pennsylvania Law Review* 929.

[23] A Schwartz, 'Security Interests and Bankruptcy Priorities: A Review of Current Theories' (1981) 10 *Journal of Legal Studies* 1, 11; see also CW Smith and JB Warner, 'Bankruptcy, Secured Debt, and Optimal Capital Structure: Comment' (1979) 34 *Journal of Finance* 247; CW Smith and JB Warner, 'On Financial Contracting: An Analysis of Bond Covenants' (1979) 7 *Journal of Financial Economics* 117, 127 where the authors note advantages of secured debt but also point out that secured debt involves opportunity costs by restricting the firm from potentially profitable dispositions of assets which are subject to the security.

[24] TH Jackson and AT Kronman, 'Secured Financing and Priorities Among Creditors' (1979) 88 *Yale Law Journal* 1143, 1149–57.

[25] RE Scott, 'The Truth About Secured Lending' (1997) 82 *Cornell Law Review* 1436.

[26] J Armour, 'Should We Redistribute in Insolvency?' in J Getzler and J Payne (eds), *Company Charges: Spectrum and Beyond* (Oxford: OUP, 2006) ch 9.

[27] F Oditah, *Legal Aspects of Receivables Financing* (London: Sweet & Maxwell, 1991) 14–18 (this provides a valuable discussion of the various economic theories used by commentators to explain secured debt); F Oditah, 'The Treatment of Claims in Insolvency' (1992) 108 LQR 459.

[28] JL Westbrook, 'The Control of Wealth in Bankruptcy' (2004) 82 *Texas Law Review* 795, 842. L LoPucki, 'The Unsecured Creditor's Bargain' (1994) 80 *Virginia Law Review* 1887; LA Bebchuk and JM Fried, 'The Uneasy Case for the Priority of Secured Claims in Bankruptcy' (1996) 105 *Yale Law Journal* 857.

may not occur. This suggests that security devices could be socially harmful because they may result in uncompensated risk falling on those creditors that are least well informed, least able to adjust loan terms, least protected in the insolvencies of their debtor companies, and least likely to be capable of absorbing financial shocks.[29] Empirical data on this issue is not conclusive but it has been argued that there is room for scepticism about whether the harmful effects of security outweigh its benefits.[30] Claims have been made for a growing international consensus that secured credit is a general social and economic good.[31]

Security has been said to be a signal of a company's creditworthiness[32] but the effectiveness of security as a signaller does not go unquestioned because there is some evidence that companies give security only when they are unable to borrow on an unsecured basis, so that whatever signal is sent out may be more negative than positive.[33] It is consistent with intuitive expectations for security to be more prevalent in relation to smaller, riskier companies where the likelihood of default is higher[34] and this is supported by empirical research showing that the principal users of secured debt are small and medium-sized firms.[35] There is evidence of a relative aversion for secured borrowing among smaller quoted companies (SQCs) but banks do tend to require security for companies of this size, especially on longer-term loans.[36] Very profitable SQCs are more able to borrow on an unsecured basis.[37] Most of large companies' debt is unsecured.[38] Special purpose vehicles (SPVs) for particular ventures often have complex financing structures that include various tiers of security.[39]

Policy—Dominance of Freedom of Contract

English law allows companies to create a wide range of security interests, including security that extends to all of their assets. The prevailing policy stance is exemplified by a comment by Lord Hoffmann in a case that raised questions about the legal validity of a particular type of security arrangement: 'In a case in which there is no threat to the consistency of the law or objection of public policy, I think that the courts should be very slow to declare a practice of the commercial community to be conceptually impossible.'[40]

---

[29] V Finch, 'Security, Insolvency and Risk: Who Pays the Price' (1999) 62 MLR 633, 668. L LoPucki, 'The Unsecured Creditor's Bargain' (1994) 80 *Virginia Law Review* 1887; LA Bebchuk and JM Fried, 'The Uneasy Case for the Priority of Secured Claims in Bankruptcy' (1996) 105 *Yale Law Journal* 857.

[30] J Armour, 'Should We Redistribute in Insolvency?' in J Getzler and J Payne (eds), *Company Charges: Spectrum and Beyond* (Oxford: OUP, 2006) ch 9; R Mokal, 'The Search for Someone to Save: A Defensive Case for the Priority of Secured Credit' (2002) 22 OJLS 687.

[31] G McCormack, 'The Priority of Secured Credit: An Anglo-American Perspective' [2003] JBL 389, 404–7 provides a review.

[32] A Schwartz, 'Security Interests and Bankruptcy Priorities: A Review of Current Theories' (1981) 10 *Journal of Legal Studies* 1, 14–21.

[33] See M Bridge, 'The *Quistclose* Trust in a World of Secured Transactions' (1992) 12 OJLS 333, 336–9.

[34] J Armour, 'Should We Redistribute in Insolvency?' in J Getzler and J Payne (eds), *Company Charges: Spectrum and Beyond* (Oxford: OUP, 2006) ch 9.

[35] J Armour, 'Should We Redistribute in Insolvency?' in J Getzler and J Payne (eds), *Company Charges: Spectrum and Beyond* (Oxford: OUP, 2006) ch 9 reviews the data.

[36] P Brierley and M Young, 'The Financing of Smaller Quoted Companies: a Survey' (Summer 2004) *Bank of England Quarterly Bulletin* 160.

[37] P Brierley and M Young, 'The Financing of Smaller Quoted Companies: a Survey' (Summer 2004) *Bank of England Quarterly Bulletin* 160.

[38] MA Lasfer, *Debt Structure, Agency Costs and Firm's Size: An Empirical Investigation*, working paper (2000); G McCormack, 'The Priority of Secured Credit: An Anglo-American Perspective' [2003] JBL 389, 404.

[39] eg *Belmont Park Investments v BNY Corporate Trustee Services* [2011] UKSC 38, [2012] 1 AC 383. PR Wood, 'Is the English Law of Security Interests Sleepwalking?' (2005) 20(6) *Butterworths Journal of International Banking and Financial Law* 211.

[40] *Re Bank of Credit and Commerce International SA (No 8)* [1998] AC 214, HL, 228. See also *Re Lehman Brothers International (Europe)* [2012] EWHC 2997 (Ch), [34].

Through its flexibility and its ability to absorb and give effect to innovative structures, English law has played an important role in the development of business by providing security mechanisms that meet the needs of both the consumers and providers of capital.[41] Practitioners, rather than the legislature, have driven the law forward, with it falling to the courts to determine the legal effects of their efforts in instances of uncertainty. In areas of doubt, the courts have certainly not simply provided a rubber-stamp endorsement for whatever new structures and schemes emerge from the ingenious minds of corporate finance practitioners. Freedom of contract is bounded by what is legally possible[42] and where those limits have been exceeded the courts do not shy away from making a decision merely because it will disappoint practitioners and disrupt existing commercial arrangements.[43] Yet, taking a long-term view, it is fair to say that over the centuries the English courts have generally been supportive of transactional lawyers' efforts to mould and develop the law so as to provide cost-effective financing solutions for the corporate sector.[44] Within the limits of what is legally possible, the parties' freedom of contract is not constrained by additional considerations of public policy.[45]

This stance can prompt fairness-related concerns.[46] By readily accommodating the preferences of creditors for security, the law permits situations in which holders of security can step in and sweep off everything, leaving nothing for unsecured creditors including, in particular, a company's employees whose wages have not been paid.[47] Such concerns have attracted the attention of the legislature but the response thus far has not been to limit freedom of contract in the creation of security.[48] Instead, the legislature has intervened by means of mandatory disclosure requirements in the companies legislation, whereby most forms of security must be registered in order to protect their legal effectiveness,[49] and of provisions in the insolvency legislation that have redistributive effects in favour of unsecured creditors of an insolvent borrower. These include provision for security interests created in the twilight period leading up to a company's insolvency to be invalidated;[50] stipulation for certain employee claims to

---

[41] *Buchler v Talbot* [2004] 2 AC 298, HL, [2] *per* Lord Nicholls.

[42] F Oditah, 'Fixed Charges and Recycling of Proceeds of Receivables' (2004) 120 LQR 533, 537–8.

[43] *Re Spectrum Plus Ltd* [2005] 2 AC 680, HL (refusal by the House of Lords to overrule earlier inconsistent authority with prospective effect only so as not to disrupt existing security arrangements); *Smith (Administrator of Cosslett (Contractors) Ltd) v Bridgend County Borough Council* [2002] 1 AC 336, HL. (The fact that a standard form document had been used for many years without anyone thinking that it created a floating charge was not a reason for holding that this was not its legal effect; Lord Hoffmann said (at [42]): 'The parties cannot therefore be supposed to have intended to create such a charge. But the intentions of the parties, as expressed in the ICE form of contract, are relevant only to establish their mutual rights and obligations. Whether such rights and obligations are characterised as a floating charge is a question of law... The answer to this question may come as a surprise to the parties but that is no reason for adopting a different characterisation.')

[44] R Nolan, 'Property in a Fund' (2004) 120 LQR 108.

[45] *Re ASRS Establishment Ltd (in administrative receivership and liquidation)* [2000] 2 BCLC 631, CA, 642.

[46] V Finch, 'Security, Insolvency and Risk: Who Pays the Price' (199) 62 MLR 633, 660–7.

[47] *Re Spectrum Plus Ltd* [2005] 2 AC 680, HL, [97] *per* Lord Scott. In *Salomon v A Salomon and Co Ltd* [1897] 2 AC 22, HL, 53 Lord Macnaghten described the sweeping effect of the floating charge as a 'great scandal.'

[48] In particular, calls for the outright abolition of the floating charge have generally not found favour: see the discussion in the *Insolvency Law and Practice* (Cmnd 8558, 1982) ch 36 (Report of the Review Committee under the Chairmanship of Sir Kenneth Cork) and AL Diamond, *A Review of Security Interests in Property* (1989) ch 16. Recent discussion on reforming the law of credit and security is surveyed at the end of this chapter.

[49] Companies Act 2006, Pt 25. In *Agnew v The Commissioner of Inland Revenue* [2001] 2 AC 710, PC, [10] Lord Millett described the benefits of registration so far as the ordinary trade creditors were concerned as 'more theoretical than real.'

[50] Insolvency Act 1986, s 238 (avoidance of transactions at an undervalue), s 239 (avoidance of voidable preferences) and s 245 (invalidity of certain floating charges) are the key sections. These sections permit a retrospective review of security for a maximum period of two years prior to the commencement of liquidation or administration. If certain conditions are satisfied, the court can order the invalidation of a security on the grounds that it is a transaction at an undervalue (eg *Hill v Spread Trustee (Re Nurkowski)* [2006] EWCA Civ 542, [2007] 1 WLR 2404; *Official Receiver for Northern Ireland v Stranaghan* [2010] NICh 8, [2010] BPIR 928) or a voidable preference. If certain conditions are satisfied, a floating charge created in the twilight period is automatically invalid under s 245.

have a preferential status over debts secured by particular types of security;[51] and provision for a prescribed part of secured assets to be set aside for unsecured creditors.[52]

Consensual Security Interests

The scope of the term 'security interest' is a matter of some uncertainty but in *Bristol Airport plc v Powdrill*[53] counsel acting for one of the parties described real security in the following terms: 'Security is created where a person ('the creditor') to whom an obligation is owed by another ('the debtor') by statute or contract, in addition to the personal promise of the debtor to discharge the obligation, obtains rights exercisable against some property in which the debtor has an interest in order to enforce the discharge of the debtor's obligation to the creditor.' Browne-Wilkinson V-C declined to hold that this was a comprehensive definition of security but confirmed that the description was certainly no wider than the ordinary meaning of the word. One way in which it may be too restrictive is that it fails to acknowledge that a third party may grant rights over its property by way of guarantee to secure the loan to the debtor.[54] The description does highlight the essence of security, namely, that it gives the creditor proprietary and not merely personal rights in respect of a debt.

The proprietary nature of security was emphasized by Lord Jauncey in *Armour v Thyssen Edelstahlwerke AG*:[55]

> A right in security is a right over property given by a debtor to a creditor whereby the latter in the event of the debtor's failure acquires priority over the property against the general body of creditors of the debtor. It is of the essence of a right in security that the debtor possesses in relation to the property a right which he can transfer to the creditor, which right must be retransferred to him upon payment of the debt.

The focus of the discussion in this chapter is security interests created by agreement of the parties. Security interests can also arise by operation of law, an example being the vendor's lien on property sold which is to secure payment of the purchase price but these types of security are not considered further in this chapter.[56]

Grant and reservation—fundamental legal distinctions

An element of these descriptions of security that merits closer examination is the emphasis on the creditor *obtaining* rights and the debtor *granting* rights. An important distinction is conventionally[57] drawn in English law between being granted an interest to secure an

---

[51] Insolvency Act 1986, ss 40, 175, 386, and Sch 6.

[52] Insolvency Act 1986, s 176A; Insolvency Act (Prescribed Part) Order 2003, SI 2003/2097. See J Armour, 'Should We Redistribute in Insolvency?' in J Getzler and J Payne (eds), *Company Charges: Spectrum and Beyond* (Oxford: OUP, 2006) ch 9; G McCormack, 'The Priority of Secured Credit: An Anglo-American Perspective' [2003] JBL 389, 416–9.

[53] [1990] Ch 744, CA, 760.

[54] A guarantor can charge its property without giving a personal undertaking to pay: *Re Conley* [1938] 2 All ER 127 CA; *Re Bank of Credit and Commerce International SA (No 8)* [1998] AC 214, HL; *Re Lehman Brothers International (Europe)* [2012] EWHC 2997 (Ch), [42].

[55] [1990] 3 All ER 481, HL, 486. It has been held that '[a]ll that is necessary is that the chargee has a specifically enforceable right to have the relevant property appropriated to the payment or discharge of the relevant debt or other obligation. It is that right of specific enforcement which transforms what might have otherwise been a purely personal right into a species of proprietary interest in the charged property': *Re Lehman Brothers International (Europe)* [2012] EWHC 2997 (Ch), [43].

[56] See S Worthington, *Proprietary Interests in Commercial Transactions* (Clarendon Press, 1996) Pt II.

[57] See L Gullifer (ed), *Goode on Legal Problems of Credit and Security* 4th edn (London: Sweet & Maxwell, 2008) paras 1-28–1-32; WJ Gough, *Company Charges* 2nd edn (London: Butterworths, 1996) 3–4; and EI Sykes and

obligation and reserving an interest for that purpose.[58] If, for example, a supplier sells goods to a customer on credit and title to those goods passes, the seller, if it wants to be secured in respect of the credit which it has advanced, must take an interest in the purchaser's, or some other person's, property. An alternative course for the seller would have been to reserve title to the goods until payment had been effected. An effective retention of title clause[59] has the same economic effect as taking a security but it falls into a different legal category for the purpose of English law and, in particular, it does not require registration under the company charges provisions of the Companies Act 2006.[60] Furthermore, although this will depend on the precise wording of the provision in question, it may fall outside a covenant not to create future security that was previously given by the company. The fact that by fitting the arrangement into one legal category rather than another, even though the economic effect is the same in either case, is a feature of English law which is open to criticism, in that form is allowed to prevail over substance.[61] Transactions which are really very similar in nature are treated in different ways and this compartmentalization leads to complexity. However, counterarguments are that English law's respect for the legal form of transactions is one of the reasons for its popularity as the governing law for international financial transactions and that the benefits of having a flexible system that can be moulded to fit business needs should not be jeopardized.[62]

At intervals, various review bodies have proposed that English law should adopt a more flexible approach and that interests retained by the creditor should be treated as security interests in the same way as interests granted by the debtor.[63] The most recent airings for this idea were in two consultation papers published by the Law Commission in 2002 and 2004.[64] Treating proprietary interests reserved by the creditor in the same way as proprietary security interests granted by the debtor would bring English law more into line with article 9 of the US Uniform Commercial Code, where the term 'security interest' is defined broadly to include any 'interest in personal property or fixtures which secures payment or the performance of an obligation' and it is clear that this encompasses retained interests as well as interests granted by the debtor. However, proposals to this effect are invariably controversial, with opponents raising technical objections as well as policy concerns about the potential adverse impact on English law's attractiveness to commerce. In 2005 the Law Commission withdrew its proposal to include title-retention devices such as finance leases, hire purchase, and conditional sale agreements within a new registration scheme but

---

S Walker, *The Law of Securities* 5th edn (Sydney: Law Book Company, 1993) 3, 12–3. Contrast F Oditah, *Legal Aspects of Receivables Financing* (London: Sweet & Maxwell, 1991) 4–11 where it is argued that consensual security need not always lie in grant and that reservation can give rise to a security interest in law.

[58] A distinction clearly established by the House of Lords in *McEntire v Crossley Brothers Ltd* [1895] AC 457, HL.

[59] There is a considerable amount of case law on when such clauses will be effective, including *Aluminium Industrie Vaassen BV v Romalpa Aluminium Ltd* [1976] 1 WLR 676, CA; *Re Peachdart Ltd* [1984] Ch 131; *Hendy Lennox Ltd v Grahame Puttick Ltd* [1984] 1 WLR 485; *Clough Mill Ltd v Martin* [1985] 1 WLR 111, CA; *Armour v Thyssen Edelstahlwerke AG* [1990] 3 All ER 481, HL; *Re CKE Engineering* [2007] BCC 975; *Sandhu (t/a Isher Fashions UK) v Jet Star Retail Ltd (t/a Mark One)* [2011] EWCA Civ 459. Generally, on retention of title agreements, see G McCormack, *Reservation of Title* 2nd edn (London: Sweet & Maxwell, 1995); S Wheeler, *Reservation of Title Claims: Impact and Implications* (Clarendon Press, 1991).

[60] *Clough Mill Ltd v Martin* [1985] 1 WLR 111, CA.

[61] RM Goode, 'The Modernisation of Personal Property Security Law' (1984) 100 LQR 234, 237–8; M Bridge, 'Form, Substance and Innovation in Personal Property Security Law' [1992] JBL 1.

[62] R Calnan, 'The Reform of Company Security Interests' (2005) 20(1) *Butterworths Journal of International Banking and Financial Law* 25.

[63] *Report of the Committee on Consumer Credit* (Cmnd 4596, 1971) paras 5.2.8–5.2.15; AL Diamond, *A Review of Security Interests in Property*, paras 3.4–3.10.

[64] Law Commission, *Registration of Security Interests: Company Charges and Property other than Land* (Law Com CP No 164, 2002); Law Commission, *Company Security Interests, A Consultative Report*, (Law Com CP No 176, 2004).

suggested that it would reconsider the issue at a later date.[65] There is scant indication that proposals for radical change will attract a consensus among interested groups or political support in the short to medium term.

There are two principles that limit the rule of English law that courts must respect the distinction between law and economics and give effect to the legal form of a transaction, notwithstanding that in economic terms it is the functional equivalent of another type of transaction that would attract a different legal treatment.[66] The first is the doctrine of 'shams'. Acts or documents are regarded as shams where the parties intend by means of those acts or documents to give to third parties or to the court the appearance of creating between the parties legal rights and obligations different from the actual legal rights and obligations (if any) which the parties intend to create.[67] An arrangement will not take legal effect in accordance with its appearance if, in fact, that appearance is a sham. The court will disregard the deceptive language by which the parties have attempted to conceal the true nature of the transaction into which they have entered and attempt by extrinsic evidence to discover what the real transaction was.[68] The doctrine of sham is not lightly invoked, however. A sham transaction has been said to be one in which there is a degree of dishonesty on the part of the parties, and the courts are generally slow to find dishonesty.[69] There is a very strong presumption that parties intend to be bound by the provisions of agreements into which they enter and intend the agreements they enter into to take effect.[70] An arrangement is not a sham merely because it is artificial or uncommercial.[71]

The second basis for disregarding the apparent form of a transaction is what may be described as the 'mislabelling' principle. Freedom of contract means that, generally speaking, contracting parties can grant each other whatever rights and obligations they like but the categorization of the transaction created by the chosen bundle of rights and obligations is a matter of law.[72] Whatever label the parties have put on their agreement is not conclusive and the court will recategorize it if its terms are inconsistent with the label that has been attached.[73]

Security interests are defeasible interests

An uncontroversial feature of a security interest is that it confers an interest in property that is defeasible or destructible on payment of the debt or performance of the obligation which was

[65] Law Commission, *Company Security Interests* (Law Com Rep No 296, 2005) para 1.29.

[66] *Bank of Tokyo Ltd v Karoon* [1986] 3 All ER 468, CA, 486 *per* Goff LJ.

[67] *Snook v London & West Riding Investments Ltd* [1967] 2 QB 786, CA, 802 *per* Diplock LJ; *Autoclenz v Belcher* [2011] UKSC 41, [2011] 4 All ER 745.

[68] *Orion Finance Ltd v Crown Financial Management Ltd* [1996] 2 BCLC 78, CA, 84 *per* Millett LJ.

[69] *National Westminster Bank plc v Jones* [2001] 1 BCLC 98, paras 39 and 46. Appeal dismissed [2001] EWCA Civ 1541.

[70] *National Westminster Bank v Jones* [2001] 1 BCLC 98, [59].

[71] *Hitch v Stone (Inspector of Taxes)* [2001] EWCA Civ 63, [2001] STC 214, [67] *per* Arden LJ; *National Westminster Bank v Jones* [2001] 1 BCLC 98, [39].

[72] *Agnew v The Commissioner of Inland Revenue* [2001] 2 AC 710, PC, [32]. This case concerned characterization of a charge as fixed or floating but the reasoning can be regarded as being of more general application and as being relevant to questions whether a transaction creates an absolute interest or a security: H Beale, M Bridge, L Gullifer, and E Lomnicka, *The Law of Security and Title-Based Financing* 2nd edn (Oxford: OUP, 2012) para 4.16. See also *Re F2G Realisations* [2010] EWHC 1772 (Ch), [2011] 1 BCLC 313.

[73] *Re George Inglefield Ltd* [1933] Ch 1, CA; *Re Curtain Dream plc* [1990] BCLC 925; *Welsh Development Agency v Export Finance Co Ltd* [1992] BCC 270, CA; *Orion Finance Ltd v Crown Financial Management Ltd* [1996] BCC 621, CA; *Re Bond Worth Ltd* [1980] Ch 228; *Borden UK Ltd v Scottish Timber Products Ltd* [1981] Ch 25, CA; *Pfeiffer E Weinkellerei-Weineinkauf GmbH & Co v Arbuthnot Factors Ltd* [1988] 1 WLR 150; *Tatung (UK) Ltd v Galex Telesure Ltd* (1989) 5 BCC 325; *A1 Lofts v Revenue and Customs* [2009] EWHC 2694 (Ch), [2010] STC 214.

secured.[74] A borrower that gives security can always obtain the release of its property from the security by repaying the loan.[75] Subject to one exception, equity renders void any attempt to restrict the borrower's right to redeem a security.[76] In equity a mortgagee has a limited title which is available only to secure satisfaction of the debt. The security is enforceable for that purpose and no other. It follows that any act by way of enforcement of the security (at least if it is purely) for a collateral purpose will be ineffective, at any rate as between mortgagor and mortgagee. The reason is that such conduct frustrates the equity of redemption which a court of equity is bound to regard with great jealousy.[77]

The exception is contained in section 739 of the Companies Act 2006, which provides that a condition contained in debentures, or in a deed for securing debentures, is not invalid by reason only that the debentures are thereby made irredeemable or redeemable only on the happening of a contingency (however remote), or on the expiration of a period (however long), any rule of equity to the contrary notwithstanding. The term 'debenture' lacks a precise definition,[78] but it is clear that for the purposes of this section it includes a mortgage on land.[79] In practice, debentures that are described as 'perpetual' or 'irredeemable' may in fact give the company an option to redeem.

A security interest is an interest in the chargor's property to secure a debt

Two distinct issues arise under this heading. The first is that a security interest is inextricably linked with the debt for which it is security. It follows from this that a creditor cannot be said to have a security interest in property at any time when there is no outstanding debt.[80] This situation could arise, for example, where the charge pre-dates the advance of the money or where it relates to a current account which fluctuates between being in credit and being overdrawn.

The second issue relates to the essential feature of a security interest that it gives the creditor an interest in the property of the person providing the security. This means that if the debtor[81] agrees to give security over property that it does not presently own but will acquire in the future, the creditor cannot be viewed as having a security interest in the debtor's property at the time when the agreement is concluded.[82] Adopting language that is familiar to that of US lawyers in the context of article 9 of the Uniform Commercial Code, the Crowther

---

[74] *Re Bond Worth Ltd* [1980] Ch 228, 248; *Brighton & Hove City Council v Audus* [2009] EWHC 340 (Ch), [2010] 1 All ER (Comm) 343, [46]: 'It is inherent in the concept of a mortgage or security interest that the borrower of money should be able to discharge the security interest, that is, to redeem the mortgage by paying the money and in that way performing the obligation performance of which is secured.'

[75] *Re George Inglefield Ltd* [1933] Ch 1, CA, 27 *per* Romer LJ. This is one characteristic which can help to distinguish a mortgage or charge from a sale.

[76] The history of this rule of equity is traced by Viscount Haldane LC in *Kreglinger v New Patagonia Meat and Cold Storage Co Ltd* [1914] AC 25, HL. In this case the House of Lords confirmed that the rule applies to floating charges, thereby dispelling doubts raised by *De Beers Consolidated Mines v British South Africa Co* [1912] AC 52, HL. 'The relevant rules are threefold. The first is that a condition which is repugnant to the contractual right to redeem and the equitable right to redeem is void. The second rule is that a condition which imposes a penalty in respect of the exercise of the equitable right to redeem, following a failure to exercise a contractual right to redeem, is void in equity. The third rule is that a provision which regulates or controls the right to redeem is invalid, if it is unconscionable': *Brighton & Hove City Council v Audus* [2009] EWHC 340 (Ch), [2010] 1 All ER (Comm) 343, [47].

[77] *Cukurova Finance International v Alfa Telecom Turkey* [2013] UKPC 2, [73].

[78] *Fons v Corporal* [2013] EWHC 1801 (Ch).   [79] *Knightsbridge Estates Trust Ltd v Byrne* [1940] AC 613, HL.

[80] 'A security for a non-existent liability is a contradiction in terms': *Serious Organised Crime Agency v Szepietowski* [2010] EWHC 2570 (Ch), [2011] 1 BCLC 458, [45].

[81] As used here, this term is intended to include a third party provider of security by way of guarantee.

[82] There are some exceptions to the rule that a debtor cannot give a valid security over another's property but these exceptions are of limited significance: see L Gullifer (ed), *Goode on Legal Problems of Credit and Security* 4th edn (London: Sweet & Maxwell, 2008) paras 2–7.

Committee, whose report containing a review of credit and security was published as a government command paper in 1971, described situations where there is an agreement for security but no outstanding loan, or where the security is not presently owned by the debtor, as being ones where the security interest has not 'attached' to the debtor's property:[83] 'The fact that there is an enforceable agreement which provides for a security interest is not by itself sufficient to make that security interest attach to a security, for the agreement may well have been entered into before the security was acquired by the debtor and/or before any advance has been made by the secured party.'

Even though attachment may not have taken place, the date of an enforceable agreement for security has considerable legal significance. It is the date from which the twenty-one-day registration period runs for the purposes of the registration requirements of the Companies Act 2006.[84] Also, as is clear from cases involving security on property not owned by the debtor at the time of the agreement but later acquired (commonly referred to as 'future property'), even though the security does not attach until the property is acquired, the creditor has more than a mere contractual right from the time when the agreement is concluded, which has important implications should the debtor become insolvent or grant someone else an interest in the same property, thereby creating a potential priority dispute.

Security on future property

The seminal authority on the effect of an agreement for security relating to future property is the decision of the House of Lords in *Holroyd v Marshall*.[85] The indenture between the lenders and the borrower in this case provided for the lenders to have security on existing premises, machinery, and other implements owned by the borrower and also on 'all machinery, implements and things, which during the continuance of this security shall be fixed or placed in or about the said mill...in addition to or substitution for the said premises or any part thereof.' When the borrower later defaulted on the loan, the lenders sold the machinery and effects that had been in existence at the date of the security agreement but this sale did not realize sufficient proceeds to discharge their loan. They therefore also sought to claim, as part of their security, machinery which had been added and substituted since the date of the security but this was also claimed by a judgment creditor. The question for the House of Lords was whether the lenders had an interest in the added and substituted machinery because, if they did, that machinery could not be taken in execution by the judgment creditor.

The House of Lords held that the lenders had an equitable interest and that their title therefore prevailed over the judgment creditor. Although the agreement to confer an interest in future property was void as law because there was nothing to convey,[86] in equity the agreement took effect so that as soon as the future property was acquired by the borrower and without the need for any new act on the part of the lenders, it became subject to the lenders' security. Lord Westbury LC said:[87]

> But if a vendor or mortgagor agrees to sell or mortgage property, real or personal, of which he is not possessed at the time, and he receives the consideration for the contract, and afterwards becomes possessed of property answering the description in the contract, there is no doubt that

---

[83] *Report of the Committee on Consumer Credit* (Cmnd 4596, 1971) para 5.6.4. See also L Gullifer (ed), *Goode on Legal Problems of Credit and Security* 4th edn (London: Sweet & Maxwell, 2008) ch 2.

[84] Companies Act 2006, s 870.

[85] (1862) 10 HLC 191, 11 ER 999, [1861–73] All ER Rep 414, HL. This case did not lay down new doctrine but contains 'the mere enunciation of elementary principles long settled in Courts of Equity': *Tailby v Official Receiver* (1888) 13 App Cas 523, HL, 535 *per* Lord Watson; see also 546 *per* Lord Macnaghten.

[86] *Robinson v Macdonnell* (1816) 5 M&S 228, 105 ER 1034.   [87] (1862) 10 HLC 191, HL, 211.

a court of equity would compel him to perform the contract, and that the contract would in equity transfer the beneficial interest to the mortgagee or purchaser immediately on the property being acquired.

Holroyd v Marshall was considered and in some respects clarified by the House of Lords in the later case of *Tailby v The Official Receiver*.[88] Here a bill of sale assigned (among other things) all of the book debts due and owing or which might during the continuance of the security become due and owing to the mortgagor. It was held that this was effective to give the creditor an equitable interest in the book debts incurred after the date of the bill of sale. The respondent's argument that the description of the security was too vague to be effective (which had found favour in the Court of Appeal) was rejected. The House of Lords took the view that the Court of Appeal (and courts in some previous cases) had proceeded on a misapprehension of some observations of Lord Westbury in *Holroyd v Marshall* which had appeared to link the doctrine enunciated in that case to the class of circumstances in which a court of equity would grant specific performance.[89] Lord Macnaghten in particular sought to correct the misunderstanding. He explained that the principle of equity underlying *Holroyd v Marshall* was that equity considers as done that which ought to be done. This principle was independent of the rules relating to the granting of specific performance and applied where there was an agreement assigning future property for value, with the result that, provided the consideration had passed, the agreement was binding on the property as soon as it was acquired.[90]

Tailby v Official Receiver indicates that the principle enunciated in *Holroyd v Marshall* will apply where a person has agreed to give a security interest to a lender in the following circumstances:

(1) There is an agreement to confer the security interest on the lender: in *Holroyd v Marshall* this took the form of an agreement to assign by way of security whilst in *Tailby v Official Receiver* this took the form of a present assignment (by way of security) of future debts. As Lord Macnaghten stated, the principle gives effect to the parties' contractual intentions.

> The truth is that cases of equitable assignment or specific lien, where the consideration has passed, depend on the real meaning of the agreement between the parties. The difficulty, generally speaking, is to ascertain the true scope and effect of the agreement.[91]

(2) The consideration for the security interest has been executed, ie the lender has advanced the money.

(3) The borrower has acquired an interest in property matching the description of the subject-matter of the security. The subject-matter of the security may be expressed in broad terms as in the *Tailby* case where it extended to all of the borrower's future book debts. Provided the clause identifying the subject-matter of the security is not so vaguely drafted as to make it impossible to ascertain to what it is applicable, the principle will apply. Two members of the House of Lords in the *Tailby* decision adverted to the possibility of equity denying effect to a purported equitable assignment on

---

[88] (1888) 13 App Cas 523, HL.

[89] (1888) 13 App Cas 523, 529 *per* Lord Hershell, 535 *per* Lord Watson. The third judge, Lord Fitzgerald did not address the point (and he neither assented to nor dissented from the decision). The opinion of the remaining judge, Lord Macnaghten, is considered next.

[90] *Metcalfe v Archbishop of York* (1836) 1 My & Cr 547.

[91] *Tailby v Official Receiver* (1888) 13 App Cas 523, HL, 547. Contrast *Carr v Allatt* (1858) 27 LJ (Ex) 385 and *Brown v Bateman* (1866–7) LR 2 CP 272 with *Reeve v Whitmore* (1864) 33 LJ (Ch) 63, *Thompson v Cohen* (1871–2) LR 7 QB 527; *Cole v Kernot* (1871–2) LR 7 QB 534n; *Collyer v Isaacs* (1881) 19 Ch D 342, CA (as explained in *Re Lind* [1915] 2 Ch 345 CA, 362–3 *per* Swinfen Eady LJ).

grounds of public policy where it included all of the present and future property of the person giving it and deprived that person of the power of maintaining himself but that possible limitation has not been applied in later cases.

The position of the creditor between the conclusion of the security agreement and the acquisition of the property by the debtor is demonstrated by *Re Lind, Industrial Finance Syndicate Ltd v Lind*.[92] Lind was presumptively entitled to a share in his mother's personal estate and he used this expectancy as security for two mortgages. Later, but before his mother's death, Lind became bankrupt and obtained his discharge. He then assigned his expectancy to a syndicate. On his mother's death, the two mortgagees claimed Lind's share of the estate in priority to the syndicate and the Court of Appeal upheld their claim. The discharge in bankruptcy had discharged Lind's personal obligations but the mortgagees had a stronger claim. Bankes LJ explained: 'it is true that the security was not enforceable until the property came into existence, but nevertheless the security was there;'[93] and Phillimore LJ stated, 'it is I think well and long settled that the right of the assignee is a higher right than the right to have specific performance of a contract, that the assignment creates an equitable charge which arises immediately upon the property coming into existence.'[94] Earlier, apparently inconsistent, authority was explained and distinguished.[95]

The precise nature of the interest held by a lender with security over future property before the property has been acquired has never been defined but some of the consequences of *Re Lind* are reasonably clear. First, a lender which has security over future property ranks as a secured creditor in the chargor's liquidation and is not required to proceed as an unsecured creditor by submitting a proof. If the chargor company is in compulsory liquidation, the creditor can enforce its rights against the property when it is acquired without infringing section 127 of the Insolvency Act 1986, which renders void any disposition of the company's property after the commencement of the winding up.[96] The reason for this is that the creditor's interest in the property pre-dates the insolvency and there is therefore no disposition of the company's property at a vulnerable time. Secondly, for the purposes of priority rules which depend on order of creation, a security over future property is created when the agreement is concluded and not at the later date when the property is acquired. Thus, in the *Re Lind* decision itself, the mortgagees held interests that took priority over a later assignment.[97]

The Subject Matter of a Security Interest—Forms of Property that Can Be Used as Security

The previous section made the point that a chargor can grant security only over its own property but including property that it may acquire in the future. Here, the question is whether there is any limitation on the type of property owned by the chargor that can be used as security.

---

[92] [1915] 2 Ch 345, CA.   [93] [1915] 2 Ch 345, 374, CA.
[94] [1915] 2 Ch 345, 365–6, CA.   [95] *Collyer v Isaacs* (1881) 19 Ch D 342, CA.
[96] *Re Androma Pty Ltd* [1987] 2 Qd 134, Q FC. Although a decision on Australian legislation, the reasoning would seem to be equally applicable to the English statute.
[97] 'At common law, it was not possible for an individual to grant an interest in property that he or she did not at that time own. However, it has long been held that equity will recognize and enforce interests which are granted in after-acquired property…The grantee's equitable interest in the property does not arise at the time the contract is executed. Rather, once the grantor acquires the property, the grantee immediately acquires an equitable interest in that property…As between competing equitable interests in after-acquired property, priority has generally been given to the first agreement to be executed…[E]quity in effect recognizes a type of inchoate proprietary interest in after-acquired property from the moment the agreement is executed': *Royal Bank of Canada v Radius Credit Union Ltd*, 2010 SCC 48, [20], Canada SC.

It is now clear that a company can use all of its present and future assets as security.[98] Land, whether freehold or leasehold, and the fixtures and fittings attaching to it, tangible personal property such as the company's stock in trade and intangible personal property, including debts owing to the company and its intellectual property, can all be used as security.

The decision in *Re Charge Card Services Ltd*,[99] in which it was held that a chargor could not use debts as security in favour of a creditor which was itself the person that owed the debts to the company—ie that a chargor could not 'charge back' debts to the debtor—because a security in that form was 'conceptually impossible,' sparked a decade of controversy. The matter was extensively debated in academic journals and elsewhere.[100] When an opportunity to consider the issue arose in *Re Bank of Credit and Commerce International SA (No 8)*,[101] the view that charge-backs were conceptually impossible was rejected by the House of Lords. Lord Hoffmann, who delivered the only reasoned speech, accepted that a charge-back lacked one of the regular features of a charge on debts—ie the chargee could not enforce the security by suing the debtor since the chargee could not sue itself—but held that the absence of this one feature did not preclude the existence of a charge. His Lordship emphasized that where there was no threat to the consistency of the law or objection of public policy, the courts should be very slow to declare a practice of the commercial community to be conceptually impossible. Although resolution of the charge-back issue was not essential to the decision in the case and Lord Hoffmann's views can therefore be regarded as technically obiter,[102] the point had been very fully argued before their Lordships and, for most practical purposes, the Opinion appears to put an end to the debate and confirm the validity of charge-backs as a form of security.[103]

Forms of Consensual Real Security

Consensual real security is conventionally divided into four categories: pledge, lien, mortgage, and charge. Pledges and liens have limited practical significance because they require the creditor to take some form of possession of the subject matter of the security. The forms of security that are in more widespread use in corporate financing are mortgages and charges. The terms 'mortgage' and 'charge' are often used interchangeably but there are some technical distinctions between them. For the purposes of the registration requirements of the Companies Act 2006, the term 'charge' includes mortgages.[104]

---

[98] *Jurong Data Centre Development v M+W Singapore* [2011] SGHC 58, [2011] 3 SLR 337, [37], Singapore HC ('the interest necessary to meet the interest requirement of a charge is to be interpreted broadly and the general principle is that most interests can be subject to a charge unless they are, inter alia, of a personal nature').

[99] [1987] Ch 150 (affirmed but without reference to the point relevant here [1989] Ch 497, CA).

[100] The leading proponent of the pro charge-back view was Philip Wood: see PR Wood, 'Three Problems of Set-off: Contingencies, Build-ups and Charge-Backs' (1987) 8 *Company Lawyer* 262. Detailed analysis of the point is also to be found in PR Wood, *English and International Set-off* (London: Sweet & Maxwell, 1989) paras 5.134–5.181.

[101] [1998] AC 214, HL. G McCormack, 'Charge Backs and Commercial Certainty in the House of Lords' [1998] CFILR 111.

[102] A point made by L Gullifer (ed), *Goode on Legal Problems of Credit and Security* 4th edn (London: Sweet & Maxwell, 2008) paras 3–12. Goode had argued that charge-backs were conceptually impossible.

[103] *Re Lehman Brothers International (Europe)* [2012] EWHC 2997 (Ch). On certain detailed questions that still remain, see H Beale, M Bridge, L Gullifer, and E Lomnicka, *The Law of Security and Title-Based Financing* 2nd edn (Oxford: OUP, 2012) para 6.25.

[104] Companies Act 2006, s 859A(7).

Pledge and lien[105]

In a pledge, assets of the debtor are delivered to the creditor as security for the debt or other obligation.[106] The creditor is said to have a special interest in the pledged property and, if the debtor fails to pay the debt when due, the creditor can sell the pledged property and use the sale proceeds to discharge the debt whilst accounting to the debtor for any surplus.[107] This distinguishes the pledge from the lien, which at common law confers on the creditor a right to detain the debtor's property but no right of sale or disposition.[108] The creditor may use the pledged assets at its own risk. The creditor may also assign his interest as pledgee and may sub-pledge that interest.[109] The debtor is entitled to the immediate possession of the assets when he has paid the debt for which they were pledged and, if the goods have been sub-pledged, the sub-pledgee may be sued in conversion if he impedes the debtor from exercising this right. In these circumstances, the debtor can also sue the creditor for breach of the contract of pledge.[110]

A valid pledge requires an agreement between the debtor and creditor and also delivery of the assets which form the subject matter of the security; agreement alone does not suffice.[111] In addition to actual delivery, the law has recognized constructive delivery as being effective for this purpose, an example of this being the delivery of the key to a warehouse in which goods are stored.[112] Negotiable instruments and securities, such as bearer bonds, can be pledged[113] but it has been held that the effect of depositing share certificates with a lender is to create an equitable mortgage rather than a pledge.[114] This distinction can be explained: delivery of bearer securities to a creditor constitutes delivery of the assets in the same way as delivery of goods; but delivery of share certificates, which are simply evidence of title to the shares,[115] does not amount to delivery of the shares and even the delivery of share certificates accompanied by executed share transfer forms does not complete delivery of the shares.[116]

A pledge requires agreement between debtor and creditor and there is no such thing as a pledge arising by operation of law. A common law lien can arise by operation of law[117] or by agreement.[118] A lien is a limited form of security which entitles the creditor to hold the assets which are the subject matter of the security but, generally, not to sell them.[119]

---

[105] H Beale, M Bridge, L Gullifer, and E Lomnicka, *The Law of Security and Title-Based Financing* 2nd edn (Oxford: OUP, 2012) ch 5.

[106] *Coggs v Barnard* (1703) 2 Ld Raym 909, Ct of Kings Bench; *Haliday v Holgate* (1868) LR 3 Exch 299, Exch Chamber.

[107] *Re Hardwick, ex p Hubbard* (1886) 17 QBD 690, CA.

[108] *Donald v Suckling* (1866) LR 1 QB 585, 604, 610, 612.

[109] *Donald v Suckling* (1866) LR 1 QB 585, 604, 610, 612.

[110] See further LS Sealy and RJA Hooley, *Commercial Law: Text, Cases and Materials* 4th edn (Oxford: OUP, 2009) 1091–106.

[111] *Official Assignee of Madras v Mercantile Bank of India Ltd* [1935] AC 53, PC.

[112] *Wrightson v McArthur and Hutchinsons (1919) Ltd* [1921] 2 KB 807.

[113] *Carter v Wake* (1877) 4 Ch D 605.   [114] *Harrold v Plenty* [1901] 2 Ch 314.

[115] Companies Act 2006, s 768. cf Companies Act 2006, s 779(2), which is concerned with share warrants, title to which does pass by delivery.

[116] *London and Midland Bank Ltd v Mitchell* [1899] 2 Ch 161; *Stubbs v Slater* [1910] 1 Ch 632, CA. It is generally considered that legal title to shares passed only when the transferee is registered in the company's books as a member of the company: *Société Générale de Paris v Walker* (1885) 11 App Cas 20, HL, 28 *per* Lord Selborne; *Colonial Bank v Hepworth* (1887) 36 Ch D 36, 54.

[117] *Re Bond Worth Ltd* [1980] Ch 228, 250 *per* Slade J; *Toll Logistics (NZ) v McKay* [2011] NZCA 188; [2011] 2 NZLR 601.

[118] *Samsun Logix Corporation v Oceantrade Corporation* [2007] EWHC 2372 (Comm), [2008] 1 All ER (Comm) 673; *Toll Logistics (NZ) v McKay* [2011] NZCA 188; [2011] 2 NZLR 601.

[119] *Hammonds v Barclay* (1802) 2 East 227, 102 ER 356; *Larner v Fawcett* [1950] 2 All ER 727, 731, CA; *Tappenden v Artus* [1964] 2 QB 185, CA. On liens see further LS Sealy and RJA Hooley, *Commercial Law: Text, Cases and Materials* 4th edn (Oxford: OUP, 2009) 1106–122.

Mortgage

Leaving aside statutory intervention, a mortgage is a transfer of ownership, legal or equitable, as security for a debt or other obligation with an express or implied proviso for redemption when the debt or obligation has been discharged.[120] A debtor may mortgage its own property as security but it is also possible for a third party to mortgage its property as security for another's debts and the third party need not itself undertake any personal obligation to pay.[121] Since 1926, mortgages of land have been subject to special statutory rules under which the creation of a mortgage does not involve a transfer of ownership. Mortgages of land and interests in land are not explored further in this chapter.

Also excluded from detailed discussion in this chapter are security interests in equitable property, such as beneficial interests under trusts. Although companies may hold equitable property, it is perhaps more common to think of the property that a company may use as its security as being property of which it is the legal owner, such as plant, machinery and equipment, stock in trade, intellectual property, book debts, and other receivables.

A legal mortgage of personal property requires the transfer to the creditor of the legal title to the assets that are to form the security. The form of the transfer depends on the nature of the assets in question. A legal mortgage of goods may be oral[122] or may be created by deed or by delivery of the goods. Whether a transaction involving the delivery of goods is a mortgage or a pledge depends on the intention of the parties.[123] Generally, a legal mortgage of a chose in action, such as a debt, must comply with section 136(1) of the Law of Property Act 1925 and, as such, must be in writing with written notice to the debtor,[124] but particular types of choses in action are subject to special rules: a legal mortgage of shares requires the mortgagee to be registered in the company's register of members in respect of the shares;[125] and a legal mortgage of negotiable instruments, such as bearer securities, can be created simply by delivery of the relevant documents. Future property cannot be the subject of a legal mortgage.[126] An assignment of part of a debt cannot be brought within section 136(1) with the result that it is not possible to create a legal mortgage of part of a debt.[127]

---

[120] *Santley v Wilde* [1899] 2 Ch 474, CA; *Noakes & Co Ltd v Rice* [1902] AC 24, HL, 28 *per* Earl of Halsbury LC; *Brighton & Hove City Council v Audus* [2009] EWHC 340 (Ch), [2010] 1 All ER (Comm) 343, [46] ('It is inherent in the concept of a mortgage or security interest that the borrower of money should be able to discharge the security interest, that is, to redeem the mortgage by paying the money and in that way performing the obligation performance of which is secured'); *Szepietowski v Serious Organised Crime Agency* [2011] EWCA Civ 856, [1] ('A legal mortgage of real property confers upon the mortgagee a title by way of security which will subsist until the redemption of the mortgage or the sale of the property. Correspondingly the mortgagor retains an equity of redemption which entitles him to redeem the property from the mortgage upon payment of the mortgage debt, interest and costs'); *Cukurova Finance International v Alfa Telecom Turkey* [2013] UKPC 2, [73] ('In equity, a mortgagee has a limited title which is available only to secure satisfaction of the debt.').

[121] *Perry v National Provincial Bank of England* [1910] 1 Ch 464, CA; *Re Conley* [1938] 2 All ER 127 CA.

[122] *Newlove v Shrewsbury* (1888) 21 QBD 41, CA.

[123] AP Bell, *Modern Law of Personal Property in England and Ireland* (London: Butterworths, 1989) 185; RW Ramage, 'Chattel Mortgages' (1971) 121 NLJ 291.

[124] Law of Property Act 1925, s 136(1) refers to 'absolute' assignments and provides that it does not apply to assignments purporting to be by way of charge only. An assignment by way of mortgage is considered to be absolute and not by way of charge only: *Burlinson v Hall* (1884) 12 QBD 347; *Tancred v Delagoa Bay Co* (1889) 23 QBD 239.

[125] *General Credit and Discount Co v Glegg* (1883) 22 Ch D 549 is an example of a legal mortgage of shares. It is generally considered that legal title to shares passed only when the transferee is registered in the company's books as a member of the company: *Société Générale de Paris v Walker* (1885) 11 App Cas 20, HL, 28 *per* Lord Selborne; *Colonial Bank v Hepworth* (1887) 36 Ch D 36, 54.

[126] *Holroyd v Marshall* (1862) 10 HLC 191; 11 ER 999, [1861–73] All ER Rep 414, HL; *Robinson v Macdonnell* (1816) 5 M&S 228, 105 ER 1034.

[127] *Durham Brothers v Robertson* [1898] 1 QB 765, CA; *Re Steel Wing Co Ltd* [1921] 1 Ch 349; *Earle v Hemsworth* (1928) 44 TLR 605; *Williams v Atlantic Assurance Co* [1933] 1 KB 81, CA. Although there are authorities to the

An equitable mortgage involves the transfer to the creditor of equitable ownership subject to a proviso for redemption. An equitable mortgage of personal property can be created in various ways. For instance, a contract to give a legal mortgage on property can give rise in equity to an equitable mortgage when the requirements for a full legal mortgage (for example, registration of the creditor in the company's register of members in the case of a legal mortgage of shares or compliance with the Law of Property Act 1925, section 136(1) in relation to the legal mortgage of a debt) have not been fulfilled.[128]

The debtor's continuing interest in mortgaged property stems from its entitlement to require the property to be redeemed on the discharge of the secured debt or other obligation. This is known as the 'equity of redemption'.[129] The equity of redemption survives default,[130] and late payment or performance will still entitle the mortgagor to redeem at least until such time as the creditor enforces its security by selling the secured assets or by foreclosure. Any provision in the terms of a mortgage which purports to remove the mortgagor's right to redeem, or which would indirectly tend to have the effect of making the mortgage irredeemable, is regarded in equity as a 'clog' or 'fetter' on the equity of redemption and, as such, it is void.[131] The principle that clogs on the equity of redemption are void applies to all types of mortgages and also to charges, including floating charges.[132] While this is a long established, and by no means obsolete, doctrine of equity,[133] it has been described as an 'unruly dog' and 'one might perhaps reasonably expect its venerable age to inhibit it from straying too far or too often from its kennel.'[134]

contrary, so that the point may not be regarded as being definitively settled, the view expressed in the text is widely regarded as being the better view: OR Marshall, *Assignment of Choses in Action* (Pitman, 1950) 173–4. In *Norman v FCT* (1963) 109 CLR 9, High Ct of Aust, 29 Windeyer J stated that the earlier inconsistent decisions must be taken to be overruled.

[128] See further LS Sealy and RJA Hooley, *Commercial Law: Text, Cases and Materials* 4th edn (Oxford: OUP, 2009) ch 26.

[129] *Dellway Investments v NAMA* [2011] IESC 14 ('A mortgagor's interest in the mortgaged property is the equity of redemption, the right at any time to redeem the mortgage. The right exists at any time during the term of the mortgage, and after the expiration of the mortgage term at any time up to the realisation of the security by the mortgagee entering into an enforceable contract for sale under the power of sale. It is a valuable interest in property and may be sold or mortgaged by way of a second or subsequent mortgage.'); *Sofaer v Anglo Irish Asset Finance* [2011] EWHC 1480 (Ch), [2011] BPIR 1736, [25] ('The equity of redemption is in effect the residual rights of the mortgagor in the mortgaged property after the mortgage has been satisfied and after the mortgagee has exercised his remedies. The bank, almost by definition, has no security over the equity of redemption because that is what remains after the security has been given effect.').

[130] This was not always the case: see AWB Simpson, *A History of the Land Law* 2nd edn (Oxford: Clarendon Press, 1986) ch X.

[131] eg *Noakes & Co Ltd v Rice* [1902] AC 24, HL, 28 *per* Earl of Halsbury LC and 30 *per* Lord Macnaghten; *Brighton & Hove City Council v Audus* [2009] EWHC 340 (Ch), [2010] 1 All ER (Comm) 343, [46] ('At common law it was possible to include in a mortgage a contractual term which had the effect that the mortgagor would lose the right to redeem if he failed to repay the monies due by a specified date. Equity regarded such a term as liable to work injustice and hardship and equity granted relief against the operation of such a contractual term by recognising an equitable right to redeem, notwithstanding non-compliance with the contractual term. It is not necessary for present purposes to describe in detail the difference between a right to redeem at law, the right to redeem in equity and the "equity of redemption." It is sufficient to turn to the rules of equity which came into existence to protect the equitable right to redeem.'); *Dellway Investments v NAMA* [2011] IESC 14 ('Any express stipulation in a mortgage which is inconsistent with the right of redemption is void. A mortgage may not be made irredeemable, nor can the right to redeem be limited to particular persons or to a particular period.').

[132] *Kreglinger v New Patagonia Meat and Cold Storage Co Ltd* [1914] AC 25, HL dispelling doubts raised by *De Beers Consolidated Mines v British South Africa Co* [1912] AC 52, HL.

[133] *Cukurova Finance International v Alfa Telecom Turkey* [2013] UKPC 2, [111]. See also *Cukurova Finance International v Alfa Telecom Turkey* [2013] UKPC 20.

[134] *Warnborough v Garmite* [2003] EWCA Civ 1544, [72]. See also *Lift Capital Partners v Merrill Lynch* [2009] NSWSC 7, [106]–[137].

Charges

Every equitable mortgage is also an equitable charge but the converse is not true:[135] a mortgage, like a charge, appropriates property for the payment of a debt or the discharge of an obligation but a mortgage goes further than a charge and also operates to transfer title to the creditor, subject to the chargor's equity of redemption.[136] A charge gives its holder rights in relation to the property which is the subject matter of the security but does not effect a transfer of title to that property.[137] Except in relation to land where, by statute, a mortgage by way of legal charge can be created,[138] a charge is a form of equitable security. A charge would normally be created by an agreement between the parties supported by consideration or in the form of a deed. Where the charge extends to future property, consideration is always required and a deed alone will not suffice.

The importance of the distinction between mortgages and charges is said to lie in the range of remedies available to the creditor in the event of default as a matter of general law. Broadly speaking, a chargee has available to it under the general law a more limited range of remedies than is available to a mortgagee.[139] However, well-drafted charges invariably expand the chargee's remedies with the result that, in practice, there is usually little difference between the remedies enjoyed by a mortgagee and by a chargee. In *Re Bond Worth Ltd* Slade LJ acknowledged that the words 'mortgage' and 'charge' are often used interchangeably.[140]

In *Buchler v Talbot*,[141] a case concerning the question of whether by virtue of section 175(2)(b) of the Insolvency Act 1986 the liquidator's costs and expenses were payable out of the proceeds of the realization of assets subject to a charge, all three members of the House of Lords who delivered reasoned speeches described a charge in terms that are more usually associated with a mortgage: 'the charged assets belong to the debenture holder to the extent of the amounts secured;'[142] 'the proceeds of the assets comprised in a floating charge which belong to the charge holder to the extent of the security;'[143] 'the company has only an equity of redemption; the right to retransfer of the assets when the debt secured by the floating charge has been paid off.'[144] The use of such language has attracted critical comment.[145] At first sight it seems impossible to think that their Lordships (including Lord Hoffmann) simply ignored the basic and very familiar differences between mortgages and charges, and this led some to argue that it is a mistake to overtheorize in abstract terms about the nature of charges because their operation depends on the statutory context to which questions relate (in the *Buchler* case, the insolvency legislation and the distribution of assets by a liquidator) and on the particular rights and obligations that the parties have granted each other in the charging documentation.[146]

---

[135] *Shea v Moore* [1894] IR 158, Ir CA.

[136] *Re Bond Worth Ltd* [1980] Ch 228, 250. However, where an equitable mortgage arises from the failure to complete the requirements for a full legal mortgage, no transfer of title occurs. Such equitable mortgage is to all intents and purposes a charge.

[137] *National Provincial and Union Bank of England v Charnley* [1924] 1 KB 431, CA, 449–50 *per* Atkin LJ; *Re Bond Worth Ltd* [1980] Ch 228, 250 *per* Slade J; *Swiss Bank Corpn v Lloyds Bank Ltd* [1982] AC 584, CA and HL, 594–5 *per* Buckley LJ; *Re Charge Card Services Ltd* [1987] Ch 150, 176 *per* Millett J; *Re BCCI (No 8)* [1998] AC 214, HL, 226 *per* Lord Hoffmann; *Re Cosslett (Contractors)* [1998] Ch 495 CA, 508 *per* Millett LJ.

[138] Law of Property Act 1925, s 87.

[139] H Beale, M Bridge, L Gullifer, and E Lomnicka, *The Law of Security and Title-Based Financing* 2nd edn (Oxford: OUP, 2012) para 6.57.

[140] [1980] Ch 228, 250.   [141] [2004] 2 AC 298, HL.   [142] At [16] *per* Lord Nicholls.

[143] At [62] *per* Lord Millett.   [144] At [29] *per* Lord Hoffmann.

[145] RJ Mokal, 'Liquidation Expenses and Floating Charges—the Separate Funds Fallacy' [2004] LMCLQ 387; RJ Mokal, 'What Liquidation Does for Secured Creditors, and What it Does for You' (2008) 71 MLR 699.

[146] J Armour and A Walters, 'Funding Liquidation: a Functional View' (2006) 122 LQR 295.

But in *National Insurance Corp v Winmark*[147] Lord Hoffmann appears to have retracted from his position in the *Buchler* case. The issue in *Winmark* was similar to that in *Buchler*. Under St Lucia law, an employer's debt due to the National Insurance Corporation, the body established to administer the National Insurance Fund, would rank as a privileged debt where any execution had been levied against the 'property of an employer,' or on the application of a secured creditor, the 'property of an employer' had been sold. At issue was whether the employer's debt due to the National Insurance Corporation would rank above or below a secured creditor holding a hypothec over the employer's real property. Unsurprisingly, the secured creditor relied on *Buchler* to argue that the National Insurance Corporation's privilege could not give the Corporation priority in respect of the proceeds of sale of the hypothecated property because the effect of the hypothec was that, at any rate when the property was sold, the proceeds were not the 'property of an employer.' The proceeds were beneficially owned by the secured creditor. But Lord Hoffmann (speaking for the Privy Council) rejected the secured creditor's argument and explained away *Buchler* in an incomprehensible manner:

> These statements [in *Buchler*] were made to explain why, if in principle the costs of realising a fund should be borne by the creditors interested in that fund, it would be wrong to make assets in the hands of a receiver, which were subject to a floating charge, bear the costs of a liquidator realising assets for the benefit of unsecured creditors ...
>
> In their Lordships' view it is dangerous to apply notions of the separate beneficial interests of the chargee and the unsecured creditors, which were used in *Buchler*'s case to explain why one fund should not have to bear costs attributable to the realisation of another, to the very different question of priorities under the civilian system of security interests in immoveable property applicable in St Lucia.[148]

But in *Buchler* the issue was almost identical. Section 115 of the Insolvency Act 1986 provides that all liquidation expenses 'are payable out of the company's assets in priority to all other claims.' Their Lordships in *Buchler* concluded that because floating charge assets belonged beneficially to the debenture holder, those assets were not the company's assets available to defray liquidation expenses. Lord Hoffmann's explanation in *Winmark* about the notion of separate funds in *Buchler* is nothing but question-begging. Properly analyzed, *Winmark* vindicates the criticisms against *Buchler*.

Fixed and Floating Charges—a Comparison of Their Key Features

Fixed charges

For companies, the category of charges has to be sub-divided into fixed charges and floating charges. A fixed charge is similar to a mortgage in that the holder immediately obtains rights in relation to the secured property and can restrict the chargor company from disposing of it or destroying it. The chargee may obtain an injunction to restrain unauthorized disposals[149] and, if property which is subject to an enforceable fixed charge is wrongfully disposed of by the chargor, the person acquiring the property will take it subject to the charge unless he can claim to be a bona fide purchaser of the legal title to the property who is without notice of the existence of the fixed charge. A fixed charge is said to fasten on the assets which are the subject matter of the security; thus in the leading case of *Illingworth v Houldsworth*[150] Lord

---

[147] [2009] UKPC 8.   [148] *National Insurance Corp v Winmark* [2009] UKPC 8, paras 19–20.
[149] *Holroyd v Marshall* (1862) 10 HL Cas 191, HL, 211–2 *per* Lord Westbury.   [150] [1904] AC 355, HL, 358.

Macnaghten described a fixed charge as 'one that without more fastens on ascertained and definite property or property capable of being ascertained or defined.' In a much more recent case Lord Walker echoed these views: 'Under a fixed charge the assets charged as security are permanently appropriated to the payment of the sum charged, in such a way as to give the chargee a proprietary interest in the assets. So long as the charge remains unredeemed, the assets can be released from the charge only with the active concurrence of the chargee.'[151] The subject matter of a fixed charge security may extend to future property in accordance with the principles in *Holroyd v Marshall*.[152]

Floating charges

In his speech in *Illingworth v Houldsworth* Lord Macnaghten described the floating charge in these terms:[153] 'a floating charge, on the other hand, is ambulatory and shifting in its nature, hovering over and so to speak floating with the property which it is intended to affect until some event occurs or some act is done which causes it to settle and fasten on the subject of the charge within its reach and grasp.'

The essence of the floating charge, and the key factor which distinguishes it from the fixed charge, is that the chargor can continue to deal with the assets which are the subject of the security and can transfer them to third parties unencumbered by the security.[154] However, as is discussed later in this chapter, some degree of restriction on dealings by the chargor with the secured assets is not incompatible with a floating charge. Whether a charge can be categorized as a fixed charge where it allows the chargor a degree of freedom to deal with the secured assets and to withdraw them from the security is much more questionable.

Floating charges can, and commonly do, extend to future property as well as to property presently owned by the chargor company. The effect of a floating charge on present and future property, such as stock in trade, is that as the stock turns over in the ordinary course of trade, items sold pass out of the security but new items come within the scope of the charge as soon as they are acquired by the company. It is not clear that a floating charge on chattels extends to the proceeds when those assets are sold by the company for its own benefit as permitted by the terms of the charge[155] but well-drafted security documentation will include express provision for the security to cover receivables and their proceeds.

Much of the wealth of a business may be tied up in raw materials, goods in process of being manufactured, or stock in trade. The floating charge is ideally suited to unlock the potential of items such as these as a valuable source of security.

Since the items comprising raw materials, goods being manufactured, or stock are circulating assets which necessarily fluctuate in the ordinary course of trade, fixed security under which the lender has power to restrain disposals tends not to be an attractive option. The floating charge was developed in the nineteenth century by practitioners and the Chancery courts[156] at a time when industrial and commercial expansion meant that the demand for

---

[151] *Re Spectrum Plus Ltd* [2005] 2 AC 680, HL, [138].
[152] (1862) 10 HLC 191, 11 ER 999, [1861–73] All ER Rep 414, HL.   [153] [1904] AC 355, HL, 358.
[154] *Re Spectrum Plus Ltd* [2005] 2 AC 680, HL, [111] *per* Lord Scott.
[155] See discussion in Law Commission, *Company Security Interests* (Law Com Rep No 296, 2005) paras 3.51–3.52.
[156] *Re Panama, New Zealand and Australia Royal Mail Co* (1870) 5 Ch App 318; *Re Florence Land and Public Works Co, ex p Moor* (1878) 10 Ch D 530, CA; *Moor v Anglo-Italian Bank* (1878) 10 Ch D 681; *Re Hamilton's Windsor Ironworks Co, ex p Pitman and Edwards* (1879) 12 Ch D 707; *Re Colonial Trusts Corp, ex p Bradshaw* (1879) 15 Ch D 465. The development of the floating charge in response to the industrial and commercial expansion of nineteenth-century Britain and the increasing need by companies for more capital is explored in *Re Spectrum Plus Ltd* [2005] 2 AC 680, HL, paras 95–6 *per* Lord Scott and in *Agnew v The Commissioner of Inland Revenue* [2001] 2 AC 710, PC, paras 5–7 *per* Lord Millett.

corporate finance was very strong and smaller companies, which were either unable or unwilling to raise it by issuing equity securities, were largely dependent on loans.[157]

There is an obvious risk to a lender who takes floating as opposed to fixed security in that the company may dispose of the subject matter of the security unprofitably, thereby undermining the value of the security and potentially putting its solvency at risk. Floating charges lack one of the important features associated with security, which is that the collateral remains with the chargor or is readily recoverable from transferees, a feature which Westbrook has labelled 'asset constraint'.[158] Furthermore, if the company does become insolvent, the lender with a floating charge may find that other lenders have taken fixed charges ranking in priority to the floating charge with the consequence that the company has insufficient assets to satisfy the debt secured by the floating charge.

There are certain devices available to strengthen the floating charge without destroying its flexibility. First, it is established that there are certain restrictions on dealings which are not incompatible with the floating nature of a floating charge and the lender can seek to include these in the charge in order to protect its interests.[159] Secondly, the lender with a floating charge can also try to protect its interest through provisions in the terms of the charge relating to crystallization. A floating charge need not continue to float forever but can convert into a fixed charge, a process normally described as crystallization. Once a floating charge crystallizes it operates from that point onwards as a fixed charge and, as such, it attaches to the company's existing assets which fall within the description of the subject matter of the security and, if the security extends to future property, to property matching that description which is subsequently acquired by the company. In other words, crystallization brings about asset constraint.[160] Certain crystallizing events are implied by law into a floating charge unless they are expressly excluded by the parties. It is possible to extend the range of crystallizing events by express provision to that effect in the terms of the charge.[161] However, devices such as these, though of some effect in priority disputes between private parties, do not override public law provisions in the insolvency legislation that have redistributive effects. Those provisions apply primarily to charges created as floating charges and can have the effect of redistributing part of the floating charge collateral to unsecured creditors.

Since the floating charge does not provide asset constraint until crystallization and it has only limited effect as a mechanism for establishing a priority claim, its importance as a type

---

[157] RR Pennington, 'The Genesis of the Floating Charge' (1960) 23 MLR 630. WJ Gough, 'The Floating Charge: Traditional Themes and New Directions' in PD Finn (ed), *Equity and Commercial Relationships* (Sydney: Law Book Company, 1987) 239 describes the floating charge as being 'one of the great legal success stories of Victorian times.'

[158] JL Westbrook, 'The Control of Wealth in Bankruptcy' (2004) 82 *Texas Law Review* 795, 808.

[159] In particular the negative pledge whereby the company covenants not to create any new security ranking in priority to or equally with the floating charge. The priority effect of the negative pledge is discussed later in this chapter.

[160] *J. D. Brian v Companies Acts* [2011] IEHC 113, [18] ('Upon crystallisation, the charge ceases to float over the assets which are subject to it, and attaches to or becomes fixed on those assets. As is sometimes said, the floating charge upon crystallisation becomes a fixed charge. However, no new charge is created by the company. The existing charge, the floating charge created by the company, changes in nature and becomes a fixed charge. The nature of the security held by the debenture holder under the floating charge created by the company upon crystallisation changes; it ceases to float, and becomes a fixed charge over the charged property. In accordance with the general principles relating to fixed charges, upon the charge becoming fixed, there is an equitable assignment of the relevant assets to the debenture holder. Nevertheless, the right of the debenture holder to the charged assets derives from the floating charge created by the Company. It is the nature of the right which is changed by the crystallisation.').

[161] *J. D. Brian v Companies Acts* [2011] IEHC 113, [56] ('there is no rule of law which precludes parties to a debenture creating a floating charge agreeing, as a matter of contract, that the floating charge will crystallise upon the happening of an event or a particular step taken by the chargee'). See further later.

of security can be called into question.[162] Moreover, changes in insolvency law[163] that have to a large extent removed the right for holders of floating charges to appoint administrative receivers and require them to look instead to the collective procedure of administration[164] deepen the doubts about its usefulness. Notwithstanding that floating charge holders enjoy certain special rights in administration, including the right to choose the administrator, the administration procedure is fundamentally different from administrative receivership because it has features of independence and altruism that did not apply to administrative receivership.[165] As the changes in the law are not retrospective, and there are various exceptional cases in which administrative receivers can still be appointed under post-15 September 2003 floating charges, it will take some time before their practical impact can be properly evaluated. However, it seems reasonable to predict some diminution in the perceived advantages associated with the floating charge by the lending community, which could affect the pricing of debt secured by a floating charge. The case for the abolition of the floating charge is becoming stronger.[166]

The Nature of the Floating Charge

The nature of the floating charge is intriguing. It is undoubtedly an immediate security interest and not merely an agreement to create a security in the future at the time of crystallization.[167] As conventionally understood, the holder of a security interest has a proprietary interest in the debtor's property and can control dealings in that property, yet where the charge is floating the debtor remains, broadly, free to deal with the assets as if they were unsecured.[168] How can this be explained? The cases do not provide a clear answer but they have provided plenty of ideas to feed a lively academic debate.

One theory on the nature of the proprietary interest created by the floating charge is that it is in essence the same as that created by a fixed charge but coupled with a license from the creditor to the debtor to continue to deal with the assets. It is now generally accepted that the floating charge is a distinct type of security and is not merely a fixed charge with a special feature.[169] However, that the nature of the interest created by a floating charge is the same as that in a fixed charge has some strong support. In particular, Worthington argues that a floating charge is best understood as giving rise to a proprietary interest that is of precisely the same type as that held by the owner of a fixed charge but which is defeasible when the charged assets are dealt with in accordance with the permitted license to deal.[170] Nolan also suggests that the standard default entitlements associated with a floating charge are that it behaves as an ordinary equitable fixed charge but he differs from Worthington by suggesting that it is

---

[162] R Mokal, 'The Floating Charge—An Elegy' in S Worthington (ed), *Commercial Law and Commercial Practice* (Hart, 2003) ch 17.

[163] By the Enterprise Act 2002, taking effect by way of amendment to the Insolvency Act 1986, with effect from September 2003.

[164] Insolvency Act 1986, Sch B1, para 14.

[165] M Simmons, 'Some Reflections on Administrations, Crown Preference and Ring-fenced Sums in the Enterprise Act' [2004] JBL 423, 425.

[166] RM Goode, 'The Case for the Abolition of the Floating Charge' in J Getzler and J Payne (eds), *Company Charges: Spectrum and Beyond* (Oxford: OUP, 2006) ch 2.

[167] Buckley LJ in *Evans v Rival Granite Quarries Ltd* [1910] 2 KB 979, CA, 999: 'A floating charge is not a future security; it is a present security which presently affects all of the assets of the company expressed to be included in it.'

[168] This apparent paradox led the US courts to deny the effectiveness of floating security: *Benedict v Ratner* 268 US 353, 45 S Ct 566, 69 L Ed 991 (1925).

[169] In particular Buckley LJ in *Evans v Rival Granite Quarries Ltd* [1910] 2 KB 979, CA, 999: 'A floating charge is not a specific mortgage of the assets, plus a licence to the mortgagor to dispose of them in the course of his business.'

[170] S Worthington, *Proprietary Interests in Commercial Transactions* (Clarendon Press, 1996) 81; S Worthington, *Personal Property Law: Text, Cases and Materials* (Hart, 2000) 129.

better to describe the floating charge not as defeasible but as an interest which is inherently limited because it can be overreached. He also emphasizes that the parties can adjust the standard terms with the consequence that the precise nature of the interest created may vary from case to case.[171]

Another view is that the floating charge, as a security interest entirely distinct from the fixed charge, gives the creditor an immediate proprietary interest of some sort in the property owned by the company from time to time but one that does not attach specifically to any of the assets until crystallization.[172] The theory enjoys considerable academic support[173] but a difficulty with it is that it does not give a clear indication of the nature and quality of the proprietary interest created by the floating charge.[174] Goode has attempted to capture the special nature of the proprietary interest created by the floating charge by suggesting that the floating charge gives the holder a present interest in a *fund* of assets which the debtor is free to manage in the ordinary course of its business.[175] The fund concept has some explanatory power in relation to landmark cases on the floating charge that emphasize that the holder of such a security does not have an interest attaching specifically to the debtor's property and it has attracted significant judicial support in modern leading cases. In *Re Spectrum Plus Ltd (in liquidation)*[176] Lord Walker said that: 'the chargee has a proprietary interest but its interest is in a fund of circulating capital, and unless and until the chargee intervenes (on crystallization of the charge) it is for the trader, and not the bank, to decide how to run its business.'[177]

This comment from Lord Walker implicitly rejects yet another theory on the nature of the floating charge. This is the view, of which the major proponent is Gough, that although the floating charge is a present equitable security, it does not give the holder any equitable proprietary interest until crystallization.[178] The floating charge, in his view, gives rise to a deferred equitable interest and, prior to crystallization, the holder of a floating charge has a personal or 'mere' equity against the chargor arising under the charge contract.

The conceptual uncertainty about the nature of the floating charge that has intrigued many commentators has not stood in the way of the floating charge becoming a commercially important element of corporate financing. Furthermore, even though they have often had to resort to using rather vague metaphors to describe the floating charge,[179] through an incremental process the courts have been able to work out answers to many questions about the floating charge to the point where many clear and well understood principles governing its operation are now established.[180] For example, the priority of the floating charge and the extent to which a prohibition

---

[171] R Nolan, 'Property in a Fund' (2004) 120 LQR 108.

[172] RR Pennington, 'The Genesis of the Floating Charge' (1960) 23 MLR 630, 646 and RR Pennington, *Company Law* 8th edn (London: Butterworths, 2001) 539–41.

[173] Although there are differences of emphasis and on points of detail, the following writers agree that the holder of an uncrystallized floating charge has some form of proprietary interest: L Gullifer (ed), *Goode on Legal Problems of Credit and Security* 4th edn (London: Sweet & Maxwell, 2008) ch 4; JH Farrar, 'World Economic Stagnation puts the Floating Charge on Trial' (1980) 1 *Company Lawyer* 83; EV Ferran, 'Floating Charges—The Nature of the Security' [1988] CLJ 213.

[174] *Re Margart Pty Ltd; Hamilton v Westpac Banking Corpn* (1984) 9 ACLR 269, NSW SC-EqD, 272 *per* Helsham CJ, 'while the charge is a floating charge that interest may or may not be an interest of the same dimension as that which he would obtain if the charge became a fixed charge.'

[175] L Gullifer (ed), *Goode on Legal Problems of Credit and Security* 4th edn (London: Sweet & Maxwell, 2008) paras 4-03–4-07.

[176] [2005] 2 AC 680, HL, [139]. See also S Atherton and RJ Mokal, 'Charges Over Chattels: Issues in the Fixed/Floating Jurisprudence' (2005) 26 *Company Lawyer* 10.

[177] See also *Agnew v The Commissioner of Inland Revenue* [2001] 2 AC 710, PC, [11] *per* Lord Millett.

[178] WJ Gough, *Company Charges* 2nd edn (London: Butterworths, 1996) 97–101 and ch 13.

[179] *Re New Bullas Trading Ltd* [1993] BCC 251, 260.

[180] *Evans v Rival Granite Quarries Ltd* [1910] 2 KB 979, CA stands out as a case where the English Court of Appeal attempted to grapple with the theoretical nature of the interest created by the floating charge before proceeding to consider its effect in a particular context (competition with a judgment creditor). The Australian courts have

in the terms of the charge on the subsequent creation of prior ranking security on any part of the charged property is effective to postpone such security to the floating charge, are well known and undisputed.[181] This makes it pertinent to ask whether pinpointing in an exact manner the abstract nature of the proprietary interest created by a floating charge actually matters that much: need we be concerned if, on the whole, the law seems to function perfectly well without it? The deficiency in the law, to the extent that there is one and this is not simply a consequence of the fact that the rights that the floating charge holder has before crystallization cannot be universally defined because they depend to some extent on the terms of the charge and the context in which questions have arisen,[182] does not appear to cause major practical problems and its significance should not be exaggerated. However, where a particular aspect of the operation of a floating charge is not clearly determined by existing authority, the lack of an authoritative general understanding of its proprietary effect makes it hard to predict how a case would be decided. For example, the proprietary consequences of a sale of assets that breaches a restriction in a floating charge has yet to be fully explained in the British cases,[183] and it is an issue on which commentators have suggested different views.[184]

Establishing Whether a Charge is Fixed or Floating

An issue of considerable practical significance is that of distinguishing between fixed and floating charges. Whether a charge is fixed or floating is relevant to questions about its priority against competing securities. It is also relevant for the purposes of many of the provisions of the Insolvency Act 1986 that have redistributive effect because these mostly affect floating, but not fixed, charges.[185] Many of the modern landmark cases on the categorization of charges arose from disputes between preferential creditors and holders of security over the

demonstrated a willingness to embark upon a discussion of the theoretical nature of the floating charge or, at least, to acknowledge the different theories that have been put forward. The authorities in support of both arguments are reviewed in *Lyford v CBA* (1995) 17 ACSR 211, Fed Ct of Aust-GenD where the Gough view is adopted and Australian cases supporting the alternative view (*Landall Holdings Ltd v Caratti* [1979] WAR 97, WA SC; *Hamilton v Hunter* (1982) 7 ACLR 295, NSW SC Eq D; *Re Margart Pty Ltd (in liquidation), Hamilton v Westpac Banking Corp* (1984) 9 ACLR 269, NSW SC Eq D) are not followed. *Lyford* was followed in *Wily v St George Partnership Banking Ltd* (1997–98) 26 ACSR 1, Fed Ct of Aust. *Westpac Banking Corporation v The Bell Group (No 3)* [2012] WASCA 157 held that the preponderant view now is that a floating charge creates an equitable interest in property.

[181] Priority rules are considered further later in this chapter. Other situations in which arise questions about the proprietary effects of a floating charge include: whether the court can appoint a receiver and manager on the application of the holder of a floating charge (*Re Victoria Steamboats Ltd, Smith v Wilkinson* [1897] 1 Ch 158 ('yes')); competing claims of floating charge holders and judgment creditors (*Evans v Rival Granite Quarries Ltd* [1910] 2 KB 979, CA); the application of particular statutory provisions (eg *Re Margart Pty Ltd; Hamilton v Westpac Banking Corp* (1984) 9 ACLR 269, NSW SC-EqD where it was held that a payment to a creditor who held an uncrystallized floating charge did not contravene the New South Wales equivalent of the Insolvency Act 1986, s 127 because that section did not apply to the process whereby a person with a beneficial interest in property obtained the property or the proceeds of its realization from the company—the floating charge conferred a beneficial interest for this purpose).

[182] R Nolan, 'Property in a Fund' (2004) 120 LQR 108; PG Turner, 'Floating Charges—A "No Theory" Theory' [2004] LMCLQ 319.

[183] As was noted in *National Westminster Bank Plc v Spectrum plus Ltd* [2004] Ch 337, CA, paras 25–30 *per* Lord Phillips MR. In *Ashborder BV v Green Gas Power Ltd* [2005] 1 BCLC 623 disposals were held to be in breach of restrictions in floating charges limiting the chargor's dealings to the ordinary course of its business but the proprietary consequences of that finding were not fully explored.

[184] However, the clearest view and most persuasive view (not following EV Ferran, 'Floating Charges—The Nature of the Security' [1988] CLJ 213, 231) is that even before crystallization, the equitable interest created by the floating charge is capable of binding a third party who has acquired property with notice of the charge and of the circumstances of the transfer: R Nolan, 'Property in a Fund' (2004) 120 LQR 108, 127. See also Law Commission, *Company Security Interests* (Law Com Rep No 296, 2005) para 3.219, which assumes that buyers will not take free of a charge if they know that the disposition is not permitted because of some explicit restriction in the charge.

[185] J Armour, 'Should We Redistribute in Insolvency?' in J Getzler and J Payne (eds), *Company Charges: Spectrum and Beyond* (Oxford: OUP, 2006) ch 9.

order of payment.[186] With the abolition of the Crown's preferential status with regard to tax claims, effected by section 251 of the Enterprise Act 2002, the classes of debt entitled to this statutory priority have been significantly reduced.[187] A consequence may be that in future there will be less controversy about this aspect of the insolvency regime and its interaction with consensual security interests.

However, other provisions of the Insolvency Act 1986 may take the place of the preferential debts regime as a key factor that drives disputes about the correct categorization of a charge. First, under section 176A of the Insolvency Act 1986, introduced by the Enterprise Act 2002, in insolvency proceedings a certain portion of a company's net property must be ring-fenced and not distributed to the holder of a floating charge except to the extent that it exceeds the amount required to satisfy unsecured debts. Secondly, the general expenses of administration (one type of insolvency proceeding) can be recouped out of assets that are subject to a floating charge but not from assets that are subject to a fixed charge.[188] This was also thought to be the position in liquidation until the decision of the House of Lords in *Buchler v Talbot*,[189] where it was held that assets secured by a floating charge were not available to meet general liquidation expenses. The more favourable position in liquidation for holders of floating charges was, however, short-lived because it was reversed by section 176ZA of the Insolvency Act 1986, inserted by the Companies Act 2006. Thirdly, floating (but not fixed) charges may be invalid if they are created within a certain period before the onset of insolvency proceedings and other specified conditions are satisfied.[190]

Fixed and floating charges are both consensual securities created by agreement between the parties. Freedom of contract prevails to the extent that the parties can choose what rights and obligations to grant each other. However, whether the particular package of rights and obligations that they have chosen amounts to a fixed or floating charge is a question of law. Any label that the parties may attach to the security documentation is not determinative of the nature of a charge: if the rights and obligations that the parties have granted each other in respect of the charged assets are inconsistent with the label attached to the charge by the parties, that description will be disregarded and, as a matter of law, the security will be categorized in accordance with the substantive rights and obligations that it creates.[191] The two-stage process—(1) ascertainment of the rights and obligations that the parties have given each other; and (2) attribution of the correct legal label to that package of rights and obligations—will be followed in any case where the nature of a charge is in doubt.

What, then, is the package of rights and obligations that the law will recognize as giving rise to a floating charge or, as the case may be, a fixed charge? Their consensual nature and the very flexible character of English law on security interests imply that neither type of charge should be expected to have a rigidly fixed set of terms that cannot be departed from in any respect. So, in considering this question, it needs to be borne in mind that what we

---

[186] Such as *Agnew v The Commissioner of Inland Revenue* [2001] 2 AC 710, PC and *Re Spectrum Plus Ltd* [2005] 2 AC 680, HL.

[187] Insolvency Act 1986, Sch 6 lists the remaining categories of preferential debts (contributions to occupational pension schemes and state pension schemes; remuneration and related payments owing to employees; and levies on coal and steel production).

[188] Insolvency Act 1986, Sch B1, para 99(3). J Armour, 'Floating Charges: All Adrift' [2004] CLJ 560, 564. However, *Buchler v Talbot*, considered next, complicated the position: R Henry, 'The New World of Priority for Floating Charge Holders' (2004) 20 *Insolvency Law and Practice* 194.

[189] [2004] 1 BCLC 281, HL.

[190] Insolvency Act 1986, s 245.

[191] *Agnew v The Commissioner of Inland Revenue* [2001] 2 AC 710, PC, [32]. Much of the debate on proper characterization has focused on whether charges carrying the label 'fixed charge' are really floating charges but the characterization issues can also run the other way: *The Russell Cooke Trust Co Ltd v Elliot* [2007] EWHC 1443 (Ch), [2007] 2 BCLC 637 (charge labelled as 'floating' held to be a fixed charge).

are seeking to identify are the standard, or default, terms from which parties may have some freedom to depart without necessarily creating a different security from that which was their original intention. As Hoffmann J said, when he noted that the floating charge could not be exhaustively defined:[192]

> All that can be done is to enumerate its standard characteristics. It does not follow that the absence of one or more of those features or the presence of others will prevent the charge from being categorised as 'floating'. There are bound to be penumbral cases in which it may be difficult to say whether the degree of deviation from the standard case is enough to make it inappropriate to use such a term. But the rights and duties which the law may or may not categorise as a floating charge are wholly derived from the agreement of the parties, supplemented by the terms implied by law. It seems to me fallacious to argue that once the parties have agreed on some terms which are thought sufficient to identify the transaction as a floating charge, they are then precluded from agreeing to any other terms which are not present in the standard case.

When seeking to establish the characteristics of the floating charge, it is usual to cite the following passage from the judgment of Romer LJ in *Re Yorkshire Woolcombers Ltd*:[193]

> ...I certainly think that if a charge has the three characteristics that I am about to mention, it is a floating charge.
> (1) If it is a charge on a class of assets of a company present and future;
> (2) if that class is one which, in the ordinary course of the business of the company, would be changing from time to time; and
> (3) if you find that by the charge it is contemplated that, until some future step is taken by or on behalf of those interested in the charge, the company may carry on its business in the ordinary way as far as concerns the particular class of assets I am dealing with.

These three characteristics are indicative of a floating charge but, as Romer LJ emphasized,[194] they do not amount to a precise definition of a floating charge. A charge can still be a floating charge even though it does not meet all of the criteria. This is evident from *Re Croftbell Ltd*[195] where a charge was held to be a floating charge notwithstanding that the secured property (shares in subsidiaries) was not expected to be the subject of regular turnover in the ordinary course of business.[196] In a similar vein, in *Re ASRS Establishment Ltd*[197] it was said to be 'irrelevant' to the determination that a charge on an escrow account was floating that the escrow moneys were not a regular source of working capital and would not thus be subject to fluctuation. In *Smith (Administrator of Cosslett (Contractors) Ltd) v Bridgend County Borough Council*[198] a clause which gave the provider of finance a right of sale in respect of constructional plant, temporary works goods, and materials (whose nature came to be tested with respect to heavy-duty coal-washing plants which were used to separate usable coal from residue) was held to be a floating charge.

Although it would be very unusual for a floating charge not to extend to future, as well as presently owned, assets of the debtor company, it has been held that a charge on present property only can be a floating charge.[199] Likewise, a charge on future property only can also be

---

[192] *Re Brightlife Ltd* [1987] Ch 200, 214–5.
[193] [1903] 2 Ch 284 CA; affirmed *sub nom Illingworth v Houldsworth* [1904] AC 355, HL.
[194] At 295. See also 298 *per* Cozens Hardy LJ.   [195] [1990] BCLC 844.
[196] See also *Welch v Bowmaker (Ireland) Ltd* [1980] IR 251, Ir SC, where the majority of the Irish Supreme Court held that a charge secured on land could be a floating charge notwithstanding that the debtor company was not in the business of property trading and the land was not a class of asset changing from time to time in the course of the company's business.
[197] [2000] 2 BCLC 631.   [198] [2002] 1 AC 336, HL.
[199] *Re Bond Worth Ltd* [1980] 1 Ch 228, 267; *Re Cimex Tissues Ltd* [1994] BCC 626, 635.

a floating charge and it is not essential to bring existing assets within the scope of the charge for it to be so classified.[200]

The most important of the three criteria is thus the third one: the extent to which the charge contemplates that the company will continue to be free to deal with the assets which are the subject matter of the security without having to refer back to the creditor for authorization.[201] In *Agnew v Commissioners of Inland Revenue* Lord Millett said of the three criteria that 'the first two characteristics are typical of a floating charge but they are not distinctive of it.'[202] His Lordship continued: 'It is the third characteristic which is the hallmark of a floating charge and serves to distinguish it from a fixed charge.'[203] In *Re Spectrum Plus Ltd*[204] Lord Scott went even further: 'Indeed if a security has Romer LJ's third characteristic I am inclined to think that it qualifies as a floating charge, and cannot be a fixed charge, whatever may be its other characteristics.' In the factual circumstances of the *Spectrum* litigation, which concerned the legal nature of a charge on book debts, which are fluctuating assets, Lord Scott's comment is noteworthy but not especially startling. However, if it is read as indicating a more general principle—that any freedom to deal with the assets that are the subject matter of security means that a security must be categorized as a floating charge regardless of its other characteristics, such as the nature of the assets secured, it takes on a more controversial character.[205] This is because a line of case law stretching back to some of the classic cases on fixed and floating charges appears to establish that some degree of license to deal with assets is not necessarily incompatible with a fixed charge and that the extent to which the license to deal is compatible with a fixed charge depends on all the circumstances of the case.[206] It has been suggested that cases that sanction a limited power to deal as being compatible with a fixed charge are now very doubtful because of *Smith (Administrator of Cosslett (Contractors) Ltd) v Bridgend County Borough Council*[207] where a charge on assets, including heavy duty machinery, was held to be a floating charge.[208] However, the case was decided on the basis that the property subject to the charge was a fluctuating body of assets which could be consumed or (subject to the approval of the engineer) removed from the site in the ordinary course of the contractor's business.[209] It may therefore still be open to argue that the case is not determinative of the position in different circumstances, such as where a charge is confined to non-fluctuating assets and the license to withdraw assets from the security is limited.

The two-stage process for ascertaining whether a charge is fixed or floating, which the *Agnew* and *Spectrum* cases firmly establish as the method for determining the legal nature of a charge, emphasizes the rights and obligations that the parties have granted to each other and the legal categorization associated with that package of rights and obligations. The nature of the asset class to which the security relates is relevant in this process as part of the factual background against which the standard process of documentary interpretation takes place.[210] It may have particular significance in certain circumstances[211]—for instance, in the

---

[200] *Re Croftbell Ltd* [1990] BCLC 844, 848.

[201] *Jurong Data Centre Development v M+W Singapore* [2011] SGHC 58, [2011] 3 SLR 337, [73], Singapore HC ('the essential element in determining whether a charge is fixed or floating is ascertaining whether the chargee or the charger is in control of the asset concerned prior to the occurrence of an event of default').

[202] [2001] 2 AC 710, PC, [13].   [203] [2001] 2 AC 710, PC, [13].   [204] [2005] 2 AC 680, HL, [107].

[205] N Frome, '*Spectrum*—An End to the Conflict or The Signal for a New Campaign?' (2005) 20 *Butterworths Journal of International Banking and Financial Law* 433, 434; N Frome and K Gibbons, '*Spectrum*—An End to the Conflict or the Signal for a New Campaign' in J Getzler and J Payne (eds), *Company Charges: Spectrum and Beyond* (Oxford: OUP, 2006) ch 5.

[206] The cases are reviewed in *Re Cimex Tissues Ltd* [1994] BCC 626, 634–40.   [207] [2002] 1 AC 336, HL.

[208] P Walton, 'Fixed Charges Over Assets Other Than Book Debts—Is Possession Nine-tenths of the Law?' (2005) 21 *Insolvency Law and Practice* 117.

[209] At [41].   [210] *Ashborder BV v Green Gas Power Ltd* [2005] 1 BCLC 623, [183].

[211] *Ashborder BV v Green Gas Power Ltd* [2005] 1 BCLC 623, [183].

absence of an express provision permitting disposals in the ordinary course of business, a charge on assets that would ordinarily fluctuate in the ordinary course of business is likely to be categorized as a floating charge, as to classify it as a fixed charge would be likely to paralyze the chargor's business and the courts will favour a commercially sensible construction if the words used can bear it.[212] However, for the purposes of characterization, asset-class character is, at best, of second-order[213] importance only and, on one view, is actually irrelevant in determining whether a charge is fixed or floating.[214]

The essence of the floating charge, on the other hand, is that the assets that are the subject matter of the security remain under the management and control of the chargor.[215] A charge does not cease to be a floating charge merely because it includes certain restrictions on dealing with the secured assets by the chargor;[216] the question remains whether overall control lies with the chargor, in which case the charge is floating, or with the chargee, in which case it may be fixed. The most familiar example of a restriction that is not incompatible with a floating charge is the covenant whereby the chargor promises not to create any subsequent security on the charged assets which would rank before or equally with the floating charge. Negative pledge covenants of this type are very common and their compatibility with a floating charge is now unquestionable.[217] Another example is provided by *Re Brightlife Ltd*[218] where a prohibition on the company selling debts which were the subject matter of the security was held to be consistent with the charge being a floating charge. This case was part of a long and complex saga on the legal categorization of charges on book debts, to which we now turn.

Classification of a Charge as Fixed or Floating and the Nature of the Secured Property—Charges on Book Debts

In *Siebe Gorman & Co Ltd v Barclays Bank Ltd*[219] the agreement between the company and its creditor Barclays Bank, charged the company's present and future book debts and other debts by way of first fixed charge. Under the terms of the charge, the company was required not to charge or assign any part of the charged property without the consent of Barclays. The company was permitted to continue to collect the proceeds of its book debts itself but was required to pay those proceeds into an account with Barclays. Slade J held that the restrictions on dealing with the debts (albeit that only certain forms of dealing were prohibited) together with the requirement to pay the proceeds into an account with Barclays from which, as the debenture was construed, Barclays could prevent withdrawals (although this right to block withdrawals was not expressly stated in the terms of the charge) were sufficient to constitute a fixed charge.

---

[212] *Mannai Investment Co Ltd v Eagle Star Life Assurance Co Ltd* [1997] AC 749 HL, 771 *per* Lord Steyn.

[213] *Re Cosslett (Contractors)* [1998] Ch 495 CA, 510 *per* Millett LJ, affirmed *Smith (Administrator of Cosslett (Contractors) Ltd) v Bridgend County Borough Council* [2002] 1 AC 336, HL.

[214] S Worthington, 'Floating Charges: Use and Abuse of Doctrinal Analysis,' in J Getzler and J Payne (eds), *Company Charges: Spectrum and Beyond* (Oxford: OUP, 2006) 25, 29.

[215] *Re Cosslett (Contractors)* [1998] Ch 495 CA, 510 *per* Millett LJ. However, any dealings by the chargor of the charged assets in breach of restrictions imposed by the chargee would not change the nature of the charge from fixed to floating. As long as the chargee does not consent to the chargor's non-observance of any restriction or waive any breach which it subsequently discovers, the chargor would not be able to rely on its own wrong to convert a fixed charge into a floating charge: *Jurong Data Centre Development v M+W Singapore* [2011] SGHC 58, [2011] 3 SLR 337, Singapore HC.

[216] *Re Cosslett (Contractors)* [1998] Ch 495 CA, 510 *per* Millett LJ.

[217] *Re Cosslett (Contractors)* [1998] Ch 495 CA, 510 *per* Millett LJ.

[218] [1987] Ch 200.   [219] [1979] 2 Lloyd's Rep 142.

Siebe Gorman [220] was a breakthrough decision. It appeared to resolve a problem that practitioners had been grappling with since the early days in the nineteenth century when the forms of security with which we are now familiar were starting to emerge, namely, that creditors need control over the secured assets if their security is to be regarded as fixed but companies need to have ready access to the proceeds of their book debts, which are an important element of their cash flow. In the *Yorkshire Woolcombers* litigation, the fact that a fixed charge on book debts could have prevented the continued operation of the company's business by depriving it of an important source of cash was regarded as significant and as pointing towards the conclusion that the parties intended to create a floating charge.[221] *Siebe Gorman* confirmed that dual control—on the debts and on the proceeds of the debts—was essential to the creation of a fixed charge on book debts and that, in relation to the proceeds of the debts, the creditor had to be able to prevent withdrawals from the account into which they were paid. The court's interpretation of the charge was the dual control requirement was satisfied. The cash flow implications of that conclusion were not explored.

After the *Siebe Gorman* case, corporate finance practice quickly embraced the fixed charge on book debts as a standard part of the package of security sought by lenders but a steady stream of cases, in England and elsewhere in common law countries, gave some indication of difficulties with the decision that were eventually to culminate in the decision of the House of Lords in *Spectrum Plus*[222] in which it was overruled. There were two core problems: the construction of the charging document used by Barclays Bank which was litigated in the *Siebe Gorman* case—did it actually give the chargee sufficient control over the proceeds of the book debts for the charge to be regarded as fixed?; and a deeper problem as to whether control over proceeds, as well as the debts themselves, was necessary for the existence of a fixed charge on book debts.

On the first issue, in *Supercool v Hoverd Industries Ltd*[223] the New Zealand High Court declined to follow *Siebe Gorman* in a case involving charging documentation that was substantially the same as that litigated in the English case and did not draw the implication found in the *Siebe Gorman* case that the company was not free to make withdrawals from the account into which the proceeds were paid without the creditor's consent. Therefore, since the company's access to the proceeds was not restricted, the charge was only a floating charge. Doubts about whether the court in *Siebe Gorman* had correctly construed the charging documentation used by Barclays Bank were further reinforced by decisions elsewhere in the common law world.[224] The *Spectrum Plus* case finally provided an opportunity for the House of Lords to consider this issue of construction because there were no material differences between the charge used by the National Westminster Bank in that case and the Barclays Bank debenture in issue in *Siebe Gorman*.[225] The seven-person House concluded, unanimously, that the charge, properly construed in the context of the matrix of facts in which it was created, placed no restrictions on the use that the company could make of the balance on the account into which the proceeds of the book debts were paid and that therefore the charge, though labelled as fixed, was in law only a floating charge. *Siebe Gorman* was overruled and the Court refused to take the exceptional step of limiting the overruling so as to have prospective effect only; the argument that the *Siebe Gorman* debenture had become

---

[220] Generally, on the development of the concept of fixed charges on book debts, see: RA Pearce, 'Fixed Charges over Book Debts' [1987] JBL 18; RR Pennington, 'Fixed Charges Over Future Assets of a Company' (1985) 6 *Company Law* 9; G McCormack, 'Fixed Charges on Future Book Debts' (1987) 8 *Company Lawyer* 3.

[221] [1903] 2 Ch 284, 288 *per* Farwell J, 296 *per* Romer LJ, and 297 *per* Cozens-Hardy LJ. See also A Berg, 'Charges Over Book Debts: A Reply' [1995] JBL 433, 436–40.

[222] *Re Spectrum Plus Ltd* [2005] 2 AC 680.   [223] [1994] 3 NZLR 300, NZ HC.

[224] *Re Holidair* [1994] 1 IR 416, Ir Sc.   [225] At [86] *per* Lord Scott.

a widely-used precedent for a fixed charge and that lenders should be shielded from the consequence of full, retrospective overruling found no favour.

The House of Lords in the *Spectrum* case also overruled the decision of the Court of Appeal in *Re New Bullas Trading Ltd*.[226] That case had involved a form of charge on book debts which differed from the standard *Siebe Gorman*-style precedent in a significant respect. Whereas the conventional form of charge treated book debts and their proceeds as indivisible, the charge in issue in the *New Bullas* case had treated the debt and its proceeds as divisible. The charge included the usual restrictions on dealings with the book debts themselves and required the chargor company to pay the proceeds of those debts into a designated bank account with a specified bank. However, the charge further stipulated that, once the proceeds had been paid in, they would be released from the fixed charge on the book debts and would be subject only to the creditor's general floating charge on the company's assets in the absence of any written directions from the creditor concerning the use of the money. The Court of Appeal had held that it was legally possible to separate a debt from its proceeds and that the debts could be the subject of a fixed charge, whilst the proceeds were subject only to a floating charge. That decision, though consistent with the English judiciary's tendency to look favourably on practitioner ingenuity in moulding the law to suit commercial needs, was widely criticized because it allowed a charge to be categorized as fixed even though assets that were the subject matter of the security would be extinguished through collection of the proceeds, an event over which the holder of the charge did not have control.[227] Shortly before the decision of the House of Lords in *Spectrum*, the *New Bullas* case was said to have been wrongly decided by the Privy Council in *Agnew v Commissioner of Inland Revenue*.[228] The Privy Council, speaking through Lord Millett, reasoned:

> While a debt and its proceeds are two separate assets, however, the latter are merely the traceable proceeds of the former and represent its entire value. A debt is a receivable; it is merely a right to receive payment from the debtor. Such a right cannot be enjoyed in specie; its value can be exploited only by exercising the right or by assigning it for value to a third party. An assignment or charge of a receivable which does not carry with it the right to the receipt has no value. It is worthless as a security. Any attempt in the present context to separate the ownership of the debts from the ownership of their proceeds (even if conceptually possible) makes no commercial sense.
>
> ...
>
> The company was left in control of the process by which the charged assets were extinguished and replaced by different assets which were not the subject of a fixed charge and were at the free disposal of the company. That is inconsistent with the nature of a fixed charge.[229]

In the *Spectrum* case the House of Lords agreed that the essential value of a book debt as a security lay in the money that could be obtained from the debtor in payment and that a security that did not allow its holder to control the proceeds of the debt should be categorized as a floating security.[230] This is not to say that a debt and its proceeds can never in law be regarded as separate assets—for example, it would be possible to take a fixed charge on proceeds without also controlling the debts themselves;[231] rather, it is simply that a chargee must control the proceeds of debts for its charge on those debts to be a fixed charge.

---

[226] [1994] BCLC 485.

[227] RM Goode, 'Charges Over Book Debts: a Missed Opportunity' (1994) 110 LQR 592; and S Worthington, 'Fixed Charges over Book Debts and other Receivables' (1997) 113 LQR 562. cf A Berg, 'Charges Over Book Debts: A Reply' [1995] JBL 433.

[228] *Agnew v The Commissioner of Inland Revenue* [2001] 2 AC 710, PC.   [229] At [49].

[230] *Re Spectrum Plus Ltd* [2005] 2 AC 680, HL, [110] *per* Lord Scott.

[231] *Re SSSL Realisations (2002) Ltd* [2005] 1 BCLC 1, [54], appeal dismissed [2006] Ch 610, CA.

Post-*Agnew* and *Spectrum* it remains conceptually possible to create a fixed security over book debts[232] but, although the heresy that it is possible in this context to separate debts and proceeds as envisaged in the *New Bullas* case has been erased, problems remain in working out exactly what minimum degree of control a chargee must have over debts and their proceeds for its security on book debts to be fixed. Concern about technical legal uncertainty overlaps with a deeper policy concern: that the control legally required to create a fixed charge over book debts may exceed what is commercially acceptable because vesting that degree of control in the providers of debt finance could paralyze businesses by depriving companies of essential access to working capital.

It is clear that if the chargee collects the proceeds of book debts for its own benefit or allows the chargor to collect them on its behalf and requires them to be paid into an account from which no withdrawals can be made without its specific consent, the charge will be fixed. However, such arrangements would be administratively burdensome and likely to be commercially unworkable.[233] On the other hand, if the chargor has complete freedom to collect and use the proceeds in the course of its business, the charge will undoubtedly be floating, which may not satisfy the chargee's desire for strong priority.[234] Commercial considerations suggest that the parties should aim for some type of middle ground, such as a standing authorization in the terms of the charge for the chargor to draw on the account when the credit balance exceeds a specified security cover. However, it is by no means certain that such an arrangement would be effective to create a fixed charge: in the *Spectrum* case Lord Walker suggested that assets could only be released from a fixed charge with the *active* concurrence of the chargee[235] and passages in speeches of other members of the House of Lords can also be read as casting doubt on whether any pre-agreed drawing rights on a supposedly blocked account in favour of the chargor can be accommodated within the terms of a fixed charge on book debts.[236] In the Court of Appeal in the *Spectrum* case Lord Phillips MR had said that it would seem to be 'beyond dispute' that a requirement to pay book debts into a blocked account would be sufficient restriction to render a charge over book debts a fixed charge, even if the chargor was permitted to overdraw on another account, into which from time to time transfers were made from the blocked account.[237] However, even this seemingly firm guidance must be treated with caution because the Court of Appeal was reversed by the House of Lords and Lord Walker, in the Lords, noted that the structure mentioned by the Master of the Rolls, although no doubt appropriate and efficacious in some commercial contexts, might not provide a simple solution in every case.[238]

Must the chargor actually block withdrawals from the account into which the proceeds of book debts are paid or are the legal requirements for a fixed charge on book debts satisfied so long as the proceeds are to be paid into an account that, on the face of the documents, is adequately blocked? Lord Millett's answer to this question in the *Agnew* case was unequivocal: 'But their Lordships would wish to make it clear that it is not enough to provide in the debenture that the account is a blocked account if it is not operated as one in

---

[232] *Spectrum*, [54] *per* Lord Hope; [136] *per* Lord Walker. See also S Worthington, 'An "Unsatisfactory Area of the Law"—Fixed and Floating Charges Yet Again' (2004) 1 *International Corporate Rescue* 175.

[233] G Yeowart, 'Spectrum Plus: The Wider Implications' (2005) 20 *Butterworths Journal of International Banking and Financial Law* 301, 302.

[234] It is irrelevant that some months after the execution of the debenture, the company finds itself restricted from freely using the proceeds of the book debts then and thereafter becoming available, as a result of the setting up of a blocked account: *Re Harmony Care Homes* [2009] EWHC 1961 (Ch), [2010] BCC 358, [19].

[235] *Re Spectrum Plus Ltd* [2005] 2 AC 680, HL, [138]. See also *Re Lehman Brothers International (Europe)* [2012] EWHC 2997 (Ch).

[236] A Berg, 'The Cuckoo in the Nest of Corporate Insolvency: Some Aspects of the Spectrum Case' [2006] JBL 22; F Oditah, 'Fixed Charges and the Recycling of Proceeds of Receivables' (2004) 120 LQR 533.

[237] *National Westminster Bank plc v Spectrum Plus Ltd* [2004] Ch 337, CA, [99].

[238] [2005] 2 AC 680, HL, [160].

fact.'[239] In *Spectrum* Lord Walker twice referred to Lord Millett's statement with evident acceptance of its correctness,[240] though with an acknowledgement that it could raise difficult questions with regard to the construction of commercial contracts. The difficulty is that conventional principles of contractual interpretation suggest that whether the account is actually operated as a blocked account is irrelevant to the question of construction because evidence of the parties' conduct after the conclusion of a contract is not generally admissible as an aid to interpretation of the terms of a contract.[241] In several cases that are part of the saga from *Siebe Gorman* to *Spectrum*, the inadmissibility of evidence relating to post-contractual conduct played a part in the courts reaching a conclusion that charges were fixed rather than floating.[242] Shams are an exception to the principle that post-contractual conduct is inadmissible but the courts are usually rather reluctant to invoke the doctrine of shams. It is not clear whether Lord Millett's warning is best interpreted merely as a reminder of the existence of the sham doctrine as conventionally understood, as signalling a departure from the traditional approach to construction, or as indicating one of the consequences of the two-stage process for the categorization of charges, with general principles of contractual interpretation[243] governing the first stage of the process (what rights and obligations have the parties granted each other?) but not the second stage (what is the legal categorization of their rights and obligations?). The third alternative—that post-charge conduct is relevant to the second stage legal categorization of the rights and obligations because it indicates that one of the legal features of a fixed charge, namely permanent appropriation of the secured assets to the payment of the sum charged,[244] is not present—has been strongly argued.[245] Whatever its precise meaning, it is not credible to suppose that a judge with such experience and distinction in this field as Lord Millett[246] would have included such a warning or that the equally eminent Lord Walker would have mentioned it specifically in the later case if they did not intend it to be taken seriously.[247] There would thus appear to be significant legal risk in corporate finance practice now proceeding on the basis that there is room for much divergence between the terms of a charge on book debts that provide for a blocked account and how that account is actually operated in practice.

Implications of *Agnew* and *Spectrum* for Other Asset Classes

Queens Moat Houses plc v Capita IRG Trustees Ltd[248] is a recent case that supports the proposition that a limited power for the chargor to release property from the security is not incompatible with a fixed charge provided the chargee remains in overall control. A portfolio of

---

[239] [2001] 2 AC 710, PC.   [240] At paras 140 and 160. See also Lord Scott, [119].

[241] *James Miller & Partners v Whitworth Street Estates (Manchester) Ltd* [1970] AC 583, HL; *Wickman Ltd v Schuler AG* [1974] AC 325, HL; *Re Armagh Shoes* [1984] BCLC 405; *Re Wogan's (Drogheda) Ltd* [1993] 1 IR 157, Ir SC; *Wimpole Theatre (a firm) v JJ Goodman* [2012] EWHC 1600 (QB) para 40. Post-contractual conduct is, of course, relevant to questions about variation of existing contracts, contractual waivers, and estoppels, eg *Newbury v Sun Microsystems* [2013] EWHC 2180 (QB), [27].

[242] In particular *Re Wogan's (Drogheda) Ltd* [1993] IR 157, Ir SC. See also *Re Keenan Bros Ltd* [1985] BCLC 302, Ir HC, [1986] BCLC 242 Ir SC, where a special blocked account was not opened for some five months after the charge documentation was concluded and during that period the company was apparently free to deal with the proceeds of its book debts. The trial judge rejected the admissibility of the evidence concerning the conduct of the parties during that five months and the Irish Supreme Court did not question that approach.

[243] On which, see *Mannai Ltd v Eagle Star Assurance Co Ltd* [1997] AC 749, HL; *Investors Compensation Scheme Ltd v West Bromwich Building Society* [1998] 1 WLR 896.

[244] *Re Spectrum Plus Ltd* [2005] 2 AC 680, HL, [138] *per* Lord Walker.

[245] A Berg, 'The Cuckoo in the Nest of Corporate Insolvency: Some Aspects of the Spectrum Case' [2006] JBL 22.

[246] On Lord Millett's contribution to the law see G McCormack, 'Lords Hoffmann and Millett and the Shaping of Credit and Insolvency Law' [2005] LMCLQ 491.

[247] A Berg, 'The Cuckoo in the Nest of Corporate Insolvency: Some Aspects of the Spectrum Case' [2006] JBL 22, 36.

[248] [2005] 2 BCLC 199.

hotels was charged as security for debenture stock. The charging deed gave the chargor power unilaterally to withdraw property from the charge in certain circumstances. It was held that the existence of this unilateral right in favour of the chargor did not change what was otherwise a fixed charge into a floating charge. Lightman J reasoned that there was a critical difference between a corporate chargor's right to deal with and dispose of property free from a charge without reference to the chargee and a chargor's right to require the chargee to release property from the charge, in that the former right was consistent only with the existence of a floating charge and was inconsistent with the existence of a fixed charge, whereas there was no inconsistency between the existence of a fixed charge and a contractual right on the part of the chargor to require the chargee to release property from the charge. However, *permanent* appropriation of the secured assets for payment of the debt and *active* concurrence of the chargee in the release of any assets from the security are emphasized in the *Spectrum* decision as being crucial to the fixed charge.[249] Whether the *Queens Moat Houses* case, which was decided before *Spectrum*, is compatible with the decision of the House of Lords is thus open to question.[250] The different nature of the assets in the two cases offers a possible line of distinction but many of the key passages in the *Spectrum* speeches are worded in general terms and do not obviously appear to be confined to charges on book debts. Furthermore, as noted earlier in this chapter, there is a strong trend in the modern cases to downgrade the significance of asset class in determining whether a charge is fixed or floating. Notwithstanding that English law on security interests has traditionally been characterized by its flexibility within the bounds of legal possibility and the cases have established the standard terms of different types of security without defining them exhaustively, the recent authorities suggest that total control of the assets secured, whatever their nature, may be necessary for a fixed charge.[251]

Whether it is possible to distinguish *Spectrum* in the context of security relating to asset classes other than book debts is relevant in relation to project financing and structured financing transactions. In a securitization, for example, income producing assets, such as mortgages, equipment leases, consumer loans, credit card receivables, commercial loans, property rents, car finance loans, or trade receivables (for example, commodities), are transferred by an originator to a special purpose vehicle (SPV) and the payment of principal and interest on the bonds issued by the SPV to fund the acquisition is met from the income stream produced by those assets. The SPV grants 'fixed' security over all of its assets and undertaking in favour of the trustee for the bonds, including its bank accounts, but the security documentation will set out the order of payments from the bank accounts (a payment waterfall), which, typically, will include the possibility of a payment to the originator after the payment of fees and expenses and of amounts due to the bondholders. Payment waterfalls, which are also common in project financing,[252] are essentially pre-agreed arrangements for withdrawals from bank accounts and the effect is that the chargee does not give consent on a drawing-by-drawing basis. There is thus a risk that the security over the bank accounts could be characterized as a floating charge. A further risk is that, applying *Agnew* and *Spectrum* reasoning, the security on the assets that have produced the income stream paid into the bank accounts could also be held to be floating. In some cases before *Spectrum* it was held that charges on income producing assets, such as leases and shares, could be fixed

---

[249] In particular by Lord Walker, [139].
[250] *Re F2G Realisations* [2010] EWHC 1772 (Ch), [2011] 1 BCLC 313, [38].
[251] *Fanshaw v Amav Industries (Re Beam Tube Products)* [2006] EWHC 486 (Ch), [2007] 2 BCLC 732; *Re Rayford Homes* [2011] EWHC 1948 (Ch), [2011] BCC 715.
[252] G Yeowart, 'Spectrum Plus: The Wider Implications' (2005) 20 *Butterworths Journal of International Banking and Financial Law* 301, 302.

even though the chargor had free use of the income but the correctness of those decisions is now in doubt.[253]

The risk of the security arrangements being recharacterized as floating rather than fixed could affect the credit rating of a structured financing. The rating agency, Fitch, has given specific advice on this matter.[254] It says that given the legal uncertainty surrounding the application of *Spectrum* to asset classes other than book debts and the factual issues surrounding the level of control exercised by the chargee in practice, in respect of each charge in the transaction structure (including those granted by bankruptcy-remote SPV issuers), Fitch will expect the transaction legal counsel to:

(1) give a clean opinion that the relevant charge constitutes a fixed (rather than a floating) charge;

(2) give a reasoned (rather than 'clean') opinion as to whether the relevant charge constitutes a fixed (rather than floating) charge. In these circumstances, Fitch and its legal counsel will review the reasonableness of the views and analysis provided. If the conclusion expressed in the opinion is that the charge is or is likely to be held to be floating, the legal consequences of this need to be clearly stated (for example any impact on enforcement rights or recoveries in an administration, or risk of avoidance) so that these consequences can be factored into Fitch's rating analysis; or

(3) in circumstances where the transaction lawyers cannot express any legal conclusion on the recharacterization risk (in which case Fitch will assume in its analysis that the charge is floating), specify clearly what the legal consequences are if the fixed charge is recharacterized as a floating charge (for example any impact on enforcement rights or recoveries in an administration, or risk of avoidance), so that these consequences can be factored into Fitch's rating.

Assessment of the Post-*Spectrum* Position

While there are different views on the extent to which the post-*Spectrum* position is uncertain, particularly with regard to asset classes other than book debts, commentators tend to agree that costly efforts will continue to be made both by transactional lawyers and, in cases of dispute, by the judiciary to establish which side of the fixed/floating boundary a particular security structure falls.[255] If the control requirements set by the judiciary for fixed charges on circulating or other assets prove to be commercially unworkable, a possible policy response would be a statutory reformulation of security interests to provide a type of security that gives lenders the benefits associated with the fixed charge and, at the same time, allows companies free use of income streams.[256] However, to date, the legislature has not shown any willingness to intervene in this way. A more likely prospect for the short and medium term is that corporate finance practitioners will seek to find constructive solutions that avoid difficulties and

---

[253] *Re Atlantic Computer Systems plc* [1992] Ch 505, CA; *Re Atlantic Medical Ltd* [1992] BCC 653; *Arthur D Little Ltd (in administration) v Ableco Finance LLC* [2003] Ch 217. cf *Royal Trust Bank v National Westminster Bank plc* [1996] BCC 613, CA, 618 *per* Millett LJ.

[254] Fitch Ratings, 'Spectrum Plus—Implications for Structured Finance Transactions?,' Special Report (December 2005) available at <http://www.fitchratings.com/corporate/reports/report_frame.cfm?rpt_id=259190&sector_flag=1&marketsector=2&detail=> (accessed May 2013).

[255] This point is made in many of the essays in J Getzler and J Payne (eds), *Company Charges: Spectrum and Beyond* (Oxford: OUP, 2006).

[256] The idea of a third category of charge because the conceptual apparatus of fixed security and floating security may be inadequate to accommodate new forms of security has been mooted: A Berg, 'Charges Over Book Debts: The Spectrum Case in the Court of Appeal' [2004] JBL 581, 608; A Berg, 'Brumark Investments Ltd and the "Innominate Charge"' [2001] JBL 532.

uncertainties in the general law.[257] One possible solution is for companies to make greater use of alternative products and systems that allow borrowers to realize the value of their book debts through outright sales (invoice discounters and factors) rather than by granting security.[258] Another is for more debt finance to be raised through SPVs that are structured so as to be bankruptcy-remote (insolvency being when the status of a charge matters most).

Crystallization of a Floating Charge

Until a floating charge crystallizes, a company can continue to deal with the assets that are the subject matter of the security in the ordinary course of its business.[259] The expression 'ordinary course of its…business' has to be given the meaning which ordinary business people in the position of the parties to the security would be expected to give it against the factual and commercial background in which the documents were made.[260] A transaction can be in the ordinary course of business even if it is exceptional or unprecedented or even if it might be a fraudulent or wrongful preference in the context of a winding up.[261] The existence of an uncrystallized floating charge does not prevent the company's debtors from claiming rights of set-off against it,[262] nor does it preclude any of the company's other creditors from enforcing judgment against its assets.[263]

When a floating charge crystallizes into a fixed charge, it attaches to the existing assets of the company within the ambit of the charge and, unless the charge excludes this, all such assets as are subsequently acquired.[264] A crystallized floating charge ranks as a fixed charge for the purposes of determining its priority against other interests in the company's property which are created or acquired after crystallization.[265] Although there is one case that suggests otherwise,[266] the better view is that crystallization does not affect the priority of a floating charge against other interests in the same property which predate crystallization. Crystallization has the effect of postponing execution creditors to the chargee's interest,[267] and once

---

[257] N Frome, 'Spectrum—An End to the Conflict or the Signal for a New Campaign' (2005) 11 *Butterworths Journal of International Banking and Financial Law* 433: 'Ultimately the lending community will always find a way of achieving their control objectives even if the law requires them to use more complex methodologies (such as off balance sheet structures) to do so. Unfortunately, in that event, the additional cost will have to be borne by the borrower community.' Also noting the potentially economically damaging consequences of additional costs: G Moss, 'Fictions and Floating Charges: some Reflections on the House of Lords' Decision in Spectrum' in J Getzler and J Payne (eds), *Company Charges: Spectrum and Beyond* (Oxford: OUP, 2006) 1.

[258] P Flood, 'Spectrum Plus: Legal and Practical Implications' (2006) 17(2) *International Company and Commercial Law Review* 78. Under a factoring arrangement, the body providing finance purchases and collects trade debts (with or without recourse to the company if debtors fail to pay). Invoice discounting involves the financier purchasing the debts, but the company collects them and the debtors are not notified.

[259] *Re Panama, New Zealand & Australia Royal Mail Co* (1870) 5 Ch App 318; *Re Florence Land & Public Works Co, ex p Moor* (1878) LR 10 Ch D 530, CA; *Wallace v Evershed* [1899] 1 Ch 189; *Re Yorkshire Woolcombers Ltd* [1903] 2 Ch 284, CA; affirmed *sub nom Illingworth v Houldsworth* [1904] AC 355, HL; *J. D. Brian v Companies Acts* [2011] IEHC 283.

[260] *Ashborder BV v Green Gas Power Ltd* [2005] 1 BCLC 623, applying *Countrywide Banking Corp Ltd v Dean* [1998] 1 BCLC 306.

[261] *Ashborder BV v Green Gas Power Ltd* [2005] 1 BCLC 623.

[262] *Biggerstaff v Rowatt's Wharf Ltd* [1896] 2 Ch 93, CA.

[263] *Evans v Rival Granite Quarries Ltd* [1910] 2 KB 979, CA, not following *Davey & Co v Williamson & Sons* [1898] 2 QB 194, CA.

[264] *NW Robbie & Co Ltd v Witney Warehouse Co Ltd* [1963] 3 All ER 613, CA. But cf *Re Dex Developments Pty Ltd* (1994) 13 ACSR 485, CT SC, criticized by CH Tan, 'Automatic Crystallisation, De-Crystallisation and Convertibility of Charges' [1998] CFILR 41, 44.

[265] This is subject to the special considerations that may apply where there is no public indication of the fact of crystallization.

[266] *Griffiths v Yorkshire Bank plc* [1994] 1 WLR 1427.

[267] *Re Standard Manufacturing Co* [1891] 1 Ch 627, CA; *Re Opera Ltd* [1891] 3 Ch 260, CA; *Taunton v Sheriff of Warwickshire* [1895] 1 Ch 734; *Norton v Yates* [1906] 1 KB 112; *Cairney v Back* [1906] 2 KB 746. This is a complex area. The difficulties lie mainly in determining whether, for the mode of execution in question, the execution

debtors of the company have notice of crystallization they are largely precluded from claiming rights of set-off.[268]

As charges are essentially consensual securities, it is for the parties to determine crystallizing events but, in the absence of any other provision, three crystallizing events will be implied.[269] These are intervention by the holder of the charge to take control of the security, such as by appointing a receiver under the terms of the charge,[270] the commencement of the winding-up of the company,[271] and the cessation of its business.[272] It is also possible for the parties to agree additional crystallizing events in the terms of the charge. For example, a floating charge may contain a provision which entitles its holder to trigger crystallization by serving a notice to that effect on the company.[273] Until the 1980s, it was uncertain whether under English law it was possible to provide for automatic crystallization upon the happening of an event that did not require intervention from the holder of the charge and which, unlike liquidation or cessation of business, did not signal the end of the company's business. Dicta in some old cases suggested that, outside situations of cessation of business, the holder of the charge had to intervene positively in order to bring about crystallization.[274] In England, the powerful dicta of Hoffmann J in *Re Brightlife Ltd*[275] and his decision in *Re Permanent Houses (Holdings) Ltd*[276] heralded the acceptance of the legal effectiveness of automatic crystallization clauses that did not require the charge holder actively to intervene. Elsewhere in the Commonwealth, it has also been held that automatic crystallization in this form is possible.[277] This acceptance of non-interventionist automatic crystallization clauses, despite certain policy objections,[278] represents a triumph for freedom of contract: a floating charge is

---

process has been completed by the time of crystallization. See further, WJ Gough, *Company Charges* 2nd edn (London: Butterworths, 1996) 319–28.

[268] *NW Robbie & Co Ltd v Witney Warehouse Co Ltd* [1963] 3 All ER 613, CA. This is another difficult area which is considered further in PR Wood, *English and International Set-Off* (London: Sweet & Maxwell, 1989) 925–9; WJ Gough, *Company Charges* 2nd edn (London: Butterworths, 1996) 281–302; EV Ferran, 'Floating Charges—The Nature of the Security' [1988] CLJ 213, 217–27.

[269] *Edward Nelson & Co Ltd v Faber & Co* [1903] 2 KB 367.

[270] *Evans v Rival Granite Quarries Ltd* [1910] 2 KB 979, CA; *NW Robbie & Co Ltd v Witney Warehouse Co Ltd* [1963] 3 All ER 613, CA. The appointment of a receiver by the court at the instance of a debenture holder would also trigger crystallization but appointment of a receiver via this route would nowadays be very unusual.

[271] *Re Panama, New Zealand and Australian Royal Mail Co* (1870) 5 Ch App 318; *Re Colonial Trusts Corp, ex p Bradshaw* (1879) 15 Ch D 465, CA, 472 *per* Jessel MR.

[272] *Re Woodroffes (Musical Instruments) Ltd* [1986] Ch 366; *William Gaskell Group Ltd v Highley* [1993] BCC 200; *Re The Real Meat Co Ltd* [1996] BCC 254.

[273] *Re Brightlife Ltd* [1987] Ch 200. The effectiveness of crystallization notices was conceded in *Re Woodroffes (Musical Instruments) Ltd* [1986] Ch 366.

[274] In particular *Evans v Rival Granite Quarries Ltd* [1910] 2 KB 979, CA, 986–7 *per* Vaughan Williams LJ and 992–3 *per* Fletcher Moulton LJ; *Reg in right of British Columbia v Consolidated Churchill Copper Corp Ltd* [1978] 5 WWR 652, BC SC.

[275] [1987] Ch 200. This case was actually about crystallization by service of a notice but there is no important difference in the legal analysis between that type of clause and 'pure' non-interventionist automatic crystallization provisions. See further, WJ Gough, *Company Charges* 2nd edn (London: Butterworths, 1996) 233.

[276] (1989) 5 BCC 151. Counsel conceded the point but Hoffmann J reiterated the view that he had expressed in the earlier case that there was no conceptual reason why parties should not agree that any specified event should cause the charge to crystallize (at 154–5).

[277] *Stein v Saywell* [1969] ALR 481, H Ct of Aust (although the point was not argued); *Fire Nymph Products Ltd v The Heating Centre Pty Ltd* (1991–92) 7 ACSR 365, NSW CA; *Re Manurewa Transport Ltd* [1971] NZLR 909, NZ SC; *DFC Financial Services Ltd v Coffey* [1991] 2 NZLR 513, PC, 518 *per* Lord Goff; *Dovey Enterprises Ltd v Guardian Assurance Public Ltd* [1993] 1 NZLR 540, NZ CA.

[278] Historically, the effect of automatic crystallization clauses on the ranking of preferential debts was one of the issues that concerned writers on this topic. Before the Insolvency Act 1986, the position was that the floating charge had to continue to float up to the date of the liquidation for preferential debts to rank for payment ahead of the debt secured by the floating charge: *Re Griffin Hotel Co Ltd* [1941] Ch 129. The Insolvency Act 1986 reversed the position so that preferential debts now rank ahead of a debt secured by a charge which, as created, was a floating charge. Generally, on policy objections to automatic crystallization see: AJ Boyle, 'The Validity of Automatic Crystallisation Clauses' [1979] JBL 231; *Insolvency Law and Practice* (Cmnd 8558, 1982) (Report of the Review Committee under

a consensual security and it is for the parties to determine its features, including the circumstances in which it will crystallize.

Drafting of automatic crystallization clauses

There are now two main recognized forms of automatic crystallization clause: the first is where crystallization is to happen upon the occurrence of specified events without positive intervention from the holder of the charge; and the second is where crystallization is to happen if and when the holder of the charge serves a notice to that effect.[279] The first type of clause places the occurrence of crystallization outside the control of the holder of the charge and, unless the clause is narrowly and carefully drafted, may result in situations where the charge crystallizes even though the charge holder is content for it to continue to exist in uncrystallized form. In anticipation of this, an automatic crystallization clause may be coupled with an express clause entitling its holder to de-crystallize it again.[280] In the absence of such a clause, it should be possible to achieve de-crystallization with the express or implied consent of the holder of the charge.[281] However, there is a risk that if the automatic crystallization clause is so widely drafted that the holder of the charge has frequently to agree to de-crystallization, this pattern of events may lead a court to conclude that the original agreement was later varied by the parties so as to exclude the automatic crystallization provision. The second form of automatic crystallization clause avoids the issue of unwanted crystallization by keeping the trigger for crystallization within the control of the holder of the charge by stipulating for crystallization on service of a notice.[282] On the other hand, automatic crystallization clauses in this form have an in-built delay factor, which could operate to the detriment of the holder of the charge in its claim to priority over other interests in the same property.[283]

The commencement of administration proceedings in respect of a company in accordance with the Insolvency Act 1986 might not constitute an implied crystallizing event. This is an example of the type of event that could be covered by an express automatic crystallization clause in either of the forms outlined in the previous paragraph.

Automatic crystallization and third parties

An argument against automatic crystallization provisions is that they are unfair because they can cause a charge to crystallize without that fact becoming apparent to others who deal with the company and advance credit to it. It has been suggested that any unfairness to third parties that results from recognizing that automatic crystallization clauses are effective may be

the Chairmanship of Sir Kenneth Cork) paras 1570–80. Academic opinion in favour of automatic crystallization clauses pre-dating the 1980s cases on the point included JH Farrar, 'The Crystallisation of a Floating Charge' (1976) 40 Conv 397.

[279] *J. D. Brian v Companies Acts* [2011] IEHC 113.

[280] As in *Covacich v Riordan* [1994] 2 NZLR 502, NZ HC.

[281] But note R Grantham, 'Refloating a Floating Charge' [1997] CFILR 53; CH Tan, 'Automatic Crystallisation, De-Crystallisation and Convertibility of Charges' [1998] CFILR 41.

[282] The court in *J. D. Brian v Companies Acts* [2011] IEHC 283 held that in deciding whether a crystallization notice is effective to convert a floating charge into a first fixed charge, the court has to adopt the same approach to fixed/floating charge classification. The court must, as a first step, construe the charge document to ascertain the intention of the parties as to the rights and obligations granted to or imposed on each other in relation to the property subject to the floating charge after the service of a crystallization notice. Once this has been ascertained, the court should embark on the second stage and determine whether such rights and obligations are consistent with a fixed charge. If so, the notice will have the effect of converting the floating charge into a fixed charge. If not, it will not have achieved the stated intention and the property will remain subject to the floating charge.

[283] However, the extent to which third parties will be affected by crystallization if they do not know, and have no means of knowing, that it has occurred is limited. See later.

mitigated by estoppel[284] or agency[285] principles: this is to say that until the fact of crystallization has been drawn to the attention of outsiders dealing with the company, the holder of the charge may be estopped from denying that the charge remains floating or, alternatively, that outsiders can continue to rely on the company's ostensible authority to deal with its assets as if they were subject only to an uncrystallized floating charge. In circumstances where a subsequent chargee is unaware of the crystallization of the earlier charge, application of either set of principles would mean that a debt secured by a floating charge that has crystallized into a fixed charge by operation of an automatic crystallization notice could lose priority to a debt secured by a subsequent fixed charge on the same property even though, in accordance with the normal priority rules that are discussed in the next section of this chapter, it would rank ahead of it.

The operation of estoppel or agency principles in relation to automatic crystallization clauses has not been litigated. In its recent work on company charges, the Law Commission for England and Wales adopted the agency reasoning suggested by Goode and concluded that it was extremely unlikely that such a device would be effective against a subsequent chargee without actual knowledge of the automatic crystallization clause because the company would still have apparent authority to dispose of its assets in the ordinary course of business.[286] Likewise, purchasers without notice would not be affected.[287] Judgment creditors would, on Goode's reasoning be in a different position because they are unsecured creditors with no interest in its assets.[288] The Law Commission has accepted that judgment creditors are at risk of automatic crystallization clauses.[289]

A system for registration of crystallization has been advocated from time to time[290] and the Companies Act 1989 contained a provision to that effect. That provision would have authorized the Secretary of State to make regulations stipulating requirements for registration of notice of crystallizing events and providing for the consequences of failure to give notice. It was specifically stated that those consequences could have included the ineffectiveness of the crystallization against such persons as might be prescribed. This provision was part of a series of measures that were intended to revise and update the requirements of the Companies Act 1985 on the registration of charges. Various difficulties in the drafting of the new provisions emerged after the passing of the legislation and they were never brought into force.

Priority Rules for Competing Interests in the Same Property

A company may use its assets as security for more than one debt. When this happens and the value of the security proves to be insufficient to pay off all of the debts that were secured on it, it becomes necessary to work out the respective priorities of the various charges. Priority disputes can also arise where a company charges property in favour of

---

[284] WJ Gough, *Company Charges* 2nd edn (London: Butterworths, 1996) 252–6 discusses the operation of estoppel in this context and its limits. See also WJ Gough, 'The Floating Charge: Traditional Themes and New Directions' in PD Finn (ed), *Equity and Commercial Relationships* (Sydney: Law Book Company, 1987), 239, 251–2.

[285] L Gullifer (ed), *Goode on Legal Problems of Credit and Security* 4th edn (London: Sweet & Maxwell, 2008) paras 4-53 and 5-50.

[286] Law Commission, *Registration of Security Interests: Company Charges and Property other than Land* (Law Com CP No 164, 2002) para 2.44.

[287] Law Commission, *Registration of Security Interests: Company Charges and Property other than Land* (Law Com CP No 164, 2002) para 4.143.

[288] L Gullifer (ed), *Goode on Legal Problems of Credit and Security* 4th edn (London: Sweet & Maxwell, 2008) para 5-50.

[289] Law Commission, *Company Security Interests* (Law Com Rep No 296, 2005) para 3.201.

[290] AJ Boyle, 'The Validity of Automatic Crystallisation Clauses' [1979] JBL 231, 240.

one person and then agrees to sell that property to someone else: here the issue is whether the purchaser takes the property subject to, or free from, the charge. The English courts worked out a series of rules for resolving priority disputes and these rules continue to apply to company charges even though certain aspects of them are affected by the statutory requirements for the registration of charges. English law on security interests in personal property differs from many other modern legal systems by not providing for a statutory system of priority based primarily on the timing of the registration of charges on a public register.[291] Reform bodies have periodically considered English law to be deficient in this respect and have called for a complete overhaul of the law relating to credit and security, including the establishment of a priority system based on filing but, to date, legislation has not been forthcoming.[292]

There follows an outline of the various rules. At the outset of this discussion, it is pertinent to note that these priority rules are default rules that apply where the parties have not made alternative provision. It is open to secured creditors to vary the priority afforded to their charges under the general law by a priority agreement. Also to be noted at the outset is that land, ship mortgages, and other asset classes where priority is affected by the requirements of specialist legislation are excluded from this discussion. The special rules that apply where there are competing interests in debts or other forms of intangible personal property are considered separately after the general rules have been outlined.

Competing interests in tangible personal property

There are two main rules.[293] The first rule is that where the equities are equal the first in time prevails.[294] This is the priority rule that governs, for example, priority disputes between two fixed equitable charges on the same property. The charge that was created first has priority unless the equities are not equal. A situation where the equities would not be equal is where the first chargee's conduct has led the second to believe that the property is unencumbered. The second rule is that a person who bona fide purchases for value a legal interest in property takes free of existing equitable interests in that property provided he or she does not have notice of their existence and there is no fraud, estoppel, or gross negligence on his or her part.[295] By application of this rule a bona fide purchaser for value without notice takes property that is subject to a fixed charge free of the charge. The creditor is obliged to pursue his remedies against the company that has disposed of the security in breach of the terms of the charge.

A key feature of the floating charge is that it allows the company to continue to deal with its assets in the ordinary course of business as if they were unsecured. This power to continue trading includes power to grant subsequent mortgages and charges and accordingly, although the security is first in time, the holder of a floating charge is estopped from denying the priority of later legal or fixed equitable interests.[296] A subsequent fixed chargee

[291] See, in particular, the Uniform Commercial Code, art 9 (US); the Uniform Personal Property Security Act 1982 (Canada), and the various Personal Property Security Acts, based on the model of art 9, adopted in the various provinces of Canada. Article 9 has also served as a basis for a new statutory system in New Zealand: Personal Property Securities Act 1999, which is described in D McLauchlan, 'Fundamentals of the PPSA: An Introduction' (2000) 6 *New Zealand Business Law Quarterly* 166.

[292] See later.

[293] For detailed treatment: J McGhee (gen ed), *Snell's Equity* 32nd edn (London: Sweet & Maxwell, 2010) ch 4.

[294] *Cave v Cave* (1880) 15 Ch D 639; *Rice v Rice* (1853) 2 Drew 73, 61 ER 646; *Naxatu v Perpetual Trustee Company* [2012] FCAFC 163, [101].

[295] *Pilcher v Rawlins* (1872) 7 Ch App 259.

[296] *Re Castell & Brown Ltd* [1898] 1 Ch 315; *Re Valletort Sanitary Steam Laundry Co Ltd* [1903] 2 Ch 654.

or purchaser takes free of an earlier floating charge even where he or she is aware of the existence of that charge.[297] This modification of the normal first-in-time rule does not apply as between two floating charges on the same property. Here, in accordance with the general principle, the first in time takes priority[298] unless the first charge expressly permits the creation of subsequent floating security ranking in priority to, or equally with, the first floating charge.[299]

It is commonplace for floating charges to contain a promise from the chargor company not to use the assets that are the subject matter of the security as security for any subsequent borrowing that would rank ahead of, or equally with, the floating charge, without the consent of the holder of that charge. This 'negative pledge' has a twofold purpose.[300] Its internal purpose is to ensure that if the promise is broken, the holder of the charge can sue the company for breach of contract. In a well-drafted agreement, this breach will be an event of default that entitles the chargee to call in the loan. Its external purpose is to reverse the ordinary priority rule applicable to floating charges by ensuring that the floating charge ranks ahead of the security created in breach of the covenant. Contractual promises do not normally affect third parties who are not party to the agreement but it is established that a person who obtains security, legal or equitable, on property that is already subject to a floating charge containing a negative pledge takes subject to that charge if he or she has notice of the existence of the negative pledge.[301] It is insufficient that the subsequent creditor has notice simply of the existence of the floating charge; he or she must have notice of the fact that it contains a negative pledge.[302] An explanation for the priority effect of a negative pledge in a floating charge is that it is an equity attached to an equitable interest which, on general principles, is binding on persons who have notice of it.[303]

Priority rules for competing interests in intangible property

The priority rules for competing interests in intangible property are relevant where, for example, a company grants a series of charges, fixed or floating, on its book debts, or sells book debts that were subject to a charge. Priority here is governed by the rule in

---

[297] *Moor v Anglo-Italian Bank* (1878) 10 Ch D 681; *Re Hamilton's Windsor Ironworks Co, ex p Pitman and Edwards* (1879) 12 Ch D 707; *Wheatley v Silkstone & Haigh Moor Coal Co* (1885) 29 Ch D 715; *English and Scottish Mercantile Investment Co v Brunton* [1892] 2 QB 700, CA; *Re Standard Rotary Machine Co Ltd* (1906) 95 LT 829.

[298] *Re Benjamin Cope & Sons Ltd* [1914] 1 Ch 800. *Griffiths v Yorkshire Bank plc* [1994] 1 WLR 1427, which is to the effect that a second floating charge can take priority by being the first to crystallize, is inconsistent with earlier authorities.

[299] *Re Automatic Bottle Makers Ltd* [1926] Ch 412, CA where a second floating charge on part of the property that was the subject matter of the security in an earlier floating charge took priority to the earlier charge. This decision turned on the terms of the first floating charge, which reserved to the company the right to create certain specific charges ranking in priority. The Court of Appeal concluded that a charge in floating form could be within the scope of the reserved power.

[300] *DBS Bank v Tam Chee Chong* [2011] SGCA 47, [2011] 4 SLR 948, [50], Singapore CA: 'A negative pledge is an undertaking by a borrower or debtor to a lender or creditor not to give security to any other present or future lender or creditor. It is a device usually employed by a borrower who has commercial bargaining power not to encumber any of its assets where its business or operations are financed by more than one lender so that it can deal with its assets freely in its own commercial interests. A negative pledge clause fulfils the function of contractually preventing any creditor from trying to obtain security over the assets of the debtor at any time, and particularly when the debtor is in deep financial distress and the creditor wants its overdue debts paid before the claims of other creditors. In such cases, a creditor who induces the debtor to breach the latter's negative pledges to other creditors may be liable for the tort of interfering with the contractual relations of the debtor with those creditors…'

[301] *Cox v Dublin City Distillery Co* [1915] 1 IR 345, Ir CA.

[302] *Re Valletort Sanitary Steam Laundry Co Ltd* [1903] 2 Ch 654; *Siebe Gorman & Co Ltd v Barclays Bank Ltd* [1979] 2 Lloyd's Rep 142.

[303] *Rother Iron Works Ltd v Canterbury Precision Engineers Ltd* [1974] QB 1, CA.

Dearle v Hall,[304] which is that priority is governed by the order in which notice is given to the debtors. Notice does not have to be in a particular form and it can be given orally.[305] Accordingly, the purchaser of the legal title to debts[306] takes them subject to an earlier fixed charge where the chargee is the first to give notice of his interest to the debtors, even though the purchaser may be unaware of the existence of the fixed charge when he acquires the debts.[307] It is axiomatic that a company that has charged its debts by way of a floating charge can continue to deal with the debts and to collect their proceeds; no notice of the existence of the floating charge will be given to the company's debtors, with the consequence that the charge will rank behind notified interests.

The rule in *Dearle v Hall* is subject to the qualification that where, at the time that a person acquires an interest, he is aware of the existence of other interests, apart from floating charges, in the same property, he takes subject to those interests irrespective of the order in which notice is given to the debtors.[308]

Priority of purchase money security interests

This is a special case of a priority conflict. The situation arises where a company which has created a charge covering future property acquires property fitting the description of the subject matter of the security but that acquisition has been funded by borrowing from a third-party lender and that lender requires an interest in the acquired property in order to secure its advance. Assuming that the bona fide purchaser rule is inapplicable, which security interest has priority: the charge that was first in time or the later purchase money security? In *Abbey National Building Society v Cann*[309] the House of Lords held that the provider of the purchase money finance took priority. Lord Jauncey stated the basis for the decision in these terms: 'a purchaser who can only complete a transaction by borrowing money...cannot in reality ever be said to have acquired even for a *scintilla temporis* the unencumbered freehold or leasehold interest in the land whereby he could grant interests having priority over the mortgage.'[310] For the after-acquired property to feed the existing charge in priority to the new charge would constitute an unwarranted windfall in favour of the holder of the existing charge.[311]

---

[304] (1823) 3 Russ 1, 38 ER 475, 492.   [305] *Lloyd v Banks* (1868) 3 Ch App 488.

[306] An assignment of the legal title to debts must comply with the formal requirements of the Law of Property Act 1925, s 136(1). These formalities include a requirement to give written notice of the assignment to the debtors. This written notice suffices for the purposes of the rule in *Dearle v Hall* but it does not override notices, in whatever form, of prior interests that were given earlier.

[307] The displacement of the rule that a bona fide purchaser for value of a legal interest who is without notice of a prior equitable interest takes free of it is supported by recent case law (*E Pfeiffer Weinkellerei-Weinenkauf GmbH & Co v Arbuthnot Factors Ltd* [1988] 1 WLR 150; *Compaq Computers Ltd v Abercorn Group Ltd* [1991] BCC 484). The contrary view in favour of the application of the bona fide purchaser rule to this situation, developed by F Oditah, (1989) OJLS 513 and restated in F Oditah, *Legal Aspects of Receivables Financing* (London: Sweet & Maxwell, 1991) 154–63 has not been accepted.

[308] *Re Holmes* (1885) 29 Ch D 786, CA; *Spencer v Clarke* (1878) 9 Ch D 137.

[309] [1991] 1 AC 56, HL. G McCormack, 'Charges and Priorities—The Death of the Scintilla Temporis' (1991) 12 *Company Lawyer* 10; RJ Smith, 'Mortgagees and Trust Beneficiaries' (1990) 106 LQR 545; R Gregory, 'Romalpa Clauses as Unregistered Charges—A Fundamental Shift?' (1990) 106 LQR 550; J de Lacy, 'The Purchase Money Security Interest: A Company Charge Conundrum' [1991] LMCLQ 531.

[310] For some doubt about the extent of the decision see L Gullifer (ed), *Goode on Legal Problems of Credit and Security* 4th edn (London: Sweet & Maxwell, 2008) para 5-64. But the *Cann* decision has been applied in various contexts, eg *Whale v Viasystems Technograph* [2002] EWCA Civ 480; *Redstone Mortgages v Welch* [2009] 3 EGLR 71; *Mortgage Business v O'Shaughnessy* [2012] EWCA Civ 17, [2012] 1 WLR 1521; *Re Lehman Brothers International (Europe)* [2012] EWHC 2997 (Ch).

[311] AL Diamond, *A Review of Security Interests in Property*, para 17.7.

Registration of Charges—Outline of Requirements

A statutory system for the registration of company charges dates back to 1900. The Law Commission for England and Wales has summarized its intended purposes in the following terms:[312]

(1) it provides information on the state of the encumbrances on a company's property to those who may be interested (for example creditors and those considering or advising on dealing with the company, including credit reference agencies, financial analysts, and potential investors);

(2) it assists companies in enabling them to give some form of assurance to potential lenders that their property is unencumbered;

(3) it provides a degree of protection to a chargee, in relation to the validity and priority of its registered charge; and

(4) it assists receivers and liquidators in deciding whether or not to acknowledge the validity of a mortgage or charge.

For a long time, the UK registration regime did not fully achieve these goals. Improving the system for the registration of charges has been much debated by reform bodies, practitioners, and academics over the years and there was even legislative intervention in the form of Part IV of the Companies Act 1989, which contained a proposed new Part XII to the 1985 Act, which would have corrected some of the deficiencies of the present law. However, potential problems with the new regime that emerged after its enactment, including its inter-relationship with other applicable registration requirements, such as those relating to registered land, meant that it could not be brought into force. The Companies Act 1989, Part IV scheme was intended to be an improvement rather than a radical change.[313]

Part 25 of the Companies Act 2006 was originally a consolidated version of the Companies Act 1985 Part XII. The substantive content of the law was not changed on consolidation (save for an extension of the legislation generally to Northern Ireland). However, the current version of Part 25 of the Companies Act 2006[314] represents a significant improvement. Its policy objectives are as follows:

- To enable the registrar of companies to make provision for lenders and companies to register charges against their assets electronically and to simplify the summary information provided;

- To increase transparency by making the whole instrument available on the public register, but to allow certain redactions in relation to personal information to guard against fraud;

- To establish a mechanism for UK-wide registration, which works with both the provisions of Scottish law on security interests and the law of England and Wales on charges;

- To remove the criminal offence for failing to register a charge, which is not necessary to secure compliance as failure to register invalidates a lender's claim against

---

[312] Law Commission, *Registration of Security Interests: Company Charges and Property other than Land* (Law Com CP No 164, 2002) para 2.21.

[313] Companies Act 1989, Part IV was to some extent based on recommendations in AL Diamond, *A Review of Security Interests in Property*, Pt III. These recommendations were made as proposed interim measures pending the complete overhaul of the general law relating to security interests in personal property that formed the main recommendation in the report.

[314] Introduced by the Companies Act 2006 (Amendment of Part 25) Regulations 2013 which came into force on 6 April 2013.

the debt in insolvency, so the commercial interests of lenders ensure registration of charges;

- To replace a piecemeal and complex list of types of registrable charges to a simple exemption based system.

In outline, the structure of Part 25 of the Companies Act 2006 is that all charges (other than those expressly exempted)[315] created by UK-registered companies[316] must be registered if prescribed statements of particulars relating to the charges are delivered to the companies registry for registration within twenty-one days of creation.[317] The fact that there remains a twenty-one-day registration period remains a key defect of the registration system. A person who searches the register can never be sure from that search alone[318] that he or she has discovered all of the charges affecting a company's property or even, because of the permitted twenty-one-day registration period, that he or she has discovered all of the existing registrable charges. When this point is considered in conjunction with the priority rule of first in time, its significance can be readily appreciated. The registrar of companies is required to maintain a register of charges and this is available for public inspection. The registrar has to check whether the requirements for registration have been complied with and, if he is satisfied that they have been, his certificate of registration in respect of the charge is conclusive. Whether the registrar of companies should carry the administrative burden of filtering out defective applications is debatable but the certainty provided by the system is valued in practice.[319] Failure to file as required by the legislation results in the charge becoming void against specified persons, including subsequent secured creditors. In this respect, the registration requirements can affect priority by withdrawing from a registrable, but unregistered, charge the priority over subsequent interests that it would have enjoyed under the first-in-time rule. However, where there is proper compliance with the filing requirements, the order of priority is not affected by order of filing. This is a complexity that many argue the system could do without: a system of priority based on date of filing would be far more straightforward than a series of rules that depend on order of creation of competing securities, equality of equities, and notice. Where the obligation to file particulars of registrable charges is overlooked, the court may authorize late filing. There is no mechanism for late filing without a court order.

Registration Requirements—Detailed Aspects

Charges requiring registration

Unless expressly exempted, all charges created by a company are registrable.[320] The term 'charge' in this context includes a 'mortgage,' but not a 'pledge.'[321] Charges arising by operation of law, as opposed to act of creation by the company, are not registrable.[322]

---

[315] Namely, a charge in favour of a landlord on a cash deposit given as a security in connection with the lease of land, a charge created by a member of Lloyd's to secure its obligations in connection with its underwriting business at Lloyd's, and a charge exempted from registration by legislation (Companies Act 2006, s 859A(6)).

[316] Pursuant to the Overseas Companies (Execution of Documents and Registration of Charges) (Amendment) Regulations 2011, charges created by overseas companies are not registrable.

[317] The date of creation of a charge is defined in s 859E of the Companies Act 2006.

[318] Inquiries of the company may elicit further information. Also, a company has to keep available for inspection a copy of every instrument creating a registrable charge (Companies Act 2006, ss 859P and 859Q).

[319] The proposal in the Companies Act 1989 to relieve the registrar of this obligation and, as a consequence, to remove the conclusive certificate of registration was one of the most controversial aspects of the proposed new regime. For a more detailed examination of the 1989 Act see G McCormack, 'Registration of Company Charges: The New Law' [1990] LMCLQ 520; EV Ferran and C Mayo, 'Registration of Company Charges—The New Regime' [1991] JBL 152.

[320] Companies Act 2006, s 859A(1).   [321] Companies Act 2006, s 859A(7).

[322] *London and Cheshire Insurance Co Ltd v Laplagrene Property Co Ltd* [1971] Ch 499.

The registration requirement

The registrar of companies must register a charge if, within twenty-one days after its date of creation, the company or any person interested in the charge delivers to the registrar for registration a prescribed statement of particulars.[323] Where a company creates a series of debentures containing a charge and the debenture holders are entitled to the benefit of the charge pari passu, any instrument creating or evidencing the charge must accompany the statement of particulars. If the charge is not created or evidenced by an instrument, a certified copy of one of the debentures in the series must accompany the statement of particulars.[324] At present, not all, but most documents may be delivered to the registrar electronically.[325]

The prescribed statement of particulars of a charge created by a company are:[326] (a) the registered name and number of the company; (b) the date of creation of the charge and, where relevant, the date of acquisition of the property or undertaking concerned; (c) where the charge is created or evidenced by an instrument, (i) the name of each of the persons in whose favour the charge has been created or of the security agents or trustees holding the charge for the benefit of one or more persons,[327] (ii) whether the instrument is expressed to contain a floating charge and, if so, whether it is expressed to cover all the property and undertaking of the company, (iii) whether any of the terms of the charge prohibit or restrict the company from creating further security that will rank equally with or ahead of the charge, (iv) whether (and if so, a short description of) any land, ship, aircraft or intellectual property that is registered or required to be registered in the United Kingdom, is subject to a charge (which is not a floating charge) or fixed security included in the instrument, (v) whether the instrument includes a charge (which is not a floating charge) or fixed security over any tangible or intangible property not already described; and (d) where the charge is not created or evidenced by an instrument, (i) a statement that there is no instrument creating or evidencing the charge, (ii) the names of each of the persons in whose favour the charge has been created or the names of any security agents or trustees holding the charge for the benefit of one or more persons, (iii) the nature of the charge, (iv) a short description of the property or undertaking charged, and (v) the obligations secured by the charge.

The role of the registrar and the issue of the certificate of registration

The role of the registrar is to check that documents received are in order.[328] If they are not and the charge is not registered, the defective filing cannot be relied upon in satisfaction of the Companies Act 2006 registration requirement and, to avoid the charge becoming void, a second, correct, set of documents must be delivered to the registrar within the original twenty-one-day filing period.[329] Once correct particulars relating to a registrable charge are filed with the registrar of companies, the statutory filing requirement is fulfilled and the charge cannot thereafter be held to be void for non-registration even if it does not actually

---

[323] Companies Act 2006, s 859A.

[324] Companies Act 2006, s 859B.

[325] See Company Charges and Mortgages FAQs published by Companies House <http://www.companieshouse.gov.uk/infoAndGuide/faq/companyCM.shtml> (accessed May 2013).

[326] Companies Act 2006, s 859D.

[327] Where there are more than four such persons, security agents, or trustees, the names of any four such persons, security agents, or trustees listed in the charge instrument, and a statement that there are other such persons, security agents, or trustees.

[328] Under the Law Commission's 2005 proposals for improvements to the system for the registration of charges, the Registrar would be relieved of this obligation and conclusive certificates would not be issued: Law Commission, *Company Security Interests* (Law Com Rep No 296, 2005).

[329] *R v Registrar, ex p Central Bank of India* [1986] QB 1114, CA.

appear on the register until sometime after the twenty-one-day period for filing. Upon registration of a charge, the registrar issues a certificate of registration to the person who delivered to the registrar the statement of particulars relating to the charge. The certificate must state (a) the registered name and number of the company in respect of which the charge was registered, and (b) the unique reference code allocated to the charge.[330] This certificate is conclusive evidence that the documents required by the section concerned were delivered to the registrar before the end of the relevant period allowed for delivery.[331] The conclusive nature of the certificate means that, with possible exceptions for manifest error on the face of the certificate or evidence that it was obtained by fraud, it cannot be challenged by any person other than the Crown.[332] Thus, for example, where the registrar issues a certificate even though the statement of particulars relating to the charge were in fact out of time, it is not open to any person (apart from the Crown) to argue that the charge is void for non-registration.[333]

Where the registrar fails to notice a mistake in filed particulars that misstates the chargee's rights in some respect, this does not estop the chargee from asserting his rights under the terms of the charge. This is illustrated by a case where the filed particulars understated the amount secured. It was held that the chargee was nevertheless entitled to enforce the charge to the full secured amount as stated in the charge.[334] This was an unfortunate outcome that further undermined the status of the register of charges as a source of useful information. But the current registration regime requires the instrument creating the charge to be included in the register.[335] Another illustration of the deficiencies of the registration system was provided by *Grove v Advantage Healthcare (T10) Ltd*[336] where, in the particulars delivered for registration, the registered number of the chargor company was incorrectly stated as being that of another company in its group and the error was not noticed, with the result that the charge was registered against the wrong company. It was held that the failure to provide the correct registered number did not constitute a failure to comply with the registration obligation because the number was not a prescribed particular. Accordingly, the charge was registered and valid even though its existence would not have been discovered by a search against the correct registered number. The court noted that this outcome could have led to the prejudice of third parties who dealt with the company and suggested that a remedy might in those circumstances have been available to the third party in the form of a claim to recover any loss occasioned from the registrar or the party who misinformed the registrar as to the registered number of the company. *Grove* would probably be decided differently today as the registration number of the chargor is now a prescribed particular.[337]

Registration and notice

Registration of a registrable charge serves to give constructive notice of the existence of that charge to such persons as can be reasonably expected to search the register.[338] The category of

[330] Companies Act 2006, s 859I.

[331] Companies Act 2006, s 859I.

[332] *R v Registrar, ex p Central Bank of India* [1986] QB 1114, CA; *Sterritt v Allied Irish Banks* [2013] NICh 6. The conclusiveness of registration applies to a challenge by way of judicial review, as well as to other forms of challenge: *Bahamas Hotel Maintenance & Allied Workers Union v Bahamas Hotel Catering & Allied Workers Union* [2011] UKPC 4, [33].

[333] *Re CL Nye* [1971] Ch 442, CA; *Re Eric Holmes Ltd* [1965] Ch 1052.

[334] *Re Mechanisations (Eaglescliffe) Ltd* [1966] Ch 20. See also *National Provincial and Union Bank of England v Charnley* [1924] 1 KB 431, CA.

[335] Companies Act 2006, s 859I(2).

[336] [2000] 1 BCLC 661, noted A Walters, 'Registration of Charges: Wrong Company Number in Particulars Submitted to the Registrar' (2000) 21 *Company Lawyer* 219.

[337] Companies Act 2006, s 859D(1)(a).

[338] *Re Standard Rotary Machine Co Ltd* (1906) 95 LT 829; *Wilson v Kelland* [1910] 2 Ch 306.

persons who can reasonably be expected to search the register includes subsequent chargees but it is doubtful whether it covers purchasers of the company's property.[339] It does not constitute notice to debtors for the purposes of the rule in *Dearle v Hall*. Constructive notice of a charge covers the prescribed particulars of a charge but it is widely accepted, and has been specifically so held in Ireland,[340] that it does not extend to information that chargees voluntarily include in the application for filing of a charge but which are not required to be there as a matter of law. It is at this point that the inclusion of the existence (or not) of a negative pledge in a floating charge in the list of prescribed particulars comes into sharp focus. Previously, the fact that the existence of a negative pledge clause was not a prescribed particular, so as to come within the scope of constructive notice, undermined the protection to the floating charge holder of including such a provision. But this is no longer the position as negative pledges are now required to be included in the statement of particulars relating to the charge.[341]

Non-registration

'Non-registration' in this context means failure to file correct particulars of a registrable charge within twenty-one days of creation of the charge. Provided filing within the twenty-one-day period has taken place, it does not matter that the charge may not actually appear on the register until sometime after the twenty-one-day registration period. Where there is non-registration in the relevant sense, the charge becomes void against the company's liquidator or administrator and also against the company's other secured creditors.[342] The reference to the charge becoming void against the liquidator or administrator means that it is void against the company in liquidation or administration or (another way of saying the same thing) against the company when acting by its liquidator or administrator.[343] Failure to register a registrable charge does not render it void against purchasers of the company's property although they may take free of it under the bona fide purchaser for value without notice rule.[344] Also, so long as it is not in liquidation or administration, the security remains valid against the company itself.[345] When a charge becomes void for want of registration, the money secured by the charge becomes immediately repayable.[346]

---

[339] Law Commission, *Registration of Security Interests: Company Charges and Property other than Land* (Law Com CP No 164, 2002) paras 2.60–2.61. See, however, *Sterritt v Allied Irish Banks* [2013] NICh 6, [27], where the court said that the purpose of registration was to provide a warning to persons (including purchasers of apartments developed by the company) dealing with the company that someone was claiming to have a charge on the company's property—to afford them the right and opportunity to ensure that their interests were properly protected and that they did not act to their detriment. Under the Law Commission's 2005 proposals for improvements to the system for the registration of charges, registration would affect purchasers: Law Commission, *Company Security Interests* (Law Com Rep No 296, 2005).

[340] *Welch v Bowmaker (Ireland) Ltd* [1980] IR 251, Ir SC.

[341] Companies Act 2006, s 859D(2).

[342] Companies Act 2006, s 859H. This section refers to 'creditors' but it is clear from case law (*Re Cardiff's Workmen's Cottage Co Ltd* [1906] 2 Ch 627) that unsecured creditors have no standing to challenge the validity of a security that has not been duly registered.

[343] *Smith (Administrator of Cosslett (Contractors) Ltd) v Bridgend County Borough Council* [2002] 1 AC 336, HL.

[344] Law Commission, *Registration of Security Interests: Company Charges and Property other than Land* (Law Com CP No 164, 2002) para 2.58.

[345] *Re Monolithic Building Co Ltd* [1915] 1 Ch 643 CA, 667 *per* Phillimore LJ.

[346] Companies Act 2006, s 859H(4). Under the Law Commission's 2005 proposals for improvements to the system for the registration of charges, there would be no time limit for registration but lenders would have strong incentives to register because priority would be determined by filing: Law Commission, *Company Security Interests* (Law Com Rep No 296, 2005).

Late registration

Section 859F of the Companies Act 2006 provides for the late registration of charges. On the application of the company, or any person interested, the court may order the extension of the time for delivery of the particulars of a registrable charge. Before making such an order the court must be satisfied that the failure to deliver in time was accidental, or due to inadvertence or some other sufficient cause, or is not of a nature to prejudice the position of creditors or shareholders of the company, or that on other grounds it is just and equitable to grant relief. The court may impose such terms and conditions as seem to it to be just and expedient. The usual form for such orders is to extend the delivery period, subject to the proviso that this 'is to be without prejudice to the rights of parties acquired during the period between the date of creation of the said charge and the date of its actual registration.'[347] Errors in, or omissions from, the registered particulars or in a statement of satisfaction may also be corrected by a court order.[348]

Clearing the register—memoranda of satisfaction

When a debt secured by a registered charge is wholly or partly repaid, or property has been released from a registered charge or is no longer part of the company's property, that fact may be publicly advertised by filing with the registrar of companies a statement of satisfaction in the prescribed form.[349]

Modification of registration requirements for financial collateral

The Companies Act 2006 registration obligations do not apply (if they would otherwise do so) in relation to a security financial collateral arrangement or any charge created or otherwise arising under a security financial collateral arrangement.[350] This modification derives from the Financial Collateral Directive,[351] which aims to safeguard financial stability and also to promote cross-border efficiency by simplifying the processes for using financial collateral. It insulates financial collateral (ie collateral in the form of cash or investment securities) from aspects of company, property, and insolvency laws that could otherwise apply.[352]

Reform[353]

In 2002, the Department of Trade and Industry asked the Law Commission for England and Wales to consider the case for reforming the law on company charges.[354] This followed a recommendation in the Final Report of the Company Law Review Steering

---

[347] This proviso is derived from the decision in *Watson v Duff Morgan & Vermont (Holdings) Ltd* [1974] 1 WLR 450. On applications under this section generally, see G McCormack, 'Extension of Time for Registration of Company Charges' [1986] JBL 282. See also *Petition of Salvesen* [2009] CSOH 161; *Peleton v Companies Acts* [2011] IEHC 479; *Sterritt v Allied Irish Banks* [2013] NICh 6.

[348] Companies Act 2006, s 859M.   [349] Companies Act 2006, s 859L.

[350] The Financial Collateral Arrangements (No 2) Regulations 2003, SI 2003/3226, reg 4(4).

[351] Directive (EC) 2002/47 of the European Parliament and of the Council of 6 June 2002 on financial collateral arrangements [2002] OJ L168/43.

[352] See further ch 15.

[353] H Beale, M Bridge, L Gullifer, and E Lomnicka, *The Law of Security and Title-Based Financing* 2nd edn (Oxford: OUP, 2012) ch 23.

[354] The Scottish Law Commission was also asked to conduct an inquiry. The two Law Commissions conducted broadly parallel but separate consultative exercises. The law of security in Scotland is different from that in England and Wales. An overview of the Scottish exercise can be found in Law Commission, *Company Security Interests* (Law Com Rep No 296, 2005) paras 1.42–1.43.

Group.[355] The Steering Group reported that it had received substantial criticism of the current system for registering charges and for deciding priority between them. However, because of lack of time for consultation, it was able itself to present only provisional conclusions in favour of reform. The Law Commission published a consultation paper in 2002,[356] and a more detailed consultative report in 2004.[357] These papers floated some radical ideas for an entirely new scheme for security interests created by companies. The Law Commission's provisional proposals included the suggestion that the floating charge should disappear and be replaced by a new form of security that would allow the debtor to dispose of collateral without specific transaction-by-transaction consent from the holder of the charge. The Commission raised the possibility of extending the new scheme to title-retention devices such as finance leases, hire purchase, and conditional sale agreements. It thought that a system of effectiveness and priority against third parties based on filing should replace the existing complicated common law rules. These proposals proved to be controversial[358] and in its report, published in August 2005, the Law Commission set out revised proposals, which were intended to remove some of the more controversial features of the provisional scheme.[359] The 2005 proposals involved preservation of the distinction between fixed and floating charges, principally because of its importance in insolvency, and the exclusion of title-retention devices from the scheme, in response to the criticism that it would be illogical to have one set of rules applying to title-retention devices entered into by companies, and another for those involving unincorporated businesses and individuals. Sales of receivables of the kind which factoring and discounting agreements cover would be brought within the scheme and would need to be registered to preserve validity on insolvency. The Law Commission continued to advocate reforms to the filing system for company charges, including electronic filing, the abolition of the conclusive certificate of registration, removal of the twenty-one-day time limit for registration, extension of the list of registrable charges, and clearer priority rules based on filing. However, in July 2005 the government launched its own consultation seeking views on the economic impact of the recommendations of the Law Commission in respect of company charges. This was followed by a Ministerial announcement in November 2005 that it was clear from the consultation that there was not a consensus of support for the Law Commission's[360] proposals and that therefore the new companies legislation would not include a specific power to implement charges measures but that the Bill would include a new power to make company law reform orders and this would provide a mechanism for implementing certain changes in respect of company charges, on matters of company law (as against property law), if wished.[361] The government said it would continue to consider and to discuss with

---

[355] *Final Report* (URN 01/942) paras 12.8–12.10.

[356] Law Commission, *Registration of Security Interests: Company Charges and Property other than Land* (Law Com CP No 164, 2002).

[357] Law Commission, *Company Security Interests, A Consultative Report* (Law Com CP No 176, 2004).

[358] One prominent group with concerns was the Financial Law Committee of the City of London Law Society, a group comprising partners of City of London international law firms: R Calnan, 'The Reform of Company Security Interests' (2005) 20(1) *Butterworths Journal of International Banking and Financial Law* 25; R Calnan, 'The Reform of the Law of Security' (2004) 19(3) *Butterworths Journal of International Banking and Financial Law* 88.

[359] Law Commission, *Company Security Interests* (Law Com Rep No 296, 2005).

[360] This rejection extended to the proposals of the Scottish Law Commission as well as those made by the Law Commission for England and Wales.

[361] Written Ministerial Statement, Alun Michael, Minister for Industry and the Regions, 3 November 2005, 'Company Law Reform Government Statement Following the White Paper and Related Consultations,' reported *Hansard*, HL, vol 675, col WS 27 (3 Nov 2005).

interested parties exactly what changes should be implemented.[362] The proposed general power to make company law reform orders was dropped from the Bill during its passage through Parliament but there has been enacted a new power for the Secretary of State to amend Part 25 by regulations.[363]

The resistance to change of English law relating to corporate security interests is remarkable given the severe criticism stretching back over many years that it has attracted, the attention it has received from law reform bodies, and also the examples provided by the generally well-received adoption of more modern systems in other countries that have a common legal heritage with Britain.[364] Yet there are some serious voices who question the value of notice filing systems[365] or who suggest that there may be good reason to draw back from convergence toward a US-inspired model that may not fit well with established local circumstances or with future EU or international initiatives in this field.[366] The fate of the company charges provisions of the Companies Act 1989, which were never implemented, demonstrates the difficult challenges involved in successfully legislating in such a technically difficult area. All in all, the most prudent course of action may be to eschew radical change in favour of incremental modest improvements to the existing regime, including making it more consonant with the electronic era,[367] and this is precisely what the Companies Act 2006 (Amendment of Part 25) Regulations 2013 have done.

---

[362] Written Ministerial Statement, Alun Michael, Minister for Industry and the Regions, 3 November 2005, 'Company Law Reform Government Statement Following the White Paper and Related Consultations,' reported *Hansard*, HL, vol 675, col WS 27 (3 Nov 2005).

[363] See Companies Act 2006, Pt 25, ch 3.

[364] Most Canadian provinces and also New Zealand have introduced schemes of notice filing and priority rules that were modelled on the American Uniform Commercial Code, art 9: Law Commission, *Company Security Interests* (Law Com Rep No 296, 2005) para 1.8.

[365] U Drobnig, 'Present and Future of Real and Personal Security' [2003] *European Review of Private Law* 623, 660; R Calnan, 'The Reform of the Law of Security' (2004) 19(3) *Butterworths Journal of Banking and Financial Law* 88.

[366] R Calnan, 'The Reform of Company Security Interests' (2005) 20(1) *Butterworths Journal of International Banking and Financial Law* 25: 'We believe that the Model Security Law produced by the European Bank for Reconstruction and Development is a much more suitable starting point than art 9 of the UCC;' G McCormack, 'The Law Commission Consultative Report on Company Security Interests: An Irreverent Riposte' (2005) 68 MLR 286, 307–9. However, see S Worthington, 'Floating Charges: Use and Abuse of Doctrinal Analysis,' in J Getzler and J Payne (eds), *Company Charges: Spectrum and Beyond* (Oxford: OUP, 2006) 25, 49 who argues that the UK might have been well advised to update its law in order to participate effectively in the making of European and international law.

[367] G McCormack, 'The Law Commission Consultative Report on Company Security Interests: An Irreverent Riposte' (2005) 68 MLR 286, 309.

PART IV

CAPITAL MARKETS FINANCE

13

Public Offers and Listings of Equity Securities

Scope of this Part

This part of the book looks at the raising of corporate finance by issuing securities directly to investors. It focuses first on issues of equity securities and then on corporate bonds.

In this chapter the main focus is the process whereby for the first time a company raises finance by offering its equity securities to investors in the market, although the regulatory requirements associated with secondary offerings by seasoned issuers, such as rights issues, are also considered.[1] Whilst not essential, the initial public offer (IPO) process is often coupled with the admission of the securities to trading on an organized trading platform so as to ensure easy access to trading and settlement facilities and coverage from investment analysts, and generally to enhance the liquidity of the securities. In considering IPOs, this chapter will generally assume that the securities are to be admitted to trading on a formal trading platform contemporaneously with the offer. It will also assume a domestic offering—that is an IPO by a UK incorporated company where the securities are to be offered to investors in the UK and admitted to trading on a UK market. Chapter 14 is about international equity offerings. Corporate bonds are considered in chapter 15.

Once a company is admitted to trading on a formal platform it will become subject to enhanced regulatory requirements, in particular mandatory periodic and episodic disclosure requirements that aim at boosting investor protection through the accuracy of securities prices. These obligations are examined in the latter part of this chapter.

Reasons for Going Public[2]

There are various reasons why the controllers of a business may consider that the time is ripe to embark on an IPO or a flotation, as this process is commonly described.[3] First, and most obviously, an IPO allows a company to raise new equity finance. Accessing the capital markets by an IPO expands the range of sources of corporate finance and reduces a company's dependence on internally generated capital, its controllers' personal resources, bank finance, trade finance (such as debt factoring), and venture capital. Whilst new funding structures for small private businesses continue to evolve, such as 'crowdfunding,' whereby large numbers of investors can put capital (sometimes quite small amounts individually) into businesses via internet-based funding platforms and social media sites, these alternatives are risky, niche operations that do not displace the more established funding options.[4] Cash raised from a

---

[1] The company law aspects of share allotments, including pre-emption rights are considered in ch 5.

[2] JC Brau, 'Why Do Firms Go Public?' in D Cumming (ed), *The Oxford Handbook of Entrepreneurial Finance* (Oxford: OUP, 2012) ch 16.

[3] T Jenkinson and A Ljungqvist, *Going Public: The Theory and Evidence on How Companies Raise Equity Finance* 2nd edn (Oxford: OUP, 2001).

[4] O Stacey, S Lovegrove, and D Murphy, 'Crowdfunding: Possibilities and Prohibitions' (2012) 23(1) PLC 18; FSA, 'Crowdfunding: Is Your Investment Protected?' <http://www.fsa.gov.uk/consumerinformation/product_news/saving_investments/crowdfunding> accessed July 2013.

Crowdcube, the first crowdfunding group to be authorized and regulated by the FSA, raised nearly £5m for small UK companies since its launch in 2011, from angel investors, putting in up to £100,000 in a single investment, and others, contributing as little as £10.

flotation will reduce gearing and, once quoted, the issuer then has the option of going back to the market for secondary issues of securities in order to raise further finance. Being quoted may also improve the rate at which a company can borrow from banks.[5] As an illustration of the impact of a flotation on capital structure we can consider the Yell Group, which floated in July 2003 and raised £433.6 million (gross proceeds) in its IPO. It used the proceeds to settle £109.5 million payable on loan notes; to pay share issue costs of £23.7 million; to pay £79.6 million of exceptional costs; to repay £48.3 million of debt under senior credit facilities; and to redeem 35 per cent (£172.5 million) of senior notes pursuant to the optional redemption features in the terms of issue. It also replaced remaining senior credit facilities with new senior credit facilities of £664 million and $596 million and a revolving credit facility of £200 million. Overall, it achieved a decrease in net debt from £2.4 billion to £1.3 billion. However, in the years following its flotation Yell once again increased its debt levels in order to finance a number of ambitious acquisitions around the world. In the difficult economic conditions that followed in the wake of the financial crisis of 2007–9, the company's capital structure again came under considerable pressure and, in 2009, it had to seek an injection of new equity from its shareholders as part of a major refinancing exercise. These efforts did not succeed in putting the company permanently onto a secure financial footing. By mid 2013, the company, by now known as Hibu plc, in default on lending covenants and having failed to make interest payments when due, was in the process of another major debt-for-equity restructuring.[6]

Exit is a second reason for the controllers of a business to consider a flotation. A flotation provides existing controllers with an opportunity to offer their existing shares to the market alongside the offer of new shares made by the company to raise new equity finance. In some cases, almost as many shares in public offerings can come from pre-IPO holders as from issuers themselves.[7] Using a flotation as an exit mechanism can be important for venture capital firms, which provide specialized finance to small and medium-sized companies with high growth potential[8] and for private equity firms that sponsor leveraged buyout transactions. However, whereas IPOs were once thought of as 'the gold standard' in venture capital success,[9] in recent years such exits have fallen off relative to exits through trade sales.[10]

Exit need not be immediate upon an IPO and may instead follow some time after. A flotation establishes a public market in the company's shares thereby providing the opportunity of exit at a later date for those controllers who choose to retain the bulk of their shares at flotation. In some instances, flotation may be a step that is taken in order to draw attention to the company as a potential takeover target and with a view to facilitating an acquisition of the company's business at a higher price than would be attracted in a private sale.[11] A flotation

---

[5] M Pagano and A Röell, 'The Choice of Stock Ownership Structure: Agency Cost, Monitoring, and the Decision to Go Public' (1998) 113 *Quarterly Journal of Economics* 187.

[6] Hibu plc, 'Interim Management Statement for the Quarter Ended 31 December 2012' (12 February 2013); R Gribben, 'Investors Try to Salvage Returns from Hibu Deal: Former Yellow Pages Group Aims to Lose Market Listing and Shed Debt' *The Daily Telegraph*, 10 June 2013, 8 (Business Section).

[7] MJ Brennan and J Franks, 'Underpricing, Ownership and Control in Initial Public Offerings of Equity Securities in the UK' (1997) 45 *Journal of Financial Economics* 391, 406.

[8] DJ Cumming and JG MacIntosh, 'The Extent of Venture Capital Exits: Evidence from Canada and the United States' in J McCahery and L Renneboog (eds), *Venture Capital Contracting and the Valuation of High Technology Firms* (Oxford: OUP, 2004) ch 15.
Venture capital can be seen as a subset of private equity investment, with its distinguishing feature being that funds are advanced to early-stage businesses rather than to more mature firms.

[9] DM Ibrahim 'The New Exit in Venture Capital' (2012) 65 *Vanderbilt Law Review* 1, 11.

[10] DM Ibrahim 'The New Exit in Venture Capital' (2012) 65 *Vanderbilt Law Review* 1, 11.

[11] L Zingales, 'Insider Ownership and the Decision to Go Public' (1995) 62 *Review of Economic Studies* 425.

may also enhance a company's position as a bidder in the takeover market by enabling it to use its shares, which post-flotation are liquid investments, as consideration for acquisitions.

Macroeconomic conditions are also relevant to flotation decisions. Market conditions, together with the stage of the firm in its life cycle, are regularly cited as an important factor in the decision to go public.[12] IPOs can be timed to take advantage of 'hot' markets, in which prices are affected by excessive investor enthusiasm.[13] For example, the so-called 'dot-com' bubble of 1999–2001 prompted a surge in IPOs in Europe, whilst in the years that followed immediately after, the different economic conditions meant less need for the corporate sector to seek external financing and, to the extent that it was required, more reliance on debt and private equity than on publicly-issued securities.[14] By the same token, IPO activity can be expected to drop when markets are depressed. Thus, the global financial crisis of 2007–9 and the Eurozone crisis of 2011 have been cited as factors in the decline in European IPO activity between 2008 and 2011.[15]

The 'market timing' theory of capital structure seeks to capture the link between firms' decisions on financing and general market conditions by positing that firms' capital structures can be understood as the cumulative result of efforts to time the equity market—that is to issue shares when market prices are high and to repurchase them when market values are low.[16] There are also economies of scope arguments, by which it is meant that smaller firms may prefer to grow by mergers, acquisitions, and trade sales, rather than to go public and remain independent.[17] Some older work found a difference between European and US markets in this respect, with smaller firms going public in Europe less than in the United States,[18] an outcome that is consistent with the hypothesis that there are country-by-country variations in the size, age, industry, and riskiness of companies that are regarded by the market as being ready to go public.[19] However, in recent years IPO activity by smaller firms has also declined in the United States.[20] The US Jumpstart Our Business Startups (JOBS) Act, which became law in 2012, was designed to generate more IPOs by smaller companies by creating a new category of issuer (the Emerging Growth Company (EGC)) and revising IPO regulatory requirements to accommodate EGC IPOs. However, one year on, it was reported that whilst the JOBS Act had brought increased flexibility, scaled disclosure, and temporary relief from some of the regulatory burdens on public companies, these improvements to the IPO process were still not widely understood by many private companies.[21]

Politics can also influence levels of IPO activity, as is most obvious in relation to the privatization and flotation of previously state-owned enterprises. Distinctive features of privatization IPOs can include incentives for employees and for retail investors to take up the offer.

---

[12] JR Ritter and I Welch, 'A Review of IPO Activity, Pricing and Allocations' (2002) 57 *Journal of Finance* 1795.

[13] A Ljungqvist, VK Nanda and R Singh, 'Hot Markets, Investor Sentiment, and IPO Pricing' (2006) 79 *Journal of Business* 1667.

[14] L Bê Duc, G de Bondt, A Calza, D Marqués Ibáñez, A van Rixtel, and S Scopel, *Financing Conditions in the Euro Area* (2005) ECB Occasional Paper Series No 37, 27–9.

[15] JR Ritter, A Signori, and S Vismara, 'Economies of Scope and IPO Activity in Europe' (30 October 2012) <http://ssrn.com/abstract=2169966> accessed July 2013.

[16] M Baker and J Wurgler, 'Market Timing and Capital Structure' (2002) 57 *Journal of Finance* 1.

[17] Ritter, Signori and Vismara, 'Economies of Scope and IPO Activity in Europe.'

[18] F Degeorge and EG Maug, 'Corporate Finance in Europe: A Survey' in X Freixas, P Hartmann and C Mayer (eds), *Handbook of European Financial Markets and Institutions*, (Oxford: OUP, 2008) ch 7.

[19] M Goergen and L Renneboog, 'Why are the Levels of Control (so) Different in German and UK Companies? Evidence from Initial Public Offerings' (2003) *Journal of Law, Economics and Organization* 141.

[20] X Gao, JR Ritter, and Z Zhu, 'Where Have All the IPOs Gone?' (13 March 2012) <http://ssrn.com/abstract=1954788> accessed July 2013.

[21] Latham & Watkins, *The JOBS Act After One Year: A Review of the New IPO Playbook* (April 2013). See generally DC Langevoort and RB Thompson, '"Publicness" in Contemporary Securities Regulation After the JOBS Act' (2013) 101 *Georgetown Law Journal* 337.

Finally, there is a myriad array of other factors that may be relevant to the going public decision, although these tend to be subsidiary to the new financing and exit considerations and associated benefits. These miscellaneous reasons include enhanced prestige, which may enable the company to attract a higher quality of professional managers and to build a higher public profile, which may, in turn, help to attract customers in product markets. In a survey conducted on behalf of the London Stock Exchange (LSE), one in ten of all respondents stated that the extra credibility and profile afforded by being traded on a stock market was the major motivator in going public.[22] Another benefit is that the liquidity associated with publicly-quoted securities provides greater scope for companies to offer remuneration packages that include shares and options.

There are drawbacks associated with going public that also need to be considered. The process of flotation is complex and costly, although underwriting and other direct IPO costs, such as lawyers' fees, are typically lower in Europe than in the US.[23] For the UK, the Association of British Insurers (ABI) has confirmed that typical fees are much lower than in the US for transactions of similar size but it has, nevertheless, drawn attention to investor concerns with overall costs and called for greater disclosure of fees in prospectuses and more control with respect to incentive fees.[24] As for complexity, the process of flotation involves a rite of passage that is likely to entail a significant corporate reorganization involving the status of the company, its constitutional framework, and its managerial structure. The status of the company may have to change because of the rules that private companies may not make public offers of their securities[25] or have their securities admitted to official listing.[26] The company's constitutional framework, as set out in its articles, will need to be reviewed so as to remove provisions, such as restrictions on the transfer of shares, which will cease to be appropriate once its shares are publicly traded.[27] Independent non-executive directors will have to be appointed in order to meet listing requirements and the expectations of the market with regard to good corporate governance; and the terms of employment of existing executive directors may need to be made more transparent, particularly with regard to remuneration entitlements and notice periods.[28] There are also significant ongoing obligations associated with going public. Once a company has become a public company with outside investors, it will be subject to more stringent legal requirements and to the discipline imposed by market forces and by increased visibility.[29]

---

[22] Eversheds, *Going Public 2: A Survey of Recently Floated Companies* (2003).

[23] L Bell, L Correia da Silva, and A Preimanis, *The Cost of Capital: An International Comparison* (City of London, 2006) presented research showing underwriting fees of 3–4 per cent on average in European transactions and underwriting fees of 6.5–7 per cent on US transactions. Legal, accounting, and advisory fees, as well as the marketing and PR costs, were found to add another 3–6 per cent. A more recent study of fees charged by investment banks for conducting IPOs confirms that European IPO fees remain roughly three percentage points lower than those in the US, despite the same banks dominating the markets in both regions and the considerable convergence in offering practices: M Abrahamson, T Jenkinson, and H Jones, 'Why Don't U.S. Issuers Demand European Fees for IPOs?' (2011) 66 *Journal of Finance* 2055.

[24] ABI, *Encouraging Equity Investment: Facilitation of Efficient Equity Capital Raising in the UK Market* (July 2013) 24–6.

[25] Companies Act 2006, s 755.

[26] Financial Services and Markets Act 2000 (Official Listing of Securities) Regulations 2001, SI 2001/2956, reg 3.

[27] The FCA *Listing Rules* provide that if an issuer seeks to list securities they must be free from 'any restriction on the right of transfer' (see *LR* 2.2.4). The FCA will permit the use of restrictions on transfer only in very limited circumstances, such as to prevent a company from falling within the scope of onerous overseas legislative requirements: UKLA *Technical Note: Restrictions on Transferability* (UKLA/TN/101.1).

[28] Generally on the corporate governance implications of going public: I Filatotchev and K Bishop, 'Board Composition, Share Ownership and "Underpricing" of UK IPO Firms' (2002) 23 *Strategic Management Journal* 941.

[29] For the purposes of the application of progressively more burdensome requirements under the Companies Act 2006, the public/private distinction is the main dividing line but in certain places the legislation contains further subdivisions (eg Pt 13 (special requirements for company meetings applicable to traded companies, ie companies admitted to trading on a regulated market); Pt 15 (certain accounting requirements applicable to quoted companies,

Fundamentally, an IPO will entail some loss of control by the existing owners of the business. An IPO is typically regarded as a watershed in the process whereby managerial control and share ownership become separated. A key feature of UK market practice that promotes this result is the prevalence of straightforward, one-share-one-vote, equity capital structures. Institutional investors in the UK markets generally expect issuers involved in IPOs to have capital structures comprising a single class of ordinary shares adhering to the 'one share—one vote' principle.[30] The strength of feeling on this matter was confirmed by a Review of the UK Equity Markets that was conducted in 2012 on behalf of the Department of Business by Professor John Kay. The Kay Report noted:[31]

> UK companies are already legally free to create different share classes with differential voting rights. Two notable recent US flotations—those of Google and Facebook—have involved such a structure, and it is less likely that the founders of these companies, who are anxious to maintain their influence on the distinctive character of their organisations, would have agreed to an IPO if such an arrangement had not been possible.
>
> However multiple share classes are viewed with considerable hostility by UK institutional investors. The ABI, which led the historic opposition to these structures—a stance which led to the virtual elimination of dual class share structures amongst UK listed companies—told us that they remain strongly opposed.

In 2013 the Financial Conduct Authority (FCA) announced that it would strengthen its top-tier premium listing regime by introducing new premium listing principles to mandate voting equality and proportionality for premium listed equity shares and classes of shares.[32] These changes are part of a package of measures that is designed primarily to ensure that premium listed companies are not improperly influenced by controlling shareholders. At the time of writing (November 2013) these changes were expected to take effect in mid-2014.

Nevertheless, as is apparent from the quoted passage from the Kay Report, there is some divergence between the UK and the United States with respect to these matters. UK practice can also be contrasted with Continental European market conditions, where institutional investors have historically played a more limited role. In some European countries, mechanisms such as dual class structures, which allow the existing owners to preserve control by weighting voting rights in their favour, remain common. According to one major study of the capital structure of European companies, which was published in 2005, only 65 per cent of the companies in the study applied the 'one share—one vote' principle to equity securities.[33] The study found the highest proportion of companies adopting this principle was in Belgium (100 per cent), followed by Germany (97 per cent) and the UK (88 per cent). 'One share—one vote' was applied by only a minority of companies in the Netherlands

---

ie a company admitted to official listing in any EEA state or to dealings on NYSE or Nasdaq)). Regulatory requirements (listing rules etc) are geared to the market or market segment on which the company's securities trade.

[30] Brennan and Franks, 'Underpricing, Ownership and Control,' 396 (none of a large sample of UK IPOs for the years 1986–89 included the issuance of dual class shares, nor did any prospectus provide super priority rights to a particular group of shareholders, or other constraints on the control rights of a particular class of shareholders); JR Franks, C Mayer, and S Rossi, 'Ownership: Evolution and Regulation' (2009) 22 *Review of Financial Studies* 4009.

[31] J Kay, *The Kay Review of UK Equity Markets and Long-term Decision Making* (BIS, July 2012) paras 8.33–8.34.

[32] FCA, *Feedback on CP12/25: Enhancing the Effectiveness of the Listing Regime and Further Consultation* (CP13/15, November 2013) paras 10.9–10.13.

[33] Deminor Rating, *Application of the One Share—One Vote Principle in Europe* (March 2005) (study commissioned by the ABI). Non-voting preference shares were not regarded in this Report as breaching the 'one share—one vote' principle because the absence of voting rights was compensated by a preferential dividend.

A later study was consistent with the Deminor Study in identifying France, the Netherlands, and Sweden as the countries in which companies make most use of multiple voting right structures: Institutional Shareholder Services, Shearman & Sterling, and European Corporate Governance Institute, *Report on the Proportionality Principle in the European Union* (May 2007) (study commissioned by the European Commission).

(14 per cent), Sweden (25 per cent), and France (31 per cent).[34] Yet dual class structures are only part of the story because complex pyramid share ownership structures, cross shareholdings, and other mechanisms can also achieve the effect of concentrating power disproportionately to the level of investment.[35] Up to thirteen different control enhancing mechanisms have been identified as being in use in Europe.[36] Pyramid ownership structures were historically common in German corporations[37] but they are no longer such a typical feature of its corporate landscape.[38] Elsewhere, pyramid structures are still widely used throughout Europe (except in Ireland, Denmark, and Finland) with particular frequency in Belgium and Sweden.[39]

Dual class, pyramid, and other functionally equivalent structures can impede the process for the separation of ownership and control because they enable pre-flotation controllers to go public whilst still maintaining control through a disproportionate say in the company's affairs. On the other hand, they can act as a counterbalance to the negative effects of short-termism in investment strategies by in effect 'rewarding' long-term holders of shares for their patience. The Kay Report summarized the position by noting that: 'the challenge is to advantage engagement by committed shareholders without undermining protections for minority shareholders.'[40] An indication of the difficulties involved in striking an appropriate balance can be gleaned from the inconclusive state of scholarship on these issues. A line of theoretical and empirical literature places discussion of the proportionality principle within a broader debate about the relationship between law and finance. One strand of literature suggests that there are links between the differences in patterns of corporate ownership around the world, including in particular the persistence of deviations from the proportionality principle, and the protections that national legal systems provide to minority shareholders: weak legal protection can be taken to imply concentrated ownership.[41] However, this explanation of ownership patterns does not go uncontested, as it is possible to point to countries such as Sweden, where concentrated ownership persists despite good law,[42] and, indeed, to the UK, where share ownership has become dispersed in spite of certain weaknesses in the legal protections afforded to minority shareholders.[43] A significant alternative suggestion emphasizes national politics as a powerful driver of concentrated ownership in many countries,[44] though this explanation has also been questioned.[45] Moreover, it has been

---

[34] On the Swedish position see also: P Högtfeldt and M Holmen, 'A Law and Finance Analysis of Initial Public Offerings' (2004) 13 *Journal of Financial Intermediation* 324. On Germany: Goergen and Renneboog, 'Why are the Levels of Control (so) Different in German and UK Companies?'

[35] A pyramid is a chain of holding companies with ultimate control based on a small total investment: High Level Group of Company Law Experts, *A Modern Regulatory Framework for Company Law in Europe* (Brussels, November 2001) 17.

[36] Institutional Shareholder Services et al, *Report on the Proportionality Principle in the European Union*.

[37] JR Franks, C Mayer, and HF Wagner, 'Ownership and Control of German Corporations' (2006) 10 *Review of Finance* 537.

[38] Institutional Shareholder Services et al, *Report on the Proportionality Principle in the European Union*, para 4.3.4.

[39] Institutional Shareholder Services et al, *Report on the Proportionality Principle in the European Union*, para 4.3.4.

[40] Kay, *The Kay Review*, paras 8.33–8.34

[41] R La Porta, F López-de-Silanes and A Shleifer, 'Corporate Ownership Around the World' (1999) 54 *Journal of Finance* 471.

[42] RJ Gilson, 'Controlling Shareholders and Corporate Governance: Complicating the Comparative Taxonomy' (2006) 119 *Harvard Law Review* 1641.

[43] BR Cheffins, 'Does Law Matter? The Separation of Ownership and Control in the United Kingdom' (2001) 30 *Journal of Legal Studies* 459.

[44] MR Roe, *Political Determinants of Corporate Governance: Political Context, Corporate Impact* (Oxford: OUP, 2003).

[45] BR Cheffins, 'Putting Britain on the Roe Map: The Emergence of the Berle-Means Corporation in the United Kingdom' in JA McCahery, P Moerland, T Raaijmakers, and L Renneboog (eds), *Corporate Governance Regimes: Convergence and Diversity* (Oxford: OUP, 2002) 147.

pointed out that a distinction between 'concentrated' and 'dispersed' share ownership is too simplistic and that a more sophisticated taxonomy is required to reflect the different con- trolling shareholder models that can be found around the world.[46] Furthermore, it has been argued compellingly that it is not clear that controlling shareholder regimes inevitably lead to the extraction of large private benefits of control at the expense of minority sharehold- ers.[47] The inconclusive state of knowledge on whether disproportional ownership creates social costs by destroying firm value[48] provides contextual justification for the decision by the European Commission in the late 2000s not to pursue the idea of intervention to regulate control enhancing mechanisms.[49]

The 'free float'—that is the minimum percentage of shares that must be put into the hands of the public on flotation is another factor that has an important bearing on the loss of control that is entailed in a flotation. Free float requirements and associated requirements relating to the position of controlling shareholders have become a key area of debate in the UK: strin- gent requirements may deter listings but relaxed requirements may lead to corporate govern- ance problems of exploitation of minority shareholders by the majority controllers in ways that supposedly independent non-executive directors are unable or unwilling to contain.[50]

Going public is not an irreversible step. Companies that are experiencing some difficulties may 'go private' in order to effect a turnaround away from the harsh gaze of the public mar- kets. Reverting to the private arena may also appeal to companies which have failed to attract significant investor interest and have thus not gained sufficient benefits from being public to outweigh the disadvantages of a heavier regulatory burden and harsh public scrutiny.[51] In particular, entrepreneurial characters who have built up companies from scratch may chafe against the constraints of the public arena. An economically significant public-to-private market has developed in the UK since the late 1990s.[52]

Where to List? International Choice

This chapter focuses mainly on domestic IPOs—ie an offer in the UK by a UK company in which the shares are listed on a formal market based in the UK ('listed' here being used in a loose sense that is synonymous with the idea of shares being admitted to trading on an organ- ized market, although, as will be seen later in this chapter, 'listing' can also be used in a more precise way to denote admission to trading on a particular market segment to which enhanced regulatory standards apply). However, whilst the conventional option for a company coming to market for the first time is to have its securities admitted to listing or trading on a stock exchange in its home country, it is pertinent to note that other listing options are also available. A primary listing in the domestic market may be supplemented, either initially or at some later date, by a secondary, or cross, listing on a foreign exchange, or the domestic jurisdiction could even be bypassed altogether. An important study of the geography of equity listings found that during the 1990s European companies that cross-listed in the United States were mainly high-tech companies motivated by the need for infusions of new equity. The authors suggested as factors contributing to the US's competitive advantage in this respect: the presence of skilled

---

[46] Gilson, 'Controlling Shareholders and Corporate Governance.'

[47] Gilson, 'Controlling Shareholders and Corporate Governance.'

[48] Institutional Shareholder Services et al, *Report on the Proportionality Principle in the European Union*, 6.

[49] C McCreevy, Speech to European Parliament Legal Affairs Committee, 3 October 2007.

[50] Free float and corporate governance issues are highlighted in ABI, *Encouraging Equity Investment*, 26–9. They are discussed in more detail later in this chapter.

[51] European Commission, *Report of Alternative Investment Group: Developing Private Equity* (July 2006) 13.

[52] L Renneboog, T Simons, and M Wright, 'Why Do Firms Go Private in the UK?' (2007) 13 *Journal of Corporate Finance* 591.

analysts and institutional investors specializing in evaluating these companies; the liquidity of American exchanges; the quality of US accounting standards and shareholder rights' protection; and the huge US product market which provided a natural springboard for foreign companies with a strong export orientation.[53] Another powerful line of analysis from the same period emphasized 'bonding'—voluntarily subjecting themselves to the United States' higher disclosure standards and greater threat of enforcement—as the reason why issuers from certain parts of the world came to the US stock markets.[54]

In the mid-2000s there was a decline in the number of European issuers listing in the US, a trend which prompted much analysis and reflection by market observers, politicians, and academic commentators. Revealing statistics included: in 2003 31 per cent of the NYSE's IPO volume came from foreign issuers (including Europe) but by 2005 foreign issuers accounted for only 8 per cent of this volume;[55] and only 5 per cent of the value of global initial public offerings (that is, IPOs done outside the issuer's home country) was raised in the US in 2005 compared to 50 per cent in 2000.[56] Overall, between 2001 and 2011, London attracted 41 per cent of all cross-border IPOs compared to 23 per cent by New York.[57] Among the many explanations for this trend that were put forward, two that attracted much attention were the impact of the stricter US regulatory requirements, epitomized by the Sarbanes-Oxley Act of 2002, that emerged in response to certain high-profile corporate collapses and scandals of that period, and the propensity for private litigation within the US system.[58] The debate was intense but the evidence was inconclusive. Some analysis in relation to foreign companies trading in the United States in the period leading up to and immediately after the adoption of the Sarbanes-Oxley Act found that the premium associated with being subject to US regulation declined during the period, an outcome that seemed to point to the conclusion that investors perceived Sarbanes-Oxley to have greater costs than benefits for cross-listed firms on average, especially for smaller firms and already well-governed firms.[59] On the other hand, other studies of the determinants and consequences of cross-listings on the New York and London stock exchanges found no deficit in cross-listing counts on US exchanges related to Sarbanes-Oxley.[60] The authors of these studies concluded that their evidence supported

[53] M Pagano, AA Röell, and J Zechner, 'The Geography of Equity Listing; Why Do Companies List Abroad?' (2002) 57 *Journal of Finance* 2651.

[54] R Stulz, 'Globalization, Corporate Finance, and the Cost of Capital' (1999) 12 *Journal of Applied Corporate Finance* 8; JC Coffee, 'Racing Towards the Top?: The Impact of Cross-Listings and Stock Market Competition on International Corporate Governance' (2002) 102 *Columbia Law Review* 1757; C Doidge, GA Karolyi, and RM Stulz, 'Why Are Foreign Firms That List in the U.S. Worth More?' (2004) 71 *Journal of Financial Economics* 205.

[55] McKinsey & Co, *Sustaining New York's and the US' Global Financial Services Leadership* (2007) 46 (report commissioned by MR Bloomberg and CE Schumer) <http://www.nyc.gov/html/om/pdf/ny_report_final.pdf> accessed July 2013.

[56] Committee on Capital Markets Regulation, *Interim Report* (November 2006) 2. This report (commonly referred to as the 'Paulson Committee Report') is available at <http://www.capmktsreg.org/pdfs/11.30Committee_Interim_ReportREV2.pdf> accessed July 2013.

[57] PWC, *Equity Sans Frontières—Trends in Cross-border IPOs and an Outlook for the Future* (November 2012); ABI, *Encouraging Equity Investment*.

[58] Some considered the Sarbanes-Oxley Act to be a serious policy blunder, which was enacted too quickly amidst a media frenzy over corporate scandal: see, eg, R Romano, 'The Sarbanes-Oxley Act and the Making of Quack Corporate Governance' (2005) 114 *Yale Law Journal* 1521.

The McKinsey Report commissioned by Schumer and Bloomberg on the potential for New York to lose its status as the financial capital of the world was also a product of this period.

[59] K Litvak, 'Sarbanes-Oxley and the Cross-Listing Premium' (2007) 105 *Michigan Law Review* 1857. See also K Litvak, 'The Effect of the Sarbanes-Oxley Act on Foreign Companies Cross-Listed in the U.S.' (2007) 13 *Journal of Corporate Finance* 195.

[60] C Doidge, GA Karolyi, K Lins, D Miller, and R Stulz, 'Private Benefits of Control, Ownership, and the Cross-listing Decision' (2009) 64 *Journal of Finance* 425; C Doidge, GA Karolyi, and R Stulz, 'Has New York Become less Competitive than London in Global Markets? Evaluating Foreign Listing Choices over Time' (2009) 91 *Journal of Financial Economics* 253.

the theory that an exchange listing in New York had unique governance benefits for foreign firms that had not been seriously eroded by Sarbanes-Oxley and which could not be replicated through a London listing.

Recent work focusing specifically on initial public offerings of firms outside their home country has confirmed the decline in the number of foreign and global IPOs issuing in the US, with the UK and Singapore being the locations that have seen the largest increase in the number of issues over time.[61] However, this study also made the point that when proceeds, rather than numbers of listings are examined, a slightly different picture emerges. While the UK had experienced a large increase in the number of foreign and global listings, these offers have tended to be significantly smaller in size than US IPO listings. This finding is consistent with the point made by other authors that the rise in numbers of cross-listings in the UK can be largely attributed to the junior tier of the London Stock Exchange, the Alternative Investment Market, which has lower listing standards and which thus fills a niche for smaller issuers that would have been unlikely candidates to cross-list on US exchanges, either before or after Sarbanes-Oxley.[62] The IPO study also found that companies making foreign (ie in one foreign country only and bypassing the home country) and global (ie simultaneously in the home country and abroad) IPOs were more likely to originate in countries with poor capital market development, few recent industry peers, and lower disclosure requirements.[63] By way of contrast, firms going public at home and then subsequently cross-listing abroad tended to originate in markets that were significantly better developed, with stronger securities laws. Larger IPOs were more likely to list in the US and stronger disclosure requirements appeared to be a strong factor in the decision to list there. Geographical proximity was a factor in decisions to list in the UK and firms listing in the UK tended to originate from countries with stronger, not weaker, disclosure requirements.

Where to List? National (UK) and Regional (EU) Choice

The creation of a pan-European securities market has for a long time featured prominently on the EU internal market agenda and much has been done to put in place a regulatory framework and a system of supervisory oversight to facilitate and support its operation. In a sense, therefore, the entire EU[64] could be regarded as the 'domestic' market for a UK company. Certainly there is competition between the major European stock exchanges for listing business from issuers. With demutualization, the concept of a national stock exchange that performs significant public interest functions has disappeared and exchanges now operate as major internationally-oriented business. For example the London Stock Exchange Group is now a cross-border group, formed by the merger in October 2007 of the London Stock Exchange and Borsa Italiana. The London Stock Exchange has tried unsuccessfully to merge with the Toronto Stock Exchange, and other possibilities, including suggestions of a link with the Singapore Exchange, continue to surface periodically in the media. One of the main rivals to the London Stock Exchange, NYSE Euronext, is also highly international in orientation, having been formed in

---

[61] C Caglio, K Weiss Hanley, and J Marietta-Westberg, 'Going Public Abroad: The Role of International Markets for IPOs' (March 2011) <http://ssrn.com/abstract=1572949> accessed July 2013. See also C Doidge, GA Karolyi, and RM Stulz, 'Financial Globalization and the Rise of IPOs Outside the U.S.' (January 2013) <http://ssrn.com/abstract=2118624> accessed July 2013.

[62] Doidge, Karolyi, and Stulz, 'Has New York Become less Competitive than London in Global Markets?'

[63] Caglio, Weiss Hanley, and Marietta-Westberg, 'Going Public Abroad.'

[64] Or even the European Economic Area because the regulatory framework in question extends beyond the EU to the EEA countries as well.

2007 by the combination of NYSE Group, Inc and Euronext NV. Ownership of organized trading platforms has become a fiercely contested business. In late December 2012 Intercontinental Exchange Inc (ICE) agreed to buy NYSE Euronext in an $8.2bn deal. This bid was approved by the European Commission, in its role as EU competition authority, in June 2013. A previous bid by ICE, jointly with Nasdaq, had failed because of opposition from US competition authorities. Competition issues also scuppered a bid by the Deutsche Börse for NYSE Euronext, which was blocked by EU competition authorities. NYSE Euronext operates markets in New York, Amsterdam, Brussels, Lisbon, and Paris and has even begun to compete with the London Stock Exchange in its home territory by establishing a London listing facility. In June 2012 Groupe Eurotunnel became the first company on the NYSE Euronext London market, transferring from the London Stock Exchange.

Yet notwithstanding the growing importance of the EU internal market, it still remains more accurate to regard the UK on its own as the domestic market for a UK incorporated company. Furthermore, for a UK company seeking to go public, one of the markets or market segments provided by the London Stock Exchange is likely to be venue of choice. Whilst there are other UK-based equity markets, these have struggled to establish and maintain a substantial market share.[65] The London Stock Exchange provides the Main Market, which, loosely, is a market aimed at larger, more established companies or companies that aspire to that status, and the Alternative Investment Market (AIM), which is a market for younger, smaller growth companies.[66] The Main Market is an EU regulated market for officially-listed securities or, with respect to its High Growth segment, opened in 2013, an EU regulated market for securities that are not admitted to the Official List. AIM, on the other hand, is an exchange-regulated market for unlisted securities. The choice for an issuer considering official listing and admission to the Main Market subdivides into 'premium' and 'standard' listing. The differences between 'EU regulated' and 'exchange-regulated,' between 'listed' and 'unlisted,' and between 'premium' and 'standard' listing all relate to the applicable regulatory standards. To make sense of this confusing array of labels and categories it is necessary, therefore, to examine the regulatory framework in some detail.

EU Capital Market Regulation

This examination must begin at EU level. Since the late 1970s, capital market regulation has been increasingly shaped by legislative intervention at EU level intended to promote the establishment of an integrated pan-European securities market. Early EU laws, in the late 1970s and early 1980s, applied to the 'officially listed' segment of the securities market.[67] Issuers that sought to raise finance by offering their securities to the public via a market for officially listed securities (usually the main stock exchange in each Member State) or which sought to facilitate the secondary market trading of their securities by their admission to such a market were required to make initial mandatory disclosures in the form of a set of listing

---

[65] Until 2012 the Plus Group offered two markets, one aimed at younger or smaller issuers, and the other for larger, more established issuers. Facing serious financial problems that threatened its survival, the Group, which managed the listings of about 140 companies with a combined market worth of £2.3bn was bought by Icap, an interbroker dealer in 2012. The new owner continues to offer two tiers, the ISDX Main Board, as a market aimed at more established companies, and the ISDX Growth Market with a regulatory framework dedicated to the needs of smaller companies.

[66] In addition, the LSE's Professional Securities Market for specialist securities is considered in ch 14 (as a market for depositary receipts of overseas issuers) and ch 15 (as a market for corporate bonds).

[67] See also A Alcock, 'The Rise and Fall of UK Quoted Company Regulation?' [2007] JBL 733.

particulars.[68] They were also subject to certain mandatory qualitative admission criteria.[69] Once officially listed, issuers were subject to certain continuing periodic disclosure and other requirements.[70] Member States were free to vest responsibility for the implementation and supervision of the regime for officially listed securities in their stock exchanges. This freedom was exploited in the UK where the London Stock Exchange was the competent authority for matters relating to official listing. The regime for officially listed securities was followed towards the end of the 1980s by further EC law whereby prospectuses became mandatory for public offers of both officially listed and other securities.[71]

Market changes during the 1990s, such as the emergence of new trading platforms, made the regulatory emphasis on the officially listed segment of securities markets increasingly anomalous. The reliance on exchanges, which were converting from not-for-profit entities to commercial companies in order to operate more effectively in a new, more competitive, environment, to perform regulatory and supervisory functions came under increasing scrutiny. Other aspects of the EU regulatory regime for official listing and public offers of securities also proved to be ill-suited to the changing market conditions.

In 1999 the European Commission adopted the Financial Services Action Plan (FSAP).[72] The FSAP was an attempt by the European Commission to equip the Community better to meet the challenges of monetary union and to capitalize on the potential benefits of a single market in financial services. It set out an ambitious plan for new legislation including a revamped regime for public offers of securities and the admission of securities to trading platforms. FSAP ideas eventually crystallized into a considerable corpus of new EU capital markets law, of which the following are key components for the purposes of regulating issuer access to capital markets:

Directive 2003/6/EC of the European Parliament and of the Council of 28 January 2003 on insider dealing and market manipulation (market abuse) (the 'Market Abuse Directive' or MAD).[73] The Market Abuse Directive is under review and will be replaced by a new Market Abuse Regulation and a Directive on Criminal Sanctions for Market Abuse.[74]

Directive 2003/71/EC of the European Parliament and of the Council of 4th November 2003 on the prospectus to be published when securities are offered to the public or admitted to trading on a regulated market (the 'Prospectus Directive').[75] The Prospectus Directive was amended by Directive 2010/73/EU to clarify a number of provisions, reduce certain administrative

---

[68] Council Directive 80/390/EEC co-ordinating the requirements for the drawing-up, scrutiny and distribution of the listing particulars to be published for the admission of securities to official stock exchange listing (Listing Particulars Directive) [1980] OJ L100/1.

[69] Council Directive 79/279/EEC co-ordinating the conditions for the admission of securities to official stock exchange listing (Admission Directive) [1979] OJ L66/21.

[70] Council Directive 82/121/EEC on information to be published on a regular basis by companies shares of which have been admitted to official stock-exchange listing (Interim Reports Directive) [1982] OJ L48/26.

[71] Council Directive 89/298/EEC co-ordinating the requirements for the drawing-up, scrutiny and distribution of the prospectus to be published when transferable securities are offered to the public (Public Offers Directive) [1989] OJ L124/8.

[72] European Commission, *Financial Services: Implementing the Framework for Financial Markets: Action Plan* (COM(1999) 232).

[73] [2003] OJ L339/70.

[74] European Commission, *Proposal for a Regulation of the European Parliament and of the Council on insider dealing and market manipulation (market abuse)* (COM(2011) 651) and *Amended Proposal* (COM(2012) 421); European Commission, *Proposal for a Directive of the European Parliament and of the Council on criminal sanctions for insider dealing and market manipulation* (COM(2011) 654) and *Amended Proposal* (COM(2012) 420). In September 2013, the European Parliament endorsed the political agreement with the Council on the Market Abuse Regulation. Final adoption of the Market Abuse Regulation will take place after a final political agreement on the revised Markets in Financial Instruments Directive (MiFID II), since aspects of the Market Abuse Regulation depend on the final text of MiFID II and these will need to be aligned. The date as of which the new market abuse rules will apply is to be aligned with that of MiFID II.

[75] [2003] OJ L435/64.

burdens and introduce a proportionate disclosure regime for particular issuers and types of capital raising;[76] and

Directive 2004/109/EC of the European Parliament and of the Council of 15 December 2004 on the harmonization of transparency requirements in relation to information about issuers whose securities are admitted to trading on a regulated market and amending Directive 2001/34/EC (the 'Transparency Obligations Directive').[77] The Transparency Obligations Directive has been reviewed and amended by Directive 2010/73/EU and Directive 2013/50/EU.[78]

The new approach heralded by the FSAP Directives has to a large extent replaced the older EU regime governing official listing. Only a limited number of relatively undemanding provisions specifying qualitative admission criteria remain extant.[79]

Under the Prospectus Directive, Member States are obliged to enact laws requiring a prospectus to be published in respect of all non-exempt offers of securities to the public. The Prospectus Directive also requires Member States to pass laws imposing the requirement for a prospectus to be published on the admission of securities to trading on a 'regulated market.' Top tier national markets such as the Main Market of the London Stock Exchange tend to be regulated markets. The category can also extend to second-tier markets but, as in the case of AIM, such markets can be deliberately organized so as to fall outside the 'regulated' category in order to avoid certain regulatory requirements that are applicable to the regulated segment and thus to preserve a more flexible regulatory regime for smaller companies. The regulatory obligations associated with being admitted to trading on a regulated market are further reinforced by the Transparency Obligations Directive. This Directive makes it obligatory for Member States to require issuers that have their securities admitted to trading on a regulated market to comply with periodic disclosure requirements. It also requires shareholders to disclose major holdings. In addition, under the Market Abuse Directive, issuers with securities admitted to trading on a regulated market are required to disclose inside information (although under the Market Abuse Regulation, which will replace the Directive, this obligation will be extended to a wider range of issuers). The issuer disclosure obligations that are imposed by the Market Abuse and Transparency Obligations Directives are considered further at the end of the chapter.

Another EU law of particular significance is Regulation (EC) No 1606/2002 of the European Parliament and of the Council of 19 July 2002 on the application of international accounting standards (IAS Regulation), which, with effect from January 2005, imposes a requirement for the consolidated accounts of EEA issuers with securities admitted to trading a regulated market to be drawn up in accordance with the standards now known as the International Financial Reporting Standards (IFRS) that have been adopted by the EU.[80]

The formal definition of a 'regulated market' is provided currently by the Markets in Financial Instruments Directive (MiFID) Art 4(1)(14) and means:

a multilateral system operated and/or managed by a market operator, which brings together or facilitates the bringing together of multiple third-party buying and selling interests in financial

---

[76] [2010] OJ L327/1.   [77] [2004] OJ L390/38.

[78] Directive 2013/50/EU of the European Parliament and of the Council of 22 October 2013 amending Directive 2004/109/EC, [2013] OJ L294/13. For background see European Commission, *Proposal for a Directive of the European Parliament and of the Council amending Directive 2004/109/EC* (COM(2011) 683). Implementation at national level by Member States is expected to take place by mid-2015.

[79] Directive 2001/34/EC of the European Parliament and of the Council of 28 May 2001 on the admission of securities to official stock exchange listing and on information to be published on those securities [2001] OJ L184/1 (known as the Consolidated Admission and Reporting Directive or CARD). CARD consolidated a number of earlier measures (the Admission Directive, the Listing Particulars Directive, and the Interim Reports Directive).

[80] [2002] OJ L243/1.

instruments—in the system and in accordance with its non-discretionary rules—in a way that results in a contract, in respect of the financial instruments admitted to trading under its rules and/or systems, and which is authorised and functions regularly and in accordance with the provisions of Title III [of the Directive].[81]

MiFID is under review, and the review includes a re-examination of the classification of different trading venues.[82] The MiFID review introduces a new regulatory subcategory of Multilateral Trading Facilities (MTF) known as SME growth markets.[83] The European Commission has suggested that this move will raise visibility and profile, and help lead to common pan-European regulatory standards for such markets that are tailored to take into account the needs of relevant issuers and investors while maintaining existing high levels of investor protection.[84] The implications of this development for existing regulated and exchange-regulated markets such as AIM (which is an MTF) remain to be seen. A balance has always to be maintained between the needs of SMEs for proportionate regulation (which may involve differentiated prospectus, disclosure, or listing requirements) and the needs of investors for an appropriate level of protection irrespective of whether they are investing in large or small entities. We return to this point later in the context of prospectus disclosure requirements, which have recently been amended to provide a more 'proportionate' disclosure regime for SMEs and issuers with reduced market capitalization in order to facilitate their access to capital markets.

Giving Effect to EU Law in the UK: An Introductory Outline

Admission to official listing, admission to trading on regulated markets, and public offers of securities are principally regulated by the Financial Services and Markets Act 2000 (FSMA), Part 6 and the FCA *Handbook*, in particular the *Prospectus Rules* (or *PR*), the *Disclosure Rules and Transparency Rules* (or *DTR*), and the *Listing Rules* (or *LR*), which in combination implement the EU Directives. Part 6 of the Financial Services and Markets Act 2000 provides the FCA with statutory authority for these matters and sets out its general duties and responsibilities in that capacity as well as an outline framework governing the listing process and the mechanisms for its enforcement. The FCA's predecessor, the Financial Services Authority (FSA), had assumed responsibility for listing matters in May 2000 as one of the consequences of the reorganization of the London Stock Exchange into a publicly-quoted commercial company. These responsibilities transferred to the FCA in 2013.

Admission to the Official List and to the Main Market of the London Stock Exchange carries with it the most onerous compliance obligations: an issuer must comply with the full panoply of regulatory requirements, although these will vary in certain respects depending on whether an issuer opts for 'premium' or 'standard' listing. An issuer admitted to the High

---

[81] Directive 2004/39/EC of the European Parliament and of the Council of 21 April 2004 on markets in financial instruments amending Council Directives 85/611/EEC and 93/6/EEC and Directive 2000/12/EC of the European Parliament and of the Council and repealing Council Directive 93/22/EEC [2004] OJ L145/1.

[82] European Commission, *Proposal for a Directive of the European Parliament and of the Council on markets in financial instruments repealing Directive 2004/39/EC* (COM(2011) 656); European Commission, *Proposal for a Regulation of the European Parliament and of the Council on markets in financial instruments and amending Regulation (EU) No 648/2012 on OTC derivatives, central counterparties and trade repositories.*

[83] COM(2011) 656, Art 35.

[84] COM(2011) 656, para 3.4.10. For a thoughtful evaluation of this argument see G Ferrarini and P Saguto, 'Reforming Securities and Derivatives Trading in the EU: From EMIR to MiFIR' [2013] *Journal of Corporate Law Studies* 319.

Growth Segment of the Main Market is not subject to the *Listing Rules* because this is not a market for listed securities, but the regulatory requirements relating to admission to an EU regulated market, including prospectus requirements and continuing disclosure obligations, will still apply.[85] The differentiated regulatory requirements that apply to the High Growth Segment reflect a policy choice to facilitate access to the UK IPO market for high-growth companies. The segment is intended to act as a 'launch pad' for companies seeking a full premium listing.

Companies that are not yet ready for the Main Market can seek admission to trading on AIM. Admission to AIM, an exchange-regulated market under the oversight of the FCA, does not trigger EU-derived mandatory prospectus disclosure requirements unless there is a public offer of the securities, in which case a public offer prospectus will be required. Issuer mandatory periodic disclosure requirements derived from EU law also do not apply directly to AIM companies because these requirements are limited in scope to regulated markets.

An issuer that seeks to have its securities admitted to trading on any organized trading platform must, of course, accept the conditions imposed by the market operator in addition to those under the general law. In the case of admission to the London Stock Exchange's Main Market, these requirements are set out in the London Stock Exchange *Admission and Disclosure Standards*[86] or, where applicable, its *High Growth Segment Rulebook*.[87] The AIM *Rules for Companies* stipulate the admission criteria and responsibilities that are applicable to AIM companies.[88] These requirements include disclosure requirements relating, among other things, to the prompt disclosure of price sensitive information and to the publication of half-yearly reports.

Official Listing—Its Continuing Significance in the UK

Premium and standard listing

It should be apparent from the preceding discussion that the regulatory significance at EU level of the officially listed segment of the market is now reduced to a shadow of its former self. The initial and ongoing EU issuer disclosure regime applies to all regulated markets, irrespective of whether or not they are also markets for officially listed securities; and the officially listed segment of regulated markets is subject only to relatively minor EU law-derived additional requirements in relation to qualitative admission criteria.[89]

Yet whilst policy at the EU level is moving firmly away from targeting regulation at the officially listed segment of the market, within UK domestic law there remains quite a significant distinct body of regulation in the Financial Services and Markets Act 2000 and the FCA *Handbook* relating to official listing. This reflects a policy decision to continue to single out the officially listed segment of the securities market and to subject it to public regulation that extends beyond the minimum that is necessary to give effect to the EU Directives. In 2004, the FCA's predecessor, the FSA, explained this policy decision in the following terms:

> However, we have applied higher standards to issuers admitted to the Official List, and our consultation has shown that market participants value many of these tougher, or super-equivalent, standards as providing additional investor protection and contributing to deep and liquid

---

[85] LSE, *High Growth Segment Rulebook* (published 27 March 2013).
[86] LSE, *Admission and Disclosure Standards* (June 2011).
[87] LSE, *High Growth Segment Rulebook* (March 2013).　　　[88] February 2010.　　　[89] [2001] OJ L184/1.

markets. We will continue to apply certain super-equivalent standards to issuers of equity securities that are admitted to the Official List.[90]

More recently, the FSA described the listing regime as 'a self-standing regime that sets out for issuers the behavioural and governance obligations that they must meet, and for investors a regime that is based on the provision of information to allow them to make active and properly informed decisions.'[91] Yet, notwithstanding a continuing emphasis on quality, thinking on the purpose of the listing regime and on the appropriate degree of stringency of its requirements has remained in a state of evolution. The FCA, as successor to the FSA as listing authority, has noted that making the regime too onerous or too complex could be detrimental to investors by leading to the reduced availability of, or access to, listed securities for investors or classes of investors.[92]

Responding to concerns about lack of clarity and scope for confusion, particularly with regard to the requirement imposed on foreign issuers admitted to listing, in 2010 the FSA reorganized the listing regime to introduce a more clearly differentiated two-tier regime: 'premium' and 'standard' listing.[93] These reforms tightened the requirements for foreign issuers in certain respects, but for UK issuers their primary significance was that they introduced the possibility of 'standard' listing—that is listing at EU directive standards rather than the higher 'premium' listing standards.[94] To this extent, therefore, the review constituted a reining in of the 'super-equivalence' philosophy. However, returning to the issues again in 2012, the FSA instigated a process of further amendments to the listing regime, in part to reinforce the requirements relating to premium listing (including introducing additional eligibility requirements and listing principles, and new continuing obligations for premium listed companies with a controlling shareholder), but also in part to reinforce the standard listing regime by expanding the application of certain listing principles to companies with a standard listing. This initiative was adopted by the FCA on the transfer of responsibility for listing and, at the time of writing (November 2013), changes resulting from it were expected to come into effect in mid-2014. The FCA contends that the application of listing principles to the standard segment is not a departure from the policy of applying EU-Directive minimum standards because the principles in question can be regarded as being derived from the existing statutory framework.[95]

In summary, the main differences between standard and premium listing in the current regime are as follows in Table 13.1.[96]

As can be seen from Table 13.1, the 25 per cent minimum free float requirement applies to both premium and standard listing. The free float requirement dilutes the control of controlling shareholders, but only to a limited extent: the controlling shareholder will still be in a position to force through key decisions, including those requiring a special resolution (ie a 75 per cent super majority). The FCA can lower the required percentage if it considers that the market will operate properly in view of the large number of shares in public hands and the extent of distribution. So far as premium listing is concerned, the FCA has indicated that in exercising this discretion it may take account of shares of the same class that are held (even though they are not listed) in states that are not EEA States, the number and nature of the public shareholders, and

---

[90] FSA, *The Listing Review and Implementation of the Prospectus Directive—Draft Rules and Feedback on CP203* (CP04/16) para 1.8.

[91] FSA, *Enhancing the Effectiveness of the Listing Regime* (CP12/25) 13.

[92] FCA, CP13/15, para 3.34.

[93] These changes were preceded by extensive reviews: FSA, DP 08/01; CP08/21; CP09/24; CP09/28; CP09/24; PS10/02.

[94] *LR* ch 6 (additional requirements for premium listing (commercial company)); ch 14 (requirements for standard listing: shares).

[95] FCA, CP13/15, para 10.5.   [96] *LR* ch 1.5.

Table 13.1 Premium and Standard Listing: Main Requirements

Listing requirements	Premium	Standard
Eligibility criteria	Equity shares	Equity shares
Minimum free float[97]	LR 6 (25%)	LR 14 (25%)
Minimum market cap	LR 2 (£700,000)	LR 2 (£700,000)
Audited historical financial information	LR 6 (3 years)[98]	PR Appendix 3 (3 years or such shorter period as issuer has been in operation)
At least 75% of business supported by 3 year historical financial information	LR 6	n/a
Control of assets for at least 3 years and independence	LR 6	n/a
Relationship agreement with controlling shareholder	LR 6	n/a
Working capital statement	LR 6 (12 months minimum)	PR Appendix 3 (information concerning issuer's capital resources, both short and long term)
Listing principles	LR 7	LR 7
Sponsor	LR 8	n/a

whether the expected value of the shares in public hands at admission exceeds £100 million.[99] However, the FCA is prepared to be more flexible with regard to standard listing so as to allow small free floats provided there will be sufficient liquidity present. This stance is intended to enhance the international competitiveness of a London standard listing.[100] In its reflections on the regulatory position with respect to free floats, the ABI has noted that the option of standard listing is generally seen as less attractive by vendors, issuers and investors because of lower valuations and corporate governance standards.[101] With regard to premium listing, it maintains that 25 per cent should be the minimum free float to provide appropriate liquidity. A minimum free float of 25 per cent is required for inclusion in FTSE indices.[102]

The introduction into the premium listing requirement of a mandatory relationship agreement between the company and any controlling shareholder (expected 2014) is also designed to address investor concerns.[103] The purpose of the agreement is to ensure that the company is able to act independently of that shareholder's influence and to trigger enhanced oversight in the event of non-compliance with its terms. Premium listed companies with controlling shareholders are also required (expected 2014) to ensure that their constitutions provide for the election of independent directors by a dual voting structure whereby independent directors must be separately approved by both the shareholders as a whole and the independent shareholders as a separate class.

Listing principles

The purpose of the listing principles is to ensure that listed companies pay due regard to their fundamental role in maintaining market confidence and ensuring fair and orderly

---

[97] One of the key features of the High Growth Segment is that the minimum free float is lowered to 10 per cent.

[98] The track record and accounts requirements are modified for mineral and scientific companies and the FCA has power also to modify or dispense with them in other cases: *LR* 6.1.8–6.1.15.

[99] FCA, CP 13/15, paras 8.4–8.17 setting out proposed changes to the *Listing Rules*, which are expected to be effective in mid-2014. The text anticipates the revised position.

[100] FSA, CP 12/25, para 7.112. The FCA has confirmed its intention to proceed in this way: CP13/15, para 8.7.

[101] ABI, *Encouraging Equity Investment*, 27.

[102] For UK companies. The requirements are more stringent for non-UK companies. See further ch 14.

[103] This paragraph draws generally on FCA, CP13/15. The changes outlined will be implemented via amendments to the *Listing Rules*, in particular *LR* 5, *LR* 6, *LR* 9, and *LR* 11.

Table 13.2 Premium Listing Principles

Principle 1	A listed company must take reasonable steps to enable its directors to understand their responsibilities and obligations as directors.
Principle 2	A listed company must act with integrity towards holders and potential holders of its listed equity shares.
Principle 3	All equity shares in a class that has been admitted to premium listing must carry an equal number of votes on any shareholder vote.
Principle 4	Where a listed company has more than one class of equity shares admitted to premium listing, the aggregate voting rights of the shares in each class should be broadly proportionate to the relative interests of those classes in the equity of the listed company.
Principle 5	A listed company must ensure that it treats all holders of the same class of its listed equity shares that are in the same position equally in respect of the rights attaching to such listed equity shares.
Principle 6	A listed company must communicate information to holders and potential holders of its listed equity securities in such a way as to avoid the creation or continuation of a false market in such listed equity shares.

markets.[104] There are two tiers of listing principles. Two listing principles apply to both the standard and premium segments.[105] These principles are that a listed company must: take reasonable steps to establish and maintain adequate procedures, systems, and controls to enable it to comply with its obligations; and must deal with the FCA in an open and cooperative manner. In addition, there are six further listing principles for the premium segment, as set out in Table 13.2.[106]

Premium listing: sponsor requirements

As can be seen from Table 13.1, another significant super-equivalent requirement in the premium listing regime is for companies to appoint a sponsor when they are applying for a primary listing of equity securities and on specified occasions thereafter.[107] The role of a sponsor, which will be an investment bank or a similar financial institution, is to ensure that premium listed issuers (and applicants for listing) understand and comply with the regulatory requirements to which they are subject. The sponsor is often a senior member of the underwriting syndicate for the issue. The sponsor will liaise with the FCA and is expected by the regulator to play a key role in overseeing issuer compliance. The sponsor regime in the *Listing Rules* is regularly reviewed and expanded. It is regarded by institutional investors as being fundamental to ensuring the effectiveness of the premium equity market.[108]

Premium listing: continuing obligations

Officially listed companies with a premium listing are subject to certain continuing obligations under the *Listing Rules* (with certain modifications for non-UK companies). These obligations are in addition to the periodic and other disclosure requirements that are imposed on all companies with securities admitted to trading on a regulated market (whether premium or standard listed) and which are contained in the *Disclosure and Transparency Rules* (discussed later in this chapter). The extensive continuing obligations in the *Listing Rules* are a manifestation of

---

[104] *LR* 7.1.2.

[105] Up to 2014, listing principles applied only to the premium segment. FSA, CP 12/25, paras 7.131–141 proposed a two-tier system of listing principles (premium and standard) for all listed companies. This recommendation was supported by the FCA: FCA, CP13/15. At the time of writing (November 2013), the changes were not formally adopted but were expected to be in operation by mid-2014. The text anticipates that result.

[106] *LR* 7.2.1A.   [107] *LR* ch 8.   [108] ABI, *Encouraging Equity Investment*, 30.

the policy choice to provide a 'gold-plated,' robust regulatory regime for the premium segment of official listing. Significant continuing obligations in the *Listing Rules* include:

- to state in the annual financial report how the issuer has applied the main principles set out in the UK Corporate Governance Code, to confirm compliance with all relevant provisions of the Code, or to indicate and explain areas of non-compliance;[109]
- to report on directors' remuneration policies and packages;[110]
- to comply with the Model Code restricting dealings in securities;[111]
- to notify shareholders of certain transactions and to provide shareholders with the opportunity to vote on larger proposed transactions.[112]

With a view to enhancing the governance function performed by the *Listing Rules* additional continuing obligations have been drawn up (at the time of writing (November 2013) these were expected to come into effect in mid-2014).[113] These new continuing obligations are primarily aimed at premium listed companies with controlling shareholders and they complement the measures to strengthen the premium listing entry criteria by, among other things, requiring a formal agreement regulating the relationship between such a shareholder and the company and insisting on a majority of independent directors on the board of such a company. The additions to the continuing obligations regime include the requirement to observe the dual voting mechanism for the election of independent directors whereby independent directors of premium listed companies with controlling shareholders must be approved by the shareholders as a whole and by the independent shareholders, to restrict voting on matters relevant to premium listing to shares that have been admitted to premium listing, and enhanced transparency as regards independence. Oversight of related party transactions is also strengthened. The requirements governing cancellation of listing are reinforced, including a requirement for separate approval by independent shareholders of a proposal to cancel a premium listing.

Enforcement of the *Listing Rules*

If the FCA considers that an issuer of officially listed securities or an applicant for listing has contravened any provision of the *Listing Rules*, including the listing principles, it can impose a financial penalty.[114] Directors of issuers or applicants are also personally at risk of having a fine imposed on them if the FCA considers that they were 'knowingly concerned' in the contravention.[115] If the FCA is entitled to impose a penalty on a person for breach of the *Listing Rules*, it may alternatively publicly censure that person.[116] Disciplinary action (including the imposition of penalties, public censure, and suspension or limitations on regulatory approval) can also be taken against sponsors.[117] In certain circumstances breach of the *Listing Rules* could also amount to market abuse contrary to the Financial Services and Markets Act 2000, Part 8. The FCA has the power to impose an unlimited fine on any person who engages in market abuse[118] and to require restitution.[119] The FCA also has power to seek restitution orders against persons who have been knowingly concerned in a contravention of the *Listing Rules* that does not involve market abuse.[120]

---

[109] *LR* 9.8.6(5)–(6)A. This requirement extends to overseas companies: *LR* 9.8.7.
[110] *LR* 9.8.8. This requirement extends to overseas companies: *LR* 9.8.6A.
[111] *LR* 9.2.7–9.2.8.   [112] *LR* ch 10.
[113] This paragraph draws generally on FSA, CP12/25 and FCA, CP13/15. The ABI reported that investors were broadly supportive of these proposals: ABI, *Encouraging Equity Investment*, 28. The changes will take effect by way of amendment to the *Listing Rules*, in particular *LR* 5, *LR* 6, *LR* 7, *LR* 9, and *LR* 11.
[114] FSMA, s 91(1).   [115] FSMA, s 91(2).   [116] FSMA, s 91(3).
[117] FSMA, s 88A–F (as substituted for s 89 by Financial Services Act 2012).
[118] FSMA, s 123.   [119] FSMA, s 384.   [120] FSMA, s 382.

Table 13.3 Enforcement of *Listing Rules*

Company	Decision Date	Breach	Sanction
Prudential plc & Prudential Assurance	27/03/2013	Failure to inform regulator of 2010 acquisition plans: breach of FSA Principles and Listing Principle 6	Company Fine 30M Public censure of CEO
Lamprell	15/03/13	Systems and controls failures, disclosure failures, and breach of dealing rules: Listing Principle 2, DTR 1.3.4R and 2.2.1R and LR 9 and Model Code	Company Fine 2.4M
Nestor Health Group	14/02/2013	Breach of Model Code: Listing Principles 1 and 2, LR 9.2.8	Company Fine 175K
Exillion Energy	26/04/12	Failure to identify payments to chairman and systems and controls failures: LR 11.1.1/2, DTR 2.2.1 and Listing Principle 2	Company Fine 292K
Cattles	28/03/12	False information: market abuse and breach of LR 1.3.3/Listing Principles 3 and 4	Public censure
BDO LLP (sponsor)	26/05/11	Failure of sponsor to act with due care and skill: LR 8.3.3 and 8.3.5	Firm Censure
JJB Sports	26/01/11	Failure to disclose inside information: DTR 2.2.1 and Listing Principle 4	Company Fine 455K
Photo-Me International plc	21/06/10	Failure to disclose inside information: DTR 2.2.1 and Listing Principle 4	Company Fine 500K
Entertainment Rights	19/01/09	Delayed announcement: DTR 2.2.1 and Listing Principle 4	Company Fine 245K
Wolfson Microelectronics	19/01/09	Delayed announcement: DTR 2.2.1 and Listing Principle 4	Company Fine 140K
Woolworths	11/06/08	Delayed announcement: DTR 2.2.1 and Listing Principle 4	Company Fine 350K
Eurodis	12/09/05	Delayed announcement: LR9.2	Company Censure
My Travel	14/07/05	Delayed announcement: LR9.2	Company Fine 240K
Pace Micro	26/01/05	Omission from the interim results and failure to announce: LR9.2 and 9.3A	Company Fine 450K
Shell	24/08/04	Market Abuse and breaches of LR	Company Fine 17M
Universal Salvage	19/05/04	Delayed announcement: LR9.1	Company Fine 19K Director Fine 10K
Sportsworld	29/03/03	Delayed announcement: LR9.2	Company Censure Director Fine 45K
SFI	11/12/03	Misleading preliminary results: LR9.3A	Company Censure
Marconi	11/04/03	Delayed announcement: LR9.2	Public Statement

The FCA's predecessor, the FSA, made only limited use of its range of sanctioning powers with respect to listed issuers and their sponsors. Its most prominent scalp was Shell Royal Dutch plc which in 2004 was fined £17 million by the FSA for market abuse and breach of the *Listing Rules* in misstating over a number of years its proved reserves of oil and gas.

Table 13.3 summarizes FSA enforcement action relating to *Listing Rules* breaches up to March 2013.

Standards for Admission to Trading on AIM

As discussed already, admission to trading on AIM falls outside the scope of mandatory issuer disclosure requirements derived from European law, unless there is also a public offer of securities. Nor must prospective AIM issuers meet minimum qualitative criteria imposed by the general law. Instead, a company wishing to be admitted to AIM must comply with the AIM *Rules for Companies*, which include that each of its directors must accept full responsibility, collectively and individually, for compliance with the AIM *Rules*.[121] The AIM *Rules* impose no requirements on the minimum percentage of shares that must be in public hands post-admission, minimum prior trading records before admission, or minimum market capitalization. There is no pre-vetting of admission documents by a regulatory agency, as there is in the listed/regulated market regimes. Instead, the AIM *Rules* require companies applying to join AIM to appoint a nominated adviser (Nomad) and to retain a Nomad at all times after admission.[122] The Nomad is responsible to the Exchange for assessing the appropriateness of an applicant for AIM, or an existing AIM company when appointed as its nominated adviser, and for advising and guiding an AIM company on its responsibilities under these rules.[123] There are detailed requirements with respect to the matters to which a Nomad should have regard in determining an applicant's suitability for admission.[124]

Notwithstanding that the disclosure requirements for regulated markets derived from EU law do not directly apply to AIM, AIM issuers are in fact subject to a range of disclosure obligations that to a large extent mimic those that apply to regulated markets under the general law. The AIM *Rules* require applicants to produce an admission document, the prescribed contents of which are less onerous than, but to a significant extent equivalent to, those that would be required in a mandatory prospectus.[125] Likewise, the ongoing disclosure requirements to which AIM-quoted companies are subject under the AIM *Rules* are, broadly speaking, a lighter version of those under the general law for issuers admitted to trading on regulated markets.[126] An AIM company incorporated in an EEA country must prepare and present its accounts in accordance with IFRS.[127] An AIM company incorporated in a non-EEA country must prepare and present its accounts in accordance with IFRS, US Generally Accepted Accounting Principles, Canadian Generally Accepted Accounting Principles, Australian International Financial Reporting Standards, or Japanese Generally Accepted Accounting Principles.[128] An AIM company must take reasonable care to ensure that any information it notifies is not misleading, false, or deceptive and does not omit anything likely to affect the import of such information.[129] There are a number of other continuing obligations following admission to AIM, including a requirement for shareholder consent before making a reverse takeover[130] or a major disposal resulting in a fundamental change of business.[131] However, one important distinction is that AIM issuers are not subject to disclosure requirements in respect of their compliance with the Corporate Governance Code. The Quoted Company Alliance, a body that champions the interests of small to medium-sized quoted companies, provides *Corporate Governance Guidelines for Smaller Quoted Companies* that AIM issuers may find suitable as an alternative.

Forms of Public Offer of Shares

There are a number of ways in which an IPO can be structured, of which some of the most important are as follows.[132]

---

[121] AIM *Rules for Companies* (AIM *Rules*) r 31.   [122] AIM *Rules*, r 1.   [123] AIM *Rules*, r 1.
[124] AIM *Rules for Nominated Advisers*.   [125] AIM *Rules*, r 3 and sch 2.
[126] AIM *Rules*, r 11 (prompt disclosure of price sensitive information), r 17 (disclosure of miscellaneous information) r 18 (half-year reports), r 19 (annual financial statements).
[127] AIM *Rules*, r 19.   [128] AIM *Rules*, r 19.   [129] AIM *Rules*, r 10.   [130] AIM *Rules*, r 14.
[131] AIM *Rules*, r 15.   [132] The definitions in this section are taken from the FCA, *Listing Rules*, Appendix 1.1.

Offer for subscription

In an offer for subscription the public are invited to subscribe directly for new securities of the issuer that are not yet in issue. An offer for subscription of new shares may be combined with an offer for sale of existing shares by vendor shareholders.

Offer for sale

In an offer for sale the public are invited to purchase securities of the issuer that are already in issue or allotted. Where this marketing method is used in an IPO, the company allots the new issue of securities to an investment bank which then invites the general public to apply for the securities. The investment bank may acquire securities from existing holders and offer them to the public at the same time.

Placings and intermediaries offers

A placing is a marketing of securities by the investment bank which is sponsoring the issue to its clients or to clients of any securities house assisting in the placing. An intermediaries offer is a marketing of securities by means of an offer by, or on behalf of, the issuer to intermediaries for them to allocate to their own clients. As selective methods of marketing, placings and intermediaries offers present potential transaction cost savings, which will be a key consideration where the costs of an offer for subscription or offer for sale would be disproportionate relative to the issuer's needs for new capital. In an international IPO a full retail offering in one country, typically the issuer's home state, may be combined with placings to institutional investors in other countries.

Determining the Issue Price—Underwriting and Bookbuilding

It is usual for companies to engage underwriters when they raise equity capital. The underwriters (often a syndicate of investment banks, and usually including firms that are already providing corporate broking services to the issuer) provide a guarantee that the issuer will receive the required capital by agreeing to purchase the shares, if they are not subscribed by anyone else, at a specified price. Underwriting services typically extend to advising the company on the capital raising generally, and performing associated administrative and distributional services. One of the principal underwriters will usually also act as the sponsor to the issue. Sub-underwriters may agree (for a fee) to meet part of the underwriter's obligation to purchase the shares. Sub-underwriting services may be provided by institutional investors, banks, and hedge funds.

Historically, UK market practice was that the price at which shares were to be offered was determined by the underwriter to the issue in consultation with the company before the commencement of the official offer period. Although the underwriter would have had an idea as to the price at which sub-underwriters would be willing to take the issue, the actual sub-underwriting and formal marketing to other institutions and the public did not take place until the offer price had been set and the primary underwriter was contractually bound to take up shares not subscribed or purchased in the offer. The underwriter and sub-underwriters would then be on risk for the offer period, typically ten days to two weeks, at the end of which allocations would be determined and shares admitted to listing. The standard fee for underwriting was 2 per cent of the proceeds of the issue.

Since the 1990s it has become common for the issue price of securities to be determined through a process known as bookbuilding. The principal difference between bookbuilding and traditional UK-style underwriting relates to the timing of the determination of the offer price relative to the underwriting and marketing of the issue. Where bookbuilding is used, the marketing of the securities effectively precedes the determination of the offer price. After some initial investigatory pre-marketing work by the bookrunner, the bookbuilding period commences with the publication by the company of a pathfinder or an approved price range prospectus which indicates a range of price and the conditions for the final determination of the price.[133] The bookrunner, acting through a network of managers, assesses the level of interest in the shares to be offered. During this period, sophisticated communications systems and computer programs enable the bookrunner to monitor and analyse the level of demand. At the end of the bookbuilding period, the price is determined by reference to the level of demand.

Various advantages have been claimed for bookbuilding over the traditional UK method of price-setting. It is said to match price with demand more accurately and reduce the risk of the underwriters being left with a large 'stick' (ie securities not taken up by investors); to create price tension between prospective investors; and to encourage investor transparency. However, the advantages of bookbuilding as a more accurate pricing mechanism come at a cost because fees tend to be higher than for the more traditional method.[134] Bookbuilding also presents potential regulatory problems because of the wide discretion (and hence scope for abuse) with regard to allocations that it gives to the investment bank that is running the book[135] and the potential for conflicts between the obligations that it owes to the issuer and those that it may owe to its investment clients,[136] or its own proprietary interests.[137]

Improvements in price-setting mechanisms aim at achieving better price discovery. A substantial body of empirical literature has examined the phenomenon of IPO 'underpricing'—meaning that the share price jumps significantly on the first day of trading.[138] The level of underpricing fluctuates over time but can be particularly high in 'hot' markets, such as the technology stocks boom at the end of the 1990s. Underpricing is a major curiosity because it implies a significant transfer of value from the existing owners to the new investors. The literature offers various explanations for underpricing, of which the most established are models based on information asymmetries, such as: that the investment bank running the transaction knows more about demand conditions than the issuer; that the issuer knows more than other key players about the true value of the firm; or that some investors are better informed than others. However, information-based models do not fully explain IPO underpricing and there is considerable ongoing debate about other causes, including behavioural theories that look at the influence of 'irrational' investors in the marketplace or biases that affect the decisions made by those in control of companies that are launching IPOs. Liability risks associated with overpricing an IPO may also play a part.

---

[133] The process is described in ABI, *Encouraging Equity Investment*, 13–4.

[134] Degeorge and Maug, 'Corporate Finance in Europe.'

[135] Systematic evidence on how investment banks use their discretion over allocations is limited: TJ Jenkinson and H Jones, 'Bids and Allocations in European IPO Bookbuilding' (2004) 59 *Journal of Finance* 2309, 2336. However, the level of fees charged in London is still below that in New York: McKinsey & Co, *Sustaining New York's and the US' Global Financial Services Leadership*, 43.

[136] FSA, *Conflicts of Interest: Investment Research and Issues of Securities. Feedback on CP171* (CP 205, October 2003) ch 5.

[137] The FSA has taken enforcement action for failure to observe proper standards of market conduct in a book-built transaction: FSA Final Notice, 10 April 2006 against Deutsche Bank.

[138] A Ljungqvist, 'IPO Underpricing: A Survey' in BE Eckbo (ed), *Handbook of Corporate Finance: Empirical Corporate Finance* (North Holland: Elsevier, Handbook of Finance Series, 2007) vol 1, ch 7.

Pricing inaccuracy can sometimes manifest itself in ways other than underpricing as was demonstrated by the notorious Facebook IPO in May 2012, where the surge in the share price on flotation was very short lived and the shares ended the first day of trading at a price only very slightly above the flotation price, with further falls thereafter. Institutional investors have suggested ways in which the information asymmetry between issuers and investors could be addressed through much earlier engagement by issuers with potential investors—up to a year or more before the proposed IPO—earlier publication of the prospectus, and the publication of more independent research.[139]

Equity underwriting fees periodically attract attention from the competition authorities. The most recent example is the Office of Fair Trading (OFT) market study in 2011.[140] This study found that there had been a significant increase in fees since the onset of the financial crisis, with average fees rising to more than 3 per cent in 2009 from around 2 to 2.5 per cent in the period from 2003 to 2007. The OFT considered that the increase in volatility and risk in the period was only a partial explanation for the higher fees. It did not have significant concerns over the number of available providers of equity underwriting services, and indicated that its analysis suggested that the trend towards higher fees and greater clustering of fees and discounts might be the result of companies not negotiating cost effective outcomes with investment banks, and shareholders not putting sufficient pressure on companies raising equity capital to reduce costs. The OFT therefore ruled out a further Market Investigation Reference as inappropriate since concerns could be tackled most effectively and efficiently by companies and institutional shareholders.

The Principle of Mandatory Prospectus Disclosure

That securities markets are relatively efficient in the sense that prices adjust quickly to new information is the cornerstone of modern securities or capital markets regulation.[141] Even though there is considerable debate in the literature about the desirability of mandatory disclosure and its value in improving both the fundamental accuracy of share prices as the best possible estimates of future risks and returns[142] and the efficient allocation of scarce resources to the most deserving projects,[143] policy and lawmakers have inclined to accept that there are connections between publicly available information, the accuracy of securities prices, and the allocation of resources and, furthermore, that there are imperfections in market mechanisms for voluntary disclosure that could lead to sub-optimal levels of disclosure in the absence of regulatory intervention, with adverse ramifications for allocative efficiency and investor protection.[144] In having a set of mandatory prospectus disclosure requirements that

---

[139] ABI, *Encouraging Equity Investment*, 17–22.

[140] OFT, *Equity Underwriting and Associated Services* (OFT1303).

[141] RJ Gilson and RH Kraakman, 'The Mechanisms of Market Efficiency' (1984) 70 *Virginia Law Review* 549.

[142] LA Stout, 'The Mechanisms of Market Inefficiency: An Introduction to the New Finance' (2003) 28 *Journal of Corporation Law* 635, 640. Gilson and Kraakman stress the need to distinguish between a market's informational efficiency and the 'fundamental' value of securities: RJ Gilson and R Kraakman, 'The Mechanisms of Market Efficiency Twenty Years Later: The Hindsight Bias' (2003) 28 *Journal of Corporation Law* 71; RJ Gilson and R Kraakman, 'Market Efficiency After the Fall: Where Do We Stand Following the Financial Crisis' in CA Hill and BH McDonnell (eds) *Research Handbook on the Economics of Corporate Law* (Cheltenham: Edward Elgar, 2012).

[143] MB Fox, R Morck, B Yeung, and A Durnev, 'Law, Share Price Accuracy, and Economic Performance: The New Evidence' (2003) 102 *Michigan Law Review* 331, pt I, reviews important contributions to the literature. See also the Summer 2003 issue of the *Journal of Corporation Law*, which contains a series of papers from a symposium that revisited the seminal 1984 Gilson and Kraakman paper.

[144] JC Coffee, 'Market Failure and the Economic Case for a Mandatory Disclosure System' (1984) 70 *Virginia Law Review* 717 remains the classic statement of the case for mandatory disclosure. A review of the literature on mandatory disclosure is provided by RA Prentice and FB Cross, *Law and Corporate Finance* (Cheltenham: Edward Elgar, 2007) 28–69.

must be satisfied by an issuer which is offering its securities to investors, the UK (giving effect to EU Directives) thus conforms to the international norm.

The Operation of the Mandatory Prospectus Disclosure Regime

When is a prospectus required?

It is unlawful to offer prescribed transferable securities to the public in the UK or to request that they be admitted to trading on a regulated market situated or operating in the UK unless an approved prospectus has been made available to the public before the offer or, as the case may be, request is made.[145] Contravention is a criminal offence[146] and is actionable as a breach of statutory duty by any person who suffers loss as a result of the contravention.[147] Shares are prescribed transferable securities for this purpose.[148] All IPOs will thus prima facie fall within the scope of the mandatory prospectus requirement for public offers, including those which are to be admitted to AIM rather than the Main Market of the London Stock Exchange. However, the mere admission of securities to AIM is not an admission to trading on a regulated market and therefore will not trigger the mandatory prospectus requirement in the absence of a public offer but the disclosure requirements under the AIM *Rules for Companies* will apply instead.

An offer of transferable securities to the public in the UK is broadly defined. There is an offer of transferable securities to the public if there is a communication in any form or by any means to any person which presents sufficient information on the securities and the terms on which they are offered to enable an investor to make an investment decision in respect of them.[149] This definition embraces secondary offers by shareholders as well as offers of new shares by issuers. A placing of securities through a financial intermediary is included[150] but communications in connection with trading on certain markets or facilities are not.[151] To the extent that an offer is made to a person in the UK, it is an offer to the public in the UK.[152]

There are certain exclusions and exemptions from the mandatory prospectus requirements that apply by reference to the amount of capital being sought, the number of investors to whom the offer is made, the nature of the investors to whom the offer is made (broadly, exemptions for offers to non-retail investors), or the minimum purchase price of the securities. The first such exclusion is that under EU law there is no need at all for a public offer prospectus where transferable securities are part of an offer for which the total consideration for the offer in the Union is less than €5 million or an equivalent amount.[153] This exclusion was introduced to enable small and medium-sized enterprises to raise finance more easily. Since offers of less than €5 million fall entirely outside the scope of the EU Prospectus Directive, in principle Member States are free to impose their own domestic prospectus law on offers below this size (subject to other exemptions) should they wish to do so. However, the UK has not chosen to make use of this facility. Producing a prospectus is a costly business, with costs impacting particularly on smaller capital-raising exercises. According to some estimates, the cost can range from 7 to 12 per cent of the funds raised for consideration levels below

---

[145] FSMA, s 85(1) and (2).   [146] FSMA, s 85(3).   [147] FSMA, s 85(4).
[148] FSMA, s 102A   [149] FSMA, s 102B(1) and (3).   [150] FSMA, s 102B(4).
[151] FSMA, s 102B(5).   [152] FSMA, s 102B(2).
[153] FSMA, s 85(5) and (6), and Sch 11A, para 9. The threshold amount was increased from €2.5m to €5m by Directive 2010/73/EU, [2010] OJ L327/1, implemented in the UK by Prospectus Regulations 2011, SI 2011/1668. Directive 2010/73/EU also clarified the geographical scope of the monetary threshold for the exclusion to apply, implemented in the UK by Prospectus Regulations 2012, SI 2012/1538.

£10 million, meaning that a prospectus for an offer of £5 million could cost in the range of £350,000 to £600,000.[154] This would be disproportionate.

An overlapping exemption provides that an offer to the public of securities is exempt from the public offer prospectus requirement where the total offer consideration in the Union cannot exceed €100,000 or an equivalent amount.[155] Where the €100,000 exemption applies, Member States are not permitted to impose prospectus requirements under their domestic law.[156] The costs involved in producing a prospectus would be highly disproportionate where such small amounts of capital are sought.

Offers made or directed at fewer than 150 people per Member State are also exempt from the public offer prospectus requirement,[157] as are offers made or directed to qualified investors only.[158] There is a further exemption from the public offers prospectus requirement for offers where an investor must pay at least €100,000 (or equivalent) to acquire the securities.[159] These exemptions facilitate non-retail offers, including IPOs made only to institutions. They are especially useful in international IPOs where, conventionally, an issuer makes a full retail offer in its home country (for which a prospectus is required) and makes selective placings of its securities to institutional investors in other countries, and in the marketing of international bond issues. These exemptions are considered further in chapter 14, on international equity offerings, and in chapter 15, on corporate bonds. A further exemption covers 'retail cascades': no new prospectus is required where shares that are being sold or placed through a financial intermediary have previously been the subject of one or more offers to the public, provided certain conditions are satisfied including that a relatively fresh prospectus is available (ie approved by the FCA no earlier than twelve months before the date of the current offer) and the issuer (or other person who was responsible for drawing up the prospectus) has given written consent to the use of the prospectus for this purpose.[160]

In the case of all the exemptions just considered, it is only the public offers prospectus requirement that is avoided. If the securities are to be admitted to trading on a regulated market, an admission prospectus will still be required unless another exemption is available. Exemptions from the admission prospectus requirement, and also further exemptions from the public offer prospectus requirement, are provided by the FCA *Prospectus Rules*.[161] The relevant exemptions under the *Prospectus Rules* have little significance so far as IPOs are concerned. For secondary offerings, ie offers by issuers that are already admitted to trading, an important exemption is that the requirement for the publication of a prospectus on the admission of securities to trading does not apply to shares representing, over a period of

---

[154] HM Treasury, *Consultation on Early Implementation of Amendments to the Prospectus Directive* (March 2011) 6.

[155] FSMA, s 86(1)(e), as amended by Prospectus Regulations 2011, SI 2011/1668 and Prospectus Regulations 2012, SI 2012/1538, implementing Directive 2010/73/EU.

[156] So if a Member State were to choose to impose prospectus requirements on offers below the €5 million threshold (which the UK has not done), the exemption for offers below €100,000 would limit its ability to do so.

[157] FSMA, s 86(1)(b), as amended by Prospectus Regulations 2011, SI 2011/1668, implementing Directive 2010/73/EU.

[158] FSMA, s 86(1)(a), as amended by Prospectus Regulations 2011, SI 2011/1668, implementing Directive 2010/73/EU. S 86(7) (as amended) defines 'qualified investor' by reference to the definitions used in MiFID.

[159] FSMA, s 86(1)(c) and (d), as amended by Prospectus Regulations 2011, SI 2011/1668, implementing Directive 2010/73/EU.

[160] FSMA, s 86(1A), as added by Prospectus Regulations 2012, SI 2012/1538, reg 2(2) and amended by Prospectus Regulations 2013, SI 2013/1125. See also Commission Delegated Regulation (EU) 862/2012 of 4 June 2012, amending the Prospectus Regulation to provide for inclusion of information regarding the issuer's consent to said use of the prospectus.

[161] *PR* 1.2.2 and *PR* 1.2.3. The statutory authority for the FCA to limit the scope of the mandatory prospectus requirement in this way is provided by FSMA, s 85(5) and (6).

twelve months, less than 10 per cent of the number of shares already admitted to trading on the same regulated market.[162] This facilitates the streamlined placing of seasoned equity with qualified investors.[163]

Prospectus form and contents

Single or tripartite prospectus

A mandatory prospectus for equity securities may be drawn up as a single or a tripartite document, the latter comprising a registration document (containing information relating to the issuer), a securities note (containing details of the securities to be offered or admitted), and a summary note.[164] Issuers contemplating an issue of securities may file a registration document with the FCA which will then be valid for twelve months. When the issuer is ready to issue securities to the public or to apply for their admission to trading on a regulated market, it will need to submit only the securities note (which will also provide information on any significant change since the registration document was approved, if this could affect the investors' assessment of the securities since the latest updated registration document was published) and the summary.[165] Having a tripartite prospectus can thus enhance the efficiency of the issuance process. The first major UK securities offering to adopt the new tripartite format was the flotation of Standard Life plc in July 2006.[166]

Prospectus Directive Regulation: schedules and building blocks

The detailed items of information that must be included in a prospectus and the order in which they must appear are prescribed by the Prospectus Directive Regulation, which, under EU law, is directly applicable in the UK.[167] The Prospectus Directive Regulation is an example of 'Level 2' legislation made under the Lamfalussy Process for EU securities lawmaking.[168] The approach adopted in the Prospectus Directive Regulation is to require a prospectus to be drawn up using a combination of schedules and building blocks, as appropriate to the type of issuer and relevant securities involved.[169] There are, inter alia, separate schedules and building blocks relating to shares, debt securities with a denomination of less than €100,000, debt securities with a denomination of at least €100,000, asset-backed securities, and derivative securities. Annex XVIII to the Prospectus Directive Regulation provides a table of combinations that is designed to enable issuers to determine the specific content requirements for a particular prospectus. As an aid to readers, the *Prospectus Rules* contained in the FCA

---

[162] FSMA, s 85(6)(b) and PR 1.2.3(1).　　　[163] See further ch 5.　　　[164] *PR 2.2.*　　　[165] *PR 2.2.5.*

[166] E Ferran, 'Cross-border Offers of Securities in the EU: The *Standard Life* Flotation' (2007) 4 *European Company and Financial Law Review* 462.

[167] Commission Regulation (EC) 809/2004 of 29 April 2004 implementing Directive (EC) 2003/71 of the European Parliament and of the Council as regards information contained in prospectuses as well as the format, incorporation by reference and publication of such prospectuses and dissemination of advertisements [2004] OJ L149/1 (Prospectus Directive Regulation or PDR). Commission Delegated Regulation (EU) No 486/2012 of 30 March 2012, [2012] OJ L150/1 amends Regulation (EC) No 809/2004 as regards the format and the content of the prospectus, the base prospectus, the summary and the final terms and as regards the disclosure requirement. Commission Delegated Regulation No 862/2012 of 4 June 2012, [2012] OJ L256/4 amends Regulation (EC) No 809/2004 as regards information on the consent to use of the prospectus, information on underlying indexes and the requirement for a report prepared by independent accountants or auditors. Commission Delegated Regulation (EU) No 759/2013 of 30 April 2013, [2013] OJ L213/1 amends Regulation (EC) No 809/2004 as regards the disclosure requirements for convertible and exchangeable debt securities.

[168] On the Lamfalussy Process generally, E Ferran, *Building an EU Securities Market* (Cambridge: CUP, 2004) 58–126.

[169] PDR, Art 21.

Handbook include lengthy extracts from the Prospectus Directive Regulation but it is the Regulation itself that is the definitive source.[170]

Proportionate disclosure—SMEs and Small Caps

The changes to the Prospectus Directive that were made in 2010 introduced a proportionate disclosure regime for certain issuers and certain types of capital raising. Small and medium-sized enterprises (SMEs) and issuers with reduced market capitalization (Small Caps) are among the beneficiaries of these changes.[171] The prospectus disclosure requirements for SMEs and Small Caps are adapted to their size and, where appropriate, shorter track record. An SME is a company that, according to its last annual or consolidated accounts, meets at least two of the following three criteria: an average of less than 250 employees during the financial year; a balance sheet not exceeding €43 million; and an annual net turnover not exceeding €50 million.[172] A Small Cap is a company listed on a regulated market with an average market capitalization of less than €100 million on the basis of end-year quotes during the last three calendar years.[173] Among the changes benefitting SMEs and Small Caps are dispensations in certain circumstances from the requirements to include an operating and financial review, details of related party transactions, and historical financial information. According to estimates cited by the Commission, the cost reduction resulting from the relaxations should be in the region of 20 per cent, meaning a reduction of €20,000 to €60,000 per prospectus.[174] Data gathered by the European Securities and Markets Authority (ESMA)[175] indicates that the costs of drawing up a prospectus can amount to over 10 per cent of the amounts raised in a small capital raising exercise (eg €5 million) and, of this, preparing the operating and financial review and the historical financial information can each cost in excess of €100,000.[176]

ESMA expressed concern about the introduction of a proportionate disclosure regime for SMEs and Small Caps on the grounds that this move would not be consistent with the perceived higher risk profile of such companies and, in the long run, could be detrimental to SMEs and Small Caps because they would not be meeting the disclosure standards required by investors.[177] ESMA recommended that in order to maintain sufficient investor protection a full prospectus should still be required on an IPO by an SME or Small Cap, the rationale being that a new entrant would be unknown to investors and, therefore, investors should be afforded maximum protection. The Commission, however, did not accept this advice.[178] Its view was that the proportionate disclosure regime should be generally applicable to avoid as far as possible the duplication in the prospectus of any information which was available elsewhere and to adjust the level of information required by the Prospectus Directive to better suit the size of SMEs and Small Caps. It considered that a general across-the-board adaptation would make a real difference in favour of easier access to the market by SMEs and Small Caps without significantly harming investor protection.

---

[170] *PR* 1.1.7. [171] Prospectus Directive, Art 7.2(e); PDR, Art 26b; Annex XXV-XXVIII.

[172] Prospectus Directive, Art 2(1)(f); Commission Recommendation 2003/361, [2003] L124/36.

[173] Prospectus Directive, Art 2(1)(ii)(t) (as amended).

[174] European Commission, *Impact Assessment* (SWD (2012) 77) 28–9.

[175] ESMA succeeded CESR (the Committee of European Securities Regulators) with effect from 1 January 2011. ESMA was established by Regulation (EU) No 1095/2010 of the European Parliament and of the Council of 24 November 2010, [2010] OJ L331/84.

[176] ESMA, *Technical Advice on Possible Delegated Acts Concerning the Prospectus Directive as Amended by the Directive 2010/73/EU* (ESMA/2011/323) para 229.

[177] ESMA, *Technical Advice on Possible Delegated Acts Concerning the Prospectus Directive as Amended by the Directive 2010/73/EU*, paras 319–33.

[178] European Commission, *Impact Assessment* (SWD (2012) 77) 28–9.

The tension between facilitating capital formation and delivering an appropriate level of investor protection runs through capital market regulation. Exemptions and exclusions for small offers, as discussed earlier in this chapter, provide one set of examples in which policymakers have come down on the side of capital formation in recognition of the potential for burdensome regulation to have a disproportionate impact where relatively small amounts of capital are involved. The proportionate disclosure regime goes in the same direction. European policymakers are, moreover, thinking along broadly the same lines as their counterparts on the other side of the Atlantic with respect to these matters: start ups and small businesses are seen to be a beacon of hope in a period of economic gloom, and removing regulatory impediments that may impede them from reaching their full potential has become a priority. This thinking underpins the US JOBS Act of 2012. The aim of the JOBS Act is to reduce the regulatory burden on smaller companies by providing exemptions for smaller transactions (eg to facilitate crowdfunding) and by relieving smaller issuers from some disclosure requirements.[179] Encouraging entrepreneurship, spurring job creation, and revitalizing the IPO market are all goals with an obvious appeal.[180] However, the ever-present risk is that well-meant deregulation of this sort may turn out to have negative unintended consequences as regards investor protection, especially in circumstances where short-term political considerations may have added to the impetus for reform.[181]

Proportionate disclosure—certain secondary issues

Seasoned issuers, that is, issuers with securities that are already publicly traded, are subject to a range of periodic and episodic disclosure obligations, and are also already under the scrutiny of investors, financial analysts, and the media. When such issuers need to return to the market to raise new capital, the costs of producing a full prospectus may not be justified given the amount of information that is already publicly available. There are thus potential efficiency gains in moving to a proportionate disclosure regime for secondary issues, although, as ever, a balance must be maintained between reducing the burden on issuers and investor protection. As ESMA noted in its technical advice to the Commission on the introduction of a simplified disclosure regime for such issuers, notwithstanding the clear arguments in favour of avoiding duplication, it is important not to 'empty prospectuses of their substance' because that would be 'contradictory to the objective of enhancing investor protection.'[182]

The Prospectus Directive, as amended, provides for a proportionate disclosure regime that seeks to strike this balance as follows.[183] The proportionate disclosure regime is available only for a 'rights issue' but, for this purpose, a rights issue is defined to include not only a full-blown statutory rights issue in accordance with the Companies Act 2006 but also issues where the statutory pre-emption rights have been disapplied and replaced with 'near identical rights.' A standard rights issue conducted in accordance with the *Listing Rules* (ie an offer to existing shareholders in proportion to existing holders made by way of a renounceable letter of allotment, with compensation for shareholders that do not take up their rights or sell them, and with special arrangements for overseas shareholders, treasury shares, and fractions) would qualify for the modified regime, as would an open offer with compensation but

---

[179] Latham & Watkins, *The JOBS Act After One Year.*
[180] JR Ritter, 'Re-energizing the IPO Market,' in M Bailey and R Herring (eds) *Restructuring to Speed Economic Recovery* (Washington: Brookings Press, 2013).
[181] JC Coffee, 'The Political Economy of Dodd-Frank' in E Ferran, N Moloney, JG Hill, and JC Coffee, *The Regulatory Aftermath of the Global Financial Crisis* (Cambridge: CUP, 2012) 301, 364–7.
[182] ESMA/2011/323, para 262.   [183] Prospectus Directive, Art 7.2(g).

not an open offer with no compensatory element that is not in accordance with Companies Act 2006 pre-emption rights.[184] To benefit from the modified disclosure regime, the class of shares proposed to be issued pursuant to the secondary issue must already be admitted to trading on a regulated market or MTF which meets certain regulatory requirements in relation to ongoing disclosure requirements and rules on market abuse.[185] The rules of the MTF (a category which includes AIM) must require issuers to publish annual financial statements and audit reports within six months after the end of each financial year, half-yearly financial statements within four months after the end of the first six months of each financial year, and inside information within the meaning of the Market Abuse Directive. Relaxations under the regime include: no requirement for an operating and financial review; only one year audited historical financial information is required; no disclosure of capital resources or selected financial information is required; details of related party transactions may be omitted if certain conditions are satisfied; and for issuers on a regulated market, no disclosure about remuneration and benefits and board practices is required. Whenever the proportionate disclosure regime for rights issues is used, the beginning of the prospectus must contain a warning to that effect.[186]

Although issuers may be eligible to draw up a prospectus under the relevant proportionate disclosure regime, an issuer may still elect to prepare a prospectus in accordance with the fuller form disclosure requirements set out in the relevant Annex(es) to the Prospectus Regulation. This election may be made where an issuer perceives there to be marketing benefits to including the additional disclosure in the prospectus or where there are concerns that the omission of certain information may lead to the prospectus as a whole being misleading. Care should be taken in this regard as, even where the proportionate disclosure regime is available to an issuer, the general duty of disclosure (discussed later) will still apply.

Maximum harmonization

The disclosure regime set by the Prospectus Directive and the Prospectus Directive Regulation is generally viewed as being one of 'maximum harmonization,' although the Directive does not use this term.[187] Maximum harmonization implies that national authorities cannot adopt general rules requiring a prospectus to contain items of information which are not included in relevant schedules and building blocks of the Prospectus Directive Regulation. Although the Prospectus Directive, Article 7 and the Prospectus Directive Regulation refer to 'minimum' information to be included in a prospectus, this is not intended to affect the level of harmonization and simply leaves room for the inclusion of further information to satisfy the general disclosure obligation (discussed later) or information going beyond the specified items that those responsible for the prospectus choose to disclose.[188] Only for a limited and precise list of issuers can competent authorities require adapted information going beyond the information items listed in the schedules and building blocks.[189] However, on a case-by-case basis as a condition of approving a prospectus, the FCA can require the inclusion in a prospectus of supplementary information that it

---

[184] See further, ch 5.   [185] PDR, Art 26a(1), as inserted by Commission Regulation 486/2012.

[186] PDR, Art 26a(3).

[187] Prospectus Directive, rec 15 and rec 20 allude to this feature although the point is not especially obvious. See further PDR, Arts 3 and 22(1), and for detailed examination of the point see P Schammo, *EU Prospectus Law* (Cambridge: CUP, 2011) 69–74.

[188] PDR, rec 5 envisages the possibility of voluntary inclusion of additional information.

[189] PDR, rec 5 and rec 22. Note also rec 23, which caters for the situation of completely new types of securities not covered in the PDR. Here the competent authority necessarily has to exercise discretion with respect to prospectus contents but 'should always try to find similarities and make use as much as possible of existing schedules.'

considers necessary for investor protection.[190] There is also scope for the FCA, on a specific basis, to authorize the omission of information that would otherwise be required where disclosure would be contrary to the public interest or seriously detrimental to the issuer (provided that, in this case, the omission would be unlikely to mislead the public) or where the information is only of minor importance.[191] Maximum harmonization of prospectus disclosure requirements does not preclude Member States from imposing other particular requirements, such as corporate governance requirements, in the context of admission to trading of securities on a regulated market.[192]

The overriding aim of maximum harmonization is standardization. Standardization of prospectus information should enable investors more easily to compare and evaluate the relative strengths and weaknesses of different investment opportunities.

ESMA recommendations and Q&A

Also in furtherance of the standardization objective, ESMA, the EU regulatory and supervisory agency for securities and markets, maintains recommendations for the consistent implementation of prospectus requirements.[193] Under the *Prospectus Rules* those responsible for drawing up a prospectus must consider the ESMA recommendations as part of the determination of prospectus contents, as this will be taken into account by the FCA in the prospectus approval process.[194] ESMA also maintains a *Questions and Answers* document on prospectuses.[195] This regularly updated document records responses to questions posed by the general public and competent authorities in relation to the practical application of the Prospectus Directive. Its purpose is to promote common supervisory approaches and practices.

General duty of disclosure

In addition to the detailed requirements derived from the Prospectus Directive Regulation, a prospectus must contain the 'necessary information,' which is defined by section 87A(2) of the Financial Services and Markets Act 2000 as information necessary to enable investors to make an informed assessment of:

(1)   the assets and liabilities, financial position, profits and losses, and prospects of the issuer of the transferable securities and of any guarantor; and

(2)   the rights attaching to the transferable securities.

The necessary information must be presented in a form which is comprehensible and easy to analyse.[196] It must be prepared having regard to the particular nature of the transferable securities and their issuer.[197]

This general disclosure obligation is not limited to information that is actually known to persons responsible for the prospectus or which it would be reasonable for them to have obtained by making inquiries. Nor does it provide an explicit concession whereby regard may be had to the fact that certain information may reasonably be expected to be within the knowledge of those professional advisers whom likely purchasers may reasonably be

[190] FSMA, s 87J.   [191] FSMA, s 87B.   [192] Prospectus Directive, rec 15.

[193] ESMA, *Update of the CESR recommendations on the consistent implementation of Commission Regulation (EC) No 809/2004 implementing the Prospectus Directive* (ESMA/2013/319).

[194] *PR* 1.1.6 and 1.1.8. The recommendations have not, however, been adopted as recommendations under ESMA Regulation No 1095/2010, Art 16 and therefore the 'comply or explain' mechanism established under that Article does not apply.

[195] ESMA/2013/1537 (October 2013 update).   [196] FSMA, s 87A(3).   [197] FSMA, s 87A(4).

expected to consult and to the fact that certain information may be otherwise available as a result of requirements imposed on the issuer by a recognized investment exchange, by listing rules, or by or under any other enactment.

An overriding principle for disclosure of all information that an investor would find material in addition to the mandatory specific disclosures is a standard feature of capital markets laws.[198] Notwithstanding the importance of standardization of prospectus contents, it would be inappropriate to allow those responsible for drawing up a prospectus to treat specific disclosure requirements as an exhaustive checklist and a requirement for a holistic assessment of the comprehensiveness of the information in the prospectus provides essential support.

Incorporation by reference

References are allowed in a prospectus to information which is contained in one or more previously or simultaneously published documents that have been approved by or filed with the competent authority of the issuer's home state (ie the FCA in the case of a UK incorporated issuer) or which has been provided to that authority in accordance with regulatory requirements.[199] Information that may be incorporated by reference includes annual accounts and reports, and half-yearly reports.[200]

Prospectus summaries

All IPO prospectuses, whether in single or tripartite form, must contain a summary.[201] In EU capital markets law, summaries are regarded as a key source of information for retail investors. A summary must be drafted in clear language and must present the key information in an easily accessible and understandable way. It should convey concisely, in non-technical language and in an appropriate structure, the key information relevant to the securities which are the subject of the prospectus and, when read with the rest of the prospectus, must be an aid to investors considering whether to invest in the securities.[202] The length of the summary should take into account the complexity of the issuer and of the securities but should not exceed seven per cent of the length of a prospectus or fifteen pages, whichever is longer.[203]

'Key information' means essential and appropriately structured information which is to be provided to investors with a view to enabling them to understand the nature and the risks of the issuer, any guarantor, and the securities that are being offered to them or admitted to trading on a regulated market and to decide which offers of securities to consider further.[204] The key information must include a short description of the risks associated with, and essential characteristics of, the issuer and any guarantor, a short description of the risk associated with, and essential characteristics of, the investment in the relevant security, the general terms of the offer, including estimated expenses charged to the investor by the issuer or the offeror, details of the admission to trading, and reasons for the offer and use of proceeds.[205] The summary must be drawn up in a common format in order to facilitate comparability with summaries of similar securities.[206] The high importance of standardization is reflected in the

---

[198] IOSCO, *International Disclosure Standards for Cross-Border Offerings and Initial Listings by Foreign Issuers* (1998) 5.

[199] *PR* 2.4.1.   [200] *PR* 2.4.2.   [201] FSMA, s 87A(5).

[202] Prospectus Directive, Art 5(2) (as amended), implemented by FSMA, s 87A(6) and 87A(9)–(10), which were added by The Prospectus Regulations 2012, SI 2012/1538.

[203] PDR, Art 24 (as amended); *PR* 2.1.4.

[204] Prospectus Directive, Art 2(1)(s) (as amended), implemented as FSMA, s 87A(9)–(10).

[205] Prospectus Directive, Art 2(1)(s) (as amended), implemented as FSMA, s 87A(9)–(10).

[206] Prospectus Directive, Art 5(2) (as amended).

evolution of the Prospectus Directive Regulation: whereas the PDR, Article 24, in its original form, provided for the issuer, offeror, or person asking for admission to trading to determine 'on its own' the detailed content of the summary, the key information items are now stipulated and it is provided that 'the order of the sections and of the elements of [the relevant Annex] shall be mandatory.'[207]

A prospectus summary must also contain risk warnings informing readers that it is only an introduction, that investment decisions should be based on the prospectus, and that certain pitfalls may be encountered in litigation arising from civil claims relating to prospectus information.[208] Incorporation by reference is not permitted in summaries.[209] Cross-references in summaries are considered to carry the risks that the summary will not be self-contained and that a cross-reference might substitute for a concise explanation.[210]

Missing details

If a prospectus for which approval is sought does not include the final offer price or the amount of transferable securities, as would be the case in a price range prospectus, the missing details must be filed with the FCA as soon as practicable,[211] whereupon limited withdrawal rights may be triggered.[212] Withdrawal rights are considered further later in this chapter.

Financial information in prospectuses

Historical financial information in prospectuses of EU issuers must generally be drawn up in accordance with IFRS that have been adopted in the Union.[213] Accordingly, for a UK-incorporated issuer, the position regarding the form and content of financial disclosures in a prospectus is relatively straightforward. For third country issuers, things are more complicated because the position is that the required financial information must be prepared according to IFRS adopted in the Union or a third country's national accounting standards, provided those standards have been assessed by the European Commission to be equivalent to IFRS adopted in the Union.[214] The requirement for foreign issuers to present financial information according to Union-adopted IFRS or an 'equivalent' accounting system was one of the most controversial features of the regime established by the Prospectus Directive—and for a period, there were serious concerns that rigid requirements for restated accounts could make the European capital market prohibitively expensive for foreign issuers.[215] However, in more recent times the equivalence determination process, in which the European Commission plays the leading role, advised by ESMA, has stabilized.[216] The Japanese and US national accounting systems (Generally Accepted Accounting Principles or GAAP) have been held to satisfy the 'equivalence' test.[217] The GAAPs of China, Canada, South Korea and India have also been found to be equivalent, although in the case of India the equivalence

[207] PDR, Art 24 and Annex XXII (as amended); *PR* 2.1.4.   [208] PDR, Annex XXII, Section A; *PR* 2.1.7.
[209] PDR, Art 24; *PR* 2.14.4.   [210] ESMA/2011/323, 63.   [211] FSMA, s 87A(7); *PR* 2.3.2.
[212] FSMA, s 87Q.   [213] PDR, Annexes.   [214] PDR, Art 35.
[215] E Ferran, *Building an EU Securities Market* (Cambridge: CUP, 2004) 160–4.
[216] Commission Regulation (EC) No 1569/2007, [2007] OJ L340/66 establishing a mechanism for the determination of equivalence of accounting standards applied by third country issuers of securities pursuant to Directives 2003/71/EC and 2004/109/EC of the European Parliament and of the Council (amended by Commission Delegated Regulation (EU) No 310/2012, [2012] OJ L103/11). The establishment of this mechanism was mandated by the Transparency Obligations Directive, Art 23(4).
[217] Commission Decision 2008/961/EC of 12 December 2008, [2008] L340/112.

determination remains temporary in order to allow more time for the implementation of an IFRS-compliant reporting system.[218] The position of foreign issuers is considered further in chapter 14.

Language requirements

Where, as is usual in an IPO, an issuer is making an offer to the public and/or applying for its securities to be admitted to trading in its home state, it must draw up its prospectus in a language accepted by its home state regulator.[219] Where the issuance activity is to extend cross-border into other states as well as the home state, the prospectus must also be made available in languages that are acceptable to the competent authorities in each of the host states or, at the issuer's choice, in a language that is customary in the sphere of international finance.[220] Where, as would be unusual in an IPO, the issuer is not directing its efforts into its home state, the language requirement is for the issuer to satisfy each of the relevant host states or else to write its prospectus in a language that is customary in the sphere of international finance.[221] Where a prospectus that has been drawn up in accordance with these language rules is used for cross-border issuance activity within the EU, host Member States can require only the summary to be translated into their official language.[222]

Historically, the EU's multi-lingual character was a significant barrier to the use of prospectuses for cross-border offers of securities because Member States could insist upon the translation of the entire prospectus into their local language. Compliance with such requests would have necessitated time-consuming, intensive cross-checking and verification exercises to counter the risk of inaccuracies creeping into disclosures via the translation process, hence adding to the overall transaction costs. This consideration helps to explain why, historically, cross-border use of prospectuses was a rare event. The language regime put in place by the Prospectus Directive is designed to address these problems. The costs involved in translating short summaries should be trivial compared to the costs of full prospectus translation.

ESMA, and its predecessor, CESR, have periodically published statistical information on the cross-border use of prospectuses. The data for the period from January 2012 to June 2012, for example, indicates that in total 2317 prospectuses were approved by national competent authorities, and 722 were passported into one or more other Member States.[223] This published statistical information does not break down these figures by reference to the type of securities (equity, debt, or hybrid) or the nature of the offer. However, it is apparent from the records maintained by the FCA (and its predecessor) of prospectuses passported into the UK from other EU jurisdictions that the passporting system is used mostly for offerings of debt or hybrid securities, and that it is rare for it to be used for an IPO. Even so, these figures provide an example of regulatory change having a powerful impact in shaping market practice. A few Member States (Luxembourg, Austria, and the Netherlands) have even dispensed with translations of prospectus summaries for prospectuses in English.[224] The operation of the prospectus passport is considered further in chapter 14.

---

[218] Commission Implementing Decision of 11 April 2012, [2012] L103/49.
[219] Prospectus Directive, Art 19.1. For the UK implementation of the language rules, see *PR* 4.1.
[220] Prospectus Directive, Art 19.3.   [221] Prospectus Directive, 19.2.
[222] Prospectus Directive, Arts 19.2 and 19.3.
[223] ESMA, *Data on Prospectuses Approved and Passported—January 2012 to June 2012* (ESMA/2012/603).
[224] UKLA Factsheet, *Passporting* (October 2008).

Supplementary prospectuses

There is a Directive-derived requirement for a supplementary prospectus where, following the approval of a prospectus and prior to the closure of the offer or admission to trading, there arises a significant new factor or a material mistake or inaccuracy is noted.[225] A factor is significant if it would be significant for the purposes of making an informed assessment of the kind mentioned in the general duty of disclosure.[226] There is, however, no express statutory test for judging materiality in this context. A supplementary prospectus must provide sufficient information to correct any mistake or inaccuracy which gave rise to the need for it.[227] Where the relevant transaction involves both an offer and admission to trading on a regulated market, the relevant period during which a supplementary prospectus may be required ends with the later of the closure of the offer or when trading of the securities on a regulated market begins.[228]

Withdrawal rights

Statutory withdrawal rights arise in relation to prospectuses relating to offers of securities to the public in certain circumstances, namely:

(a) where a person has agreed to buy or subscribe for transferable securities where the final offer price or the amount of transferable securities on offer was not included in the prospectus, unless the prospectus disclosed the criteria and/or the conditions in accordance with which these elements will be determined;[229] or

(b) where a supplementary prospectus has been published, provided the factor that triggered the need for the supplementary prospectus arose before the delivery of the securities.[230]

The exercise of withdrawal rights could have a destabilizing effect on the market. Since price-range prospectuses stating the indicative offer price range should not give rise to withdrawal right complications so long as the criteria/conditions for the determination of the offer price are disclosed and the final price is within the range, this risk pertains primarily to the possibility of withdrawal rights arising from the publication of a supplementary prospectus. Amendments to the Prospectus Directive in 2010 have clarified some uncertainties that had arisen in practice about the operation of withdrawal rights in these circumstances. In particular, it is now clear that withdrawal rights arise only in relation to prospectuses relating to public offers and that they do not survive the delivery of the securities. The withdrawal period in this situation is further restricted by a time limit of two working days from the date of the supplementary prospectus or such later time as may be specified in the supplementary prospectus.

Prospectus approval

A prospectus must be approved by the competent authority of the issuer's home state and then made available to the public before an offer of securities to the public or a request for

---

[225] FSMA, s 87G.   [226] FSMA, s 87G(4).   [227] FSMA, s 87G(6).

[228] FSMA, s 87G(3A), as amended by Prospectus Regulations 2012, SI 2012/1538, implementing Directive 2010/73/EU.

[229] FSMA, s 87Q(1)–(2). The withdrawal period in this case is two working days from the date the competent authority is informed of the information.

[230] FSMA, s 87Q(4)–(6) as amended by Prospectus Regulations 2012 SI 2012/1538, implementing Directive 2010/73/EU.

admission of securities to trading on a regulated market.[231] Regulatory approval must precede publication. The scheme for establishing an issuer's home state is established by the Prospectus Directive.[232] For a Community issuer its home state for approval of share prospectuses is the state in which it has its registered office. Thus a UK issuer has to apply to the FCA for prospectus approval.[233] A foreign (non-EEA) issuer has a one-off opportunity to choose its EU home state.[234]

The rigidity of the approval regime has generated some controversy. Before the Prospectus Directive, issuers were tied to their home state only where an element of their securities issuance or listing activity was taking place there.[235] If the home state was not involved, an issuer could seek regulatory approvals from any one of the states in which that activity was occurring. The reduction of issuer mobility in this respect is based on the assumption that home states are assumed to be in the best position to regulate and supervise those issuers that have their registered office within their jurisdiction. However, tying issuers in this way means that, in effect, national regulators are shielded from competition by their monopoly with regard to their home issuers. This removes some incentives for national regulators to improve their efficiency and effectiveness.

An approved prospectus has Community scope, which means that it is valid for public offers or the admission of the securities to trading on a regulated market in any number of the states within the EU.[236] The only permissible additional formalities are that the home state must notify host states that the prospectus has been approved in accordance with the Prospectus Directive and send a copy of the prospectus, and host states may require translation of the summary into their official language. Host states cannot impose their own approval requirements.[237] The cross-border use of approved prospectuses is considered further in chapter 14.

Prospectus publication

An approved prospectus must be filed with the competent authority and made available to the public.[238] The requirement for 'publication' does not mean that a prospectus must be sent directly to prospective investors. Instead, under the *Prospectus Rules*, and giving effect to the Prospectus Directive,[239] a prospectus is deemed to be made available to the public when it has been published in any one of the following ways:

(1) inserted in one or more newspapers, circulated throughout, or widely circulated in, the states in which the securities are to be offered or admitted to trading;[240]

(2) in printed form, free of charge to the public at the offices of the regulated market on which the securities are being admitted to trading, or at the registered office of the issuer and at the offices of the financial intermediaries placing or selling the securities, including paying agents;[241]

---

[231] Prospectus Directive, Art 13. UK implementation: FSMA, s 85 and *PR* 3.
[232] Prospectus Directive, Art 2(1)(m). [233] FSMA, s 87A. [234] Prospectus Directive, Art 2(1)(m)(iii).
[235] CARD, Art 37 and Public Offers Directive, Art 20. [236] Prospectus Directive, Art 17.
[237] Prospectus Directive, Art 18.
[238] Prospectus Directive, Art 14 (as amended). For UK implementation, see *PR* 3.2.
[239] Prospectus Directive, Art 14 (as amended).
[240] *PR* 3.2.4(1). Note PDR, rec 32 provides that where a newspaper is used for the publication of a prospectus it should have a wide area of distribution and circulation. For further requirements on publication in newspapers, see PDR, Art 30.
[241] *PR* 3.2.4(2).

(3) in electronic form on the issuer's website or, if applicable, on the website of the financial intermediaries placing or selling the securities, including paying agents;[242] or

(4) in an electronic form on the website of the regulated market where admission to trading is sought.[243]

Where a prospectus is published by one of the electronic methods, a paper copy must be delivered free of charge to those investors who request it.[244]

There is provision in the Prospectus Directive for the publication requirement to be satisfied by publication in electronic form on the website of the home state competent authority if the said authority has decided to offer this service.[245] The FCA does not offer this service and is therefore required by the Prospectus Directive to publish on its website a list of all the prospectuses it has approved.[246] The FCA has implemented this by providing a list of approved prospectuses with a hyperlink, where applicable, to the websites of the specific issuers.[247] Approved prospectuses are also available for public inspection via Morningstar, the UK's National Storage Mechanism.

In general a prospectus must be filed with the FCA and made available to the public as soon as practicable, and in any case at a reasonable time in advance of, and at the latest at the beginning of, the offer.[248] However, in the case of an IPO of securities that are to be admitted to trading on a regulated market for the first time, the timing requirements are more precise: the prospectus must be made available to the public at least six working days before the end of the offer.[249] Once published, a prospectus is valid for twelve months provided it is updated by supplementary prospectuses as required.[250] Once the registration document for a tripartite prospectus has been approved, it will remain valid for twelve months and can be combined with a new or updated securities note and summary note for future issues of securities during that period.[251]

Advertisements, pathfinder prospectuses, and mini prospectuses

The *Prospectus Rules* impose specific constraints relating to advertisements.[252] An advertisement relating to an offer or to an admission to trading on a regulated market must not be issued unless:

(1) it states that a prospectus has been or will be published and indicates where investors are, or will be, able to obtain it;

(2) it is clearly recognizable as an advertisement;

(3) information in the advertisement is not inaccurate or misleading; and

(4) information in the advertisement is consistent with the information contained in the prospectus, if already published, or with the information required to be in the prospectus, if the prospectus is published afterwards.[253]

---

[242] *PR* 3.2.4(3). For further requirements on publication in electronic form, see PDR, Art 29.
[243] *PR* 3.2.4(4).   [244] *PR* 3.2.6.   [245] Prospectus Directive, Art 14.2(e).
[246] Prospectus Directive, Art 14.4.
[247] *PR* 3.2.7. See <http://www.fsa.gov.uk/ukla/officialPublicationOfProspectuses.do?view=true&listType=publ icationOfProspectuses> and <http://www.fsa.gov.uk/ukla/officialProspectusesPassported.do?view=true&listType =prospectusesPassported> accessed July 2013.
[248] *PR* 3.2.2, implementing Prospectus Directive, Art 14.1.
[249] *PR* 3.2.3, implementing Prospectus Directive, Art 14.1
[250] *PR* 5.1.1 and Prospectus Directive, Art 9 (as amended).
[251] *PR* 5.1.4 and Prospectus Directive, Art 9.4 (as amended).
[252] PR 3.3 implementing Prospectus Directive, Art 15.   [253] *PR* 3.3.2.

To comply with this requirement, a written advertisement should also contain a bold and prominent statement to the effect that it is not a prospectus but an advertisement and that investors should not subscribe for any transferable securities referred to in the advertisement except on the basis of information in the prospectus.[254] All information concerning an offer or an admission to trading disclosed in an oral or written form (even if not for advertising purposes) must be consistent with that contained in the prospectus.[255]

An advertisement for this purpose means an announcement:

(1) relating to a specific offer to the public of securities or to an admission to trading on a regulated market; and

(2) aiming to specifically promote the potential subscription or acquisition of securities.[256]

Article 34 of the Prospectus Directive Regulation sets out a non-exhaustive list of the types of document or event that could amount to an advertisement as so defined. The list is very wide and includes standard letters, newspaper advertising (with or without an order form), seminars and presentations, posters, brochures, and faxes. FCA technical guidance emphasizes that the scope of the advertisement regime is wide and can include investor presentations, audiocasts, analyst conference calls, and even comments made by an issuer to the media.[257] Whether investment research issued in the context of a new issue triggers the advertisement regime will depend on the facts and circumstances of the particular case.[258]

Pathfinder prospectuses, which are draft prospectuses not yet formally approved by the FCA, can be issued as advertisements in accordance with the *Prospectus Rules*.[259] Pathfinders are only likely to be used where an offer is exempt from the public offers prospectus requirement, as in an institutional offering. In IPOs that have a retail as well as an institutional element, issuers are likely to prefer FCA-approved price range prospectuses so as to start the six-day publication period required under the *Prospectus Rules* as soon as possible.

The Financial Services and Markets Act 2000 contains a general prohibition on the communication of invitations or inducements to engage in investment activity in the course of business otherwise than by authorized persons or with their approval of the contents.[260] This is known as the 'financial promotion' regime. The restriction on financial promotions does not apply to FCA-approved prospectuses and certain related documents.[261] However, advertisements produced under the *Prospectus Rules* are not covered by these exemptions and will therefore require approval under the financial promotion regime unless some other exemption applies.

It used to be a common practice to issue mini prospectuses to prospective retail investors. Under the regime that is now in force, an old-style mini prospectus would be an advertisement and, as such, would be subject to the *Prospectus Rules* and, unless an exemption can be found, the financial promotions regime. The current regime furnishes issuers with the alternative of circulating the summary of a tripartite prospectus. An advantage of this route is that, under the requirements relating to summaries, it will contain a statement that any investment decision should be based on the prospectus as a whole[262] and that civil liability will arise only where the summary (when read together with the other

---

[254] *PR* 3.3.3. [255] *PR* 3.3.4. [256] PDR, Art 2(9).
[257] UKLA Technical Note, *PD Advertisement Regime* (UKLA/TN/604.1).
[258] UKLA Technical Note, *PD Advertisement Regime*. [259] UKLA Technical Note, *PD Advertisement Regime*
[260] FSMA, s 21.
[261] Financial Services and Markets Act 2000 (Financial Promotion) Order 2005, SI 2005/1529, regs 70–71.
[262] *PR* 2.1.7.

parts of the prospectus) is misleading, inaccurate, or inconsistent, or does not provide key information.[263]

Enforcement of Securities Laws Regulating Public Issues and Admission to Trading—Overview

UK law employs a mix of public and private enforcement strategies to underpin the regulatory framework governing public issues of securities and the admission of securities to trading on organized markets. On the private side, investors have available to them the rights under the general law of tort and contract to sue where they have acquired information on the basis of false information. Additionally, the securities legislation not only mandates a broader range of disclosures than would be required of issuers under the general law but also gives investors a special right to sue, which is more favourable in certain respects than claims based on tort or contract. The strategy of combining regulatory intervention to establish the disclosure rules for securities issuance with private enforcement of those rules by investors has been commended by commentators, who point out that it may be easier, and therefore cheaper, for investors to establish in a trial that the issuer has failed to reveal specific information, disclosure of which was mandated by law, than to prove the issuer's negligence in the absence of a statute, and that subversion of judges becomes more difficult when a statute describes precisely what facts need to be established for a claim to succeed.[264] In one line of study the development of stock markets has been found to be strongly associated with measures of private enforcement, such as extensive disclosure requirements and a relatively low burden of proof on investors seeking to recover damages resulting from inaccurate or incomplete prospectuses.[265] However, this analysis is challenged by other research that stresses the importance of oversight and enforcement by public authorities.[266] The reputational fallout resulting from being the target of public enforcement action must also be factored in.[267] It is also recognized in the literature that private enforcement mechanisms also have at least the potential to damage a securities market, where the checks and balances to curb manipulation of the system simply in order to extract settlements rather than to obtain redress for genuine grievances are inadequate. During the mid-2000s the propensity for civil litigation in the US featured significantly in important reports as a threat to the international competitiveness of its capital markets.[268]

As yet there is no meaningful degree of EU-wide harmonization of the mechanisms of private enforcement of securities laws.[269] This is a specific aspect of a much broader point, namely, that the EU still remains far away from being a genuine European area of justice in

---

[263] FSMA, s 90(12) as amended by Prospectus Regulations 2012, SI 2012/1538, implementing Directive 2010/73/EU.

[264] S Djankov, EL Glaeser, R La Porta, F López de Silanes, and A Shleifer, 'The New Comparative Economics' (2003) 31 *Journal of Comparative Economics* 595.

[265] R La Porta, F López de Silanes, and A Shleifer, 'What Works in Securities Laws?' (2006) 61 *Journal of Finance* 1. Further on the relationship between (private and public) enforcement of securities laws and market development: U Bhattacharya, 'Enforcement and its Impact on Cost of Equity and Liquidity of the Market', Study Commissioned by the Task Force to Modernize Securities Legislation in Canada (May 2006).

[266] HE Jackson and MJ Roe, 'Public and Private Enforcement of Securities Laws: Resource-based Evidence' (2009) 93 *Journal of Financial Economics* 207.

[267] J Armour, C Mayer, and A Polo, 'Regulatory Sanctions and Reputational Damage in Financial Markets' Oxford Legal Studies Research Paper No 62/2010 <http://ssrn.com/abstract=1678028> accessed July 2013.

[268] McKinsey & Co, *Sustaining New York's and the US' Global Financial Services Leadership*, 73–5; Committee on Capital Markets Regulation, *Interim Report*, 71–91.

[269] But groundwork for possible future harmonization is being done: in response to a European Commission mandate, ESMA has compiled a comparative table of Member States' liability regimes in relation to the Prospectus Directive: ESMA, *Comparison of Liability Regimes in Member States in relation to the Prospectus Directive* (ESMA/2013/619).

civil and commercial matters in which people can approach courts and authorities in any other Member State as easily as in their own. Mutual recognition of judgments and judicial cooperation, rather than harmonization, serve as the focus for the as yet tentative policy initiatives in the field of EU civil justice.[270] Although the capital markets directives are not completely silent on civil liability in that they do contain provisions requiring Member States to apply their national laws on civil liability, they do not prescribe the contents of those laws or regulate the process by which they are to be applied.[271] This means that those engaging in share issuance activity on a cross-border basis within Europe must still take account of multiple, potentially quite divergent, liability regimes. Potential liability risks associated with cross-border offerings of securities are considered further in chapter 14.

On the public side of enforcement, the FCA is equipped with a wide array of tools. It can impose administrative sanctions, including fines and public censure, and can seek restitution of profits. It can suspend or prohibit issuance or listing activity and can instigate criminal proceedings. Pan-European coordination of public enforcement in the area of issuer disclosure is more advanced than with regard to private mechanisms of enforcement.[272] The capital markets directives contain provisions requiring Member States to impose 'effective, proportionate and dissuasive' administrative measures or sanctions.[273] They also stipulate a minimum range of investigative tools that national securities regulators must have at their disposal[274] and provide for information sharing and cooperation.[275] In a significant breakthrough, harmonization of criminal sanctions will be introduced into the market abuse regime.[276] This will be the first legislative measure based on the Treaty on Functioning of the European Union, Article 83, which provides for the adoption of directives to establish minimum rules concerning the definition of criminal offences and sanctions in the areas of particularly serious crime with a cross-border dimension resulting from the nature or impact of such offences or from a special need to combat them on a common basis. Measures adopted under Article 83 will only apply to the UK on the basis of an opt-in. The current government does not intend to opt into the market abuse criminal sanctions regime.

The IAS Regulation also provides for the development of a common approach in financial reporting, an aim that ESMA is seeking to foster through the updating and upgrading of CESR standards from 2003/4 to ESMA guidelines.[277] This will result in enforcers of financial information coming under a comply or explain obligation with respect to the guidelines.[278] ESMA's view is that investor protection requires the extension of the scope of enforcement to the whole financial reporting framework applicable to listed issuers, including national GAAPs from EU jurisdictions (which as discussed in chapter 9 may still be used for individual accounts, for example, for the purposes of identifying profits available for distribution) and third country GAAPs that have been declared equivalent to EU-adopted IFRS.[279] It stresses the need for a common European approach to the enforcement of financial information in

---

[270] M Andenas, 'National Paradigms of Civil Enforcement: Mutual Recognition or Harmonization in Europe?' (2006) 17 *European Business Law Review* 529.

[271] Prospectus Directive, Art 6.2; Transparency Obligations Directive, rec 10 and Art 7.

[272] Prospectus Directive, Art 23; Transparency Obligations Directive, Art 22. However, the Market Abuse Directive is more territorially based (rec 35).

[273] Prospectus Directive, Art 25; Transparency Obligations Directive, Art 24; Market Abuse Directive, Art 14.

[274] Prospectus Directive, Art 21; Transparency Obligations Directive, Art 20; Market Abuse Directive, Art 12.

[275] Prospectus Directive, Art 22; Transparency Obligations Directive, Art 21; Market Abuse Directive, Art 16.

[276] As proposed in COM(2011) 654 and COM(2012) 420. As part of the background work, ESMA (following up on work done previously by its predecessor CESR) conducted a mapping exercise and reported on the actual use of MAD sanctioning powers: ESMA/2012/270.

[277] ESMA, *Consultation Paper: Guidelines on Enforcement of Financial Information* (ESMA/2013/1013).

[278] In accordance with the ESMA founding regulation, Regulation (EU) No 1095/2010, Art 16.

[279] ESMA/2013/1013.

order to avoid regulatory arbitrage by issuers, that is situations in which an issuer's choice of the market on which to list its securities may be influenced by different approaches to enforcement being applied in different European jurisdictions.

Civil Liability in the UK for Defective Prospectuses—Rescission of Contracts

An investor who is induced[280] to acquire securities on the basis of factual information provided by or on behalf of the other party which later turns out to have been false or misleading can seek rescission of the contract by which he acquired the securities. It is clear from case law that a company is unlikely to be able to distance itself from statements in a prospectus issued by or on its behalf, even where those statements are the work of specialists who have contributed to the compilation of the prospectus.[281] The statement complained of must have been a statement of fact not of law, intention, or opinion, but a prospectus that states that it is the company's intention to do something which it has, in fact, no intention of doing contains a false statement of fact.[282] Silence is not actionable as a general rule, but a claim may lie if the effect of an omission is to render what is said false or misleading.[283] In cases on the prospectus requirements of older companies legislation, it was held that a mere failure to comply with the mandatory disclosure requirements relating to prospectuses did not entitle an investor to rescind a contract to take shares.[284] These cases still appear to represent the law. An ambiguous statement may be actionable but it is for the claimant to prove that he interpreted the words in their false sense and was thereby induced to take the securities.[285] A person who was unaware of the false statement or who did not rely on it cannot claim that he was induced to acquire the shares by reason of it.[286]

The person claiming rescission must be within the class of persons to whom the false statement was addressed.[287] Where shares are offered to the public generally, this requirement should be easily satisfied since everyone is within the category of addressee. Identifying the class of person to whom the statement was addressed is more problematic where the offer is directed to particular investors as, for example, in a rights issue where the offer is to the company's existing shareholders. In a typically structured rights issue, the company's offer of new securities to its existing shareholders is in a form whereby it can be renounced by those shareholders in favour of other investors. A sensible interpretation of this structure is that the offer, and the documentation supporting it, is addressed to existing shareholders and to persons in whose favour they renounce their entitlements, although there is no clear modern authority in support of this view.[288]

Rescission involves unwinding the contract and putting the parties back into their pre-contractual position. Its great advantage from an investor's perspective is that it enables

---

[280] The false statement need not be the sole inducement: *Re Royal British Bank, Nicol's Case* (1859) 3 De G&J 387. If a statement would have influenced a reasonable person in deciding to acquire the securities, the court will readily infer that the claimant was induced: *Smith v Chadwick* (1883) 9 App Cas 187, HL, 196 *per* Lord Blackburn.

[281] *Lynde v Anglo-Italian Hemp Co* [1896] 1 Ch 178; *Mair v Rio Grande Rubber Estates* [1913] AC 853, HL.

[282] *Edgington v Fitzmaurice* (1885) 29 Ch D 459, CA.

[283] *Derry v Peek* (1889) 14 App Cas 337, HL. See also *R v Kylsant* [1932] 1 KB 442, CCA.

[284] *Re Wimbledon Olympia Ltd* [1910] 1 Ch 630; *Re South of England Natural Gas and Petroleum Co Ltd* [1911] 1 Ch 573. In *Re Wimbledon Olympia Ltd* at 632 Neville J said: 'I cannot attribute to the Legislature the intention that the mere fact of the omission of any of the facts required by this section to be stated should give the shareholders the right to get rid of their shares.'

[285] *Smith v Chadwick* (1883) 9 App Cas 187, HL.

[286] *Smith v Chadwick* (1883) 9 App Cas 187, HL.

[287] *Peek v Gurney* (1873) LR 6 HL 377; *Al Nakib Investments (Jersey) Ltd v Longcroft* [1990] 1 WLR 1390.

[288] The situation described in the text is different from that considered in the cases such as the *Al Nakib* decision, where an investor who acquired shares in the secondary market could not base a claim on false statements contained in a prospectus issued in connection with an offer of new shares.

the investor simply to hand back the shares and recover all of the money that was paid for them.[289] The investor does not need to become embroiled in the complications that can arise in relation to the assessment of compensation for deceit, misrepresentation, or negligence. The operation of rescission in relation to modern securities markets has not produced much case law, but whether this is because the remedy is little used or rarely leads to argument when it is invoked is hard to tell.[290] Older cases suggest that the remedy of rescission may have limited practical significance in this context. As a general rule, a party seeking rescission must act promptly after the discovery of the fraud or misrepresentation, and the need for swift action is particularly emphasized in nineteenth-century cases concerning contracts to take shares:

> Where a person has contracted to take shares in a company and his name has been placed on the register, it has always been held that he must exercise his right of repudiation with extreme promptness after the discovery of the fraud or misrepresentation.[291]
>
> If a man claims to rescind his contract to take shares in a company on the ground that he has been induced to enter into it by misrepresentation he must rescind it as soon as he learns the facts, or else he forfeits all claims to relief.[292]
>
> The delay of a fortnight in repudiating shares makes it to my mind doubtful whether the repudiation in the case of a going concern would have been in time. No doubt where investigation is necessary some time must be allowed... But where, as in the present case, the shareholder is at once fully informed of the circumstances he ought to lose no time in repudiating.[293]

If, after learning of an entitlement to reject, the investor does something which amounts to accepting ownership of the shares, this will bar the right to rescind. The following acts have been held to have this effect: trying to sell the shares;[294] attending company meetings;[295] and signing proxies, paying calls, or accepting dividends.[296] There are conflicting authorities on whether it is possible to rescind if some of the shares originally acquired have since been sold.[297] Since shares are fungible securities, it is doubtful in principle whether disposal of part of the original holding should bar rescission: the investor can always go into the market to buy substitute shares and in that way put himself into a position to give back the full portion of what he acquired in return for his money back.[298] If the acquirer of the shares has used them as security for its own borrowings, or third parties have otherwise acquired an interest in them, this may bar rescission unless those rights can be unwound or arguments based on fungibility are accepted. Rescission cannot be sought against a company that has gone into liquidation because, at that point, the rights of the creditors of the company intervene.[299] This bar applies even though the company which is in liquidation may be solvent.[300]

---

[289] *Re Scottish Petroleum Co* (1883) 23 Ch D 413, CA. The investor may also recover interest: *Karberg's Case* [1892] 3 Ch 1, CA.

[290] *Smith New Court Securities Ltd v Scrimgeour Vickers (Asset Management) Ltd* [1997] AC 254, HL, 262 *per* Lord Browne-Wilkinson.

[291] *Aaron's Reefs v Twiss* [1896] AC 273, HL, 294 *per* Lord Davey.

[292] *Sharpley v Louth and East Coast Rly* (1876) 2 Ch D 663, CA, 685 *per* James LJ.

[293] *Re Scottish Petroleum Co* (1883) 23 Ch D 413, CA, 434 *per* Baggallay LJ.

[294] *Ex parte Briggs* (1866) LR 1 Eq 483.   [295] *Sharpley v Louth and East Coast Rly* (1876) 2 Ch D 663.

[296] *Scholey v Central Rly of Venezuela* (1869) LR 9 Eq 266n.

[297] *Re Metropolitan Coal Consumers' Association Ltd* (1890) 6 TLR 416 (no rescission if part sold); *Re Mount Morgan (West) Gold Mines Ltd* (1887) 3 TLR 556 (rescission still possible despite sale of part).

[298] *Smith New Court Securities Ltd v Scrimgeour Vickers (Asset Management) Ltd* [1997] AC 254, HL, 262 *per* Lord Browne-Wilkinson.

[299] *Tennent v City of Glasgow Bank* (1879) 4 App Cas 615, HL; *Oakes v Turquand* LR 2 HL 325, HL. The investor must have repudiated the shares and taken active steps to be relieved of them (or reached some agreement with the company whereby that particular investor is dispensed from having to take active steps (eg where another investor has taken action and the result of that case will determine whether other claims stand or fall)) before the commencement of the winding up: *Re Scottish Petroleum Co* (1883) 23 Ch D 413, CA, 433–4 *per* Baggallay LJ.

[300] *Re Hull and County Bank, Burgess's Case* (1880) 15 Ch D 507.

The mechanics of rescission of a contract to subscribe shares are that the investor must notify the company that the shares are repudiated and take steps to have his name removed from the register[301] or some other equivalent action.[302]

In some offering structures, an investor may acquire shares otherwise than from the company directly. Indeed the company may have no direct involvement in the offer or the prospectus documentation relating to it, such as where it is an offer for sale by a major shareholder. In such a case the investor's claim for rescission for false information in the prospectus would lie against the vendor of the shares rather than the company. The investor must first establish that there is an actionable misrepresentation of fact for which the vendor is responsible and must then give notice to the vendor of the intention to repudiate the shares.[303] If the vendor does not accept the claim, the investor may seek an order for rescission from the court. The investor may have been registered by the company as the owner of shares but this does not preclude rescission[304] and the investor can seek to have the register rectified. Section 125 of the Companies Act 2006 provides a summary mode of rectifying the register in any circumstance where the name of a person is, without sufficient cause, entered in the company's register of members. This power, which is discretionary,[305] is a general one and it can be exercised in circumstances where shares have been improperly transferred as well as in cases of improper allotments.[306] However, the summary procedure should not be used in complicated cases, such as where an investor's right to seek rectification is disputed.[307] The bars to rescission of a contract to purchase shares from a vendor shareholder should, on general principles, be the same as those that apply to a contract to subscribe for shares and would thus include failing promptly to take steps to rescind once the false statement has been discovered or, in those circumstances, acting in a way which amounts to affirmation of the contract.

Civil Liability for Defective Prospectuses—Compensation Claims

An investor who has acquired shares on the basis of a false prospectus may seek financial compensation in addition to, or instead of, rescission. There are various different claims that are potentially available to the aggrieved investor. Anyone who is induced to enter into a contract by false statements that were addressed to him can sue those who were responsible for those statements in tort for deceit. If there is a contractual relationship between the maker of the statements and the person seeking compensation, the innocent party may be able to seek

---

[301] *Re Scottish Petroleum Co* (1883) 23 Ch D 413 CA. The company may agree to rectify the register (as in *Re London and Mediterranean Bank* (1871–72) 7 LR Ch App 55) but if the company disputes the claim, the investor may apply to the court for rectification. It has been said that a court order should normally be obtained: *Re Derham and Allen Ltd* [1946] 1 Ch 31, 36 *per* Cohen J.

[302] *Re General Rly Syndicate* [1900] 1 Ch 365, CA (the investor, when sued for unpaid calls, filed a counterclaim for rescission; this was held to be sufficient). Contrast *First National Reinsurance Co v Greenfield* [1921] 2 KB 260 where the defendant claimed, as a defence to an action for unpaid calls, that he was entitled to rescission but he did not, because it fell outside the jurisdiction of the court, claim rescission or rectification; his action was held to be insufficient and he was therefore liable for the calls.

[303] Giving notice of the intention to rescind to the other contracting party is a general requirement although it may be waived in unusual circumstances: *Car and Universal Finance Co Ltd v Caldwell* [1965] 1 QB 525, CA.

[304] See eg *Cory v Cory* [1923] 1 Ch 90 where the possibility of the register being rectified where a transfer which has been registered has been shown to have been induced by fraud or misrepresentation was considered, although the judgment related only to procedural questions concerning discovery against the company.

[305] *Re Piccadilly Radio plc* [1989] BCLC 683.

[306] *Re London, Hamburgh and Continental Exchange Bank, Ward and Henry's Case* (1867) 2 Ch App 431; *Ex parte Shaw, Re Diamond Rock Boring Co* (1877) 2 QBD 463, CA; *Re Tahiti Cotton Co, ex p Sargent* (1874) 17 Eq 273.

[307] *Reese River Co v Smith* (1869) LR 4 HL 64, HL, 80 *per* Lord Cairns; *Re Greater Britain Products Development Corp Ltd* (1924) 40 TLR 488; *Re Hoicrest Ltd* [1998] 2 BCLC 175.

compensation under the Misrepresentation Act 1967 and may also have a claim for breach of contract. Another possible claim is for the investor to allege that the maker of the statements is in breach of a duty of care and is liable to pay damages under the tort of negligence. These remedies are generally available and they are not unique to securities transactions. Under the Financial Services and Markets Act 2000, there is, in addition, a statutory claim for compensation that is exclusive to prospectuses and listing particulars (which is a type of securities disclosure document that now has limited significance).[308]

The following text concentrates on the statutory claim under the Financial Services and Markets Act 2000 because, when it is compared to the general financial remedies for deceit, misrepresentation, or breach of duty of care, it is the remedy that is likely usually to produce the most favourable result for the investor. In outline, there are various reasons why this is so. The statutory claim under the Financial Services and Markets Act 2000 can be made in relation to the omission of information and, unlike other claims, is not limited to positive misstatements. It is also available to a potentially wider range of aggrieved investors than other claims. The persons against whom a claim under the Financial Services and Markets Act 2000 can be brought are clearly set out. The elements that an investor must establish in order to succeed are softer than with other claims; in particular, there is no need to show that the inaccuracies were included knowingly or negligently (though lack of knowledge and proper care can be a defence) or that the investor positively relied on the inaccurate information (though, again, the fact that an investor did not rely on the prospectus can operate as a defence). The statutory claim is, however, only available in respect of false or incomplete information in a prospectus or set of listing particulars. Where the allegedly false information is contained in another document, such as a broker's circular, this is a situation where the investor will need to look outside the Financial Services and Markets Act 2000 for a remedy.[309]

Potential claimants

Any person who has acquired, or agreed to acquire, securities to which a prospectus applies or any interest in them and who has suffered loss in respect of them as a result of untrue or misleading statements in the prospectus or the omission of any matter required to be included can bring the statutory claim.[310] Likewise, a person who has suffered loss in respect of such securities because of a failure to publish a required supplementary prospectus can sue.[311] The claim should therefore be open not only to original subscribers but also to subsequent purchasers in the market so long as they can show that the securities they acquired were ones to which the prospectus applied.[312] The requirement for a causal link between the inaccurate prospectus and the loss will, however, serve to exclude purchasers whose acquisition occurs after the distorting effect of the wrong information has been exhausted.

---

[308] FSMA, s 90. For the application of this provision to prospectuses see in particular s 90(11). Listing particulars are required for admission to official listing where no mandatory prospectus is required: *LR* 4.1. This situation could occur in the context of the Professional Securities Market (PSM). The PSM run by the London Stock Exchange is a market for officially listed securities but it is not an EU regulated market. Accordingly, so long as the securities are not being offered to the public, an admission of securities to this market would not trigger a mandatory prospectus requirement. The PSM is considered further in chs 14–15.

[309] *Hall v Cable and Wireless plc* [2010] 1 BCLC 95, QBD.   [310] FSMA, s 90(1).   [311] FSMA, s 90(4).

[312] *Hall v Cable and Wireless plc* [2010] 1 BCLC 95, QBD, [20]. Note *Possfund Custodian Trustee Ltd v Diamond* [1996] 2 All ER 774 where it is suggested that a reference to the 'person who has acquired the securities to which the prospectus relates' refers only to the placee in respect of the shares originally allotted to him, thereby excluding secondary purchasers. This interpretation, which was not decisive to the decision in question, appears to be unduly narrow. See also J Cartwright, *Misrepresentation, Mistake and Non-Disclosure* 3rd edn (London: Sweet & Maxwell, 2012) para 7.52; P Davies, *Review of Issuer Liability: Final Report* (HM Treasury, June 2007), para 2, n 4.

In allowing claims by persons other than initial subscribers or purchasers, the statutory remedy under the Financial Services and Markets Act 2000 compares favourably to the civil remedies available under the general law. In an action based on deceit, the claimant must show that the false statement was made with the intention that it should be acted on by the claimant or by a class of persons of whom the claimant is a member. A deceit claim brought by a market purchaser of shares in respect of which a false prospectus had been issued failed on this ground because the House of Lords held that the purpose of the prospectus had been exhausted when the initial allotment was complete.[313] In a deceit claim it is for the investor to establish that the purpose for which a prospectus was issued was to induce purchasers in the market to acquire the shares as well as initial subscribers.[314] A claim for compensation under the Misrepresentation Act 1967 also compares unfavourably in this respect because it depends on there being a contractual nexus between the parties and is only for loss resulting from that contract.[315] Whilst it is the case that an investor who acquires shares in the secondary market becomes a party to a statutory contract with the company under the Companies Act 2006, section 33 when he is registered as a member, loss suffered by the investor because of a false prospectus results from the purchase contract rather than the statutory contract.[316] In a claim based on breach of duty of care the claimant must establish that the defendant owed him a duty of care and is in breach of that duty. In the leading case of *Caparo Industries Ltd v Dickman*[317] the House of Lords held that for such a duty to arise, the following must be established: (a) foreseeability of damage to the claimant; (b) a relationship of proximity between the claimant and the defendant; and (c) that the situation is one in which it is fair, just, and reasonable to impose a duty of care. The concept of 'proximity' is not one that is precisely defined: in the words of Lord Oliver of Aylmerton in the *Caparo* decision,[318] 'it is no more than a label which embraces not a definable concept but merely a description of circumstances from which, pragmatically, the courts conclude that a duty of care exists.' As such, it can overlap with, and shade into, the third criterion, which explicitly acknowledges that the existence or otherwise of a duty of care is not a matter of scientific deduction and can be affected by policy considerations as perceived by the courts. In a later case, *Henderson v Merrett Syndicates Ltd*,[319] Lord Goff thought that tortious liability for misstatements could be explained on the basis of an 'assumption of responsibility' by the person making the statement. The assumption of responsibility criterion has been found helpful in some subsequent cases.[320]

The English courts are generally reluctant to impose a duty of care on the makers of statements to persons who rely on those statements and suffer economic loss. One consideration that the court regards as important in limiting the duty of care in these circumstances is the 'floodgates' argument: it is said that if the maker of a statement put into general circulation were to be held to owe a duty of care to everyone who relied on it, this would open up 'liability in an indeterminate amount for an indeterminate time to an indeterminate class.'[321] Another argument against the imposition of a duty of care is that persons who are concerned about the accuracy of statements on which they seek to rely should protect themselves by obtaining

---

[313] *Peek v Gurney* (1873) LR 6 HL 377, HL.

[314] *Andrews v Mockford* [1896] 1 QB 372, CA; *Peek v Gurney* (1873) LR 6 HL 377, HL, 412–3 *per* Lord Cairns.

[315] Under the Misrepresentation Act 1967, s 2(1) a claim lies 'where a person has entered into a contract after a misrepresentation has been made to him by another party thereto and as a result thereof he has suffered loss…'; the claim is against the other party. Under the Misrepresentation Act 1967, s 2(2) the court may in its discretion order damages in lieu of rescission of the contract between the parties.

[316] *Hall v Cable and Wireless plc* [2010] 1 BCLC 95, QBD.   [317] [1990] 2 AC 605, HL.

[318] [1990] 2 AC 605, 633, HL.   [319] [1995] 2 AC 145, HL.

[320] See in particular *Williams v Natural Life Health Foods Ltd* [1998] BCC 428.

[321] *Ultramares Corp v Touche* (1931) 174 NE 441, 444 *per* Cardozo CJ.

contractual warranties from the maker or by taking out insurance, and that it is beyond the proper ambit of the law of negligence to provide a claim in such circumstances.

A claim involving an allegedly false rights issue prospectus based on duty of care largely failed in *Al-Nakib Investments (Jersey) Ltd v Longcroft*.[322] The claim was brought by an existing shareholder in the company but it was struck out in so far as it related to the acquisition of shares in the market over and above its rights issue entitlement. The court held that the purpose of the prospectus was to do no more than to encourage shareholders to take up their rights and there was not sufficient proximity between the directors and those who bought shares in the secondary market. This is not to say that investors in the market who rely, for example, on statements in a prospectus relating to an offer for sale could never succeed in a claim based on a duty of care—indeed, in a case decided after the *Al Nakib* decision the court held that there was an arguable case for the existence of such a duty of care owed by a company, its directors, auditors, and financial advisers to purchasers in the market and that the issues merited full consideration at trial.[323] However, the onus is on the investor who is seeking compensation to establish that there exists the necessary proximity for such a duty to arise.

Persons who can be sued

The range of potential defendants also puts the claim under the Financial Services and Markets Act 2000 into a favourable light because of its clarity compared to other civil law remedies.

The *Prospectus Rules* set out a list of persons who are responsible for a prospectus and, as such, potentially liable to compensate investors.[324] The persons responsible for a prospectus relating to equity shares, warrants, or options to subscribe for equity shares that are issued by the issuer of the equity shares or other transferable securities with similar characteristics are:

(a) the issuer;

(b) if the issuer is a body corporate:
   (i) each person who is a director of that body corporate when the prospectus is published; and
   (ii) each person who has authorized himself to be named, and is named, in the prospectus as a director or as having agreed to become a director of that body corporate either immediately or at a future time;

(c) each person who accepts, and is stated in the prospectus as accepting, responsibility for the prospectus;

(d) in relation to an offer:
   (i) the offeror, if this is not the issuer; and
   (ii) if the offeror is a body corporate and is not the issuer, each person who is a director of the body corporate when the prospectus is published;

(e) in relation to a request for the admission to trading of transferable securities:
   (i) the person requesting admission, if this is not the issuer; and
   (ii) if the person requesting admission is a body corporate and is not the issuer, each person who is a director of the body corporate when the prospectus is published; and

---

[322] [1990] 1 WLR 1390.   [323] *Possfund Custodian Trustee Ltd v Diamond* [1996] 2 All ER 774.
[324] PR 5.5.

(f)   each person not falling within any of the previous paragraphs who has authorized the contents of the prospectus.[325]

An issuer and its directors are not responsible persons for this purpose if the issuer has not made or authorized the offer or the request for admission to trading in relation to which the prospectus was published.[326] A director is not responsible for a prospectus if it is published without his knowledge or consent and on becoming aware of its publication he, as soon as practicable, gives reasonable public notice that it was published without his knowledge or consent.[327] An offeror is not responsible for a prospectus where the issuer is responsible for it, the prospectus was drawn up primarily by or on behalf of the issuer, and the offeror is making the offer in association with the issuer.[328] Where, for example, employees seek to realize their holding in their company by offering their shares for purchase in conjunction with a public offer of new securities by the company itself, this rule protects the employees from personal statutory liability relating to the prospectus information. This is a reasonable outcome since those employees are unlikely to have played a significant role in the preparation and pro- duction of the prospectus. This approach is supported by the ESMA *Questions and Answers* guidance on prospectuses.[329] A person who accepts responsibility for a prospectus or who authorizes the contents of a prospectus may state that they do so only in relation to specified parts of the prospectus, or only in specified respects, and in that case the person is responsible only to the extent specified and only if the material in question is included in (or substantially in) the form and context to which the person has agreed.[330] The inclusion of persons who have accepted responsibility for the prospectus in the list of responsible persons has to be read together with the requirements of the Prospectus Directive Regulation on prospectus contents, which mandate a declaration from the persons responsible for the information in the prospectus (whether legal persons or natural persons, whose names are to be listed in the prospectus) that to the best of their knowledge information contained therein (or informa- tion contained in the parts for which they are responsible) is in accordance with the facts and contains no omission likely to affect its import.[331] In the UK, the reporting accountants are required to take responsibility for the historical financial information in a prospectus. Not surprisingly, their standard practice is to limit their responsibility to that part only.

A person is not responsible for any prospectus by reason *only* of giving advice about its contents in a professional capacity.[332] The FCA does not expect the investment banks that act as sponsors to flotations and the lawyers who advise on them to give express prospectus responsibility statements. For responsibility to arise in these cases it would therefore have to be on the basis that such individuals have 'authorized' the contents of the prospectus.

Controlling shareholders are also not a specific category of responsible person. The ABI has suggested that the list should be extended to include them on the grounds that discourag- ing controlling shareholders who are not willing to take on such liability from listing would be a good outcome for the quality of companies listing in London.[333]

The existence of this detailed code of responsibility relieves investors from having to show that statements are attributable to particular persons and that they are legally responsible for them. Whilst investors cannot recover compensation in respect of the same loss from more than one responsible person, the fact that various persons are clearly identified as being liable, subject to defences, may increase the chances of finding a sufficiently deep financial pocket to cover the amount of the claim. In a deceit claim or a claim based on breach of duty

---

[325] *PR* 5.5.3.   [326] *PR* 5.5.5.   [327] *PR* 5.5.6.   [328] *PR* 5.5.7.   [329] ESMA/2013/1537, Q47.
[330] *PR* 5.5.8.   [331] PDR, Annex I, item 1 and Annex III, item 1.
[332] *PR* 5.5.9.   [333] ABI, *Encouraging Equity Investment*, 28.

of care, investors have a heavier burden because they must establish that the defendants were legally responsible for the making of the offending statement in accordance with common law rules. So far as deceit claims are concerned, directors have been held personally liable for common law deceit, alongside their company, for knowingly or recklessly issuing a false prospectus[334] and more recent authority has confirmed that the courts will not look kindly on directors who attempt to use the company's separate legal personality as a shield against liability for fraudulent behaviour.[335] In principle, directors, reporting accountants, financial advisers, and other professional intermediaries could be liable for negligent misstatements contained in a prospectus but the rules on duty of care liability mean that it would be necessary to establish that such persons have assumed personal responsibility for that information, which may not be easy.[336] The position under the Misrepresentation Act 1967 is that there must be a contractual nexus between the claimant and the defendant.

Defences to liability

A responsible person may escape liability under section 90 of the Financial Services and Markets Act 2000 by establishing that one of the exemptions from liability specified in Schedule 10 to the Act is applicable. The exemptions are:

(1) that the responsible person reasonably believed, having made reasonable enquiries, in the accuracy of the prospectus or, in the case of the omission of information, that the omission was proper, at the time when the prospectus was submitted to the FCA and any one of the following applies—

    a. that he continued to hold that belief until the time when the securities were acquired; or

    b. that the securities were acquired before it was reasonably practicable to bring a correction to the attention of likely purchasers; or

    c. that he had already taken all steps that were reasonably practicable to bring a correction to the attention of likely purchasers; or

    d. that he continued in the belief until after the securities were admitted to trading on a regulated market and dealings in them had commenced and further, that the securities were acquired after such a lapse of time that he ought to be reasonably excused; this exemption will limit the potential liability of responsible persons to a chain of market purchasers but it should be noted that it is a discretionary exemption, not available as of right;[337]

(2) if the loss in question is incurred as a result of an incorrect statement by an expert,[338] other responsible persons may claim an exemption on the grounds that they reasonably believed that the expert was competent and had consented to the inclusion of the statement in its particular form and context at the time when the prospectus was submitted to the FCA and that any one of the conditions equivalent to those specified in (1)(a) to (d) is satisfied;[339]

(3) irrespective of the responsible person's original belief, he is exempt if he satisfies the court that he had published a correction in a manner calculated to bring it to the

---

[334] *Edgington v Fitzmaurice* (1885) 29 Ch D 459.
[335] *Standard Chartered Bank v Pakistan National Shipping Corp and ors (Nos 2 and 4)* [2003] 1 AC 959, HL.
[336] *Al Nakib Investments (Jersey) Ltd v Longcroft* [1990] 1 WLR 1390.   [337] FSMA, sch 10, para 1.
[338] Defined in FSMA, sch 10, para 8.   [339] FSMA, sch 10, para 2.

attention of likely purchasers before the acquisition or had taken all reasonable steps to secure such publication and reasonably believed that it had in fact taken place;[340]

(4) liability is not incurred in respect of an incorrect statement made by an official person or stated in an official public document provided it is accurately and fairly reproduced in the prospectus;[341]

(5) no liability arises in relation to any person who acquired the securities in the knowledge that the prospectus was inaccurate;[342] and

(6) a responsible person is exempt from liability for failure to comply with the obligation to produce a supplementary prospectus if he satisfies the court that he reasonably believed that a supplementary prospectus was not required.[343]

It should also be noted that statutory liability for summaries is regulated.

Liability in respect of prospectus summaries

Special provision is made with respect to liability in respect of information contained in a prospectus summary. A person is not to be subject to civil liability solely on the basis of a summary in a prospectus unless the summary, when read with the rest of the prospectus, is misleading, inaccurate or inconsistent; or does not provide key information.[344]

Elements of the claim

Loss causation

Section 90 of the Financial Services and Markets Act 2000 allows an investor to claim compensation for the distortion of the operation of the market through the provision of false information. The investor must establish a causal link between the inaccurate prospectus and the loss suffered; this means that an investor must establish that the loss was suffered as a consequence of the fact that the price at which he acquired the shares was distorted by the wrong information. However, there is no further requirement that the investor should have been specifically aware of the false information and have relied upon it in making an investment decision. In a deceit claim or a claim under the Misrepresentation Act 1967, the investor must show that he was induced to act by the false statement[345] (although an inference as to reliance can be drawn from the facts);[346] if the evidence positively shows that the investor was unaware of the statement or took no notice of it, the claim will not succeed.[347]

Investor's knowledge of falsehood

A claim brought by an investor who knows that the information contained in a prospectus is false is likely to fail irrespective of the particular remedy pursued. An investor who knows that information is false cannot claim to have been induced to act on it and a deceit or misrepresentation claim will fail for that reason.[348] Equally, in a case based on breach of a duty of

---

[340] FSMA, sch 10, paras 3–4.   [341] FSMA, sch 10, para 5.   [342] FSMA, sch 10, para 6.
[343] FSMA, sch 10, para 7.   [344] FSMA, s 90(12).
[345] *Edgington v Fitzmaurice* (1885) 29 Ch D 459, CA.
[346] *Smith v Chadwick* (1881) 9 App Cas 187, HL, 196 *per* Lord Blackburn.
[347] *Smith v Chadwick* (1881) 9 App Cas 187, HL.
[348] But the investor is not required to make inquiries to verify the accuracy of information: *Aaron's Reefs Ltd v Twiss* [1896] AC 273, HL, 279 *per* Lord Halsbury LC.

care, an investor could not credibly claim that the mistaken advice caused the loss when he or she was actually aware of the mistake and proceeded anyway. Under the Financial Services and Markets Act 2000, a person who would otherwise be a responsible person can defend the claim by showing that the investor acquired the shares with knowledge of the inaccuracy.[349]

Knowledge of falsehood by the persons responsible for the statement

An investor bringing a claim under section 90 is not required to show that the responsible persons knew that the offending statements were wrong. Lack of such knowledge on the part of responsible persons is relevant only to the extent that this may provide the basis for a defence where they can establish that they believed on reasonable grounds that the information was true. There are some similarities in this respect with the claim for compensation under the Misrepresentation Act 1967. There the claimant is not required to prove negligence but the defendant can escape liability by establishing that he or she reasonably believed that the statements were true.[350] The mental element is important in an action for deceit where the claimant must establish that the maker of a statement knew that it was false, did not have an honest belief in its truth, or was reckless as to its veracity.[351] In a claim based on breach of duty of care, it is for the claimant to show that the maker of the statement failed to act with sufficient care.

Liability for silence

The general law regarding liability for silence or failure to warn is restrictive. Keeping quiet does not, as a general rule, amount to deceit and the law of tort does not readily impose a duty of care to warn others of potential dangers.[352] Equally, unless silence has the effect of making what is said untrue, there is no claim for misrepresentation under the Misrepresentation Act 1967. Under the Financial Services and Markets Act 2000, however, inadequate information can give rise to liability even if it does not render what is said inaccurate. The omission of information required in order to satisfy the prospectus disclosure requirements is actionable, as is the failure to produce a supplementary prospectus when required.[353]

Amount of compensation

The rules relating to the amount of damages that may be awarded to a successful claimant are more generous in deceit claims than those based on breach of duty of care because the latter are subject to remoteness rules limiting liability only to foreseeable losses resulting from the breach of duty, whereas a person who can establish that he was deceived can claim all losses flowing directly from the transaction induced by the fraud whether or not those losses were foreseeable.[354] The deceit rules have also been held to apply to claims under the Misrepresentation Act 1967.[355] The Financial Services and Markets Act 2000 provides no

---

[349] FSMA, sch 10, para 6.
[350] Misrepresentation Act 1967, s 2(1). *Howard Marine & Dredging Co Ltd v A Ogden & Sons (Excavations) Ltd* [1978] QB 574, CA.
[351] *Derry v Peek* (1889) 14 App Cas 337, HL.   [352] *Smith v Littlewoods Organization Ltd* [1987] 2 AC 241, HL.
[353] FSMA, s 90(1)(b)(ii) and (11).   [354] *Doyle v Olby (Ironmongers) Ltd* [1969] 2 QB 158, CA.
[355] *Royscot Trust Ltd v Rogerson* [1991] 2 QB 297, CA. This extension of the deceit rules to circumstances where the defendant has not deliberately misled the claimant has been criticized: RJA Hooley, 'Damages and the Misrepresentation Act 1967' (1991) 107 LQR 547. In *Smith New Court Securities Ltd v Scrimgeour Vickers (Asset Management) Ltd* [1997] AC 254, HL, 282–3 Lord Steyn noted that there was a question whether the loose wording of the Misrepresentation Act 1967 compelled the court so to extend the deceit rules, but he expressly refrained from giving a concluded view on the correctness of the *Royscot* decision. Lord Browne-Wilkinson was equally restrained (at 267).

explicit guidance on the basis upon which statutory compensation is to be assessed. Cases on older companies legislation provisions that provided for compensation for untrue prospectuses applied the deceit rules.[356] Whilst the different statutory context means that such cases need to be treated with some caution, there is sufficient similarity between the modern statutory regime and its predecessors in this respect to suggest that the courts may continue to apply the deceit rules.[357]

In *Smith New Court Securities Ltd v Scrimgeour Vickers (Asset Management) Ltd*[358] the House of Lords reviewed the rules governing the assessment of damages in tort for deceit. This case involved a sale and purchase of shares that had been induced by deliberate misstatement. The House of Lords rejected a simple but inflexible rule to the effect that the claimant's basic measure of damages was the difference between the price paid for the shares and the market price that the shares would have had on the date of purchase if the market had not been distorted by the false information as being both wrong in principle and liable to produce manifest injustice. The overriding principle was that the victim of the tort was entitled to be compensated for all actual loss flowing directly from the transaction induced by the wrongdoer. In some circumstances, the difference between the price paid for property and the market price that it would have had on the date of the transaction but for the tort might be the appropriate measure of this loss, but in others a different measure, such as the difference between the price paid for the property and the price at which it was later disposed of, might be required in order to give the claimant full compensation in accordance with the general principle.

An issue that is likely to concern an investor is whether he can recover for the decline in the value of the shares that reflect post-acquisition movements in the market generally. An inflexible date of transaction rule would preclude recovery for losses resulting from post-acquisition market movements, but under the more flexible approach adopted in the *Smith New Court* case they are potentially recoverable. However, even though this measure is quite generous (more so than the measure in the tort of negligence), the investor must still show that the loss was attributable to the transaction induced by the misstatement and was a direct consequence of it. Establishing causation is a complex issue of which it has been said that: 'no satisfactory theory capable of solving the infinite variety of practical problems has been found.'[359] Where an investor has acquired shares at a price that is distorted by a misstatement and still holds those shares when the market subsequently crashes, the correct conclusion, depending on an assessment of the circumstances, could be that the additional loss flows from the investor's decision to retain those shares rather than being a direct consequence of the original transaction.[360]

---

[356] *Clark v Urquhart* [1930] AC 28, HL. Viscount Sumner (at 56) explained that the statutory action was intended to give the remedy which in *Derry v Peek* the House of Lords had limited to those who could prove deceit. See also Lord Tomlin (at 76): 'the effect of the section is to create a statutory tort having within the ambit prescribed by the section the same characteristics and consequence as the corresponding common law tort based on misrepresentation except that the complainant is relieved of the necessity of alleging and proving fraud.'

[357] P Davies, *Liability for Misstatements to the Market: A Discussion Paper* (HM Treasury, March 2007) para 107 takes the view that 'It seems likely that the courts would apply the same approach as is followed in the case of common law claims for deceit, since the section is closely modelled on the common law tort.' But compare A Alcock, 'Liability for Misinforming the Market' [2011] JBL 243. Cartwright contends that it is entirely possible that the Supreme Court could depart from the deceit measure: Cartwright, *Misrepresentation, Mistake and Non-Disclosure*, para 7-62.

[358] [1997] AC 254, HL.

[359] *Smith New Court Securities Ltd v Scrimgeour Vickers (Asset Management) Ltd* [1997] AC 254, HL, 284–5 *per* Lord Steyn.

[360] For discussion of breaks in the chain of causation in a fraud case see *Invertec Limited v De Mol Holding BV, Henricus Albertus de Mol* [2009] EWHC 2471 (Ch) at [381]–[386].

It is usually said that speculation about alternative transactions that an investor might have entered into but for the fraud is out of place in the assessment of damages for fraud.[361] However, this view has been questioned: it has been argued that since case law establishes that there are circumstances in which a claimant's compensation can include a sum representing a profit that would have been obtained from entering into some other transaction, it must in principle be equally relevant to take account of any hypothetical alternative loss; not to do so 'would be not merely difficult but impossible to defend.'[362]

Under section 74(2)(f) of the Insolvency Act 1986 a sum due to any member of a company in his character of a member by way of dividends, profits, or otherwise is not deemed to be a debt of the company payable to that member in a case of competition between himself and any other creditor not a member of a company. This statutory subordination in liquidation does not apply to claims for damages for misrepresentation by a purchaser of shares but the position of a subscriber for shares is more uncertain.[363]

Civil Liability for False Prospectuses—Assessment

Standards of accuracy in relation to prospectuses are perceived to be high in the UK and this has been linked in part to civil liability standards.[364] The background threat of civil sanctions may hold in check the incentives for corporate managers to fabricate prospectus information and/or for financial and professional intermediaries to take risks in verifying its accuracy and completeness. Yet if, or to the extent that, this is so it is noteworthy that the low level of actual enforcement activity has not compromised the deterrent force of civil sanctions. One of the most striking features of the UK position is the paucity of modern cases in which investors have pursued civil claims, statutory or otherwise, relating to allegedly false prospectuses. There is no reported case of an investor succeeding in bringing a claim for compensation under the special statutory regime in the Financial Services and Markets Act 2000 or its predecessor, the Financial Services Act 1986. Nor is there much evidence in the reported decisions of investors even commencing such claims—the LexisNexis database from 1986 onwards reveals just one case where the statutory claim was directly in point: aggrieved investors in a rights issue tainted by an inaccurate set of listing particulars sought orders for discovery to obtain documentary evidence and information with a view to establishing whether it would be worthwhile to sue the issuer's accountants under the equivalent provision in the Financial Services Act 1986 or for common law negligence. The application was rejected on grounds relating to civil procedure rules on discovery.[365] (The investors' case against the accountants and the company's banks was eventually settled out of court; the company's managing director was convicted of fraud and given an eight-year prison sentence.[366]) In one other case, claims for compensation under the relevant provision of the Financial Services Act 1986

---

[361] *Smith New Court*, 283F-G *per* Lord Steyn.

[362] *Yam Seng Pte Limited (A company registered in Singapore) v International Trade Corporation Limited* [2013] EWHC 111 (QB), [209]–[217].

[363] *Soden v British & Commonwealth Holdings plc* [1998] AC 298, HL. The interface between shareholder and creditor hierarchy, capital maintenance and investor compensation claims in respect of false disclosures has been brought before the Court of Justice: Case C-174/12 *Alfred Hirmann v Immofinanz AG*. The Advocate General's opinion (September 2013) does not consider an obligation to repay investors who acquired shares on the basis of false information to be an infringement of maintenance of capital principles.

[364] Davies, *Discussion Paper*, para 71 reporting the views of respondents consulted by Professor Davies in the first stage of his review.

[365] *Axa Equity and Law Life Assurance Society plc and others v National Westminster Bank plc* Chancery Division, 2 February 1998, Court of Appeal, 7 May 1998.

[366] J, Willcock, 'Resort Hotels Chief Jailed for Eight Years,' *The Independent* (London), 2 April 1997, Business Section, 21.

were relevant but the litigation was primarily about a compromise of claims in insolvency.[367] Section 90 itself was considered briefly in a case reported in 2010, but the allegedly false statements in the case were not contained in a prospectus or listing particulars and, accordingly, the court did not hesitate to hold that section 90 (which, in any event, was not one of the pleaded causes of action) did not assist the claimants.[368] Historically, it has been relatively uncommon even to find newspaper stories to the effect that investors are considering suing for having been sold securities on the basis of a false prospectus.

However, investor attitudes could be starting to change.[369] In particular, one part of the fallout from the financial crisis of 2007–9 has been an attempt by a coordinated group of investors who acquired shares in a rescue rights issue by the Royal Bank of Scotland to seek compensation from the bank and its directors for misleading statements in the rights issue prospectus and related documentation. This action has the potential to become a landmark decision on the role of civil litigation in the regulation of primary capital market activity. However, there are significant civil procedure hurdles to collective suits that will have to be overcome for this potential to be realized. Also striking by their absence are modern cases relating to prospectus inaccuracies in which companies, or shareholders acting on their behalf, have sought to hold directors liable for breach of the general duty of care and skill owed to the company under section 174 of the Companies Act 2006. As discussed further later in this chapter, in general, litigation against directors plays a quite limited role as a mechanism of corporate governance control in the UK.

Administrative Sanctions for Defective Prospectuses

The FCA has a range of enforcement powers at its disposal in respect of breaches of the *Prospectus Rules*. The basic framework is the same as that already discussed in this chapter in the context of the *Listing Rules*. The powers include: ordering the suspension or prohibition of an offer to the public or admission to trading on a regulated market of transferable securities[370] issuing public censure notices;[371] and imposing fines.[372] Restitution can also be sought in respect of profits made or losses or other adverse effects resulting from requirements imposed by or under the Act, which would include the *Prospectus Rules*.[373] If the contravention also amounts to market abuse, the FCA may itself order restitution without the need for court proceedings.[374] Where there is market abuse, the FCA may also impose penalties including the possibility of unlimited fines.[375]

When the FSA (the FCA's predecessor) was first established, there was considerable concern about how it would use its large armoury of enforcement powers.[376] As things turned out, the FSA never actually exercised its general enforcement powers in relation to information contained in a published prospectus. Part of the explanation for the absence of ex post enforcement could be that pre-publication regulatory scrutiny of prospectuses provides an alternative control mechanism. The potential for administrative actions to play an important role in relation to the quality of information in prospectuses is illustrated by the use that the FSA made of the extended range of disciplinary powers that it has with respect to regulated firms and persons performing significant influence functions within them. These powers

---

[367] *Re Barings plc* [2001] 2 BCLC 159.   [368] *Hall v Cable and Wireless plc* [2010] 1 BCLC 95, QBD.
[369] On whether there are grounds for thinking that things are changing in the UK in the direction of an increasing propensity for civil litigation see Davies, *Final Report*, paras 12–18.
[370] FSMA, ss 87K and 87L.   [371] FSMA, ss 87M and 91(3).   [372] FSMA, s 91(1A).
[373] FSMA, ss 382–6.   [374] FSMA, s 384.   [375] FSMA, Pt 8.
[376] E Ferran, 'Examining the United Kingdom's Experience in Adopting the Single Financial Regulator Model' (2003) 28 *Brooklyn Journal of International Law* 257.

were used by the FSA to impose a fine (under section 67 of the Financial Services and Markets Act 2000) on the former finance director of a bank that collapsed in 2008 who had failed to update the board on the bank's deteriorating financial position. This oversight had resulted in the publication of inaccurate rights issue documentation, which had to be corrected by an updated trading statement amounting to a profits warning, and may have contributed to the eventual failure of the rights issue. The director's attempt to challenge the FSA's action by way of judicial review of its procedures was unsuccessful.[377]

Action taken by the Hong Kong Securities and Futures Commission (SFC) against Hontex International Holdings Company Limited in respect of a false and misleading prospectus provides another strong illustration of the role that administrative sanctions can play in this context.[378] Hontex was listed on the Hong Kong Stock Exchange on 24 December 2009 at an IPO price of HK$2.15 per share. On 30 March 2010, trading in Hontex shares was suspended at the direction of the SFC. The closing price of Hontex shares on 30 March 2010 was HK$2.06 per share. On 20 June 2012, the SFC and Hontex agreed a set of facts whereby Hontex acknowledged that it had been reckless in allowing materially false and misleading information to be included in its prospectus which induced investors to subscribe and purchase its shares. On the basis of the admitted facts, Hontex was ordered to make an offer to public shareholders who had subscribed for Hontex shares in the IPO or purchased them in the secondary market to repurchase the shares at HK$2.06 per share, amounting in total to a HK$1.03 billion buy-back offer. In addition, Hontex was ordered to pay the SFC's costs fixed in the sum of HK$7 million.

Criminal Liability for Defective Prospectuses

Issuing a prospectus that contains false information, promises, or forecasts, or which conceals material facts, could be an offence under the Financial Services Act 2012, sections 89–90. Section 89 makes it an offence for a person knowingly or recklessly to make a statement which they know to be false or misleading in a material respect, or dishonestly to conceal any material facts if they do so with the intention of inducing, or being reckless as to whether their action may induce, another person to enter into a relevant agreement. Section 90 provides for the offence of intentionally creating misleading impressions as to the market or price or value of investments in order to induce an investment decision. A person who is found guilty of any of these offences is liable to a maximum penalty of seven years' imprisonment plus a fine.[379] The application of this type of sanction in relation to public offers of securities is illustrated by *R v Feld*[380] where the Court of Appeal upheld a six-year sentence against a director for offences relating to a rights issue prospectus under a statutory predecessor offence. The prospectus had contained serious misinformation that overstated profits and understated liabilities. The figures had been supported by forged documents supplied to the company's auditors by its managing director, Feld. The company had raised over £20 million by the rights issue but went into insolvent liquidation the following year. In upholding the length of the conviction, the court emphasized the vital importance of maintaining the confidence of the City and financial institutions in the veracity of information contained in prospectuses and similar documents.

The issuance of a false prospectus may be part of a broader scheme that falls within the scope of a number of criminal offences. For example, in 2003, two directors, Nicolaides and Atkins,

---

[377] *R (on the application of Christopher Willford) v FSA* [2013] EWCA 677.
[378] Securities and Futures Commission, 'Hontex Ordered to Make $1.03 Billion Buy-back Order over Untrue IPO Prospectus', 20 June 2012.
[379] Financial Services Act 2012, s 92.   [380] 6 April 1998, CCA.

were convicted under section 12 of the Criminal Justice Act 1987 of defrauding shareholders of two companies. The companies were supposedly established to provide internet access to subscribers and low-cost telephone calls and were promoted, in various prospectuses, as attractive investment opportunities in a new and apparently lucrative technology market. In fact the companies were used as vehicles by which the defendants fraudulently enriched themselves using a variety of intermediate companies and businesses which were controlled by the defendants. However, Atkins and another director were found not guilty of an offence under the statutory predecessor to the Financial Services Act 2012, sections 89–90.[381]

The Fraud Act 2006, in force from 15 January 2007, provides for a general statutory criminal offence of fraud that can be committed by false representation, by failure to disclose information, or by abuse of position. In each case the act must be done dishonestly and with the intention of making a gain or causing a loss or risk of loss to another, but the gain or loss does not actually have to take place. On conviction a defendant may be sentenced to up to ten years in prison and/or a fine. This new fraud offence has been enacted with a view to removing the complications that can be encountered in prosecuting fraudulent activity. It may be used alongside or in preference to other existing offences.

The high burden of proof in criminal cases is a factor that militates against extensive reliance on the criminal law as a mechanism for curbing abuse. The challenges facing public authorities in seeking to prosecute company directors and others for misleading statements are vividly illustrated by the circumstances surrounding the collapse in July 2013 of the FCA's prosecution of former directors of iSoft, a healthcare software provider, for alleged conspiracy to make misleading statements to the market about the company's financial results.[382] The FCA, and its predecessor, the FSA, had spent seven years and around £5 million investigating the facts but abandoned the prosecution after the first criminal trial resulted in a hung jury and the second collapsed because of irresolvable procedural issues.

Public Offers of Securities by Private Companies

The Companies Act 2006 provides that private limited companies that have a share capital must not offer their securities to the public or allot or agree to allot their securities with a view to their being offered to the public.[383] A statutory prohibition on private companies offering their securities to the public long pre-dates the very detailed regulation of public offers now contained in the Financial Services and Markets Act 2000. The approach to defining an offer of securities to the public in the companies legislation is not the same as that in section 102B of the Financial Services and Markets Act 2000. Although it would be superficially appealing to align the definitions, in the debates in Parliament on the Bill that became the Companies Act 2006 the government maintained the view that the two statutes were directed at different things and that this precluded making the definitions exactly the same.[384]

The Companies Act 2006 does not contain a comprehensive definition of an 'offer to the public' but the essence of the approach in that legislation is that it is an offer that does not have a private character because there is no close connection between the company and the

---

[381] FSA/PN/091/2005 (18 August 2005) and FSA/PN/106/2005 (7 October 2005).

[382] J Rankin, 'Blow to city Watchdog as iSoft Case Collapses' *Guardian*, 23 July 2013, 23.

[383] Companies Act 2006, s 755. There is a presumption that an allotment or an agreement to allot is made with a view to a public offer if that offer is made within six months of the allotment or agreement or before the company receives the whole of the consideration due to it in respect of the securities (s 755(2)).

[384] The evolution of the debate on this issue is traced briefly by Lord McKenzie, speaking on behalf of the government in the Lords: *Hansard*, vol 679, GC 455–6 (14 March 2006), *Hansard*, vol 679, GC 471–3 (15 March 2006). The debate on the point in the House of Commons is at *Hansard*, Standing Committee D, cols 819–25 (18 July 2006).

persons to whom the offer is made.[385] Thus an offer to the public includes an offer to any section of the public, however selected.[386] However, an offer is not regarded as an offer to the public if it can properly be regarded, in all the circumstances, as not being calculated to result, directly or indirectly, in securities of the company becoming available to persons other than those receiving the offer, or otherwise being a private concern of the person receiving it and the person making it.[387] An offer is to be regarded (unless the contrary is proved) as being a private concern of the person receiving it and the person making it if:

(a) it is made to a person already connected with the company and, where it is made on terms allowing that person to renounce his rights, the rights may only be renounced in favour of another person already connected with the company; or

(b) it is an offer to subscribe for securities to be held under an employees' share scheme and, where it is made on terms allowing that person to renounce his rights, the rights may only be renounced in favour of another person entitled to hold securities under the scheme, or a person already connected with the company.[388]

Persons already connected with the company for this purpose are existing members or employees of the company, members of the family of members or employees, widows, widowers, or surviving civil partners of members or employees, existing debenture holders, and trustees of trusts of which the principal beneficiaries are persons in the preceding categories.[389]

The meaning of 'securities' for the prohibition on public offers by private companies is limited to shares or debentures.[390] It is possible that an offer of other securities, such as options or warrants, could be caught as amounting to an indirect offer of shares or debentures.[391]

The prohibition on public offers of securities by private companies could impinge upon preparatory steps taken by a private company that is intending to convert to a public company in order to make an IPO. However, the Companies Act 2006 provides a carve-out that should be helpful in this situation: a company is not in breach if either it acts in good faith in pursuance of arrangements under which it is to re-register as a public company before the securities are allotted, or as part of the terms of the offer it undertakes to re-register as a public company within a specified period of not more than six months, and that undertaking is complied with.[392]

Under the predecessor legislation to the Companies Act 2006, it was an offence for a private company to infringe the prohibition on offers to the public. Criminal sanctions are no longer used in this context. On the application by any member or creditor of the company or the Secretary of State, the court can restrain a proposed contravention.[393] If the contravention has already occurred, the court must require the company to re-register as a public company unless it does not meet the requirements for re-registration or it would be impractical or undesirable to require it to do so.[394] In those circumstances, the court may make a remedial order (which may require a person knowingly concerned in the contravention to purchase the securities) and/or order the compulsory winding up of the company.[395]

---

[385] As indicated by Lord McKenzie on behalf of the government in Parliamentary debate during the passage of the Companies Bill 2006: *Hansard*, vol 679, GC col 472 (15 March 2006).

[386] Companies Act 2006, s 756(2).   [387] Companies Act 2006, s 756(3).

[388] Companies Act 2006, s 756(4).   [389] Companies Act 2006, s 756(5)–(6).

[390] Companies Act 2006, s 755(5).

[391] This was suggested by Lord McKenzie, the government spokesperson, in Parliamentary debate during the passage of the Companies Bill 2006: *Hansard*, vol 679, GC col 453 (14 March 2006).

[392] Companies Act 2006, s 755(3)–(4).   [393] Companies Act 2006, s 757.

[394] Companies Act 2006, s 758.   [395] Companies Act 2006, ss 758(3)–(4) and 759.

The persons who have standing to apply for a post-contravention order are those who were members or creditors at the time of the offer, those who became members as a result of the offer, and the Secretary of State.[396] Contravention does not affect the validity of an allotment of securities.[397]

Crowdfunding

The restrictions on private companies making public offers of their securities have implications for crowdfunding, that is the provision of often small sums of finance by large numbers of investors to start-ups and growing business.[398] One structure that may sidestep this concern is for private companies seeking equity funding to become subsidiaries of a crowdfunding vehicle that is established as a public company. Another option is for crowdfunding projects to be structured as collective investment schemes.[399] In addition to the restrictions on capital raising by private companies, due account must be taken of the requirements relating to financial promotions and public offer prospectus requirements. Dedicated crowdfunding regulatory exemptions could be useful but, as ever, questions arise about striking a balance between facilitating issuer access to finance and investor protection.[400]

Periodic and Episodic Disclosure Obligations of Listed and Quoted Companies

Companies that have taken the key step of opening up to outside investors by having their securities admitted to trading on an organized trading platform become subject to enhanced regulatory requirements. This is a factor that companies that are considering going public must factor into their evaluation of the pros and cons. Some of the continuing obligations that the UK of its own volition has chosen to impose on premium listed issuers via the FCA *Listing Rules* have been considered already. This section deals mainly with continuing obligations with respect to disclosure derived principally from the Transparency Obligations Directive and the Market Abuse Directive/expected Regulation. Corporate governance disclosure requirements derived from the Accounting Directives are also mentioned. The Transparency Obligations Directive also contains requirements for major shareholders to disclose their holdings and entitlements to shares when they cross certain thresholds and for issuers, in turn, to disclose this information to the markets. The disclosure obligations with respect to major holdings are touched on briefly, as are certain other continuing obligations for issuers not previously examined.[401]

---

[396] Companies Act 2006, s 758(4). [397] Companies Act 2006, s 760.

[398] O Stacey, S Lovegrove, and D Murphy, 'Crowdfunding: Possibilities and Prohibitions' (2012) 23(1) PLC 18.

[399] Association for UK Interactive Entertainment, *UKIE Crowd Funding Report: A Proposal to Facilitate Crowd Funding in the UK* (February 2012).

[400] The protracted process involved in drafting the regulatory rules needed to make the crowdfunding exemption in the US JOBS Act operational indicates that striking this balance is not necessarily a straightforward exercise. See J Eaglesham, 'Crowdfunding Efforts Draw Suspicion' *Wall Street Journal Online*, 17 January 2013. The SEC published proposed rules to permit companies to offer and sell securities through crowdfunding in October 2013. Immediate media commentary on the proposed rules noted that the exemption differed greatly from earlier proposals and ideas, and doubted whether it achieved the right balance between investor protection and minimizing red tape.

[401] Continuing obligations with respect to the structure of secondary offerings by listed issuers (rights issues, placings etc) are examined in detail in ch 5.

Issuer Disclosure Obligations Derived from the Transparency Obligations Directive

Periodic financial reporting obligations

The Transparency Obligations Directive sets out requirements on the content and timing of annual and half-yearly financial reports.[402] In its original form, the Transparency Obligations Directive in addition introduced the concept of mandatory interim management statements (IMS) for issuers of shares that did not produce quarterly reports. Mandatory quarterly or interim reporting quickly attracted criticism, however, because it was perceived to have had the unintended side effect of fostering undue short-termism.[403] It came to be understood that quarterly earnings figures could be dominated by random fluctuations or worse, managed to avoid them.[404] Abolishing this requirement was put forward by the European Commission as a streamlining measure that, it was thought, would not compromise investor protection. Member States will not be permitted to continue to impose the requirement to publish periodic financial information on a more frequent basis and to this extent, the revised Transparency Obligations Directive thus becomes maximal in its approach. However, this restriction on Member State autonomy is qualified: Member States may nevertheless require issuers to publish additional periodic financial information if such requirement does not constitute a significant financial burden and if the additional information required is proportionate to the factors that contribute to investment decisions. Furthermore, the restriction is without prejudice to any additional information that may be required by sectorial European legislation and, in particular, Member States may require the publication of additional periodic financial information by financial institutions. Moreover, a regulated market may require issuers which have their securities admitted to trading on that regulated market to publish additional periodic financial information in all or some of its market segments.

The periodic disclosure requirements in the Transparency Obligations Directive must be applied (with certain exceptions) to all issuers that have securities admitted to trading on a regulated market situated or operating within a Member State. For an issuer of shares, the home state for the purposes of this Directive is the state in which it has its registered office.[405] In the UK, implementation of the Transparency Obligations Directive was effected by means of changes to the Financial Services and Markets Act 2000 that were inserted by the Companies Act 2006 and by regulatory rules made under the new statutory powers.[406]

Under the FCA's *DTR* issuers whose transferable securities are admitted to trading on a regulated market and whose home state is the UK, whether premium or standard listed or admitted to the High Growth Segment, are required to make public their annual financial reports at the latest four months after the end of each financial year and to ensure that they remain publicly available for at least five years.[407] The annual financial report must include the audited financial statements, a management report, and responsibility statements.[408]

---

[402] Transparency Obligations Directive, Arts 4–5. The text discusses amendments made by Directive 2013/50/EU which are expected to become effective in the UK during 2014.

[403] COM(2011) 683; Kay, *The Kay Review*, paras 10.1–10.19.   [404] Kay, *The Kay Review*, para 10.19.

[405] Transparency Obligations Directive, Art 2(1)(i).

[406] FSMA, ss 89A–89N (inserted by Companies Act 2006, ss 1266–1268), and FSMA, ss 90A and 90B (inserted by Companies Act 2006, s 1270), FSMA, s 100 (inserted by Companies Act 2006, s 1271) and FSMA, s 103(1) (amended by Companies Act 2006, s 1265). The Companies Act 2006 also made certain minor and consequential amendments: (Companies Act 2006, s 1272 and Sch 15). The relevant rules are in the FCA *Handbook, Disclosure Rules and Transparency Rules* (*DTR*).

[407] *DTR* 4.1.1R–4.1.4. Under the revised Transparency Obligations Directive, Art 6, annual reports must remain publicly available for at least ten years.

[408] *DTR* 4.1.5.

For EU-incorporated issuers, consolidated financial statements will normally be prepared in accordance with IFRS.[409] The signed audit report must be disclosed in full to the public together with the annual financial report.[410] The management report must contain a fair review of the issuer's business and a description of the principal risks and uncertainties facing the issuer.[411] Other information required to be included in the management report includes an indication of important events that have occurred since the end of the financial year, the issuer's likely development, activities in the field of research and development, information on own share acquisitions, the existence of branches, financial risk management objectives and policies, and exposure to financial risks.[412]

Responsibility statements must be made by the persons responsible within the issuer and in respect of each such person must set out to the best of his or her knowledge that: the financial statements give a true and fair view of the assets, liabilities, financial position and profit or loss of the issuer and the undertakings included in the consolidation taken as a whole; and that the management report includes a fair review of the development and performance of the business and the position of the issuer and the undertakings included in the consolidation taken as a whole, together with a description of the principal risks and uncertainties that they face.[413]

Half-yearly financial reports must be made public as soon as possible, but no later than two months after the end of the period to which the report relates and they must remain available to the public for at least five years.[414] Half-yearly financial reports must include a condensed set of financial statements, an interim management report, and responsibility statements.[415] For an issuer of shares, the half-yearly report must also include a fair review of major related party transactions.[416]

There is provision for non-EU issuers that are incorporated in countries whose relevant laws are considered 'equivalent' to be exempted from the rules on annual financial reports and half-yearly financial reports.[417] The issue of equivalence of accounting standards has been discussed already in this chapter in relation to prospectuses. More generally, the FCA considers the issuer continuing disclosure regimes of Switzerland, the United States, and Canada to be equivalent in many respects to the *DTR* requirements and therefore exempts issuers from those countries from compliance with those UK domestic requirements.[418]

Other continuing obligations derived from the Transparency Obligations Directive

The Transparency Obligations Directive contains provisions relating to the notification obligations in respect of the acquisition or disposal of major holdings in shares and certain other financial instruments. These requirements, which apply to issuers that have the UK as their home state, are implemented in the UK by chapter 5 of the FCA *DTR*.[419] Chapter 5 imposes obligations on holders to notify the issuer and, in the case of a notification relating to shares admitted to trading on a regulated market, the FCA. The issuer must then make public all of the information contained in the notification through a Regulated Information Service (RIS). An issuer must also, at the end of each calendar month during which an increase or

---

[409] *DTR* 4.1.6. [410] *DTR* 4.1.7(3). [411] *DTR* 4.1.8–4.1.10.
[412] *DTR* 4.1.11. [413] *DTR* 4.1.12.
[414] *DTR* 4.2.2. Under the revised Transparency Obligations Directive, the publication period is extended to three months. Reports must remain publicly available for at least ten years.
[415] *DTR* 4.2.3. [416] *DTR* 4.2.8. [417] Transparency Obligations Directive, Art 23.
[418] *DTR* 4.4.8–4.4.9. For detail of the scope of the exemptions, see <http://www.fca.org.uk/firms/markets/ukla/information-for-issuers/non-eea-regimes> accessed July 2013.
[419] Under statutory authority provided by FSMA, ss 89A and 89B–89D (inserted by the Companies Act 2006).

decrease has occurred, disclose to the public the total number of voting rights and capital in respect of each class of share in issue and the total number of voting rights attaching to shares of the issuer which are held by it in treasury. There are also disclosure obligations in respect of the acquisition or disposal by an issuer of its own shares.

Chapter 6 of the FCA *DTR* implements other continuing obligations under the Transparency Obligations Directive for issuers whose home state is the UK.[420] These include an obligation to ensure equal treatment for all holders of shares who are in the same position.[421] Other continuing obligations in this chapter are concerned with ensuring that holders of securities can exercise their rights, including using proxies, and with ensuring that they are informed of changes in the rights attaching to securities and about arrangements for meetings, issues of new shares, and the payment of dividends.

Annual Corporate Governance Disclosures by Issuers Admitted to Trading on a Regulated Market

All UK companies that are admitted to trading on a regulated market are required by the *DTR* to provide a corporate governance statement in their annual report.[422] To avoid duplication, premium listed issuers that discharge the comply or explain rule in relation to the UK Corporate Governance Code imposed by the continuing obligations regime in the *Listing Rules* are deemed to satisfy certain *DTR* requirements.[423] The *DTR* requirements with respect to corporate governance (and the deeming provision with respect to comply or explain) are extended to overseas companies with a premium or standard listing.[424]

Periodic Disclosure by AIM Issuers

AIM issuers are required by the AIM *Rules for Companies* to produce annual and half-yearly reports. EU incorporated issuers must prepare and present their accounts in accordance with IFRS but other issuers are not required to reconcile accounts that have been drawn up under US GAAP, Canadian GAAP, Australian IFRS, or Japanese GAAP.[425] The *LR* and most of the *DTR* do not apply to AIM issuers.[426] AIM issuers are not formally subject to the UK Corporate Governance Code but it is regarded as an aspirational standard.

Episodic Disclosure Obligations

Article 6 of the Market Abuse Directive currently completes the EU regulatory framework for disclosure by issuers by obliging Member States to require an issuer of financial instruments to inform the public as soon as possible of inside information which directly concerns the said issuer, save where this would prejudice its legitimate interests. The Directive applies to all issuers with securities admitted to trading on a regulated market. The Directive provides that each Member State must apply the requirements provided for in the Directive to (a) actions carried out on its territory or abroad concerning financial instruments that are

---

[420] Under statutory authority provided by FSMA, ss 89A and 89E (inserted by the Companies Act 2006).
[421] *DTR* 6.1.3.
[422] *DTR* 7.2. FSMA, s 89O and *DTR* 7 are the vehicle for giving effect to Directive 2013/34/EU of the European Parliament and of the Council of 26 June 2013 on the annual financial statements, consolidated financial statements and related reports of certain types of undertakings, amending Directive 2006/43/EC of the European Parliament and of the Council and repealing Council Directives 78/660/EEC and 83/349/EEC, [2013] OJ L182/19, Art 20.
[423] *DTR* 7.2.4.   [424] *LR* 9.8.7–9.8.7A (premium); *LR* 14.3.24R (standard).   [425] *AIM Rules*, r 19.
[426] *DTR* 5 (vote holder and issuer notification rules) does apply.

admitted to trading on a regulated market situated or operating within its territory or for which a request for admission to trading on such a market has been made; and (b) actions carried out on its territory concerning financial instruments that are admitted to trading on a regulated market in a Member State or for which a request for admission to trading on such market has been made.[427] So far as issuer disclosure required by Article 6 is concerned, UK implementation is effected by chapter 1 of the FCA *DTR*. The *DTR* provide that a listed issuer must notify an RIS as soon as possible of any inside information which directly concerns the issuer unless an exception applies.[428] Exceptionally, an issuer may, under its own responsibility, delay the public disclosure of inside information, such as not to prejudice its legitimate interests provided that: (1) such omission would not be likely to mislead the public; (2) any person receiving the information owes the issuer a duty of confidentiality; and (3) the issuer is able to ensure the confidentiality of that information.[429] The duty of public disclosure of inside information is retained in the new Market Abuse Regulation (Article 12, according to the numbering in the consolidated version of the text endorsed by the European Parliament in September 2013).

AIM issuers are currently subject to a duty of general disclosure of price-sensitive information under the AIM *Rules*.[430] Under the new Market Abuse Regulation, which will replace the Market Abuse Directive, the existing requirement for public disclosure of inside information requirement will be extended to financial instruments traded on an MTF (which AIM is) or on an Organized Trading Facility (OTF).[431] This is intended to promote a level playing field among trading venues and facilities and to assist in the prevention and detection of market abuse. Nevertheless, the disclosure framework will be adapted to the characteristics and needs of issuers, whose financial instruments are admitted to trading on SME growth markets so as not to deter smaller issuers from raising capital on the capital markets.[432]

Civil Liability for Periodic and Episodic Disclosures

The Financial Services and Markets Act 2000, section 90A and schedule 10A (as substituted by the Financial Services and Markets Act 2000 (Liability of Issuers) Regulations 2010)[433] provide investors (purchasers, sellers, and holders of securities) with a claim for compensation in respect of misleading statements in, or omissions from, periodic and episodic disclosures (including voluntary disclosures), and for disclosure delays. The statutory liability regime applies to all issuers of securities admitted to trading on a securities market situated or operating in the UK (this would include AIM as well as the various segments of the LSE Main Market) and also to UK home state issuers[434] with securities admitted to trading on a securities market elsewhere.[435] The statutory regime applies to all information published by an issuer by means of a recognized information service or whose availability has been announced by means of such a service.[436]

The statutory liability regime in respect of issuer disclosures is intended to provide certainty in an area where it was previously unclear whether any common law duty was owed by issuers and their directors to investors. Resolution of that uncertainty became an issue during

---

[427] Market Abuse Directive, Art 10.   [428] *DTR* 2.2.1.   [429] *DTR* 2.5.   [430] AIM *Rules*, r 11.
[431] Market Abuse Regulation, Art 12 (numbered from September 2013 legislative text).
[432] COM(2011) 651, para 3.4.3.3.   [433] SI 2010/1192.
[434] FSMA, sch 10A, para 1(3) explains how the home state of an issuer is to be identified.
[435] FSMA, sch 10A, para 1.Choice of law rules will determine whether the UK statutory regime applies in a case with international dimensions: W-G Ringe and A Hellgardt, 'The International Dimension of Issuer Liability— Liability and Choice of Law from a Transatlantic Perspective' (2011) 31 *Oxford Journal of Legal Studies* 23.
[436] FSMA, sch 10A, para 2.

the mid 2000s because the Transparency Obligations Directive imposed an obligation on Member States to have in their national laws a liability regime in respect of periodic disclosures. The first version of the statutory regime, which was inserted into the Financial Services and Markets Act 2000 by the Companies Act 2006, did not go far beyond the minimum that the government at the time felt that it needed to do to discharge the UK's Community obligations. However, it was always recognized that this was an interim step taken in a hurry, and that the issues required closer examination. Thereafter, following a review by Professor Paul Davies of Oxford University, in 2010 the original statutory framework was substituted by the more wide-ranging issuer disclosures liability regime that is now in operation.[437]

In the revised version of the regime, the category of potential claimants is widely drawn: not only purchasers but also sellers and those who continue to hold securities are within its scope.[438] The claimant must establish a loss in respect of the securities that is attributable to the inaccurate disclosure or disclosure delay (loss causation).[439] As discussed earlier in this chapter, loss causation is also an element of the prospectus liability regime under section 90 of the Financial Services and Markets Act 2000. However, in contrast to section 90 liability, in a section 90A/schedule 10A claim that is based on inaccuracies in, or omissions from, published information (but not a claim based on delayed disclosure), the claimant must also demonstrate that in acquiring, disposing of, or continuing to hold the securities it acted in reliance on the published information and that this reliance was reasonable. Authorities in the English law on misrepresentation establish that an inference of reliance may be drawn from the facts.[440] A similar approach may be adopted in relation to section 90A/schedule 10A liability. An inference drawn from the facts is to be distinguished from a legal presumption of reliance. The classic 'fraud on the market' theory developed in US securities law, which affords investors trading in efficient markets a rebuttable legal presumption of reliance,[441] has not been adopted in section 90A/schedule 10A.

Liability standards in the section 90A/schedule 10A regime are high. For liability to arise in respect of a positive misstatement, the claimant must show that a person carrying managerial responsibility within the issuer in relation to the publication knew about the inaccuracy or was reckless as to its accuracy.[442] 'Recklessness' involves deliberately disregarding an obvious risk and it is not to be equated with negligence or even gross negligence. In respect of an omission from published information, the disclosure failure must amount to a dishonest concealment and a person with managerial responsibility must have known this to be the case.[443] In a delayed disclosure case, there must again be dishonesty on the part of a person with managerial responsibility.[444] For these purposes, the test of dishonesty is that the conduct in question would be regarded as dishonest by persons who regularly trade on the securities market in question, and the person was aware (or must be taken to have been aware) that it was so regarded.[445]

Section 90A/schedule 10 is an issuer-only liability regime. This is strikingly different from the position under the section 90 prospectus liability regime where the issuer, its directors, and other persons who accept responsibility for a prospectus are potentially on the hook.[446] Furthermore, issuers are afforded a (limited) safe harbour: except as specified in schedule 10A issuers are not subject to any liability in respect of disclosure failures to which the schedule applies.[447] This safe harbour is subject to a number of significant

---

[437] Davies, *Discussion Paper*; Davies, *Final Report*. See also: P Davies, 'Liability for Misstatements to the Market: Some Reflections' [2009] *Journal of Corporate Law Studies* 295.

[438] FSMA, sch 10A, paras 3(1) and 5(1).   [439] FSMA, sch 10A, paras 3(1)(b) and 5(1)(b).

[440] *Smith v Chadwick* (1884) 9 App Cas 187 HL.   [441] *Basic v Levinson* 485 US 224 (1988).

[442] FSMA, sch 10A, para 3(2). Directors are among those discharging managerial functions: FSMA, sch 10A, para 8(5).

[443] FSMA, sch 10A, para 3(3).   [444] FSMA, sch 10A, para 5(2).

[445] FSMA, sch 10A, para 5.   [446] *PR* 5.5.   [447] FSMA, sch 10A, para 7.

carveouts that rein in its effect.[448] It does not affect civil liability: (i) under section 90 of the Financial Services and Market Act 2000; (ii) under rules made by virtue of section 954 of the Companies Act 2006;[449] (iii) for breach of contract; (iv) under the Misrepresentation Act 1967; or (v) arising from a person's having assumed responsibility, to a particular person for a particular purpose, for the accuracy or completeness of the information concerned. Nor does it affect liability to a civil penalty or criminal liability. Likewise, it does not affect the FCA's powers to require restitution or to seek a court order for restitution.[450]

Directors and others who may have actually contributed to the disclosure failure are not subject to any liability other than to the issuer in respect of losses within the scope of section 90A/schedule 10 (although this safe harbour is also subject to the qualifications mentioned in the previous paragraph). Why issuer-only liability? Not to include the directors of an issuer within the scope of a dedicated civil liability regime for issuer disclosures could be thought controversial.[451] At first blush, issuer-only liability does not appear to be well suited to the task of making sure that the individuals who are responsible for putting together corporate disclosures take the appropriate degree of care to prevent the dissemination of false information and to keep the market updated on new developments. However, it is a feature of the regime that attracted considerable attention, both on enactment of the original section 90A regime and in the Davies Review that led to the substitution of the now-current regime. That it has been maintained in spite of such close attention suggests that there are strong arguments in its favour.[452]

The reasoning behind this approach depends on placing civil liability for issuer disclosures within a broader frame of reference.[453] A civil liability regime can play a role in deterring careless reporting but it need not do all of the heavy lifting. The view advocated in the Davies Review and broadly accepted by the government was that public enforcement with its lower liability standards (negligence rather than fraud) and its broader scope (sanctions capable of being imposed on directors as well as on issuers) could be expected to do the bulk of the work in deterring careless reporting. Davies noted that public enforcement would be supplemented by the company's ability to seek compensation from its directors for breach of duty, or from advisers or others. He also referred to the possibility of shareholders bringing an action against directors under the new derivative action procedures in the Companies Act 2006. Davies suggested that the adoption of a negligence standard in the private law civil claim could adversely affect disclosure practices by inducing undesirable caution in order to avoid liability. He noted that the fact that directors and officers (D&O) liability insurance could have the effect of shifting loss from directors back to the company as a further factor militating in favour of an issuer-only liability regime.

---

[448] FSMA, sch 10A, para 7(3)–(5). There are some uncertainties about the scope of these carveouts: Alcock, 'Liability for Misinforming the Market'. There was an element of swings and roundabouts in the revisions to the regime by the 2010 Regulations in that the statutory liability and its safe harbour were extended to a wider range of disclosures but at the same time additional qualifications to the safe harbour were applied.

[449] Compensation in respect of breaches of takeover rules.   [450] Under FSMA, s 382 and s 384.

[451] E Ferran, 'Are US-style Investor Suits Coming to the UK?' [2009] *Journal of Corporate Law Studies* 315.

[452] However, the safe harbour is less extensive than as originally enacted.

[453] This paragraph draws on a summary of the arguments in Davies, *Final Report*, 4–5. A further argument, not examined closely by Davies but put forward since in the academic literature is that issuer liability increases the incentives for controlling shareholders (who, as long-term holders, are exposed to the loss-shifting that would result from issuer liability) to monitor management to control fraud risk and, as such, may have a particularly strong deterrent effect in countries where the presence of controlling shareholders continues to be a common feature of corporate ownership: M Gelter, 'Risk-shifting through Issuer Liability and Corporate Monitoring' (2014) 15 *European Business Organization Law Review* (forthcoming).

It is indisputable that opening the floodgates to extensive private enforcement could create more problems than it would solve. However, the credibility of the strategy of preferring public enforcement over a broad expansion of private enforcement is crucially dependent on the effective operation of public enforcement mechanisms.

Administrative and Criminal Sanctions

The FCA's standard range of disciplinary and sanctioning powers is available in respect of issuer disclosure failures with respect to the *DTR*. In addition, disclosure failures could amount to market abuse and/or criminal offences under the Financial Services Act 2012, sections 89–90 (misleading statements and impressions) or the Fraud Act 2006. The FCA's powers include public censure of issuers and directors,[454] and the imposition of civil penalties.[455] As is apparent from Table 13.3, breach of *DTR* disclosure obligations by a premium listed issuer may also contravene the listing principles, in particular the principle relating to the communication of information in such a way as to avoid a false market. The standard applied by the FCA with respect to fulfilment of disclosure obligations is one of reasonable care on the part of the issuer.[456] Only those directors (or others) who were 'knowingly concerned' in a contravention can be fined or publicly censured.[457]

The data in Table 13.3 indicate that the imposition of stringent administrative sanctions for disclosure failures is not commonplace. In view of the thrust of the discussion in the Davies Review, it is particularly striking that sanctions against directors personally are relatively rare. Formal sanctions never tell the whole story[458] but a lingering sense of sub-optimality in overall levels of enforcement is hard to shake off. The FCA's vision for enforcement is based around 'credible deterrence' and it is envisaged that it will involve more preparedness to use formal tools than was the norm for its predecessor.[459] The need for a more effective enforcement regime for financial activity in the UK commands wide and powerful support.[460] The financial services industry will bear the brunt of a more vigorous public enforcement strategy, but publicly-traded commercial companies, and their directors, can also be expected to feel its effects.[461]

The amended version of the Transparency Obligations Directive amplifies the harmonized requirement for effective, proportionate, and dissuasive sanctions by prescribing minimum sanctions. Failure by an issuer to make required disclosures will attract minimum fines set as the higher of (i) up to €10 million or 5% of annual turnover, or (ii) up to twice the profits gained or losses avoided because of the breach.

---

[454] FSMA, s 89K and s 91(3).   [455] FSMA, s 91(1ZA) and (1B).

[456] *DTR* 1.3.4 and 1A.3.2; *LR* 1.3.3.   [457] FSMA, s 91(2)–(3).

[458] E Ferran, 'Capital Market Competitiveness and Enforcement' (April 2008) <http://ssrn.com/abstract=1127245> accessed July 2013; J Armour, 'Enforcement Strategies in UK Corporate Governance: A Roadmap and Empirical Assessment' in J Armour and J Payne (eds), *Rationality in Company Law* (Oxford: Hart Publishing, 2009) 71; K Cearns and E Ferran, 'Non-Enforcement Led Public Oversight of Financial and Corporate Governance Disclosures and of Auditors' [2008] *Journal of Corporate Law Studies* 191; J Armour, C Mayer, and A Polo, 'Regulatory Sanctions and Reputational Damage in Financial Markets'.

[459] M Wheatley, 'The FCA—Our Vision for Enforcement,' speech at FSA's Enforcement Conference, 2 July 2012.

[460] eg, Parliamentary Commission on Banking Standards, *Changing Banking for Good* (HL Paper 27, HC Paper 175, June 2013). The Commission was appointed by both Houses of Parliament to consider and report on professional standards and culture of the UK banking sector.

[461] Banks and other institutions that are publicly listed are, of course, subject to the disclosure obligations examined in this chapter as well as their more specialized regulatory obligations. For example, the allegations against JPMorgan Chase arising from the derivatives trading out of its London office in 2012 that was on a scale so large as to destabilize world financial markets (known as the 'London Whale' trades) and which resulted in JPMorgan eventually reporting a $2 billion loss included that the bank failed to comply with required disclosures under US securities laws. In October JPMorgan Chase agreed to pay US$100 million and admitted wrongdoing to settle the investigation.

14

International Equity Offerings and Listings

Introduction

An issuer makes an international (or global) offering when it offers its securities directly to investors outside its home market. The international offer may be made alongside an offering to investors in the home market or, less commonly, instead of it. The modern market for international equity offerings emerged in the 1980s, driven by political and economic changes that included the emergence of market economies in the formerly communist countries of Eastern Europe, the privatization of large utility companies that had been state-owned and which typically had capital needs that were too large to be absorbed easily by their domestic market, reforms in developing countries that led to the abolition of exchange controls and the creation of emerging markets attractive to international investment funds, and a deepening investor appetite for foreign securities as part of portfolio diversification strategies.[1] This segment of the market is now of considerable economic significance. Cross-border activity as a proportion of total IPO issuance activity rose steadily during the 2000s, reaching a peak of 14 per cent of the total volume in 2007.[2] IPO activity slumped generally during the global financial crisis of 2007–9 but recovered thereafter.[3] A landmark event was the flotation of Jersey-incorporated Glencore International plc (formerly Marc Rich & Co, a Swiss company, and from May 2013, GlencoreXstrata) on the London Stock Exchange in 2011, accompanied by a dual listing in Hong Kong.[4] Glencore raised $10 billion in London's largest ever IPO and the largest ever premium listed IPO.

Each issuer will have its own reasons for making an equity offering outside its home jurisdiction, but the following are commonly mentioned: to establish access to well-developed foreign capital markets for immediate and future financing needs; to overcome limited investor appetite in the home market and/or to tap into foreign investor interest; to achieve a desired investor base in a particular foreign country for strategic/business reasons; to gain attention from analysts; to benchmark against a more appropriate peer group, for example, by being included in specialist funds or indices; to bond voluntarily with the regulatory regimes in which the offer is made (this reason is considered to be of particular relevance to issuers whose home regimes are regarded as being relatively weak by international standards);[5] and to gain publicity or to enhance international prestige.[6] These reasons overlap and for any particular issuer a combination of factors is likely to influence any decision to make an international offering. Prominent among the factors militating against an international offering will be the extra costs involved in making a multijurisdictional offer, which will embrace both the costs of the offering itself and on-going costs associated with having a

---

[1] The importance of wide portfolio diversification is a central element of modern finance theory: M Rubinstein, 'Markowitz's "Portfolio Selection": A Fifty-Year Retrospective' (2002) 57 *Journal of Finance* 1041.

[2] PwC, *Equity Sans Frontières: Trends in Cross-border IPOs and An Outlook for the Future* (November 2012). This study defines a cross-border IPO as an IPO in which 50 per cent or more of the proceeds are raised on a non-domestic exchange (counting listings from Mainland China into Hong Kong as domestic transactions).

[3] PwC, *Equity Sans Frontières*.

[4] London Stock Exchange, 'Glencore Raises $10bn in London's Largest Ever IPO,' 24 May 2011.

[5] JC Coffee, 'Racing Towards the Top?: The Impact of Cross-listings and Stock Market Competition on International Corporate Governance' (2000) 102 *Columbia Law Review* 1757.

[6] PwC, *Equity Sans Frontières*.

presence in several different securities markets and being subject to local regulation in each of those markets.

Market infrastructure providers compete globally to attract cross-border IPO business. Until the 2000s the US markets were the undisputed top destination for issuers in search of international capital,[7] but indicators of the more competitive nature of the contemporary markets include the London Stock Exchange, being the destination for 41 per cent of all cross-border IPOs between 2002 and 2011 against 23 per cent taking place in New York, and the increasing market share attracted by Singapore and Hong Kong as hubs for the Asia-Pacific region.[8] Numerous factors have contributed to the shaping of cross-border IPO trends, including the changing preferences of issuers from rising economies (for example, London has dominated as the listing venue of choice for Russian issuers), geographical proximity, and more intense competition between exchanges facilitated by technological improvements and by financial globalization that has enabled capital to flow unimpeded by geographical or political borders. Regulation is another relevant factor, although, as discussed in chapter 13, exactly how regulation affects issuers' choice of listing venue is a matter for considerable debate.

Strategies for Developing a Regulatory Framework for International Offerings

International offerings of securities, in common with other types of cross-border capital market activity, present profound challenges for regulators and policymakers. On the one hand, removing local regulatory barriers that deter foreign issuers from entering a market could bring in business and boost the domestic economy. If a country sticks rigidly to a national treatment approach—that is, applying the same regulations to foreign issuers and firms as to nationals—it risks damaging the international competitiveness of its capital markets. Furthermore, by limiting the choice that is available to investors in their 'home' market, such a strategy could have precisely the opposite effect to that which was intended, by forcing investors either to restrict their portfolio diversification strategies or to bear in full the risks and costs involved in fending for themselves in seeking out foreign investment opportunities. Writing in a personal capacity, two then-senior SEC officials acknowledged in an important article published in 2007 that a purely domestic focus does not these days fulfil regulators' investor protection mandate because of the increasing ease with which investors can move their capital from jurisdiction to jurisdiction in search of higher returns.[9] The authors remarked: 'our markets are now interconnected and viewing them in isolation—as we have for so long—is no longer the best approach to protecting our investors, promoting an efficient and transparent U.S. market, or facilitating capital formation for U.S. issuers.'[10] On the other hand, waiving requirements for foreign issuers touches upon sensitive issues relating to national sovereignty, the mission of national regulatory authorities to protect their own markets from fraud or other destabilizing activities and to ensure investor protection, and the equal treatment of all market participants whether they be domestic or foreign.

---

[7] McKinsey & Co, *Sustaining New York's and the US' Global Financial Services Leadership* (January 2007) 45 (report commissioned by MR Bloomberg and CE Schumer) notes that a listing on a US exchange used to be considered de rigueur for a non-US company that wanted to capitalize on the deepest and most liquid market in the world.

[8] PwC, *Equity Sans Frontières*.

[9] E Tafara and RJ Peterson, 'A Blueprint for Cross-Border Access to U.S. Investors: A New International Framework' (2007) 48 *Harvard International Law Journal* 31.

[10] E Tafara and RJ Peterson, 'A Blueprint for Cross-Border Access to U.S. Investors: A New International Framework,' 32.

There are a number of conceptual approaches to the development of a regulatory framework that is suitable for the modern reality of mobile capital and seamless markets. The following paragraphs discuss these concepts in general terms before moving on in the next sections to examine in more detail some specific initiatives to improve international capital market regulation and to consider the application of the various conceptual tools in practical settings. Countries differ in how far they are prepared to go in opening up their markets to foreign actors otherwise than on a full national treatment basis and many of the conceptual approaches are deployed in varying combinations.

Convergence

Convergence in the context of international financial regulation means reducing or eliminating differences between sets of national or regional requirements.[11] 'Harmonization' is another term that is sometimes used interchangeably with convergence but 'convergence' has come to be preferred because it is thought to capture the idea of an exercise that is designed to arrive at the 'best' standard, whereas, for some, harmonization suggests a compromise where differences exist.[12] Full convergence implies a single, generally applicable, set of standards. The EU has achieved this level of cross-border uniformity within the internal market for prospectus disclosures and consolidated financial reporting by a significant segment of EU issuers but this achievement has to be set in the context of the overall EU market integration project.[13] The regulatory framework governing a cross-border offer of securities within the EU and the extensive supervisory architecture that supports it are considered further later in this chapter. Such an extensive array of regulatory and institutional arrangements to support cross-border activity is unique to the EU.

Total uniformity is not often realistically achievable at the global level for political reasons, nor is it necessarily optimal anyway. Whilst a single set of uniform standards would have certain advantages in terms of facilitating issuer access and comparability by investors, these advantages cannot be viewed in isolation and need to be set against possible disadvantages, including unwieldiness and lack of receptiveness to important regional variations in market conditions and legal environments. In any case, without global bodies with the worldwide authority to interpret and apply standards and a globally-consistent system of private enforcement, considerable divergence between the level of standardization on paper and in actual practice would be inevitable.[14] Variations in other supporting institutions and broader compliance incentives around regulatory standards could also result in differences in capital market outcomes.[15]

Numerous international bodies are involved in setting and maintaining non-binding international financial regulatory standards of varying degrees of specificity that influence, but do not dictate, the content of regional (EU) and national laws. In the capital markets sphere, the two most significant international bodies are the International Organization

[11] G Whittington, 'The Adoption of International Accounting Standards in the European Union' (2005) 14(1) *European Accounting Review* 127, 133.

[12] Tafara and Peterson, 'A Blueprint for Cross-Border Access to U.S. Investors'; DT Nicolaisen, 'A Securities Regulator Looks at Convergence' (2005) 25 *Northwestern Journal of International Law and Business* 661, 672.

[13] PH Verdier, 'Mutual Recognition in International Finance' (2011) 52 *Harvard International Law Journal* 55; E Ferran, 'EU Financial Supervision in the Context of Global Financial Governance' in D Mügge (ed) *Europe's Place in Global Financial Governance* (Oxford: OUP, 2014).

[14] HS Scott, 'Internationalization of Primary Public Securities Markets' (2000) 63 *Law and Contemporary Problems* 71.

[15] H Daske, C Leuz, and RS Verdi, 'Adopting a Label: Heterogeneity in the Economic Consequences Around IAS/IFRS Adoptions' (2013) 51 *Journal of Accounting Research* 495.

of Securities Commissions (IOSCO) and the International Accounting Standards Board (IASB). The functions performed by these bodies and certain standard for which they are responsible are considered in more detail later in this chapter.

Equivalence, mutual recognition, and substituted compliance

At the global level it often makes more sense to think about 'substantial' rather than 'full' convergence. Substantial convergence is about achieving a robust degree of similarity between different sets of standards but not necessarily making them identical.[16] Non-binding international standards can assist in the achievement of this goal by establishing agreed minimum norms that may serve as a focal point for substantial convergence.[17]

In principle, comparability should foster trust and confidence in the quality of foreign regulatory systems and, as such, should facilitate the granting of concessions to those engaging in cross-border activity from full compliance with the domestic requirements of each of the jurisdictions in which they operate.[18] To be workable, comparability should embrace not only the content of regulatory rules but also the mechanisms for oversight and enforcement as well. Since making concessions for foreign issuers could mean placing considerable reliance on the foreign regulator to apply foreign regulatory requirements properly, a country is unlikely to be willing to proceed in that direction unless it is confident that the quality of the foreign oversight and enforcement is at least as good as its own.[19] Furthermore, if confidence in the quality of foreign oversight and enforcement erodes, that is likely to undermine support for the continuance or extension of such arrangements.[20]

Equivalence

The term 'equivalence' is often used to describe the foundational degree of similarity that is needed for concessionary access arrangements to function. A number of different interpretations of the term are possible[21] but, in principle, equivalence is best understood as implying a holistic test with benchmarks that focus on high comparability between regulatory and supervisory outcomes, rather than rigid line-by-line examinations of similarities and differences and a quest for exact mirroring of practices and philosophies. International standards set by global bodies may be called into use as the benchmark for equivalency of outcomes. This is the approach that has been adopted, for example, in Australia where the Australian Corporations Act 2001 uses the phrase 'sufficient equivalence' in its third country access provisions and the Australian Securities and Investments Commission (ASIC)

---

[16] Nicolaisen, 'A Securities Regulator Looks at Convergence,' 672–3.

[17] AM Slaughter, *A New World Order* (Princeton: Princeton University Press, 2004), 180; E Ferran and K Alexander, 'Can Soft Law Bodies Be Effective? The Special Case of the European Systemic Risk Board' [2010] *European Law Review* 751.

[18] Tafara and Peterson, 'A Blueprint for Cross-Border Access to U.S. Investors.'

[19] Various authors have made the point that the mutual recognition agreement between the USA and Canada, noted later in the text, was only possible because of the similarity of their standards: SJ Choi and AT Guzman, 'Portable Reciprocity: Rethinking the International Reach of Securities Regulation' (1998) 71 *South California Law Review* 903, 920; DS Ruder, 'Reconciling U.S. Disclosure Practices with International Accounting and Disclosure Standards' (1996) 17 *Northwestern Journal of International Law and Business* 1, 11.

[20] W Hicks, 'Harmonisation of Disclosure Standards for Cross-Border Share Offerings: Approaching an "International Passport" to Capital Markets?' (2002) 9 *Indiana Journal of Global Legal Studies* 361, 377 outlines problems with the Canadian/US mutual recognition agreement for issuer disclosure which, it is said, nearly collapsed because of eroding US confidence in the quality of Canadian oversight.

[21] TB Wei, 'The Equivalence Approach to Securities Regulation' (2007) 27 *Northwestern Journal of International Law & Business* 255.

has supplemented the statutory framework by setting out equivalence principles whereby an equivalent regulatory regime is understood to be one that (i) is clear, transparent, and certain; (ii) is consistent with IOSCO's Objectives and Principles of Securities Regulation; (iii) is adequately enforced in the home jurisdiction; and (iv) achieves equivalent outcomes to the Australian regulatory regime.[22] The relevant regulatory and supervisory authorities are expected to make enhanced commitments to cross-border supervisory cooperation and information-sharing arrangements.

Mutual recognition

Mutual recognition involves at least two countries agreeing on an essentially reciprocal basis to allow participants from the other into their markets on condition of adherence to foreign regulatory requirements and with a waiver of some local requirements.[23] Pre-conditions as regards the comparability of each other's standards and with respect to enhanced cross-border cooperation are likely. It has been said that mutual recognition depends for traction on there being sufficient similarity, or equivalence, between systems to foster the development of the cross-border trust.[24] In theory, it would be open to a country unilaterally to grant concessions to foreign actors seeking to conduct cross-border business within its territory. Unilateral recognition might appeal as a way of making available to domestic investors a wider range of diverse financial products and services, or a way of introducing more competition or innovation in the domestic financial sector. However, unilateral recognition touches on sensitivities about giving foreign actors a 'better deal' than domestic players. Mutual recognition should be less contentious because it offers domestic players at least the opportunity of reciprocal advantages.

Mutual recognition is a cornerstone principle of EU law and it has been instrumental in the building of the EU internal market.[25] Historically, mutual recognition within EU capital markets law relied on relatively low-level standardization of Member States' domestic regulatory requirements; as such, capital markets law mirrored the 'minimum harmonization' approach commonly deployed for internal market measures in general.[26] More recently and under the pressure of needing to reinforce the entire EU financial regulatory structure to deal more effectively with the cross-border ramifications of financial shocks, a much greater level of regulatory uniformity has been imposed on Member States by EU financial market laws. In this respect the EU experience tends to suggest that the more successful mutual recognition is at stripping down national barriers, the more serious the potential side effects that need to be countered by more regulatory convergence at the cross-border level. However, the dangers of negative side effects should not loom so large where the underlying aim is merely to achieve a degree of consistency and coordination in international dealings rather than the creation of a fully integrated market. Mutual recognition still commands considerable support as a viable way of dealing efficiently and effectively with cross-border capital market issues at a global level.[27]

---

[22] ASIC, *Regulatory Guide 54: Principles for Cross-border Financial Regulation* (2012) principles 7–10.

[23] Choi and Guzman, 'Portable Reciprocity' 907 use the term 'normal reciprocity' to describe such arrangements.

[24] K Nicolaïdis, 'Trusting the Poles? Constructing Europe through Mutual Recognition' (2007) 14 *Journal of European Public Policy* 682; K Nicolaïdis and G Schaffer, 'Transnational Mutual Recognition Regimes: Governance Without Global Government' (2005) 68 *Michigan Review of International Law* 267.

[25] K Armstrong, 'Mutual Recognition' in C Barnard and J Scott (eds), *The Law of the Single European Market* (Oxford: Hart Publishing, 2002).

[26] M Dougan, 'Minimum Harmonisation and the Internal Market' (2000) 37 *Common Market Law Review* 853.

[27] Ferran, 'EU Financial Supervision in the Context of Global Financial Governance.'

Substituted compliance

'Substituted compliance' has much in common with mutual recognition. One practical difference between the phrases is that substituted compliance tends to be used more by US regulators and officials, whilst mutual recognition and equivalence are terms that are strongly associated with European discourse. Substituted compliance has been described by US commentators as a system in which instead of being subject to direct SEC supervision and US federal securities regulations and rules, foreign actors would apply for an exemption from SEC registration based on their compliance with substantively comparable foreign securities regulations and laws and supervision by a foreign securities regulator with oversight powers and a regulatory and enforcement philosophy substantively similar to the SEC's.[28] The SEC would still retain jurisdiction to pursue violations of the anti-fraud provisions of the U.S. federal securities laws. The comparability finding would need to be complemented by an arrangement between the SEC and its foreign counterpart to share extensive enforcement and supervisory-related information.

Regulatory competition

Convergence, equivalence, mutual recognition, and substituted compliance all have in common the central idea that some level of regulatory standardization is conducive to the development of a well-functioning system of international financial regulation. However, it is the differences between systems that serve as the foundation for another conceptual approach, namely regulatory competition.

Some authors have written strongly in favour of opening up capital market activity to 'regulatory competition', whereby, in essence, financial market actors would be free to operate internationally on the basis of adherence to a national regulatory regime of their choice. Some supporters of regulatory competition argue that if issuers, for example, are free to choose the regulatory regime governing their issuance activity, this will promote a 'race to the top' because issuers have incentives to select disclosure regimes that offer good investor protection laws because such choices lower the cost of capital.[29] In turn, governmental responsiveness to regulatory competition should mean that countries around the world will adapt their standards so as to bring them into line with issuer and investor preferences.[30] In other words, although similar standards are not a prerequisite, regulatory competition could lead eventually to convergence, but a convergence that is market-driven and therefore arguably more in tune with market preferences and needs.[31]

---

[28] Tafara and Peterson, 'A Blueprint for Cross-Border Access to U.S. Investors,' 32.

[29] Fierce debate has raged among leading scholars on the merits of regulatory competition in securities market regulation. Key articles include: R Romano, 'Empowering Investors: A Market Approach to Securities Regulation' (1998) 107 *Yale Law Journal* 2359; R Romano, 'The Need for Competition in International Securities Regulation' (2001) 2 *Theoretical Inquiries in Law* 387; Choi and Guzman, 'Portable Reciprocity'; MB Fox, 'Securities Disclosure in a Globalizing Market: Who Should Regulate Whom' (1997) 95 *Michigan Law Review* 2498; MB Fox, 'Retaining Mandatory Securities Disclosure: Why Issuer Choice is Not Investor Empowerment' (1999) 85 *Virginia Law Review* 1335; MB Fox, 'The Issuer Choice Debate' (2001) 2 *Theoretical Inquiries in Law* 563. HE Jackson, 'Centralization, Competition, and Privatization in Financial Regulation' (2001) 2 *Theoretical Inquiries in Law* 649, 659–62 provides a valuable overview of the debate.

[30] HE Jackson and E Pan, 'Regulatory Competition in International Securities Markets: Evidence from Europe in 1999—Part I' (2001) 56 *Business Lawyer* 653 note that an implicit assumption in the debate over regulatory competition is that at least some governments will make meaningful changes in their legal regimes in order to preserve or expand the number of entities under their regulatory oversight.

[31] One of the most commonly cited benefits of regulatory competition is that it provides a market-driven mechanism for discovering what people want: JM Sun and J Pelkmans, 'Regulatory Competition in the Single Market' (1995) 33 *Journal of Common Market Studies* 67.

From other quarters, however, come doubts about issuers' incentives to select regimes with good investor protection laws[32] and about investors' ability to collect and process all of the information that would be needed to make meaningful assessments of differences in quality between different investor protection regimes and to reflect these accurately in the cost of capital.[33] Whether there are sufficient regulatory jurisdictions to engage in meaningful competition is questioned.[34] Some commentators have identified enforcement as a likely weak spot in that issuer freedom of choice as regards investor protection could imply highly contentious extraterritorial enforcement by the securities regulatory agency of the chosen national regime or unskilled and inexperienced enforcement of that regime by the agencies of other countries.[35] Fraud concerns, in particular, lead regulators to question whether regulatory competition is capable of promoting a race to the top.[36]

Private placement exemptions

The final conceptual approach is the use of private placements. Chapter 13 discussed the use of private placement exemptions in a range of contexts, including their usefulness in small-scale capital raising exercises by SMEs. In the area of international financial regulation, private placement exemptions are a particularly useful mechanism for larger issuers that have a sufficiently strong international profile to be able credibly to seek capital outside their domestic markets. Private placements exemptions enable such capital formation to occur without the burden of full compliance with foreign capital markets law. International issuers will rely principally on exemptions for offers that are targeted at sophisticated investors. One not uncommon structure for an international equity offer is for the issuer to make a full retail and wholesale prospectus offer in its home country, accompanied by cross-border private placements to wholesale investors in selected foreign jurisdictions.

Private placement exemptions are convenient and popular. One measure of their significance is that in 2006 more equity financing was raised via one of the most heavily used exemptions from US securities law than the combined total raised that year in IPOs listed on the New York Stock Exchange, NASDAQ, and the American Stock Exchange.[37] Moreover, in principle, they appear to be relatively uncontentious: why not dispense with the panoply of mandatory disclosure requirements where all the parties involved should be able to look after their own interests without the help of the state? In addition, for larger listed issuers that are already subject to demanding periodic and episodic disclosure requirements, having to comply with (potentially) multiple sets of prospectus disclosure requirements in order

---

[32] JC Coffee, 'Law and Regulatory Competition: Can They Co-exist?' (2002) 80 *Texas Law Review* 1729.

[33] JD Cox, 'Regulatory Duopoly in U.S. Securities Markets' (1999) 99 *Columbia Law Review* 1200, 1234: 'Before we embrace multiple standards in the belief that a disclosure hierarchy will develop among the securities of a particular market, we need better evidence that securities markets are capable of making discrete judgments among issuers using different disclosure standards.' Being fully informed is one of the conditions which, according to the classic theory of regulatory competition (the 'Tiebout model' from C Tiebout, 'A Pure Theory of Local Expenditures' (1956) 64 *Journal of Political Economy* 416), needs to be satisfied for it to operate effectively: JP Trachtman, 'Regulatory Competition and Regulatory Jurisdiction in International Securities Regulation' in DC Esty and D Geradin (eds), *Regulatory Competition and Economic Integration* (Oxford: OUP, 2001) 289–310. However, this exacting condition can never be fully met (JP Trachtman, 'Regulatory Competition and Regulatory Jurisdiction in International Securities Regulation'); Scott, 'Internationalization of Primary Public Securities Markets.'

[34] Cox, 'Regulatory Duopoly in U.S. Securities Markets,' 1232–3.

[35] Cox, 'Regulatory Duopoly in U.S. Securities Markets,' 1239–44; Coffee, 'Law and Regulatory Competition.'

[36] Tafara and Peterson, 'A Blueprint for Cross-Border Access to U.S. Investors.'

[37] WK Sjostrom, 'The Birth of Rule 144A Equity Offerings' (2008) 56 *UCLA Law Review* 409, 412. See also L Zingales, 'The Future of Securities Regulation' (2009) 47 *Journal of Accounting Research* 391.

to raise a fresh tranche of capital may involve an unwarranted costs burden. However, private placements run the risk of becoming 'a regulatory black hole'.[38] The absence of specific disclosure-based regulation underscores the importance of ensuring that formal definitions of 'sophisticated' investors in private placement exemptions are tightly drawn so that those who should not be expected to fend for themselves really are excluded.[39] The need to consider potential systemic risks has also been identified.[40] The systemic significance of the 'unregulated' nature of private placements markets has increased in tandem with the growth in size of these markets and in the range of exotic types of financial instrument that are placed through them.[41]

Developing a Regulatory Framework for International Equity Issuance Activity: The Practical Application of International Standards

IOSCO international disclosure standards for non-financial information

The International Organization of Securities Commissions (IOSCO) was formed in 1983, from the transformation of an inter-American regional association (created in 1974), to facilitate cooperation between securities regulators.[42] Its members include over 120 securities regulators and 80 other securities markets from around the world. IOSCO's membership regulates more than 95 per cent of the world's securities markets. The IOSCO objectives are: to cooperate in developing, implementing, and promoting adherence to internationally recognized and consistent standards of regulation, oversight and enforcement in order to protect investors, maintain fair, efficient, and transparent markets, and seek to address systemic risks; to enhance investor protection and promote investor confidence in the integrity of securities markets, through strengthened information exchange and cooperation in enforcement against misconduct and in supervision of markets and market intermediaries; and to exchange information at both global and regional levels on their respective experiences in order to assist the development of markets, strengthen market infrastructure, and implement appropriate regulation. IOSCO has distilled the fundamental elements of the regulation of capital markets in an international standard *Objectives and Principles of Securities Regulation*.[43] This standard identifies the objectives of securities regulation as being to protect investors, ensure that markets are fair, efficient, and transparent, and reduce systemic risk. The thirty-eight principles relate to the organization of supervision, the enforcement of securities regulation, cooperation in regulation, principles for issuers, principles for auditors, credit rating agencies, and other information service providers, principles for collective investment schemes, principles for market intermediaries, and principles for secondary markets.

Cross-border offers of equity securities are specifically addressed by the IOSCO International Disclosure Standards (IDS) for cross-border offerings and initial listings of equity securities by foreign issuers. The underlying aim of the IDS is to facilitate cross-border

---

[38] JJ Johnson, 'Private Placements: A Regulatory Black Hole' (2010) 35 *Delaware Journal of Corporate Law* 151.
[39] Anti-fraud rules will still apply. In the US context it has been suggested that, in addition, a dedicated civil liability for private placements should be developed: WK Sjostrom, 'Rebalancing Private Placement Regulation' (2013) 36 *Seattle University Law Review* 1143. As discussed in ch 13, the role of civil liability in capital market regulation is more developed in the US than elsewhere.
[40] AI Anand, 'Is Systemic Risk Relevant to Securities Regulation?' (2010) 60 *University of Toronto Law Journal* 941.
[41] Zingales, 'The Future of Securities Regulation.'
[42] This paragraph draws on IOSCO, *Fact Sheet* (May 2013). [43] Last updated June 2010.

offerings and listings by multinational issuers by enhancing comparability of information while ensuring a high level of investor protection.[44] The IDS are designed to apply to international listings and public offers and sales of equity securities for cash.[45] They set out disclosure requirements for prospectuses, offering and initial listing documents, and registration statements relating to such listings and offerings.[46] The IDS are non-binding but were issued by IOSCO with a recommendation to members to give effect to them in their domestic jurisdictions. In 1999, the US adopted revised disclosure requirements for foreign issuers that were based on the IOSCO model.[47] Within the EU, the IDS were the starting point for the disclosure requirements in the Prospectus Directive.[48]

However, the IDS are not comprehensive: in particular, in relation to financial information, whilst the IDS identify the types of financial statements that are required to be included, specify the periods that they should cover, and impose independent audit requirements, they do not prescribe the contents of financial statements.[49] It is left open to individual countries to choose whether or not to require profit forecasts or other forward looking statements.[50] Another noticeable gap in the coverage of the IDS relates to 'materiality'. As well as specific disclosure requirements, most countries rely on an overriding principle of disclosure of material information in prospectuses or other offering documents. Thus, for example, section 87A of the UK Financial Services and Markets Act 2000 provides that a prospectus must contain the 'necessary information', which means 'the information necessary to enable investors to make an informed assessment of (a) the assets and liabilities, financial position, profits and losses, and prospects of the issuer of the transferable securities and of any guarantor, and (b) the rights attaching to the transferable securities.' Different countries interpret the concept of materiality in different ways. The IDS note this divergence of approach but they do not seek to challenge it directly.[51] This means that there is still room for considerable divergence in the disclosure expectations of countries that have adopted the IDS for international offerings, a feature that undermines their role as a single set of common disclosure requirements for international offerings. Another tricky issue that can act as an obstacle to cross-border issuance and listing activity that is side-stepped in the IDS is the language of non-financial information: it is simply assumed that all information contained in a document will be provided in a language acceptable to the host country,[52] which means that issuers may have to contend with onerous translation burdens. More generally, the IDS envisage host states having considerable room to tailor international disclosure requirements to their home market, which, again, lessens their impact as a standardizing force.[53] The IDS may be best regarded as containing the 'seeds of true harmonisation'[54] but clearly they are not a fully grown plant. In a more recent project to develop common standards for debt issuance activity, IOSCO's Technical Committee itself was relatively modest about the achievements of the IDS.[55] It referred to the IDS as being *broadly* accepted as a

---

[44] IOSCO, IDS, 3.   [45] IOSCO, IDS, 3.   [46] IOSCO, IDS, 3.

[47] HS Scott and A Gelpern, *International Finance: Law and Regulation* 3rd edn (London: Sweet & Maxwell, 2012) 192.

[48] Directive 2003/71/EC of the European Parliament and of the Council of 4 November 2003 on the prospectus to be published when securities are offered to the public or admitted to trading on a regulated market [2003] OJ L435/64 (Prospectus Directive), rec 22. Directive 2003/71/EC was amended by Directive 2010/73/EU, [2010] L327/1.

[49] IOSCO, IDS, 20–3, Standard VIII (Financial Information).   [50] IOSCO, IDS, 14.

[51] IOSCO, IDS, 5 and Pt II-2.   [52] IOSCO, IDS, 6.

[53] Hicks, 'Harmonisation of Disclosure Standards for Cross-Border Share Offerings,' 372.

[54] TG Siew, 'Regulatory Challenges in the Development of a Global Securities Market—Harmonisation of Mandatory Disclosure Rules' [2004] *Singapore Journal of Legal Studies* 173, 186.

[55] IOSCO, *International Disclosure Principles for Cross-border Offerings and Listings of Debt Securities by Foreign Issuers* (Final Report, 2007).

disclosure *benchmark*, and it notes that the equity disclosure regimes of many IOSCO members are *based* on them (emphasis added).[56]

More recently still, IOSCO has produced *Principles for Periodic Disclosure by Listed Entities*.[57] It suggests that these *Principles* should provide a useful framework for any jurisdiction seeking to establish or review its periodic disclosure regime but acknowledges that individual jurisdictions may conclude that other disclosures are needed to address the specific concerns of their markets.

The International Accounting Standards Board and International Financial Reporting Standards

The International Accounting Standards Committee was created in 1973 to set international accounting standards and issue discussion documents on international accounting issues.[58] Its objectives were to harmonize existing diverse standards, to formulate and publish in the public interest accounting standards to be observed in the presentation of financial statements, and to promote a common international approach. Over the years the organizational structure developed into an independent, not-for-profit private sector body, the International Financial Reporting Standards (IFRS) Foundation, of which the International Accounting Standards Board (IASB) is now the standard setting body. The objectives of the IFRS Foundation are to:

(1) develop in the public interest a single set of high quality, understandable, and enforceable and globally accepted accounting standards based upon clearly articulated principles. These standards should require high quality, transparent, and comparable information in financial statements, and other financial reporting, to help investors, other participants in the world's capital markets, and other users make economic decisions;

(2) promote the use and rigorous application of those standards;

(3) in fulfilling the objectives associated with (1) and (2), to take account of, as appropriate, the needs of a range of sizes and types of entities in diverse economic settings; (4) to promote and facilitate adoption of International Financial Reporting Standards (IFRS), being the standards and interpretations issued by the IASB, through the convergence of national accounting standards and IFRS.

Standards produced under this system were known as International Accounting Standards (IAS) up to April 2001. Standards made since then are known as International Financial Reporting Standards (IFRS). As elsewhere in the book, this chapter uses 'IFRS' as a composite term except where the particular context calls for a specific reference to IAS.

The IASB and the IFRS Foundation are not regulatory bodies with formal powers at their disposal. They cannot enforce international standards or require compliance. Like the IOSCO standards, IFRS are international 'soft law' standards that achieve legal force only when, either by a process of transposition of IFRS or by convergence of the contents of national

---

[56] IOSCO, *International Disclosure Principles for Cross-border Offerings and Listings of Debt Securities by Foreign Issuers*, 1.

[57] IOSCO (2010).

[58] This paragraph draws on information available for the IASB website: <http://www.iasb.co.uk/>. For a more detailed explanation of the structure and how it operates in practice see Whittington, 'The Adoption of International Accounting Standards in the European Union.'

standards towards IFRS, they become part of national (or in the EU, regional) law or when market participants adopt them in particular transactional contexts.[59]

Transatlantic adoption of IFRS

Notwithstanding their soft law origins, IFRS have acquired considerable hard significance.[60] By January 2013 almost 120 countries had required or permitted the use of IFRS, including three-quarters of the G20 member countries.[61] One of strongest endorsements of the IFRS as a set of enforceable disclosure standards came from Europe in June 2000, when the European Commission announced a new proposed law that by January 2005 would require all companies listed on regulated markets within the EU to prepare consolidated accounts using IASB accounting standards.[62] This goal was realized with the adoption of Regulation (EC) 1606/2002 of the European Parliament and of the Council of 19 July 2002 on the application of international accounting standards.[63] The IAS Regulation stipulates that for each financial year starting on or after 1 January 2005, companies governed by the law of a Member State must prepare their annual consolidated accounts in conformity with EU-adopted IFRS if, at their balance sheet date, their securities are admitted to trading on a regulated market of any Member State.[64] This Regulation applies to EEA countries not in the EU as well as EU Member States. Issuers that are subject to the IAS Regulation must present historical financial information in any prospectus they issue in conformity with IFRS[65] and, for such issuers, periodic financial disclosures required by the Transparency Obligations Directive must also conform to EU-adopted IFRS.[66] The Prospectus and Transparency Obligations Directives also in principle extend the mandatory use of IFRS to issuers from third countries but make provision for non-EU issuers to use financial statements prepared otherwise than in accordance with these IFRS, provided the accounting standards under which they have been drawn up have been deemed 'equivalent' in accordance with EC mechanisms.[67]

It is important to note that the effect of the IAS Regulation is to impose an EU filter on the mandatory application of IFRS. The Regulation provides a procedure for Community adoption of IFRS and obliges listed companies to draw up their consolidated accounts in accordance with only those IFRS that have been so endorsed. The endorsement mechanism

---

[59] Whittington, 'The Adoption of International Accounting Standards in the European Union,' notes that the initial success of international standards was market based and that arguably it was because of their established importance in practice that governments were forced to take a position in relation to them.

[60] Whittington, 'The Adoption of International Accounting Standards in the European Union,' 127–8 provides background on the adoption of international standards around the world.

[61] IFRS Foundation & IASB, *Who We Are and What We Do* <http://www.ifrs.org/The-organisation/Documents/2013/Who-We-Are-English-2013.pdf> accessed May 2013.

[62] European Commission Communication, *EU Financial Reporting Strategy* (COM(2000) 359). This step was described by a former SEC Chief Accountant as the primary driver of significantly expanded use of IFRS: Nicolaisen, 'A Securities Regulator Looks at Convergence.'

[63] [2002] OJ L243/1 (IAS Regulation).

[64] IAS Regulation, Art 4.

[65] Commission Regulation (EC) 809/2004 of 29 April 2004 implementing Directive 2003/71 (EC) of the European Parliament and of the Council as regards information contained in prospectuses as well as the format, incorporation by reference and publication of such prospectuses and dissemination of advertisements [2004] OJ L149/1 (Prospectus Directive Regulation) Annex 1, para 20.

[66] Directive 2004/109/EC of the European Parliament and of the Council of 15 December 2004 on the harmonisation of transparency requirements in relation to information about issuers whose securities are admitted to trading on a regulated market and amending Directive (EC) 2001/34 [2004] OJ L390/38 (Transparency Obligations Directive) Arts 4–5. Amended by Directive 2010/73/EU, [2010] OJ L327/1 and Directive 2013/50/EU, [2013] OJ L294/13.

[67] Prospectus Directive Regulation, Annex 1, para 20.1 and Transparency Obligations Directive, Art 23. The debate on equivalence is considered in more detail later in this chapter.

thus provides for EU oversight and control over the application of IFRS. Constitutionally and politically this screening procedure addresses sensitivities associated with giving de facto rule-writing authority to a third party, but there are drawbacks as well. Although the European Commission has said that the role of the mechanism is not to reformulate or replace IFRS, but to oversee the adoption of new standards and interpretations, intervening only when these contain material deficiencies or have failed to cater for features specific to the EU environment,[68] the existence of filters of this nature gives rise to the possibility of regional variant forms of IFRS whose existence could impede broader international efforts to establish common accounting standards.[69] Practical experience to July 2013 has not provided wide-scale evidence to feed this concern but one specific area, hedge accounting requirements in IAS 39, *Financial Instruments: Recognition and Measurement*, is the outlier. Controversy over the accounting treatment of derivatives and other complex financial instruments by IAS 39 has a long history. In 2003–4 the European Commission's efforts to secure changes to IAS 39 before its endorsement was seen by US regulators as potentially jeopardizing efforts to achieve convergence between IAS/IFRS and US generally accepted accounting principles (US GAAP). In the end, the EU voted to adopt a version of IAS 39 that had two carveouts from the Standard as published by the IASB.[70] The justification for the first carveout, relating to fair value, concerned in particular its use with respect to financial assets that were not traded in active and liquid markets.[71] On hedge accounting, the subject of the second carveout, the issue was whether IAS 39 sufficiently took into account the way in which many European banks operated their asset/liability management operations.[72] The IASB subsequently revised IAS 39 in respect of fair value issues and thereafter the Commission adopted the revised IASB Standard in respect of that matter.[73] Certain of the IAS 39 hedge accounting requirements remained unendorsed.[74] IAS 39 is in the process of being superseded by IFRS 9, *Financial Instruments*, for annual periods beginning on or after 1 January 2015. As of July 2013 IFRS 9 had not yet been endorsed by the European Commission.

The United States, on the other hand, has thus far resisted full implementation of IFRS for domestic issuers but it has granted significant concessions for foreign issuers. Its strategy in the early 2000s was to focus on the promotion of convergence in financial reporting standards. Since October 2002 the IASB and the US Financial Accounting Standards Board ('FASB') have been engaged in a long-term project on the convergence of IFRS and US GAAP. This project, known as the 'Norwalk Agreement,' committed both sides to using their best efforts to make their existing financial reporting standards fully compatible as soon as practicable and to coordinate their future work programmes to ensure that, once achieved, compatibility would be maintained.[75] The Norwalk Agreement embraced both relatively straightforward short-term projects to remove technical detailed differences between different standards and

---

[68] COM(2000) 359 7.

[69] SEC, *Work Plan for the Consideration of Incorporating International Financial Reporting Standards into the Financial Reporting System for U.S. Issuers* (13 July 2012) 3.

[70] Commission Regulation (EC) 2086/2004 of 19 November 2004 amending Regulation (EC) 1725/2003 on the adoption of certain international accounting standards in accordance with Regulation (EC) 1606/2002 of the European Parliament and of the Council as regards the insertion of IAS 39 [2004] OJ L363/1.

[71] Commission Regulation (EC) No 2086/2004, recital 5.

[72] Commission Regulation (EC) No 2086/2004, recital 7.

[73] Commission Regulation (EC) 2106/2005 of 21 December 2005 amending Regulation (EC) 1725/2003 adopting certain international accounting standards in accordance with Regulation (EC) 1606/2002 of the European Parliament and of the Council as regards International Accounting Standard (IAS) 39 [2005] OJ L337/16.

[74] European Financial Reporting Advisory Group, *The EU Endorsement Status Report: position as at 21 May 2013* <http://www.efrag.org/WebSites/UploadFolder/1/CMS/Files/Endorsement%20status%20report/EFRAG_Endorsement_Status_Report_21_May_2013.pdf> accessed July 2013.

[75] IASB and FASB, *Memorandum of Understanding* (October 2002).

thereby reduce the need for reconciliation and also longer term, more ambitious, projects to find common solutions on issues of principle. According to an IASB-FASB memorandum of understanding published in February 2006, the goal was to reach a conclusion on some short term convergence issues by 2008.[76] Since then, progress has faltered and timetables have slipped. An SEC Staff Report in July 2012 noted that whilst commendable progress had been made on some priority projects: 'The Boards have, at times, struggled to reach converged conclusions in some areas, which has contributed to delays in project timing and, for several projects, to total suspension of efforts. The Boards' efforts have been further complicated by a number of challenges during the last several years, including a financial crisis and shifting priorities of investors and regulators.'[77]

Notwithstanding the complications associated with the Norwalk convergence project, there was a breakthrough in the US stance with regard to IFRS when in November 2007 the SEC voted to adopt rules to allow foreign private issuers to file financial statements prepared in accordance with IFRS without reconciliation.[78] This momentous decision, attributable in part to pressure exerted by the EU in a complex transatlantic dialogue regarding financial market access,[79] and also in part a product of an era in which US capital markets appeared to be losing their global competitive edge,[80] took effect from March 2008. This was a watershed moment in international financial regulation. In the 1980s, the US had adopted a position with regard to foreign issuers that were subject to US reporting requirements that allowed them to prepare their financial statements using a body of generally accepted accounting principles other than US GAAP but, if they did so, they had also to include a reconciliation of significant variations from US GAAP. When it was introduced, reconciliation was intended to be a concession in favour of foreign issuers but it came to be regarded as an expensive and time-consuming process that served as a barrier against foreign issuers entering the US markets.[81] Some relatively modest relaxations of the reconciliation requirements for accounts drawn up in accordance with IAS/IFRS were made in 1994 but deepening demand from market participants for a single set of high-quality international accounting standards that would facilitate both the comparability of issuers by investors and issuer access to pools of capital kept the spotlight on this issue.

The SEC went further towards an embrace of IFRS in November 2008 with a formal proposal for a phased-in mandatory introduction of IFRS for US issuers, beginning from financial years from December 2014 onwards.[82] As with the Norwalk Agreement on convergence, this timetable has since been affected by the reassessment of policies and priorities in the aftermath of the global financial crisis, which has been shaped by profound changes in financial markets and economies. The SEC Staff Report of July 2012 refrained from answering the fundamental question whether transitioning to IFRS was in the best interests of the US

---

[76] FASB and IASB, *A Roadmap for Convergence between IFRSs and US GAAP—2006-2008* (February 2006).

[77] SEC, *Work Plan*, 10–13.

[78] SEC, *Acceptance from Foreign Private Issuers of Financial Statements Prepared in Accordance with International Financial Reporting Standards Without Reconciliation to U.S. GAAP*, Release Nos 33-8879; 34-57026; International Series Release No 1306; File No S7-13-07. This permission relates only to accounts they are prepared using IFRS as issued by the IASB, not regional variants thereof.

[79] This dialogue is discussed in detail in E Ferran, 'Capital Market Openness After Financial Turmoil' in P Koutrakos and M Evans (eds) *Beyond the Established Orders* (Oxford: Hart Publishing, 2010). As discussed later in this chapter, the equivalence mechanisms in the Prospectus and Transparency Obligations Directives gave the EU a powerful lever with which to exert influence over the EU.

[80] LA Cunningham, 'The SEC's Global Accounting Vision: A Realistic Appraisal of a Quixotic Quest' (2008) 87 *North Carolina Law Review* 1.

[81] Scott and Gelpern, *International Finance*, 193–4.

[82] SEC, *Roadmap for the Potential Use of Financial Statements Prepared in Accordance with International Financial Reporting Standards by U.S. Issuers*, Release Nos. 33-8982; 34-58960; File No S7-27-08.

securities markets generally and US investors specifically.[83] It determined that additional analysis and consideration of this threshold policy question would be necessary before any decision by the Commission concerning the incorporation of IFRS into the financial reporting system for US issuers could occur.

This faltering progress is indicative of the magnitude of the challenges involved in achieving full convergence around a single set of universal standards. As well as the myriad of technical and conceptual issues on which accounting and regulatory specialists may disagree, for a sovereign state in effect to allow a third party the de facto authority to write rules governing significant activity within its territory (even if moderated by an endorsement mechanism) would be a step of high political significance that could never be taken lightly. These sensitivities are especially acute for the US, given its historic position as the global financial market hegemon. Another factor is that the salience of issues relating to the independence, legitimacy, transparency, and accountability of a standard-setter inevitably grows in tandem with the expansion of the importance of its role: increasingly intense scrutiny of the governance structure, processes, and funding of the IFRS Foundation bears this out.[84] At a fundamental level, questions arise about whether a single universal set of financial reporting standards is desirable in any event or whether there is something to be said for having some competitive tension between at least a small number of alternatives, each of which may be more, or less, suited to national particularities.[85]

IFRS and equivalence

Cross-border accommodations based on equivalence can avoid some of the problems associated with ambitious initiatives that aim at uniformity, although they come with their own challenges as well. An equivalency-based approach for financial disclosures by issuers engaging in cross-border capital market activity has been actively pursued by the EU. This activity merits closer examination.

The disclosure regimes established by the Prospectus and Transparency Obligations Directives require third country issuers to use IFRS or an equivalent system of accounting disclosure.[86] The equivalence mechanism involves a determination made by the European Commission after consultation with the European Securities and Markets Authority (ESMA) with regard to technical aspects.[87] The equivalency standard is that a third country's accounting standards (Generally Accepted Accounting Principles or GAAP) may be considered equivalent to IFRS adopted in the EU if those standards enable investors to make a similar assessment of the assets and liabilities, financial position, profit and losses, and prospects of the issuer as financial statements drawn up in accordance with IFRS, with the result that investors are likely to make the same decisions about the acquisition, retention, or disposal of securities of an issuer.[88] In addition, the third country must have made a public and actively pursued commitment to converge its standards with IFRS.[89]

Initially, equivalency of financial reporting standards was one of the most controversial features of these disclosure regimes. The transatlantic dialogue regarding the position of

---

[83] SEC, *Work Plan*, executive summary.   [84] SEC, *Work Plan*, 34–70.

[85] Scott and Gelpern, *International Finance*, 200.

[86] Prospectus Directive Regulation, Annex 1, para 20; Transparency Obligations Directive, Art 23.

[87] Regulation (EC) No 1569/2007 establishing a mechanism for the determination of equivalence of accounting standards applied by third country issuers of securities [2007] OJ/340/66, as amended by Commission Delegated Regulation (EU) No 310/2012, [2012] OJ L103/1.

[88] Regulation (EC) No 1569/2007, as amended by Commission Delegated Regulation (EU) No 310/2012.

[89] Regulation (EC) No 1569/2007, as amended by Commission Delegated Regulation (EU) No 310/2012.

issuers that reported in accordance with US GAAP was particularly intense but there were also some internal tensions within the EU as regards the respective roles of supranational and national authorities. However, things have since settled down. The Japanese and US GAAPs have been held to satisfy the equivalence test.[90] The GAAPs of China, Canada, South Korea, and India have also been found to be equivalent, although in the case of India the equivalence determination remains temporary in order to allow more time for the implementation of an IFRS-compliant reporting system.[91] Discussions with other countries continue.

Other examples of equivalence and mutual recognition/substituted compliance arrangements

The idea of allowing an issuer to offer or list securities on the basis of home country disclosure rules is not confined to the specific area of financial reporting standards. Within the EU framework, there is also provision in Article 20 of the Prospectus Directive for a third country issuer to use a prospectus for an offer to the public or for admission to trading on a regulated market that has been drawn up in accordance with the legislation of a third country.[92] The competent authority of the Member State that is the issuer's home state for this purpose is responsible for approving the prospectus. The Commission is empowered by the Directive to adopt delegated acts to establish general equivalence criteria but, as yet, has not exercised this power.[93] However, ESMA, which has responsibility for ensuring a uniform application of the Prospectus Directive, has published an assessment framework under which it is for ESMA to decide what additional information must be included in a wrap to the third country prospectus to make it equivalent.[94] Equivalence in this context is seemingly based on a literal interpretation of the words used.[95]

Under Article 4(1)(e) of the Prospectus Directive (as amended) there is an equivalency-based exemption from the requirement for a prospectus for employee share schemes of companies established outside the European Union whose securities are admitted to trading on a third country market.[96] In this context, the Commission is to adopt an equivalence decision stating whether the regulatory (legal and supervisory) framework of that third country ensures that market is authorized in that third country, it complies with legally binding requirements which are, for the purpose of the application of this exemption, equivalent to the requirements resulting from specified EU capital markets law, and it is subject to effective supervision and enforcement in that third country. In its mandate to ESMA requesting technical advice on elaboration of the equivalence criteria, the Commission emphasized the need for a 'global and holistic assessment' that focuses on the materiality of differences; but the signals as to how far it will be prepared to go in being satisfied by similarity of outcomes are mixed because, at the same time, the Commission also emphasized that the EU Directives 'have set up a strict legal and supervisory framework in the Union, which should be preserved by all actors and market participants in order to underpin confidence in the financial markets'.[97]

---

[90] Commission Decision 2008/961/EC of 12 December 2008, [2008] L 340/112, amended by Commission Implementing Decision of 11 April 2012, [2012] OJ L103/49.

[91] Commission Implementing Decision of 11 April 2012.

[92] This regime is discussed in detail in P Schammo, *EU Prospectus Law* (Cambridge: CUP, 2011) ch 4.

[93] Article 20(3) (as amended).

[94] ESMA, *Framework for the Assessment of Third Country Prospectuses under Article 20 of the Prospectus Directive* (ESMA/2013/317).

[95] ESMA, *Framework for the Assessment of Third Country Prospectuses under Article 20 of the Prospectus Directive*.

[96] P Schammo, *EU Prospectus Law* (Cambridge: CUP, 2011) ch 4.

[97] European Commission, *Formal Request to ESMA for Technical Advice on Possible Delegated Acts Concerning the Amended Prospectus Directive* (Ares(2011)56961—19/01/2011).

Equivalence mechanisms for third country access are also found in other aspects of EU financial services and company law, and more (or less) rigid interpretations of equivalence, and also different equivalence determination mechanisms, are found in different contexts.[98] For example, under the Statutory Audit Directive,[99] there is provision for derogations for third country auditors from EU quality assurance reviews and from the system of investigations and penalties on the basis of reciprocity subject to an equivalence test to be performed by the Commission in cooperation with Member States.[100] In 2011, the European Commission adopted a decision recognizing the equivalence of the auditor oversight systems of ten third countries, namely Australia, Canada, China, Croatia, Japan, Singapore, South Africa, South Korea, Switzerland, and the US.[101] A further twenty countries were added in 2013.[102]

For certain purposes under the Transparency Obligations Directive the Commission has taken the view that equivalence should be able to be declared when general disclosure rules of third countries provide users with understandable and broadly equivalent assessments of issuers' positions that enable them to make similar decisions as if they were provided with the information according to requirements under the Transparency Obligations Directive, even if the requirements are not identical.[103] This has enabled national regulatory agencies to make their own determinations of equivalence for certain Transparency Obligations Directives purposes. For example, the UK FCA considers that the laws of the USA, Japan, Israel, and Switzerland on major shareholdings are equivalent to the notifications required under its rules implementing the Transparency Obligations Directive and issuers with securities admitted to trading on a regulated market in the UK that are incorporated in any of these countries are exempt from the FCA's requirements.[104] Swiss, US, and Canadian issuers also enjoy further equivalency-based exemptions in respect of periodic disclosure requirements.[105]

Nor is the idea of granting concessions to avoid wasteful duplication where two systems of regulation and supervision are substantially similar one on which the EU has a monopoly. Another prominent use of these concepts is the Multijurisdictional Disclosure System (MJDS) between the US and Canada whereby Canadian companies can issue securities into the US on the basis of Canadian disclosure rules and US companies can issue securities into Canada on the basis of US rules.[106] The MJDS, used mainly by Canadian issuers, is considered to have furthered market integration, although periodically there are reports of its future being in doubt.[107] Also notable is the Trans-Tasman Mutual Recognition of Securities Offerings (MRSO) scheme whereby Australian and New Zealand issuers may offer shares, debentures, or interests in managed or collective investment schemes in both countries. The MRSO enables issuers of securities to use one disclosure document to offer financial instruments to investors on both sides of the Tasman, subject to meeting certain requirements. The scheme is considered to have brought significant cost savings for issuers

---

[98] E Ferran, 'EU Financial Supervision in the Context of Global Financial Governance.'

[99] Directive 2006/43/EC of the European Parliament and of the Council of 17 May 2006 on statutory audits of annual accounts and consolidated accounts [2006] OJ L157/87.

[100] Art 46(1).

[101] Commission Decision of 19 January 2011 on the equivalence of certain third country public oversight, quality assurance, investigation and penalty systems for auditors and audit entities and a transitional period for audit activities of certain third country auditors and audit entities in the European Union [2011] OJ L15/12.

[102] Commission implementing decision of 13 June 2013 amending Decision 2011/30/EU, [2013] OJ L 163/26.

[103] Commission Directive 2007/14/EC, [2007] L69/27, rec 18 and Arts 13–23.

[104] <http://www.fca.org.uk/firms/markets/ukla/information-for-issuers/non-eea-regimes> accessed July 2013.

[105] <http://www.fca.org.uk/firms/markets/ukla/information-for-issuers/non-eea-regimes> accessed July 2013.

[106] Securities Act Release No 6902 (21 June 1991).

[107] Hicks, 'Harmonisation of Disclosure Standards for Cross-Border Share Offerings.'

offering securities and also benefits investors by providing them with a wider range of investments.[108]

Notwithstanding doubts about the value of the MJDS, in the period immediately prior to the financial crisis of 2007–9 it appeared that US authorities were about to embrace more fully the concept of mutual recognition (or substituted compliance) when it was announced, in August 2008, that the SEC had entered into a mutual recognition agreement with the Australian government and ASIC.[109] The agreement provided a framework for the SEC, the Australian government, and ASIC to consider regulatory exemptions that would permit eligible US and Australian stock exchanges and broker-dealers to operate in both jurisdictions in respect of certain types of investor, without the need for these entities (in certain aspects) to be separately regulated in both countries.[110] Enhanced arrangements for more supervisory and enforcement cooperation and coordination between the SEC and ASIC were built into the mutual recognition arrangement. When it was first announced much appeared to be expected of the SEC's new venture, with Australia being just the first of a series of jurisdictions with which the SEC expected to conclude similar arrangements. Steps were taken to pave the way for discussions on a potential US-Canada mutual recognition arrangement for exchanges and financial firms.[111] The SEC also indicated that it envisaged the European Union being part of this initiative.[112]

These developments were heralded by some as key breakthroughs that would finally dismantle barriers to global investment.[113] The focus on broker-dealers rather than issuers appeared to be in tune with market developments that were facilitating the trading of international securities and thereby reducing the need for issuers positively to seek out foreign investors by offering their securities cross-border.[114] However, these initiatives also prompted concerns about the potential dangers involved in entrusting, at least in part, the fate of ordinary retail investors to foreign agencies, as well as about the creation of an uneven playing field in which foreign issuers might (or might appear to have) access to the US markets on better terms than US issuers.[115] The turmoil in financial markets from 2007 onwards fed the concerns because one of the main lessons from that period was that in a crisis national authorities put national interests first. This was so even within the EU, where the 'beggar-thy-neighbour' consequences of unilateral and uncoordinated stabilizing action taken by Member States in the immediate aftermath of the collapse of the Lehman Brothers investment bank in September 2008 eventually led policymakers to the conclusion that more pan-European standardization of both regulation in its narrow rule-making sense and of the accompanying supervisory architecture was inevitable in order to avoid a retreat from single market freedoms. Outside the EU single market context, however, sentiments moved in a different direction. As awareness deepened of just how difficult it is to strike the right balance between achieving a system of international

---

[108] Securities Commission New Zealand & ASIC, *Offering Securities in New Zealand and Australia under Mutual Recognition* (RG 190, March 2011).

[109] This paragraph draws heavily from the relevant SEC Press Release: 'SEC, Australian Authorities Sign Mutual Recognition Agreement,' Washington, 25 August 2008.

[110] *Mutual Recognition Arrangement Between the United States Securities and Exchange Commission and the Australian Securities and Investments Commission, Together with the Australian Minister for Superannuation and Corporate Law* (August 2008). Discussed in P Schammo, 'Regulating Stock Exchanges' (2008) 57 *International and Comparative Law Quarterly* 827.

[111] SEC Release 2008-49 (24 March 2008).   [112] SEC Release 2008-49 (24 March 2008).

[113] EF Greene, 'Beyond Borders: Time to Tear Down the Barriers to Global Investing' (2007) 48 *Harvard International Law Journal* 85.

[114] HE Jackson, 'A System of Selective Substitute Compliance' (2007) 48 *Harvard Journal of International Law* 105.

[115] DC Langevoort, 'The SEC, Retail Investors, and the Institutionalization of the Securities Markets' (2009) 95 *Virginia Law Review* 1025.

regulation that, on the one hand, is coordinated and efficient, and, on the other, does not compromise on safety and stability, arguments against depriving domestic investors of the full protections of their domestic laws acquired more salience.

A Genuine Single Regulatory Regime for Cross-border Offers and Listings of Securities: The EU Passport

The EU regulatory framework for cross-border offers and listings of securities has evolved from one of mutual recognition between similar systems to one of identical rules and increasing standardization (but not yet denationalization) of supervision. As such, it has become the world's most advanced example of barrier-dismantling to facilitate international issuance activity. As it has evolved to meet the needs of a single regional market, this system has become increasingly unsuitable as a global template. The EU system aims at an objective (ie the single market) that does not apply at the global level and it depends on regional institutions that do not have global counterparts.[116] Nevertheless, the EU regime for cross-border offers and listings of securities is still a valuable case study from the viewpoint of international financial governance because it reveals the 'price' that must be paid for a genuinely common system. Countries that are not linked together in a close regional grouping can use the EU experience as a benchmark even though their own aspirations for economic integration are likely to be considerably more modest than those of the EU Member States.

Under the regulatory framework that preceded the current disclosure regime, there was provision for mutual recognition by other Member States of any prospectus that had been approved by the securities regulator in one state. However, very few issuers took advantage of these arrangements. They came to be seen as being flawed because host Member States could require prospectuses to include additional information for their local market and could insist on full translation of the documents. The additional costly complexity involved in tailoring documentation so as to satisfy various different sets of national regulatory requirements undermined the appeal of the mutual recognition procedures.

Under the current Prospectus Directive, these design flaws have been addressed. The basic idea that once a prospectus has been approved in one state it can then be used for issuance and listing activity in other EEA states without the need for any further approvals is retained but the ability of host states to require additional local information and to insist on full translation is removed. This system has 'worked': in 2012, for example, of the 4113 prospectuses that were approved by Member States' competent authorities, 967 were passported into other Member States. It therefore merits closer examination.

Obtaining a passport

As discussed in chapter 13, an issuer that is proposing to offer its securities to the public and/or apply for admission of its securities to trading on a regulated market within the EEA must draw up a prospectus that, in form and content, complies with the requirements of the Prospectus Directive and the Prospectus Directive Regulation. An issuer must apply to the competent authority of its home state for regulatory approval of the prospectus before it is published.[117] For European issuers, the home state is the Member State in which their registered office is located.[118] Issuers from third countries are also entitled to a passport in respect

---

[116] PH Verdier, 'Mutual Recognition in International Finance.'   [117] Prospectus Directive, Art 13.
[118] Prospectus Directive, Art 2.1(m)(i).

of any prospectus that has been approved by the issuer's home state. For a third country issuer of equity securities, the home state is the Member State where the securities are intended to be offered to the public for the first time after the date of entry into force of the Prospectus Directive or where the first application for admission to trading on a regulated market is made, at the choice of the issuer.[119] For an EU issuer, the contents of the prospectus are as discussed in chapter 13. For a third country issuer, the contents of the prospectus are determined by reference to the Prospectus Directive regime, subject to concessions on grounds of equivalence discussed earlier in this chapter.

Once a prospectus is approved, it has Community scope, which means that it is valid for public offers or the admission of securities to trading on a regulated market in any number of states within the EU.[120] The home state authority must, if so requested by the issuer or the person drawing up the prospectus, notify host state authorities with a certificate of approval attesting that the prospectus has been approved in accordance with the Prospectus Directive and with a copy of the prospectus.[121] Host states have only a right to be notified that the home state has approved the prospectus and they cannot impose their own approval process.[122] If applicable, the notification must be accompanied by the translation of the summary that, as discussed in chapter 13, must be included in equity prospectuses. The language rules for a prospectus that is to be used for cross-border issuance or listing activity are that where an offer to the public is made or admission to trading on a regulated market is sought in more than one Member State, including the home Member State, the prospectus shall be drawn up in a language accepted by the competent authority of the home Member State and shall also be made available either in a language accepted by the competent authorities of each host Member State or in a language customary in the sphere of international finance, at the choice of the issuer, offeror, or person asking for admission to trading, as the case may be.[123] Where an offer to the public is made or admission to trading on a regulated market is sought in one or more Member States, excluding the home Member State, the prospectus shall be drawn up either in a language accepted by the competent authorities of those Member States or in a language customary in the sphere of international finance, at the choice of the issuer, offeror, or person asking for admission, as the case may be.[124] In either case, the competent authority of each host Member State may only require that the summary be translated into its official language(s). Approved prospectuses must be made available to the public in the relevant Member States in any one of a number of prescribed ways, which must include electronic publication.[125] The design of this regime reflects lessons learnt from past experience: the disclosure requirements are standardized, host states cannot require the inclusion of additional local information for the home market, and translation burdens have been significantly lightened.

Public oversight of EU prospectus requirements: ensuring cross-border supervisory consistency

The EU prospectus disclosure regime has also to be seen in the context of the institutional framework for its implementation and supervision. Oversight of prospectuses takes place at national level and is primarily the responsibility of the issuer's home state securities regulator. Where a host state into which a prospectus has been passported finds irregularities,

---

[119] Prospectus Directive, Art 2.1(m)(iii).   [120] Prospectus Directive, Art 17.
[121] Prospectus Directive, Art 18 (as amended).   [122] Prospectus Directive, Art 17.
[123] Prospectus Directive, Art 18(3).   [124] Prospectus Directive, Art 18(2).
[125] Prospectus Directive, Art 14 (as amended).

it must refer these findings to the competent authority of the home Member State and it is only where irregularities persist, despite the measures taken by the competent authority of the home Member State or because such measures prove inadequate, that the host state can itself take all the appropriate measures in order to protect investors.[126] This fragmentation of responsibility carries the risk that standardization objectives will not be met because they are undermined by differences in the way that national regulators interpret and apply the rules.

One strategy for addressing this risk is to draft the rules in such a way as to leave little room for differing interpretations. The very detailed nature of the prospectus disclosure requirements applies this strategy to some extent. It is reflected also in the choice of legal instrument in which the requirements are contained: the Prospectus Directive *Regulation* applies directly in Member States without the need for transposition via a domestic instrument, as would be required for a Directive and which could provide opportunities for differences to creep in via the transposition process. However, excessive detail carries its own dangers and thus this strategy for drafting the content of rules cannot be taken too far. Nor can too much reliance be placed on the choice of legal instruments because regulations may often be inappropriate, perhaps because there are legitimate local specificities of which account needs to be taken.[127]

Another way in principle of addressing the problem of different national authorities taking different views is to vest the responsibility for oversight in a dedicated supra-national pan-European securities agency. However, whatever the merits of a Euro-SEC in principle,[128] the establishment of such authority is not a viable short-term proposition because it would be met by formidable political, legal, and practical objections. Instead, a different approach has been pursued whereby national agencies retain oversight responsibilities but a supranational institutional framework has been put in place to foster convergence in the way that they perform these tasks. ESMA now performs the function of steering EU supervision towards a standardized approach. The emergence of a centralized dimension to the supervision of capital market activity in the EU, including but not limited to prospectuses, has been a gradual and incremental process, and it continues to evolve. A Euro SEC is still not on the cards as an immediate prospect but that ESMA will eventually assume that role is becoming an increasingly plausible scenario. This issue merits closer examination.

EU-level supervision of capital market activity: a brief overview of its development from 2000[129]

In July 2000, the European Council (in its Economic and Finance Ministers formation ('ECOFIN')) appointed a Committee of 'Wise Men,' under the chairmanship of Baron

---

[126] Prospectus Directive, Art 23.

[127] Inter-institutional Monitoring Group, *Second Interim Report Monitoring the Lamfalussy Process* (January 2007) para 34.

[128] The extensive debate on this topic is reviewed in E Ferran, *Building an EU Securities Market* (Cambridge: CUP, 2004) 119–22.

[129] The seminal work on EU capital market regulation is N Moloney, *EU Securities and Markets Regulation* 3rd edn (Oxford: OUP, expected 2014). Articles and chapters examining the transition from the Lamfalussy committees of supervisors to the European Supervisory Authorities include: N Moloney, 'EU Financial Market Regulation after the Global Financial Crisis: "More Europe" or More Risks?' (2010) 47 *Common Market Law Review* 1317; N Moloney, 'The European Securities and Markets Authority and Institutional Design for the EU Financial Market—a Tale of Two Competences: Part 1: Rule-making' (2011) *European Business Organization Law Review* 41; N Moloney, 'The European Securities and Markets Authority and Institutional Design for the EU Financial Market—a Tale of Two Competences: Part 2: Rules in Action' (2011) 12 *European Business Organization Law Review* 177; E Ferran, 'Understanding the New Institutional Architecture of EU Financial Market Supervision' in G Ferrarini, KJ Hopt,

Alexandre Lamfalussy, to conduct a broad examination of the mechanisms for regulating and supervising EU securities markets.[130] The work of the Lamfalussy Committee was very influential. It led to the adoption of a new structure for rule-making and supervision of securities market activity (generally known as the 'Lamfalussy Process') involving four levels:

- Level 1 (in essence primary legislation decided upon by the Council and Parliament in accordance with established lawmaking procedures—of which the Prospectus Directive is an example);

- Level 2 (implementing measures, or more detailed rules, decided upon by the Commission acting in accordance with EU comitology procedures—of which the Prospectus Directive Regulation is an example);

- Level 3 (a drive towards consistent implementation and transposition of legislation at Member State level); and

- Level 4 (greater emphasis on monitoring and enforcement).

The Committee of European Securities Regulators (CESR) was formally established by the Commission in June 2001 (although it could trace its origins back to the Forum of European Securities Commissions which was established on an informal basis in 1997) to perform the Level 3 role of promoting the drive towards consistency, as well as providing technical advice to the Commission on legislative proposals. Sister coordinating committees were also established for banking and for insurance. As part of its Level 3 role, CESR performed a standard-setting function, ie it issued standards, rules, and guidance that were not binding EU laws but which, in a manner akin to the 'enforceability' of other forms of international 'soft law', were underpinned by loose commitments from CESR members to give effect to them in their national regulatory systems. CESR also played a peer review role, monitoring regulatory practices within the single market. CESR was also charged with keeping an eye on global developments in securities regulation and considering their impact on the regulation of the single market for financial services.

A pertinent example of CESR's 'soft' standard-setting role was provided by its recommendations for the consistent implementation of prospectus requirements. The CESR recommendations provided clarification in relation to issues such as working capital disclosure, profit forecasts, capitalization, and indebtedness, and also on the detailed disclosure items under the Prospectus Directive Regulation. These recommendations were not binding as a matter of European law but CESR members introduced them into their national requirements on a voluntary basis. Also especially relevant to the discussion in this chapter were the CESR 'Q&A' publications on prospectuses and on transparency obligations, which outlined common positions agreed by CESR members and also some points where views diverged.

The *de Larosière Report*, published in February 2009, marked the start of a bolder phase in the organization of EU-wide financial market supervision.[131] While continuing to give due respect to the distribution of competences (which are bolstered by the Treaty-enshrined principles of subsidiarity and proportionality) whereby day-to-day supervision of firms is a matter

and E Wymeersch (eds), *Rethinking Financial Regulation and Supervision in Times of Crisis* (Oxford: OUP, 2012); E Ferran, 'Crisis Driven Regulatory Reform' in E Ferran, N Moloney, Jennifer G Hill, John C Coffee, *The Regulatory Aftermath of the Global Financial Crisis* (Cambridge: CUP 2012); P Schammo, 'EU Day-to-day Supervision or Intervention-based Supervision: Which Way Forward for the European System of Financial Supervision?' (2012) *Oxford Journal of Legal Studies* 771; E Wymeersch, 'The Reforms of the European Financial Supervisory System: An Overview' (2010) 7 *European Company and Financial Law Review* 240.

[130] *Regulation of European Securities Markets: Final Report* (Brussels, 15 February 2001).
[131] High Level Group on Financial Supervision in the EU, *Report* (February 2009) (*de Larosière Report*).

for national supervisory authorities, the de Larosière Group, exploiting the crisis-driven receptive political mood of the time, put forward a significant innovation by proposing to upgrade CESR and its sister committees to European Supervisory Authorities (ESAs) with formal legal personality and enhanced powers, including powers to impose binding decisions in certain circumstances.[132] These recommendations were broadly accepted: ESMA was established by a Regulation of the European Parliament and of the Council in November 2010 and became operational from January 2011.[133]

ESMA assumed responsibility for CESR's existing and on-going tasks, including its guidelines, recommendations, standards, and other Level 3 material. With regard specifically to matters concerning prospectuses, ESMA has reissued (and periodically updated) CESR's recommendations for the consistent implementation of prospectus requirements.[134] It has also maintained the Q&A on prospectuses[135] and on transparency.[136] ESMA describes the Q&A mechanism as a practical convergence tool used to promote common supervisory approaches and practices.[137] As detailed earlier in this chapter, ESMA has also been centrally involved in the operation of equivalence mechanisms, and it has maintained statistical data on the use of prospectus passports. Another important part of its role has been to provide advice to the Commission on regulatory matters, including reform of the issuer disclosure directives and with respect to the content of the delegated acts and technical standards required for the disclosure regime to be fully effective.[138] ESMA has certain enforcement powers and guidelines adopted under Article 16 of its founding instrument are underpinned by a 'comply or explain' disclosure mechanism that is applicable to national competent authorities.

Liability for issuer disclosures—gradual closing of a gap in the cross-border standardization agenda?

Many national legal systems provide a special civil remedy to investors who have acquired securities on the basis of a false prospectus.[139] This dedicated remedy is often more favourable to investors than claims that are available under the general law, for example, because there is less that the investor needs to prove in order to win the claim or because the range of defendants against whom the claim can be brought is wider. Section 90 of the UK Financial Services and Markets Act 2000, considered in chapter 13, provides an example of such a claim. Chapter 13 also examines the UK Financial Services and Markets Act 2000, section 90A/schedule 10A, which provide another special liability regime for issuer disclosures (excluding prospectuses): the section 90A/schedule 10A regime clarifies the law but in a fashion that is noticeably less favourable to investors than section 90.

The Prospectus Directive and the Transparency Obligations Directive impinge only lightly on civil liability. They require that such liability should exist under national laws and that responsibility should attach at least to the issuer or its administrative, management, or

---

[132] High Level Group on Financial Supervision in the EU, *Report* (February 2009) (*de Larosière Report*).

[133] Regulation (EU) No 1095/2010, [2010] OJ L331/84.

[134] Most recently: ESMA, *Update of the CESR Recommendations: The Consistent Implementation of Commission Regulation (EC) No 809/2004 Implementing the Prospectus Directive* (ESMA/2013/319). The recommendations have not, however, been adopted as recommendations under ESMA Regulation, Art 16 and therefore the 'comply or explain' mechanism established under that Article does not apply.

[135] Most recently: ESMA/2013/1537 (October 2013).   [136] Most recently: ESMA/2012/198 (April 2012).

[137] ESMA/2012/198 (April 2012) para 7.   [138] See summary in ESMA, *Annual Report 2012*, 48–50.

[139] ESMA, *Comparison of Liability Regimes in Member States in relation to the Prospectus Directive* (ESMA/2013/619), para 26 (15 Member States have specific prospectus civil liability regimes).

supervisory bodies,[140] but do not otherwise prescribe the contents of civil liability (save with respect to a safe harbour from civil liability in respect of prospectus summaries).[141] The UK's decision to enact section 90A/schedule 10A because of uncertainty whether existing laws would satisfy the Transparency Obligations Directive demonstrates that even light steering can have a catalytic effect.[142]

However, this relatively light touch form of intervention means that there is considerable room for variations between the liability regimes of different Member States. ESMA has noted that a common approach to civil liability is generally lacking.[143] This remark is included in a report on the prospectus liability regimes applied by Member States that was drawn up by ESMA in response to a mandate from the European Commission. Information-gathering work of this sort may have a conditioning effect, whereby harmonization of issuer disclosure civil liability regimes gradually shifts from being an over-ambitious policy choice to a viable option.[144]

It is already clear that the diversity of approach within the EU with regard to civil liability has potentially adverse implications for those engaged in cross-border securities issuance or listing activity when it is combined with applicable conflict of laws rules, and that it may therefore discourage such activity. Civil jurisdiction within the EU is regulated by the Brussels Regulation,[145] which, as a general rule, allocates jurisdiction on the basis of domicile of the defendant[146] but which, in tort claims (ie claims where a defendant's non-contractual civil liability is in question), provides also for jurisdiction in the courts of the location of the harmful event.[147] The place where the damage occurs is the general rule for the choice of law governing a tort claim under the Rome II Regulation governing non-contractual obligations.[148] Applying these rules, there is a risk that participants in cross-border issuance activity on the basis of a prospectus passport could face the possibility of multiple prospectus liability suits in the various countries in which the prospectus is used; if so, liability could fall to be

---

[140] Or, in the case of a prospectus, the offeror, the person asking for the admission to trading on a regulated market, or the guarantor, as the case may be.

[141] Prospectus Directive, Art 6; Transparency Obligations Directive, Art 7.

[142] Chapter 13 provides further detail on the background to the enactment of FSMA, s 90A/sch 10A.

[143] ESMA/2013/619, para 125.

[144] The Impact Assessment for the proposed revisions to the Prospectus Directive (SEC(2009)1223) ruled out harmonization of civil liability regimes as a goal that exceeded the Prospectus Directive.

[145] Regulation (EU) No 1215/2012 of the European Parliament and of the Council of 12 December 2012 on jurisdiction and the recognition and enforcement of judgments in civil and commercial matters [2012] OJ 351/1 (a recast of Council Regulation No 44/2001).

[146] Brussels Regulation (recast), Art 4. The domicile of legal persons is determined by Art 63, which provides three possible solutions: the statutory seat, or the place of the central administration or the principal place of business of the company.

[147] Brussels Regulation (recast), Art 7 (2). This place can be either where the harm was directly suffered or where the acts giving rise to the harm were done (Case C-21/76 *Bier v Mines de Potasse* [1976] ECR 1735). The claimant has a free choice between these two (or more) courts as an alternative to the courts of the defendant's domicile. Locating financial loss can be challenging (see eg Case C-364/93 *Marinari v Lloyds Bank* [1995] ECR I-2719 and Case C-220/88 *Dumez France v Hessische Landesbank* [1990] ECR I-49). These add to the uncertainties which an issuer may face in determining where a suit might be brought. However, there is a movement towards limiting the jurisdiction of the court under Art 7(2) to the damage suffered within that jurisdiction (Case C-68/93 *Shevill v Presse Alliance* [1995] ECR I-415). That may prevent parallel litigation on the same damage, but will permit a claimant to split up the claim to pursue an issuer in several jurisdictions.

[148] Regulation (EC) 864/2007 of the European Parliament and of the Council of 11 July 2007 on the law applicable to non-contractual obligations (Rome II) [2007] OJ L199/40, Art 4(1) applies the law of that country 'irrespective of the country in which the event giving rise to the damage occurred and irrespective of the country or countries in which the indirect consequences of that event occur.' There are exceptions to the general rule, including one where there is a 'manifestly closer connection' with another country, which could be based in a pre-existing relationship or a contract between the parties to the litigation. The limits and applicability of the exception will require elucidation from the Court of Justice if the experience follows that of the similar wording in the equivalent EU measure relating to contractual obligations.

determined under different national laws and in accordance with different civil procedure rules. Some groups could find themselves within one country's list of responsible persons to whom liability can attach but outwith another country's list. Overall, the lack of standardization with regard to the civil liability position could quite significantly undermine the appeal of the prospectus passport. As ESMA has said: 'particularly in case of cross-border transactions, the diversity in the different jurisdictions could make it difficult for market participants to assess their risks and rights in accordance with the applicable prospectus liability regimes'.[149]

The position regarding the liabilities of issuers with respect to periodic and episodic disclosure is potentially even more serious. Under the Prospectus Directive, an issuer can pick and choose: it is not required to make an offer on the basis of a passported prospectus into all Member States. However, under the Transparency Obligations Directive, issuers with securities admitted to trading on a regulated market are required to disseminate regulated information effectively to the public throughout the Community.[150] An implementing measure made under the Transparency Obligations Directive fleshes out what this means:

> Directive 2004/109/EC sets high-level requirements in the area of dissemination of regulated information. The mere availability of information, which means that investors must actively seek it out, is therefore not sufficient for the purposes of that Directive. Accordingly, dissemination should involve the active distribution of information from the issuers to the media, with a view to reaching investors.
>
> Minimum quality standards for the dissemination of regulated information are necessary to ensure that investors, even if situated in a Member State other than that of the issuer, have equal access to regulated information...
>
> Additionally, by way of minimum standards, regulated information should be disseminated in a way that ensures the widest possible public access, and where possible reaching the public simultaneously inside and outside the issuer's home Member State...[151]

Once admitted to a regulated market, issuers must therefore contend with the possibility of multi-jurisdictional litigation in respect of their periodic disclosures, as liability could arise in each of the jurisdictions in which the information is received and acted upon.[152] Of course, in a sense there is nothing new here because, even before the Transparency Obligations Directive, issuers with publicly quoted shares faced the risk that investors in various countries might acquire their securities and later sue in their local courts. However, the Transparency Obligations Directive has led to fears in some quarters of an increased risk of multiple civil liability suits under different national laws, for example, because, even though national laws may remain the same, investors may find it easier to establish the factors (such as receipt of information within the jurisdiction) on which liability depends or because the Directive may have a dynamic effect on Member States' liability laws and result in the enactment of new remedies that are more favourable to investors.

---

[149] ESMA/2013/619, para 136.   [150] Transparency Obligations Directive, Art 21.

[151] Commission Directive (EC) 2007/14 of 8 March 2007 laying down detailed rules for the implementation of certain provisions of Directive (EC) 2004/109 on the harmonisation of transparency requirements in relation to information about issuers whose securities are admitted to trading on a regulated market [2007] L69/27, recs 15–17.

[152] This issue has been considered in some detail by the UK Financial Markets Law Committee (FMLC), which identifies issues of legal uncertainty in the framework of the wholesale financial markets and considers how such issues should be addressed. See *Issue 76—Transparency Obligations Directive (January 2004); Issue 76—Transparency Obligations Directive* (October 2004), and *Issue 76—Transparency Obligations Directive* (September 2006). These memoranda, together with an exchange of correspondence between Lord Woolf (FMLC) and Alexander Schaub (European Commission), are available via the FMLC website at <http://www.fmlc.org> accessed July 2013.

Listing Requirements and Concessions for Foreign Issuers

Cross-listing may enhance liquidity and raise the issuer's profile in the jurisdiction in question. However, it will bring with it an enhanced regulatory burden by reason of the need to comply with listing and related continuing obligations. This section outlines the listing options available to foreign issuers considering listing in the UK on the London Stock Exchange and identifies some of the key regulatory implications of those choices.

Listing of shares or depositary receipts

Depositary receipts (DRs) are negotiable instruments issued by a depositary (usually a bank) certifying that a stated number of securities have been deposited with it by an issuer. DRs confer tradeable ownership rights in the shares on the holder, which are easy and convenient from a clearing and settlement perspective. American depositary receipts (ADRs) are used by non-US companies to attract investment from US investors via US stock exchanges, whilst global depositary receipts (GDRs) are commonly listed on European exchanges. Both ADRs and GDRs are typically denominated in currencies that are attractive to international investors such as US dollars or the euro.

Category of listing and market segment

The FCA will not admit shares of a company incorporated outside the EEA to the Official List that are not listed in its country of incorporation (or country in which the majority of shares are held) unless the FCA is satisfied that the absence of the listing is not due to the need to protect investors.[153] This requirement applies to both premium and standard listings.[154]

Only equity shares are eligible for premium listing on the LSE Main Market.[155] Should a foreign company opt for premium listing of its shares, it will become subject to onerous continuing obligations including corporate governance requirements. Certain requirements are modified in their application to foreign companies (including the equivalency-based dispensations from disclosure requirements derived from the Transparency Obligations Directive that were discussed earlier in this chapter) but these modifications are now relatively narrow in scope. In particular, premium listed foreign companies must now include a statement in their annual accounts of how they have applied the main principles set out in the UK Corporate Governance Code, in a manner that would enable shareholders to evaluate how the principles have been applied.[156] They must also state whether they have complied with the relevant provisions set out in the UK Corporate Governance Code and explain where they have not so complied. Premium listed foreign companies must also comply with the provisions regarding offering pre-emption rights to existing shareholders.[157]

Shares and DRs are eligible for standard listing on the LSE Main Market. The disclosure requirements applicable to a standard listed foreign company include that it must make a corporate governance statement in its directors' report explaining the corporate governance code to which it is subject or which it has voluntarily decided to apply.[158] A distinction

---

[153] *LR* 6.1.21 and *LR* 14.2.4.
[154] The significance of 'premium' listing and how it differs from 'standard' listing are considered in ch 13.
[155] *LR* ch 6.   [156] *LR* 9.8.7.   [157] *LR* 9.3.11–9.3.12.
[158] *DTR* 7.2, applied to foreign standard listed companies by *LR* 14.3.24 (shares) and *LR* 18.4 (depositary receipts).

between a standard listing of shares and of DRs is that requirements to produce half-yearly reports do not apply in respect of DRs.[159]

DRs are also eligible for admission to trading on the LSE Professional Securities Market (PSM). The PSM is the LSE's market for the listing and trading of specialist securities, including debt, depositary receipts, and convertible securities. The PSM is a market for officially listed securities but it is not an EU regulated market. One of the advantages of PSM listing for a foreign issuer is that there is no requirement to report financial information under IRFS or equivalent. The operation of the PSM is considered further in chapter 15 (bonds).

FTSE UK Index Series

A further factor that may be relevant to a foreign company's decision of what and where to list may be eligibility for inclusion in the FTSE UK Index Series in order to secure greater liquidity.[160] This Series is designed to provide investors with a comprehensive and complementary set of indices which measure the performance of the major capital and industry segments of the UK market. The FTSE UK Index Series includes the FTSE 100, FTSE 250, FTSE 350 and the FTSE All-Share. Only premium listed equity shares are eligible for inclusion in these indices. Companies that are not incorporated in the UK are eligible for inclusion provided they publicly acknowledge adherence to the principles of the UK Corporate Governance Code, pre-emption rights, and the UK Takeover Code as far as practicable, and have a free float greater than 50 per cent. Certain sensitivities around free float requirements are examined in chapter 13. Some of the main recent controversies have involved international issuers.

Controversial London listings of foreign-based companies

In July 2010 Vallar plc, a Jersey-incorporated investment vehicle raised £707.2 million in an IPO and standard listing on the London Stock Exchange. In November 2010, Vallar announced the acquisition of stakes in two Indonesian thermal coal producers, in effect allowing the Indonesian companies to achieve a London listing via an LSE-listed cash shell. These acquisitions were completed by April 2011. Thereafter, Vallar's shareholders approved a scheme of arrangement to put in place a new parent company, Bumi plc, for the Bumi group. Bumi was listed on the premium listing segment of the Official List. At the time, the Director of Equity Premium Markets at the LSE was fulsome in welcoming Bumi plc: 'We are delighted to welcome Bumi to the Main Market today. A London flotation affords the company access to the broadest pool of international capital in the world, listing and trading alongside its global peers. A Premium Listing ensures it is subject to the highest regulatory standards, and makes it eligible for inclusion in the internationally recognised and tracked FTSE indices.'[161] However, this positive mood did not last long. In September 2012 the company announced that it was looking into possible financial irregularities in its Indonesian operations. This was followed by the delayed publication of the 2012 financial results, which showed a US$200m (£133m) black hole and high-profile boardroom disputes. The shares were suspended in April 2013 at the request of the company pending clarification of its financial position.

---

[159] *LR* 18.4.3.

[160] This paragraph draws on FTSE, *Ground Rules for the Management of the FTSE UK Index Series* (Version 11.6, June 2013).

[161] <http://www.londonstockexchange.com/about-the-exchange/media-relations/press-releases/2011/bumi-plc.htm> accessed July 2013.

In late 2007 the Eurasian Natural Resources Corporation plc (ENRC), a Kazakhstan-based, but formally UK incorporated, holding company was floated on the London Stock Exchange. Thereafter, as a premium listed company and a constituent of the FTSE 100 Index, ENRC embarked on a series of major acquisitions in natural resources and energy, becoming a major contributor to Kazakhstan GDP. At the time of flotation, the government of Kazakhstan was ENRC's biggest shareholder. The other major shareholders were another Kazakh company and the three businessmen who had founded ENRC. Those individuals had been subjects of a long-running Belgian criminal investigation into the source of funds used in some property dealings. ENRC's listing was dogged by controversy from the beginning. One feature that caused concern was the waiver by the FSA of the normal 25 per cent free float requirement: less than 20 per cent of the equity was in public hands at the time of flotation, which the FSA considered to be acceptable because it considered the company was sufficiently large for its shares to be liquid. That fears had not been unfounded was confirmed in the years following the flotation by a series of scandals and boardroom spats including the ousting of non-executive directors who had been appointed to meet governance concerns. In April 2013 the Serious Fraud Office announced the launch of an investigation into ENRC based on allegations of fraud, bribery, and corruption. By then ENRC was also facing probes from the FCA (as successor to the FSA as UK Listing Authority) and the Takeover Panel. By June 2013 ENRC was the target of a take-private bid from its oligarch founders.

The problems surrounding ENRC and Bumi have led to probing questions about whether London listing standards are too lax or are applied with insufficient stringency.[162] As discussed in chapter 13, new requirements are to be introduced into the *Listing Rules* in 2014, amongst other things, to impose more demanding requirements for independence from controlling shareholders, mandatory rules (as opposed to corporate governance code 'comply or explain' provisions) regarding the composition of the board of companies that have controlling shareholders, and mandatory dual voting structures for the election of independent directors of premium-listed companies with a controlling shareholder.[163] The circumstances in which the FCA will consider allowing companies seeking a premium listing to receive a waiver from meeting the requirement for a minimum free float of 25 per cent will also be clarified. Certain listing principles will also be applied to the standard listing segment but, on the other hand, other conditions for standard listing may be relaxed in certain respects.[164] The issues put into sharp focus the delicacy of the balancing act involved in providing a listing regime that is simultaneously internationally competitive and of appropriate quality.[165]

Cross-border Share Issuance Activity Without a Passport—Making Use of Exemptions in EU Law

As an alternative to a full public offer in a number of countries made on the basis of a prospectus passport, the Prospectus Directive provides a number of exemptions that enable an issuer to conduct cross-border share issuance activity without a prospectus. This may be an attractive option where the issuer's need for capital or likely international investor interest

---

[162] J Guthrie and D Oakley, 'Listing Rules to be Tightened', *Financial Times*, 18 May 2013, 10.

[163] FSA, *Enhancing the Effectiveness of the Listing Regime* (CP12/25); FCA, *Feedback on CP12/25: Enhancing the Effectiveness of the Listing Regime and Further Consultation* (CP13/15, November 2013).

[164] FSA, CP12/25; FCA, CP13/15. In particular small percentage free floats may be permitted provided sufficient liquidity is present. See further ch 13.

[165] J Gapper, 'The City Drive to Help Small Investors Goes Much Too Far', *Financial Times*, 27 June 2013, 9.

in its offering is limited or where considerations such as the risk of facing multiple prospectus liability suits under a number of different legal systems are seen to outweigh the benefits of making an offering to a widely-drawn group of investors. A study of capital raising practices in the EU in 1999 found that prospectus passports were rarely used by European issuers to make offerings in European capital markets and that the much more common structure was for the home element of the offering to be made on a basis of a prospectus but for the cross-border element to be structured so as to come within exemptions.[166] That study pre-dated the current Prospectus Directive and the significant improvements to the design of the passport regime that have been made. However, some considerations, such as prospectus liability concerns, that militate against using the passport remain. The option of a full retail offer to investors in the home market which is accompanied by a prospectus, combined with an exempt wholesale offer to professional investors in other countries, may thus continue to hold considerable attraction.

Cross-border private placements within the EU have to be structured so as to comply with local requirements relating to investment advertisements and resale restrictions that are designed to prevent seepage into the retail market of securities sold on a prospectus-exempt basis to professionals only. The exact scope of the relevant exemptions under the local law in each of the Member States in which they are to be relied upon also needs to be checked. As the exemptions are derived from the Prospectus Directive, which is a maximum harmonization measure, in theory they should be identical across the EU but, as noted earlier in this chapter, differences in interpretation can creep in as part of the process whereby directives are incorporated into national laws. The wording of the exemptions in the current EU prospectus disclosure regime has been progressively refined with a view to minimizing divergence. ESMA's Guidance and Q&A relating to prospectuses also reduce the risk of inconsistent interpretations.

EU prospectus exemptions for international private placements

The exemptions in respect of public offer prospectuses that are of most relevance for cross-border equity issuance activity are those relating to offers of securities addressed solely to qualified investors; and offers of securities addressed to fewer than 150 natural or legal persons per Member State, other than qualified investors.[167] So long as the issuer is not seeking to list its securities on a regulated market in any of the territories in which the offer is made (in which case a prospectus obligation under that heading would arise unless a relevant exemption is available),[168] it can rely on these exemptions to make its offering. The category of qualified investors in the Prospectus Directive is now consistent with the definition in MiFID, namely, professional clients and eligible counterparties.[169] Standardization of the definition should reduce complexity and costs in respect of private placements.

A subsequent resale of securities to which an exemption applied is regarded as a separate offer and may require a prospectus unless an exemption applies.[170] However, a retail cascade (whereby securities are sold first to an intermediary, such as an investment bank, and then on to retail distributors) does not require a separate prospectus so long as a valid prospectus

---

[166] Jackson and Pan, 'Regulatory Competition in International Securities Markets: Evidence from Europe in 1999—Part I'.

[167] Prospectus Directive, Art 3(2).

[168] A point specifically confirmed in the ESMA Q&A on prospectuses (Q44).

[169] Prospectus Directive, Art 2.1(e).

[170] Prospectus Directive Art 3(2) (as amended).

is available and the issuer or the person responsible for drawing up the prospectus has consented to its use.[171]

A Brief Transatlantic Comparison[172]

The US and EU regulatory frameworks for public offers and listings of securities are, at a high level, broadly similar. On both sides of the Atlantic, public offers and listings of equity securities trigger extensive disclosure requirements; listed issuers are subject to an array of demanding regulatory requirements; these requirements are modified in certain respects for foreign issuers; and there are numerous exemptions from the general disclosure and other requirements that, among other things, facilitate international offerings of securities targeted at sophisticated investors who can fend for themselves. This section provides a very brief overview of the treatment of foreign private issuers in US securities regulation and examines the exemptions that are most pertinent for international issuance activity in a little more detail.[173]

Public offers and listings

In outline, the US Securities Act of 1933, section 5 generally prohibits an issuer from making any public offer or sale of any security in the US unless a registration statement with respect to that security filed with the SEC has become effective and delivery of a prospectus forming a part of such registration statement accompanies (or precedes) confirmation of the sale. The prohibition may in certain circumstances extend to the sale of securities outside the US to US persons. A US listing triggers registration under the Securities Exchange Act of 1934, section 12.[174] The disclosure requirements for making a public offering and for listing are substantially identical. A listed issuer also becomes subject to the periodic reporting and other requirements of the Exchange Act of 1934, section 13 and section 15. Foreign private issuers use SEC Form 20-F for their original registration and for subsequent annual filings, and Form 6-K for other periodic filings. A foreign company is a 'foreign private issuer' for this purpose unless more than 50 per cent of its outstanding voting securities are owned directly or indirectly by US residents, and any of the following conditions is satisfied: (a) the majority of executive officers/directors are US citizens or residents; (b) more than 50 per cent of the assets of the issuer are located in the US; or (c) the business is administered principally in the US. In 1999 the SEC adopted a complete revision of Form 20-F that replaced most of the other requirements with IOSCO international disclosure standards. As discussed earlier in this chapter, since 2008 foreign issuers have been permitted to use IFRS to satisfy financial reporting requirements. Certain other requirements of the US securities regulatory regime are also modified for foreign issuers.[175] These accommodations reflect efforts by the SEC to balance investor protection considerations and an interest in maintaining the international competitiveness of the US securities markets.

---

[171] Prospectus Directive Art 3(2) (as amended).

[172] SEC, *Accessing the U.S. Capital Markets—A Brief Overview for Foreign Private Issuers* <http://www.sec.gov/divisions/corpfin/internatl/foreign-private-issuers-overview.shtml> accessed July 2013.

[173] On the topic generally: KB Davis, 'The SEC and Foreign Companies—A Balance of Competing Interests' (2010) 71 *University of Pittsburgh Law Review* 457.

[174] In certain circumstances foreign private issuers may also be required to register a class of equity securities under the Exchange Act based upon the size of the company and the nature of its share ownership, both globally and within the United States: SEC, *Accessing the U.S. Capital Markets*.

[175] R de la Mater, 'Recent Trends in SEC Regulation of Foreign Issuers: How the U.S. Regulatory Regime is Affecting the United States' Historic Position as the World's Principal Capital Market' (2006) 39 *Cornell International Law Journal* 109 provides an overview.

The Sarbanes-Oxley Act of 2002, which is concerned with corporate governance matters including senior officer certification of financial statements, independent audit committees, audit partner rotation and auditor oversight, applies to foreign issuers that are listed in the United States as well as to domestic issuers. The Act, as originally enacted, treated domestic and foreign companies in the same way but accommodations had to be made in order to avoid conflicts with corporate governance requirements and practices under foreign issuers' domestic laws.[176] Even so, compliance with the Sarbanes-Oxley Act remains a concern for foreign issuers. The enhanced regulatory burdens associated with Sarbanes-Oxley are regarded by many as a factor that has undermined the attractiveness of a US listing for foreign issuers.

It is relatively easy for an issuer to delist its securities in the US but this does not terminate registration and obligations that are associated with registration. Until 2007 an issuer was not entitled to terminate its registration of a class of securities not listed on a US exchange unless the class was held by fewer than 300 US residents. The '300 US resident holders' test had not kept pace with the internationalization of investment portfolios, which had meant that many foreign issuers had well in excess of that number of US investors. In 2007 the SEC accepted that the test was inadequate and amended its rules so as to permit foreign private issuers to deregister on the basis of specified criteria designed to measure US market interest for any class of securities by reference principally to the US trading volume of that class as compared to the trading volume in the primary trading market for that class.[177] Under the amended rules, a foreign private issuer is eligible to terminate its Exchange Act registration and reporting obligations regarding a class of equity securities if the US average daily trading volume of the class of securities has been no greater than 5 per cent of the average daily trading volume of that same class of securities on a worldwide basis during a recent 12-month period and certain other conditions are met.

The new category of registrant for listing known as an 'emerging growth company' (EGC) created by the Jumpstart Our Business Startups Act (the JOBS Act) of 2012 does not exclude foreign companies. Foreign EGCs considering an SEC-registered IPO can therefore benefit from the scaled-back requirements that are now in place for smaller issuers, including modified disclosure requirements.[178]

US exemptions for international private placements

There are several exemptions from the section 5 registration requirements. The exemptions that are of most significance in relation to international equity offerings are: sales of securities outside the US (Regulation S); private placements (Section 4(a)(2) and Regulation D); and resales to qualified institutional buyers (Rule 144A).

Regulation S: sales and resales outside the US[179]

The SEC adopted Regulation S in 1990 in order to clarify the circumstances under which the Securities Act 1933, section 5 registration requirements would not be applied extraterritorially. Regulation S replaced a complicated set of selling restrictions with a more territorial

---

[176] Coffee, 'Racing Towards the Top?' 1824–6.

[177] SEC, *Termination of a Foreign Private Issuer's Registration of a Class of Securities under Section 12(g) and Duty to File Reports under Section 13(a) or 15(f) of the Securities Exchange Act of 1934*, 17 CFR Parts 200, 232, 240, and 249 (2007).

[178] SEC, *Accessing the U.S. Capital Markets*.   [179] Scott and Gelpern, *International Finance*, 94–9.

approach to the application of US law. Where the requirements of Regulation S are met, US registration requirements will not apply. Regulation S does not affect the extraterritorial application of the anti-fraud provisions of the US federal securities laws.

The effect of Regulation S is that for the purposes of the registration requirements of the Securities Act of 1933, the terms 'offer' and 'sale' are deemed to exclude offers and sales that occur 'outside the United States.' By way of non-exclusive safe harbours, an offer or sale is deemed to take place outside the US when two general conditions are satisfied: (a) it is an 'off-shore' transaction, and (b) there are no directed selling efforts in the US. In addition, there is a further condition on the Regulation S safe harbour for primary offerings, which operates by reference to whether there is substantial US market interest (SUSMI) in the issuer's securities.

An offshore transaction is one where the offer is made outside the US and the buyer is, or is reasonably believed by the seller to be, outside the US at the time of origination of the buy order. Alternatively, it is a transaction where the offer is made outside the US and the transaction is executed through a securities exchange located outside the US (for a primary offer) or the facilities of a designated offshore securities market (in the case of a resale). Offshore transactions are not restricted to sales to non-US residents.

Directed selling efforts are any activities that could reasonably be expected to have the effect of conditioning the market in the US for any of the securities being offered. Directed selling efforts could include advertisements with television or radio stations reaching the US (though there are certain specific exemptions for particular types of advertisement). Marketing efforts in the US for an offering that is otherwise exempt from the registration requirements of the Securities Act will not generally be treated as directed selling efforts of a simultaneous offering outside the US under Regulation S.

The primary offer safe harbour in Regulation S distinguishes between three categories of offerings. The thinking that underlies this three-tier structure is that there is a risk that securities that have been sold initially on an exempt basis could flow back into the US markets by unregulated routes and the more the issuer is connected with the US the greater the risk of flow back.

Category I offerings include offerings of equity securities of foreign issuers for which there is no substantial US market interest. Whether there is a substantial US market interest is determined by reference to whether the US represents the largest single market for such securities of the issuer or to a comparison of the percentage of dealings in that class of securities that takes place via US market facilities and of dealings via the facilities of the securities market of a single foreign country. As a matter of practice, the view generally taken is that there will be a substantial US market interest for very few foreign issuers, including even those foreign issuers that have obtained a listing on a securities exchange in the US. Category I offerings need only comply with the general conditions discussed earlier.

Category II offerings include equity offerings by foreign issuers that are subject to periodic reporting requirements under US securities law that do not fit within Category I because there is substantial US market interest. For Category II offerings, in addition to satisfying the offshore transaction and directed selling efforts requirements, the issuer must also comply with certain selling restrictions. Offers and sales of the securities in the US or to US persons (defined by reference to residency rather than nationality) are prohibited during a restricted period lasting forty days. There are also certain procedural requirements relating to legends that must appear on all offering material and agreements that must be obtained from distributors on their efforts to conform to the safe harbour.

Category III offerings include equity offerings of foreign issuers not subject to the periodic reporting requirements under US securities law that do not fit into Category I because there is a substantial US market interest for the class of securities being offered. Very few offerings of foreign issuers will fall into this category. Equity offerings by US issuers also fall into this category. The most rigorous restrictions apply in this case: in addition to the general conditions, selling restrictions apply for a period of one year for offerings of equity securities, and there are additional procedural requirements.

Securities may also be re-sold under Regulation S so long as the transaction is offshore and there are no directed selling efforts in the US. The resale provisions are not limited to securities originally sold under the Regulation. Securities privately placed in the US or acquired in another exempt sale can be re-sold offshore in reliance on Regulation S. Equally, securities offered outside the US using the Regulation S exemption can then be immediately re-sold in the US using the Rule 144A exemption, considered later.

Private placements and Regulation D[180]

Section 4(a)(2) of the Securities Act of 1933 exempts from registration requirements transactions by an issuer not involving any 'public offering.' In Regulation D the SEC addressed uncertainties in determining whether a 'public offering' has occurred by providing a non-exclusive safe harbour for offerings made under section 4(a)(2). The background to the adoption of Regulation D was Congressional demands for a relaxation of the registration burden on smaller issuers. However, for the purposes of this chapter it is the safe harbours that Rule 506 of Regulation D provides for private offerings that is most important.[181] Rule 506(b) of Regulation D allows offers and sales not involving any public offering to an unlimited number of accredited investors. The category of 'accredited investor' includes banks, insurance companies, registered and small business investment companies, certain business development companies, certain employer benefit plans, and organizations and individuals that meet certain minimum net worth thresholds. Rule 506(b) of Regulation D also allows sales to no more than 35 non-accredited investors who meet certain sophistication standards. Reliance on Rule 506(b) is subject to the condition that the issuers and persons acting on its behalf must not offer or sell the securities through any form of general solicitation. In addition, Rule 506(c) of Regulation D, added in 2013 to implement rule changes mandated by the JOBS Act, permits, on certain conditions, the use of general solicitation to offer and sell securities under Rule 506. The conditions include that the issuer must take reasonable steps to verify that the purchasers of the securities are accredited investors, and all purchasers of the securities must be accredited investors.[182]

Rule 144A: resales of restricted securities to qualified institutional buyers[183]

Rule 144A is a non-exclusive safe harbour that exempts from registration requirements resales to qualified institutional buyers (QIBs) of securities issued in a non-public offering that are not of the same class or fungible with securities listed or quoted on a US national securities exchange or automated inter-dealer quotation system. As such, the rule addresses the circumstances in which a person who has purchased securities from an issuer in a transaction which was itself exempt from registration under the Securities Act of 1933, such as an offshore transaction made in accordance with Regulation S or a private placement made in

---

[180] Scott and Gelpern, *International Finance*, 91–2.   [181] Under Rule 506.
[182] SEC, *Eliminating the Prohibition Against General Solicitation and General Advertising in Rule 506 and Rule 144A Offerings* (Release No 22-9415, July 2013).
[183] Scott and Gelpern, *International Finance*, 99–101.

reliance on Regulation D, may resell those securities without destroying the original exemption or otherwise being subject to the Securities Act registration requirements. The rationale behind the Rule 144A exemption is that the benefit of disclosure-based investor protection is outweighed by the benefit of more rapid access to capital markets when securities are exclusively placed with experienced, sophisticated investors.

Under Rule 144A, a person may resell securities to any QIB provided that the securities are not of the same class when issued as securities of the issuer listed on a US national securities exchange or quoted on a US automated inter-dealer quotation system (the fungibility prohibition) and certain notice and informational requirements are fulfilled. Rules enacted to implement the JOBS Act have given more flexibility to publicize a Rule 144A offering by permitting general solicitation and general advertising provided that actual sales are made only to persons that are reasonably believed to be QIBs.[184] A QIB is (a) an institution that owns and invests on a discretionary basis at least US$100 million in qualifying securities (US$10 million if the person is a US broker-dealer), or (b) an entity owned by a QIB, or (c) a US broker-dealer buying as agent for, or in a riskless principal transaction for resale to, a QIB. In addition, banks and savings and loan associations with a net worth of at least US$25 million are also QIBs.

The fungibility prohibition means, for example, that common stock of US listed companies cannot be sold under Rule 144A. The goal of this requirement is to prevent trading of essentially the same securities simultaneously in public and private markets.

Rule 144A sales are not subject to the stringent liability provisions that apply to registered public offers. However, Rule 10b-5 liability under the Exchange Act of 1934 is applicable. This is the basic anti-fraud provision of the federal securities law. It prohibits fraudulent devices, schemes, and practices, and also misstatements/omissions of material facts (but negligence is not enough). It gives rise to a private remedy in the hands of injured investors.

The more favourable position with regard to potential liability is commonly cited as a factor with explanatory force with regard to the spectacular growth of the Rule 144A market. Surveying the decade from the mid-1990s, Howell Jackson and Eric Pan note that, around the world, foreign issuers increasingly have available to them a menu of choices as to how to access the US capital markets and that for many foreign issuers the Rule 144A alternative has emerged as the option of choice.[185] The observation by Hal Scott and Anna Gelpern that by 2010 over three-quarters of all capital raised by foreign firms in US IPOs was raised in the Rule 144A market supports this claim.[186] Jackson and Pan acknowledge that the trend can be attributed to a number of factors, including improvements in the relative quality of foreign trading markets, a narrowing of the gap distinguishing US and European disclosure standards and increasing investor mobility, but they also stress the salience of US litigation risks for foreign issuers.

---

[184] SEC, *Eliminating the Prohibition Against General Solicitation and General Advertising*.

[185] HE Jackson and EJ Pan, 'Regulatory Competition in International Securities Markets: Evidence from Europe—Part II' (2008) 3 *Virginia Law & Business Review* 207.

[186] Scott and Gelpern, *International Finance*, 101.

15

Corporate Bonds

Introduction

Bond markets are a source of debt financing for companies. The economic benefits that can flow from well-functioning corporate bond markets include:[1]

(1) diversification of sources of funds for the corporate sector, thereby making it less vulnerable to collapses in bank lending;

(2) increased choice and flexibility, which enhance the ability of firms to raise finance that is a good match for the timing and currency of their cash flows;

(3) strengthening of the balance sheets of pension funds and life insurance companies by providing institutional investors with instruments that satisfy demand for fixed-income assets with long maturities, higher returns than government bonds, and less risk than equity;

(4) internationalization of funding sources;

(5) enhancement of corporate transparency and disclosure; and

(6) risk management benefits.

Noting their many benefits, the International Organization of Securities Commissions (IOSCO), in collaboration with the World Bank, has emphasized the need for deeper and broader corporate bond markets in emerging economies in order to reduce reliance on bank financing and to improve efficiency.[2] With respect to developed economies, the bond markets have been described as 'a core sector of the capital markets in the UK... a major financing tool for the private sector.'[3] Historically, the bond markets played a less significant role in the financing of the Continental European, especially German, corporate sector[4] but political and economic developments since the 1990s, including the introduction of the euro, have changed the market environment.[5] Bank loans and other advances still accounted for 85 per cent of total non-financial corporate debt outstanding in the euro area and in the UK in 2011, while non-financial corporate bonds accounted for only 15 per cent.[6] (By contrast, the equivalent proportions in the United States were 53 per cent to 47 per cent.[7]) Nevertheless, commentators on the European position noted that corporate bonds are 'developing into a meaningful alternative to bank loans.'[8]

---

[1] ICMA (International Capital Market Association), *Economic Importance of the Corporate Bond Markets* (March 2013); IMF, *Global Financial Stability Report* (September 2005) ch IV (Development of Corporate Bond Markets in Emerging Countries).

[2] IOSCO, *Development of Corporate Bond Markets in the Emerging Economies* (FR10/11, November 2011).

[3] FSA, *Trading Transparency in the UK Secondary Bond Markets* (Discussion Paper 05/5) para 2.3.

[4] ECB, *The Euro Bond Market Study* (December 2004) 45.

[5] M Pagano and EL von Thadden, 'The European Bond Markets under EMU' (2004) 20 *Oxford Review of Economic Policy* 531; G de Bondt and JD Lichtenberger, 'The Euro Area Corporate Bond Market: Where Do We Stand Since the Introduction of the Euro?' (2003) 4 *European Business Organization Law Review* 517.

[6] European Commission, *European Financial Stability and Integration Report 2012* (April 2013) 5.

[7] European Commission, *European Financial Stability and Integration Report 2012* (April 2013) 5.

[8] Deutsche Bank, 'Corporate Bond Issuance in Europe' (January 2013) *EU Monitor* 13.

This trend was already evident in the years prior to the financial crisis of 2007–9 and the later euro area sovereign debt crisis. During the pre-crisis years, euro area issuers increasingly sought to expand their range of funding sources by issuing bonds, including euro denominated bonds.[9] According to one study, the overall euro area bond market achieved a growth rate of 283 per cent between 1994 and 2004, outstripping its US equivalent, where the market grew by 35 per cent over the same period.[10] Private-sector debt issuance in the euro area rose from US$124 billion to US$273 billion between 1994 and 1998 and, after the introduction of the euro, increased to US$657 in 1999.[11] By 2004, private-sector bond issuance in the euro area was about US$550 billion.[12] Bond issues played a significant part in the financing of the wave of mergers and acquisitions that swept across Europe in the 2000s.[13] Issuers found a rapidly growing community of investors pursuing internationally-diversified investment strategies for bonds, especially within the euro area. The financial services industry responded quickly to new business opportunities and helped to push forward changes in the market through more aggressive competition for underwriting and other intermediary services, and the provision of more standardized electronic trading services.[14] Continuous product development, including innovative asset-backed securitization structures and credit derivative products, also played a role in broadening and deepening the European corporate bond market.[15]

In the aftermath of the financial and sovereign debt crises, bond market growth helped to counterbalance the decline in bank lending to the corporate sector.[16] According to Dealogic, a financial data provider, all time high issuance volumes in 2009 were followed by a record high in investment grade bond issuance in 2012. Quantitative easing programmes by central banks (involving the creation of new money in the economy in order to bring down interest rates faced by corporate and individual borrowers) helped to fuel the demand. The corporate sector's high dependency on bond issues as a source of finance is expected to continue as banks cut back on lending in order to restructure their balance sheets so as to comply with more demanding capital requirements. In addition, with sovereign bonds offering historically low returns, the expansion of the corporate bond market is also being driven by high levels of interest from investors in search of yield.[17] However, as the search for yield takes investors further away from investment grade opportunities, the dangers of a market 'bubble' increase. At the time of writing (mid-2013) fears that the corporate bond market may be overheating are being openly discussed.

Institutional investors are the major investors in bonds and they are especially dominant in the UK market.[18] Sovereign wealth funds and hedge funds are also significant players in the bond capital markets. Direct retail investment in bonds was rare historically in the UK but more common elsewhere in Europe.[19] However, the situation is fluid: in response to growing UK retail investor interest in bond market investments, in 2010 the London Stock Exchange

---

[9] ECB, *The Euro Bond Market Study*, 21–2.

[10] JP Casey and K Lannoo, *Europe's Hidden Capital Markets* (Centre for European Policy Studies, Brussels, 2005) 8.

[11] Pagano and von Thadden, 'The European Bond Markets under EMU.'

[12] Pagano and von Thadden, 'The European Bond Markets under EMU.'

[13] ECB, *The Euro Bond Market Study*, 22.

[14] Pagano and von Thadden, 'The European Bond Markets under EMU.'

[15] ECB, *The Euro Bond Market Study*, 6.

[16] Deutsche Bank, *Corporate Bond Issuance in Europe* (*EU Monitor*, January 2013) 7–8.

[17] Deutsche Bank, *Corporate Bond Issuance in Europe*, 9–10.

[18] FSA, *Trading Transparency in the UK Secondary Bond Markets*, paras 2.12–2.13. See also IOSCO, *Transparency of Bond Markets*, (Report of the Technical Committee of the International Organization of Securities Commissions, May 2004) section B.2.

[19] FSA, *Trading Transparency in the UK Secondary Bond Markets*, para 2.14.

(LSE) launched an electronic Order book for Retail Bonds (ORB), a new initiative based on the successful Borsa Italiana's MOT retail fixed market, on which there was €230 billion worth of trading in 2009. This was followed in 2013 by the establishment of the FTSE ORB Index Series, measuring the performance of corporate bonds trading on the ORB across different industry sectors and maturity bands. Retail bonds traded on the ORB must be tradable in units of no larger than £10,000, and the bond issue must meet the requirements of both the listing regime and the disclosure framework set by the Prospectus Directive, discussed further later in this chapter.[20] ORB listed bonds tend to be characterized by simple structures, and to have trading denominations of under £1,000, typically £100 but with a minimum upfront investment of £2,000.[21] By October 2012 £2.5 billion had been raised via ORB but secondary market trading activity remained sluggish.[22] Retail bonds are potentially much more lucrative in terms of yield than bank deposits but are correspondingly riskier investments because principal can be lost and they are not covered by deposit protection or financial compensation schemes.

Bonds and Issuers' Capital Structure and Financing Choices

Corporate bonds are regarded as providing predictable cash flows for issuers and investors: they provide issuers with an investment of capital when the bonds are issued; and they afford investors regular interest payments and repayment of capital at maturity.[23] Bonds may be secured, unsecured or unsubordinated; hence ranking in insolvency depends on the terms of issue. However, bonds will always rank ahead of equity. For this reason, and also because interest payments have greater certainty and predictability than dividends, bond financing is generally cheaper than equity. At the same time, bonds usually offer potentially higher rates of return than bank deposits, which increases their attractiveness (but also risk) to investors. Bonds can trade on secondary markets, where prices will fluctuate according to general interest expectations and issues relating specifically to the issuer's creditworthiness. Bond prices tend to be in an inverse relationship with interest rates. Secondary market turnover in bond markets is lower than in equity markets as many institutional investors buy bonds to hold to maturity in order to fund long-term cash flow commitments such as pensions.[24] In 2013 the International Capital Market Association (ICMA) noted that average bond trade size was in the region of €1 to 2 million, with many trades above €5 million; that unlike equities, in which trading takes place mostly on stock exchanges and other multilateral trading facilities, most secondary market trading in the international bond market took place bilaterally over the counter; and that only about 2 per cent of issues traded once a day or more.[25]

Bonds are a very flexible form of financing for companies because the terms of issue are infinitely adaptable to the individual issuer's circumstances and the prevailing market conditions at the time of issue. Large corporate issuers are best placed to exploit the flexibility that bond markets provide. Such issuers have the widest choice, including, for example, being able to raise financing for very large projects directly from the corporate bond market

---

[20] LSE, *Listing and Admitting Retail Bonds* (2010).

[21] LSE, 'Retail Bonds' <http://www.londonstockexchange.com/specialist-issuers/retail-bonds/retail-bonds.htm> accessed July 2013.

[22] M Stothard, 'UK Market for Retail Bonds on Track to Top £1 billion of Issues' *Financial Times*, 30 October 2012, 20.

[23] ICMA, *Economic Importance of the Corporate Bond Markets*, 7; H Bessembinder and W Maxwell, 'Transparency and the Corporate Bond Markets' (2008) 22 *The Journal of Economic Perspectives* 217.

[24] ICMA, *Economic Importance of the Corporate Bond Markets*, 8.

[25] ICMA, *Economic Importance of the Corporate Bond Markets*, 13.

and/or indirectly from banks via the syndicated loan market.[26] Raising finance directly from the bond markets via direct issuance is generally not an option for small and medium-sized companies because of their relatively small size, their limited financing needs, and the corresponding disproportionality of issuance costs.[27] Smaller quoted companies can also be effectively shut out of the bond markets by reason of their size and needs, and by the fact that they are not rated.[28] The opening of the LSE's retail bond market (ORB, discussed earlier) was accompanied by efforts to encourage rating agencies to extend their coverage to a wider range of companies in order to facilitate the marketing of Mid-Cap bonds to investors. However, the UK Quoted Companies Alliance/BDO Small and Mid-Cap Sentiment Index (2013) reported that small and mid-cap quoted companies and their advisors continued to know little about the ORB and that significant obstacles to the issuance of corporate bonds, including lack of past experience and relevant knowledge of the potential value of this form of financing, remained.[29]

As hinted at in the previous paragraph, credit rating agencies (CRAs) perform a central function in modern capital markets by assigning ratings to debt instruments, including the more exotic derivative and structured products that proliferated up to the 2007–9 financial crisis.[30] The common description of bonds as 'investment grade' or 'speculative grade'/'junk' derives from the ratings assigned to them by CRAs.[31] The ratings industry's origins lay in bridging information gaps between buyers and sellers of financial instruments. The correction of informational asymmetries in the market continues to be an important part of their modern role. Ratings are also widely used in contractual provisions governing the availability of credit. In addition, ratings have acquired considerable direct regulatory significance because of a trend (now in the process of being reversed) for bank capital regulatory requirements to incorporate references to ratings in the treatment of financial instruments. Partnoy captured the pre-crisis market and regulatory significance of the ratings industry by describing the business of CRAs as having changed over time from the selling of information to that of being the distributors of 'keys that unlocked the financial markets.'[32]

Terms of Bonds[33]

Bonds generally have three basic features—the par value (which will normally also be the redemption value), the interest rate, (or coupon), and the length of time to maturity—but these can be freely added to or varied, so as most effectively to meet particular investor preferences and market conditions at the time of issue. Accounting and regulatory considerations

[26] Y Altunbaş, A Kara, and D Marqués-Ibáñez, 'Large Debt Financing: Syndicated Loans versus Corporate Bonds' (ECB Working Papers Series No 1028, March 2009).

[27] Department for Business Innovation and Skills, *SME Access to External Finance* (BIS Economics Paper No 16, January 2012).

[28] P Brierley and M Young, 'The Financing of Smaller Quoted Companies: A Survey' (2004) *Bank of England Quarterly Bulletin* 160.

[29] <http://theqca.com/news/briefs/68507/confidence-improves-but-access-to-funding-deteriorates-in-qcabdo-index.thtml> accessed July 2013.

[30] Joint Forum, *Stocktaking on the Use of Credit Ratings* (June 2009). The Joint Forum is established under the aegis of the Basel Committee on Banking Supervision (BCBS), IOSCO and the International Association of Insurance Supervisors (IAIS) to deal with issues common to the banking, securities, and insurance sectors.

[31] For Moody's, Aaa-Baa3 is investment grade; Ba1-C is speculative. For Standard and Poors, the equivalents are AAA-BBB- and BB+-C.

[32] F Partnoy, 'Historical Perspectives on the Financial Crisis: Ivar Kreuger, The Credit Rating Agencies, and Two Theories about the Function, and Dysfunction, of Markets' (2009) 26 *Yale Journal on Regulation* 431, 432. See also JC Coffee, 'The Ratings Agencies' in JC Coffee, *Gatekeepers* (Oxford: OUP, 2006), 283.

[33] WL Megginson, SB Smart, and BM Lucey, *An Introduction to Corporate Finance* (London: South-Western Cengate Learning, 2008) 131–7.

can have a significant impact on the terms included in bond issues, as in the case of some hybrid securities, which are debt instruments that replicate some features of equity with a view to securing the interest-deductibility tax benefits of debt whilst at the same time being treated as equivalent to equity for accounting purposes or for the purposes of bank capital adequacy requirements.[34] For example, contingent convertible bonds (CoCos), which are bonds that are designed automatically to convert to equity upon the occurrence of a speci-fied trigger event, are being developed by banks with a view to satisfying the more stringent capital requirements that are being put in place in the aftermath of the financial crisis.[35] The Basel Committee, which is the body responsible for the international capital adequacy stand-ards, divides capital into tiers, of which the top category is Common Equity Tier 1, and the second is Additional Tier 1.[36] The Basel Committee has considered whether 'high trigger' CoCos, which are instruments designed to convert to equity whilst the bank remains a going concern, could be considered to be so similar to common equity as to be capable of satisfying new capital surcharges aimed at addressing the 'too-big-to-fail' problem posed by the largest international banks, but, thus far, has declined to give the green light to the use of CoCos for this purpose.[37] However, it has allowed 'low trigger' debt financial instruments that provide for conversion to common shares at the point of non-viability, ie when the bank is no longer to support itself in the market, to count as Additional Tier 1 capital.[38]

Another relevant factor for the drawing up of issuance terms can be the views of rating agencies, which, as noted earlier, perform an information gathering, evaluation, and dis-semination function by assigning ratings to bonds when they are issued. The terms and con-ditions attaching to a particular issue of bonds can affect the rating assigned and may result in a difference between the rating applied to the issue and the general credit rating applied to the issuer itself. An illustration of the importance of the role played by rating agencies in driving the structure of bond issue documentation is provided by the development of the European market for corporate hybrid bonds, which began around 2003 but took off significantly in 2005 after the rating agencies clarified their methodologies for rating these instruments.[39]

Interest

The rate of interest on a bond may be fixed or floating. In floating rate bonds the coupon is set at a predetermined margin above a specified money market rate. The London Interbank Offered Rate (LIBOR), which is meant to be a representation of unsecured interbank term borrowing costs in the London markets, is one of the most common indices used for floating rate bonds. The Wheatley Review in 2012 noted that LIBOR was the most frequently utilized benchmark for interest rates globally, referenced in transactions with a notional outstanding

---

[34] eg the subordinated bonds considered by the High Court in *Kaupthing Singer & Friedlander Limited (in Administration)* [2010] EWHC 316 (Ch), which contained subordination terms that were specifically intended to ensure that they would qualify for inclusion in the issuer's regulatory capital.

[35] R Bax and P Athanassiou, 'Contingent Debt Instruments and Their Challenges: Some Insights' (2011) 26 *Butterworths Journal of International Banking and Financial Law* 20; C Pazarbasioglu, J Zhou, V le Leslé, and M Moore, 'Contingent Capital: Economic Rationale and Design Features' IMF Staff Discussion Note, No SDN/11/01 (January 2011); Goldman Sachs, *Contingent Capital: Possibilities, Problems and Opportunities* (March 2011).

[36] Basel Committee on Banking Supervision, *Basel III: A Global Regulatory Framework for More Resilient Banks and Banking Systems* (June 2011).

[37] Basel Committee on Banking Supervision, *Global Systemically Important Banks: Assessment Methodology and the Additional Loss Absorbency Requirement* (November 2011).

[38] GL Lyons, PM Rodel, and E Ligere, 'Hot CoCos from Basel III—the Next Bank Hybrid' (2011) 26 *Journal of International Banking Law and Supervision* 412.

[39] D Andrews, 'Corporate Hybrids Edge Towards Mainstream' (2006) 25(3) *International Financial Law Review* 7; B Maiden, 'Moody's Defends Hybrid Securities' (2006) 25(4) *International Financial Law Review* 68.

value of at least $300 trillion.[40] This Review was prompted by reports of manipulation of the data submitted by banks for the purposes of compiling the rate, and it has led to reform initiatives including the establishment of new arrangements for the administration of LIBOR and tighter regulation.[41]

Also possible are deep discount bonds, which typically offer a zero coupon but allow the investor to make a return by acquiring the securities at a significant discount to their redemption price. Another possibility is the step-up bond, which gives investors a higher coupon after an initial period. The step-up may be coupled with an issuer call option to enable the issuer to redeem the bond before it matures; the increase in the interest charge will act as an incentive for the issuer to exercise that option.

Ordinarily, interest on bonds is payable whether or not the issuer is profitable. However, in some types of hybrid bonds, which seek to replicate equity instruments, interest payments may be deferred until maturity in certain circumstances, such as where certain preset financial ratios are not met. Payment-in-kind or PIK bonds (or notes) are junior debt instruments that do not pay any interest until they mature.[42]

Maturity

Most bonds have an original maturity of at least a year, but this can range up to thirty years, and beyond for some issues. (Debt financial instruments with a maturity of less than one year may be described as 'notes' but bonds and notes are essentially the same type of instrument from a legal perspective.) Hybrid bonds may have a very long maturity or be perpetual, so as to replicate the permanence which is a feature of equity capital. Issuer call options are likely to be included in long-dated bonds so as to bolster their appeal to investors. Bonds may include bondholder put options, which allow bondholders to force redemption in certain circumstances, such as a change of ownership or a restructuring event within the issuer that triggers a ratings downgrade.

Ranking

Corporate bonds are normally unsecured. A major exception is the securitization, including the collateralized debt obligations (CDOs), segment of the market: bonds issued by special purpose vehicles that are secured on a pool of income-producing assets, such as mortgages, leases, credit card debts, bonds, or loans.[43] Collateralized bond issues tend to involve several tranches of debt with 'senior secured' securities on top, followed by 'second lien' securities, and then more 'junior' securities.[44] Unsecured bonds may also be subordinated so as to rank behind other unsecured debts in the event of the issuer's insolvency. Subordination is a feature of hybrid bonds that seek to mimic equity instruments whilst retaining the favourable tax deductibility status of debt. Historically, there was some doubt about the

---

[40] M Wheatley, *The Wheatley Review of LIBOR: Initial Discussion Paper* (August 2012) 9–11.

[41] M Wheatley, *The Wheatley Review of LIBOR: Final Report* (September 2012). In July 2013 the British Bankers Association announced that it would appoint NYSE Euronext Rate Administration Limited (NYSE Euronext Rate) as the new LIBOR administrator. NYSE Euronext Rate will be regulated by the FCA and expects to take over the administration of LIBOR in early 2014 after a period of transition from the current administrator, BBA LIBOR Ltd.

[42] M Stothard, 'Boom-era Debt Securities Stage Return in Europe' *Financial Times*, 24 November 2012, 14.

[43] ECB, *The Euro Bond Market Study*, 41–2. Generally on secured debt, see ch 12.

[44] S Whitehead, 'Managing Demand for Debt Puts Documentation Issues in the Spotlight' (2006) 25(1) *International Financial Law Review Private Equity Supplement* 17; G Fuller and F Ranero, 'Collateralised Debt Obligations' (2005) 20(9) *Butterworths Journal of International Banking and Financial Law* 343.

legal effectiveness under English law of contractual subordination of unsecured debt and rather complex structures were developed to safeguard against that legal risk.[45] However, concerns have receded because straightforward subordination clauses have been upheld in recent cases,[46] although issues as to the correct interpretation of subordination terms can still arise.[47] In particular circumstances, more complex subordination structures may still be employed, such as where multiple layers of unsecured subordination are sought.[48]

Covenants

The covenants that are included in bond issues tend to be less extensive than those in term loans,[49] although the emergence of 'covenant-lite' (or cov-lite) loans has narrowed the gap. Cov-lite loans were strongly associated with the boom in private-equity financed leveraged buyout activity up to 2007.[50] In more recent years, the growing popularity of cov-lite loans has been linked to investors' search for yield and to the trade-off between restrictive contractual terms and the rate of return.[51] Lower levels of covenant protection in bonds is also conventionally associated with potential renegotiation difficulties that could arise with respect to publicly-traded instruments held by a large, dispersed group of investors.[52] Some have gone as far as to suggest that covenants written into public debt instruments are virtually impossible to renegotiate with the consequence that all but the standard boilerplate covenants are useless in the public debt market.[53] The rise of secondary markets in loan participations generates a similar coordination problem and again brings the lending market closer to bond markets in this respect.

Common types of protective covenants in bonds are restrictions on additional debt, payout constraints, asset sale restrictions, investment restrictions, restrictions on changes of control, negative pledges, and restrictions on transactions with affiliates.[54] Close attention has to be paid to the drafting of the covenants in each individual case as this may reveal that

---

[45] E Ferran, *Company Law and Corporate Finance* (OUP, 1999) ch 16.

[46] *Manning v AIG Europe UK Ltd* [2006] Ch 610, CA; *Re Maxwell Communications Corporation plc* [1993] 1 WLR 1402. See also ch 11.

[47] eg, *Kaupthing Singer & Friedlander Limited (in Administration)* [2010] EWHC 316 (Ch).

[48] eg a trust may be used in a turnover subordination where the junior creditor is permitted to prove in the liquidation of the debtor but is required to account to specified senior creditors for liquidation dividends. By requiring the junior creditor to hold the liquidation dividends on trust, the arrangement is shielded from the effects of the junior creditor's own insolvency.

[49] WW Bratton, 'Bond Covenants and Creditor Protection: Economics and Law, Theory and Practice, Substance and Process' (2006) 9 *European Business Organization Law Review* 39; F Bazzana and M Palmieri, 'How to Increase the Efficiency of Bond Covenants: A Proposal for the Italian Corporate Market' (2012) 34 *European Journal of Law & Economics* 327. Regarding the tightness of covenants in loan agreements: C Demiroglu and C James, 'The Information Content of Bank Loan Covenants' (2010) 23 *The Review of Financial Studies* 3700.

[50] 'Markets and Operations' (2007) *Bank of England Quarterly Bulletin* Q2, 188, 195.

[51] S Foley, 'Covenant-lite Loans Lose Their Stigma in Hunt for Yield' *Financial Times*, 1 June 2013, 12.

[52] PR Wood, *International Loans, Bonds, Guarantees, Legal Opinions* 2nd edn (London: Sweet & Maxwell, 2007) ch 5.

[53] MH Bradley and MR Roberts, 'The Structure and Pricing of Corporate Debt Covenants' (13 May 2004) available at SSRN <http://ssrn.com/abstract=466240> accessed July 2013.

[54] DP Miller and N Reisel, 'Do Country-level Investor Protections Affect Security-level Contract Design? Evidence from Foreign Bond Covenants' (2012) 25 *Review of Financial Studies* 408; N Reisel, 'On the Value of Restrictive Covenants: An Empirical Investigation of Public Bond Issues' (January 2007) available at SSRN <http://ssrn.com/abstract=644522> accessed July 2013; WW Bratton, 'Bond Covenants and Creditor Protection: Economics and Law, Theory and Practice, Substance and Process' (2006) 9 *European Business Organization Law Review* 39; M Kahan and B Tuckman, 'Private Versus Public Lending: Evidence from Covenants' in JD Finnerty and MS Fridson (eds), *The Yearbook of Fixed Income Investing 1995* (Burr Ridge: Irwin Professional Publishing, 1996) 253 comparing covenants in private and public debt; K Lehn and A Poulsen, 'Contractual Resolution of Bondholder-Stockholder Conflicts in Leveraged Buyouts' (1991) 34 *Journal of Law and Economics* 645; CW Smith, Jr and JB Warner, 'On Financial Contracting: An Analysis of Bond Covenants' (1979) 7 *Journal of Financial Economics* 117.

the protection actually afford to the holders is weaker than first impressions suggest. For example, a negative pledge clause may be diluted by carveouts permitting the creation of security at subsidiary level or allowing security for specified types of new indebtedness or within certain parameters.[55] Similarly, covenants restricting an issuer from taking on additional debt may be undermined where those restrictions do not extend to the issuer's subsidiaries. For subsidiaries of an issuer of bonds to be free to incur new debt is potentially harmful to the issuer's bondholders because the parent's claims, as shareholder, to the subsidiary's assets rank behind (or, putting it another way, are structurally subordinated to) those of the subsidiaries' creditors. Institutional investors have responded to concern about weaknesses in the standards of protection for bondholders by producing a set of model covenants in sterling and euro bond issues.[56] The model form negative pledge covenant applies to all financial indebtedness, includes restrictions on structurally senior debt at subsidiary level, and applies to all group companies and to all types of assets. It also includes sale and leasebacks within its scope. The model form documentation also includes a change of control bondholder put event, which is a provision entitling holders to require the bonds to be redeemed in specified circumstances.[57] The trigger events in the model form documentation are: a disposal of all or substantially all of the assets of the group; any person or group of persons acting in concert acquiring over 50 per cent of the voting shares in the issuer; or any person or group of persons acting in concert acquiring control of the board of the issuer, or otherwise acquiring control of its operations. Language is provided to cater for issues where it is agreed that a ratings downgrade should trigger a put event. Wording for a covenant restricting disposals is also suggested. Where a disposals covenant is included, a disposal of all or substantially all of the assets would be both an event of default and a put event.

The immediate reaction of corporate treasurers to the model covenants was not enthusiastic. Their Association described the model covenants document as 'a missed opportunity for an initiative supportable by both investors and issuers that would have assisted the smooth running and efficiency of the bond markets.'[58] The surge in 'cov-lite' deals since its publication is an indication of limited market impact. The economic conditions of the period and, in particular, the growing number of investors searching for higher yields have moved the market in the opposite direction.

Conversion rights

Restrictive covenants limit the future actions of the issuer and thereby protect bondholders from opportunistic conduct by management and controlling shareholders. An alternative (or additional) mechanism for protecting bondholders from conduct that is favourable to shareholders but potentially disadvantageous for them is the inclusion of provisions for conversion into equity at the option of the holder.[59] ('Reverse' convertibles, in which the

---

[55] Fitch Ratings, 'Jumping The Queue: Ineffective European Bond Documentation's Negative Pledge and Structural Subordination-Related Provisions: Ratings Cliffs Waiting to Happen,' *European Corporates Special Report* (2003) 3–4; The Bond Covenant Group, *Model Covenants in Sterling and Euro Bond Issues* (June 2010) para 1.1.

[56] <http://www.treasurers.org/node/6044> accessed July 2013. This document was drawn up and published in 2010 by The Bond Covenant Group, comprising the Association of British Insurers (ABI), BVI Bundesverband Investment and Asset Management (BVI), the Investment Management Association (IMA), and the National Association of Pension Funds (NAPF).

[57] M Hartley, 'Beyond Change of Control' (2006) 21(11) *Butterworths Journal of International Banking and Financial Law* 475.

[58] <http://www.treasurers.org/node/6043> accessed July 2013.

[59] M Jensen and W Meckling, 'Theory of the Firm: Managerial Behavior, Agency Costs and Ownership Structure' (1976) 3 *Journal of Financial Economics* 305; CW Smith, Jr and JB Warner, 'On Financial Contracting: An Analysis of Bond Covenants' (1979) 7 *Journal of Financial Economics* 117.

delivery of equity is at the option of the issuer, are also possible.[60]) Conversion terms entitle bondholders to force conversion of their debt instruments into equity securities of the issuer or of another company in its group. Empirical data provides some evidence of conversion mechanisms and restrictive covenants acting as substitutes for each other.[61]

Convertible bonds work by giving the holder the option to convert the bonds into a fixed number of shares at a conversion price which is determined at the time of issue of the bonds. The conversion price is typically at a significant premium (around 25 to 30 per cent) to the market price of the shares at the time of issue. The coupon on convertible bonds tends to be lower than on 'plain vanilla' bonds of the same issuer because investors can trade interest expectations against the benefit of equity linkage. Should the market price of the conversion shares fail to rise to a level that makes the conversion price commercially attractive, bondholders can retain the bond and are not obliged to exercise the option to convert. Exercise of the conversion option has the effect of releasing the debt and converting it into equity capital. A variant on the convertible bond structure is the bond with warrant, which gives investors a debt instrument and also an entitlement to subscribe for shares. The warrant is usually detachable from the bond and can be traded separately; exercise of the warrant results in an injection of new equity capital and the bonds remain in issue. Also broadly similar to convertible bonds are exchangeable bonds, which are exchangeable into shares of another company, which need not be part of the bond issuer's corporate group.[62] Publicly issued convertible bonds usually contain special covenants that are intended to protect bondholders against actions by the issuer that would dilute the economic value of the conversion option.[63] Dilution could result from actions that result in value leaving the company, such as distributions to existing shareholders or disposals of assets at an undervalue. An issue of new shares could also cause economic dilution where the offer price of the shares is at a significant discount to the market price because the aggregate assets of the issuer would not increase sufficiently to compensate for the additional number of shares in issue. Capital reorganizations, such as share splits, could also be prejudicial to convertible bondholders, as where, for example, a company sub-divides its shares, but the conversion price remains unchanged—in effect the bondholder would have to pay the 'full' price for only part of the original assets. In overall terms, anti-dilution provisions will address voluntary action by the issuer of the bonds that could decrease the value of the equity into which the bonds are to be converted.[64] Catering for some possible future events, such as share splits, is a relatively straightforward matter of making mechanical adjustments but other possible future events can present more complex drafting challenges as well as questions of principle about how restrictive the covenants should be.[65] In publicly issued convertible bonds, anti-dilution provisions are usually limited to voluntary corporate actions in which there are clear agency problems flowing from divergence of interests between shareholders and bondholders: thus, typically, rights issues, bonus issues, disposals of assets to shareholders, and so forth are addressed but not transactions with outsiders in the ordinary course

---

[60] M Szymanowska, R Ter Horst, and CH Veld, 'Reverse Convertible Bonds Analyzed' (2009) 29 *Journal of Futures Markets* 895.

[61] M Kahan and D Yermack, 'Investment Opportunities and the Design of Debt Securities' (1998) 14 *Journal of Law, Economics and Organization* 136.

[62] M Asmar and J Cowan, 'Convertible and Exchangeable Bonds' (2001) 12(5) *Practical Law for Companies* 21.

[63] MA Woronoff and JA Rosen, 'Understanding Anti-dilution Provisions in Convertible Securities' (2005) 74 *Fordham Law Review* 129, 133; M Kahan, 'Anti-dilution Provisions in Convertible Securities' (1995) 2 *Stanford Journal of Law, Business and Finance* 147; PR Wood, 'International Convertible Bond Issues' [1986] *Journal of International Banking Law* 69. For an overview of formulae used in anti-dilution covenants, see Asmar and Cowan, 'Convertible and Exchangeable Bonds,' 27.

[64] Woronoff and Rosen, 'Understanding Anti-dilution Provisions in Convertible Securities,' 133.

[65] SI Glover, 'Solving Dilution Problems' (1996) 51 *Business Lawyer* 1241.

of business.[66] Furthermore, convertible bonds do not usually provide for adjustment on the payment of ordinary cash dividends or straightforward share buy-backs, as such restrictions would hamper routine corporate activity.[67]

Takeovers leading to the end of an active market in the shares into which bonds are convertible represent a significant potential threat to the interests of convertible bondholders. There are various ways in which the terms of the bonds can safeguard against this risk, such as by permitting bondholders to convert their bonds at an adjusted conversion price on a change of control of the issuer or to exercise a put option, or by imposing an obligation on the issuer to procure that the bidder extends its offer to the bondholders. Under the UK Takeover Code, contractual provisions in bond terms are bolstered by a specific requirement whereby a bidder is obliged to make an appropriate offer or proposal to the bondholders to ensure that their interests are safeguarded and that they receive equal treatment.[68]

Structure of Bond Issues

Various parties are usually involved in a bond issue, including, as well as the issuer, a lead manager to coordinate arrangements among the managers of the issue for the subscription and distribution of the bonds, a trustee to act as the intermediary between the issuer and the bondholders, a listing agent to assist with the listing process (for bonds that are to be admitted to listing), and fiscal, or paying, agents through which are channelled interest and other payments to bondholders and which, in the case of convertible bonds, will have responsibility for conversion mechanics.[69] The appointment of a trustee for a bond issue is not mandatory under English law,[70] but is a useful feature that centralizes the administration and enforcement of bonds, thereby promoting effectiveness and enhancing the liquidity of the bonds.[71] A bond issue trustee is typically empowered to make certain, usually largely immaterial, changes to the bond issue terms and is responsible for convening meetings of bondholders to consider matters affecting their interests, including changes to the terms, and for taking enforcement action in response to the occurrence of an event of default.[72]

In *Elektrim SA v Vivendi Holdings 1 Corpn*[73] a bondholder commenced proceedings in Florida claiming fraud against the issuer company and breach of fiduciary duty against the trustee of the bond issue. Anti-suit injunctions were granted in favour of Elektrim and the trustee. The injunction granted in favour of Elektrim was to enforce a no-action clause in the trust deed and bond conditions, whereby only the trustee of the issue was entitled to take enforcement action against the issuer, and bondholders could not proceed directly against the issuer unless the trustee failed to take action in accordance with the bond documentation. The Court of Appeal upheld the decision to grant the injunctions reasoning that the commercial purpose of the no-action clause led to the conclusion that the no-action clause

---

[66] If the terms of the bonds include an investor put option this may be triggered by an extraordinary transaction, such as the sale or cessation of the principal part of the issuer's business followed by a credit rating downgrade.

[67] Asmar and Cowan, 'Convertible and Exchangeable Bonds', 27 note the extension of protective provisions to special (ie exception one-off) cash dividends and share repurchases at a significant premium.

[68] Rule 15.

[69] Asmar and Cowan, 'Convertible and Exchangeable Bonds'; A Carmichael and T Wells, 'Eurobonds' (1996) 7(7) *Practical Law for Companies* 41.

[70] cf the mandatory requirements under the US Trust Indenture Act 1939.

[71] *Elektrim SA v Vivendi Holdings 1 Corpn* [2008] EWCA Civ 1178.

[72] On the role of the trustee with regard to enforcement, see *Concord Trust v Law Debenture Trust Corp plc* [2005] 2 Lloyd's Rep 221, HL; *Elektrim SA v Vivendi Holdings 1 Corpn* [2008] EWCA Civ 1178. See also P Rawlings, 'The Changing Role of the Trustee in International Bond Issues' [2007] JBL 43.

[73] [2008] EWCA Civ 1178.

applied to claims which were in substance claims to enforce the trust deed or the bonds, as well as to claims which were in terms claims to enforce them. The no-action clause should be construed, to the extent reasonably possible, as an effective bar to individual bondholders pursuing, for their own account, what were in substance class claims. That could apply to tortious claims as well as to contractual claims. Furthermore, the Court of Appeal held that the judge was right that an injunction would have been appropriate on the ground of vexation/ oppression even if the no-action clause had not applied.

The documents will include a subscription agreement, which is the agreement in which the managers agree to purchase the bonds and the issuer agrees to issue them, a trust deed, and a paying agency agreement.[74] There will also be an offering circular, the contents and arrangements for approval of which will depend on whether the mandatory requirements for prospectuses relating to public offers or admission of securities to trading on a regulated market are applicable.

In committing their company to a bond issue, the responsible officers of the issuer must, of course, ensure that they are acting within their authority and in accordance with their duties. Particular restrictions that need to be checked are borrowing limits in articles, which limit the debt that the directors can add to the capital structure without reverting to the shareholders for approval, and covenants in existing loans whereby lenders limit the amount of additional debt that can be taken on. Issues of equity-linked debt, such as convertible bonds, also attract company law requirements that protect existing shareholders. These are, first, that directors must be specifically authorized, either by the company's articles or an ordinary resolution of the shareholders, to allot shares or securities with equity subscription or conversion rights.[75] An allotment authority must state the maximum number of shares that may be allotted, which, in the case of equity-linked securities, means the maximum number of shares that may be allotted pursuant to the subscription or conversion rights.[76] The authority must also specify an expiry date, which must be not more than five years from the date when it is given.[77] The allotment of shares on the exercise of subscription or conversion rights does not, however, need to be separately authorized and may take place after the authority for the issue of the equity-linked securities has expired.[78] Secondly, equity-linked securities are 'equity securities' for the purposes of statutory pre-emption rights, which means that prima facie equity-linked securities must be offered first to existing shareholders.[79] Pre-emption rights may, however, be disapplied, usually by special resolution.[80] Ordinary resolutions authorizing directors within limits to allot shares and equity-linked securities and special resolutions disapplying within limits pre-emption rights are routine, but would need to be carefully checked to ensure that a proposed bond issue does not exceed the limits. Another company law point that may be noted in relation to equity-linked securities is the rule that shares may not be allotted at less than their nominal value, which could be infringed, for instance, by the issue of a convertible bond at a discount to its nominal value of £1 which entitles the holder immediately to convert it into a £1 nominal value share.[81] However, this point is unlikely to have much practical significance because shares tend to trade at a price which is far in excess of their par value and the conversion price is set by reference to, and above, the market price of the shares. Company law rules on the valuation of non-cash consideration[82]

---

[74] [2008] EWCA Civ 1178.
[75] Companies Act 2006, s 551. The text assumes that the issuer is a public company.
[76] Companies Act 2006, s 551(3)(a) and (6).   [77] Companies Act 2006, s 551(3)(b).
[78] Companies Act 2006, s 551(7).
[79] Companies Act 2006, s 561. For the meaning of equity securities see Companies Act 2006, s 560.
[80] Companies Act 2006, ss 570–1.   [81] *Mosely v Koffyfontein Mines* [1904] 2 Ch 108, CA.
[82] Companies Act 2006, s 593.

do not apply where convertible bonds are converted into shares of the issuer of the bonds because, technically, the shares are issued for cash in this case;[83] but they would need to be considered where bonds are convertible into newly-issued shares of, say, the parent company of the issuer of the bonds.[84]

Listing and Issuance of Bonds

Listing of bonds

Bond issues may be listed or unlisted. A factor that is relevant to the decision of whether or not to list is that listing may attract institutional investors that are subject to regulatory or mandate constraints that limit their holdings of unlisted securities. The London Stock Exchange and the Luxembourg Stock Exchange dominate the market for listing of international bond issuance activity in Europe.[85]

Regulation of the issuance process

In 1963, the US government introduced a tax regime that discouraged foreign issuers from raising dollar-denominated finance directly from US investors. This step was a catalyst for the development in Europe of an offshore market for US dollar-denominated bonds, which was originally known as the 'eurobond' market but which has since come to be known as the international securities market. The international securities market has become a very successful and economically significant part of the European economy. It now provides a facility for public and private-sector issuers around the world to raise capital in many different currencies by issuing a diverse range of financial instruments.[86]

The origins of the international securities market, as an entrepreneurial response by sophisticated practitioners to an opportunity created by a restrictive regulatory step, and its inherently international character has left a lasting imprint on the way in which it is regulated. It has been suggested that the 'hidden' nature of the market—with trading mostly taking place off-exchange—meant that in its early days it largely escaped the attention of national regulators within Europe, who were, understandably, more concerned with activities that could more directly affect retail investor protection in local, domestic markets.[87] Initiatives at national and at Community level to upgrade securities market regulation brought the international securities market onto the regulatory radar screen during the 1980s but, broadly speaking, it continued to enjoy light-touch regulation, a stance that could be justified in policy terms because issuers tended to be public authorities and highly-rated private sector entities, and investors tended to be sophisticated professionals who could be expected to look after themselves. The adoption of the Financial Services Action Plan (FSAP, 1999) by the European Commission marked the start of a more interventionist phase at EU level in relation to the regulation of financial markets generally and led to the adoption of a series of new EU-wide laws affecting the issuance and trading of securities. The application of this legal

---

[83] Companies Act 2006, s 583(3)(c) provides that shares are deemed paid up in cash where the consideration is a release of a liability of the company for a liquidated sum.

[84] In this case, the liability released belongs to the subsidiary rather than the parent which is issuing the shares and therefore s 583(3)(c) is not satisfied.

[85] Casey and Lannoo, *Europe's Hidden Capital Markets*, 33.

[86] P Krijgsman, *A Brief History: IPMA's Role in Harmonising International Capital Markets 1984–1994* (International Primary Market Association, 2000).

[87] P Krijgsman, *A Brief History: IPMA's Role in Harmonising International Capital Markets 1984–1994*.

framework to equity issuance activity is discussed in detail in chapters 13 and 14. However, the new approach continued to recognize the highly international nature of large segments of the debt capital markets and the sophistication of typical investors by modifying the regime for debt issuance activity in important ways.

To recap the general regulatory framework for equity securities briefly, the Prospectus Directive[88] now sets the pan-European framework for prospectus disclosure. The general scheme is that a prospectus must be published when securities are offered to the public or admitted to trading on a regulated market. The contents of a prospectus are exhaustively prescribed by Community law and Member States do not have discretion to set additional 'super-equivalent' prospectus disclosure requirements. Some incorporation of information by reference is permitted. Financial information in a prospectus must be compiled in accordance with International Financial Reporting Standards (IFRS) or, for foreign (non-EU) issuers, in accordance with another accounting system, so long as it has been deemed 'equivalent' to IFRS by the EU. A prospectus must be approved before publication by the issuer's home state securities regulator; for EU issuers, the home state is the state of their registered office and for non-EU issuers it is the state that they have chosen as their EU home state by offering securities or having them admitted to trading on a regulated market in that jurisdiction (but once that choice is made by a non-EU issuer it cannot subsequently be changed for new issues). An approved prospectus can be used throughout the EU without any need to obtain local approvals from host state regulators. A prospectus can be in the form of a single document or separate documents comprising a registration statement, a securities note, and (where relevant) a summary. Where securities are offered cross-border, the whole prospectus need not be translated into local languages so long as it is written in a language customary in the sphere of international finance, such as English.

There are the general exemptions whereby the requirement to publish a prospectus does not apply to certain offers securities (assuming the securities are not also being admitted to trading on a regulated market).[89] The category of excluded unlisted offers includes offers to 'qualified investors,'[90] offers to fewer than 150 people per Member State (other than qualified investors),[91] offers of large denominated securities (minimum €100,000),[92] and offers with high minimum subscriptions (minimum €100,000 per investor).[93] The high-denomination exemptions are of particular significance for bond issuance activity.

For bond issues where a prospectus is required—such as where securities are to be admitted to trading on a regulated market (as they may well be in order to enhance their attractiveness to institutional investors)—the prospectus form and content requirements are modified in certain respects, again particularly for bond issues that have a minimum denomination of €100,000.[94] Base prospectuses are allowed for non-equity securities, including warrants in any form, issued under an offering programme.[95] A base prospectus consists of the required information relating to the issuer and the securities but not the final terms of the offer. A base prospectus, which is valid for one year, is typically used for multiple issues of bonds as the

---

[88] Directive (EC) 2003/71 of the European Parliament and of the Council of 4 November 2003 on the prospectus to be published when securities are offered to the public or admitted to trading and amending Directive (EC) 2001/34, [2003] OJ L345/64. Amended by Directive 2010/73/EU, [2010] OJ L327/1.

[89] Prospectus Directive, Art 3(2). [90] Prospectus Directive, Art 3(2)(a).

[91] Prospectus Directive, Art 3(2)(b). [92] Prospectus Directive, Art 3(2)(c).

[93] Prospectus Directive, Art 3(2)(d).

[94] Prospectus Directive, Art 7(2)(b); Prospectus Directive Regulation (Commission Regulation (EC) No 809/2004 of 29 April 2004 [2004] OJ L149/1, as amended) rec 14 and Arts 7–8, and Annexes IV–V (under €100,000), Arts 12, 16, and 21, and Annexes IX, XIII (€100,000 or above).

[95] Prospectus Directive, Art 5(4).

securities to which the prospectus relates may be issued from time to time under a debt issuance programme by the production of final terms.[96]

An important difference between debt and equity issuance is that the requirement for prospectuses to give financial information drawn up under IFRS, or an equivalent set of accounting standards, is disapplied for non-EU issuers of large denominated securities (minimum €100,000) of non-equity securities. Non-EU issuers can instead use accounts based on other accounting standards so long as the prospectus contains an appropriate warning and provides a narrative description of the differences between the standards in question and IFRS.[97] Debt securities that are convertible into new shares of the issuer of the debt instruments or of another company in its group would be equity securities for this purpose and thus would not benefit from this modification. Another modification is that the requirement for prospectus summaries does not apply to bond issues with a minimum denomination of €100,000.[98] Prospectus summaries are an element of retail investor protection and would be an out of place requirement in high denomination bonds.

The requirement tying issuers to their home states for regulatory approvals does not apply to issues of non-equity securities. Instead, the issuer (whether EU incorporated or non-EU) can choose to obtain its regulatory approvals from either its home state or the Member State where the securities are offered to the public or admitted to trading on a regulated market.[99] Debt securities that are convertible into equity of the company that issued the debt securities or equity of another company in its group do not benefit from this modification because they are classified as equity securities for this purpose. The Prospectus Directive limits this modification to debt instruments denominated in units of least €1,000. The inclusion of this minimum threshold was a compromise between those who argued that, as with equity issues, issuers should be tied to their home state because their home state could be presumed to be in the best position to regulate and supervise them, and others who argued that this rule should not apply to bond issues because of the concentration of relevant supervisory expertise in London and Luxembourg, which are the principal centres for bond issuance and listing activity in the EU. Experience of several years of operation led the European Commission to suggest that for reasons of reduction of administrative burdens and effectiveness it would be preferable to extend issuer choice to all issues of non-equity securities.[100] It argued that the threshold was causing practical problems for issuers of non-equity securities that sometimes found that they needed to draw up several prospectuses for a single issue, ie one to cover a debt issuance programme within the threshold and another for the remaining debt issuance activities which might exceed that threshold. Moreover, the threshold could not apply to certain structured products which were not denominated. The Commission's view was that removing the threshold would not create concrete risks in terms of investor protection because the characteristics of, and the risks associated with, debt securities did not depend on the denomination of the securities offered or traded in a regulated market. Notwithstanding the strength of these arguments, the 2010 amendments to the Prospectus Directive did not include removal of the threshold. Instead, the Commission was mandated to undertake a review and, following that review, to consider whether the provision should be maintained or revoked.[101]

---

[96] The final terms published when the securities are issued would not require separate regulatory approval. The 2010 amendments to the Prospectus Directive clarified the distinction between final terms and material updates that would need to be published in an approved supplement and which would therefore trigger withdrawal rights. Withdrawal rights are considered in ch 13.

[97] Prospectus Directive Regulation, Annex IX, para 11.1.

[98] Prospectus Directive, Art 5(2) (as amended).   [99] Prospectus Directive, Art 2(1)(m)(ii).

[100] European Commission, *Proposal for a Directive Amending Directive 2003/71/EC and Directive 2004/109/EC* (COM(2009) 491) 6.

[101] Directive 2010/73/EU, rec 8.

A further difference in the capital market issuer disclosure regime generally is that issuers of 'wholesale' bonds with a minimum denomination of €100,000, that are admitted to trading on a regulated market, are exempt from the obligations under the Transparency Obligations Directive to publish periodic financial reports.[102] Exemption from the ongoing financial reporting requirements under the Transparency Obligations Directive is an especially important element of the wholesale regime.

Exchange-regulated markets for bonds

Markets have the capacity to work flexibly and creatively around regulatory requirements, as the very origins of the Eurobond market demonstrate. The bifurcation of the EU prospectus and ongoing disclosure regime for bonds into retail and wholesale segments, with a threshold of (now) €100,000 as the dividing line, gives rise to the possibility of essentially wholesale-oriented bond issuance activity that does not meet the minimum denomination threshold migrating from EU markets.[103] In response to this risk, in July 2005 the London Stock Exchange opened a new trading platform called the Professional Securities Market (PSM). The PSM is a market for officially listed debt securities and depository receipts, hence securities trading on it can be freely acquired by institutional investors that are constrained from buying unlisted securities. For tax purposes, bonds quoted on the PSM are 'quoted eurobonds' that qualify for a withholding tax exemption.[104] However, the PSM is not a 'regulated market' for the purposes of the Prospectus and Transparency Obligations Directives. Accordingly, securities that are admitted to trading on the PSM fall outside the scope of the EU-wide mandatory requirements for IFRS (or equivalent) financial information (provided that they are not the subject of a public offer). The disclosure requirements for listing particulars (the term used in this context for the offering circular rather than 'prospectus') relating to securities that are to be admitted to the PSM are set and monitored by the Financial Conduct Authority, as the UK listing authority.[105] The requirements for PSM listing particulars are substantially based on Prospectus Directive disclosure requirements for wholesale debt—in effect, 'cherry picking' those parts of the EU-wide regime that fit comfortably with the international securities market and, to that extent, meeting investor preferences for information standardization, and dispensing with those that do not. The desire of the British players to maintain a competitive position as an international market for listed securities is, unsurprisingly, also evident elsewhere within the EU. In July 2005, the Luxembourg Stock Exchange launched a similarly structured platform, the Euro MTF.

Listing particulars prepared for the purposes of having bonds admitted to trading on the PSM or the Euro MTF market do not benefit from the European passport for prospectuses. However, this is not a major problem because the principal purpose of having international bonds admitted to trading on a formal market is not to open up direct investor access but rather to ensure their acceptability to investors that must invest in 'listed securities' and to obtain favourable tax treatment. Secondary market trading of bonds listed on the PSM, Euro

---

[102] Directive (EC) 2004/109 of the European Parliament and of the Council of 15 December 2004 on the harmonisation of transparency requirements in relation to information about issuers whose securities are admitted to trading on a regulated market and amending Directive (EC) 2001/34 [2004] OJ L390/38.

[103] FH Kung, 'The Regulation of Corporate Bond Offerings: A Comparative Analysis' (2005) 26 *University of Pennsylvania Journal of International Economic Law* 409, 427.

[104] During 2012 the government consulted on a proposal to restrict this exemption but in the light of the responses from the consultation, which were largely against the changes as they would make it more difficult to raise funds and therefore make the UK less competitive than other jurisdictions, decided not to proceed: HMRC, *Possible Changes to Income Tax Rules on Interest: Summary of Responses* (October 2012).

[105] *Listing Rules*, ch 4.

MTF, or any similarly organized platform can take place on a cross-border basis through intermediaries which themselves hold passports to operate across the EU. Secondary market trading will not trigger a requirement to produce a prospectus so long as it remains within the public offer exemptions provided by the Prospectus Directive.

Stabilization

It is common for the bond issuance process to include some stabilization activity to maintain and support the price of the bonds in the immediate post-issuance period. In policy terms, a degree of stabilization is permissible because it alleviates sales pressure generated by short-term investors and maintains an orderly market in the relevant securities.[106] Stabilization can thus contribute to greater confidence of investors and issuers in the financial markets.[107] However, stabilization needs to be carefully controlled to avoid infringing laws prohibiting market abuse. An EU Regulation provides a safe harbour from infringement of the market abuse laws that give effect to the Market Abuse Directive.[108] As it currently stands, the EU regime is limited in scope to financial instruments admitted to trading on a regulated market in at least one Member State, or for which a request for admission to trading on such a market has been made, and to financial instruments not admitted to trading on a regulated market in a Member State, but whose value depends on a financial instrument so admitted or for which admission has been sought.[109] The UK in its domestic regime has been more expansive and includes conduct occurring in relation to securities listed on the PSM, which is a market established under the rules of a UK recognized investment exchange, within its scope.[110] The Market Abuse Directive is in the process of being overhauled and, amongst other things, the reforms will extend the scope of the EU framework to apply to any financial instrument admitted to trading on an MTF or organized trading facility, as well as to any related financial instruments traded over the counter (OTC) which can have an effect on the covered underlying market.[111] Consequential changes to the UK domestic position will follow.

Restrictions on general solicitation

In the bond issuance process it is also necessary to pay attention to general solicitation controls on advertisements and other promotional materials. In the UK, the principal control is section 21 of the Financial Services and Markets Act 2000, which requires 'financial promotions' in the course of business to be made only by authorized persons or with the contents having been approved by an authorized person. This requirement does not apply to exempt communications, which include certain communications to overseas recipients, investment professionals, high net worth individuals, companies and firms, and sophisticated

---

[106] Commission Regulation (EC) 2273/2003 of 22 December 2003 implementing Directive (EC) 2003/6 of the European Parliament and of the Council as regards exemptions for buy-back programmes and stabilisation of financial instruments [2003] OJ L336/33, rec 11.

[107] Commission Regulation (EC) 2273/2003 of 22 December 2003.

[108] Commission Regulation (EC) 2273/2003 of 22 December 2003.

[109] Directive (EC) 2003/6 of the European Parliament and of the Council of 28 January 2003 on insider dealing and market manipulation (market abuse) [2003] OJ L96/16, Art 9.

[110] Financial Services and Markets Act 2000, s 118 and Financial Services and Markets Act 2000 (Prescribed Markets and Qualifying Investments) Order 2001, SI 2001/996 (as amended); FCA *Handbook*, MAR 2 (Stabilisation).

[111] In September 2013, the European Parliament endorsed the political agreement with the Council on the Market Abuse Regulation. Final adoption of the Market Abuse Regulation will take place after a final political agreement on the revised Markets in Financial Instruments Directive (MiFID II), since aspects of the Market Abuse Regulation depend on the final text of MiFID II and these will need to be aligned. The date as of which the new market abuse rules will apply is to be aligned with that of MiFID II.

investors.[112] Prospectuses and listing particulars are also within the scope of an exemption under the financial promotions regime.[113] The Prospectus Directive, implemented in the UK in the FCA *Handbook*, also regulates advertisements relating to public offers of securities or the admission of securities to trading on a regulated market by requiring advertisements to be accurate, complete, and consistent with the prospectus and to alert people to the fact that there is a prospectus containing the information that investors should use as the basis for their investment decisions.[114] As bonds tend to be targeted at an international community of investors, foreign (in particular US) selling restrictions, discussed in chapter 14 with respect to equity offerings, must also be considered. Debt issuance is, by far, the largest component of the Rule 144A market.[115]

Secondary Market Trading of Bonds: A Brief Note on Topical Issues

OTC trading

Secondary market trading of bonds, including listed bonds, generally takes place outside formal exchanges. The International Capital Market Association gives three reasons why wholesale bonds tend to trade over the counter:[116]

- First, there is a very large population of debt securities compared with equities. For example, there were 6,810 shares admitted to trading on regulated markets in the EU on 22 July 2009 whereas Xtrakter's CUPID database contains information on over 150,000 debt securities in issue. Therefore, debt markets are far less concentrated than equity markets.

- Second, the average size of a bond trade tends to be substantially greater than for an equity trade. Xtrakter data indicates that average bond trade sizes are between €1m and €2m while trades in excess of €2m–€5m are common. Prior to the crisis, even trades of €100m or more were not uncommon. The average trade size for equities on the London Stock Exchange, on the other hand, is in the region of £43,000 and European legislation defines the typical retail trade in equities as €7500 or less.

- Third, unlike equities almost all bonds trade very infrequently so there is rarely a constant supply of buyers and sellers looking to trade sufficient to sustain a central pool of investor provided liquidity. Only 3,000 of the top bonds (by volume) traded at least once a day on average. Of the top 100 bonds by volume traded the highest trade count bond traded 10,000 times in the year whilst others traded only 6 times in the year. This contrasts significantly to liquidity in the equity market. Under MiFID a share is considered to be liquid if it is traded daily, with a free float of less than EUR 500 million, and either the average daily number of transactions in the share is not less than 500 or the average daily turnover for the share is not less than EUR 2 million.

Developments such as the LSE ORB are intended to provide bond investors with organized trading platforms.[117] Furthermore, the expansion of trading venues under the Markets in

---

[112] The exemptions are provided by the Financial Services and Markets Act 2000 (Financial Promotion) Order 2005, SI 2005/1529.

[113] Financial Services and Markets Act 2000 (Financial Promotion) Order 2005, regs 70–1.

[114] Prospectus Directive, Art 15 and FCA *Handbook, PR* 3.3.

[115] P Carayannopoulos and S Nayak, 'Debt Issuance Under Rule 144A and Equity Valuation Effects' (2013) 16 *Review of Pacific Basin Financial Markets and Policies.*

[116] <http://www.icmagroup.org/Regulatory-Policy-and-Market-Practice/Secondary-Markets/Bond-Market-Transparency-Wholesale-Retail/So-why-do-bonds-trade-OTC-/>, accessed July 2013.

[117] <http://www.icmagroup.org/Regulatory-Policy-and-Market-Practice/Secondary-Markets/Bond-Market-Transparency-Wholesale-Retail/So-why-do-bonds-trade-OTC-/>, 49–53.

Financial Instruments Directive (MiFID) II package[118] to include not only regulated markets and multilateral trading facilities but also the new category of organized trading facilities represents another potential squeeze on OTC trading activity.

Transparency of secondary bond markets

The growing significance of the bond markets as a source of capital for the corporate sector, the complexity of these markets, and increased retail participation in bond market investments have together resulted in bond market transparency becoming an increasingly pressing policy concern.[119] The predominance of OTC trading means that there is not the flow of readily available pricing information in relation to bond trades that there is in respect of equity securities. However, the introduction of more transparency via regulatory intervention is a controversial matter and the issues are hotly contested.[120] A tension between transparency and liquidity lies at the heart of the controversy: there is said to be a risk that increased mandatory transparency requirements could lead dealers, on whom the market is heavily reliant for liquidity, to withdraw their capital from the market. Nevertheless, MiFID II reforms will move the EU position towards greater transparency. The MiFID II package will require all organized trading to be conducted on regulated trading venues (regulated markets, multilateral trading facilities, and organized trading facilities) and will introduce identical pre and post-trade transparency requirements to all of these venues, although the transparency requirements will be calibrated for different types of instruments, notably equity, bonds, and derivatives, and for different types of trading, notably order book and quote driven systems.[121] In announcing these changes, the European Commission asserted that the extension of transparency requirements was considered justified because the existing level of transparency was not always sufficient.[122] However, concerns that these moves threaten to harm bond market efficiency and liquidity have not abated.[123]

Clearing and settlement

Clearing and settlement are the processes of identifying the rights and obligations resulting from securities trading (clearing) and effecting the payment and transfer of ownership (settlement). Central counterparties that perform clearing services are now within the scope of the EU European Market Infrastructure Regulation (EMIR).[124]

So far as settlement is concerned, there are over 30 central securities depositories in the EU (CSDs), generally one in each country, and two 'international' CSDs (ICSDs),[125] namely,

---

[118] European Commission, *Proposal for a Directive on Markets in Financial Instruments repealing Directive 2004/39/EC* (COM(2011) 656); European Commission, *Proposal for a Regulation on Markets in Financial Instruments and Amending Regulation (EU) No 648/2012 on OTC derivatives, central counterparties and trade repositories* (COM(2011) 652).

[119] FH Kung, 'The Regulation of Corporate Bond Offerings: a Comparative Analysis' (2005) 26 *University of Pennsylvania Journal of International Economic Law* 409, 410–1; IOSCO, *Transparency of Corporate Bond Markets*.

[120] GA Ferrarini, 'Market Transparency and Best Execution: Bond Trading under MiFID' in M Tison et al (eds), *Perspectives in Company Law and Financial Regulation* (Cambridge: CUP, 2009).

[121] COM(2011) 656; COM(2011) 652, 7–9.

[122] COM(2011) 652, 7–9.

[123] R Healey, *MiFID II and Fixed-Income Price Transparency: Panacea or Problem?* (TABB Group, 2012).

[124] Regulation (EU) No 648/2012 of the European Parliament and of the Council of 4 July 2012 on OTC derivatives, central counterparties and trade repositories [2012] OJ L201/1.

[125] European Commission, *Proposal for a Regulation on Improving Securities Settlement in the European Union and on Central Securities Depositories (CSDs)* (COM(2012) 73).

Euroclear Bank SA/NV[126] and Clearstream Banking Luxembourg.[127] In most cases, bonds admitted to trading on the LSE ORB must be settlable in CREST, which is the central settlement depositary for the UK and which is owned by Euroclear.[128] Securities settlement systems in the EU settled approximately €920 trillion worth of transactions in 2010, and held almost €39 trillion of securities at the end of 2010.[129] The EU took initial steps to harmonize the law relating to settlement in 1998.[130] However, in the aftermath of the financial crisis of 2007–9, concerns about lack of safety and efficiency of securities settlement and the resulting obstacles to the functioning of the internal market resulting from the divergent national rules regulating securities settlement and the activities of the CSDs intensified. This greater sense of danger has led to the proposed introduction of more harmonized rules concerning certain aspects of the settlement cycle and discipline, as well as a set of common prudential requirements addressing the resilience of and access to CSDs.[131] The new EU Regulation, as proposed by the European Commission, will, among other things, impose dematerialization/immobilization of securities (ie issuance of securities in book entry form only), harmonize the settlement period for securities transactions across the EU, and harmonize settlement discipline measures across the EU. The key objectives of dematerialization, which will mainly affect the UK and Ireland as these are the Member States where the holding of certain securities in paper form is still common, is to ensure a quicker settlement, to enhance safety, and to reduce costs. Also in the legislative pipeline is a Directive on securities law to enhance security by providing harmonized rules on the rights of investors who are not officially registered as the holders of securities and who hold them via intermediaries. Alongside these legislative developments, Target2-Securities (T2S) is a large infrastructure project that was launched by the Eurosystem in 2007 to stimulate cross-border settlement harmonization. T2S is expected to reshape the European post-trading industry by providing a single pan-European platform for securities settlement in central bank money.[132]

[126] <http://www.euroclear.com/en.html>, accessed July 2013.
[127] <http://www.clearstream.com/ci/dispatch/en/kir/ci_nav/home>, accessed July 2013.
[128] LSE, *Listing and Admitting Retail Bonds*.
[129] European Commission, *Proposal for a Regulation on Improving Securities Settlement in the European Union and on Central Securities Depositories (CSDs)* (COM(2012) 73).
[130] Directive (EC) 98/26 of the European Parliament and of the Council of 19 May 1998 on settlement finality in payment and securities settlement systems [1998] OJ L166/45 (amended in certain respects by Directive 2009/44/EC, [2009] OJ L156/37).
[131] European Commission, *Proposal for a Regulation on Improving Securities Settlement in the European Union and on Central Securities Depositories (CSDs)* (COM(2012) 73).
[132] <http://www.ecb.int/paym/t2s/html/index.en.html>, accessed July 2013.

Index